Library Use Only

Encyclopedia of Domestic Violence and Abuse

Encyclopedia of Domestic Violence and Abuse

Volume 1: A–R

LAURA L. FINLEY, EDITOR

ABC-CLIO

Santa Barbara, California • Denver, Colorado • Oxford, England

Copyright 2013 by ABC-CLIO, LLC.

All rights reserved. No part of this publication may be reproduced, stored in a retrieval system, or transmitted, in any form or by any means, electronic, mechanical, photocopying, recording, or otherwise, except for the inclusion of brief quotations in a review, without prior permission in writing from the publisher.

Library of Congress Cataloging-in-Publication Data

Encyclopedia of domestic violence and abuse / Laura L. Finley, editor.
   volumes cm
Includes bibliographical references and index.
ISBN 978–1–61069–001–0 (hard copy : alk. paper) — ISBN 978–1–61069–002–7 (ebook) 1. Family violence—Encyclopedias. 2. Abused women—Encyclopedias. 3. Older people—Abuse of—Encyclopedias. 4. Child abuse—Encyclopedias. 5. Family violence—United States—Encyclopedias. 6. Abused women—United States—Encyclopedias. 7. Older people—Abuse of—United States—Encyclopedias. 8. Child abuse—United States—Encyclopedias. I. Finley, Laura L., editor of compilation.
HV6626.E535 2013
362.82′9203—dc23   2012048843

ISBN: 978–1–61069–001–0
EISBN: 978–1–61069–002–7

17 16 15 14 13   1 2 3 4 5

This book is also available on the World Wide Web as an eBook.
Visit www.abc-clio.com for details.

ABC-CLIO, LLC
130 Cremona Drive, P.O. Box 1911
Santa Barbara, California 93116-1911

This book is printed on acid-free paper ∞

Manufactured in the United States of America

Contents

Alphabetical List of Entries	vii
Topical List of Entries	xi
Preface	xv
Acknowledgments	xvii
Introduction	xix
Timeline of Significant Events Related to Domestic Violence and Abuse	xxxiii
Encyclopedia Entries	1
Appendix 1: Primary Documents	571
1. Convention on the Elimination of All Forms of Discrimination Against Women	571
2. Report of the Inter-American Commission on Human Rights re: *Jessica Lenahan (Gonzales) et al. v. United States*	585
3. Trafficking Victims Protection Act of 2000	661
4. Violence Against Women Act	756
Appendix 2: State, National, and International Organizations Related to Domestic Abuse	815
Glossary	835
Recommended Resources: Books, Journals, Articles, and Videos	841
About the Editor and Contributors	851
Index	857

Alphabetical List of Entries

Acid Throwing
Africa and Domestic Abuse
AIDS and Domestic Violence
Alaska Natives and Domestic Abuse
Alcohol and Domestic Abuse
Ali, Somy
American Medical Association (AMA)
Amnesty International
Anger Management and Domestic Abuse
Animal Abuse and Domestic Abuse
Asia and Domestic Abuse
Athletes and Domestic Abuse
Avon Corporation

Battered Woman Syndrome
Batterer Intervention Programs
Beijing Declaration and Platform for Action
Biological and Psychological Theories about Domestic Abuse
The Body Shop
Break the Cycle
Brides Walk
Bullying and Domestic Abuse
Bystander Intervention Programs

The Caribbean and Domestic Abuse
Castle Rock v. Gonzales Case
Celebrities and Domestic Abuse
Centers for Disease Control and Prevention (CDC)
Child Abuse and Domestic Abuse
Children, Impact of Domestic Abuse on
Christianity and Domestic Abuse
College-Aged Victims
Convention on the Elimination of All Forms of Discrimination Against Women (CEDAW)
Courts and Domestic Abuse
Crisis Lines

Culturally Competent Services
Cycle of Violence

Demographic and Health Surveys
DeShaney v. Winnebago County Department of Social Services Case
Disabilities and Domestic Abuse
Disasters and Domestic Violence
Domestic Violence Prevention Enhancement and Leadership Through Alliances (DELTA) Program
Dowry Killings
Drugs and Domestic Abuse
Duluth Model

Economic Recession and Domestic Abuse
Educational Programs
Effects of Domestic Violence
Elder Abuse
End Violence Against Women (EVAW) International
Equality Now
Europe and Domestic Abuse

Failure to Protect
Family Structure and Domestic Abuse
Family Violence, Risk Factors for
Female Genital Mutilation (FGM)
Female Perpetrators
Feminism and Domestic Abuse
Films and Domestic Abuse
Financial Abuse
Forced Marriage and Domestic Abuse
Funding for Domestic Violence Services
Futures Without Violence

Gender-Related Theories
Global Fund for Women
Grassroots Movements

Health Effects of Domestic Abuse
History of U.S. Domestic Violence before 1970
History of U.S. Domestic Violence Developments, 1970s
History of U.S. Domestic Violence Developments, 1980s
History of U.S. Domestic Violence Developments, 1990s
History of U.S. Domestic Violence Developments, 2000s
Honor Killings
Hospital and Medical Records and Domestic Abuse
Housing and Domestic Abuse
Hughes, Francine
Human Trafficking

Immigrant Victims of Domestic Abuse
Incite!
India and Domestic Abuse
International Violence Against Women Act (I-VAWA)
Islam and Domestic Abuse

Judaism and Domestic Abuse

Katz, Jackson
Kimmel, Michael
Kivel, Paul
Kristof, Nicholas and Sheryl WuDunn

Latin America and Domestic Abuse
Legislation and Policies, Dating Violence
Legislation and Policies, Domestic Abuse
Lesbian, Gay, Bisexual, and Transgendered (LGBT) Victims
Linguistic Analysis of Verbal Abuse
Liz Claiborne Inc.

Mai, Mukhtar
Male Victims of Domestic Abuse
Mam, Somaly
Mandatory Arrest Policies
Mary Kay Corporation
Mediation and Domestic Abuse
Men's Efforts against Domestic Abuse

Middle and Upper Classes and Domestic Abuse
The Middle East and Domestic Abuse
The Military and Domestic Violence
Minneapolis Domestic Violence Experiment
Mortality Review Boards and Domestic Abuse
Music and Domestic Abuse

National Coalition Against Domestic Violence (NCADV)
National Crime Victimization Survey (NCVS)
National Domestic Violence Hotline
National Family Violence Survey
National Network to End Domestic Violence (NNEDV)
National Organization for Men Against Sexism (NOMAS)
National Organization for Women (NOW)
National Teen Dating Abuse Helpline
Native Americans and Domestic Abuse
News Media and Domestic Abuse
Nongovernmental Organizations (NGOs) and Domestic Abuse
Nonprofit Organizations and Domestic Abuse
Nonviolence Theories and Domestic Abuse
North America and Domestic Abuse

Outreach Services

Patriarchy and Domestic Abuse
Personal Narrative: Kristin Franklin
Personal Narrative: Lauren Pilnick
Personal Narrative: Patricia
Personal Narrative: Sabrina
Physicians, Health-Care Providers, and Domestic Abuse
Pizzey, Erin
Policing Domestic Abuse
Pregnancy and Domestic Abuse
Prevention Institute
Prisons and Domestic Abuse
Psychological Effects of Domestic Abuse

Reproductive Coercion
Restraining Orders and Personal Protection Orders
Runaway and Homeless Youth

Schechter, Susan
Self-Defense, Homicides, and Domestic Abuse
Self-Defense, Legal Issues
Shelters for Domestic Abuse Victims
Simpson, O. J. Case
Social and Societal Effects of Domestic Abuse
Social Change Movements
Sociological Theories about Domestic Abuse
South America and Domestic Abuse
South and Southeast Asia and Domestic Abuse
Spiritual Abuse
Stalking
Straus, Murray
Support Groups for Victims of Domestic Abuse

Technology and Domestic Abuse
Teen Victims of Domestic Abuse
Therapy and Counseling for Domestic Abuse
Thurman, Tracey Case
Trafficking Victims Protection Act (TVPA)
Traumatic Brain Injury and Domestic Abuse
Tribal Law and Justice Act
Types of Domestic Abuse

UNIFEM and UN Women
Uniform Crime Reports
The United Nations and Domestic Abuse
U.S. Government Responses to Domestic Violence
United States v. Morrison Case

Verizon Foundation
Violence Against Women Act (VAWA)
Vital Voices

Walker, Lenore
War and Domestic Violence
Warning Signs of Abuse
Welfare and Domestic Abuse
White Ribbon Campaign
Women's Aid Federation of England
Women's Rights Movement
Women Thrive Worldwide
Workplace Violence and Domestic Abuse
World Health Organization (WHO)

Topical List of Entries

HISTORICAL INFORMATION

History of U.S. Domestic Violence before 1970
History of U.S. Domestic Violence Developments, 1970s
History of U.S. Domestic Violence Developments, 1980s
History of U.S. Domestic Violence Developments, 1990s
History of U.S. Domestic Violence Developments, 2000s
Women's Rights Movement

FORMS OF ABUSE

Acid Throwing
Christianity and Domestic Abuse
Dowry Killings
Female Genital Mutilation (FGM)
Financial Abuse
Forced Marriage and Domestic Abuse
Honor Killings
Human Trafficking
Islam and Domestic Abuse
Judaism and Domestic Abuse
Linguistic Analysis of Verbal Abuse
Reproductive Coercion
Spiritual Abuse
Stalking
Technology and Domestic Abuse
Types of Domestic Abuse
Workplace Violence and Domestic Abuse

VICTIMS AND OFFENDERS

Africa and Domestic Abuse
Alaska Natives and Domestic Abuse
Asia and Domestic Abuse
Athletes and Domestic Abuse
The Caribbean and Domestic Abuse
Celebrities and Domestic Abuse
Child Abuse and Domestic Abuse
College-Aged Victims
Disabilities and Domestic Abuse
Elder Abuse
Europe and Domestic Abuse
Female Perpetrators
Immigrant Victims of Domestic Abuse
India and Domestic Abuse
Latin America and Domestic Abuse
Lesbian, Gay, Bisexual, and Transgendered (LGBT) Victims
Male Victims of Domestic Abuse

MIDDLE AND UPPER CLASSES AND DOMESTIC ABUSE

The Middle East and Domestic Abuse
The Military and Domestic Violence
Native Americans and Domestic Abuse
North America and Domestic Abuse
Pregnancy and Domestic Abuse
Runaway and Homeless Youth

Self-Defense, Legal Issues
South America and Domestic Abuse
South and Southeast Asian and Domestic Abuse
Teen Victims of Domestic Abuse

UNDERSTANDING AND EXPLAINING ABUSE

Battered Woman Syndrome
Biological and Psychological Theories about Domestic Abuse
Cycle of Violence
Demographic and Health Surveys
Duluth Model
Family Structure and Domestic Abuse
Family Violence, Risk Factors for
Feminism and Domestic Abuse
Films and Domestic Abuse
Gender-Related Theories
Hospital and Medical Records and Domestic Abuse
Mortality Review Boards and Domestic Abuse
Music and Domestic Abuse
National Crime Victimization Survey (NCVS)
National Family Violence Survey
News Media and Domestic Abuse
Nonviolence Theories and Domestic Abuse
Patriarchy and Domestic Abuse
Psychological Effects of Domestic Abuse
Sociological Theories about Domestic Abuse
Uniform Crime Reports (UCR)
Warning Signs of Abuse

EFFECT OF ABUSE

Children, Impact of Domestic Abuse on
Effects of Domestic Violence
Health Effects of Domestic Abuse
Psychological Effects of Domestic Abuse
Self-Defense, Homicides, and Domestic Abuse
Social and Societal Effects of Domestic Abuse
Traumatic Brain Injury and Domestic Abuse
Welfare and Domestic Abuse

CORRELATES OF ABUSE

AIDS and Domestic Violence
Alcohol and Domestic Abuse
Animal Abuse and Domestic Abuse
Bullying and Domestic Abuse
Disasters and Domestic Violence
Drugs and Domestic Abuse
Economic Recession and Domestic Abuse
Housing and Domestic Abuse
Poverty and Domestic Abuse
Prisons and Domestic Abuse
War and Domestic Violence

KEY PEOPLE

Ali, Somy
Hughes, Francine
Katz, Jackson
Kimmel, Michael
Kivel, Paul
Kristof, Nicholas and Sheryl WuDunn
Mai, Mukhtar
Mam, Somaly
Personal Narrative: Kristin Franklin
Personal Narrative: Lauren Pilnick
Personal Narrative: Patricia
Personal Narrative: Sabrina
Pizzey, Erin
Schechter, Susan

Simpson, O. J. Case
Straus, Murray
Thurman, Tracey Case
Walker, Lenore

LAWS, COURT DECISIONS, AND POLICIES

Beijing Declaration and Platform for Action
Castle Rock v. Gonzales Case
Convention on the Elimination of All Forms of Discrimination Against Women (CEDAW)
DeShaney v. Winnebago County Department of Social Services Case
International Violence Against Women Act (I-VAWA)
Legislation and Policies, Dating Violence
Legislation and Policies, Domestic Abuse
Tribal Law and Justice Act
Trafficking Victims Protection Act (TVPA)
United States v. Morrison Case
Violence Against Women Act (VAWA)

INTERVENTIONS

Anger Management and Domestic Abuse
Batterer Intervention Programs
Bystander Intervention Programs
Courts and Domestic Abuse
Crisis Lines
Culturally Competent Services
Failure to Protect
Funding for Domestic Violence Services
Grassroots Movements
Mandatory Arrest Policies
Mediation and Domestic Abuse
Minneapolis Domestic Violence Experiment
National Domestic Violence Hotline
National Network to End Domestic Violence (NNEDV)
National Organization for Men Against Sexism (NOMAS)
National Organization for Women (NOW)
National Teen Dating Abuse Helpline
Outreach Services
Physicians, Health-Care Providers, and Domestic Abuse
Policing Domestic Abuse
Restraining Orders and Personal Protection Orders
Shelters for Domestic Abuse Victims
Support Groups for Victims of Domestic Abuse
Therapy and Counseling for Domestic Abuse
U.S. Government Responses to Domestic Violence

PREVENTION

Brides Walk
Domestic Violence Prevention Enhancement and Leadership Through Alliances (DELTA) Program
Educational Programs
Men's Efforts against Domestic Abuse
Social Change Movements

ORGANIZATIONS AND RESOURCES

American Medical Association (AMA)
Amnesty International
Avon Corporation
The Body Shop
Break the Cycle

Centers for Disease Control and Prevention (CDC)
End Violence Against Women (EVAW) International
Equality Now
Futures Without Violence
Global Fund for Women
Incite!
Liz Claiborne Inc.
Mary Kay Corporation
National Coalition Against Domestic Violence (NCADV)
Nongovernmental Organizations (NGOs) and Domestic Abuse
Nonprofit Organizations and Domestic Abuse
Prevention Institute
UNIFEM and UN Women
The United Nations and Domestic Abuse
Verizon Foundation
Vital Voices
White Ribbon Campaign
Women's Aid Federation of England
Women Thrive Worldwide
World Health Organization (WHO)

Preface

The *Encyclopedia of Domestic Violence and Abuse* is intended to be one component in the effort to prevent and educate about domestic violence, not only in the United States but worldwide. Providing information about abuse to scholars, practitioners, and students can help not just educate but hopefully inspire action to end the many forms of violence addressed herein.

These volumes, authored by 60 experts in the field, from scholars to practitioners to survivors of abuse, include 173 alphabetically arranged entries that describe the scope and extent of various forms of this abuse, occurring globally. The encyclopedia provides information about the people from the most vulnerable demographics and those who are most likely to perpetrate abuse. Entries are also included to help explain why abuse occurs and the impact it has, both on individuals and on society. Readers can find entries on global laws and policies devoted to addressing abuse; histories of the movement to end abuse; and information about groups, organizations, and corporations involved in those efforts. Key people and court cases are highlighted, as are important correlates, such as animal abuse and substance abuse.

Special Features

A timeline of important events related to domestic abuse, from ancient Rome to the present day, is featured at the beginning of the encyclopedia. At the end of volume two, following the entries, is Appendix 1, giving complete text of and introductions to primary source documents related to critical court decisions, legislation, and international treaties. Included are four documents: (1) Convention on the Elimination of All Forms of Discrimination Against Women (CEDAW), the international human rights treaty first adopted by the United Nations in 1979, which the United States has still not ratified; (2) the Report of the Inter-American Commission on Human Rights re: *Jessica Lenahan (Gonzales) et al. v. United States,* which was based on a U.S. court case where a woman sued a city in Colorado for not enforcing the order of protection against her husband, who subsequently murdered their three daughters; (3) the Trafficking Victims Protection Act of 2000 passed by the U.S. Congress; and (4) the Violence Against Women Act (VAWA) passed in Congress in 1994, which is up for reauthorization in 2012. Following that is Appendix 2, a list of recommended, helpful websites for state, national and international resources. After are is a glossary of key terms relating to domestic violence; a selected bibliography of recommended books, journals, journal articles, and multimedia sources; and brief contributor biographies. The comprehensive index will help readers navigate this timely and important volume, as will the lists of all entries at the beginning of the book, which are arranged both alphabetically and topically.

Acknowledgments

This project was truly a labor of love. Having worked in the field of domestic violence in some capacity for the last seven years, I am thrilled to have been able to share insights I have gained and to draw on the expertise of the many scholars, practitioners, and survivors whose work is included in this volume.

Tremendous thanks go to all the contributors whose entries will surely inform readers about the important topic of domestic abuse. It was a pleasure to work with such a diverse group of authors. Contributors to this volume include advocates, scholars of sociology, psychology, social work, women's issues, theology, and health care, as well as survivors themselves. To the survivors who shared their personal stories, I offer my deepest gratitude. Your courage and resilience are amazing.

Throughout the process of writing and editing, I was able to work with many great people at ABC-CLIO. First Sandy Towers and then Anne Thompson offered timely and useful suggestions and provided needed support. It was a pleasure to work with such professional editors.

I also want to thank my family for their continued support of my work. My husband Peter and daughter Anya also volunteer with a domestic violence center and are always helpful when mom needs her "writing time." I dedicate this volume to my amazing family and hope that it in some way helps ensure that when Anya is old enough to date, she is in nothing but healthy, happy relationships as she has witnessed with her parents.

Finally, I want to acknowledge the many people, including some close friends, who work daily to assist victims and to raise awareness about abuse. I am happy to devote 50 percent of royalties for this book to No More Tears, which offers assistance to victims. Led courageously and creatively by Somy Ali, one of my best friends, No More Tears truly is a model of what is best about humanity.

Introduction

Although this volume is focused on domestic abuse, entries cover topics relevant to broader human rights issues that disproportionately impact women. Examining the broader issues allows readers to attain a more thoughtful and critical understanding of domestic abuse, its causes, its impact, and possible solutions.

Domestic Abuse: A Global Human Rights Epidemic

Domestic abuse involves multiple types of violent and degrading behavior. Although any type of violence and humiliation is painful, domestic abuse is acutely so because it is perpetrated by someone who is supposed to provide love and respect. It is but one example of the many forms of violence women are most likely to endure across the globe. It is important to note, however, that men too are victims of abuse and that it is unacceptable in any form.

Scope and Extent of the Problem

Accurate statistics on domestic abuse are difficult to obtain because many victims never report the abuse. Victims do not report for many reasons, including shame, embarrassment, fear of retaliation, feeling as though the abuse is their fault, language barriers, the feeling that no one will believe them, lack of familiarity with laws and help services, distrust of authorities, and more.

It is estimated that one-third of the world's women will endure an abusive relationship during their lifetime. According to a major global study coordinated by the World Health Organization in 2005, 20 to 50 percent of the world's women had endured one or more form of gender-based violence, and 40 to 70 percent of the homicides of women across the world are committed by intimate partners. In 2005, Amnesty International reported that nearly one woman per hour is killed from domestic violence in the Russian Federation. This totals approximately 14,000 women annually. An estimated 70 percent of Russian women report being subjected to psychological, physical, sexual, or economic abuse. As of 2005, Russia had no law prohibiting domestic violence (Russia: One woman an hour being killed…, 2005).

In many South Asian countries, domestic violence is common and stems from traditional cultural beliefs that stress that women should be submissive to men. In Cambodia, for instance, women may still be encouraged to follow Chbab Srey, a code which teaches them to obey and respect their husbands and that, if he becomes violent, it is her fault because she failed in her wifely duties. Although Cambodia criminalized domestic violence in 2005, the law provides no specific penalty for violations. In China, domestic violence may be the result of women earning a higher level of education than men, Indian society remains quite patriarchal, with girls and women suffering numerous forms of oppression and violence. Even in Western Europe, generally a more developed region, the World Health Organization found in 2001 that between 20 and 50 percent of women have suffered from at least one form of abuse. In South Africa, Amnesty International reported that every six hours, a woman is killed by a husband or boyfriend (Amnesty International, 2005).

The 2005 World Health Organization study was the first major multicountry examination of domestic abuse. Researchers interviewed 24,000 women in 10 countries: Bangladesh, Brazil, Ethiopia, Japan, Namibia, Peru, Samoa, Serbia and Montenegro, Thailand, and the United Republic of Tanzania. In addition to identifying shockingly high rates of abuse all over, the study found specific risk factors. Individual factors placing women at risk included education, financial autonomy, previous victimization, social supports, and personal empowerment. Male partners' level of communication, substance use and abuse, employment status, and history of violence were risk factors. Socially, the degree of economic inequality between men and women, women's mobility and autonomy, attitudes about gender roles, level of male-to-male aggression, and family and community attitudes toward domestic violence were connected to rates of abuse. Twenty percent of the women interviewed had never spoken about the abuse before.

Risk Factor=Female

Anyone can be a victim of domestic abuse. Yet, as Heise (1989) explained, "This is not random violence; the risk factor is being female" (p. 13). That is, women and girls are at greatest risk. Typical estimates are that females constitute 85 percent of domestic violence victims in the United States. The remaining 15 percent of victims includes males being abused by females and males being abused by other males in gay relationships. In some years, domestic violence accounts for 20 percent of all nonfatal violent crime experienced by women in the United States. Rates of abuse are similar among homosexual relationships. Studies vary as to whether specific racial or ethnic groups are at greater risk to experience abuse, but it is clear that societal racism impacts victims' abilities to receive help. Victims of color may endure racism in the legal system, in health care, in education, and even in social services and shelters. They may fear that reporting the abuse will reinforce negative stereotypes about their racial or ethnic group. Some may endure additional pressure to keep their family together because of stereotypes about one-parent households. A historical lack of trust of authorities may increase the likelihood that victims of color will not report abuse to police. Similarly, classism affects the likelihood that victims will receive the support they need to remain safe from abuse. People making less money lack financial opportunities to leave abusers and support themselves. Studies have repeatedly shown that significant portions of women receiving welfare benefits have experienced abuse, with figures ranging from 19 to 33 percent. Affluent women may face very different but no less challenging barriers to reporting abuse and receiving help. Research has shown that this group is least likely to report abuse due to shame and embarrassment related to their position in society. Many blame themselves, asserting that abuse does not happen to people like them. Often, affluent victims are totally financially dependent on their partners. Negative stereotypes about the poor may result in heightened shame and self-blame, however, those with more resources may believe that it is only the poor who endure abuse.

Research has repeatedly shown that immigrants as a whole are at greater risk to endure abuse in intimate partner relationships, although data are not clear as to whether people from any particular region or country are more at risk. Immigrant victims may find it difficult to report abuse due to language barriers, financial instability, lack of knowledge of legal rights, fear of deportation, cultural values, and other reasons. Native Americans living on reservations are also at increased risk. Located largely in rural areas spread out over miles, victims may find reporting abuse and leaving abusers challenging due to lack of transportation, scarcity of resources, and complex jurisdictional issues.

Elder victims also suffer unique difficulties. Some were raised with the idea that abuse is normal and something people must learn to live with. They may have no financial resources of their own and may endure pressures from adult children to keep the relationship with an abusive spouse or partner together. Dating violence among young people, or abuse involving two people ages 14 to 22 in a dating relationship, is one of the fastest-growing types of abuse. Estimates are that 30 percent of teen relationships are abusive. Teenagers may not know that what they are experiencing is abuse, mistaking jealousy or even violence for love. A growing body of literature has documented the difficulties for victims with disabilities who have suffered domestic violence. Some may have a hard time communicating, and stereotypes about those with disabilities may make it difficult for victims to be believed. Shelters and other social services may not have made appropriate accommodations for victims with mental or physical disabilities.

Global Gender Inequalities

Far from just an individual or private matter, domestic abuse occurs within the context of a world in which women are still oppressed. Kirk and Okazawa-Rey (2007) explain that "macro-level inequalities are present in violence at the micro level" (p. 250). Violence against women begins before birth, as in the sex-selective abortions that are not uncommon (albeit illegal) in China, India, and the Republic of Korea. Female infanticide, emotional and physical abuse, and differential access to food, vaccinations, and medical care are another form of violence against women. Young girls suffer when they are forced into marriages or must undergo painful female genital mutilation, endure sexual or physical abuse by family members, or are sold or pushed into prostitution. In adolescence, girls suffer abuse, sexual violence, sexual harassment, forced prostitution, and are disproportionately the victims of human traffickers. Women of reproductive age (and increasingly, young girls) may endure marital rape, acid attacks, honor killings, dowry abuse, and more, while elderly women suffer from elder abuse and neglect.

Worldwide, women still lack equal rights and may be exploited in the home, workplace, schools, and in other institutions. Abuse of women by their husbands is usually deeply rooted in patriarchy. Men have traditionally been viewed as the rulers of their homes and women were to obey. It wasn't until the 1970s in the United States and the United Kingdom that activists were able to kick off a movement that began to counter the patriarchal norms and raise awareness about abuse. Yet societal patriarchy remains, to lesser and larger degrees, virtually everywhere across the globe. It manifests itself in many ways—gender inequalities in pay, access to work, political representation, educational opportunities, for instance—and is particularly acute in women's global access to justice, or at least, to justice that protects them and holds assailants and abusers accountable. Take this example: In 1992, an 18-year-old Italian woman alleged that a 45-year-old driving instructor took her to a remote location outside of Naples and raped her. According to the Third Division of the Italian Supreme Court, she could not actually have been raped because she was wearing blue jeans, which, according to the court "cannot be easily removed and certainly it is impossible to pull them off if the victim is fighting against her attacker with all her available force" (In Rowland, 2004, p. 596). And thus no justice for her; instead, like so many other women, she was blamed for her own assault.

Even before birth, females face tremendous discrimination. Globally, more than 100 million women are missing, according to Nobel Prize–winning economist Amartya Sen. Other studies put the number between 60 million and 101 million. That is, babies known to be females are never brought into the world. While females outnumber males in more developed nations because they tend to live longer, in poorer regions of the world males outnumber females by significant margins. For instance, China has 107 males for every 100 females. The ratio in India is 108 to 100 and in Pakistan, 111 to 100. These disparities are the result of several factors. Parents may be less likely to take infant daughters to doctors or for vaccinations. Sons are considered economically indispensable, while females are not. Since ultrasound technology has been available in these regions, women are finding out the sex of their babies and aborting girls. Sex-selective abortion is illegal, and laws in China and India prohibit doctors and ultrasound technicians from telling pregnant women the sex of their child, but some still do. In sum, more girls have been killed due to abortion and infanticide in the last 50 years simply because of their sex than all the men killed in all the battles of the twentieth century (Kristof & WuDunn, 2009).

Women suffer in childbirth, in part because in many regions of the world, they are left alone, with no prenatal or labor care, to endure the process. This, too, may result in fistulas that leave the women incontinent. Kristof and WuDunn (2009) tell the story of Mahabouba, who was just 14 when she was pregnant and couldn't afford a midwife and so tried to have her baby herself. Her pelvis was undeveloped, however, and after seven days of labor she was unconscious. The baby's head was stuck, and the result was that Mahabouba had lost circulation in her pelvis, a part of which had rotted. When she regained consciousness, Mahabouba found her baby was dead, and she had no control over her bladder or bowels. She was told by locals that she was cursed and was forced to live in a tent on the outside of the village, purposely left with the door off so the hyenas would eat her. She managed to crawl in the direction of a missionary village, and a day later was rushed to Addis Ababa's Fistula Hospital, where many other women waited for repair of the same problem. While it costs just $300 to repair a fistula, and about 90 percent are repairable, many women never see a doctor. Instead, these women find their lives basically over, as they are forced to live by themselves, ostracized because of their smell, and many die of infection or starve to death.

There are so many female circumcisions, that approximately every ten seconds, a different girl somewhere in the world endures this painful process. The girl is typically pinned down, her legs pulled apart, and someone with no training and no anesthetics uses a knife or razor blade to slice off a portion or all of her genitals. This practice is found in parts of Africa and is designed to minimize women's sexual pleasure, thus supposedly making her less promiscuous. In the late 1970s and 1980s, laws against female genital mutilation (FGM) were passed in 15 African countries. Yet, despite a law passed in Guinea in the 1960s, no one has ever been prosecuted for the offense, and some 99 percent of Guinean women have endured FGM. While Sudan prohibited the practice since 1946, more than 90 percent of Sudanese girls are estimated to have been cut (UNICEF, 2008).

In some parts of the world, rape and sexual assault are used as tools of control. Rape itself is widespread across the globe, with estimates that 21 percent of Ghanian women's first introduction to sex was via rape. In Nigeria, 17 percent of women have endured rape or an attempted rape by the age of 19, while 21 percent of South African women have been raped by age 15. In Ethiopia, if a young man doesn't have a bride price (like a dowry paid by men) but is interested in a young girl, or if he thinks her family won't accept him, he and some friends might kidnap and rape her. She will be considered "ruined," which improves the young man's bargaining position, and the chance that he will suffer any legal consequences is minimal (Kristof & WuDunn, 2009).

In Darfur, the Janjaweed militias gang-raped women, then cut off their ears or otherwise mutilated them to mark them as rape victims. Women who report the rapes may suffer punishment, as in the cases when women are penalized for fornication because they engaged in sex before marriage and could not produce the required four eyewitnesses to testify they were raped. The United Nations estimates that 90 percent of girls over the age of three were sexually assaulted during the civil war in Liberia. Doctors who treat these women often advise them not to report to police, as the police are likely to rape them as well. Women in refugee camps in Rwanda, Darfur, and elsewhere fear being raped whenever they leave their camps, which they must do to get firewood and water. The Democratic Republic of Congo is perhaps the world capital of rape, as militias "discovered that the most cost-effective way to terrorize civilian populations is to conduct rapes of stunning brutality. Frequently the Congolese militias rape women with sticks or knives or bayonets, or else they fire their guns into the women's vaginas" (Kristof & WuDunn, 2009, p. 84). Among the many ways these victims suffer, they often endure painful and degrading fistulas, or tears in their bodies that leave them leaking urine and feces. As Kristof and WuDunn (2009) note, "Mass rape is as effective as slaughtering people, yet it doesn't leave corpses that lead to human rights prosecutions. And rape tends to undermine the victim groups' tribal structures, because leaders lose authority when they can't protect the women. In short, rape becomes a tool of war in conservative societies precisely because female sexuality is so sacred. Codes of sexual honor, in which women are valued based on their chastity, ostensibly protect women, but in fact they create an environment in which women are systematically dishonored" (p. 83). The threat of rape is also a tool of control. For example, in Kenya, women must pay for round-the-clock security because political enemies often have them raped.

Although honor killings are illegal, they are not uncommon in the Middle East, South, and Southeast Asia. The UN Population Fund has estimated some 5,000 honor killings occur each year, although it is likely much more because so many are considered suicides. Kristof and WuDunn (2009) offer the story of Du'a Aswad, a Kurdish girl from the north of Iraq. At age 17, she fell in love with a Sunni Arab boy. While no one knows if they slept together, her family assumed they did, and, with the encouragement of religious leaders, eight men stoned her to death in front of a large crowd that included security forces who did nothing to stop it. Honor rapes are also common. These are rapes intended to disgrace or demean the victim or as a way to punish entire families for real or perceived indiscretions, as in the case of Mukhtar Mai (included in this volume), who was gang-raped as a way to punish her brother.

The first documented acid attack occurred in Bangladesh in 1967, and while specific data documenting the frequency of such attacks is hard to find, it is by no means uncommon in South and Southeast Asia. Globally, the "cult of virginity" is widespread. Numerous religious texts advocate stoning girls to death if they fail to bleed on their wedding night or selling them into slavery if they lose their virginity.

It is not just men who are culpable for these forms of violence. In fact, research has shown that women may choose to have their female babies aborted out of fear their husbands will leave them or concern that baby girls are less prestigious. Women are the ones who make decisions about getting their daughters vaccinated. Women own or at least manage many brothels, and reports have shown women were involved in at least one-quarter of the gang rapes during the Sierra Leone civil war, typically luring women and girls to the rape site and restraining them during the act. Similar participation has been documented in Iraq and Haiti. Data have shown that in some places, women pledge support for domestic violence. One study found 62 percent of women in an Indian village supporting the practice. Globally, it is often mothers-in-law who use cruel corporal punishment against females and who participate in or even orchestrate honor killings and acid attacks. As Kristof and WuDunn (2009) pointed out, "women themselves absorb and transmit misogynistic values, just as men do. This is not a tidy world of tyrannical men and victimized women, but a messier realm of oppressive social customs adhered to by men and women alike" (p. 69).

Yet, as Kristof and WuDunn note, women are not the problem—they are the solution. Numerous studies show women to be the linchpins of economic development. When girls are educated and offered opportunities for work, it pays off. These girls delay marriage and pregnancy, resulting in lowered population. Since women tend to raise the children, more educated women do so in ways that are more progressive, resulting in offspring that are less likely to commit violent acts. And, importantly, they are less likely to be involved in abusive relationships.

Explaining Domestic Abuse

There are numerous explanations for abuse. Some focus on biological or psychological factors, while others address more sociological issues such as patriarchal systems and rigid gender roles. Most agree, however, that domestic abuse is generally the result of abusers' desire to obtain and maintain power and control over victims.Some have proposed that abusers suffer from certain types of personality disorders, such as borderline personality or antisocial personality disorders. Some studies have found almost 90 percent of batterers to have elevated scores on the Miller Clinical Multiaxial Inventory (MCMI), which indicates the likelihood that they suffer from a personality disorder, while others have found far lower rates. Dutton and Bodnarchuck (2005) contend that there is an "abusive personality," similar to borderline personality disorder, which is characterized by shame-based rage, a tendency to blame others, attachment anxiety, and sustained outbursts. They believe that abusers become violent when they fear abandonment, as they are excessively dependent on their partners for attention. Many have pointed to alcohol and drugs as a reason for abuse. Most experts recognize that there is a high correlation between abuse and alcohol, with alcohol being present in anywhere from 48 to 70 percent of cases. Rather than causal, however, researchers believe that abusers use the alcohol as an excuse. Alcohol may exacerbate the abuse, causing abusers to blow real or imagined problems out of proportion and lowering inhibitions. Because abuse is not caused by alcohol or drugs, though, it is incorrect to assume that sending abusers to rehabilitation or substance abuse interventions will stop it. Too often, however, courts do just that when sentencing abusers.

Social learning theories remain popular as a way of explaining abuse. According to these theories, males become abusers because they learned this behavior in their homes, while women seek out abusive partners because they learned the role of victim from their mothers. Social learning theories also emphasize that perpetrators and victims learn stereotypical gender roles and violence behavior from other sources, including media, athletic activities, and popular culture. There is no doubt that media plays a large role in perpetuating dangerous gender role stereotypes, as in advertisements that use images of beaten women to promote alcohol brands, video games in which the goal is to rape or murder, or music lyrics suggesting that "she had it coming." News media tends to describe abuse in passive terms and often uses language that blames victims for the abuse. Although experiencing abuse in the home does increase the risk that young people will later become involved in abusive relationships, many do not. Likewise, most people are exposed to similar media yet respond differently. Clearly, other explanations are required.

Other theories focus on biological explanations, asserting that abuse is either hereditary or the result of brain injuries. Genetic explanations have not been proven, but recent studies have found a difference between the brains of batterers who were abused as children and those who were not, suggesting that sustaining trauma as a child may alter the brain in ways that is connected to later violent behavior.

Family systems theory views the family as a dynamic organization made up of interdependent parts. Thus the behavior of one family member is affected by the response of other family members. According to this theory, the communication styles, conflict resolution techniques, and problem-solving skills of all family members must be addressed in order to truly understand why abuse occurs. Many feminists take issue with family systems theory, however, contending that it serves to blame victims. Feminists focus their explanation of domestic abuse on gender inequalities that occur in patriarchal cultures.

Forms of Abuse

Abuse can and does take many forms. In virtually all cases, abusers emotionally control their victims through such tactics as insults (at both the victim and loved ones), making hostile jokes, ignoring the victim's feelings, withholding approval, yelling, calling the victim derogatory names, blaming, minimizing, accusations, and more. Victims are typically isolated from family and friends. Abusers may isolate victims by literally imprisoning them in their homes, by moving them far away from supporters, by alienating those who might help the victim, and other tactics. Isolation is particularly acute for rural, Native American, and immigrant victims. Many victims endure sexual abuse, which can include but is not limited sexual assault, extreme criticism of sexual performance, constant demands for sexual activity, and chronic infidelity. In approximately 50 percent of abuse cases, victims endure physical abuse, which might include pinches, slaps, punches, bites, and more. Abusers may attempt to kill victims. In far too many cases, they succeed. Each year in the United States, an estimated 1,300 to 1,800 people are murdered as a result of domestic violence.

Who Are the Abusers?

Just as victims can be either female or male and come from any racial, ethnic, national, age, socioeconomic, religious, or educational group, so too can abusers. Most abusers do not have criminal records and may even be well liked and well established outside of the home. Common traits among male abusers include negative attitudes toward women, adherence to stereotypical gender roles, and a tendency to minimize or blame others for their violence. Research has shown that more patriarchal families experience more domestic abuse, whereas relationships that are more egalitarian in terms of power structure typically have the least.

Impact of Abuse

Victims of domestic abuse suffer in myriad ways. Psychologically, victims may experience lowered self-esteem and depression. Many develop unhealthy behaviors, such as substance abuse, unsafe sexual activity, and eating disorders. Physically, victims suffer from a host of problems, including ulcers, hypertension, skin disorders, chronic fatigue, back ailments, migraines, reproductive problems, and more. Some researchers, including psychologist Lenore Walker, believe victims suffer from learned helplessness. That is, victims feel helpless due to the repeated abuse and develop a distorted sense of reality that makes it difficult for them to leave abusers. In some cases, victims may suffer from post-traumatic stress disorder (PTSD), a condition characterized by feelings of reexperiencing a traumatic incident through recurrent dreams, recollections, or flashbacks. PTSD may involve sleep disturbances, outbursts of anger, difficulty concentrating, hypervigilance, exaggerated responses, and physiological reactions. Some believe that victims suffer from something like the Stockholm Syndrome, which is named after a situation in 1973 when four people who were held captive in a Stockholm bank vault for six days became attached to their captors and began to see them as friends. Yet others point out that abuse is far different from being held hostage, in that hostages tend not to have an intimate relationship with their captors and typically know that someone is helping advocate for them, trying to effect their release. In some cases, victims fight back. Occasionally, a victim kills his or her abuser. Although typically the victim is acting in self-defense, many are still arrested, prosecuted, and convicted. In about one-quarter of cases in which victims kill their abusers, they are in no imminent threat. This makes it difficult for legal professionals to believe they acted in self-defense. For instance, after years of enduring physical and verbal abuse, Judy Norman shot her husband while he was sleeping. Her lawyers argued she suffered from battered woman syndrome, but the judge refused to allow this defense, and Norman was convicted of manslaughter.

Domestic abuse impacts the entire community as well. It is the number one cause of women's homelessness. Victims use emergency health-care services eight times more often than do nonvictims, resulting in higher medical costs for everyone. Abuse breaks up families and disrupts communities. Children who witness or experience abuse are more likely to struggle in school and may eventually drop out. Those same children are at greater risk for involvement in delinquency. As Kristof and WuDunn (2009) point out, the failure to fully utilize half the world's skills and expertise because of global gender discrimination is, simply put, abominable.

Barriers to Leaving Abusers

One of the most frequently asked questions about abuse is why victims stay. In the 1920s, many people believed that only unintelligent victims stayed with abusers. In the 1930s and 1940s, it was believed that victims stayed because they were masochistic. Since the 1970s, most people have begun to realize that victims find it difficult to leave abusers and to remain free for many complex reasons, although simply asking the question puts the responsibility for ending abuse on the victim. Instead, we should be asking why abusers continue to beat, harass, and demean their victims.

Many victims fear retaliation by their abusers, a fear that is all too real given that the most dangerous time in an abusive relationship is when the victim is planning to leave, is leaving, or has just left the abuser. Abusers see this as a threat to the power and control they had maintained and may respond by increasing the frequency or severity of the abuse. It is at these times—for instance, when the abuser is served paperwork notifying him or her that the victim has a protection order, or when divorce papers are filed—that abusers may violently attack or even try to kill their victims.

Movement to End Abuse

Although women (and some men) had long spoken out about abuse and provided needed shelter and support to others who were enduring it, the battered women's movement gained steam in the 1970s in both the United Kingdom and the United States. An important part of the women's liberation movement, these women (and sometimes men) critiqued patriarchal systems that resulted in abuse of women. They called out law enforcement for their failure to respond to women, and they organized support systems. In the 1970s, 1980s, and 1990s, the world saw media attention to abuse; the development of crisis line, shelters, and other victim services; and the emergence of laws and training that helped police apprehend batterers and courts hold them accountable. More recent efforts have been made to address other forms of violence against women, including laws to prohibit female genital mutilation, human trafficking, acid attacks, honor killings, and more. As the movement has grown and evolved, greater effort has been placed on recognizing the unique needs of all types of victims, from children to elders, heterosexual to homosexual, poor to affluent, rural to urban, and more.

Although tragic, high-profile examples like the O. J. Simpson case in 1995 have called much-needed attention to the issue of domestic abuse. Simpson was acquitted of the June 13, 1994, murders of his former wife Nicole Brown Simpson and her friend Ronald Goldman, but the trial brought to light a lengthy history of domestic abuse. Nicole had made numerous calls to police, and O. J. was convicted and served two years' probation for a 1989 incident of abuse. In the week following Simpson's arrest for the murders, calls about domestic violence in Los Angeles increased 80 percent. States sought to enhance or add new legislation, such as New York's law that mandated arrest for persons committing domestic assault and required training for police. Colorado's new law, enacted in 1995, required police to take abusers into custody at the scene of violence and mandated arrest for the first violation of a restraining order, followed by jail time for subsequent violations. A bill that passed in California in 1995 increased by 10 times the funding for shelters and domestic abuse prosecutions.

One of the most celebrated pieces of legislation related to domestic abuse in the United States is the Violence Against Women Act (VAWA), which was initially signed into law by President Bill Clinton as part of the 1994 Crime Bill. One provision of VAWA is that women who are in the country illegally may self-petition for residency status or they can document a legitimate relationship and a history of abuse. This is essential for immigrant women, as many times abusers falsely promise to petition for their residency or use the threat of deportation as a tool of control. Passage of VAWA resulted in an almost immediate spike in calls from victims seeking help. The National Domestic Violence Hotline, which was established with VAWA, continues to receive some 22,000 calls per month (Strasser, 2012).

What More Is Needed?

Some 125 countries have enacted domestic violence laws, yet 603 million women live in the countries lacking legal protection from abuse. An average of 50 percent of surveyed men and women in countries without domestic violence legislation think it is sometimes justifiable for a man to beat his wife. In the countries that have laws, only 22 percent of people think it is acceptable. According to UN Women, 117 countries have equal pay laws, but on average, women are paid 10 to 30 percent less than men. There are 117 countries that outlaw sexual harassment in the workplace, yet 311 million women still work in places where there are no such protections. A third of women in the developing world are married or in some union by age 18, putting them at risk for early pregnancies and dangerous abuse. Only 52 countries have prohibited marital rape.

Although services for victims are far more extensive than they once were, many victims are still turned away from shelters or centers. Approximately 10 to 40 percent of those seeking assistance at a domestic violence shelter are turned away. Shelter staff believe that for every woman who calls a hotline or enters a shelter, 10 others are enduring abuse without seeking that help. Further, many shelters are not adequately prepared to deal with the unique needs of all victims. Elders, teens, persons with disabilities, LGBT persons, immigrants, and others might find that shelters do not make appropriate accommodations in regard to physical premises, training of staff, and/or services offered. There is still a huge shortage of shelters for male victims, which means that men suffering in abusive relationships either continue to suffer, find refuge with friends or family, or become homeless. Homeless shelters are not appropriate for victims of domestic violence in that they are open and well marked, not confidential, and not in secure, secret locations.

Victims in every state can obtain protective orders or restraining orders, although the process can be daunting. A 2005 study by the Department of Justice Bureau of Justice Statistics found that half of all protective orders are violated at least once, and many are violated routinely with no consequence.

Because many police agencies in the United States today use mandatory arrest policies, victims may be reluctant to call law enforcement out of fear that they too will be arrested. Despite decades of attention to these issues, it is still not uncommon to find police issuing minor warnings to abusers rather than taking abuse allegations seriously.

Although they can be a great place to identify abuse and to put victims in touch with needed support service, health-care providers still do not screen for abuse as often as they should. Courts sometimes fail to believe victims and thus do not hold abusers accountable. The entire legal process has often been said to revictimize.

Data from outside the United States is still inconsistent and insufficient, as many countries have yet to criminalize abuse or, if they have, do not enforce legislation. Many cultures still see abuse as a private matter, and thus victims are hesitant to report it. Research has shown abuse to be rampant in Latin America and the Caribbean, exacerbated by high rates of poverty, especially among indigenous women. Mexico only criminalized domestic violence in 2007, and significant gaps exist in much of the Latin American legislation. For instance, Peruvian law only covers those who are living together, and marital rape is not prohibited. Similarly, domestic abuse is a major problem in the Middle East and North Africa, where no country to date has criminalized all forms of domestic abuse. In some countries such as Iran, Syria, and Yemen, perpetrators of so-called honor crimes are treated leniently, if they are held accountable at all.

Since the mid-1980s, victim advocates have been emphasizing the need for coordinated community responses to abuse. Such responses accept that abuse is a community, not just personal, problem and thus requires a community-based intervention. Efforts involve bringing together key people and institutions with whom victims and abusers interact, including educators, law enforcement agencies, advocates, health-care providers, child protection services, social services, the business community, faith-based leaders, and more. In the 1990s and 2000s, efforts became more focused on prevention. There are three levels or tiers of prevention: (1) Primary prevention refers to stopping abuse before it occurs. This might include educational programs aimed at children to teach them about fair and healthy treatment of others, parenting support, and efforts to challenge gender role stereotypes. Primary prevention also includes advocacy and political action aimed at changing laws related to domestic abuse and promoting gender equality and human rights. (2) Secondary prevention involves targeting services to at-risk populations so as to reduce known risk factors. (3) Tertiary prevention, also known as intervention, involves minimizing the effects of abuse by supporting victims and their children and holding abusers accountable.

Increasingly, people are coming to see domestic violence as a human rights issue. States are required under international law to provide equal protection to all of their citizens. Domestic violence has also been viewed as a form of torture prohibited under international law. Specific treaties are applicable to domestic abuse. For instance, the International Covenant on Economic, Social, and Cultural Rights (ICESCR), passed by the UN General Assembly in 1966, prohibits sex discrimination, while the Convention on the Elimination of All Forms of Discrimination Against Women (CEDAW), adopted by the General Assembly in 1979, prohibits gender-based violence, including "physical, sexual and psychological violence occurring in the family, including battering, sexual abuse of female children in the household, dowry-related violence, marital rape, female genital mutilation and other traditional practices harmful to women." In 1994, the UN Commission on Human Rights appointed a special rapporteur on violence against women, its causes, and consequences. This special rapporteur is required to collect information about violence against women from multiple private and public sources, to disseminate that data, to make recommendations about measures and actions that can eliminate violence against women, and to work with other special rapporteurs, representatives, working groups, and independent experts of the UN Commission on Human Rights. In September 1995, the Fourth World Conference on Women adopted the Beijing Declaration and Platform of Action, which also addressed domestic abuse. The Beijing Platform has prompted some countries to make significant changes. For instance, Austria, Belarus, Bhutan, Hungary, Mexico, Portugal, and the Seychelles have all passed laws prohibiting marital rape, while Belarus, Russia, Poland and Zimbabwe have introduced shelters, refuges, and hotlines for victims. In April 1997, the UN Commission on Human Rights reiterated that governments cannot perpetrate any form of violence against women and have a duty to prevent, respond to, and punish perpetrators.

In their 2011–12 report, UN Women found 186 countries have ratified CEDAW to date, although 42 of them issued one or more reservation. Although the United States was actively involved in drafting CEDAW and President Jimmy Carter signed it on July 17, 1980, repeated attempts to ratify it have failed. A minimum of two-thirds of the Senate must vote to ratify for CEDAW to become binding on the United States. Opponents maintain that ratification would give the international community too much control over U.S. affairs. They maintain that CEDAW defines discrimination too broadly, which could result in frivolous lawsuits. Further, critics feel as though CEDAW would redefine "family," thus destroying the traditional family structure, and would interfere with parents' rights regarding how to raise their children. Proponents assert that CEDAW does none of these things but would instead be an important step, both in reality and symbolically, toward affirming gender equality.

In 2007, then-Senators Joseph Biden and Richard Lugar introduced into Congress the International Violence Against Women Act (IVAWA), which would provide funds for foreign aid devoted to preventing honor killings, bride burnings, acid attacks, mass rapes, genital cutting, and domestic violence. It would create an Office of Women's Global Initiatives within the Secretary of State's office in order to make gender violence a global priority.

Nonprofit organizations and nongovernmental organizations (NGOs) play a huge role in providing services to victims globally, as well as raising awareness through educational campaigns and outreach efforts. HEAL Africa, for instance, helps rape victims in the Congo. CARE fights FGM in Africa. While these efforts are both noble and important, sometimes they obscure the responsibility of governments to take action to end the many forms of violence, including domestic violence, that impact so many people across the globe. It is essential, then, that both efforts—the grassroots and the government-led—continue to occur and do so in ways that complement, not compete with, each other.

Kristof and WuDunn (2009) recommend that a modern movement for gender equality incorporate the following:

- Building a broad coalition that crosses liberal and conservative lines;
- Carefully and accurately publicizing results and challenges;
- Ensuring that helping women is not exclusive of helping men;
- Ensuring that American feminism focuses on these essential global human rights issues, not just civil rights concerns.

Taken seriously, these suggestions can improve the plight of not just women, but everyone.

Further Reading

Amnesty International. (2005). The impact of guns on women's lives. Retrieved September 17, 2012, from http://amnesty.ie/sites/default/files/report/2010/04/The%20Impact%20of%20Guns%20on%20Women%27s%20Lives.pdf

Dutton, D.G, & Bodnarchuk, M. (2005). Through a psychological lens: Personality disorder and spouse assault. In R. J. Gelles, D. R. Loseke, & M. Cavanaugh (Eds.), *Current controversies on family violence* (2nd ed., pp. 5–18). Newbury Park, CA: Sage.

Heise, L. (1989). International dimensions of violence against women. *Response*, 12 (1), pp. 3–11

Kirk, G., & Okazawa-Rey, M. (2007). *Women's lives, multicultural perspectives* (4th ed.). New York: McGraw-Hill.

Kristof, N., & WuDunn, S. (2009). *Half the sky: Turning oppression into opportunity for women worldwide*. New York, NY: Alfred A. Knopf.

Russia: One woman an hour being killed through domestic violence—new report calls for action. *Amnesty International UK*. Retrieved September 17, 2012, from http://www.amnesty.org.uk/news_details.asp?NewsID=16671

Strasser, A-R. (2012, September 13). After 18 years, Violence Against Women Act has saved countless lives. Retrieved September 17, 2012, from http://thinkprogress.org/justice/2012/09/13/844011/vawa-18-anniversary/?mobile=nc

UN Women (2012). 2011-12 Progress of the World's Women: In Pursuit of Justice. Retrieved June 17, 2012, from http://progress.unwomen.org/wp-content/uploads/2011/06/EN-Factsheet-Global-Progress-of-the-Worlds-Women.pdf

UNICEF. (2008). *Changing a harmful social convention: Female genital mutilation/cutting*. Retrieved September 17, 2012, from http://www.unicef-irc.org/publications/pdf/fgm_eng.pdf

Timeline of Significant Events Related to Domestic Violence and Abuse

753 BCE   Romulus, founder of Rome, formalizes the first law of marriage requiring women to obey their husbands and husbands to rule their wives as possessions.

200 BCE   The end of the Punic Wars sees advances for wealthy women, who were able to pursue politics, study philosophy, and join new religious movements while men were away. Husbands cannot beat wives without sufficient evidence for divorce. Those convicted of striking without reason must provide their wives monetary compensation.

300 CE   The Church fathers reestablish the husband's patriarchal authority and the patriarchal values of Roman and Jewish law. The Roman Emperor, Constantine the Great, has his wife burned alive when she is no longer of use to him.

               Excessive violence from either marital partner is grounds for divorce in the Roman Empire, although women had to prove the charge. Women are not considered men's property if the behavior is sufficiently terrible.

900–1300   Women in Medieval Europe are viewed as subhuman. All classes of men regularly beat their wives, with the support of the Church, which advised men to castigate their wives and beat them if they need correction.

1400s   Numerous documents advise "chivalrous" men to brutally beat their wives for committing any offense, not out of rage but from concern for her.

1500s   Lord Hale, an English Jurist, sets the tradition of nonrecognition of marital rape. He states that when women married, they "gave themselves to their husbands in contract, and could not withdraw that consent until they divorced. The husband cannot be guilty of a rape committed by himself upon his lawful wife, for by their mutual matrimonial consent a contract with wife hath given herself in this

1500s (*cont.*)	kind unto her husband, which she cannot retract." This is the basis of the "contractual consent" theory. Lord Hale burned women at the stake as witches and has been characterized as a misogynist.
Late 1500s	During the reign of Ivan the Terrible in Russia, the State Church sanctions the oppression of women by issuing a Household Ordinance that describes when and how a man might most effectively beat his wife. He is allowed to kill a wife or serf for disciplinary purposes. A half a century later, many Russian women fight back. When they kill their husbands for all the injustices they have been forced to endure, their punishment is to be buried alive with only their heads above the ground and left to die. It is not against the law for a husband to kill his wife.
1531	European religious reformer Martin Luther described women's place as in the home. Because men have broad shoulders and more narrow hips, Luther declared they possess intelligence that women lack.
1609	King James I of England declares that kings are like fathers who must be obeyed.
1641	The Puritans in Massachusetts establish the code of law called the Body of Liberties, which denounced husbands beating their wives unless they were under attack. Divorce is allowed, but physical cruelty is not ample evidence. Women seeking divorce must show they were dutiful and have not provoked their husbands.
1740	Concerted efforts made in the American colonies to protect citizens from violent crime outside of the home. Concern about wife and child abuse recedes.
1760s	English jurist William Blackstone's *Commentaries on the Laws of England* declares crime an act that produces mischief in civil society and proclaims private acts as outside the domain of law. Blackstone specifically addresses wife-beating, referring to it as necessary for chastising women but recommending it be done in moderation.
1776	Abigail Adams tells her husband, President John Adams, to "remember the ladies."
1792	In *A Vindication of the Rights of Women*, Mary Wollstonecraft calls for more education and for improvements in the way men treat women.
1800s	Based partly on a belief that there is a connection between alcohol and wife-beating, the American temperance movement begins.

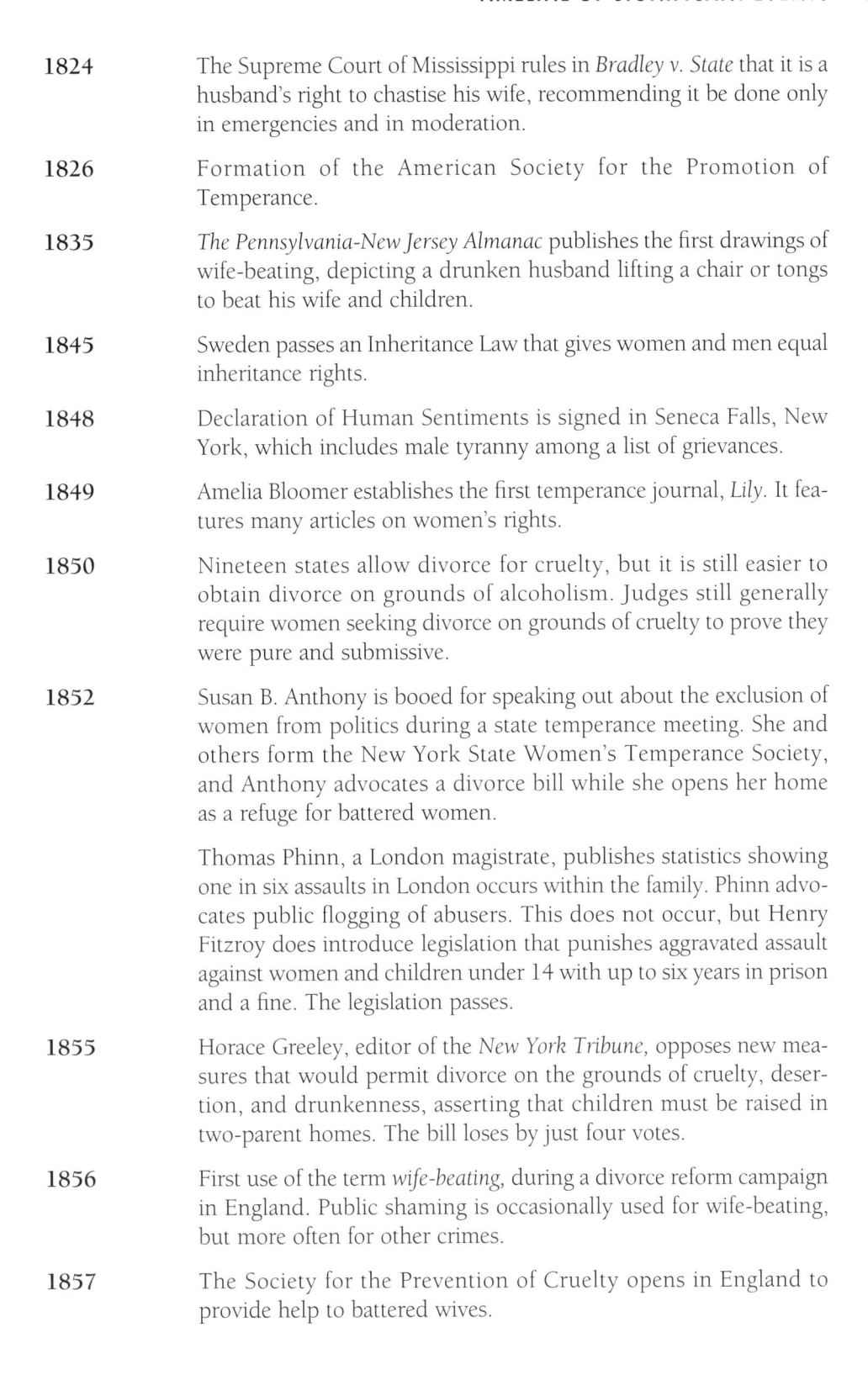

1824	The Supreme Court of Mississippi rules in *Bradley v. State* that it is a husband's right to chastise his wife, recommending it be done only in emergencies and in moderation.
1826	Formation of the American Society for the Promotion of Temperance.
1835	*The Pennsylvania-New Jersey Almanac* publishes the first drawings of wife-beating, depicting a drunken husband lifting a chair or tongs to beat his wife and children.
1845	Sweden passes an Inheritance Law that gives women and men equal inheritance rights.
1848	Declaration of Human Sentiments is signed in Seneca Falls, New York, which includes male tyranny among a list of grievances.
1849	Amelia Bloomer establishes the first temperance journal, *Lily*. It features many articles on women's rights.
1850	Nineteen states allow divorce for cruelty, but it is still easier to obtain divorce on grounds of alcoholism. Judges still generally require women seeking divorce on grounds of cruelty to prove they were pure and submissive.
1852	Susan B. Anthony is booed for speaking out about the exclusion of women from politics during a state temperance meeting. She and others form the New York State Women's Temperance Society, and Anthony advocates a divorce bill while she opens her home as a refuge for battered women.
	Thomas Phinn, a London magistrate, publishes statistics showing one in six assaults in London occurs within the family. Phinn advocates public flogging of abusers. This does not occur, but Henry Fitzroy does introduce legislation that punishes aggravated assault against women and children under 14 with up to six years in prison and a fine. The legislation passes.
1855	Horace Greeley, editor of the *New York Tribune*, opposes new measures that would permit divorce on the grounds of cruelty, desertion, and drunkenness, asserting that children must be raised in two-parent homes. The bill loses by just four votes.
1856	First use of the term *wife-beating*, during a divorce reform campaign in England. Public shaming is occasionally used for wife-beating, but more often for other crimes.
1857	The Society for the Prevention of Cruelty opens in England to provide help to battered wives.

1860	Susan B. Anthony helps the wife of a Massachusetts legislator escape abuse, which prompts Elizabeth Cady Stanton to introduce 10 new resolutions at the 1860 New York state convention in support of a new divorce bill. The onset of the Civil War in 1861 kills her proposals.
1864	A North Carolina court declares that a husband was allowed to choke his wife in order to make her behave, as no permanent damage was inflicted and the violence was not "excessive."
1866	A North Carolina court amends the law to allow a man to beat his wife with a stick as large as his finger but not larger than his thumb, which is promoted as progressive because it limits the violence a husband can perpetrate against his wife.
	The American Society for the Prevention of Cruelty to Animals is formed. It predates the founding of the Society for the Prevention of Cruelty to Children, established in 1875. Both predate any organization aimed at preventing cruelty to women.
1870	England's Married Women's Property Act allows women to keep their property when they divorce.
1871	Through a court decision, Alabama becomes the first state to rescind the legal right of men to beat their wives.
1874	A North Carolina court follows Alabama's lead but only allows courts to intervene when permanent injury has been inflicted.
1876	Lucy Stone, editor of *Woman's Journal,* a Boston newspaper, begins publishing a list of crimes against women and denouncing the leniency with which wife-beating is treated.
1878	In her article "Wife Torture in England," suffragist Frances Power Cobbe shocks readers with graphic depictions of wife-beating and lobbies for a bill allowing legal separation and child custody to women who have been beaten. The Matrimonial Causes Act passes but only allows divorce when the husband has been convicted of aggravated assault and the wife is considered to be in grave danger. Women who have committed adultery are not eligible for separation or child custody.
1880	Lucy Stone and her husband Henry Blackwell lobby for a bill similar to England's Matrimonial Causes Act. Stone and Blackwell join the movement for women's right to vote, believing that divorce reform and the reduction of abuse will occur when women vote off the bench those judges who treated abusers leniently.

1885	Founding of Chicago's Protective Agency for Women and Children, which provides legal and personal assistance to victims.
1896	Foundation of the National Association of Colored Women.
1900–1920	Establishment of family or domestic relations courts across the United States. Many see each partner as equally at fault in domestic abuse cases.
1911	The first family court is created in Buffalo, New York.
1912	Founding of U.S. Children's Bureau.
1919	U.S. women earn the right to vote with passage of the Nineteenth Amendment.
1921	In Sweden, marriage legislation gives women legal independence and equal rights as parents.
1923	England's Matrimonial Causes Act allows men and women to use the same grounds for divorce.
1930s	Beginning of era of influence of Freudian psychology. Helene Deutsch, a Freudian disciple, argues that women are masochistic, which explains that women secretly enjoy the pain of abuse and hence stay with violent husbands. Deutsch's views dominate the discourse about domestic abuse through the 1950s.
1931	Jane Addams wins the Nobel Peace Prize.
1945	Eleanor Roosevelt advocates for women's issues as part of the U.S. delegation to the United Nations.
1946	United Nations establishes the Commission on the Status of Women.
1960s	Pediatrician C. Henry Kempe and four colleagues publish "The Battered-Child Syndrome," which draws much attention to child abuse. Violence against wives is not addressed.
1960	*Palmer v. State* finds a woman responsible for involuntary manslaughter because she did not remove her toddler from an abusive domestic situation.
1961	Founding of human rights watchdog Amnesty International in London.
	President John F. Kennedy creates the President's Commission on the Status of Women. He appoints Eleanor Roosevelt as chair.

1962	New York State transfers domestic violence cases to civil court, where convicted wife-beaters receive shorter sentences than those assaulting strangers.
1963	Foundation of Mary Kay Cosmetics Inc.
	Congress passes Equal Pay Act.
1964	John Snell, Richard Rosenwald, and Ames Robey's "The Wife-Beater's Wife: A Study of Family Interaction" calls women who claim to have been assaulted by their husbands "castrating," "masculine," "frigid," "passive," and "masochistic."
	The first battered women's shelter in the world, Refuge House, opens in London.
	Sex discrimination in employment is prohibited by the Civil Rights Act.
1966	Formation of National Organization for Women (NOW).
1967	Affirmative Action is expanded to include gender.
1969	San Diego State offers the first BA program in women's studies.
	California adopts "no fault" divorce.
1971	Erin Pizzey establishes the Chiswick Centre in London, starting the shelter movement.
	First *Ms.* magazine is published.
	Copenhagen's first shelter, Kvindehuset (The Women's House), is opened by the Red Stockings, the Danish Women's Liberation organization.
1972	Female activists from the United States visit the Chiswick Centre in London and establish Women's Advocates in St. Paul, Minnesota, as the first U.S. shelter for battered women.
	Title IX prohibits gender discrimination in federally funded education programs.
1973	A survivor of 10 years of marital abuse, Nancy Kirk-Gormley establishes the National Organization for Women (NOW) task force on battered women.
	Rita Simon publishes her work about the Liberation Hypothesis, arguing women will become more criminal as they have greater opportunities in society.
	Roe v. Wade decision ends prohibition on abortion.

TIMELINE OF SIGNIFICANT EVENTS

1973–1976 Opening of shelters across the United States. Twenty battered women's shelters in operation by the end of 1976.

1974 With funds from the General Aid Office of the Netherlands, the first battered women's shelter is opened in Rotterdam.

After two women refuse to stop squatting in two abandoned houses, Elsie is opened as the first battered women's shelter in Australia.

Erin Pizzey publishes the first book about domestic abuse, *Scream Quietly or the Neighbours Will Hear*.

Former prime minister of Japan Eisaku Sato wins the Nobel Peace Prize, despite his wife saying he beats her weekly.

1975 First National Family Violence Survey.

Susan Brownmiller authors her book *Against Our Will: Men, Women, and Rape*.

Brazil passes a penal code that prohibits husbands from selling, renting, or gambling away their wives.

1976 The first International Tribunal on Crimes Against Women convenes in Brussels, attracting 8,200 women from 33 countries.

A series of lawsuits against police are filed, demanding police receive training specific to domestic violence.

England's Domestic Violence and Matrimonial Proceedings Act gives women the right to obtain civil protection orders for domestic violence.

Del Martin's *Battered Wives* attributes abuse to societal sexism, a position that is widely adopted by the battered women's movement.

Pennsylvania establishes the first statewide domestic violence coalition.

Nebraska passes first law prohibiting marital rape.

La Casa de la Madres in San Francisco, California, is opened as the first battered women's shelter established by women of color.

1977 On March 9, after enduring more than 13 years of horrific abuse by husband Mickey, Francine Hughes sets fire to their bedroom while he sleeps. She is found not guilty by reason of temporary insanity. The story is later made into the film *The Burning Bed*, which aired on national television in 1987.

The first rape crisis center opens in London.

1977 *(cont.)*	Oregon is the first state to mandate arrest for domestic violence through its Family Abuse Prevention Act. The Act also includes provisions for women to obtain restraining orders.
	In England, the Homeless Persons Act is passed, which gives a battered woman priority in obtaining housing. Many women live in refuges for up to nine months due to housing shortages.
1978	During the U.S Commission on Civil Rights' Consultation on Battered Women: Issues of Public Policy, the National Coalition Against Domestic Violence (NCADV) is organized with the goal of increasing financial aid to shelters, sharing information, and supporting research about abuse.
	Florida becomes the first state to levy a tax on marriage licenses to support battered women's shelters.
	Enactment of Pregnancy Protection Act.
	Foundation of the Women's Aid Federation of Northern Ireland.
	Captain Nancy Raiha and others start a domestic violence program at Fort Campbell, Kentucky, the first of its kind of a military facility.
	Minnesota is the first state to allow probable cause, or warrantless, arrest in cases of domestic abuse.
	John Rideout is the first person indicted for marital rape in Oregon. He is acquitted.
	Lenore Walker authors *The Battered Woman*.
1979	President Jimmy Carter establishes the Office of Domestic Violence, with a budget of $90,000 for grants, research, and dissemination of information.
	First U.S. Congressional hearings on domestic violence.
	UN General Assembly adopts the Convention on the Elimination of All Forms of Violence Against Women (CEDAW).
Late 1970s	By 1980, all but six states have laws addressing domestic violence.
1980	First NCADV national conference in Washington, D.C.
	Duluth, Minnesota, begins its Domestic Abuse Intervention Project, which involves a coordinated system of intervention including police, prosecutors, civil and criminal court judges, and probation officers. It also involves a batterer's intervention component and

parenting education programs. The Duluth program becomes a model for domestic violence intervention around the United States.

The Air Force establishes the Office on Family Matters to address domestic violence.

California becomes the first state to mandate treatment for convicted batterers.

1981 President Ronald Reagan cuts the Office of Domestic Violence due to budget cuts and a lack of support soon after taking office.

The first shelter for Asian women, Everywoman's Shelter, is established in Los Angeles by a Filipina victim, Nilda Rimote.

NCADV declares October 17 a Day of Unity on behalf of battered women, which eventually expands to Domestic Violence Awareness Month.

1981–82 Minneapolis domestic violence experiment finds that arrest is the best strategy in domestic violence cases.

1982 Founding of National Organization of Men Against Sexism (NOMAS).

1983 Federal funding for shelters is included in the Child Abuse and Prevention Treatment Act (CAPTA), but less than one-fourth of the original request is funded.

Publication of the Minneapolis Domestic Violence Experiment (MDVE), funded by the National institute of Justice, shows that arrest is more effective than other alternatives in reducing the likelihood of repeat violence. The study prompts many police departments to establish pro-arrest policies.

1984 Florida becomes the first state to mandate consideration of spousal abuse in child custody determinations.

The federal Family Violence Prevention and Services Act earmarks funding for domestic violence services.

1985 U.S. Surgeon General C. Everett Koop calls domestic violence a public health problem. His pronouncement and subsequent work prompt the Centers for Disease Control to include domestic violence research and eventually prevention in its body of work.

Tracey Thurman, who had called numerous times for help from the City of Torrington, Connecticut, police and who was left permanently disfigured and partially paralyzed by her ex-husband when he attacked her in the presence of police officers, wins a lawsuit that sparks more pro-arrest policies across the nation.

1985 (cont.)	The *Wall Street Journal* publishes a series of articles about the more than 19 years of abuse Charlotte Fedders experienced at the hands of her husband, John Fedders, Chief of the Enforcement Division of the Securities and Exchange Commission for the Reagan administration.
	First book about domestic violence and African American women, *Chain, Chain, Change,* is published by Evelyn White.
	In Seattle, the first support group for battered lesbians is started.
1986	India includes dowry killing as a form of domestic violence.
	Susan Schechter founds first program in the United States devoted to child abuse among families in which domestic violence occurs.
1987	NCADV established a national domestic violence hotline, using funds from Johnson & Johnson and from a national fund-raising effort called Shelter Aid.
	Naming the Violence by Kerry Lobel is the first book about lesbian battering.
	Expert testimony to explain the mental state and behavior of rape victims is allowed for the first time in *State v. Ciskie* to show why the victim did not call the police immediately. The defendant was convicted on four counts of rape.
	Founding of Global Fund for Women.
1988	Congress amends the Victims of Crime Act to require state victim compensation plans to include victims of domestic violence.
1989	Marc Lepine kills 14 women at Canada's Ecole Polytechnique.
1990	The U.S. Immigration and Naturalization Service first recognizes domestic violence as grounds for asylum.
	Democratic Governor Richard F. Celeste of Ohio grants clemency to 25 women who were convicted of killing or assaulting their abusive husbands or companions.
	Senator Joe Biden of Delaware and Representative Barbara Boxer introduced the Violence Against Women Act in the 101st Congress.
	The Cape Cod Women's Agenda hangs 31 painted t-shirts on a clothesline in Hyannis, Massachusetts, giving birth to the Clothesline Project.
1991	The American Medical Association (AMA) announces the beginning of its public health campaign addressing family violence.

Founding of White Ribbon Campaign in Canada.

In England, Southall Black Sisters launch the "Free Kiranjit Ahluwalia" campaign after she was given a life sentence for setting her abusive husband on fire. She is released in 1992 after her conviction is changed to manslaughter.

Liz Claiborne Inc. begins providing funding and support related to domestic violence.

Israel passes the Israeli Law for Prevention of Family Violence that allows for protection orders for physical, sexual, or psychological abuse.

Anita Hill testifies before Congress about the sexual harassment she endured from now Supreme Court Justice Clarence Thomas.

Israel is the first Middle Eastern country to enact domestic violence legislation by passing the Israeli Law for Prevention of Family Violence.

1992	Roman Catholic bishops in the United States issue the Church's first statement that the Bible does not condone spousal abuse.
	The AMA's Council on Scientific Affairs recommends that physicians routinely screen female patients to identify abuse.
	Domestic violence law enacted in the Cayman Islands.
	Systematic rape of women used by Bosnian Serbs.
	Belize passes law addressing domestic violence.
1993	Beginning July 5, all states now prohibit marital rape.
	The United Nations issues the Declaration on the Elimination of Violence Against Women.
	President Bill Clinton signs the Family Medical Leave Act (FMLA).
	After a study by the Family Violence Prevention Fund finds that emergency department staff are not adequately trained regarding domestic violence screening and protocols, California passes AB 890 requiring training of health care providers.
	Jackson Katz founds Mentors in Violence Prevention, a bystander empowerment program targeted at athletes but used with other populations to empower action to stop domestic violence.
1994	*Defending Our Lives,* a documentary about women who are in prison for killing their abusers, wins the Academy Award for best documentary.

TIMELINE OF SIGNIFICANT EVENTS

1994 *(cont.)*   Nicole Brown Simpson and Ronald Goldman are murdered on June 13 in Brentwood, California.

President Bill Clinton signs into law the Violence Against Women Act.

England prohibits marital rape.

The United Nations appoints a special rapporteur on Violence Against Women.

International Criminal Tribunals in the former Yugoslavia and Rwanda are established and include sexual violence.

Inter-American Convention on the Prevention, Punishment and Eradication of Violence against Women (known as the Convention of Belem do Para) is adopted.

Chile adopts domestic violence law.

Argentina prohibits domestic violence.

1995   President Clinton opens the Violence Against Women Office at the Department of Justice and appoints Bonnie Campbell as its first director.

UN Fourth World Conference on Women in Beijing.

Australia passes Family Law Reform Act.

Bolivia passes law on domestic violence.

Ecuador enacts legislation on domestic violence.

Panama passes law defining crimes of intrafamily violence.

O. J. Simpson is acquitted of the murders of Nicole Brown Simpson and Ronald Goldman.

World Health Organization (WHO) establishes working group on female genital mutilation (FGM).

National Alliance to End Sexual Violence forms.

1996   Congress passes the Personal Responsibility and Work Opportunity Reconciliation Act, reforming the "welfare" system. Provisions are included to allow flexibility for victims of domestic violence.

Ireland adopts domestic violence legislation.

Costa Rica adopts domestic violence legislation.

Guatemala adopts domestic violence legislation.

El Salvador enacts legislation related to domestic violence.

Enactment of Austria's federal law on protection against family violence.

Two members of Congress propose legislation requiring professional athletes to lead a campaign against domestic violence. The legislation is not passed, in part due to opposition from the National Collegiate Athletic Association (NCAA).

Break the Cycle, focusing on teen dating violence awareness, education, prevention, and resources, is formed in Los Angeles.

1997 O. J. Simpson is found liable for the deaths of Nicole Brown Simpson and Ronald Goldman and ordered to pay $33 million to their families.

Belgium passes law addressing couples violence.

Bermuda passes law addressing domestic violence protection orders.

Honduras enacts legislation related to domestic violence.

President Clinton signs an antistalking law.

First Lady Hillary Clinton and Secretary of State Madeleine Albright found Vital Voices.

Founding of Prevention Institute.

Hong Kong adopts domestic violence legislation.

1998 Jordan is the first Arab nation to enact domestic violence legislation.

Taiwan adopts domestic violence legislation.

The International Criminal Court is established to prosecute sexual violence and gender crimes within the context of war crimes, crimes against humanity, and genocide and establishes a Gender and Children's Unit to improve investigation and prosecution of crimes related to gender inequality, including rape and other forms of sexual violence perpetrated against women and children.

1999 November 25th is designated as United Nations International Day for the elimination of violence against women.

Members of the National Task Force on Violence Against Women protest outside of Eric Clapton's Washington D.C. performance because of lyrics that glorify domestic violence.

1999 *(cont.)*		Jessica Gonzales's abusive husband kidnaps and murders her three daughters. Police fail to respond to repeated attempts to get them to enforce the restraining order against her husband.

Brunei passes Married Women Act.

2000 Beijing Plus Five conference held in New York to address domestic violence, trafficking, forced marriage, female circumcision, and honor killings.

U.S. Supreme Court invalidates part of VAWA that gave victims the right to sue their attackers.

Founding of Incite! Women of Color Against Violence.

Colombia adopts a series of laws related to domestic violence.

Commonwealth of the Northern Marianas adopts domestic violence laws.

Passage of UN Security Council Resolution 1325, which calls for special protective measures for women and girls in armed conflict and emphasized the responsibility of all nations to put an end to impunity for perpetrators.

2001 China adopts domestic violence legislation.

Germany enacts legislation providing civil law protection against domestic violence and harassment.

2002 President Clinton signs the 2000 Violence Against Women Act.

The Office on Violence Against women becomes a unit separate from the Department of Justice, allowing higher priority and visibility.

CDC issues its Costs of Intimate Partner Violence Against Women in the United States report.

The U.S. Postal Service issues a Stop Family Violence Stamp to help raise funds for prevention.

CDC's DELTA Project begins focusing on primary prevention of domestic violence.

Bangladesh passes two laws addressing acid attacks.

Chad passes a law on reproductive health that includes domestic violence.

2003 Establishment of End Violence Against Women (EVAW) International.

England prohibits female genital mutilation.

	Dominican Republic adopts legislation establishing shelters for men, women, children, and adolescent victims of domestic violence.
	The World Health Organization releases the report *The Economic Dimensions of Interpersonal Violence,* finding, among other things, that in some countries, 70 percent of female murder victims were killed by a current or former husband or partner.
	The New York Court of Appeals finds that the child welfare system cannot remove a child from the home simply because domestic violence is occurring.
	Brazil law requires the establishment of domestic violence hotlines.
2004	Turkey mandates life sentences for those convicted of honor killings.
	The Commission on Human Rights appoints a special rapporteur on trafficking in persons, focused largely on women and children.
2005	New CDC report finds that homicide is the second leading cause of traumatic death for pregnant and postpartum women.
	U.S. Supreme Court rules in *Town of Castle Rock, Colorado v. Jessica Gonzales* that victims cannot sue police departments for failing to enforce restraining orders.
	World Health Organization study documents widespread domestic violence globally.
	U.S. Supreme Court rules that victims are not entitled to enforcement of their restraining orders.
	Mexico passes legislation related to medical professionals' detection of domestic violence.
	Bosnia and Herzegovina pass law on protection from domestic violence.
2006	President Bush signs the Violence Against Women Act of 2005 into law.
	Congress declares the first full week in February Teen Dating Violence Awareness Week.
	Albania passes legislation addressing family violence.
	Greece passes legislation related to domestic violence.
	Release of the UN Secretary-General's study on All Forms of Violence Against Women. It is the UN's first comprehensive report on the issue.

2008	Egypt prohibits female genital mutilation.
	Andorra amends its penal code to address domestic violence.
	The UN Secretary-General launches UNiTE to End Violence Against Women, a global campaign.
2009	East Timor's Penal Code addresses domestic violence.
	Hungary passes law on domestic violence.
	Obama administration creates "czar" of Violence Against Women.
2010	Congress declares February Teen Dating Violence Awareness Month.
	Obama administration grants asylum to a Mexican woman with a history of domestic violence from her common-law husband.
	Tribal Law and Justice Act enacted.
	The United Nations launches UN Women.
	The UN Secretary-General appoints a Special Representative on Sexual Violence in Conflict.
2011	Inter-American Commission on Human Rights determines the U.S. Supreme Court erred in stating there is no entitlement to enforcement of restraining orders.
	Affordable Care Act prohibits insurance companies from considering domestic violence a preexisting condition.
2012	Leaders in the European Union meet to create the Cadiz Declaration, which reiterated the commitment to enforce CEDAW.
	Congress debates reauthorization of VAWA.

A

ACID THROWING

Acid throwing is the deliberate use of different types of acid to attack another human being by throwing or pouring, with the intent to seriously maim, disfigure, torture, or kill the victim. Acid throwing is a worldwide phenomenon that is not confined to a particular race, religion, or geographical location. These acid attacks happen in many countries but are particularly prevalent in Bangladesh, Pakistan, India, and Cambodia. They are predominantly perpetrated by men toward women and children as a result of shame, loss of face, or perceived dishonor. Acid violence rarely kills but causes severe physical, psychological, and social scarring. In many countries, acid attacks constitute a hidden form of violence against women and children that often goes unreported.

Attempting to calculate the frequency of acid attacks and the demographics of acid attack survivors is a difficult task. Most statistical information pertaining to acid attack violence is related to survivors rather than perpetrators. Countries in which acid attacks are prominent have nongovernmental organizations (NGOs) that work on keeping statistical information on the people that they help through newspaper articles and through public court cases.

Acids

There are three different types of acid that are predominantly used in these attacks: sulfuric, hydrochloric, and nitric acid. Sulfuric acid is the world's largest-volume industrial chemical used to manufacture explosives, dyes, glue, wood preservatives, weaving, amphetamine, and automobile batteries. Nitric acid is used by goldsmiths, jewelers, and brass makers to purify gold and metals. Hydrochloric acid is used to make soy sauce, cosmetics, traditional medicine, and amphetamine and to polish jewelry. All of these acids are fairly cheap and readily available. Anyone can purchase them from mechanic shops and jewelry shops between US$.40 to US$1.50 per liter or have it on hand in their cars.

Where

The first recorded acid attack happened in France during the seventeenth century. On the rise, 99 court cases were recorded by the late nineteenth century. These attacks were reported as "crimes of passion," fueled by jealousy, vengeance, insanity, betrayal, or disappointment, and were generally perpetrated by women against women. These attacks spread over the rest of Europe but declined during World War II due to acid becoming scarce. Acid attacks have been reported habitually in

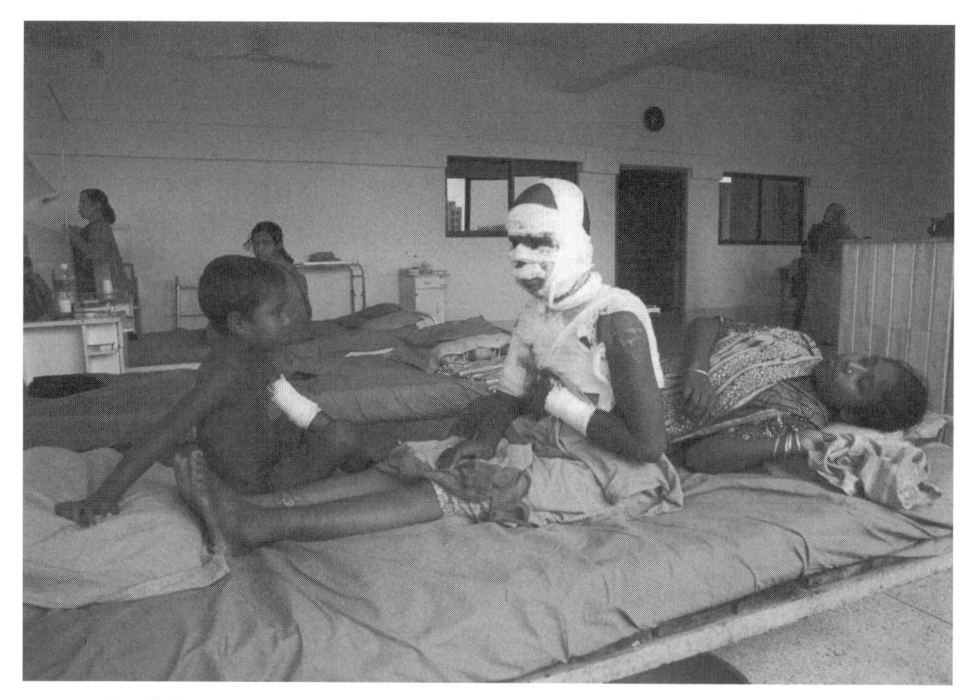

Victim of acid throwing recovers in Bangladesh. (AP Photo/Pavel Rahman)

Bangladesh, India, Pakistan, Nepal, Cambodia, Vietnam, Laos, Hong Kong, China, the United Kingdom, Kenya, South Africa, Uganda, and Ethiopia; while in Indonesia, Malaysia, Myanmar, Thailand, Taipei, Sri Lanka, Afghanistan, Iraq, Turkey, Egypt, Yemen, Saudi Arabia, Nigeria, Gabon, Italy, France, Bulgaria, the United States, Canada, Australia, Argentina, Cuba, and Jamaica cases are less habitual. There are anecdotal cases of acid attacks in other countries as well around the globe. In each country, the reasons behind these attacks, the perpetrator, and the victims are different in each case.

Bangladesh

The highest incidence of acid attacks is reportedly in Bangladesh, making up 9 percent of all reported cases worldwide, according to Acid Survivors Foundation Bangladesh (ASF) (2011). These attacks started in the 1960s and peaked in 2002, when more than 487 men, women, and children were attacked. By 2010, that figure fell to 153, with help stemming from two laws passed by the Bangladeshi government, the Acid Crimes Law, and Acid Control Law of 2002. Great work is being done by three NGOs to reduce the incident of acid attacks: Naripokkho, UNICEF, and the ASF Bangladesh. Reasons for attacks in Bangladesh include rejection of sex and marriage, marital disputes, land/money disputes, family-related incidents, and over the dowry. In 2010, the ASF Bangladesh (2011) listed land disputes as the number one reason behind these attacks with 37 percent of all cases reported, with clashes occurring between neighbors. Sex and marriage rejection, coming in second, is reported at 22 percent, all stemming from men. Women make up the majority of the victims at 69 percent. Only 7 perpetrators were convicted out of the 153 cases in 2010.

Cambodia

Cambodia's acid attacks were first recorded in 1985 and peaked in 2000 when 40 people were attacked. From 1985 to 2009, Cambodian Acid Survivors Charity (CASC) (2010) has recorded a total of 263 attacks with a total of 315 victims. According to CASC (2010), of all reported incidents in Cambodia, approximately 52 percent are female and 48 percent are males. The reasons for these attacks in Cambodia include jealousy; accidents; extramarital affair; robberies; and business, family, and land disputes. The number one cause for these attacks in Cambodia is accident at 37 percent and the second is jealousy at 28 percent. According to CASC (2010), within a three-year period, out of a total of 44 reported acid attacks, 23 cases involved female perpetrators, 17 involved male perpetrators, and 4 were by unreported assailants. Most of the attacks, 32 out of 44 cases, were purportedly committed because of familial relationship problems. The most common type of attack was a wife throwing acid on a suspected mistress or second wife, while attacks by husbands against their wives or former wives were the next most common. These husbands usually have a history of abusing their wives. Husbands also throw acid as punishment for a separation or divorce.

Uganda

Acid Survivors Foundation Uganda (ASF) (2007), an NGO collecting information on acid throwing in Uganda, states that the number of registered cases rose to 275 by the end of 2007. Of all reported incidents in Uganda, approximately 55 percent are females and 45 percent are males. ASF Uganda (2007) says that the root causes of acid attacks include "social problems as well as widespread discrimination against women." Many people have resorted to acid violence as a way of settling relationship and property disputes. It has been reported that some individuals have been hired for as little as US$10 to pour acid on an intended victim. Relationship disputes are the number one cause for these attacks in Uganda at 33 percent, and property conflicts come in second at 8 percent. ASF Uganda (2007) states that 11 percent of all the victims in Uganda are innocent bystanders. Due to cultural and societal norms, women have little power to stop the misconduct of their husbands or even seek legal redress. In these circumstances, women have used acid violence to resolve conflicts. Another problem, according to ASF Uganda (2007), is Uganda's "weak police and court system, which is corrupt, ineffective and poorly resourced." In many cases, acid throwers may be able to avoid justice, especially if they are richer or more powerful than their victims.

Perpetrators

The majority of perpetrators are adult men, but adult women are assailants also. Most NGOs use common identifying methods in reporting perpetrators and victims by showing the relationship between the two, such as husband against wife, wife against husband, wife against mistress, husband against former wife, divorced husband against new husband, father against daughter, child against parent, parent-in-law against daughter-in-law, coworker against coworker, unknown person against perceived lover, and neighbor against neighbor. Because victims are hesitant at times to report the perpetrator or lie because they are afraid of reprisal, more information is needed on perpetrators.

Victims

The victims of acid violence are overwhelmingly women and children; however, men and the elderly are also attacked. Many bystanders are accidentally burned as well. This high number of accidental burns is due to the fact that acid is thrown at individuals, and since it is a liquid substance, it tends to bounce off the intended victim, or the intended victim moves out of the way and the acid hits someone else.

Why

Countries have reported an increase in attacks in the past five years due to the physical availability, the cost, and the fact that acid is not illegal to buy, sell, or store. Unlike other weapons such as guns, knives, and grenades that are illegal, hard to find, or too expensive, acid is easy to acquire. Victims of acid violence are attacked for many reasons, and the patterns of attack vary from country to country. There are four main reasons behind attacks: cultural, societal, situational, and personal reasons. Cultural attacks stem from gender, economic, or class inequalities; the culture of revenge; "taming the wild"; morality; to shame and to calm misogyny. Societal attacks stem from impunity toward perpetrators, social permissiveness, corruption of government, history of punishments toward women, media influences, and male-dominated resources. Situational attacks are seen with family conflicts, low family education, the emotional state of individuals, geographic location, peer association, cost of acid, and the murder rate within the district. Personal attacks stem from interpersonal feelings such as male shame, powerlessness, entitlement, the age of the perpetrator or victim, poor anger management skills, attachment disorders, low educational levels or income, childhood neglect, antisocial behaviors, controlling behavior, or as a way of constructing masculinity.

Acid attacks have a catastrophic impact on the lives of the victims physically, psychologically, and financially. Victims usually do not die; the aim of nearly all acid attacks is not to kill but to injure and disfigure. Physically, acid has a devastating effect on the human body; it causes skin tissue to melt exposing bones and, in severe cases, even dissolves bones. The severity of the injury results from a variety of factors, including the type of acid used and how long it touched the skin. Victims sustain a variety of injuries, including melting of the nose, closing of the nostrils, shriveling of the ears, and burning of the eyelids and lips. Many victims are left blind. Because it is thrown at the face, the victim's hands usually sustain damage because they try to block the substance flying at their face. These burns cause numerous discomforts such as skin tightening and severe itching where the acid lands. The most salient danger for victims is that inhaling the acid vapors will result in breathing problems or even complete failure.

The psychological scars may be less visible, but they are just as traumatic and long-lasting as the physical ailments. It has been reported that survivors often suffer from depression, insomnia, nightmares, and fear that the perpetrator will harm them again. Many survivors deal with severe isolation as they are ostracized from their communities and families. From the social standpoint, survivors often become forlorn and ashamed because the community may stare at them and blame them for what happened. They may not want to go outside their homes because of the stigma from these attacks, leaving them helpless and dependent on others. Many lose the ability to earn a living and the independence they once had, which causes additional struggles. Unmarried survivors may never marry or have children. These adverse psychological effects such as depression and low self-esteem lead to many people deciding not to resume work.

Due to the disfigurement, disability, and social stigma associated with acid injuries, many survivors have lost employment. The financial consequences are even more overwhelming when the victim is a wage earner. Spouses are often humiliated by their partners, leading to separation and/or divorce. Because many women are financially dependent on their husbands, they are often left homeless and impoverished without a way of meeting their basic needs. In these circumstances, children are left with their mother, who lacks a source of income. Once the acid attack happens, survivors usually have to spend weeks or months in hospital, until their wounds begin to heal and the risk of infection is gone. Survivors often have to pay for their medical treatment and need multiple surgical operations and treatment lasting for years to come. The quality of treatment they receive may depend on how much money they have and where they are located. In sum, survivors of acid attacks face a long road to recovery, not just from the physical damage but from the resulting societal response to their disfigurement.

See also: Health Effects of Domestic Abuse; Honor Killings; India and Domestic Abuse; The Middle East and Domestic Abuse; Psychological Effects of Domestic Abuse; South and Southeast Asia and Domestic Abuse; Types of Domestic Abuse

Further Reading

Acid Survivors Foundation: http://www.acidsurvivors.org/index.html
Acid Survivors Foundation Bangladesh (2011). Statistics. Retrieved from http://www.acidsurvivors.org/statistics.html
Acid Survivors Foundation Uganda. (2007). 4th Annual Report. Retrieved from http://www.asf.be/en/asf-uganda
Acid Survivors Trust International. (2005). http://www.acidviolence.org/
Cambodian Acid Survivors Charity: http://www.cambodianacidsurvivorscharity.org/
Cambodian Acid Survivors Charity (2010). Annual report 2010. Retrieved January 26, 2013 from http://www.cambodianacidsurvivorscharity.org/Annual%20Report%202010.pdf
Walsh, Jane (2009). "It was like burning in hell": A comparative exploration of acid attack violence. Center for Global Initiatives: Caroline Papers on International Health, No 2.

Brandon Fryman

AFRICA AND DOMESTIC ABUSE

Domestic violence is said to have no cultural linkage. The kinds and causes are universal, and thus Africans (victims and perpetrators), like their counterparts elsewhere in the world, experience emotional, psychological, and physical abuses in their relationships. However, some causes for domestic violence have been attributed more to Africans than to those living on most other continents. These causes include poverty, lack of access to education and information, lack of property ownership, power inequality, the patriarchal nature of African societies, and others. Many believe that all these issues fall under the umbrella of patriarchy, which is almost universally accepted in traditional African culture. Of course, many societies outside Africa are also affected by this factor, but its preeminence in Africa is distinctive. It is seen by many as the most outstanding cause of domestic violence among Africans.

Causes

The views of Lynne Harne and Jill Radford about the meaning and nature of domestic violence are useful here. "Domestic violence is a broad concept incorporating many forms of physical violence, sexual violence and a range of coercive, intimidating and controlling behaviors. It is damaging physically and socially" (Harne & Radford, 2010). On its nature, they say that: "Domestic violence can occur in any intimate or familial relationship, irrespective of whether the parties are living together or not, whether they are married or cohabiting or living in three-generational extended families. It is this relational element, rather than location that defines the violence as 'domestic,' because while it commonly occurs in the home, it can spill out into the streets, bus stops, bars or even result in road traffic 'accidents'" (Harne & Radford, 2010).

Given this description of domestic violence, several questions come to mind. How do such acts occur given Africans' identification with the communalistic principle of "I am because we are"? Who are the victims, and who are the perpetrators? Is it the rich or poor? Rural or urban dwellers? The educated or uneducated? Male or female? And in which class do such acts of domestic violence occur? Scholars are of the opinion that domestic violence acts are not class-sensitive. That means that they can occur across every class of persons regardless of educational, economic, and social status, as well as gender and even age.

Exploring the causes, then, of African domestic violence brings us back to the critical question of whether it occurs more in the urban or rural areas. Many Western scholars have focused more on statistics based on cases in courts and law agencies, leading them to argue that there are more cases of abuse and violence in the urban areas than in the rural areas. But McCue (2008) disagrees: "The primary reason for the belief that battering occurs more in urban areas than in rural ones is that domestic violence in rural areas is vastly underreported. Fewer domestic violence resources are available to battered women in rural areas. Shelters and social service programs are scarce, and law enforcement and medical responses to domestic violence may be inadequate. Therefore, few reports are filed and relatively little data regarding domestic violence in rural settings can be gathered."

This theory speaks volumes about the victims of domestic violence in Africa, especially in the rural areas. This is largely due to the relegation of women to the traditional role of housewife, wherein her knowledge is limited to the kitchen. Except for a few ethnic groups like the Akan of Ghana, most African communities are patrilineal. In such chauvinistic societies, women who dare try to get involved in men's "serious" business may become victims of violent acts. The legendary novelist Chinua Achebe's *Things Fall Apart* captures this phenomenon when the women do not appear with the men in their community's meeting and Okonkwo's wives do not talk whenever he talks, especially when he is angry. A woman who violates this cultural norm risks being battered by her partner. In the urban areas, however, such divisions of roles have gradually been on the wane, thanks to various enlightenment programs on egalitarianism toward gender issues. Although the consciousness of male domination is still there and sometimes results in domestic violence, it is not as prevalent as among those living in the rural areas. The restriction applies not only to women but to children, who are considered too immature to make contributions on issues. Cultural norms demand that children do not speak when elders speak; otherwise, they may become victims of domestic violence.

Another kind of domestic abuse that occurs more in the rural areas is the emotional kind that men exhibit in withdrawing from their female partners when the latter are having their menstrual periods and also within a certain number of days after menstrual periods, or at the early stage of child delivery. There is a traditional belief that men who are even near their female partners within these periods lose protection and guidance from the spiritual world, especially of the ancestors. This culminates in the withdrawal of sex and emotional support from the female partners during these times. In extreme cases among the strict religious traditionalists, men will not eat the food prepared by their female partners at these times, let alone dine together. Unfortunately, most women, especially in the rural settings, have accepted that fact.

Poverty is another factor that is touted as a cause of domestic violence among Africans. But what is the link between poverty and domestic violence? Before attempting to answer this question, let us discuss the basic meaning of poverty. In McNamara's view, poverty is "a condition of life so characterized by malnutrition, illiteracy, diseases and squalid surroundings, high infant mortality and loss of life expectancy" (McNamara, 1976). Some scholars believe that poverty does not cause domestic violence but rather aggravates it. However, others believe that "a hungry man is an angry man." A minor and unexpected problem often angers someone experiencing abject poverty. Experience has shown that women and children are most often at the receiving end of such anger. Men may also have their fair share of emotional problems when women resort to withdrawal of sex and other forms of care for their male partners as protest against the latter for not fulfilling his parental responsibilities.

How does the above scenario play out within the patriarchal nature of African societies? Some statistics about selected African communities in Nigeria, the home country of the writer of this work, shed light here. In a 2010 field research project by Alumona on the level of poverty among Nigerian rural dwellers using communities in Delta and Kogi states, "A total of 1980 persons returned the questionnaires distributed to 2000 persons. Those within the age bracket of 25–59 years include 601 males, representing 30.35% of the respondents; 506 females, representing 25.56% while those from 60 years and above comprise 442 males which is 22.32% and 413 females or 21.77%. From the table generated, 82.37% of our respondents live below US$ 1.1–1.6 daily. Women share a larger percentage; accounting for 88.37% of those living within that range" (Alumona, 2010).

This is not to generalize all African communities, but the variations on the level of poverty are not markedly different across Africa. The above statistics show that women are worse off in Africa in terms of poverty. African men capitalize on this lopsidedness in holding down their female partners, even after serial abuses. Knowing that the female partners are incapacitated economically, educationally, and socially, many males have the confidence to continue the violence.

Resources

It is clear that both men and women are victims and perpetrators of domestic violence in Africa, but women are more likely to be victims than men. As discussed, reasons include that women have less access to education in Africa, the recognition of the patriarchal nature of African societies, men's power to isolate abused women and children, and poverty, which may cause and aggravate domestic violence in Africa.

What is important is how to help not only the victims but also the perpetrators. While the "Duluth" approach is mostly adopted in the West, a communalistic approach has been suggested in Africa for the perpetrators of domestic violence. Here, individuals are reminded of the bond of "I am because we are," with the elders and family members playing the roles of police and court services of the Duluth programs. This approach is believed to expose the consciousness of people, even in the cities, to the need for recognizing the sanctity of human lives, regardless of gender.

Enlightenment programs have also been encouraged across African communities to allow African women equal access to education as their male counterparts receive. This seems to be yielding results now compared with the traditional "kitchen role" that a woman was supposed to play in the past. It was seen as a waste to send a girl child to school in the past, but that has changed. Still, more needs to be done in that direction.

See also: Duluth Model; Patriarchy and Domestic Abuse; Poverty and Domestic Abuse

Further Reading

Alumona, N. O. (2010). *Ethics of healthcare for Nigerian rural dwellers*. Submitted for assessment, *Uja: Journal of Philosophy and Religious Studies*.

Harne, L., & Radford, J. (2010). *Domestic violence: Theories, policies and practice*. New York, NY: McGraw-Hill.

McCue, M. L. (2008). *Domestic violence*. Santa Barbara, CA: ABC-CLIO.

McNamara, R. (1976). *Summary proceedings of the Annual Meeting of the World Bank IFC/IDA*.

Mark Ikeke

AIDS AND DOMESTIC VIOLENCE

According to research, 12 percent of HIV/AIDS among women in romantic relationships is related to violence or abuse, and women whose partners are violent are three times more likely to get HIV/AIDS (Sareen, 2009). Women are more likely than men to get HIV/AIDS when having sex, whether consensual or coerced. Data shows that men who rape, force sex, or are violent have more sexual partners and have sex more often. This may make having sex with them risky for contracting HIV/AIDS.

The Connection between Domestic Abuse and AIDS

Domestic violence contributes to the spread of HIV/AIDS and other sexually transmitted diseases (STDs) in various ways. Fear of economic dependence, stigma and shame, ostracism, and lack of voice all affect women's ability to protect their sexual health. Abusers may rape or sexually assault their victims as part of their pattern of control, making it unlikely that the abuser will use a condom. Some abusers may even intentionally infect their partners with HIV in an attempt to keep them from leaving. Abusive partners who engage in sexual activity outside the relationship potentially expose victims to STDs including HIV. Abusive partners may also force victims to engage in sexual activities with others (Domestic violence and HIV/AIDS, 2010). Trafficked victims may be particularly vulnerable to infection, especially those who are forced into sex work.

Further, victims of domestic violence often suffer a wide range of health-related problems caused or exacerbated by the abuse. Sometimes abusers prohibit or make it difficult for victims to receive needed medical attention for those issues. These health conditions, and failure to treat them in a timely fashion, may increase their risk of HIV infection by their impact on victim's immune system.

Underlying all these issues are powerful gender inequalities. For instance, social and cultural norms that tell men they are in control of sexual decisions can preclude a woman from being able to negotiate safe sex with her partner. Thus, women may feel little power to insist on their partner's fidelity, to demand use of condoms, or to even refuse sexual relations when they know or suspect their partner is infected. Since many women lack the economic power to leave a relationship, they are financially dependent on abusers from whom they may get infected. Some victims are on a fixed income and thus are unable to access care without the financial support of the abuser. Women in abusive relationships who are unable to negotiate contraceptives sometimes attempt to use contraceptives covertly. This strategy may be effective but can backfire in the event that the abuser finds out about the deception.

Gender inequalities that result in lesser power to women also reduce the chance that a woman will seek diagnosis or treatment for HIV/AIDS, as doing so may put her at tremendous risk for ostracism. In particular, sex workers have been treated horribly by communities when they have disclosed their HIV status, in some cases resulting in abandonment, shunning, dismissal from work, assault, and even murder. Thus, women may fail to seek prevention or health-care information, thereby jeopardizing not only their safety but that of other family members to whom the virus might be spread.

When disclosed to an abuser, a positive test may result in increased or more severe abuse. One survey of providers of HIV-related health care in the United States found 24 percent of physicians had at least one female patient who experienced physical violence after disclosing her HIV status to her partner, and 45 percent had patients who feared such a reaction (Gielen et al. 2000). In Nairobi, Kenya, of a group of 66 women who disclosed their status to their partners, 11 were chased away from their homes, 7 were beaten up, and 1 committed suicide (Temmerman, Ndinya-Achola, Ambani & Piot, 1995).

Abusers can also use victims' HIV-positive status as a tool of control. Abusers may use the victim's HIV-positive status as an excuse for their violence. They may threaten to reveal the victim's HIV-positive status to children, family, friends, employers, or others in the community. Abusers might threaten to use the victim's status as grounds for child custody or as a means to increase victims' guilt about children who are also HIV positive. Victims may be hesitant to leave abusers out of fear of what will happen to them if they are incapacitated by the disease.

Additionally, abusers will degrade or verbally abuse victims for having HIV, telling the victim she is dirty or undesirable. Given that abusers are often isolating victims from family and friends, HIV-positive status can be used as another justification for this isolation. Abusers can threaten to withhold treatment or assistance. Victims may feel that no one else would want them or even provide care for them, and thus they must stay with their abusive partner. In the case of gay or lesbian relationships, a lack of family or social support might prevent victims from leaving abusers. Domestic violence shelters may not be thoroughly prepared to deal with HIV-positive victims.

Resources

There are some safe ways to get tested for AIDS. First, it is possible to be tested anonymously. Victims can also ask the testing center not to notify their partner about his/her status until s/he is in a safe place.

Educational campaigns are needed to raise awareness about domestic violence, HIV/AIDS, and the connections between the two. Advocates caution against using the traditional approach of Abstinence, Be Faithful, and Condom Use (ABC), as it emphasizes measures largely controlled by men (in particular, condom use). A reproductive justice framework is recommended. Reproductive justice provides a framework for understanding the intersections of gender, race, poverty, economics, politics, and other oppressions.

Domestic violence center staff should receive training on the connections between domestic violence and AIDS. Such training should also cover local resources to help infected persons.

See also: Health Effects of Domestic Abuse; Physicians, Health Care Providers, and Domestic Abuse; Pregnancy and Domestic Abuse; Reproductive Coercion; Types of Domestic Abuse

Further Reading

Abrahams, N., Jewkes, R., Hoffman, M., & Laubascher, R. (2004). Sexual violence against intimate partners in Cape Town: Prevalence and risk factors reported by men. *Bulletin of the World Health Organization*, 82, 330–337.

Asian and Pacific Islander American Health Forum. (2011). The intersection between HIV/AIDS and domestic violence in Asian American, Native Hawaiian, and Pacific Islander Women. Retrieved March 15, 2012, from http://www.apiahf.org/sites/default/files/APIAHF-HIV-DV-05-2011.pdf

Campbell, J., Baty, M., Ghandour, R., Stockman, J., Francisco, L., & Wagmen, J. (2008). The intersection of intimate partner violence against women and HIV/AIDS: A review. *International Journal of Injury Control and Safety Promotion*, 23(12), 1694–1712.

Domestic violence and HIV/AIDS. (2010). New York Office for the Prevention of Domestic Violence. Retrieved July 19, 2012, from http://www.opdv.ny.gov/professionals/health/hivaids.html

Domestic violence, HIV/AIDS, and other STIs. (2006). *The Advocates for Human Rights*. Retrieved March 15, 2012, from http://www.stopvaw.org/domestic_violence_hiv_aids_and_other_stis.html

Dunkle, K., Jewkes, R., Nduna, et al. (2006, Oct. 24). Connections between perpetration of partner violence and HIV risk behavior among young men in the rural Eastern Cape province of South Africa. *AIDS*, 20(16), 2107–2114.

Garcia-Moreno C. (2000). Violence against women: Its importance for HIV/AIDS, *AIDS* 14(supplement 3), 5253–5265.

Gielen, A. C., Fogarty, L., O'Campo, P., Anderson, J., Keller, J., & Faden, R. (2000). Women living with HIV: Disclosure, violence, and social support. *Journal of Urban Health*, 77(3), 480–491. doi: 10.1007/BF02386755

Intimate partner violence and HIV/AIDS. (n.d.). National Coalition Against Domestic Violence. Retrieved March 15, 2012, from http://www.ncadv.org/learn/DV%20and%20HIV%20AIDS.php

Jewkes R., Levin J., & Penn-Kenana L. (2003, January). Gender inequalities, intimate partner violence and HIV preventative practices. *Social Science and Medicine*, 56, 125–134.

Leserman, J. (2008). Role of depression, stress, and trauma in HIV disease progression. *Psychosomatic Medicine*, 70(5), 539–545.

Sareen, J., Pagura, J., & Grant, B. (2009, February). Is intimate partner violence associated with HIV infection among women in the U.S.? *Science Direct*. Retrieved from http://www.cfah.org/hbns/archives/viewSupportDoc.cfm?supportingDocID=782

Temmerman, M., Ndinya-Achola, J., Ambani, J., & Piot, P. (1995). The right not to know HIV-test results. *Lancet*, 345, 696–970.

Laura L. Finley

ALASKA NATIVES AND DOMESTIC ABUSE

Domestic violence is a long-standing and pervasive issue in the Alaska Native populations. Domestic violence rates are some of the highest of any race/ethnic group and a common experience for Alaska Native women. However, domestic violence, such as stalking and sexual assault in the Alaska Native populations, based on available data, differs from that kind of abuse seen against Native American women. The Alaska Native perpetrator of sexual assault is not a person of a different race/ethnic group as is often found in sexual violence directed at Native Americans women. The differences in the aggregated groups of Alaska Native and Native Americans suggests the need to collect data for each group, so as to better understand domestic violence causes and consequences in these diverse groups. Presently, these differences are generally attributed to how the data was collected as well as the lack of data specific to the Alaska Native population.

Defining Alaska Natives

The definition of Alaska Natives includes many culturally distinct tribes into one category which has the potential to disguise the distinctiveness within the groups. Collectively, there are at least 226 federally recognized Alaska Native villages, five unrecognized Tlingit tribes, and multiple tribes that lack federal recognition.

The population of Alaska Natives based on self-identifying with one tribal grouping is at approximately 97,000. The total Alaska Native population is estimated at approximately 120,000 when including bi- or multirace/ethnicity groupings. Just under half of Alaska Natives live off the road system in rural and remote areas of the state of Alaska. The main Alaska Native groups are: (1) Inuit/Eskimo (47,000); (2) Aleut/Unangan (12,000); and (3) Athabaskan (30,000). Alaska Natives are predominantly concentrated in Alaska.

An important distinction between Alaska Native and Native Americans is that they are located in five geographic regions and are not part of a reservation system. Another difference between the two groups is that most Alaska Natives are "shareholders" in one of 13 regional corporations rather than a tribal member. Most Alaska Natives are also organized under a Native village. Alaska Native and Native Americans are frequently aggregated into one group; however, these groups have very different lived experiences.

Stalking in Alaska

Reports of stalking by Alaska Natives are lower than the national average of American Indian/Alaska Native combined. Based on report data from the Alaska State Troopers, Alaska white women are 6.6 times more likely to be stalked than Alaska Native women. In particular, the rate of Alaska white women reporting being stalked is 109.3 per 100,000, and for Alaska Native women it is 16.6 per 100,000. Rosay and Henry (2007b) claimed the low stalking rate is due to underreporting of Alaska Native women and the reason for the findings not matching national data findings is because it is a state trooper data based on reports rather than self-disclosure. Alternative theories for the incidence/prevalence rates were not advanced.

Assaults Reported to Law Enforcement

Since 1996, Alaska has been under a mandatory arrest policy for domestic violence cases. Based on Alaska State Trooper data, 96 percent of domestic violence cases were closed and referred for prosecution. The conviction rates for these cases were 54 percent. The Bureau of Vital Statistics (2006) found that between 2000 and 2003, approximately 36 percent of domestic violence victims and 44 percent sexual assault victims were Alaska Native. Unlike Native Americans, Alaska Natives domestic violence assaults are more likely to be from the same race/ethnic group. Eighty-six percent of domestic violence incidents in Alaska occurred between offenders and victims of the same race/ethnicity. Being under the influence of alcohol was a factor in 59 percent of the domestic violence incidents.

Sexual Assaults Reported to Law Enforcement

Alaska's forcible rape rate is 2.3 times higher than the national average (73.3 per 100,000 vs. 31.78 per 100,000). According to the Anchorage Police Department data from 2009, Alaska Native account for about 45 percent of the reported sexual assaults, but only make up about 8 percent of the Anchorage population. In 2008, the organization Standing Together Against Rape (STAR) provided services to 651 primary sexual assault victims, with approximately 215 or 31.3 percent being Alaska Native. Based on data from 1996 to 2004, 56 percent of sexual assault victims receiving medical-forensic examinations were Alaska Native women. Unlike Native Americans, who are more likely to be assaulted by a member of a different race/ethnic group, Alaska Native women are more likely to be assaulted by another Alaska Native. Ninety-one percent of Alaska Native women were assaulted by another Alaska Native. Only 9 percent of Alaska Native women were assaulted by a person other than Alaska Native. Alaska white women were slightly more likely to be assaulted by a person of another race/ethnic group than Alaska Natives. Eighty-four percent of white victims were assaulted by a white suspect, while 16 percent of white women were assaulted by another race/ethnic group. The sexual assault perpetrator being under the influence alcohol was involved in under half the incidences (e.g., 43 percent).

Intimate Partner Violence

In 2006, a convenience sample study of a subgroup of Alaska Natives (n = 91) found that 63.7 percent of Ahtna (Athabaskan) women had experienced intimate partner violence during their lifetime. Over seventeen percent (17.6) reported having been physically assaulted by an intimate partner during the past 12 months. The Ahtna sample results were higher than that of national studies and a recent 2010 Alaska Victimization Survey based on a representative sample, which found that 47.6 percent of all Alaska women had experienced intimate partner violence over their lifetime.

Problems with the Domestic Violence Data

The data for Alaska Natives is mostly found at the state (e.g., Alaska) and community levels (e.g., Anchorage), and it is aggregated. This does not allow determining subgroup differences in domestic violence incidence/prevalence rates. Subpopulation data is necessary for formulating effective policies and evaluating the effectiveness of programs and interventions. Most of the Alaska Native domestic violence data is from Alaska State Trooper reports, convenience samples, and medical examinations. Each of these data sources have limitations. Presently, basic Regional and Village Corporations or even community-level data is lacking, making it difficult to distinguish between the three predominant Alaska Native groups. The population-level data aggregates Alaska Natives with Native Americans making it difficult to ascertain whether the data is representative or accurate of Alaska Natives or Native Americans or both. Whether these are actually differences or simply an artifact of underreporting or dissimilar data collection processes is not known.

Alaska Natives differ enough from Native Americans that research specific to the Alaska Natives is necessary. Alaska Native women, based on available domestic violence data such as stalking and sexual assault, differ from Native American women. These differences are attributed to how the data was collected, underreporting, as well as the lack of data specific to the Alaska Native population. Obtaining valid and reliable data on domestic violence in Alaska Native populations will provide insight into the magnitude of the problem and subgroup incidence/prevalence rate. The lack of data impedes policy decisions as well as the allocation of state and federal funds to address the issue in the Alaska Native populations, and without the social and political will to address the issue, domestic violence will continue to be a long-standing and pervasive issue.

See also: Native Americans and Domestic Abuse; Tribal Law and Justice Act; U.S. Government Responses to Domestic Violence; Violence Against Women Act (VAWA)

Further Reading

Alaska Bureau of Vital Statistics. (2006). Health profiles 1995–2004. Department of Health and Social Services, Division of Public Health, Bureau of Vital Statistics. Available at http://hss.state.ak.us/dph/bvs/Profiles/default.htm

Alaska Network on Domestic Violence and Sexual Assault (ANDVSA): http://www.andvsa.org

Indian Health Services (IHS) Violence against Native Women: Patient information: http://www.ihs.gov/MedicalPrograms/MCH/V/DV11.cfm

Mending the Sacred Hoop. (2011). http://www.mshoop.org/

National Sexual Violence Resource Center. (2012) http://www.nsvrc.org/

Rosay, A. B., & Henry, T. (2007a). *Alaska sexual assault nurse examiner study: Final report.* Report prepared under Grant No. 2004-WG-BX-0003 awarded by the National Institute of Justice, Office of Justice Programs, U.S. Department of Justice. Anchorage, AK: Justice Center, University of Alaska, Anchorage. Retrieved from http://justice.uaa.alaska.edu/research/2000/0501sexualassaults/0501.07.final.html

Rosay, A. B., & Henry, T. (2007b). *Reporting sexual assault victimizations to law enforcement.* Report prepared under Grant No. 2004-WG-BX-0003 awarded by the National Institute of Justice, Office of Justice Programs, U.S. Department of Justice. Anchorage, AK: Justice Center, University of Alaska, Anchorage. Retrieved from http://justice.uaa.alaska.edu/research/2000/0501sexualassaults/0501.06.reportsexoffense.pdf

Rosay, A. B., Samaniego, S., Rivera, M., Myrstol, B., Wood, D. S., & Morton, L. (2010, September 30). 2010 Alaska Victimization Survey (Powerpoint slide presentation). Presented at University of Alaska, Anchorage. Anchorage, AK: Justice Center,

University of Alaska, Anchorage; Council on Domestic Violence and Sexual Assault, Alaska Department of Public Safety. Retrieved from http://justice.uaa.alaska.edu/research/2010/1004.victimization/1004.01.avs.pdf

Andrew Hund

ALCOHOL AND DOMESTIC ABUSE

Various reports have found a connection between alcohol abuse and domestic violence, but it remains unclear the degree to which there is a causal relationship. While is it well known that alcohol use is linked to impaired judgment, reduced inhibition, and increased aggression, some argue that no real research exists to indicate that alcohol abuse causes domestic violence. Some suggest that the use of alcohol may actually be adaptive and may facilitate stress relief, increase conjugal relationships, and potentially improve mood states. However, the more prevalent and accepted hypothesis is that alcohol consumption is maladaptive, increases dissatisfaction, and may provoke domestic violence. Basically, this school of thought suggests that alcohol acts as a chronic stressor, causing negative family interactions, marital violence, and conjugal dissolution.

Prevalence

In a study in the *Journal of the American Medical Association* (JAMA), Brookoff and colleagues (1997) described the characteristics of assailants and victims of domestic violence. Most (78 percent) of the assailants were male, while most of victims (72 percent) were female. Of the victims who were male, 45 percent were the children of female victims who had tried to intervene in the assault of their mothers. Of the responding assailants, 86 percent acknowledged using alcohol on the day of the assault; while victims and family members reported that 92 percent of assailants used drugs or alcohol the day of the assault. Further, 45 percent of victims and family members reported that assailants used alcohol or drugs to the point of intoxication, on a daily basis, during the prior month; with 19 percent being classified as alcoholics and 14 percent dually diagnosed as drug addicts and alcoholics. Although to a lesser extent (42 percent), victims were reported to have been using alcohol or drugs the day of the assault.

According to the National Institute on Alcohol Abuse and Alcoholism study by Caetano and colleagues (2001), results from a 1995 national study indicated domestic violence rates were higher among black and Hispanic couples than among white couples for both male-female and female-male perpetrations. While the authors state no single factor is able to explain the higher prevalence, alcohol plays an important part, with 30–40 percent of men and 27–34 percent of women perpetrating violence against their partners drinking at the time of the assault.

Cause and Effect

There have been studies showing a correlation between increased alcohol consumption and domestic violence, even when the abuser is sober. Alcohol has been shown to impair neural processing, which could impact executive functioning such as inhibition and social interaction. Alcohol impedes a person's ability to consider the consequences of his or her actions and increased the likelihood that a person will act out in anger and rage.

On the other hand, some researchers claim that this correlation is nothing more than a coincidence. It's the age-old chicken-egg argument: Researchers question whether abusers use alcohol-fueled rage as an excuse for abuse, or if alcoholism and domestic violence are two separate social problems with considerable overlap. Both alcoholism and domestic violence share similarities. For example, both focus on power and control; are laden with denial and avoidance of the problem; may involve segregation, isolation, and seclusion; and could be perpetuated throughout generations.

Kyriacou and colleagues (1999) found that while alcohol abuse by men was associated with an increased likelihood of inflicting injury in a domestic violence situation, and there was a clear dose–response effect for the three measures of alcohol consumption that were evaluated, the precise mechanism by which alcohol acts to increase the risk of injury from domestic violence was not clear. The authors suggested that physiologic, psychological, and environmental factors may all play an important role in domestic abuse perpetration. Further, the fact that a large proportion of women in the study did not endorse alcohol use by men cannot account for all injuries from domestic violence and cannot be considered either a necessary or a sufficient condition for domestic violence.

Alcohol and Physical Violence

For most people, alcohol increases the inhibitory signaling in the brain, making them feel laid-back, relaxed, sedate, or calm. However, some people exhibit a completely different reaction to alcohol, becoming angry, depressed, agitated, and even violent.

One study (Fals-Stewart, 2003) suggests that men who drink alcohol and have a predisposition for physical violence toward their female partners are more likely to be violent on the days they drink alcohol. Utilizing a combination of structured interviews and drinking and physical aggression logs over a 15-month period, the authors found that for men entering a domestic violence treatment program, the odds of any level of male-to-female physical aggression was eight times higher on days when they drank alcohol than on days no alcohol was consumed. For men entering alcohol treatment programs, male-to-female physical aggression was 11 times more likely on days alcohol was consumed. Further, for both groups, the likelihood of severe male-to-female physical aggression on drinking days was more than 11 times higher. As alcohol severity increased (e.g., heavy drinking days), the likelihood of any violence and severe violence also increased in both groups (17–19 times). Of note, the likelihood of male-to-female violence was still higher on days male partners drank versus days they did not drink, even after controlling for levels of relationship disharmony and alcohol severity.

Societal Contributions

Several studies have reported a relationship between the density of alcohol outlets and negative behavioral outcomes, such as higher levels of alcohol consumption among youth and adults, and a greater prevalence of alcohol-related crime, violence, and injury. Research suggests that areas of increased alcohol outlet density may be signals of lowered normative constraints regarding general violence within the neighborhood, promote problematic drinking, and suggest more tolerant attitudes, norms, and behaviors regarding domestic violence (Alcohol and domestic violence, 2003).

See also: Drugs and Domestic Abuse; Types of Domestic Abuse

Further Reading

Alcohol and domestic violence. (2003). Minnesota Advocates for Human Rights. http://www1.umn.edu/humanrts/svaw/domestic/link/alcohol.htm

Brookoff, D., O'Brien, K., Cook, C., Thompson, T., & Williams, C. (1997). Characteristics of participants in domestic violence: Assessment at the scene of domestic assault. *JAMA: Journal of the American Medical Association, 277*(17), 1369–1373.

Caetano, R., Schafer, J., & Cunradi, Carol B. (2001). Alcohol-related intimate partner violence among white, black, and Hispanic couples in the United States. *Alcohol Research and Health, 25*(1). http://pubs.niaaa.nih.gov/publications/arh25-1/58-65.pdf

Domestic abuse and alcohol: Some doubt the role alcohol plays. http://alcoholism.about.com/cs/abuse/a/aa990331.htm

Fals-Stewart, W. (2003). The occurrence of partner physical aggression on days of alcohol consumption: A longitudinal diary study. *Journal of Consulting and Clinical Psychology, 71*(1), 41–52.

Hanson, P. J. (2012). Alcohol linked to partner violence? Alcohol problems and solutions. http://www2.potsdam.edu/hansondj/HealthIssues/1055873025.html

Kyriacou, D., Anglin, D., Taliaferro, E., Stone, S., Tubb, T., Linden, J. A., Muelleman, R., Barton, E., & Kraus, J. F. (1999). Risk factors for injury to women from domestic violence. *New England Journal of Medicine, 341*(25), 1892–1898.

McCrady, B. (1982). Marital dysfunction: Alcoholism and marriage. In E. Pattison & E. Kaufman (Eds.), *Encyclopedic handbook of alcoholism* (pp. 673–685). New York, NY: Gardner Press.

Sullivan, T., Ashare, R., Jaquier, V., & Tennen, H. (2012). Risk factors for alcohol-related problems among victims of partner violence. *Substance Use & Misuse, 47*(6), 673–685.

Stephanie A. Kolakowsky-Hayner and Kimberly Bellon

ALI, SOMY

Former Bollywood actress and model turned activist, Somy Ali is an award-winning advocate for domestic violence victims.

Born in Karachi, Pakistan, Ali grew up watching her father abuse her mother. She saw women of all ages, educational levels, ethnic groups, and religions being abused

Somy Ali's t-shirt line helps fund services for victims of domestic violence. (AP Photo/Lynne Sladky)

and was repeatedly told it was simply what women had to endure. When she was nine, she called her uncle in America after her father's abuse resulted in a broken arm for her mom. The uncle arranged for Somy, her mother, and her brother to move to the United States. Her mother continued to communicate with her father, who also supported the family financially. In 1992, at the age of 15, Ali moved from Florida to Mumbai, India, with the dream of meeting Bollywood star Salman Khan and hopefully marrying him some day. When she arrived in India, Ali had celebrated photographer Gautam Rajadhyaksha shoot portfolio pictures. She was approached by an agent in a hotel lobby, asking her to screen-test for a project. Salman Khan somehow came upon her photographs at a modeling agency and contacted Ali, offering her a role in one of his films. Throughout the 1990s, Somy Ali acted in nine Bollywood films. Her dream seemed to be close to reality, as Khan broke up with then-girlfriend Sangeeta Bijlani to date Ali, and then the two became engaged. Ali moved back to Florida in 2000, however, when Khan left her for Aishwarya Rai.

Although she was depressed, Ali determined that she would return to school. She graduated with a degree in psychology from Nova Southeastern University and then studied filmmaking in New York. She produced several short documentaries, including one about Pakistani gang rape victim Mukhtar Mai. Ali also realized that she wanted to do something to help society, but was unsure where to focus at first. Then a Bangladeshi woman living five houses down from her showed up at

Ali's door. She was bleeding badly and told Ali that her father-in-law had just raped her and that she had been beaten for 10 years. Ali helped her contact the police and find safe housing. The woman has since graduated from nursing school. Ali still carries the woman's picture in her wallet. From that point on, with the advice of her younger brother, Ali decided to help victims of domestic violence.

She started the nonprofit organization No More Tears (NMT), a name her mother suggested, in December 2006. The organization's mission is to provide individualized assistance to victims of domestic violence in the United States. NMT assists all victims, but is particularly well suited to help those who have been brought to the U.S. via arranged marriages. Ali speaks Hindi, Urdu, and can understand some Arabic and Farsi, and thus is able to communicate with women from many Middle Eastern or South Asian counties who have limited English proficiency. Knowing that many times women from these cultures are very isolated, Ali and volunteers place brochures in ethnic food stores and restaurants as well as clothing and beauty supply locations, as these might be the only places women are allowed to go without their husbands. Not all of NMT's survivors are immigrants from these countries, however. Additional outreach efforts include presentations, coordinated by Ali, board members, and volunteers, to local high schools, colleges, and community groups in order to raise awareness about abuse, ensure victims know about NMT's services, and encourage additional volunteers and donors.

Not knowing exactly how to proceed, Somy Ali began by funding the charity herself, and has since used almost $300,000 of her own savings. The organization, like so many other nonprofits, is continually hosting fund-raisers and reaching out to potential donors to support the cause. Ali and Salman Khan remain friends, and he has even convinced several of his friends to make sizable donations to NMT. Additional funds for NMT are raised through sales of the humanitarian clothing line Ali started called So-Me Designs. T-shirts feature messages about peace, social justice, and human rights and are available at NMT's website.

Ali operates NMT for no salary, devoting herself completely to this full-time work. She personally assists each victim, from the initial intake process to accompanying them to appointments, even to watching their children. She insists that no one else at NMT makes a salary either, so all the work of helping victims obtain and maintain safety and transforming their lives is coordinated by Ali and a team of student interns and other volunteers. NMT provides a "one-stop shop," as Ali likes to call it, ensuring that victims will be assisted with anything they need—pending funding, of course—to transform their lives. Services might include paying for legal assistance; medical, dental, and vision care; transportation assistance; help identifying, moving into, and paying for safe housing; English instruction; driving classes; and more. NMT also provides services not-typical of most entities. The organization regularly hosts birthday parties for survivors and their kids, and has coordinated baby showers for pregnant victims. Additionally, unlike many domestic violence services, NMT transports victims to appointments. Although this can be risky, NMT does it because most victims lack reliable transportation.

One of the most common requests is for an immigration lawyer. Many victims are undocumented because their abusers promise to petition for their residency status but do not. A provision of the Violence Against Women Act (VAWA) allows victims to self-petition for residency, so NMT collaborates with immigration lawyers, who assist with filing the VAWA applications for a reduced fee.

NMT also collaborates with family lawyers, who assist the women seeking divorce and/or child custody. Other partners include pediatricians, obstetric and gynecological practitioners, dentists, eye doctors, therapists, and other service providers. NMT also works with police victim advocates to ensure that victims know where to go for help.

To date, No More Tears has assisted almost 300 women and more than 600 children. Only one victim is known to have returned to an abuser. Given that the average victim returns seven times before she is able to leave for good, that is a remarkable achievement. One of NMT's first survivors, graduated in May 2011 with a doctoral degree in and is now working in her field of study. Many others have gone on to happier relationships and career pursuits.

Somy Ali has received numerous awards for her humanitarian efforts. Her alma mater, Nova Southeastern University, honored her with a Distinguished Alumni Achievement award in 2008, and in 2011 she received the American Heritage Award from the American Immigration Council as well as recognition from the Asian American Advisory Board of Miami Dade County, among others.

See also: Immigrant Victims of Domestic Abuse; Mai, Mukhtar

Further Reading

Khan, S. (2012, February 23). From Bollywood starlet to Florida women's rights champion. *New York Times*. Retrieved June 22, 2012, from http://india.blogs.nytimes.com/2012/02/23/from-bollywood-starlet-to-florida-womens-rights-champion/

No More Tears. (2012). http://www.nmtproject.org

Laura L. Finley

AMERICAN MEDICAL ASSOCIATION (AMA)

The American Medical Association (AMA) was founded in 1847 at the National Medical Convention in Philadelphia, Pennsylvania. With its founding, the AMA adopted a medical code of ethics and a standard of education for the MD degree. Today, the AMA is the largest professional medical association in the United States. It consists of a number of committees and councils, two of the most important of which are the Council on Science and Public Health and the Council on Ethical and Judicial Affairs. For the purposes of this article, an important council is the AMA National Advisory Council on Violence and Abuse.

The mission of the AMA is to promote the art and science of the medical profession and to improve public health. For the year 2011, the AMA identified five strategic issues of great importance: cost of health care, quality of care, access and workforce, next-generation physician payment, and prevention and wellness. To accomplish these goals, the AMA engages in a number of activities.

One of these activities is the publication of the *Journal of the American Medical Association* (*JAMA*), which has been published continuously since 1883. It is an international, peer-reviewed, professional medical journal published 48 times a year. It contains articles on all areas of interest to the medical profession.

Although the AMA devotes much of their resources to helping physicians with practical matters, such as payment for services and employment, and representing the medical community in legislative concerns, one of the primary activities of the AMA is the development and adoption of reports and policies to guide the profession. These reports and policies are intended to provide physicians with the most current ideas for the proper medical treatment of patients. They are not legally binding on health-care practitioners but do offer guidance in the field of health care and treatment.

The Council of Science and Public Health has researched a number of issues related to domestic abuse. A number of these reports have been adopted by the AMA. Examples include CSA Report 5 (A-94) Memories of Childhood Abuse; CSA Report 9 (I-94) Violence Toward Men: Fact or Fiction?; CSA Report 1 (I-00) Domestic Violence Information and Movie Theaters; CSAPH Report 7 (A-05) Diagnosis and Management of Family Violence.

The Council on Ethical and Judicial Affairs (CEJA) is responsible for establishing ethics policy for the AMA. Not only does the CEJA prepare reports for the AMA, it also issues ethical opinions to guide the AMA in the attainment of its goals. One of the CEJA's more important ethics opinions relating to domestic abuse is CEJA Opinion 2.02: Abuse of Spouses, Children, Elderly Persons, and Others at Risk.

Part of the AMA is the National Advisory Council on Violence and Abuse (NACVA). Through the AMA, the NACVA publishes a compendium of excerpts of policies on topics related to violence and abuse on its website. These excerpts in the Compendium are not the complete policies. The last update to this policy was April 2008. This Compendium is available online. Examples of some the topics in the AMA's Policy Compendium include child abuse and neglect, child sexual abuse, suicide, family violence, and elder abuse.

The AMA has been the subject of criticism as being too partisan and protective of the interests of the medical community, to the detriment of patients and those in need of medical care, especially in the area of medically related legislation that might have a negative impact on the profits of medical providers and in the area of alternative medicine. However, the AMA is a professional organization and does have responsibilities to its membership, and this issue does not detract from the value of many of its other activities. Membership in the AMA is voluntary and is not required for health-care providers by any legal authority in the United States.

Regardless, the AMA is significant source of research and information concerning the issue of domestic violence in the United States. The fact that the AMA devotes a not insignificant portion of their activities and research to the issue of domestic abuse illustrates that, in the last several decades, domestic abuse has, rightfully, become a major focus of public health. Additionally, the AMA has been a leader in recommending routine screening of patients for domestic violence. Such screening has been shown to result in greater identification of victims.

See also: Centers for Disease Control and Prevention (CDC); Health Effects of Domestic Abuse; Hospital and Medical Records and Domestic Abuse; Physicians,

Health-Care Providers, and Domestic Abuse; Social and Societal Effects of Domestic Abuse

Further Reading

American Medical Association: http://www.ama-assn.org

McAfee, R. (1995). Physicians and domestic violence: Can we make a difference? *Journal of the American Medical Association*, 273(22), 1790–1791.

Promoting healthy lifestyles. (n.d.). American Medical Association. Retrieved from http://www.ama-assn.org/ama/pub/physician-resources/public-health/promoting-healthy-lifestyles/violence-prevention.page

William Plouffe Jr.

AMNESTY INTERNATIONAL

Amnesty International (AI) is a global human rights watchdog. Founded in 1961, the organization now boasts more than 2.8 million members in 150 countries. Amnesty's main international office is in London. Sections located in specific regions or countries operate with guidance and support from the international secretariat.

Initially, AI was concerned only with prisoners of conscience. Today, however, AI works on numerous human rights issues. Campaigns include stopping violence against women, defending the rights of those who are trapped in poverty and live in slums, abolishing the death penalty, security with justice (opposing torture), protecting migrants and refugees, regulating the global arms trade, corporate responsibility, and more.

From 2004 to 2010, AI coordinated a Stop Violence Against Women global campaign. Although AI officially ended the campaign in March 2010, the issue has been incorporated into other relevant campaigns. On their website, AI notes that violence against women is pervasive and yet is often ignored and rarely punished.

Current efforts include stopping the silencing of Syrian women activists; supporting Saudi Arabian women, who cannot travel, undertake paid work or higher education, or marry without a male guardian's permission; ending discrimination against women in Yemen; helping free Iranian human rights lawyer Nasrin Sotoudeh, who was convicted of "propaganda against the system" in January 2011; seeking justice for Egyptian women who were forced to undergo "virginity tests"; and standing with women human rights defenders around the globe.

AI researchers have also completed reports about various forms of violence against women. These reports are used to educate the public and to leverage community and political support to make social and policy changes. AI's report on maternal mortality, called *Deadly Delivery: The Maternal Healthcare Crisis in the United States*, helped elevate the issue of women's access to maternal care. Included in the report is the issue of domestic violence as a factor for maternal mortality.

A January 2011 report focused on sexual violence against women in Haiti's makeshift camps. More than 250 cases of rape were reported in just 150 days after the deadly earthquake of January 2010. The report tells the story of one 14-year-old girl, Machou, who lives in a makeshift camp for displaced people in Carrefour Feuilles, southwest Port-au-Prince. She was raped in March when she went to the toilet. "A boy came in after me and opened the door. He gagged me with his hand and did what he wanted to do . . . He hit me. He punched me. I didn't go to the police because I don't know the boy, it wouldn't help. I feel really sad all the time . . . I'm afraid it will happen again," Machou told Amnesty International.

The Canadian section has stressed violence against women as a human rights issue, focusing on the fact that one in three women will endure an abusive relationships during their lifetime. AI Canada has also emphasized the importance of safe schools for girls, as young women across the globe endure abuse and assault on the way to school and on school grounds, often forcing them to drop out.

AIUSA continues to advocate for women and girls. In does so in a number of ways. AIUSA helped craft and promote the International Violence Against Women Act (I-VAWA), which was introduced several times in Congress but has yet to pass. AIUSA has also activated its membership to lobby Congress to support reauthorization of the Violence Against Women Act (VAWA) and to demand that President Obama promote ratification of the Convention on the Elimination of All Forms of Discrimination Against Women (CEDAW), something he promised during the 2008 presidential campaign.

See also: Alaska Natives and Domestic Abuse; Convention on the Elimination of All Forms of Discrimination Against Women (CEDAW); International Violence Against Women Act (I-VAWA); Native Americans and Domestic Abuse; Violence Against Women Act (VAWA); War and Domestic Violence.

Further Reading

Amnesty International. (2010). *Deadly delivery: The maternal health care crisis in the USA*. Retrieved March 15, 2012, from http://www.amnestyusa.org/sites/default/files/pdfs/deadlydelivery.pdf

Haiti: Sexual violence against women increasing. (2011, January). Amnesty International. Retrieved March 15, 2012, from http://www.amnesty.org/en/news-and-updates/report/haiti-sexual-violence-against-women-increasing-2011-01-06

Laura L. Finley

ANGER MANAGEMENT AND DOMESTIC ABUSE

In anger management courses, participants are taught to see things through the eyes of others. They are taught to understand the triggers that make them feel angry and to be in tune with the physical and psychological ways that anger manifests. Courses also teach participants a variety of ways to diffuse or manage anger when it arises, and typically offer a supportive environment in which individuals can practice or role-play those strategies.

Many people mistakenly believe that domestic abuse is caused by anger. That is, abusers must have problems with anger control and thus need to develop anger management strategies. Courts often operate on this premise, assigning abusers to attend anger management courses as a condition of their sentence. Given that domestic violence is not really an anger control issue, however, this intervention has had limited effectiveness in changing abusers' behavior. Critics note that attributing domestic violence to an anger control problem fails to hold batterers accountable for the choices they make. It may reinforce insidious stereotypes that blame victims, suggesting that it is the victim who somehow "provoked" the abuser's anger. Advocates maintain that batterers' behavior is very controlled—that is, they control to whom they will direct their anger (their victim), when they will do it, how they will do it, and who will witness it. Further, attributing domestic violence to anger control issues places the focus of abuse solely on the individual, rather than allowing for a broader view of the societal norms, gender roles, and other practices that form the basis for abuse. Anger management is a quick-fix solution to a complex community problem. A 2004 New York Times article stated that anger management may not help at all (Carey, 2004). The article emphasized that anger management programs vary tremendously and that there is no specific set of criteria to guide these programs. In 2004, the Office on Violence Against Women prohibited domestic violence grant money from being used to support anger management programs for offenders, instead favoring more complex and extensive programs.

Some studies have found that teaching anger management skills to specific groups of offenders might be effective. Lundeberg, Stith, Penn, and Ward (2004) found that the male college students with less effective anger management skills who abuse their dating partners were most likely to be psychologically and physically violent.

Although it is questionable whether anger management has any impact on batterers, it has been recommended for use with children who are exposed to abuse. Children may be angry at both the abuser and the victim, who they see as not protecting them. Several resources suggest that parents and practitioners teach young people that it is okay to be angry, but that there are acceptable and unacceptable ways to show their anger. As a prevention tool, teaching all young people to recognize how they feel when they are getting angry and what they can do to respond to that anger nonviolently is a key focus of many antibullying programs. Young people can be taught strategies like counting to ten, taking deep breaths, and expressing themselves in "I" statements as opposed to personal attacks.

Increasingly, domestic violence centers are offering anger management classes for survivors of abuse. Victims often harbor great anger, not just against their abuser but against others who may not have supported them. Anger management classes, sometimes offered right at a local domestic violence center, may be useful in helping victims come to terms with their anger and identify ways to feel more at peace. A number of workbooks and guides are available for this purpose.

The literature suggests that the most successful, holistic anger management programs are focused on the following 12 core concepts: (1) open mind, or a willingness to listen to different viewpoints; (2) anger does not equal "bad," that is, feeling angry does not make someone a bad person; (3) responsibility for anger management—each individual is personally responsible for how s/he responds when upset; (4) identifying physical cues of anger; (5) relaxation; (6) understanding the underlying emotions that cause an angry response; (7) identifying the connection between anger and negative thoughts; (8) the importance of physical activity; (9) reasoned assertive responses, or the use of "I" language to describe how one is feeling; (10) building self-esteem; (11) addressing each person's "should" system, or their understanding of how the world "should" operate; and (12) addressing resentment, which leads to anger.

See also: Batterer Intervention Programs; Children, Effects of Domestic Abuse on

Further Reading

Adults and Children Together Against Violence. (2001). Violence prevention for families of young children. Retrieved March 15, 2012, from http://actagainstviolence.apa.org/materials/publications/act/violenceprevention_families.pdf

Carey, B. (2004, November 24). Anger management may not help at all. *New York Times*. Retrieved March 15, 2012, from http://www.ncdsv.org/images/AngerManagementMayNotHelpAtAll.pdf

Dunbar, B. (2004). Anger management: A holistic approach. *Journal of the American Psychiatric Nurses Association, 10*(1), 16–23.

Gondolff, E., & Russell, D. (1986). The case against anger control for batterers. Retrieved March 15, 2012, from http://www.biscmi.org/documents/Anger%20Control%20For%20Batterers.html

Lundeberg, K., Stith, S., Penn, C., & Ward, D. (2004). A comparison of nonviolent, psychologically violent, and physically violent male college daters. *Journal of Interpersonal Violence, 19*, 1191–1199.

Potter-Effron, R. (2005). *Handbook of anger management*. London, England: Routledge.

Rosenthal, L., & McDonald, S. (2003). Seeking justice: A review of the second report of the Defense Task Force on Domestic Violence. *Violence Against Women, 9*, 1153–1161.

Laura L. Finley

ANIMAL ABUSE AND DOMESTIC ABUSE

According to the Humane Society of the United States, more American households have pets than have children, and Americans spend more money on pet food than on baby food. Clearly, our pets are many and very dear to us. Sadly, the fact that we love them so much makes them vulnerable to violence. In particular, those who seek to control their partners or family members may manipulate or harm loved pets as a means of doing so.

There are many examples of the connection between animal cruelty and abuse of or violence toward humans. For instance, Patrick Sherrill, who killed 14 coworkers at a post office before shooting himself, had a history of stealing pets and allowing his own dog to mutilate them. Albert DeSalvo, the Boston Strangler, used to abuse cats and dogs by setting their tails on fire. He raped and killed 13 women. Serial killer Jeffrey Dahmer frequently abused dogs, cats, and frogs. School shooters Kip Kinkel, Luke Woodham, Dylan Klebold, and Eric Harris all had bragged about mutilating animals before they went on their shooting sprees.

Pet abuse is related to domestic violence in many ways. A study of 11 major cities found animal abuse to be one of the four most significant indicators of domestic violence. The Humane Society of the United States reported in 2000 that 13 percent of intentional animal abuse cases involved domestic violence. The National Coalition Against Domestic Violence reported in 2007 that 71 percent of victims who own pets and who entered domestic violence shelters claimed that abusers had threatened, injured, or killed their pets. Most incidents of pet abuse occur in front of victims and children as a means of demonstrating the abuser's power and control over all living things.

Several studies have found that batterers who abuse animals are more physically violent than other batterers. Batterers may threaten, injure, or kill their partner's or children's pets. Many victims refuse to leave abusers out of fear of what might happen to family pets. Abusers may harm pets as a way to punish victims who try to leave or in an attempt to coerce the victim back. Abusers may also harm pets as a means of retaliation for some form of self-determination made by the victim, such as enrolling in classes or filing a restraining order. Victims without children are significantly more likely to delay seeking shelter out of concern for their pets than are those with children, 33.3 percent versus 19.5 percent.

Families reporting pet abuse and domestic violence are also twice as likely to report child abuse than are those families in which only domestic violence, not pet abuse, is occurring. Batterers may abuse family pets as a way of coercing children into sexual abuse or as a way of forcing them to be silent about the abuse they are witnessing. Those who abuse animals are also more likely to have been arrested for other violent crimes and drug-related offenses. Children who are exposed to domestic violence are more than three times more likely to abuse pets.

For a long time, this issue was not one that shelter staff were prepared to address. Much has improved, however, One study found 85 percent of domestic violence shelter staff reporting that they frequently help women who discuss pet abuse (Noonan, 2010).

Unfortunately, simply asking about pet abuse is not enough. Most shelters do not have on-site space for animals. According to the ASPCA, only 12 percent of domestic violence programs shelter pets, and less than one quarter (24 percent) even provide referral services to local animal welfare groups. Some research shows victims living in their cars as long as four months while waiting for a pet-friendly space to become available. Women who leave pets behind report feeling tremendous anxiety and fear, which is detrimental to their healing.

Arkow (2003) reported that animal abuse investigations are often the first point of intervention for families experiencing domestic violence. The ASPCA provides training for district attorneys in prosecuting animal cruelty cases, and assists veterinarians in providing expert testimony on the connection between animal cruelty and domestic violence. They have also worked with domestic violence shelters to establish safe locations for pets, as well as lobbying for pet protection orders (restraining orders that protect pets). As of 2012, 22 states as well as Washington, D.C., and Puerto Rico have enacted some form of pet protection order.

Suggestions for victims who have made arrangements to leave abusers and take pets with them include ensuring that all vaccinations and licenses are up-to-date and that they have proper documentation

It is recommended that shelter advocates:

- Ask questions about pets and pet abuse during intake processes;
- Work with animal shelters, veterinarians, and rescue groups to help establish or enhance "safe havens" for pets;
- Include discussion of pets during safety planning;
- Include pets in restraining orders;
- Help victims retrieve and care for pets they have had to leave behind;
- Help victims find pet-friendly housing;
- Work in coalition with animal rights advocates to promote violence-free communities.

See also: Types of Domestic Abuse

Further Reading

Arkow, P. (2003). *Breaking the cycles of violence: A guide to multi-disciplinary interventions. A handbook for child protection, domestic violence and animal protection agencies.* Alameda, CA: Latham Foundation.

Ascione, F. (2000). *Safe havens for pets: Guidelines for programs sheltering pets for women who are battered.* Logan, UT: Utah State University.

Ascione, F., & Arkow, P. (Eds.). (1999). *Child abuse, domestic violence and animal abuse: Linking the circles of compassion for prevention and intervention.* West Lafayette, IN: Purdue University Press.

Ascione, F., Weber, C., Thompson, T., Heath, J., Maruyama, M., & Hayashi. K. (2007). Battered pets and domestic violence: Animal abuse reported by women experiencing intimate violence and by non-abused women. *Violence Against Women, 13*(4), 354–373.

Ascione, F., Weber, C., & Wood, D. (1997). The abuse of animals and domestic violence: A national survey of shelters for women who are battered. *Society and Animals, 5*(3), 205–218.

The connection between domestic violence and animal cruelty. (2012). ASPCA. Retrieved May 31, 2012, from http://www.aspca.org/Fight-Animal-Cruelty/domestic-violence-and-animal-cruelty

Cruelty Connections (n.d.). Petabuse.com. Retrieved May 31, 2012, from http://www.pet-abuse.com/pages/abuse_connection.php

Duel, D. (2004). *Violence prevention & intervention: A directory of animal-related programs.* Washington, DC: Humane Society of the U.S.

Facts about animal abuse and domestic violence. (2006). American Humane Association. Retrieved May 31, 2012, from http://www.americanhumane.org/interaction/support-the-bond/fact-sheets/animal-abuse-domestic-violence.html

Faver, C., & Strand, E. (2003). Domestic violence and animal cruelty: Untangling the web of abuse. *Journal of Social Work Education, 39*(2), 237–253.

Flynn, C. (2000). Woman's best friend: Pet abuse and the role of companion animals in the lives of battered women. *Violence Against Women, 6*(2), 162–177.

Maxwell, M., & O'Rourke, K. (2000). *Domestic violence: A competency-based training manual for Florida's Animal Abuse Investigators.* Tallahassee, FL: Florida State University Institute for Family Violence Studies.

National Crime Prevention Council. (2003). *50 strategies to prevent violent domestic crimes: Screening animal cruelty cases for domestic violence.* Washington, DC.

Noonan. E. (2010, June 18). DA's training links domestic violence, animal abuse. Boston.com. Retrieved July 19, 2012, from http://www.boston.com/yourtown/news/wellesley/2010/06/middlesex_da_adresses_ties_bet.html

Laura L. Finley

ASIA AND DOMESTIC ABUSE

National Geographic lists the following countries in Asia: Afghanistan, Armenia, Azerbaijan, Bahrain, Bangladesh, Bhutan, Cambodia, China, Georgia, India, Indonesia, Iran, Iraq, Israel, Japan, Jordan, Kazakhstan, Kuwait, Kyrgyzstan, Laos, Lebanon, Malaysia, Maldives, Mongolia, Myanmar (Burma), Nepal, North Korea, Oman, Pakistan, Philippines, Qatar, Russia (parts in Europe and Asia), Saudi Arabia, Singapore, South Korea, Sri Lanka, Syria, Tajikistan, Thailand, Timor-Leste (East Timor), Turkey (parts in Europe and Asia), Turkmenistan, United Arab Emirates (UAE), Uzbekistan, Vietnam, and Yemen.

In the 2010 census, approximately 14.7 million people (about 5 percent of all respondents) identified their race as Asian alone. The Asian-alone population grew faster than any other major race group between 2000 and 2010, increasing by 43 percent. The smallest major race group was Native Hawaiian and Other Pacific Islander alone (0.5 million), which represented 0.2 percent of the total population. For more information, see http://2010.census.gov/2010census/data/.

This entry focuses on China, Japan, Singapore, Korea and Taiwan. The entry on **South and Southeast Asia and Domestic Abuse** addresses domestic violence in many of the other countries listed above.

China

A report from the All China Women's Federation released in 2010 found that 64 percent of Chinese adults had experienced some form of violence from a partner. Another study by the China Law Institute found approximately one-third of women had experienced domestic abuse. Experts say these are probably underestimates, as abuse is still considered largely a family affair and thus not discussed publicly in China. Abuse is seen as "normal," such that just 5 percent of both male and female respondents said that their marriage was unhappy. Suicides are very common in China, with an estimated 157,000 Chinese women killing themselves each year. It is believed that approximately two-thirds of those women had been domestic violence victims. Traditional beliefs that males are of greater value than females and the subordination of women economically, politically, and in other realms help explain the high rates of abuse. Higher-income families in China also experience abuse. A survey conducted by the Guangdong Municipal Women's Federation found that of 548 cases of domestic violence, 111 involved people with college diplomas and 88 were in households with incomes above $2,000 yuan ($298 dollars) per month.

China passed its first domestic violence law in 2001, via an amendment to the General Provisions of the Marriage Law. Since then, China has also signed on to the Convention on the Elimination of All Forms of Discrimination Against Women (CEDAW). In 2008, a court in Jiangsu province issued the first protection order in China.

Japan

The National Police Agency of Japan reported a spike in domestic violence incidents in 2012, recording 33,745 incidents, which was the highest since 2003 and an almost 7 percent increase over the previous year. Child abuse complaints also increased, while stalking complaints fell slightly. Previous reports from the National Police Agency have shown that more than 98 percent of the complaints are from women. Although the increases are not good, it does show that more people are willing to seek help.

Japan passed the Act on the Prevention of Spousal Violence Law in 2001. It criminalized domestic violence and incorporated provisions for restraining orders. In 2002, the government started funding domestic violence shelters across the country. Today, according to Makino (2009), there are approximately 117 secure shelters in Japan offering housing as well as counseling. A survey conducted in October/November 2008 by the Cabinet Office found approximately one-third (33.2 percent) of all married women have experienced abuse. Few sought help: 3 percent contacted police or hospitals, and only 1 percent went to shelters or sought legal counsel (Makino, 2009). Advocates say that courts tend to side with men and that those victims who do bring charges are often mistreated by police, lawyers, and judges (Makino, 2009).

Korea

Korea enacted two pieces of domestic violence legislation in 1997: the Special Act on Domestic Violence and the Prevention of Domestic Violence and Victim Protection Act. Advocates say that these laws have not reduced the number of domestic violence incidents, however, although they know that some of the increase in reported incidents is because women are simply more likely to report abuse than they were before. A second survey was administered in 2007. The 2004 survey found 44.6 percent of households had experienced some form of domestic violence in the previous year, with almost 16 percent reporting physical violence between a husband and wife.

Taiwan

The Taiwanese Ministry of the Interior (MOI) reported 79,874 cases of domestic violence in 2008, with 16 victims murdered by abusers. This was a 10 percent increase from the previous year. Experts attribute the increase to the bad economy as well as to increased reporting due to awareness campaigns enacted after Taiwan passed a domestic violence prevention law in 1998. Women still fear reporting abuse, however, because they worry about economic issues, are concerned about losing their children, fear revenge by the abusers, and don't want to tarnish their family's reputation.

A major challenge in Taiwan is the lack of resources for victims. Taiwan has just one social worker for every 3,000 citizens, a far lower rate than the United States (1 to 450), Germany (1 to 650), Hong Kong (1 to 900), and France (1 to 1,000). This means each case worker handles about 70 cases at a time.

Asian Immigrants

Dabby, Patel, and Poore (2010) found that there were 160 instances involving 226 fatalities of Asian immigrants. Of those, 78 percent of victims were women and girls.

One concern for Asian immigrants to the United States is the language barrier. According to the 2010 census, approximately 10 million Americans speak one of the 33 Asian languages categorized by the U.S. Census. Nearly three-quarters (71 percent) of Asian Americans speak a language other than English at home. Language barriers make it difficult for victims to find help and to communicate with service agencies.

According to the Asian and Pacific Islander Institute (API Institute), abuse among Asian immigrants takes generally the same forms as does abuse of other groups. There are a few key differences, however. According to the API, these are:

- Perpetrators can include marital family members: husbands, mothers-in-law, fathers-in-law, brothers-in-law, sisters-in-law, ex-wives, new wives; and/or members of a woman's natal family—her parents, aunts, uncles, adult siblings.
- Multiple batterers may act separately, each using different types of abuse.
- Multiple batterers can act together, playing different roles in one incident.
- In-laws may encourage or support domestic violence, but not perpetrate it themselves.
- Multiple abusers may use coercive control tactics; exercise micro-controls on her movements—monitoring, tracking, and reporting on them; exert power and control from afar through texting, webcams, other technologies.

Additionally, Asian women are more likely to report being pushed out of the home or relationship, whereas in some cultures abusers use "pull" tactics more frequently; that is, they promise not to reoffend in order to pull the victim back once she has left. Another difference is that Asian immigrants may experience different forms of homicides, such as honor killings, dowry killings, or contract killings that are not typical in many other cultures. Because Asian cultures tend to have more rigid gender roles, women who are perceived to have dishonored the family may become victims.

Two resources for Asian immigrants are the Asian Task Force Against Domestic Violence and the Asian & Pacific Islander Institute on Domestic Violence. The Asian Task Force Against Domestic Violence works in Massachusetts and the northeast part of the United States: http://www.atask.org/site/. The Asian & Pacific Islander Institute on Domestic Violence at http://www.apiidv.org/ "works to eliminate domestic violence in Asian and Pacific Islander communities by

- increasing awareness about the extent and depth of the problem;
- making culturally and linguistically specific issues visible;
- strengthening community models of prevention and intervention;

- identifying and expanding resources;
- informing and promoting research and policy; and
- deepening understanding and analyses of the issues surrounding violence against women."

See also: Immigrant Victims of Domestic Abuse; South and Southeast Asian Victims

Further Reading

Byun, W. (2007). Violence against women in Korea and its indicators. *United Nations*. Retrieved January 26, 2013, from http://www.un.org/womenwatch/daw/egm/vaw_indicators_2007/papers/Invited%20Paper%20Korea%20Whasoon%20Byun.pdf

Dabby, C., Patel, H., & Poore, G. (2010, February). Shattered lives: Homicides, domestic violence, and Asian families. Retrieved June 24, 2012, from http://www.apiidv.org/files/Homicides.DV.AsianFamilies-APIIDV-2010.pdf

Domestic violence complaints jump. (2012, April 13). *Japan Times*. Retrieved June 25, 2012, from http://www.japantimes.co.jp/text/nn20120413b1.html#.T-hsqpHl8xM

Makino. C. (2009, August 14). In Japan, more women report domestic crimes. *Women's enews*. Retrieved June 25, 2012, from http://womensenews.org/story/090814/in-japan-more-women-report-domestic-crimes

McLaughlin, K. (2011, September 14). China's domestic violence problem. *Salon*. Retrieved January 26, 2013 from http://www.salon.com/2011/09/14/china_domestic_violence/

Moxley, M. (2010, October 5). For too many, domestic violence part of family life. *Inter Press Service*. Retrieved June 25, 2012, from http://www.ipsnews.net/2010/10/rights-china-for-too-many-domestic-violence-part-of-family-life/

Wang, F. (2009, June 7). Taiwan sees rise in domestic violence. *China Post*. Retrieved June 25, 2012, from http://www.chinapost.com.tw/taiwan/national/national-news/2009/06/07/211190/p1/Taiwan-sees.htm

Laura L. Finley

ATHLETES AND DOMESTIC ABUSE

It wasn't until the mid-1990s, when a series of high-profile athletes were accused of domestic violence, that this issue received much attention publicly or in terms of scholarship. Between 1990 and 1996, 150 formal complaints were issued against Division I or professional athletes for domestic violence, with 77 of those complaints filed in 1995 and 1996. All but seven of the allegations involved football or basketball players. In seven of the cases, the victims were pregnant. Convictions were obtained in only 28 of the 150 cases, although many of those involved plea bargains. Jeff Benedict researched criminal complaints of domestic violence involving National Basketball Association (NBA) players for his 2004 book, *Out of Bounds: Inside the NBA's Culture of Rape, Violence & Crime*. He found 33 complaints against professional basketball players during the 2001–2002 season, but suggested that was a significant underreport. Although most of the data presented here is from the United States, athletes in other countries have perpetrated domestic abuse as well. Between September 11, 2001, and January 2002, the White Ribbon Campaign, a Canada-based, male-led movement to end domestic violence documented 11 allegations involving athletes.

Women's Action Coalition members wear Nicole Brown Simpson masks while protesting against spousal abuse during the O. J. Simpson murder trial in Los Angeles on January 23, 1995. (Vince Bucci/AFP/Getty Images)

The following high-profile cases illustrate the scope of the problem, although this is by no means a comprehensive list. In June 1988, just four months after former heavyweight champion Mike Tyson married Robin Givens, the actress and her family accused Tyson of abuse, and on September 20, 1988, Givens said on national television that she feared her husband. Givens filed for divorce a week later. Tyson's problems escalated when, in 1991, Miss Black America pageant contestant Desiree Washington accused Tyson of rape. He was convicted in 1992 and sentenced to 10 years in prison, with 4 years suspended. He served 3 years total.

Former NFL Man of the Year Warren Moon publicly apologized for repeatedly assaulting his wife. This was after the police arrived at the Moon's home in 1995 in response to a 911 call from their eight-year-old son, who was crying and saying that they needed to hurry because his daddy was going to hit his mommy, Felicia Moon had previously obtained a restraining order against Warren, and court records document at least three prior physical attacks during their marriage.

Perhaps the most well-publicized case of domestic violence involving an athlete was that of O. J. Simpson. In 1995, Simpson was found not guilty of murdering his former wife, Nicole Brown Simpson, and her friend Ronald Goldman. Throughout the investigation and during the trial, evidence emerged that Simpson had battered his former wife. Jurors heard a 911 tape made by Nicole Brown Simpson in which O. J. shouted at her while she pleaded for help. They also saw pictures of Nicole with her face terribly bruised. Many domestic violence advocates found the case to be full of mixed messages. While it did succeed in drawing the public's attention to domestic violence in general, as well as abuse perpetrated by athletes, Simpson's acquittal may have sent the message that battering men can get away with it. In San Diego, Sgt. Anne O'Dell reported batterers threatening their partners by saying, "I'll O. J. you" (Edmonds, 1996).

In 2001, New Jersey Nets star Jason Kidd pleaded guilty to assaulting his wife. Kidd was fined $200 and ordered to take anger management classes. His record was later expunged. Afterwards, he was heckled on the court as a wife beater, but the NBA did not reprimand him. In 2007, Kidd shocked sports fans when he took out a restraining order against his wife, Joumana Kidd. He accused Joumana of extreme cruelty and alleged she physically and mentally abused him over the course of their 10-year marriage. In addition, Kidd alleged that his wife's behavior negatively impacted their children.

In 2002, Milwaukee Bucks All-Star forward Glenn Robinson, suspecting his ex-fiancee Jonta French had been with another man, arrived at the home she shared with their three-year-old daughter visibly drunk, and badgered French to let him in. Upon entering the home, Robinson grabbed her hair, dragged her through the home, slammed her head against a wall, and banged her body against other objects. He then forced her onto the bed and left her, terrified, while he went to the master bedroom to obtain the gun he had left at the home a week earlier. French had hidden the weapon so the toddler wouldn't find it, which enraged Robinson. French managed to run out of the home, screaming, and Robinson was arrested. Little news media coverage addressed the case because, according to author Jeff Benedict, it was more concerned with the domestic violence allegations against an even bigger star. Only three days before Robinson's arrest, Philadelphia police arrested the NBA's Most Valuable Player Allen Iverson based on a call they received from a man stating that Iverson had thrown his wife, Tawanna, out of their home, naked. Iverson was also accused of entering the home later that same evening, gun in the waist of his pants, and threatening the same man who had called the police earlier and demanding to know where his wife was. Iverson was charged with 14 counts, including false imprisonment, criminal trespass, conspiracy, making terroristic threats, and a variety of gun offenses. At trial, the judge dismissed 12 of the 14 charges, then later the remaining 2.

In March 2003, former heavyweight champion Riddick Bowe was arrested on charges of second-degree assault against his wife. This was less than a week before Bowe was to begin serving prison time for abducting his first wife and their five children. Former Junior lightweight and lightweight champion Diego Corrales, who died in May 2007, served 14 months in prison for beating his pregnant wife. In 2002, Filmmaker Spike Lee released his second HBO documentary, this one on football great Jim Brown, who once threw a woman he was dating off a balcony during an argument and, at the time of filming, was serving a six-month sentence for domestic violence.

Some believe that athletes may be targeted by women seeking money or fame, and thus the number of allegations against athletes is inflated. Many fans refuse to believe that their favorite star could be an abuser. Former Boston Celtics star

Robert Parrish was abusive to his wife, Nancy, who kept quiet about it for years. Nancy said she thought no one would believe her, since Robert was considered to be a "gentleman" on the court.

Explanations

One reason athletes may be more likely to perpetrate domestic violence (if indeed they do) is that they may have a difficult time differentiating how to behave in private life from the hyperviolent culture in which they are immersed. This theory has been supported by the research of Jeff Benedict, who has studied college football, professional football, and professional basketball. Gender-role norms teach males to be masculine and tough, and nowhere is this norm more stressed than in sports. The male-peer culture that forms in sports, in particular those with some element of contact, has been found to reinforce antifemale attitudes. Research has shown that it is athletes involved in what sport sociologists call "power and performance sports" (largely football, basketball, boxing, and wrestling) who are most associated with abuse. These cultures also encourage silence, so that athletes who hear their peers denigrating women or know about abusive behavior generally do not speak up.

Athletes might also receive far more leniency from the criminal justice system than do others accused of criminal offenses. While the average male arrested for domestic violence typically goes through the criminal justice system, many times athletes are able to avoid serious sanctions based on their finances, fame, and connections.

Resources

In 1996, two members of Congress proposed legislation requiring athletes to spearhead a national campaign against domestic violence. The NCAA opposed the legislation, arguing it unfairly suggests that athletes bear responsibility for the problem. One NCAA official even called the legislation racist, suggesting that it was a way to target blacks, who are overrepresented in college and professional athletics. The legislation did not pass. The NFL expressed that it was committed to helping reduce the problem of domestic violence, but did not feel this bill was the best way to do so.

Given that athletes are overrepresented in allegations of domestic violence, many professional sport leagues and nonprofit organizations have created programming to show that athletes can also be part of the solution. Some of these programs are targeted specifically at athletes, while others are broader in scope. Most include a focus on gender-role norms, male socialization, and the importance of bystander intervention. Four key factors shape whether bystanders will intervene: (1) awareness that a problem exists and recognition of the negative consequences of the problem for victims; (2) cultivation of a commitment or responsibility to intervene; (3) viewing the victim as not responsible for the incident; and (4) a model for how to intervene and skills to do so.

One of the most successful programs is Mentors in Violence Prevention (MVP), which uses a bystander approach and realistic scenarios relevant to both students and athletes to empower people to intervene in helpful ways when they hear about or witness abuse. (The bystander approach teaches community members how to intervene safely in situations where there is risk for a sexual assault or to support a survivor after an incident.) The Family Violence Prevention Fund offers great materials on Coaching Boys Into Men, including curricula and downloadable posters. In 2001, Green Bay Packers guard Marco Rivera and his wife Michelle worked with Verizon Wireless to create a domestic violence public service announcement (PSA). In 2002, New York Yankees manager Joe Torre founded the Joe Torre Safe at Home Foundation, which provides educational programs to help end the cycle of domestic violence. The National Coalition against Violent Athletes (NCAVA) has a program called INTERCEPT, which "involves administrators, coaches, community leaders and behavioral professionals in a comprehensive effort to end violence by athletes and reassess the role of sport in our society. This program looks to promote sports as a vehicle for developing values such as fairness, accountability, leadership and tolerance. Mindful of the program's mission to promote proactive strategies to provide for the common good by fostering personal accountability to cultivate universal leadership, this program will become a powerful agency in combating athletes and violence while producing moral exemplars of society."

See also: Bystander Intervention Programs; Katz, Jackson; Simpson, O. J. Case

Further Reading

Benedict, J. (1997). *Public Heroes, Private Felons*. Boston, MA: Northeastern University Press.
Benedict, J. (1998). *Athletes and Acquaintance Rape*. Thousand Oaks, CA: Sage.
Benedict, J. (1998). *Pros and Cons: The Criminals Who Play in the NFL*. New York: Grand Central Publishing.
Benedict, J. (2004). *Out of bounds: Inside the NBA's culture of rape, violence & crime*. New York, NY: HarperCollins.
Benedict, J. (2010). A double standard when it comes to athletes and domestic violence. *Sports Illustrated*. Retrieved March 16, 2012, from http://sportsillustrated.cnn.com/2010/writers/jeff_benedict/08/18/krod.stephenson/index.html
Cissner, A. (2009). Evaluating the Mentors in Violence Prevention program. Retrieved March 16, 2012, from http://www.courtinnovation.org/sites/default/files/MVP_evaluation.pdf
Coaching Boys Into Men: http://www.coachescorner.org/index.asp?page=22
Edmonds, P. (1996, October 18). Messages mixed on domestic violence. *USA Today*. Retrieved July 19, 2012, from http://www.usatoday.com/news/index/nns091.htm
Finley, P., Fountain, J., & Finley, L. (2008). *Sport scandals*. Westport, CT: Praeger.
Joe Torre Safe at Home Foundation. http://www.joetorre.org/
Katz, J. (2006). *The Macho Paradox*. Naperville, IL: Sourcebooks.
Kimmel, M., & Messner, M. (Eds.). (2001). *Men's Lives*. Boston, MA: Allyn & Bacon.
McBride, J. (1995). *War, battering, and other sports: The gulf between American men and women*. New York: Humanities Press.

Moynihan, N., Banyard, V., Arnold, J., Eckstein, R., & Stapleton, J. (2010), Engaging intercollegiate athletes in preventing and intervening in sexual and intimate partner violence. *Journal of American College Health*, 59(3), 197–204.

National Coalition against Violent Athletes: http://www.ncava.org/Prevention.html

O'Neil. D. (2010, October 14). Athletes part of problem, solution. *ESPN*. Retrieved March 16, 2012, from http://sports.espn.go.com/ncaa/columns/story?columnist=oneil_dana&id=5680182

Laura L. Finley

AVON CORPORATION

Founded in 1955 by the cosmetic company Avon Products Inc., the Avon Foundation aims to improve the lives of women. Currently, the foundation focuses on two initiatives: breast cancer research and access to care, and ending gender violence, in particular, domestic violence. The foundation also provides disaster relief. Through 2011, it has raised more than $850 million, which has been donated to groups and organizations around the world. This makes it the largest corporate philanthropy effort devoted to women's causes.

In 2004, the foundation established its Speak Out against Domestic Violence campaign to raise awareness, educate, and serve victims of abuse. Through the end of 2011, more than $28 million was raised for domestic violence programs. Avon Foundation partners with "m.powerment by Mark" to raise funds through jewelry sales in order to help break the cycle of abuse. Since 2008, that effort has raised more than $1 million. Current celebrity spokesperson Ashley Greene helped kick of Teen Dating Violence Awareness Month in February 2012.

In 2012, Avon Foundation sponsored a global domestic violence prevention app challenge. It called on activists and developers to create apps that educate about abuse and/or assist victims. In honor of International Women's Day, Avon Global Ambassador and Honorary Chairman of the Avon Foundation for Women, actress Reese

Avon Global Ambassador Reese Witherspoon and Avon Chairman and CEO Andrea Jung celebrate International Women's Day on March 4, 2008. (PRNewsFoto/Avon Products, Inc./Larry Busacca)

Witherspoon, and Avon Chairman and CEO Andrea Jung, announced 10 $60,000 grants to support women's domestic violence shelters and agencies from around the world. The 2012 grantees are from Australia, Canada, Chile, Colombia, Ecuador, Ukraine, Slovakia, Romania, Italy, and Greece. These grants are part of the Global Believe Fund, which was created in 2011 to expand the company's work on domestic violence globally.

On February 28, 2012, at the 2nd World Conference on Women's Shelters in Washington, D.C., Witherspoon and Jung presented four organizations with Speaking Out about Violence against Women awards. Women's Aid of the UK won the award for storytelling for its CUT movie campaign, which featured actress Keira Knightley enduring brutal attacks. Within six days of the launch of the film online, it had received over a half million hits. The Innovation award was presented to YWCA Canada for its Safety Siren app, which has been downloaded more than 4,000 times. The Rwanda Women Network won the Break the Silence award for its poster campaign depicting abuse as a societal problem. Breakthrough India was awarded the prize for Excellence in Communications for its "Bell Bajao!" (Ring the Bell!) campaign, which helped to motivate neighbors to take action against abuse.

On its website, the Avon Foundation also provides numerous resources for victims and service providers. It features facts about abuse and a downloadable domestic abuse resource guide (available in English and Spanish). Also available is an online learning module called Honor Our Voices that teaches about abuse through the eyes of children ranging from infants to age 18. Campuses can use Avon Foundation's free downloadable "Beyond Title IX: Guidelines for Preventing and Responding to Gender-Based Violence in Higher Education." Through partnership with the National Family Justice Center Alliance and state Family Justice Centers, Avon Foundation's website features a 4:28-minute video. Other videos are available by clicking on the domestic violence video library link on the website. From the website, interested persons can link to another awareness campaign called No More, which provides additional information, toolkits, videos, and products. Finally, the website features links to ideas for survivors and friends and families to speak out and get involved.

Avon Foundation also encourages its sales associates to make personal donations to domestic violence organizations and will match donations of $25 to $15,000, per associate, per calendar year.

Further Reading

Avon Foundation: http://www.avonfoundation.org/
No More: Together We Can End Domestic Violence and Sexual Assault: http://www.nomore.org

Laura L. Finley

B

BATTERED WOMAN SYNDROME

The battered woman syndrome (BWS) was originally developed by Lenore E. A. Walker, EdD, as a research proposal funded by the National Institute of Mental Health in 1977 that included data collection from over 400 battered women. BWS is used to describe the signs and symptoms that battered women may experience as a result of violent and abusive relationships. BWS research is based on the theories of learned helplessness and the Walker cycle of violence. It includes data analysis from assessment instruments such as the Battered Woman Syndrome Questionnaire (BWSQ). According to the research, battering occurs in every demographic group studied, resulting in the syndrome being found across demographic groups. The most common risk factors for men becoming batterers was learned violent behavior, usually from exposure to violence in the childhood home. However, Dr. Walker found the risk factor for women becoming battering victims was simply being a woman. In 1998, Dr. Walker revisited the BWS study and continues to collect data in order to achieve multicultural inclusivity and generalizability and further specify BWS. Her current research includes data collected from battered women from different cultures and countries, women within the prison system, as well as battered women with substance abuse issues.

The battered woman syndrome originally "consisted of the pattern of signs and symptoms that have been found to occur after a woman has been physically, sexually, and/or psychologically abused in an intimate relationship, when the partner (usually, but not always, a man) exerted power and control over the woman to coerce her into doing whatever he wanted, without regard to her rights or feelings" (Walker, 2009, p. 42). However, current research has specifically identified BWS by six groups of criteria. The first three groups of criteria include intrusive recollection of the traumatic event(s), hyperarousal and high levels of anxiety, and avoidance behavior and emotional numbing. Avoidance behaviors and emotional numbing may include depression and dissociation, and the individual may engage in minimization, repression, and denial as coping mechanisms. These criteria are consistent with those present for the diagnosis of post-traumatic stress disorder (PTSD) as the experience of abuse in intimate relationships may result in the trauma symptomatology. The three remaining criteria are specific to intimate partner victims (IPV) and include disrupted interpersonal relationships resulting from the batterer's power and control, body image distortion and/or somatic or physical complaints, and sexual intimacy issues. Interpersonal partner violence refers to the battering of an individual in an intimate relationship and is considered learned behavior used for the acquisition and maintenance of power and control. A batterer may use physical violence, sexual coercion, and/or many forms of manipulation including isolation, following his rules, sex, degradation, jealousy, unpredictability, and direct and indirect threats of more violence. Although the limited research suggests that there may be some differences in same-sex violence and heterosexual violence, the use of power and control over one's partner is still primary.

The theories behind the BWS include learned helplessness, or the battered woman's perception of loss of control over events that occur, and the Walker cycle theory of violence, or distinct phases within a battering cycle based on tension-reduction theory. According to the theory of learned helplessness, the battered woman's belief that she is unable to control what happens to her or escape the batterer is reinforced by the batterer's power and control. This perceived lack of control or influence over one's life results in feelings of helplessness.

Critics have argued that this theory perpetuates stereotypes of battered women as helpless and powerless victims, thus further preventing the actualization of autonomous control and power in their lives. Further, some take issue with the word "syndrome," as it seems to imply some form of mental illness or deficiency. However, the concept of learned helplessness, conceptualized as cognitive and behavioral mechanisms that contribute to the perceived lack of control that battered women may experience in abusive intimate relationships, assists in the understanding of why these women may feel helpless to change or leave an abusive relationship. Furthermore, learned helplessness as applied to the BWS suggests that the perceived lack of control may result in the development of coping strategies by battered women that are essential for survival. According to Walker, the "battered woman is not helpless at all but rather skilled in staying alive and minimizing her physical and psychological injuries in a brutal environment" (Walker, 2009, p. 8). The second theory of the BWS includes the Walker cycle theory of violence, a tension-reduction theory that includes three distinct phases associated with a recurring battering cycle. The three phases include tension-building accompanied with rising sense of danger, the acute battering incident, and the loving-contrition phase.

The BWS research includes data collection via multiple assessment instruments, including the BWSQ, Trauma Symptom Inventory (TSI), the Detailed Assessment of Postraumatic Stress (DAPS), and the Posttraumatic Stress Disorder (PTSD) checklist. The BWSQ consists of participants' responses to both open-ended and forced-choice questions and descriptions of four battering incidents. The BWSQ assessed for the participants' endorsement of their subjective experience of symptoms associated with trauma and BWS resulting from battering relationships. In 2002, the BWSQ was revised to include questions that assessed for symptoms specifically associated with BWS. The current research takes into account multicultural issues and diversity to include women from other countries and cultures, as well as those within the prison system and those with substance abuse issues. In addition, the current research does not confine the definition of battering to physical abuse, as psychological abuse is the most significant factor causing painful memories.

According to Dr. Walker, there has been much controversy throughout the years about how to help battered women heal.

I have always taken the side that should they need professional services, it should be available and it should be the best professional services (psychotherapy, assessment), not because they're mentally ill but because mentally ill women do get battered and it's across all demographic groups and for some people it does cause mental illness. Some people it does not [cause mental illness]. Today it (BWS) is much more considered PTSD, and not every woman has BWS. It is defined as psychological characteristics that develop and not all women have all of the criteria but a lot of women have at least some of the characteristics. (Dr. Walker, personal communication, October 18, 2011)

BWS has also been used in cases of self-defense to explain why battered women use violent means to defend themselves against their battering partners. It was the case of Francine Hughes, who burned her husband in his bed after enduring years of abuse, that first popularized the concept of BWS. The case was popularized in the 1984 film starring Farrah Fawcett, *The Burning Bed*. The concept of the battered woman syndrome assists others in understanding that the abuse that battered women experience may cause them to reexperience trauma previous to the current battering incident.

See also: Cycle of Violence; Hughes, Francine; Self-Defense, Legal Issues; Walker, Lenore

Further Reading

Battered woman syndrome. (n.d.). Rape, Abuse, and Incest National Network. Retrieved from http://www.rainn.org/get-information/effects-of-sexual-assault/battered-woman-syndrome

Dowd, M. (1999). The "battered woman's defense": Its history and future. *Findlaw*. Retrieved March 16, 2012, from http://library.findlaw.com/1999/Dec/1/130513.html

Russell, B. (2010). *Battered woman syndrome as a legal defense: History, effectiveness, and implications*. Jefferson, NC: McFarland.

Walker, L. E. (1979). *The battered woman*. New York, NY: Harper & Row.

Walker, L. E. A. (2009). *The battered woman syndrome* (3rd ed.). New York, NY: Springer.

Kathryn Goesel

BATTERER INTERVENTION PROGRAMS

Domestic violence is a catastrophic and pervasive social problem that currently affects one out of four women living in the United States, according to the U.S. Department of Justice. The earliest response to domestic violence was developed in the 1970s by grassroots domestic violence organizations through the establishment of safe housing for women and children. By 1978, the National Coalition against Domestic Violence (http://www.ncadv.org) was formed to raise financial aid for shelters and services throughout the United States. Domestic violence agencies quickly grew in numbers as women from an array of backgrounds began reaching out for assistance; however, despite the rapid growth of support services, these agencies were only providing reactive interventions and not mitigating the abusive behaviors of perpetrators. In order to reduce these abusive behaviors, advocates began to design and promote batterer intervention programs. In 1980,

California became the first state to mandate treatment for men convicted of domestic violence, and throughout the 1980s, many states began enacting mandatory arrest laws that required police officers to arrest offenders in domestic violence incidents. Consequently, as the number of abusers entering the criminal justice system increased, the number of batterer intervention programs skyrocketed.

Batterers Intervention Modalities

The first batterer intervention programs rose out of consciousness-raising groups operating out of women's shelters. These peer-provided, self-help groups were grounded in a feminist framework and focused on identifying and eliminating behaviors that men utilize to control women. In 1980, the Domestic Abuse Intervention Programs (DAIP) were created to reform the criminal justice system in Duluth, Minnesota, which later became known as The Duluth Model (http://www.theduluthmodel.org). The Duluth Model was founded on feminist theories that highlighted the use of abusive behaviors by perpetrators to gain power and control over victims. This model includes a "Power and Control Wheel" that illustrates the variety of behaviors used by abusers; including minimization, denial, blame, intimidation, emotional abuse, isolation, male privilege, economic abuse, coercion, and threats. The Duluth Model includes a curriculum focused around eight themes: nonviolence, nonthreatening behavior, respect, support and trust, honesty and accountability, sexual respect, partnership and negotiation, and fairness. Through this curriculum, men are taught to identify their hierarchical beliefs and to reconceptualize men and women as equals. The Duluth Model became a widely acknowledged batterer intervention program and, as a result, is currently the required curriculum for many states' mandatory intervention laws.

Although the Duluth Model is the most recognized batterer intervention program, in practice, most intervention approaches encompass a blend of the Duluth Model and cognitive behavioral techniques. Cognitive behavioral therapy (CBT) was developed in the 1960s by Dr. Aaron Beck for the treatment of depression. When applied to the field of domestic violence, the aim is to examine the ways in which perpetrators' thoughts and emotions lead to their abusive behaviors. Perpetrators are taught how to identify triggers of their abusive episodes and how to use healthy coping skills to challenge their abusive thoughts and behaviors. These coping skills are practiced in group sessions and include time-outs, self-talk, and relaxation techniques.

In addition to the Duluth Model and CBT, anger management is a frequently used model for intervention treatment. Anger management classes are derived from cognitive-behavioral (CBT) approaches and emphasize the belief that abusive behaviors are attributed to out-of-control anger. The focus of treatment is to teach strategies such as relaxation, cognitive restructuring, problem solving, and communication skills. However, feminist advocates are highly critical of anger management classes because the assumption is that abuse occurs when the perpetrator is out of control. This view minimizes responsibility for abusive behaviors. In contrast, the feminist model argues that perpetrators choose to engage in abusive behaviors to gain power and control over victims.

The last treatment modality used is couples therapy. The foundation of couples therapy is the belief that both partners contribute to the strengths and problems of the relationship. The goals of therapy are to locate problems in the interactions of the couple and focus on finding ways to effectively solve the issues. Sessions are used to improve communication and conflict resolution skills. This modality is also highly criticized by feminist advocates. Similar to anger management approaches, couples therapy minimizes the responsibility of the perpetrator for his (or her) actions and places blame on the victim. In some situations, couples counseling can be dangerous for victims. For example, if the victim is encouraged in sessions to voice her or his concerns with the relationship or to identify abusive behaviors of the perpetrator, then the perpetrator may become angry and seek revenge outside of the session. For this reason, some states explicitly prohibit the use of couples therapy as a court-mandated intervention for domestic violence.

Batterer's Intervention Procedures

Each batterer intervention group is different depending on the theoretical framework, the organization providing the treatment, and the group leader running the sessions. To summarize a typical framework, most groups include similar components such as the initial assessment, victim contacts, orientation, group sessions, termination, and follow-up.

During the initial intake, the client meets with an individual counselor to assess the client's history of abusive behavior and to screen for co-occurring disorders such as mental health issues and/or substance abuse. The domestic violence assessment examines a broad range of behaviors including emotional, physical, sexual, and financial abuse. Education is provided to explain the ways in which these behaviors are abusive and how the behaviors illustrate control strategies. Mandated clients are required to sign a release for the counselor to speak with the client's probation officer and partner. If the client displays symptoms of mental health and/or substance abuse, a referral is provided for additional treatment by an outside psychiatrist and/or therapist. This referral is not a replacement for batterer intervention but rather an addition to the program.

Following the initial intake, each program differs on their protocol regarding contact with the victim. Some states require that batterer programs contact the victim, while other states have no requirement. Counselors often notify a victim that the perpetrator has started the program, inform the victim whether or not the perpetrator completes the program, and inform the victim if the perpetrator is terminated for noncompliance. A victim will always be notified if he or she is in immediate, imminent danger. When a call is made to the victim, an advocate may provide information on domestic violence services and safety planning if needed.

The goal of the orientation is to develop a therapeutic relationship with the client and to explain the rules and expectations for the program. The number one rule for group members is that they are to refrain from engaging in abusive behaviors.

Counselors provide information on the definition of abuse and the different types of abuse including emotional, physical, sexual, and financial abuse. The counselor also identifies ways in which abusive behavior affects the clients' partners and family. Many programs require that the client verbally take responsibility for his abusive behaviors in order to continue the program.

Program structures can vary from a strict curriculum focus to a more open-ended discussion. The counselor supports clients by holding them accountable to their abusive behaviors and challenging group members that are minimizing/denying the abuse or blaming the victim. Perpetrators are educated on the Power and Control Wheel and the ways in which abusive behaviors are used to gain power over the victims. Perpetrators are taught how to identify triggers and thought patterns that lead to abusive behaviors and are instructed on coping skills to intervene with their pattern of abuse.

Depending on the clients attending the group, there are also ethnic and cultural differences that must be taken into consideration. For example, among African American communities, an environment of poverty and crime can foster an association between manhood and violence. Therefore, treatment needs to address concepts of cultural self-hatred, anger, black-on-black violence, and cultural codes such as "disrespect." Similarly, among Latino groups, discussing the perception of "machismo" and possible glorification of abusive behavior as an expression of manhood needs to occur.

Batterer intervention can also utilize the strengths of ethnic communities to better facilitate change in the perpetrator. For example, among African American and Latino clients, providing information on the ways in which the perpetrator's abusive behaviors impact not only the victim but also the community can provide additional motivation for change. Batterer intervention programs that focus on Asian American perpetrators may emphasize the laws surrounding domestic violence in the United States. Counselors need to be aware that some Asian immigrant perpetrators may hold beliefs that domestic violence is an acceptable behavior. Providing education on the U.S. cultural and legal perspective is therefore imperative.

Following the completion of the batterer intervention program, many programs offer a graduation ceremony. A graduation ceremony provides an opportunity for the group members to process their accomplishments and to invite family members to celebrate. Participants are provided information for follow-up care if necessary. The partners and the probation officers are contacted and informed that the participant completed program. Some programs provide follow-up calls to the participants to periodically check in and verify whether or not the participant is succeeding. During a follow-up call, if the participant shares he has continued to engage in abusive behaviors, a recommendation is made to the participant to reenroll in the batterer intervention program.

In sum, batterer intervention groups are run differently depending on the agency that is offering the program. Some programs differ based on theoretical foundations, where others differ in the deliverance of the curriculum. There are also programs designed specifically to meet the needs in the community, as is the case with culturally competent programs.

Program Effectiveness

The effectiveness of batterer intervention programs in eliminating or decreasing the behaviors of abusers is a highly debated topic in the field of domestic violence. Most states require that perpetrators attend batterer intervention programs, but there is little evidence on the impact of these programs. Babcock, Green, and Robie (2004) analyzed 22 batterer intervention studies and concluded that there was only a 5 percent decrease in abusive behaviors for men who were arrested and referred to batterer intervention programs compared with men who were arrested and sanctioned without intervention. Similarly, Feder and Wilson (2005) conducted an analysis of the most rigorous research studies and found that there was a 7 percent decrease in recidivism in cases in which interventions were mandated. However, this 7 percent decrease was based on documented abusive behaviors. When taking into account the partner reports of abusive behavior, there was no difference in abusive behaviors between men that were mandated to treatment and men who were not mandated.

Stuart, Temple, and Moore (2007) identified four reasons why batterer interventions are unsuccessful in changing perpetrators' abusive behaviors. The first reason is that batterer interventions primarily serve mandated clients. When a client is mandated to treatment, the client's readiness and willingness to change is lower than if a perpetrator enters treatment on his own accord. If the perpetrator is not committed to change, then no treatment program will be successful. Furthermore, research has indicated that many batterers minimize and/or deny their abusive behaviors. Treatment will not be effective until the perpetrator accepts full responsibility for his behaviors. Second, there is not sufficient funding for batterer intervention-programs. A shortage of funds leads to a lack of resources, limited training of counselors, and professional burnout. Third, there are few interventions that are tailored to the specific needs of the client. For example, there is little emphasis on mental health and/or substance abuse issues among batterer intervention programs. Fourth, the rapid growth of batterer intervention programs and laws mandating batterer intervention treatment has created a rush for programs to be developed but has left little time to focus on evaluating program effectiveness. Scholarly research should continue to evaluate the effectiveness of batterer intervention programs.

As many work to address violence in their communities, most counselors and therapists agree it is essential to continue to evaluate the effectiveness of batterer intervention programs and to design programs that meet the needs of individual batterers. It is not enough to provide services to victims of abuse; there must be ways to prevent abuse from occurring.

See also: Anger Management and Domestic Abuse; Duluth Model; Feminism and Domestic Violence

Further Reading

Babcock, J. C., Green, C. E., & Robie, C. (2004). Does batterers' treatment work? A meta-analytic review of domestic violence treatment. *Clinical Psychological Review, 23,* 1023–1053.

Feder, L., & Wilson, D. B. (2005). A meta-analytic review of court-mandated batterer intervention programs: Can courts affect abusers' behavior? *Journal of Experimental Criminology, 1*, 239–262.

Healey, K., Smith, C., & O'Sullivan, C. (2009). *Batterer intervention: Program approaches and criminal justice strategies.* Washington, DC: U.S. Department of Justice.

Henning, K., & Holdford, R. (2006). Minimization, denial and victim blaming by batterers: How much does the truth matter? *Criminal Justice and Behavior, 33*(1), 110–130.

Stuart, G. I., Temple, J. R., & Moore, T. M. (2007). Improving batterer intervention programs through theory-based research. *Journal of the American Medical Association, 2*(5), 560–562.

Williams, O. (1992). Ethnically sensitive practice to enhance treatment participation of African American men who batter. *Families in Society: The Journal of Contemporary Human Services, 12*, 588–595.

Williams, O. (1995). Treatment for African-American men who batter. *CURA Reporter: Bulletin of the Center for Urban and Regional Affairs, 25*(3), 12–16. Minneapolis, MN: University of Minnesota.

Amanda Mathisen Stylianou

BEIJING DECLARATION AND PLATFORM FOR ACTION

The Beijing Declaration and Platform for Action emerged from the Fourth World Conference on Women's Rights held in September 1995 in Beijing, China. Previous World Conferences were held in Mexico City in 1975, Copenhagen in 1980, and Nairobi in 1985. In 1985, participants adopted the Nairobi Forward-looking Strategies for the Advancement of Women, to be implemented by the year 2000. Reviews in 2000, 2005, and 2010 assessed the degree to which these strategies were implemented, the results showing mixed success.

Nineteen seventy-five was proclaimed International Women's Year by the UN General Assembly, a move that is considered a turning point because it put women's issues on the agenda. It was followed by the United Nations Decade for Women, from 1976 to 1985, "a world-wide effort to examine the status and rights of women and to bring women into decision-making at all levels." Those efforts coalesced in the adoption of the Convention on the Elimination of All Forms of Discrimination against Women (CEDAW) in 1979 by the UN General Assembly. CEDAW entered into force in 1981, the first international human rights treaty to specifically address gender equality.

In Beijing, 189 governments, more than 5,000 representatives from some 2,100 nongovernmental organizations (NGOs), some 5,000 members of media, and more than 30,000 individuals attended. Hillary Clinton, then first lady, was an outspoken advocate for women's human rights and even criticized the host Chinese government for its failures. She famously pronounced "it is no longer acceptable to discuss women's rights as separate from human rights" (Tyler, 1995).

The goal of the Platform for Action is "removing all the obstacles to women's active participation in all spheres of public and private life through a full and equal share in economic, social, cultural and political decision-making." This should involve a partnership, based on equality, between women and men. The platform reiterated that women's rights and the rights of female children are inalienable and indivisible from universal human rights. Further, it acknowledged the diversity of women's conditions and experiences and recognized that some women face unique barriers to their empowerment.

A review of the status of women globally identified progress made since Nairobi. Many governments enacted legislation to promote equality between women and men, and international groups and organizations focused greater attention on gender equality. The role of nongovernmental organizations and feminist groups as catalysts in promoting the status of women was specifically noted, as were increases in knowledge about the status of women and men, greater entrance of women into formerly male-dominated areas of work, and additional acceptance of traditionally domestic tasks such as child care by men.

The review also noted significant challenges. (1) continued use of violence against women as a weapon of war; (2) excessive military expenditures resulting in a reduction in resources for social development; (3) poorly designed structural adjustment policies that keep countries in debt and thus unable to build critical infrastructures needed to ensure human rights; (4) an increase in the number of people in poverty, an overwhelming number of whom are women; (5) unequal political participation by women, such that only 10 percent of elected legislators worldwide were women and the continued underrepresentation of women in the UN itself; (6) the increasing fragility of the environment; (7) widespread unemployment or employment of women in ways that lack long-term job security; (8) failure of macro- and micro-level economic policies and programs to take into account their impact on women and girls; (9) inadequate attention to the pivotal role women play in the economy and in combating poverty; (10) wage discrimination, family disintegration, migration, war, and internal displacements that contribute to the rising number of female-headed households; (11) unequal participation of women in the movements for peace; (12) the freedom have or adopt a religion or belief and to practice it without discrimination; (13) restrictions on the ability of nongovernmental organizations, so key in advancing women's rights, in certain countries; (14) failure in some countries to see gender differences as largely socially constructed rather than biological differences; (15) lack of acceptance of the rights, capabilities, and responsibilities of all members of a family, including the significance of motherhood and the role of women in procreation; (16) inadequate recognition of the role women play as caretakers of children, the sick, and the elderly; (17) the continued marginalization of women of color and poor women; (18) the barriers to empowerment for indigenous women; (19) use of new technologies and communication systems to disseminate stereotypical and demeaning images of women and girls; (20) environmental degradation, including exposure to pollution and toxic wastes, that disproportionately impact women and girls; (21) the connections between environmental degradation and poverty, fueled largely by unsustainable consumption and production; (22) increased rural to urban migration, leading to population density concerns, among others; (23) women's greater risk for being infected with HIV and AIDs; (24) continued prenatal sex selection, higher mortality of female infants and young girls, and girls' lesser school enrollment, indicating continued son preference; (25) failure of many nations to ratify the Convention on the Rights of the Child; (26) exposure of women and girls to sexual and economic exploitation; and (27) the need to ensure that girls have the life skills for effective participation in the social, cultural, political, and economic realms.

Specifically, the platform called on governments, NGOs, and civil society to address the following:

- The persistent and increasing burden of poverty on women
- Inequalities and inadequacies in and unequal access to education and training
- Inequalities and inadequacies in and unequal access to health care and related services
- Violence against women
- The effects of armed or other kinds of conflict on women, including those living under foreign occupation
- Inequality in economic structures and policies, in all forms of productive activities and in access to resources
- Inequality between men and women in the sharing of power and decision making at all levels
- Insufficient mechanisms at all levels to promote the advancement of women
- Lack of respect for and inadequate promotion and protection of the human rights of women
- Stereotyping of women and inequality in women's access to and participation in all communication systems, especially in the media
- Gender inequalities in the management of natural resources and in the safeguarding of the environment
- Persistent discrimination against and violation of the rights of the girl child

In order to be successful, the platform requires strong commitment from governments and international organizations and institutions. The mobilization of resources—in particular, financial contributions—is essential. Subsequent reviews of achievements would continue to highlight the need for investment in gender equality beyond simple lip service.

In 2000, a five-year follow-up known as Beijing +5 was coordinated. It included a series of special sessions and meetings to review the progress made toward the Beijing Platform and offered additional recommendations. The review emphasized the continued need for women's access to decision making, in particular as it related to peacekeeping in conflict regions, HIV/AIDS and humanitarian crisis responses that are gender-sensitive, new patterns of migration that impact women's lives, new technologies that must be widely available to women and girls, violence against women and the trafficking of women and girls, and the challenges presented by globalization. Several new goals were articulated. These are listed on UN Women's website and included:

a. Closure of the gender gap in primary and secondary education by 2005, and free and compulsory and universal primary education for both girls and boys by 2015;
b. The achievement of a 50 percent improvement in levels of adult literacy, especially for women, by 2015;
c. The creation and maintenance of a nondiscriminatory, as well as gender-sensitive legal environment through reviewing legislation with a view to striving to remove discriminatory provisions as soon as possible, preferably by 2005;

d. Universal access to high-quality primary health care, throughout the life cycle, including sexual and reproductive health care, not later than 2015.

In 2005, the 10-year review of the Beijing Platform noted that women still lacked adequate representation in public- and private-sector decision making, unequal employment opportunities and economic participation, inadequate access to education and health-care systems, disproportionate impact of environmental degradation and crises on women and girls, violence in the form of domestic abuse, trafficking and sexual exploitation, higher levels of poverty for women, and the high rate of HIV/AIDS infections. It noted that while many governments and organizations had committed to implementing the platform's recommendations, there were gaps between their rhetoric and their action. Specifically, the review found only limited progress had been made in mainstreaming gender into the policy decision making of both private and public sectors. Further, the review highlighted the continued need to improve the availability and quality of data on gender inequalities, such as maternal mortality, infant mortality, adult morbidity, school enrollment, economic opportunity, and more. While noting the increased attention to the role of men and boys in achieving gender equality, the review called on still greater efforts. Noting the important role women's organizations and NGOs play in effecting gender equality, the 10-year review called for still more and more effective collaboration between governments and these groups. The continued need to recognize the diversity of women's experiences based on age, race, ethnicity, culture, and disability, among other factors, was noted as well.

March 2010 saw the 15-year review of the Beijing Platform.

See also: Convention on the Elimination of All Forms of Discrimination Against Women (CEDAW); The United Nations and Domestic Abuse

Further Reading

Beijing at ten and beyond: http://www.un.org/womenwatch/daw/beijing/beijingat10/index.html
Beijing plus fifteen: http://www.un.org/womenwatch/daw/beijing15/index.html
Five-year review of the implementation of the Beijing Declaration and Platform for Action: http://www.un.org/womenwatch/daw/followup/beijing+5.htm
Fourth World Conference on Women: http://www.un.org/womenwatch/daw/beijing/fwcwn.html
Tyler, P. (1995, September 6). Hillary Clinton, in China, details abuse of women. *New York Times*. Retrieved June 15, 2012, from http://www.nytimes.com/1995/09/06/world/hillary-clinton-in-china-details-abuse-of-women.html?pa

Laura L. Finley

BIOLOGICAL AND PSYCHOLOGICAL THEORIES ABOUT DOMESTIC ABUSE

Over time, numerous criminological theories have been applied to help explain the behavior of abusers as well as victims of abuse. The biological theories generally see crime or violence as being the result of heritable traits or of changes in brain or other bodily chemistry due to injuries. Psychological theories tend to place the onus for abuse on mental illness or other forms of psychopathology. Both theoretical perspectives have been found to have some explanatory power as well as a number of limitations. Theories are important because they not only help explain why a phenomenon occurs, but they are also crucial in shaping prevention efforts and treatment programs.

Biological Theories

The biological theories first emerged in the mid-nineteenth century, largely fueled by Charles Darwin's ideas about evolution and his concept of survival of the fittest. Gene-based evolutionary theories are based on the assumption that people inherit behaviors that were adaptive over time. That is, behaviors that help organisms respond to their environment and allow them to reproduce will be passed on via one's genes. Evolutionary perspectives suggest that males will attempt to obtain and retain young, fertile mates who can produce healthy offspring. One biological theory is that males' abuse based on sexual jealousy and their innate need to retain a mate with whom they can procreate and reproduce. Thus abusive behavior is used when men feel a threat, such as when a man believes his wife or partner might find someone else. Cunningham et al. (1998) explained:

> It is highly undesirable, genetically speaking, for a man to invest long-term parental care in offspring not carrying his genes. Females, on the other hand, will be inclined towards high status mates who can provide shelter and care for the offspring they produce. If males perceive themselves to be of a lower status than their mates (e.g., for humans, if they cannot find a job or if they suddenly lose their job), or if they perceive their mate to be very attractive to other males and therefore likely to be unfaithful or leave them altogether, gene-based internal mechanisms can trigger the use of mate retention tactics to ensure females do not leave or become impregnated by another male.

Another biological theory posits that head injuries lead men to abuse their partners. Rosenbaum and Hoge (1989), Rosenbaum (1991), and Rosenbaum et al. (1994) published a series of studies showing that many abusive men had histories of head trauma. They maintained that the correlation could actually be a causal link between the brain dysfunction and neurological damage resulting from the head trauma and abusive behavior. The argument is that head trauma leads to impulse control problems, distorted judgment, communication difficulties, and hypersensitivity to alcohol, as well as increased stress among families. Some point to the fact that military personnel are overrepresented among those with brain injuries who are also perpetrators of abuse as evidence of the link. An estimated 20 percent of U.S. combat troops leaving conflict situations suffer from a traumatic brain injury (TBI). Other research, however, has not shown that head-injured men were more physically aggressive at home than other men (Warnken, Rosenbaum, Fletcher, Hoge, & Adelman, 1994).

Several biochemical theories have been suggested to explain not just domestic violence but other forms of male violence. The most commonly cited of these is the link between testosterone and male aggression. Some research has found that men with more testosterone perpetrate more violence.

A challenge for all the biological perspectives is to ensure that other social and contextual factors are eliminated. That is, research investigating biological causes must isolate those as the predominant factor. Additionally, biological perspectives tend not to be popular among domestic violence advocates, as they see these explanations as taking away from men's personal responsibility for their actions. Another challenge is that the biological theories are often criticized as deterministic, or presuming that because a behavior has a genetic link it will inevitably be manifest by all who carry that gene. Modern biological theorists, however, maintain a more socio-biological perspective, asserting that genetics may predispose one to certain behavior, but those behaviors are exhibited only in specific social or cultural contexts.

Psychological Theories

Psychological theories focus on the individual personality characteristics of offenders. Dutton (1995) asserts that a psychological perspective is needed, as feminist explanations that it is men's patriarchal desire to obtain and maintain power and control over their partners fails to explain lesbian battering and why most men raised in a patriarchal society do not abuse their partners.

Psychological theories have also been used to explain women's behavior in abusive relationships. Women who endured abuse were also said to be mentally ill. Some studies supported this conclusion, although these studies were later discredited because the research involved women who were in mental hospitals and their batterers were asked to explain why they were abusive, giving them license to minimize and blame. Most studies have not shown that women who endure abuse suffer from any mental illness before the abuse, although enduring violence in a relationship can lead to a host of psychological effects.

Psychologist Lenore Walker, building on previous work, tested the theory of "learned helplessness" in 1979 to explain why women stay in abusive relationships. A perceived absence of control over a traumatic situation or series of events results in victims' inability to respond despite repeated threats to their safety.

Critics note, however, that this perspective minimizes or ignores the many social, economic, or cultural reasons why women may sometime choose to stay in abusive relationships. Others note that women are very well aware of the threats they face with abusers but must make active, conscious decisions about their survival. Leaving an abuser might not be the best answer at all times and in all situations. Further, critics have pointed out that Walker's theory was based on the presumption that battered women have low self-esteem, are withdrawn, and perceive a loss of control. This fails to take into account the fact that those issues might actually be the result of the abuse. Others have argued that abused women suffer from personality disorders that make them seek out abusers as a form of punishment.

Walker also contributed the idea of the "cycle of violence." The basic idea is that men's inability to express their frustrations, derived from rigid gender roles, results in a building of tensions. Eventually, the man explodes, acting violently toward his partner. After the tension is released, the man apologizes in what Walker calls the honeymoon period, only to become violent again. Critics have noted that this theory is not consistent with women's experiences, given that many experience random and unpredictable violence and no honeymoon period.

Another theory Walker produced was that some victims develop battered woman syndrome (BWS). BWS describes the signs and symptoms that battered women may experience as a result of violent and abusive relationships that result in their difficulty leaving abusers. BWS remains controversial, primarily because it has been used as a defense in cases in which women hurt or kill their abusive partners. It was popularized in the 1984 film *The Burning Bed*, which featured Farrah Fawcett as Francine Hughes, a woman who set fire to her abusive husband while he slept and was subsequently found not guilty by reason of temporary insanity.

In the early 1970s when the battered women's movement began, the prevailing explanation for men's battering was psychopathology. Abusive men were said to suffer from mental illness and thus required either therapeutic intervention, medication, or both. Most research has not, however, found a significant link between mental illness and abuse. For instance, those who suffer from schizophrenia or other mental illnesses tend, when they do act out violently, not to limit their abuse to their partners. There is some research to show that men suffering from antisocial personality disorder or borderline personality disorder are overrepresented as batterers (See for instance Greene, Coles, & Johnson, 1994). These studies have generally involved administering a battery of psychological tests such as the Minnesota Multiphasic Personality Inventory, the Millon Clinical Multiaxial Inventory (MCMI) Borderline Personality Organization, and the Conflict Tactics Scale to fairly large samples that are representative of North American men, thus suggesting the findings may be generalizable. Dutton & Starzomski (1994) studied 78 self-referred and court-referred men in treatment for wife assault. They found that more than 79 percent of the entire sample had clinically significant personality disorders, and 37 percent had borderline personalities, a rate far exceeding that in the general population (typically 11–15 percent). Persons with borderline personality disorder suffer from mood instability, black-and-white thinking, difficulty in social settings, self-harm, and trouble maintaining relationships. The patterns of behavior typical among those with borderline personality disorder parallel Walker's cycle of violence.

Other psychological theorists focus on childhood experiences that lead men to batter. Dutton and Golant (1995) have asserted that it is early childhood attachment issues that result in borderline personality disorder. Those who experience real or imagined loss or abandonment or ambivalent attachments may become angry and detached as adolescents. Their feelings of inferiority at this time of social cues about gender roles and aggressive masculinity produce a person at great risk for abusing women. Those with borderline personality disorders tend to see the world as either good or bad, and thus see women as either "madonnas or whores." Simultaneously, these people suffer from unexpressed hostile dependency needs. They look to others to meet these needs but at the same time resent them for the dependency. Yet the individual "is now afraid of needing another because he perceives a potential of being abandoned yet again. He will act to reduce the likelihood of experiencing the pain of abandonment. In psychiatric terms, these behaviours are often referred to as the means of avoiding 'narcissistic injury'" (Cunningham et al., 1998).

Walker's final phase of the cycle of violence abusers promises a violence-free relationship. This is impossible for people suffering from borderline personality disorder, as they "lack the ability to learn appropriately from life experiences. They also fear the very outcome a positive response to their promises could achieve for them: intimate attachment to another" (Cunningham et al., 1998).

Hockenberry (1995) believes that abusers suffer from what he called "grandiose narcissistic personality disorder." Narcissism also develops from childhood abandonment or attachment issues, and narcissists suffer from chronic and intense shame. Grandiose narcissists hide this shame by acting like "big men" and project their frustration and self-doubt on others. Hockenberry (1995) further argues that victims may suffer from a different type of narcissism, which he calls symbiotic narcissism. These people also suffer from shame, but theirs is self-deprecating and tends to be turned inward such that they become martyrs, enduring abusive situations because they feel responsible for the other's pain and anger.

A concern about the psychological theories is that they may divert attention from macro-level factors such as broader gender inequalities. Further, psychology is an inexact science. It is difficult to accurately diagnose someone with a mental illness, thus making it even more challenging to presume that it was this that led to abuse.

See also: Battered Woman Syndrome; Cycle of Violence; Psychological Effects of Domestic Abuse; Traumatic Brain Injury and Domestic Abuse; Walker, Lenore

Further Reading

Bell, K., & Naugle, A. (2008). Intimate partner violence theoretical considerations: Moving towards a contextual framework. *Clinical Psychology Review, 28*(7), 1096–1107.

Booth, A., & Dabbs, J. (1993). Testosterone and men's marriages. *Social Forces, 72*(2), 463–477.

Cohen, R., Rosenbaum, A., Kane, R., Warnken, W., & Benjamin, S. (1999). Neuropsychological correlates of domestic violence. *Violence and Victims, 14*(4), 397–411.

Cunningham, A., Jaffe, P., Baker, L., Dick, T., Malla, S., Mazaheri, N., & Poisson, S. (1998, September). Theory-derived explanations of male violence against female partners: Literature update and related implications for treatment and evaluation. London Family Court Clinic, London, Ontario. Retrieved June 11, 2012, from http://www.lfcc.on.ca/maleviolence.pdf

Dutton, D. (1995). Male abusiveness in intimate relationships. *Clinical Psychology Review, 15*, 567–581.

Dutton, D., & Golant, S. (1995). *The batterer: A psychological profile*. New York: Basic Books.

Dutton, D., & Starzomski, A. (1994). Psychological differences between court-referred and self-referred wife assaulters. *Criminal Justice and Behavior, 21*, 203–222.

Greene, A., Coles, C., & Johnson, E. (1994). Psychopathology and anger in interpersonal violence offenders. *Journal of Clinical Psychology, 50*, 906–912.

Hines, D., & Saudino, K. (2004). Genetic and environmental influences on intimate partner aggression: A preliminary study. *Violence and Victims, 19*(6), 701–718.

Hockenberry, S. (1995). Dyadic violence, shame, and narcissism. *Contemporary Psychoanalysis*, *31*(2).
Kwong, M., Bartholomew, K., Henderson, A., & Trinke, S. (2003). The intergenerational transmission of relationship violence. *Journal of Family Psychology*, *17*(3), 288–301.
Marsh, N. V., & Martinovich, W. M. (2006). Executive dysfunction and domestic violence. *Brain Injury*, *20*(1), 61–66.
McKenry, P., Julian, T., & Gavazzi, S. (1995). Toward a biopsychosocial theory of domestic violence. *Journal of Marriage and Family*, *57*(2), 307–320.
Pinto, L., Sullivan, E., Rosenbaum, A., Wyngarden, N., Umhau, J., Miller, M., & Taft, C. (2010). *Aggression and Violent Behavior*, *15*, 387–398.
Rosenbaum, A. (1991). The neuropsychology of marital aggression. In J. S. Milner (ed.), *Neuropsychology of aggression*. Boston: Kluwer Academic Publishers.
Rosenbaum, A., Abend, S., Gearan, P., Fletcher, K, Raine, A., Brennan, P., et al. (1997). *Serotonergic functioning in partner-abusive men: Biosocial bases of violence* (pp. 329–332). New York, NY: Plenum Press.
Rosenbaum, A., & Hoge, S. (1989). Head injury and marital aggression. *American Journal of Psychiatry*, *146*(8), 1048–1051.
Rosenbaum, A., Hoge, S., Adelman, S., Warnken, W., Fletcher, K., & Kane, R. (1994). Head injury in partner-abusive men. *Journal of Consulting and Clinical Psychology*, *62*(6), 1187–1193.
Walker, L. (2009). *The battered woman syndrome* (3rd ed.). New York, NY: Springer.
Walker, L. (1979). *The battered woman*. New York, NY: Harper & Row.
Warnken, W., Rosenbaum, A., Fletcher, K., Hoge, S., & Adelman, S. (1994). Head-injured males: A population at risk for relationship aggression? *Violence and Victims*, *9*(2), 153–166.

Laura L. Finley

THE BODY SHOP

The Body Shop began its Stop Violence in the Home campaign in 2003. The mission of the campaign was to "highlight the issue, raise money to support the work of groups helping victims of violence, and ensure that customers and employees are provided with information on sources of advice and help" (The Body Shop: About Us, 2011). The company has raised over £4 million since 2004, which it donates to already-established organizations that protect and support victims of abuse, and to those who work to prevent domestic violence.

Part of L'Oréal, The Body Shop is a body-care company that focuses on using natural ingredients and environmentally and socially conscious methods of creating its products. Beyond the products it sells, the company has five core values that promote change: "Defend Human Rights, Activate Self-Esteem, Support Community Trade, Against Animal Testing, and Protect Our Planet."

The Body Shop was started by the late Dame Anita Roddick, a human rights activist. She made campaigning on many social, environmental and animal rights causes a large part of the company's goals. The Body Shop Foundation was started in 1990 to donate money to organizations that further the core values of The Body

Shop, mostly funding programs that are grassroots and cannot get financed from many traditional sources.

Involvement is also expected of The Body Shop's employees. The company encourages its staff to volunteer through its global volunteering policy. This program gives staff members three paid days per year to dedicate to volunteering. Also, Anita Roddick said "working for The Body Shop should not just be selling bars of soap, but working for the community, lobbying for social change, campaigning for the environment—working in fact, for the greater good. (The Body Shop Activist, 2008) The employees receive benefits such as the Learning is of Value to Everyone (LOVE) training and wellness activities to encourage positive self-esteem and well-being.

The Body Shop holds retail space in shopping centers all over the world. This socially-conscious company supports a number of causes, one of which is the defense of human rights. (Syamin/Dreamstime.com)

Through independent research within 11 countries commissioned by The Body Shop, more women reported that they would go to a friend when faced with physical or mental abuse than would go for help to the police, their families, or support groups. In response to this finding, The Body Shop made the theme of its 2008 Stop Violence in the Home campaign based around the goal of encouraging people to help their friends affected by domestic abuse.

The Body Shop helps abused women through numerous grassroots campaigns throughout the world, many of which are centered locally around each store, while some go to a larger level. The company works with governments around the world to try to change laws to help women in domestic abuse situations. On a smaller level, it began a training program in the stores for employees to campaign to customers.

In the United States, the company has teamed up with the National Coalition against Domestic Violence since 2003. It has raised money for this organization, helped spread knowledge on domestic violence, and has created partnerships through its worldwide stores to fight domestic abuse on a local level. Part of the money raised for this organization goes toward facial reconstructive surgery for victims. In 2002, The Body Shop teamed up with the National Coalition against Domestic Violence (NCADV) and the Wireless Foundation to collect cell phones that could go toward victims of abuse.

In Canada, The Body Shop works with the Canadian Women's Foundation by donating money to their causes. In the United Kingdom, The Body Shop provides support by donating money and through education. Also, in 2009, employees from 80 stores in the United Kingdom volunteered with local women's refuges through the Women's Aid charity. In Seoul, Korea, the company set up a march and petition to collect customer signatures, which resulted in the government increasing programs against domestic violence. The Body Shop also tries to educate the public, as it did in classrooms in Switzerland to teach children about domestic abuse.

The Body Shop teamed up with the UN Secretary-General's Study on Violence against Children and UNICEF. The partnership was to look into how children are affected by domestic violence in the home. Through a 2007 report by The Body Shop and UNICEF, it discovered that domestic abuse affects 375 million children throughout the world. After this finding, The Body Shop worked to raise money and spread information to combat this problem.

The Body Shop also campaigns through its products. In 2008, it created the "For Me, For You" Special Edition Shea Lip Care Duo that came with the message "Break the Silence on Domestic Violence." The product served the purpose of letting a friend know she can count on the giver if she ever needs help. Further, all proceeds from this product are used to support the work of The Body Shop's partners against domestic abuse. In 2007, the company began selling tote bags, called the "New Bag for Life," with some of the profits being donated to domestic violence organizations.

Further Reading

The Body Shop. (2011). About us. Retrieved October 4, 2011, from http://www.thebodyshop-usa.com/about-us/aboutus.aspx

The Body Shop. (2011). Break the silence on domestic violence—Talk to a friend. Retrieved October 24, 2011, from http://www.thebodyshop-usa.com/values-campaigns/stop-violence.aspx

The Body Shop. (2011). How do we make our customers and employees feel good about themselves? Retrieved October 4, 2011, from http://www.thebodyshop.com/_en/_ww/values-campaigns/self-esteem.aspx

The Body Shop. (2011). What do we achieve by campaigning? Retrieved October 4, 2011, from http://www.thebodyshop.com/_en/_ww/values-campaigns/defend-human-right.aspx

The Body Shop Activist. (2008). Break the silence on domestic violence. Retrieved October 28, 2011, from http://blog.thebodyshop.com.au/2008/07/break-silence-on-domestic-violence_21.html

National Coalition against Domestic Violence. (2011). NCADV Sponsors. Retrieved October 24, 2011, from http://www.ncadv.org/sponsors.php

Sharon Thiel

BREAK THE CYCLE

Break the Cycle is an organization devoted to empowering young people to end dating violence. Calling dating violence a "silent epidemic," Break the Cycle emphasizes that knowledge is key. In addition to educational programming, the organization advocates for legal and policy changes and provides legal services to teens in need. Further, Break the Cycle has developed a series of curricula that they offer on their website and use to train administrators and educators. In 2010, Break the Cycle received the bulk of its funding from hosting special events. Funding was also acquired from corporations, individual donations, and grants and foundations.

Break the Cycle was founded in Los Angeles in 1996 because, while there were numerous organizations providing services for adult victims of domestic violence and to children being abused by adults, there was nothing focusing specifically on teen victims of dating violence. In 2004, Break the Cycle began to work on these issues nationally and now has another office in Washington, D.C. As of January 2012, 15 people are employed by Break the Cycle. Break the Cycle collaborates with the federal government, the National Network to End Domestic Violence, Mary Kay Inc., and the Girl Scouts, among other regional and local partners. Additionally, Break the Cycle collaborates with the National Dating Abuse Helpline to provide the online resource http://www.loveisrespect.org

On its website, the organization details its values, which include: (1) trusting young people as experts of their own experiences and needs; (2) providing services that meet the needs of a culturally diverse society; (3) evolving and collaborating to create long-term solutions; and (4) seeking and implementing new ideas.

Break the Cycle's prevention programs include school-based presentations as well as a School Policy Kit, the Safe Dates program, their Ending Violence curriculum, and their "Speak.Act.Change" service-learning program. They call this the four-step approach, which includes: (1) developing a comprehensive school policy on dating violence; (2) educating students about dating violence, how to recognize the signs of abusive relationships, and how to build healthy ones; (3) reinforcing that learning through interactive activities that teach young people about their rights and responsibilities in dating relationships; and (4) activating student leadership through service learning that engages young people in making change in their communities. Break the Cycle provides live training, web-based sessions, and technical assistance to schools utilizing these programs.

Legal services are provided on the website as well as via links. Young people in need can also contact representatives for personalized assistance.

Policy programs focus on three broad political and legislative priorities: (1) increasing access to essential information, services, safety, and justice; (2) ensuring confidentiality so that youth in need will seek help; and (3) ensuring a healthy environment that allows youth to escape abusive relationships. The organization's website also includes a link for users to assess their state's ranking in terms of policy and programs. The State Law Report Card is updated annually. In 2010, six states plus the District of Columbia received an "A" grade (California, Illinois, New Hampshire, Rhode Island, Oklahoma, and Washington).

Another feature of the Break the Cycle website is that it provides extensive information about the scope and extent of dating violence. Under a link for "What Is Dating Violence," the site explains that dating violence is patterned behavior that often involves a cycle in which there is a building of tensions, an explosion, and then a honeymoon period. The site also includes the widely used "wheel" of abuse to highlight that dating violence is about an abuser wanting to obtain and maintain power and control over their victim and to illustrate the many forms abuse may take. Ten warning signs are listed, which includes the fact that many abusive partners utilize technology to control their victims. Links are also provided for youth to engage in safety planning. In addition to basic tips on creating a safety plan, downloadable tools are available for teens and for college-aged populations.

In addition to the wealth of information Break the Cycle makes available on their website and through their programming, their website also features videos that can be utilized to educate young people about abuse. The public service announcement (PSA) Break the Cycle has won several awards. Through their Let Your Heart Rule link (http://www.letyourheartrule.com), they sponsor an annual youth PSA contest. Break the Cycle was also the first national organization to feature a dating violence prevention campaign specifically tailored to the Lesbian, Gay, Bisexual, Transgendered, and Questioning (LGBTQ) community through their Hear My Voice program.

Break the Cycle claims to have reached more than one million teens through sharing of information and resources and through the provision of direct legal services. Finally, Break the Cycle invites interested persons to get involved by volunteering, spreading the word, attending events, and making donations to support their work. One suggestion for supporting the organization's work is to host a Valentine's Party. Users can register on the site to receive information on how to host a party that coincides with Teen Dating Violence Awareness Week.

See also: Legislation and Policies, Dating Violence; Teen Victims of Domestic Abuse

Further Reading
Break the Cycle: http://www.breakthecycle.org
Let Your Heart Rule: http://www.letyourheartrule.org
Safe Dates Curriculum: http://www.hazelden.org/web/go/safedates

Laura L. Finley

BRIDES WALK

The Brides Walk is an annual event that is hosted by different communities across the nation as a way of promoting awareness about domestic abuse. Female participants wear wedding dresses to symbolize the lost life of a woman, Gladys Ricart, who was murdered on her wedding day while posing for photographs in her wedding dress. Participants walk to represent Ricart and others who have died or experienced abuse at the hand of another. Mothers and fathers, daughters and sons, sisters and brothers, friends and neighbors walk together in support of those who have been affected by domestic abuse.

Ricart, an immigrant from the Dominican Republic, was shot to death on September 26, 1999, at the age of 38. Ricart had dreamed of her magical wedding day, which she had been planning since she was a child, like so many little girls. Before heading to the church, her ex-lover gained access to the home in which she was preparing, shot her in the face, and then tried to turn the gun on himself.

Founder of the Brides Walk, Josie Ashton, at one of the South Florida events. (AP Photo/J Pat Carter)

Gladys's brother stopped him from committing suicide. When the police realized who the killer was, they were surprised to find out that this murderer, Agustin Garcia, was a well-respected and successful self-made business man who was seen as community leader.

Many people were outraged by this news. One woman by the name of Myhosi "Josie" Ashton sought to do something positive about this horrible tragedy and initiated the first Brides Walk. She was determined to bring people's attention to this issue. With the blessing of Ricart's family, Ashton quit her job, got organized, and set a goal to march across the country to promote awareness about domestic abuse. She accomplished her goal, challenged others to join the fight against abuse, and continues to speak out and organize Brides Walks.

Many people have a misconception that domestic abuse cannot happen to them, but in truth, anybody can be a victim of this behavioral cycle. Statistically, one out of every four women will be physically abused or raped by an intimate partner in their lifetime according to the U.S. Department of Justice. Domestic abuse is the leading cause of injury among U.S. women ages 15 to 44, where every nine seconds a women is struck. It is estimated that nearly six million women are abused annually in the United States. In fact, 75 percent of domestic violence confrontations go unreported. A person who has been abused is more likely to attempt suicide than is a person who has not. At least three women are killed every week by abusers (Domestic Violence Facts, n.d.).

One of the many goals of the Brides Walk is to educate others that abuse is not acceptable. It also is intended to let those who have suffered from domestic abuse know that there are centers and people who can help and that hope is still alive and readily available for those who seek it.

Some marchers at the walk chant positive slogans such as, "1, 2, 3, 4, we won't take it anymore, 5, 6, 7, 8, domestic violence equals hate." It is common to see participants holding up posters that say they were survivors of domestic abuse. Marchers hold signs in English and in Spanish with strong spoken words of encouragement saying "you are not alone," "end the silence," and "love shouldn't hurt."

A fair number of men also participate in the walk, alongside their wives or partners to show support for the fact that "real men don't hit women" another common phrase along with "Men Who Matter Never Batter" and bring about positive change and a sense of necessity that, as one young male bystander said, "Women need to be respected; men should be out here doing this [march] not women . . .," implying that men need to lend support to this cause since they are part of this issue.

In 2011, Josie Ashton joined activists in South Florida to coordinate the first College Bride's Walk. Recognizing that college-aged students are particularly vulnerable to abuse, the College Brides Walk is intended to unite South Florida colleges and universities in raising awareness about domestic violence. The event is held annually on the Friday before Valentine's Day.

Abuse rarely stops; rather, it is an ongoing cycle that will only continue to worsen. The chances are that if a person was struck once, it will happen again because domestic abuse is a behavior, not a random act. Abusers often threaten that if their partner leaves them, they will never see their kids again, no one will love them, or the abuser will kill them. The three most common forms of abuse are physical, emotional, and sexual violence. People in an abusive situation are forced to pretend that everything is okay, often hiding the fact that they are in an abusive situation from their friends and family, in the same way that Gladys Ricart hid the horrors of her domestic abuse from her loved ones. Many women blame themselves for their situation and can feel less of a woman because this has happened to them. This march is dedicated to all of those victims and survivors who have been in an abusive relationship.

See also: The Caribbean and Domestic Abuse; Educational Programs

Further Resources

College Bride's Walk: http://www.collegebrideswalk.com
Death of a bride. (2002). [Film]. A&E Home Video.
Domestic Violence Facts. (n.d.). National Coalition against Domestic Violence. Retrieved from http://www.ncadv.org
Scenes from Bride's March September 26, 2009 (New York). Retrieved from http://www.youtube.com/watch?v=7sQKRpY428U&feature=colike

Natasha A. Abdin

BULLYING AND DOMESTIC ABUSE

Both bullying and dating violence are common among school-aged youth; it is estimated that 30 percent of young people experience bullying in the United States. In 2001–2002, the World Health Organization conducted an international survey of bullying. The United States was in the middle of the group, with 17.9 percent of boys and 11.5 percent of girls reporting that they engaged in two or more incidents of bullying in the previous month. Rates were highest in Lithuania (43.6 percent of boys and 29.5 percent of girls) and lowest in Sweden (5.2 percent of boys and 2.3 percent of girls). Bullying is also common among the college-aged population, where it may occur between two students, between a student and a teacher, or between two teachers. One study found more than 60 percent of college students reported witnessing a peer being bullied by another student, and more than 45 percent reported witnessing a student being bullied by a teacher. In another study, almost 25 percent of respondents reported having been bullied by another student, and 19 percent reported having been bullied by a teacher.

Similarly, it is estimated that between 25 percent and 30 percent of teens have been involved in an abusive dating relationship. Some studies have shown rates as high as 57 percent. Rates are similar for lesbian, gay, bisexual, and transgendered (LGBT) youth in relationships. One in three teenage girls in a relationship reported being pressured to perform oral sex or engage in intercourse.

Both are, at root, about the need one person feels to obtain and maintain power and control over another. Perpetrators of dating violence and bullies both use a variety of tactics to do so, including but not limited to verbal harassment, emotional abuse, intimidation, unwanted sexual behavior or harassment, cyber threats, use of peer pressure, and more. Far from isolated incidents, bullying and dating violence are patterned behaviors.

Although not exclusively, both dating violence and bullying often enter the school walls, yet too often educators are not adequately prepared to respond due to inadequate or nonexistent training. Additionally, peers are witness to the abuse and bullying in the majority of cases, although many young people are hesitant to speak out. Victims of both problems can suffer emotionally and physically, and many experience great difficulty in school. Victims may be isolated from peers, have difficulty concentrating, and may act out or withdraw as a way of dealing with the abuse. Common symptoms that a person has been either bullied or abused include anxiety, depression, stress, hopelessness, and low self-esteem. Victims of both behaviors are more likely to skip school, have lower grades, and engage in risky behaviors (smoking, drinking, sexual promiscuity, self-mutilation), including suicide.

In fact, several studies have found bullying to be predictive of later involvement in abusive dating and/or domestic relationships. In particular, sexual bullying has been shown to be an antecedent of more severe relationship abuse.

Useful strategies to address both phenomena involve training educators to recognize warning signs and to know the school's protocol once either form of abuse is identified. Also important is the training of students to understand how they can help if a friend or peer is being abused or bullied. Research has repeatedly documented the effectiveness of the bystander approach. This approach addresses students not as would-be victims or perpetrators, which tends to alienate young people, but rather as would-be bystanders who can stop bullies or abusers by speaking up and interrupting the behavior. The Humanity Project is based on a bystander approach, which is the key to its success.

See also: Children, Impact of Domestic Abuse on; Runaway and Homeless Youth; Teen Victims of Domestic Abuse.

Further Reading

Chapell, M., Casey, D., De la Cruz, C., Ferrell, J., Forman, J., Lipkin, R., et al. (2004). Bullying in college by students and teachers. *Adolescence*, 39(153), 54–64.

Chapell, M., Hasselman, S., Kitchin, T., Lomon, S., MacIver, K., & Sarullo, P. (2006). Bullying in elementary school, high school, and college. *Adolescence*, 41(164), 633–648.

Fredland, M. (2008). Sexual bullying: Addressing the gap between bullying and dating violence. *ANS Advanced Nursing Science*, 2, 95–105.

Gruber, J., & Fineran, S. (2008). Comparing the impact of bullying and sexual harassment victimization on the mental and physical health of adolescents. *Sex roles*, 59, 1–13.

O'Keefe, M. (2011). Teen dating violence: A review of risk factors and prevention efforts. *Violence against Women Net (VAWnet)*. Retrieved March 16, 2012, from http://www.vawnet.org/applied-research-papers/print-document.php?doc_id=409

Olweus, D., (2004). *Bullying at school: What we know and what we can do*. Cambridge, MA: Blackwell.

Teens Experiencing Abusive Relationships: http://www.teensagainstabuse.org/index.php?q=statistics

Laura L. Finley

BYSTANDER INTERVENTION PROGRAMS

In most acts of violence, there are bystanders, or other people in the vicinity. These bystanders may be passive or active. Passive bystanders are those who watch or witness the incident quietly and do not get involved or attempt to disrupt it. Active bystanders tend to be vocal or involved in some way. Too often, however, active bystanders do not use their power to disrupt the incident. Instead, they may egg it on by cheering or otherwise encouraging the behavior.

Bystander approaches emphasize that individuals can be trained to be active bystanders that interrupt certain social problems like bullying, sexual assault, and domestic violence. Programs emphasizing bystander intervention approach participants not as would-be batterers or would-be victims but rather as potential witnesses to situations who can take an active role in ending them. Bystander intervention programs build on social norms theory. According to social norms theory, people behave according to the way they perceive others behave. Many times, individuals misperceive others' attitudes or behavior, or misunderstand their approval or disapproval of behavior. People tend to overestimate the amount of risk-taking behavior occurring and underestimate the amount of pro-social behavior. This dissonance between the perceived and actual occurrence may lead individuals to feel as though they should conform to the risk-taking behavior they believe to be common or not conform to the more healthy behaviors they perceive as less common. The applicability of social norms theory to IPV was recently supported by Neighbors et al. (2010). In their study with 124 batterers, they found the men commonly overestimated the prevalence of violent behaviors committed by other men, and that they behaved abusively due in part to these misperceptions.

Many bystander intervention programs are directed at males. The idea is to draw on the powerful male subculture to empower males to say or do something that would discourage a peer who was acting aggressively or inappropriately. Research has found that men in general are less likely to intervene than are women (Banyard, Moynihan, & Plante, 2007; McMahon, Postmus, & Koenick, 2011). Those most immersed in hegemonic masculinity—the conception that males must be tough, aggressive, and in control—are least likely to challenge violence against women for fear of being seen as weak or gay, according to research by Fabiano, Perkins, Berkowitz, Linkenbach, and Stark (2004) and Carlson (2008).

Successful interventions based on social norms theory can challenge men to partake in healthy relationships and encourage their peers to do the same by providing accurate information about people's behaviors. These include programs that encourage and support those exhibiting prosocial attitudes and behavior to be more vocal.

Evaluations of bystander intervention programs have generally supported their effectiveness. Yet research has also shown that males find it difficult to transfer the skills they learn in bystander intervention programs to real-life social settings and that they would like more opportunities to discuss and practice in a way that is safe and nonthreatening. Additionally, many times the participants do not get involved voluntarily, as some programs are mandatory for certain groups like college athletes. Greater efforts should be made to involve men of all types and in a variety of settings.

Some research has even found long-term changes in men's attitudes and behaviors. Foubert's (2000) The Men's Program has been found to decrease men's acceptance of rape myths, increase empathy toward rape victims, and increase men's willingness to speak out when others are making sexist comments (Foubert, 2000; Foubert & LaVoy, 2000; Foubert & Perry, 2007).

One of the most widely recognized bystander intervention programs is Jackson Katz's Mentors in Violence Prevention (MVP). MVP targets student-athletes and leaders and has been used with the military as well. Evaluations have found that students who complete the program feel more capable at intervening in cases of violence against women, perhaps by telling a friend to stop speaking derogatorily to his girlfriend. Katz's films *Tough Guise* and *Wrestling with Manhood* also challenge hegemonic masculinity and call on men to be active bystanders.

Banyard, Moynihan, and Plante (2007) found that a sexual violence bystander intervention program increased prosocial attitudes among diverse groups of participants, including athletes, sorority and fraternity members, student leaders, and the general student population.

See also: Athletes and Domestic Abuse; College-Aged Victims; Educational Programs; Katz, Jackson; Men's Efforts against Domestic Abuse

Further Reading

Banyard, V. L. (2008). Measurement and correlates of prosocial bystander behavior: The case of interpersonal violence. *Violence and Victims*, 23(1), 83–97.

Banyard, V., Moynihan, M., & Crossman, M. (2009). Reducing sexual violence on campus: The role of student leaders as empowered bystanders. *Journal of College Student Development*, 50(4), 446–457.

Banyard, V., Moynihan, M., & Plante, E. (2007). Sexual violence prevention through bystander education: An experimental evaluation. *Journal of Community Psychology*, 35(4), 463–481.

Berkowitz, A. (2005). An overview of the social norms approach. In L. Lederman & P. Stewart (Eds.), *Changing the culture of college drinking* (pp. 193–214). Cresskill, NJ: Hampton Press.

Carlson, M. (2008). I'd rather go along and be considered a man: Masculinity and bystander intervention. *Journal of Men's Studies*, 16(1), 3–17.

Dick, A., & McMahon, S. (2011). "Being in a room with like-minded men": An exploratory study of men's participation in a bystander intervention program to prevent intimate partner violence. *Journal of Men's Studies*, 19(1), 3.

Fabiano, P., Perkins, H. W., Berkowitz, A., Linkenbach, J., & Stark, C. (2004). Engaging men as social justice allies in ending violence against women: Evidence for a social norms approach. *Journal of American College Health*, 52(3), 105–112.

Foubert, J. (2000). The longitudinal effects of a rape-prevention program on fraternity members' attitudes, behavioral intent, and behavior. *Journal of American College Health*, 48(4), 158–163.

Foubert, J., & LaVoy, S. (2000). A qualitative assessment of "The Men's Program": The impact of a rape prevention program on fraternity men. *NASPA*, 30(1), 18–30.

Foubert, J., & Perry, B. (2007). Creating lasting attitude and behavior changes in fraternity members and male student athletes. *Violence Against Women*, 13(1), 70–86.

Katz, J. (2006). *The macho paradox*. Naperville, IL: Sourcebooks.

McMahon, S., Postmus, J. L., & Koenick, R. A. (2011). Conceptualizing the engaging bystander approach to sexual violence prevention on college campuses. *Journal of College Student Development*, 52(1), 115–130.

Neighbors, C., Walker, D., Mbilinyi, L., O'Rourke, A., Edeison, J., Zegree, J., et al. (2010). Normative misperceptions of abuse among perpetrators of Intimate Partner Violence. *Violence Against Women*, 16(4), 370–386.

Laura L. Finley

THE CARIBBEAN AND DOMESTIC ABUSE

Studies have found that rates of abuse in the Caribbean are quite high. According to UN Women's Fact Sheet: Latin America and the Caribbean (2012), 97 percent of countries in those regions have laws on domestic violence. However, fewer than half of those countries explicitly outlaw marital rape. Based on prevalence surveys in 11 countries in the region, up to a third of women have experienced physical violence, and up to 16 percent of women have been targeted for sexual violence in their lifetime.

Yet women in these countries say that abuse is still something that is rarely discussed. While some organizations are available to assist victims, they tend to be underfunded, and many women still lack access. In Antigua, for instance, there is only one shelter. Women say they are reluctant to report abuse to police because they believe nothing will happen. Police also get frustrated because the women who do lodge complaints sometimes refuse to go through with actions to arrest and/or prosecute the abusers. In some countries in the region, new legislation has helped. Trinidad and Tobago, for instance, passed the Domestic Violence Act, which gives police more power to investigate and arrest domestic violence cases. The result has been increased reports of domestic violence. Like elsewhere, however, more affluent and educated women still tend not to report, as they often feel embarrassed and thus either endure the abuse or rely on family and friends for support. Barbados has also increased attention to domestic abuse, providing more training for police officers on how to work with both victims and offenders.

Some posit that the high rates of abuse in the Caribbean are linked with other forms of societal violence common to the region. Research conducted by the World Bank found that the overall murder rate in the Caribbean was four times that of North America. The region is accustomed to violence, having emerged from a very conflictual past of slavery. Such violence becomes normalized. Corporal punishment of children, in schools and in homes, is common and accepted. Corporal punishment has been linked to higher rates of child and domestic abuse. Advocates also note that children are not taught nonviolence and kindness but instead rigid adherence to gender roles that reinforce male superiority. The Caribbean islands have higher rates of sexual violence than the world average, and one in four women in Guyana has been physically abused in a relationship. Approximately 30 percent of women in Trinidad & Tobago have experienced domestic violence, 67 percent of women in Suriname have experienced violence in an intimate partnership, and 30 percent of adult women in Antigua & Barbuda and Barbados have experienced some form of domestic abuse ("Domestic, sexual violence rates soaring in Caribbean—Wiltshire," 2010).

One organization that is raising awareness about and assisting Caribbean victims is Caribbean American Domestic Violence Awareness (http://www.cadva.org/). Another organization is the National Forum against Domestic Violence, which has held seminars and conferences on the issue for police and for the general public. Hot Peach Pages also features links to resources in the Caribbean at http://www.hotpeachpages.net/camerica/caribbean1.html. The Caribbean has also been a region of focus for the United Nations UNiTE to End Violence against Women campaign. In 2005, the Regional Coordinating Unit of the Centre for Gender and Development Studies (CGDS) and the other by the UNIFEM Caribbean Office completed an annotated bibliography of studies related to domestic violence in the Caribbean. It is available at http://www.unifemcar.org/photos/GENDER-BASED%20VIOLENCE%20IN%20THE%20COMMONWEALTH%20CARIBBEAN.pdf.

Caribbean immigrants to the United States also suffer from domestic violence. One case that received a great deal of media attention is the murder of Gladys Ricart, an immigrant from the Dominican Republic. Ricart was murdered on September 26, 1999, by her ex-boyfriend, Agustin Garcia, also a Dominican immigrant. The murder occurred just moments before she was to be married to another man, in front of her family and friends while Ricart posed for photographs. Garcia was arrested immediately, but many in the immigrant community in New Jersey believed Ricart to be at least partly to blame. Agustin Garcia's attorneys maintained that not only was he an upstanding citizen but that Gladys had led him to believe that the relationship was not over. When he found that she was marrying someone else, he responded in a fit of rage. Garcia made this "passion provocation" defense during his trial. The jury did not believe it, instead seeing enough evidence of prior abuse to find Garcia guilty of second-degree murder. He is serving a life sentence. Garcia's murder of his ex-girlfriend spawned a movement called the Bride's Walk. Shortly after the murder, a Miami-area activist named Myhosi "Josie" Ashton, also a Dominican immigrant, heard about the case. Appalled at what she saw as victim-blaming among the media and much of the immigrant community, Ashton approached the Ricart family asking if there was something she could do to raise awareness about domestic violence and correct the many misconceptions. With the family's permission, Ricart donned her own wedding gown, carried signs, and walked from shelter to shelter between New Jersey and Miami. Her efforts inspired other walks in Gladys Ricart's honor, and now New York, Milwaukee, and other cities hold annual Bride's Walks. In 2011, Ashton joined with area activists and educators in South Florida to sponsor the first College Bride's Walk at Barry University in Miami Shores. Intended to raise awareness and inspire college-aged students, the group most at risk for abuse, the College Bride's Walk has become an annual event.

Another incident that raised awareness about abuse among Caribbean women was when pop music star Rihanna (born Robin Rihanna Fenty), who is from Barbados, was punched by her boyfriend, musician Chris Brown. Rihanna spoke out about the abuse and recorded a song about violent relationships, "Love the

Way You Lie," with rapper Eminem. The song and video can be used to begin a discussion about dating violence; however, they do present some problematic images and should be used with caution.

See also: Bride's Walk; Celebrities and Domestic Abuse; Latin America and Domestic Abuse; The United Nations and Domestic Abuse

Further Reading

College Bride's Walk: http://www.collegebrideswalk.com
Domestic, sexual violence rates soaring in Caribbean—Wiltshire. (2010, September 28). Stabroek News. http://www.stabroeknews.com/2010/archives/09/28/domestic-sexual-violence-rates-soaring-in-caribbean-wiltshire/
Domestic violence a big Caribbean problem. (2011, March 2). BBC Caribbean. Retrieved June 11, 2012, from http://www.bbc.co.uk/caribbean/news/story/2011/03/110302_arch_s_domestic-violence.shtml
Fact Sheet: Latin America and the Caribbean. (2012). UN Women. Retrieved June 11, 2012, from http://progress.unwomen.org/wp-content/uploads/2011/06/EN-Factsheet-LAC-Progress-of-the-Worlds-Women.pdf

Laura L. Finley

CASTLE ROCK V. GONZALES CASE

In August 2011, the Inter-American Commission on Human Rights (IACHR) issued a landmark ruling in the case of Jessica Lenahan (formerly Gonzales). In its ruling, the IACHR determined that domestic violence is a human rights issue and that police are obligated to enforce restraining orders to protect victims from abusers. Although it does not have the power to overturn a U.S. Supreme Court decision, the IACHR ruling opposed the 2005 decision of the Supreme Court in *Castle Rock v. Gonzales*. The IACHR is a regional body whose recommendations will hopefully help shape future legislation and policies related to victim protection in the United States and beyond.

Jessica Lenahan married Simon Gonzales in 1990, and the two resided in Castle Rock, Colorado. Jessica Gonzales recalls the first abuse occurring in 1996, with Simon Gonzales targeting not just her but their three daughters, Leslie (7), Katheryn (8), and Rebecca (10) as well. After Simon attempted to commit suicide in 1999, Jessica filed for divorce and started living separately from him. Simon continued his violence and unpredictable behavior after the two separated. Between January and May 1999, Simon had several altercations with the Castle Rock Police Department, including a road rage incident while his daughters were in the car, trespassing on private property, and obstructing the work of the police department. Twice he broke into Jessica's house. According to Jessica and her attorneys, by June 22, 1999, the Castle Rock Police Department had to be quite familiar with how dangerous Simon Gonzales was.

On May 21, 1999, Jessica Gonzales obtained a temporary restraining order that restricted Simon Gonzales from the home and ordered him to remain at least 100 yards from it at all times. The order directed police to take every reasonable

An investigator with the Colorado Bureau of Investigation, right, stands over the body of Simon Gonzales in Castle Rock, Colorado on June 23, 1999. (AP Photo/Ed Andrieski)

means to enforce its provisions, and it was, as is typical, entered into the Colorado Bureau of Investigation's central registry of restraining orders and thus was accessible by any state or local law enforcement agency. Things did not change, however, and Simon continued to harass Jessica and the kids. When Jessica called to report his repeated violations, she said police were not helpful, but instead "they would be dismissive of me, and they scolded me for calling them and asking for help" (Report No. 80/11, 2011). The state court made the temporary restraining order permanent on June 4, 1999. The permanent order gave Jessica sole physical custody of the girls and allowed Simon only occasional visits. The judge allowed Simon to see the girls just once per week for dinner.

On June 22, 1999, in violation of the restraining order, Simon Gonzales abducted his three daughters and their friend from the street outside of Jessica's home. Over the next 10 hours, Jessica repeatedly contacted the Castle Rock Police Department about her missing children and reminded them about the restraining order. She expressed her clear distress and fear for the children's lives, but police repeatedly ignored her requests for help. Approximately two hours after her first call, Officer Brink and Sergeant Ruisi arrived at Jessica's home. She showed them a copy of the order, but according to Jessica, Officer Brink told her there was nothing they could do because the kids were with their father, despite the fact that it was not one of the prearranged visits the court ordered. The officers did tell Jessica they would drive to Simon's apartment to see if he was there with the girls. Sometime later, Jessica was able to talk to Simon on the phone. He said he was with the girls at an amusement park in Denver, some 40 minutes away. Simon's girlfriend, Rosemary Young, also called, asking Jessica about his mental health history, whether he was capable of harming himself or the children, and whether he had weapons. She also told Jessica that Simon had threatened to commit suicide earlier that day. Alarmed, Jessica called the Castle Rock Police Department again and was told by the dispatcher that an officer would be sent to her house. No one came, but Officer Brink called, and Jessica again explained the situation and described how worried she was. Before 10 p.m. Jessica called two more times, requesting an officer be dispatched to find Simon and the girls, that the Denver police be contacted, and that a statewide all-points bulletin (APB) be issued. She also asked that Officer Brink call Rosemary Young. He refused, instead asking her to keep waiting to see if Simon would return the girls. He even told her to stay calm because the girls were with their father and that she should deal with these things in the divorce court.

Jessica Gonzales called the police again around 10 p.m. reporting that the girls were still not home. This time the dispatcher scolded her and told her to call back on a nonemergency line. At midnight Jessica called a seventh time. She had gone to Simon's apartment, but no one was home. Again the dispatcher promised to send someone, and again, no one came. Jessica then drove to the Castle Rock Police Department and met with Detective Ahlfinger. She again described the situation and expressed that she feared Simon was suicidal. She filed an incident report, but was told that it was perfectly logical that the children's father might want to spend more time with them.

At approximately 3:15 a.m., Simon Gonzales drove up and parked outside of the police station. After sitting for approximately 15 minutes, he began shooting at the station. Police returned fire and Simon was killed. They then discovered the bodies of Leslie, Katheryn, and Rebecca in the back of Simon's truck. All had been shot to death. Jessica learned about the shooting from Rosemary Young and drove to the police station. Officers refused to give her any information about her girls for 12 hours. Jessica still does not know exactly how, when, and where her daughters died. Jessica also alleged to the IACHR that she has never received any information as to why Simon Gonzales was approved to purchase a gun that night by the Federal Bureau of Investigation. Gun dealers are prohibited from selling guns to individuals who are subject to a restraining order in the United States. The investigations of the death centered on Simon Gonzales, summarily concluding that he murdered his three daughters but not citing proof.

An activist for domestic violence victims, Jessica remarried (she is now Jessica Lenahan) but remains deeply traumatized by the deaths of her three daughters. The lack of adequate investigation into the cause of their deaths remains difficult.

The ACLU Women's Rights Project supported Jessica and coordinated nine friend-of-the-court briefs on her behalf. "Jessica's case illustrates the critical need for police enforcement of domestic violence orders of protection," said Lenora Lapidus, director of the ACLU Women's Rights Project. "Without systems of accountability in place, women and children are subjected to the whims of local police departments and may suffer grievous harm." Jessica received legal support in the case before the IACHR from the University of Miami Human Rights Law Clinic.

The case highlighted that domestic violence is indeed a human rights issue. Outside of the United States, a human rights framework has long been used to explain and analyze domestic violence. The IACHR issued a number of recommendations to the U.S. government. It recommended training for police regarding enforcing domestic violence restraining orders and a full investigation into the cause of death for Jessica's daughters, among other things.

See also: Restraining Orders/Personal Protection Orders; U.S. Government Responses to Domestic Violence

Further Reading

Castle Rock v. Gonzales: Making the court's protection real. ACLU. Retrieved June 29, 2012, from http://www.aclu.org/womens-rights/castle-rock-v-gonzales-making-courts-protection-real

International commission finds United States denied justice to domestic violence survivor. (2011, August 17). ACLU. Retrieved June 29, 2012, from http://www.aclu.org/womens-rights/international-commission-finds-united-states-denied-justice-domestic-violence-survivor

Jessica Gonzales v. USA. ACLU. (2011, October 24). Retrieved June 29. 2012, from http://www.aclu.org/human-rights-womens-rights/jessica-gonzales-v-usa

Report No. 80/11. (2011, July 21). *Inter-American Commission on Human Rights.* Retrieved from http://www.aclu.org/womens-rights/jessica-gonzales-v-usa-iachr-final-report

Laura L. Finley

CELEBRITIES AND DOMESTIC ABUSE

Former *American Idol* star Adam Lambert. Major League Baseball player Manny Ramirez. *Green Hornet* and *Terminator 2* actor Eddie Furlong. Country singer Rodney Atkins. Former rap-star Tone Loc. What do all those celebrities have in common? All were arrested in 2011 for some type of domestic violence charge. Furlong violated a court order requiring him to stay at least 100 yards from his ex-girlfriend, Ramirez assaulted his wife in Weston, Florida, and Lambert fought with his boyfriend at a bar in Finland. Atkins filed for divorce just days after his arrest for allegedly trying to smother his wife with a pillow, while Loc eventually pleaded no contest to using physical violence with the mother of one of his children. Those are just a few of the celebrity domestic violence arrests in 2011, and the list goes on and on: On April 3, 2012, Lisa Robin Kelly, who starred as the sister of Eric (played by Topher Grace) on *That '70s Show*, was arrested for domestic violence, and on April 23, 2012, it was former *Prison Break* star Lane Garrison's turn. Very few in the United States can forget the sordid past of actor Charlie Sheen, who has been arrested multiple times for domestic violence.

Numerous other famous people have been accused of domestic violence, many of them repeatedly. During boxer Mike Tyson's trial on rape charges, his former wife Robin Givens alleged that Tyson had repeatedly assaulted her. Former rap star

Bobby Brown was arrested seven times for assaulting his wife, now-deceased star Whitney Houston. Actor Mel Gibson caught national attention in 2010 not for his films but for his racist rants and the abuse he perpetrated against his then girlfriend, Oksiana Grigorieva. In 2009, pop star Chris Brown punched his girlfriend, fellow pop star Rihanna, on the evening of the Grammy Awards. Sports celebrities arrested for domestic violence are, unfortunately, too numerous to mention (additional information is included in the entry on **Athletes and Domestic Abuse**). Perhaps the most widely known is O. J. Simpson, whose repeated abuse of former wife Nicole Brown Simpson was revealed during his criminal trial on charges that he murdered her and her friend Ronald Goldman (for which he was acquitted). It is not just male celebrities who perpetrate domestic abuse. On April 25, 2012, the wife of former baseball star Deion Sanders, Pilar, was arrested.

Former *American Idol* star Adam Lambert and his partner were arrested for domestic violence in Helsinki in 2011. (Dziurek/Dreamstime.com)

Is it that famous people are more likely to be involved in abusive relationships? Or are there are other relevant factors? Surely celebrity relationships are challenging, but that is far from an adequate explanation. It could be that people are more prone to accuse celebrities as a way of gaining fame or perhaps even financially benefit. Yet in many of the above-listed cases, *both* parties are celebrities. Many of the incidents cited above occurred during the economic recession, which has long been tied to an increase in abuse. Yet the list above is just a small portion of celebrity-involved incidents, many occurring during the better financial times of the 1990s.

One study suggests that perhaps it is simply that the public receives far more information about celebrities' personal lives today. Levin, Fox, and Mazaik (2005) analyzed *People* cover stories and found a shift between 1974 and 1998 in which coverage moved from focusing on stars' careers to a preoccupation with their personal lives and problems, most of which was presented negatively. The authors noted: "Prior to a spate of scandals beginning in the 1970s including Watergate, IranGate, S&L, Helmsley, Milken, Crane, Packwood, Whitewater, Clinton/Lewinsky, Condit/Levy, Enron, and Martha Stewart, many reporters and producers lived by a code of ethics that excluded divulging certain acts that might have destroyed the career of a public figure—e.g., homosexuality, drug abuse, or alcoholism. During recent years, however, intense competition has helped inspire a 'no holds barred' attitude from journalists and producers of popular culture who go out of their way to report every ugly detail of their subjects private and public lives" (p. 14).

The public bears responsibility as well. As Levin et al. (2005) explained, "we have become infatuated with infamy." Some have suggested that scandalous celebrities serve a social comparison function for audience members who work out their own moral issues by speculating about the personal lives of the "stars" (p. 15). One danger of this is that when we give "villain status" an exciting role, we may be inadvertently encouraging young people to emulate this behavior.

It is possible, however, that celebrity cases help raise awareness about abuse among the general public and prompt victims to seek help. After O. J. Simpson's abuse of his former wife Nicole Brown Simpson was made public, advocates reported greater attention to the issue and an increase in crisis calls.

Unfortunately, sometimes the opposite occurs, where victims are blamed for their abuse and the incident increases the public's belief in stereotypes about abuse. After Chris Brown attacked Rihanna, many of his fans defended him and blamed her. Her song "Love the Way You Lie," with rapper Eminem, muddies the waters still further, as it seems to make the abuse seem mutual. Ironically, before his abusive behavior became public, Brown had an appearance on *The Tyra Banks Show* where he spoke about his experience growing up with domestic violence. Brown said he witnessed his mother suffer abuse from the time he was 7 years old until he was 13. Chris also told Tyra, "I treat women differently because I know I never want to go through the same thing or put a woman through the same thing this person put my mom through." Rihanna's later collaboration with Brown for the racy song "Birthday Cake" fueled the rumors that she was never really a victim. Girls were reported to make such comments as "I'd let Chris Brown beat me up" when it was announced that Brown won a Grammy in 2012.

Many famous people have themselves been victims of some form of abuse, most of whom are now actively involved in efforts to end abuse. Eve Ensler, best known for the *Vagina Monologues*, was a victim of child abuse, as was Tyler Perry, writer and producer of the "Madea" films, and feminist and founder of *Ms.* magazine Gloria Steinem. Singer Christina Aguilera is a victim of abuse who has become a spokesperson for the cause, working with the Women's Center & Shelter of Greater Pittsburgh and Lifetime's End Violence against Women campaign. Former Major League Baseball player and coach Joe Torre has been a vocal advocate of help services for child victims and started his own, the Joe Torre Safe at Home Foundation. Many celebrities support or have even started various causes or organizations devoted to assisting victims and raising awareness. The Pixel Project, which started the 16 Days of Activism against Gender Violence, made a list of the 16 top celebrities contributing to the cause. They are, in order:

(1) Annie Lennox, who has written letters to the UK government demanding they pledge to end violence against women and has presented a series of reports about abuse in Africa; (2) Charlize Theron, a UN Ambassador for Peace applauded for her work with Stop Rape Now; (3) Daniel Craig, who appeared in a short film showing his support for the cause; (4) David Schwimmer, who serves on the Board of the Rape Foundation in Santa Monica and has made a film, *Trust*, about the rape of a

14-year-old who was wooed via the Internet; (5) *Vampire Diaries* star Ian Somerhalder, who has taken part in "The Real Man" campaign led by Women's Aid UK; (6) R&B star Jamelia, whose song "Thank You" chronicles her experience with abuse; (7) *High School Musical* star Monique Coleman, a UN Youth champion whose active role on social media has helped raise awareness about abuse; (8) Nicole Kidman, a UN Women Goodwill Ambassador; (9) Oprah Winfrey, who has not only covered the issue extensively on her programs but herself starred as an abused woman in *The Color Purple;* (10) singer Peter Gabriel, who has long been involved with efforts to end violence against women through Amnesty International and through Witness, a nonprofit organization he cofounded that uses video to document human rights abuses; (11) Reese Witherspoon, honorary chair of the Avon Foundation, which provides resources and funding to end domestic violence; (12) Robin Wright Penn, who is active in the fight against genocide and has documented the rape of women in the Congo; (13) Salma Hayek, whose charity the Salma Hayek Foundation supports organizations that give aid to victims and raise awareness about abuse; (14) country singer Tim McGraw, who received the True Ally Award at the 2010 Men Stopping Violence Annual Awards Ceremony; (15) supermodel Waris Dirie, from Somalia, a victim of female genital mutilation (FGM) who has taken up that cause; and (16) former pop idol Will Young, an ambassador for Women's Aid.

See also: Athletes and Domestic Abuse; Avon Corporation; Films and Domestic Abuse; Music and Domestic Abuse; Simpson, O. J. Case

Further Reading

Benedict, H. (1992). *Virgin or vamp: How the press covers sex crimes.* New York, NY: Oxford UP.

Bird, E. (1997). Understanding the audience for scandal. In J. Hull & S. Hinerman (Eds.), *Media scandals: Morality and desire in the popular culture marketplace.* New York, NY: Columbia University Press.

Gitlin, T. (1998). The culture of celebrity. *Dissent, 45,* 81–83.

Johansson, S. (2006). "Sometimes you wanna hate celebrities": Tabloid readers and celebrity coverage. In S. Holmes & S. Redmond (Eds.), *Framing celebrity: New directions in celebrity culture* (pp. 343–361). London, England: Routledge, 2006.

Levin, J., Fox, J., & Mazaik, J. (2005). Blurring fame and infamy: A content analysis of cover-story trends in *People* magazine. *Internet Journal of Criminology.* Retrieved January 26, 2013 from http://www.internetjournalofcriminology.com/Levin,%20Fox%20&%20Mazaik%20%20Blurring%20Fame%20&%20Infamy.pdf

Mosk, M. (1994, June 26). Simpson case sets off domestic abuse alarm: Safety: Calls for help are increasing ominously. Counselors and police say current media attention will focus concern. *Los Angeles Times.* Retrieved June 19, 2012, from http://articles.latimes.com/1994-06-26/local/me-8745_1_domestic-violence-cases

Patterson, N., & Sears, C. (2011). Letting men off the hook? Domestic violence and postfeminist celebrity culture. *Genders, 53.*

The Pixel Project's "16 for 16 Campaign." (2011, December 10). Retrieved June 19, 2012, from http://16days.thepixelproject.net/16-celebrities-supporting-and-fighting-for-the-cause-to-end-violence-against-women/

Rihanna Attack: The Official Blow-by-Blow. (2009, August 25). TMZ.com. Retrieved from http://www.tmz.com/2009/08/25/rihanna-attack-the-official-blow-by-blow/

Torris, L. (2012, February 20). Chris Brown and Miranda Lambert twitter feud continues. *ABC News*. Retrieved June 19, 2012, from http://abcnews.go.com/blogs/entertainment/2012/02/chris-brown-and-miranda-lambert-twitter-feud-continues/

Williams, A. (2008, February). Boys will be boys, girls will be hounded by the media. Retrieved June 19, 2012, from http://www.nytimes.com/2008/02/17/fashion/17celeb.html

Fatima Zimichi

CENTERS FOR DISEASE CONTROL AND PREVENTION (CDC)

The Centers for Disease Control and Prevention (CDC) is the U.S. federal agency whose primary purposes are the research, identification, prevention, and treatment of diseases and other threats to health. Some of these purposes are accomplished through education and publication of health-related media and working with other government agencies, both foreign and domestic. It is also tasked with creating, publishing, and maintaining statistics on national health and addressing the problems of international diseases and bioterrorism. Today, the CDC is a part of the Department of Health and Human Services and has thousands of personnel with offices across the United States and in over 25 foreign nations. The agency began in 1946 with approximately 400 personnel in Atlanta, Georgia; and was originally a federal agency called Malaria Control in War Areas. The CDC focused primarily on battling malaria in its early years.

The name CDC seems to suggest that it is only concerned with naturally occurring diseases. However, the scope of the CDC's activities is, in practice, much broader and includes injuries and deaths that are initiated or caused by human agency, including domestic violence.

The U.S. Surgeon General identified violence as a key public health priority in 1979. Subsequently, in 1980, the CDC began formal studies and research into the problem of violence in the United States. In 1982, the CDC established the National Center for Injury Prevention and Control. The NCIPC has three divisions, one of which is the Division of Violence Prevention. The primary mission of the DVP is to prevent injuries and deaths caused by violence. To accomplish this mission, the DVP focuses on the following activities: monitoring violence-related injuries; conducting research on the factors that place people at risk or protect them from violence; creating and evaluating the effectiveness of violence prevention programs; assisting other agencies, including state and local agencies, plan, implement, and evaluate violence prevention programs; and conducting research on the effective adoption and dissemination of violence prevention strategies.

The CDC/DVP recognizes domestic abuse as a significant public health problem in the United States. Domestic abuse can and does occur in many forms. The CDC/DVP has classified domestic abuse into three general categories: intimate partner violence, child maltreatment, and elder maltreatment.

Child maltreatment is defined by the CDC/DVP as all types of abuse or neglect of a child less than 18 years of age by a parent, caregiver, or other person with a custodial role over the child. It can include physical, sexual, or emotional abuse or neglect. The publications and programs offered by the CDC/DVP concerning child maltreatment include the facts concerning child maltreatment, definition of child maltreatment, identification of indicators of child maltreatment, long-term effects of child maltreatment, parental training, prevention of child maltreatment, and promotion of safe and nurturing relationships. The CDC/DVP also maintains a list of other agencies that can provide assistance for child maltreatment.

Elder maltreatment is defined by the CDC/DVP as all types of abuse or neglect of a person more than 60 years of age by a caregiver or another person in a relationship having an expectation of trust. It can include physical abuse, sexual abuse or contact, emotional or psychological abuse, financial abuse or exploitation, abandonment, or neglect. Information concerning elder maltreatment offered by the CDC/DVP includes: definition and explanation of elder maltreatment, risk factors for elder maltreatment, and strategies for the prevention of elder maltreatment. The CDC/DVP also publishes a hotline for the reporting of elder maltreatment.

Intimate partner violence is defined by the CDC/DVOP as any physical, sexual, or psychological harm by a current or former spouse or partner, which includes both heterosexual and homosexual people. It can include physical violence, sexual violence, threats of physical or sexual violence, and psychological or emotional violence. The CDC/DVOP maintains numerous publications on its website addressing the problem of intimate partner violence. The CDC/DVP also publishes a national hotline for the reporting of intimate partner violence.

One of the most important federal laws concerning domestic abuse is the Family Violence Prevention and Services Act. This act provides for domestic abuse programs at the local level. Through it and its amendments, nonprofit organizations that provide domestic abuse intervention and prevention at the local level receive funding. Through the auspices of the CDC, these most important programs are funded and supported. In 2010, these programs were renamed the Domestic Violence Prevention Enhancement and Leadership Through Alliances. This program is more commonly referred to as DELTA.

The programs that DELTA supports and funds are commonly called CCRs. They occur in both formal and informal organizations. Formal organizations that are supported and funded by DELTA include social service agencies, law enforcement agencies, and faith-based organizations. The primary purpose of these programs is prevention. The core principles devoted by the CDC and DELTA are preventing first-time perpetration and first-time victimization; reducing risk factors associated with intimate partner violence; promoting protective factors that reduce the likelihood of intimate partner violence; implement evidence-supported strategies that incorporate behavior and social change theories; and evaluating prevention strategies and using results to form future plans.

Thus, the CDC is one of the leading organizations in the United States in the prevention of domestic abuse. It not only supports and funds other agencies in solving this problem but also conducts extensive research into the causes, result, and prevention of domestic abuse.

See also: Domestic Violence Prevention Enhancement and Leadership Through Alliances (DELTA) Program

Further Reading

Centers for Disease Control and Prevention: http://www.cdc.gov/ViolencePrevention

Dahlberg, L., & Krug, E. (2002). *Violence: A global public health problem in world report on violence and health.* Geneva, Switzerland: World Health Organization.

Saltzman, L. E., Fanslow, J. L., McMahon, P. M., & Shelley, G. A. (2002). *Intimate partner violence: Uniform definitions and recommended data elements.* Atlanta, Georgia: Centers for Disease Control, National Center for Injury Prevention.

William Plouffe Jr.

CHILD ABUSE AND DOMESTIC ABUSE

Each state has its own definitions of child abuse and neglect, which they developed based on federal standards and mandates. The federal Child Abuse Prevention and Treatment Act (CAPTA), as amended by the Keeping Children and Families Safe Act of 2003, defines child abse and neglect as "any recent act or failure to act on the part of a parent or caretaker which results in death, serious physical or emotional harm, sexual abuse or exploitation or an act or failure to act which presents an imminent risk of serious harm." Most states identify four types of child maltreatment: neglect, physical abuse, sexual abuse, and emotional abuse.

There is clearly a connection between child abuse and domestic abuse. In an estimated 30 to 60 percent of families in which domestic violence is occurring, child abuse, neglect, or maltreatment is also occurring. Murray Straus's (1983) nationally representative survey found half the men who battered their wives also abused their children, with abuse defined as violence more severe than a slap or spanking. Although harder to measure accurately, emotional abuse of children is probably even more likely. Men who abuse women and children are also more likely to abuse alcohol and drugs and tend to have negative or hostile communication styles. The more severe the domestic abuse, the more severe is the child abuse as well, according to several studies. Other research has shown that battered women are more likely to abuse their children than women in nonabusive relationships.

While battered mothers are generally advised to take their children away from the abuse, research does not necessarily show that parental separation or divorce prevents child abuse or domestic violence. On the contrary, Hardesty and Chung (2006) found that physical abuse, harassment, and stalking of women continued at high rates after separation and divorce. In some cases, such severe behavior only began after the separation or termination of marriage. As many as 35 percent of abuse survivors endure homicidal threats, stalking, and other forms of harassment, while Liss and Stahly (1993) found that one-quarter of battered women reported their ex-partner threatening to hurt or kidnap the children. Data is clear that separation is the highest risk time for victims of abuse, as it is perceived by abusers as a threat to the power and control they had maintained.

A factor that increases the likelihood that one will become a child abuser is enduring abuse as a child, with rates slightly higher among men who were child abuse victims. While child abusers are not likely to have severe mental disorders like schizophrenia or bipolar, they are more likely to have antisocial and narcissistic personalities, according to Holtzworth-Munroe and Stuart (1994).

Those who were abused as children are significantly more likely to physically abuse their own children. Between 3.3 million and 10 million children each year are at risk for witnessing or being exposed to domestic abuse. Some 80 to 90 percent of children who grow up in homes where domestic violence occurs can recall detailed accounts of the abuse. Children who live with domestic violence demonstrate higher levels of aggression, anger, hostility, oppositional behavior, and disobedience. They tend to be more fearful, anxious, withdrawn, and depressed. Often child victims experience poor peer, sibling, and social relationships and suffer from low self-esteem. Additionally, child witnesses often demonstrate lower cognitive functioning, poor school performance, lack of conflict resolution skills, inadequate problem-solving skills, acceptance of violent behaviors and attitudes, and belief in rigid gender-role stereotypes. Long-term problems may include adult depression, symptoms of trauma, and increased tolerance for use of violence. Infants and toddlers exposed to abuse may experience developmental delays, such as delayed potty training or language acquisition. Children may regress developmentally as well; for instance, once they witness a traumatic incident, they may return to wetting the bed regularly despite having mastered potty training. Children who experience abuse in the home may become bullies, modeling the behaviors they see from abusers. Such children are then at greater risk for involvement in abusive teen relationships. In general, boys are more likely to externalize the impact of witnessing abuse while girls are more likely to internalize it. Thus, boys are more prone to acting out, while girls may be more depressed or withdrawn. Specifically, children exposed to abuse often experience:

- Sleeplessness, fear of going to bed, and nightmares;
- Headaches and stomachaches;
- Hypervigilance to danger or harm;
- Fighting or hurting other children or animals;
- Defiant behavior or temper tantrums;
- Withdrawal from people or normal activities;
- Listlessness, depression, or abnormally low energy;
- Perpetual feelings of loneliness or isolation;
- Substance abuse or risky substance use;
- Engaging in personally injurious behavior, such as eating disorders, smoking, and self-mutilation;
- Poor school performance;
- Difficulty concentrating;
- Fear of separation;
- Taking on adult or parental responsibilities;

- Excessive worrying;
- Dissociation; and
- Identifying with or mirroring the behavior of abusers.

Studies show a number of factors that protect young people who witness or are exposed to abuse from suffering the most difficult consequences. These include social competence, intelligence, high self-esteem, outgoing temperament, strong sibling and peer relationships, and supportive adult relationships, all of which can foster resilience. The younger the age at which children begin being exposed to abuse, the more likely the impact will be more severe and longer lasting.

Historically, child protection and domestic violence programs have operated separately and, in some cases, in opposition to one another. Employees of child protective services may view their work protecting children as requiring the immediate removal of children found to be living in homes in which domestic violence is occurring. Domestic violence advocates, while agreeing that it is harmful for children to grow up in abusive homes, find it problematic when child protective services give victims ultimatums: leave the abusive home right away, or your children will be removed from the home. This, they assert, serves to revictimize, as many find it impossible to leave abuse immediately due to financial or other reasons. Focus groups held by the Women of Color Network found that women of color, in particular poor women, faced additional barriers in receiving help from child welfare authorities.

The two systems do not need to work in opposition, however. Both entities can and should remember that they have much in common: (1) both wish to end domestic violence and child maltreatment; (2) both want to ensure the safety of children; and (3) both believe in supporting parents' strengths.

Joint custody arrangements, which are common in the U.S today, may increase the risk of child abuse or of abusers manipulating children as a means of continuing their control over the victim. After reviewing the research, Johnston (1995) concluded that very conflictual parents were not likely to become cooperative parents upon divorce. Studies have shown that domestic violence is often not detected or documented in child custody proceedings. Kernic, Monary-Ernsdorff, Koepsell, and Holt (2005) found that battered and nonbattered women were equally likely to be awarded custody and that offenders and nonoffenders were equally likely to be ordered to hold supervised visits. Studies have shown that gender bias in the courts is likely a factor. Negative stereotypes about women, in particular those who claim to have endured abuse, may prompt judges and juries to disbelieve women's allegations about child abuse. Father's rights groups have promoted joint custody and have raised questions about women's claims of abuse, arguing that many women unfairly claim they have endured domestic violence as a ploy for child custody. The Model Code State Statute of the National Council of Juvenile and Family Court Judges has advocated for a presumption that it is detrimental to children to be placed in sole or joint custody with a perpetrator of domestic violence. They recommend that the perpetrator's history of threats, intimidation, and violence be considered and that victims who choose a safe location for themselves and their children, even if it is another state, should not be considered uncooperative or impulsive. Further, noncustodial parents should be denied access to the children's medical and educational records if that information can be used to locate the custodial parent. The model statute recommends that visitation only be granted to domestic violence perpetrators if adequate safety provisions for both the adult and child victim have been arranged.

Domestic violence shelters must make clear policies related to child abuse, as shelter staff are mandatory reporters of abuse. Staff must be trained to identify signs of child abuse and must inform shelter residents that they are mandatory reporters. In the last two decades, the issue of whether spanking or other forms of corporal punishment are akin to child abuse has arisen in the United States. The Child Welfare Information Gateway provides a number of resources related to identifying the differences between corporal punishment and abuse at http://www.childwelfare.gov/can/defining/disc_abuse.cfm#cultural.

There is much research to show the detrimental effects of spanking, regardless of whether it rises to the level of being considered child abuse. Typically, domestic violence shelters prohibit victims from using any form of corporal punishment while on shelter premises. In 2007, New Zealand, Venezuela, Uruguay, and Chile prohibited all forms of corporal punishment and in 2008, a majority of the Council of Europe member states agreed toward elimination.

See also: Children, Impact of Domestic Abuse on; Courts and Domestic Abuse

Further Reading

Ascione, P., & Arkow, P. (1999). *Child abuse, domestic violence, and animal abuse: Linking the circles of compassion for prevention and intervention.* West Lafayette, IN: Purdue University Press.

Bancroft, L., Silverman, J., & Ritchie, D. (2011). *The batterer as parent: Addressing the impact of domestic violence on family dynamics.* Thousand Oaks, CA: Sage.

Campbell, J. (2007). *Assessing dangerousness: Violence by batterers and child abusers* (2nd ed.) New York: Springer.

Carter, J. (2011). Domestic violence, child abuse, and youth violence: Strategies for prevention and early intervention. Retrieved May 31, 2012, from http://www.mincava.umn.edu/link/documents/fvpf2/fvpf2.shtml

Carter, N. (2003). Forging new collaborations between domestic violence programs, child welfare services, and communities of color. Retrieved May 31, 2012, from http://www.vawnet.org/domestic-violence/summary.php?doc_id=856&find_type=web_desc_NRCDV

Child abuse information. (2012). National Council on Child Abuse and Family Violence. Retrieved May 31, 2012, from http://www.nccafv.org/child.htm

Cross, T., Matthews, B., Tonmyr, L., Scott, D., & Oimet, C. (2012, March). Child welfare policy and practice on children's exposure to domestic violence. *Child Abuse & Neglect, 36*(3), 210–216.

Europe is moving toward a total ban of domestic violence against children. (2008, January 21). *Council of Europe.* Retrieved June 4, 2012, from http://www.coe.int/t/commissioner/viewpoints/080121_en.asp

Groves, B. (2003). *Children who see too much: Lessons from the child witness to violence project.* Boston, MA: Beacon.

Guille, L. (2004). Men who batter and their children: An integrated review. *Aggression & Violent Behavior, 9*(2), 129–163.

Hannah, M., & Goldstein, B. (Eds.). (2010). *Domestic violence, abuse, and child custody: Legal strategies and policy issues.* Kingston, NJ: Civic Research Institute.

Hardesty, J., & Chung, G. (2006). Intimate partner violence, parental divorce, and child custody: Directions for intervention and future research. *Family Relations, 55*(2), 200–210.

Holtzworth-Munroe, A., & Stuart, G. (1994). Typologies of male batterers: Three subtypes and the differences among them. *Psychological Bulletin, 116* (3), 476–497.

Johnston, J. (1995). Research update: Children's adjustment in sole custody compared to joint custody families and principles for custody decision making. *Family and Conciliation Courts Review, 33,* 415–425.

Kernic, M., Monary-Ernsdorff, D., Koepsell, J., & Holt, V. (2005). Children in the crossfire: Child custody determinations among couples with a history of intimate partner violence. *Violence Against Women, 11*(8), 991–1021.

Liss, M., & Stahly, G. (1993). Domestic violence and child custody. In M. Hansen, & M. Harway (Eds.), *Battering and family therapy: A feminist perspective* (175–187). Thousand Oaks, CA: Sage.

Straus, M. (2001). *Beating the devil out of them: Corporal punishment in American families and its effects on children.* New York, NY: Transaction.

Straus, M. (1983). Ordinary violence, child abuse and wife beating: What do they have in common? In D. Finkelhor, R. Gelles, G. Hotaling, & M. Straus (Eds.), *The dark side of families: Current family violence research* (pp. 213–234). Newbury Park, CA: Sage.

Laura L. Finley

CHILDREN, IMPACT OF DOMESTIC ABUSE ON

While children involved in domestic violence relationships may not have actually been abused themselves, they are often negatively affected by witnessing a parent be abused. It can have a tremendous impact on their well-being and developmental growth. In 2009, It was estimated that as many as 14 million children have been exposed to domestic violence in the United States (Edleson, Ellerton, Seagren, Kirchberg, & Ambrose, 2007). Many children who have witnessed domestic violence blame themselves and live in a perpetual state of fear. Children who are exposed to violence in their home often exhibit problems in their emotional and social adjustment (Hughes, 1988). Signs and symptoms of children who have been exposed to domestic violence often appear in multiple domains, including emotional, social, behavioral, and physical.

Children who have witnessed domestic violence often experience an array of emotions after watching their parent be abused. They typically have conflicting feelings toward the abusive parent; feeling anger and distrust, but also love and affection. The child will also usually become very protective of the abused parent and feel sorry for what he or she has endured.

Psychological Symptoms

Children who witness domestic violence in their homes are at risk of developing psychological disorders. For instance, they may develop symptoms of anxiety. They may experience a free-floating anxiety and fear; a fear they may become a victim of the abuse, a fear of abandonment, or a fear for the safety of the abused parent. In many cases children will blame themselves and also become embarrassed or ashamed of the abuse occurring in their home. This can also negatively impact a child's self-esteem, changing how they view themselves. Children may also develop depressive symptoms, believing things are not safe and they are not worthy of being protected. In severe cases, a child may develop post-traumatic stress disorder and experience nightmares, hypervigilance, difficulty focusing and concentrating, and problems sleeping.

Role Reversal

Children of an abused parent will usually assume more adult responsibilities (Riger, Raja & Camacho, 2002). The abused parent and child will often experience a complete role reversal. The child is forced to mature faster, often completing household chores such as cooking, cleaning, and caring for siblings. The parent who is being victimized may treat his or her children as confidants and seek emotional support from them. The child may become *over-parentified* and begin to take care of their parents, in an effort to reduce the tension in the household (Walker, 2009). All of these responsibilities are beyond the scope of "normal" household chores and duties, and the possibility for these children to have a normal childhood is taken away. Some of these children grow up and choose not to marry, citing the fact that they have already raised one family and are not inclined to do it again (Walker, 2009).

Physical Symptoms

In addition to the emotional wounds, children who observe their parents in an abusive relationship may also experience many physical symptoms as well. These physical symptoms can begin as early as when the mother is pregnant. Physical abuse of the pregnant mother, coupled with the emotional strain caused by the abuse, can lead to low birth weights. In some physically abusive situations, the fetus can sustain serious injuries including premature birth and, in severe cases, death. Small children may also become the unintended victims of physical abuse, getting caught in the middle of a dangerous situation. The perpetrator may accidentally hit the child as he or she is being held, or hit the child with an object thrown at the abused parent. These children may also experience gastrointestinal problems, reporting stomach aches and diarrhea. It is not uncommon for children to complain of headaches or general aches and pains, and in some cases they may engage in bedwetting. Children who have witnessed domestic violence have difficulty comprehending and communicating what they experience, and as such, their symptoms manifest as somatic complaints or problems. Research has shown that 60 percent of perpetrators of domestic violence will also abuse the children in the home. Children may present with an array of physical symptoms as a result of witnessing violence; the most deleterious of physical consequences of living in a house with domestic violence, is the possibility that the child may one day become the victim as well.

Behavioral Problems

After witnessing a parent being abused, a child may exhibit some behavioral problems as well. Domestic violence may cause a child to regress and present with out-of-control behavior (Edleson et al., 2007). These children may also imitate the behaviors they have observed. They will internalize the idea that violence is acceptable in relationships and become either the aggressor or the victim of abuse. Bandura's social learning theory states that people learn by observing others' behavior, attitudes, and outcomes of their behavior. It proved its utility when attempting to predict future violent behavior, as boys who witness their mothers being abused are 700 times more likely to become perpetrators of violence than boys who never observed domestic violence in their homes (Walker, 2009).

Children and adolescents may also exhibit behavioral problems in school, becoming disruptive, disrespectful, or getting into fights. They run the risk of getting suspended, expelled, and in some cases they may drop out. In an effort to cope with what they have experienced, some may begin using illicit substances. Others, particularly girls, may engage in risky sexual behaviors. Some teens may not be able to cope with the violence and run away from home. Observing a parent being abused can also have long-term emotional consequences. The child who has never learned how to be in a healthy relationship may also grow up and enter into dysfunctional abusive relationships perpetuating this cycle for generations to come. Girls who witness abuse are more likely to grow up and become victims, while boys are more likely to grow up and become perpetrators. It is also thought that witnessing their mothers being abused is more harmful to children than being abused themselves (Walker, 2009).

Observing and hearing family violence often affects a child's ability to develop empathy, which is the ability to put one's self in another's shoes. Children who watch others being hurt without being able to do anything about it often must not only shut off their own feelings of pain and suffering but also learn to shut off their feelings of compassion and empathy for the pain and suffering of the other persons being hurt. Over time, children exposed to violence become desensitized, making it easier for them to victimize others. In many cases where juveniles find themselves in legal trouble, there was previous identifiable violence in their families (Walker, 2009). In 1997, juveniles accounted for one out of five of all arrests, one out of six of all violent crimes arrests, and one out of three of property crimes arrests (Walker, 2009). This demonstrates that the effects of domestic violence extend beyond the perpetrator and victim; children observing then become offenders, and society as a whole is negatively impacted.

Attachment and Interpersonal Relationships

Witnessing domestic violence will inevitably affect a child's interpersonal relationships. They may isolate themselves from family and close friends, having lost the ability to trust. Being exposed to domestic violence early in life can disrupt a child's attachment to their parents. Not being able to successfully attach and form healthy bonds will affect how they connect and interact with others later in life. Older children may try to avoid their violent home situations by getting involved in extracurricular activities and staying out of the house. Some may yearn for a sense of family and belonging, and become involved in gang activity. Although this can be a dangerous and violent environment, it can make the child feel needed, included, and important; many of the things they are not receiving at home. Another common consequence of violence is "permanent or temporary loss of child custody" (Riger, Raja, & Camacho, 2002, p. 193).

Parental Custody

Being abused can affect an individual's ability to parent his or her children and can result in relinquishing custody. Victims of domestic violence often suffer severe emotional and psychological consequences, and this can overshadow their parental responsibilities. Many victims of domestic violence stay in the relationship because they believe their children will benefit from being raised by both parents. However, research has shown that living with one parent in a household free of violence is better for the child than living with both parents in an abusive household (Walker, 2009). Historically, judges have awarded custody to mothers, particularly of young children. This was to protect the mother-child bond, which was considered of paramount importance for development. In the 1970s, the "best interest of the child" became the standard for awarding custody, and was essentially neutral regarding parental rights. Exposure to domestic violence was not originally considered when determining custody, but over time states began to recognize the need to consider this factor when making custody decisions. Many states have adopted the Model Code of the Family Violence Project of the National Council of Juvenile and Family Courts. These statutes make clear that it is detrimental to a child, and not in their best interest, to be placed in sole custody or joint legal/physical custody with the perpetrator of domestic violence (NCJFCJ, 1998).

Treatment

There are many things parents can do to help children who have witnessed violence. Counseling and therapy services play a vital role in a child's healing after being exposed to violence. Some children may experience more severe consequences, and there are a range of services available. Age will also play a role in determining which services are appropriate, as some younger children may benefit more from play therapy. Some children may do better with individual or group therapy. For children who exhibit more anger and aggression, anger management classes may be necessary to teach them more appropriate coping skills. After a child has witnessed or experienced violence, it is imperative to provide a safe and consistent environment. This can be done by scheduling meals at a regular time and setting aside specific time for family, homework, and socializing. Routines can provide consistency that children can count on and begin to rebuild trust. Parents should also modify their parenting styles to remove violence in any form, and this would include any form of physical or verbal aggression. Parents should not use physical punishment, name-calling, or yelling when disciplining children. Whatever the method, it is important to intervene early to counteract the effects of abuse and promote resiliency in children.

See also: Child Abuse; Effects of Domestic Violence

Further Reading

Edleson, J. L., Ellerton, A. L., Seagren, A. E., Kirchberg, S. O., & Ambrose, A. T. (2007). Assessing child exposure to adult domestic violence. *Children and Youth Services Review, 29*(7), 961–971.

Family Violence Project, National Council of Juvenile and Family Court Judges (NCJFCJ). (1998). *Family violence: Legislative update* (Vol. 3). Reno, NV: NCJFCJ.

Hughes, H. M. (1988). Psychological and behavioral correlates of family violence in child witnesses and victims. *American Journal of Orthopsychiatry, 58*, 77–90.

Riger, S., Raja, S., & Camacho, J. (2002). The radiating impact of intimate partner violence. *Journal of Interpersonal Violence, 17*, 184–205.

Walker, L. (2009). *The battered woman syndrome* (3rd ed.). New York, NY: Springer.

Alison Mulcahy

CHRISTIANITY AND DOMESTIC ABUSE

The relationship between domestic violence and Christianity has been as multilayered and dynamic as Christianity itself. The correlation between religion and domestic violence has been a highly contentious debate, at times pitting religious adherents against each other with academic scholars and domestic violence advocates on both sides. Due to the fact that adherents of Christianity, like all other religions, interpret the scriptures in different ways and perhaps on a continuum, based on the extent of literal belief in the Bible, church leaders continue to debate whether Christianity is a tool of the abuser or a necessary coping mechanism for victims. Moreover, Christians and their religious leaders are also at odds over whether or not the Bible allows the victim to divorce the perpetrator of domestic violence. Both perpetrators and victims of intimate partner violence have used Christianity to inhibit their actions and to give credence to their actions.

It has been argued that due to the patriarchal history and inherent nature of Christianity, many victims of domestic violence are forced into a wall of silence that extends far beyond the walls of the home where the violence and abuse take place. Scripture passages have been used to support the interpretation of Christianity as a tool for the subjugation of women. The argument is that scripture leads some men to commit acts of violence due to their "natural" and "heavenly ordained" place in the social hierarchy.

Some argue that Christianity upholds traditional patriarchal ideals regarding male and female roles and thus that men are given God-granted power over women. The belief is that domestic violence arises when those traditional roles are questioned or broken. In fact, Pastor John Piper of the Bethlehem Baptist Church argues that Christianity requires the victim to remain married through the abuse and to seek help from God and the church. He contends, "If it's not requiring her (a wife) to sin but simply hurting her, then I think she endures verbal abuse for a season, and she endures perhaps being smacked for one night and then she seeks help from the church" (Piper, 2011).

Some in the Christian faith tradition place the blame for abuse on the victim rather than the abuser. Bruce Ware, a Christian theology professor at Southern Baptist Theological Seminary, believes that a woman's refusal to submit to her husband is the cause for abuse. Debi Pearl, author of *Created to Be His Help Meet* (2004), argues that some men demand respect and therefore abuse occurs when his wife is not obedient and subservient to him. In some cases, Pearl (2004) argues, some men will be cruel and abusive even when she "serves" and "obeys" as a good "help mate" should. In those cases, she suggests that the victim call the police.

However, Jocelyn Anderson believes the root of domestic violence in Christian homes lies with the religious argument supporting female subordination that Pearl (2004) espouses. Anderson states: "The premise is despotic and abusive in and of itself. Gender abuse, which includes domestic abuse and the hate crime of domestic violence among Christians will never be eradicated until gender equality for Christian women is acknowledged and practically implemented within our homes and churches."

Others argue that religion, based on love and forgiveness, negates violence from occurring in and outside the home and that scripture does not condone domestic violence, but rather forbids it. The argument is that Christianity forbids violence in the home; therefore, they argue that Christians are less apt to be perpetrators or victims of domestic violence. Moreover, they dispel the notion that scripture advocates subjugation of women or domestic violence and argue that Christianity reduces the incidences of domestic abuse.

Pastor Gary Freel (2011), writing for the Fundamental Evangelistic Association, does not see an inherent bias against women in the scripture. Rather, he interprets Genesis 1–2 as evidence that men and women are complements and their formation made creation whole. He also argues that Galatians 3:28 demonstrates the significance of women. Freel states, "Throughout the text of Holy Writ, women are exalted in terms of value and importance (Prov. 31)." Barbara Roberts, in her book *Not Under Bondage* (2008), echoes Pastor Freel's sentiments by arguing that women have the God-given right to divorce for abuse, adultery, and desertion.

Further studies need to be done regarding religion and domestic violence. Many studies dispel the notion of any correlation between the two. However, one problem appears to be the ability to measure religiosity. It seems problematic to attempt to ensure that one's stated religion, values, and beliefs are a reflection of their actions. Another major problem is with the accuracy of domestic violence reporting. Many victims are so caught in the web of power dynamics that they often mistake dominance and subjugation for love, therefore they are less apt to readily if ever report incidences of domestic violence.

It has been argued that this phenomenon occurs more often with religious victims and perpetrators, yet the studies do not demonstrate this precisely because victims tend not to self-report. Moreover, many victims may be too scared and embarrassed and many of the perpetrators and victims, due to their religious beliefs, do not view the abuse as domestic violence, but rather as the necessary order of a patriarchal household.

Further studies also need to be done regarding whether religious people attend church because they are less prone to violence or if those likely to commit acts of violence might stay away from religious clergy and religious institutions because they are more prone to violence. If, as the studies appear to demonstrate, attending church services lowers domestic violence rates, is it because those experiencing domestic violence might stay out of church to hide scars, wounds, emotional breakdowns or because those perpetuating or suffering from intimate partner violence might be attending church but not disclosing their involvement with domestic violence?

See also: Spiritual Abuse; Types of Domestic Abuse

Further Reading

Anderson, J. (2012). Women submit! Christians and domestic violence. Retrieved from http://www.womansubmit.blogspot.com/

Anonymous (n.d.). Through the eyes of a battered woman. Retrieved from http://www.notunderbondage.com/resources/Throughtheeyesofabatteredwomanvideo.html

Bauman-Maritn, B. (2004). Women on the edge: New perspectives on women in the Petrine Haustafal. *Journal of Biblical Literature, 123*(2), 253–279.

Brinkerhoff, M. B., Lupri, E., & Grandin, E. (1992). Religious involvement and spousal violence: The Canadian case. *Journal for the Scientific Study of Religion, 31*(1), 15–31.

Carter, J. (2009). The words of God do not justify cruelty to women. *The Guardian.* Retrieved from http://www.guardian.co.uk/commentisfree/2009/jul/12/jimmy-carter-womens-rights-equality

Ellison, C. G., & Anderson, K. L. (2001). Religious involvement and domestic violence among U.S. couples. *Journal for the Scientific Study of Religion, 40*(2), 269–286.

Ellison, C. G., Bartkowski, J. P., & Anderson, K. L. (1999). Are there religious variations in domestic violence? *Journal of Family Issues, 20*(1), 87–113.

Ellison, C. G., Trinitapoli, J. A., Anderson, K. L., & Johnson, B. R. (2007). Race/ethnicity, religious involvement, and domestic violence. *Violence Against Women, 13*(11), 1094–1112.

Freel, G. (2011). Is Christianity a cause for domestic violence? *Fundamental Evangelistic Association.* Retrieved from https://www.feasite.org/christianity_and_domestic_violence

McCollom, J. (2011). Religious right-wing rationalizes beating of wives by husbands. *Examiner.* Retrieved from http://www.examiner.com/article/religious-right-wing-rationalizes-beating-of-wives-by-husbands

Nason-Clark, N. (2000). Making the sacred safe: Woman abuse and communities of faith. *Sociology of Religion, 61*(4), 349–368.

Nason-Clark, N. (2004). When terror strikes at home: The interface between religion and domestic violence. *Journal for the Scientific Study of Religion, 43*(3), 303–310.

Pearl, D. (2004). *Created to be his help meet: Discover how God can make your marriage glorious*. Pleasantville, TN: No Greater Joy Ministries.
Piper, J. (2011). The new priestly class: Pastors that advocate submission to abuse. *The Reformed Traveler*. Retrieved from http://thereformedtraveler.wordpress.com/2011/11/04/the-new-priestly-class-pastors-that-advocate-submission-to-abuse/
Roberts, B. (2008). Not under bondage: Biblical divorce for abuse, adultery, and desertion. Australia: Maschil Press. Retrieved from http://www.notunderbondage.com/book.html
Todhunter, R. G., & Deaton, J. (2010). The relationship between religious and spiritual factors and the perpetration of intimate personal violence. *Journal of Family Violence, 2*, 745–753.
UNIFEM. (2008). Religious leaders of different faiths "say no to violence against women." *Religions for Peace*. Retrieved from http://religionsforpeace.org/news/press/press-release-religious-5.html
Weaver, J. D. (2001). Violence in Christian theology. *Cross Currents*, 150–176.
Wendt, S. (2008). Christianity and domestic violence: Feminist poststructuralist perspectives. *Journal of Women and Social Work, 23*(2), 144–155.
Wilcox, W. B. (2004). *Soft patriarchs, new men: How Christianity shapes fathers and husbands*. Chicago, IL: University of Chicago Press.
Woodman, B. (2000). How religion supports societal violence. *Free Inquiry, 21*, 16–17.

Chuck Goesel

COLLEGE-AGED VICTIMS

Rates of dating violence are difficult to precisely calculate. This difficulty stems from the low number of incidents reported to police. Many individuals who experience dating violence do not report their experiences because of embarrassment, self-blame, and fear. It has also been suggested that the general lack of understanding of the nature of dating violence creates some confusion around the labeling of abuse. As a result of this ambiguity, many incidents of intimate partner abuse go unreported because they are not recognized as dating violence, but rather, as noncriminal acts.

In addition to these issues, some scholars have argued that because various forms of dating violence are often studied in isolation, it is difficult to formulate an overall estimate of the prevalence of dating violence. Research does seem clear, however, that college students are at particular risk to experience abuse.

Fisher, Cullen, and Turner (2000) found that one in three college women experience sexual assault by their male partners. Further, Fisher et al. (2000) found that approximately 42 percent of college students sampled reported experiencing some type of coerced or forced kissing or fondling. Twenty-two percent reported some type of coerced or forced oral-genital contact, 23 percent reported vaginal or anal intercourse as a result of continuous arguments or pressure. 6 percent reported having someone attempt vaginal or anal intercourse by use of threat or some degree of force. Nine percent reported having anal or vaginal intercourse under those same conditions In 2002, Leonard, Quigley, and Collins found that approximately 30–40 percent of both male and female college students had experienced some form of abuse with a dating partner. Stalking, a significant predictor of very serious and potentially lethal dating violence, is also prevalent on college campuses. In one 7-month period in 2001, 13.1 percent of college women reported being stalked, and more than 40 percent of the known stalkers were a boyfriend or ex-boyfriend (Fisher, Cullen, & Turner, 2000). In 1999, Mustaine and Tewksbury found 10 percent of women attending nine colleges had been stalked in the previous six months. The Feminist Majority Foundation reported in 2005 that 32 percent of college students are domestic violence victims. Research has indicated that violence in dating relationships for university and college students is extremely common and is, in fact, on the rise. Klein (2006) found 35 percent of male college students indicated some likelihood that they would commit a violent rape against a woman who had fended off an advance if they were sure they would not be punished.

Within college samples, several studies have found sorority members more at risk for dating violence than the general population of college women. Sorority members, particularly those who live in sorority houses, are also three times as likely to be sexually assaulted while intoxicated than the general population of collegiate women who live on campus.

Research is clear that dating violence is common among college students outside the United States as well. A 2007 study involving 13,601 students from 32 universities across the globe that participated in the International Dating Violence Study found high rates of both minor and major assault perpetrated by men and women. The author of the study, Murray Straus, has maintained that most abuse among this age group is bidirectional, that is, both parties are involved in the perpetrating abusive behavior.

Sometimes, abusers kill their victims. This is true across the nation, as well as specific to South Florida. In January 2002, Michael Holmes shot and killed his girlfriend, Moriah Pierce, before killing himself on the Broward Community College Central Campus. In 2005, a student was killed on the campus of Nova Southeastern University. Approximately 20 percent of homicides are the result of dating violence. Two-thirds of the homicides in this study were planned, and most were preceded by abusive behaviors like stalking. Often, the abusive relationship began in high school and continued into college.

Causes

Many scholars have studied the causes of dating violence. Much of this research has focused specifically on the roots of male-perpetrated dating violence. Several scholars have suggested that participation in aggressive sports, beliefs in male dominance, and hostility toward women are all connected to aggressive male behavior within college dating relationships. Male sexual aggression, more specifically, has been discussed by some researchers as being the result of traditional notions of gender roles and a belief in male authority and control. Some researchers have argued that in addition to these explanations, the predominance of media highlighting sexual, and sometimes violent, imagery of women as well as the prevalent media representations of male aggression and female sexuality contribute to sexual violence within dating relationships. Stith (2007) identified problems such as stress, inability to control anger, and very intense relationships as common triggers for domestic violence in college. Many times, boys or men who are rejected by a girl or girlfriend resort to violence.

Little academic research has been directed toward female-perpetrated dating violence. Scholars have suggested that substance abuse, childhood victimization, and relationship conflict all contribute to increased rates of female dating violence.

Impact

Researchers have found that college women and men who experience dating violence often suffer from various levels of post-traumatic stress disorder, increased substance abuse, lowered self-esteem, and forms of cognitive impairment.

Dating violence has been shown to negatively affect the scholastic performance of university and college students who experience it. Having classes in common with an abuser may increase opportunities for unwanted contact and stalking. Stalking victims must often change their routines, alter their daily travel routes, quit their jobs, relocate, and restrict leaving their homes. This may significantly affect their ability to successfully complete classes.

Abuse in dating relationships has also been illustrated to have harmful effects on other individuals besides the victim. Friends and family members who are informed about the violence often experience severe distress.

On many campuses, students receive little in the way of education or training about dating violence. Rarely does coursework directly address how a person can identify the signs of an abusive relationship and what are local resources for help. Nor do all campuses have drop-in centers where victims can go to get support or assistance. Because there is so little direct attention given to these topics, many students hold misconceptions about abuse. Most notably, research has demonstrated that college students are prone to blame victims for their abuse. Victim-blaming and other myths about abuse contribute to the problem, as they prevent many victims from obtaining help. Many campuses lack clear policies on dating and domestic violence.

Recommendations

Literature suggests the following for college campuses:

(1) Including information on dating violence in freshman orientations and training of residence hall staff; (2) Distributing literature across campus about the signs of abuse and help available; (3) Specific campus programming for high risk groups, including sororities/fraternities and athletes; (4) Development of gender-specific programming; (5) Collaborations with local domestic violence agencies; (6) Peer-led efforts to change beliefs about abuse and to challenge harmful gender-role norms; (7) Opportunities for males and females to get involved to end abuse; (8) Wider access to self-defense and empowerment classes; (9) Specific training for campus medical, health care, social work, and mental health professionals; (10) Training for staff and faculty on recognizing the signs of abuse and how to help; (11) Assignment of a specific victim advocate to campus.

See also: Bystander Intervention Programs; Educational Programs; Teen Victims of Domestic Abuse.

Further Reading

Anderson, K., & Danis, F. (2007). Collegiate sororities and dating violence: An exploratory study of informal and formal helping strategies. *Violence Against Women, 13*(1), 87–100.

Boeringer, S. B. (1996). Influences of fraternity membership, athletics, and male living arrangements on sexual aggression. *Violence Against Women, 2,* 134–147.

Fisher, S., Cullen, F., & Turner, M. (2000). *The sexual victimization of college women.* Washington, DC: U.S. Department of Justice.

Fisher, S., Cullen, F., & Turner, M. (2009). *Unsafe in the ivory tower: The sexual victimization of college women.* Thousand Oaks, CA: Sage.

Klein, J. (2006). An invisible problem: Everyday violence against girls in schools. *Theoretical Criminology, 10,* 147–177.

Koss, K. P. (1998). Hidden rape: Incident, prevalence and descriptive characteristics of sexual aggression and victimization in a national sample of college students. In E. Burgess (Ed.), *Rape and sexual assault* (Vol. 2). New York, NY: Garland.

Leonard, K., Quigley, B., & Collins, R. (2002). Physical aggression in the lives of young adults: Prevalence, location, and severity among college and community samples. *Journal of Interpersonal Violence, 17,* 533–550

Marx, B. P., Nichols-Anderson, C., Messman-Moore, T., Miranda, R., & Porter, C. (2000). Alcohol consumption outcomes expectations and victimization status among female college students. *Journal of Applied Psychology, 30*(5), 1056–1070.

Mustaine, E., & Tewksbury, R. (1999). A routine activity theory explanation for women's stalking victimizations. *Violence Against Women, 5*(1), 43–62.

Paludi, M. (2008). *Understanding and preventing campus violence.* Greenwood, CT: Praeger.

Schwartz, M. D., Leggett, M. S. (1999). Bad dates or emotional trauma? The aftermath of campus sexual assault. *Violence Against Women, 5,* 251–271.

Smith, P. H., White, J. W., & Holland, L. J. (2003). A longitudinal perspective on dating violence among adolescent and college age women. *American Journal of Public Health, 93* (7), 1104–1109.

Stith, S. (2007, September 13). K-State domestic violence expert looks at dating among high school, college students. Retrieved January 26, 2013 from http://www.he.k-state.edu/news/2007/09/13/k-state-domestic-violence-expert-looks-at-dating-violence-among-high-school-college-students/

Straus, M. (2008). Dominance and symmetry in partner violence by male and female university students in 32 nations. *Children and Youth Services Review, 30,* 252–275.

Laura L. Finley

CONVENTION ON THE ELIMINATION OF ALL FORMS OF DISCRIMINATION AGAINST WOMEN (CEDAW)

The Convention on the Elimination of All Forms of Discrimination against Women (CEDAW) is an international human rights document adopted by the UN General Assembly in 1979. CEDAW promotes state responsibility to ensure human rights and equality for women and eliminate discrimination and gender-based violence. CEDAW defines discrimination against women as "any distinction, exclusion or restriction made on the basis of sex which has the effect or purpose of impairing or nullifying the recognition, enjoyment or exercise by women, irrespective of their marital status, on a basis of equality of men and women, of human rights and fundamental freedoms in the political, economic, social, cultural, civil or any other field." State signatories to CEDAW must implement measures to end discrimination and violence against women under international law.

In addition, countries must submit reports at least every four years outlining measures that have been implemented to meet the terms of CEDAW. However, CEDAW has not been ratified by all countries, and parties that have signed the international human rights treaty may do so with reservations, allowing self-determination for interpretation based on cultural, social, and political relativism for agreement and adherence. Similarly, there has been difficulty regarding the enforcement of CEDAW as with other international human rights documents and efforts. The United Nations has put forth many treaties and conventions aimed at ensuring the fundamental freedoms and human rights of all individuals without distinction based on sex. These include the Universal Declaration of Human Rights; the International Covenant on Economic, Social, and Cultural Rights; and the International Covenant on Civil and Political Rights. However, women's ability to enjoy freedom and human rights based on the universality of their humanity proved insufficient. As a result, the Commission on the Status of Women (CSW) worked on the development and implementation of treaties to promote women's human rights by examining documents from a gender perspective. The work of the CSW, women's activists, as well as consciousness-raising within a dynamic social climate precluded the development of a convention that specifically targeted the discriminatory practices of states preventing women's realization of fundamental human rights.

States that ratify this human rights document must ensure recognition and legal responsibility to end discriminatory practices against women. These measures include ending discriminatory practices within the legal system, creating institutional protection for women, and ensuring that women do not experience discrimination or exploitation at the micro, meso, or macro level. Specifically, CEDAW emphasizes women's equal access to political equality and the right to vote and run for public office, equal employment and access to education and health services, and protection of the reproductive rights of women. Countries that ratify CEDAW must take measures to ensure the safety and freedom of women from exploitation and trafficking. This treaty also obligates signatory states to ensure the rights of women to be free from discrimination and violence in the private sphere, including discriminatory gender roles within the family system and domestic violence. According to the *Harvard International Law Journal*, "The CEDAW declares that 'under general international law and specific human rights covenants, states may also be responsible for private acts if they fail to act with due diligence to prevent violations of rights, or to investigate and punish acts of violence, and provide compensation" (Culliton, 1993, p. 514).

States that do not prevent or investigate battering incidents are in violation of the CEDAW treaty in taking appropriate measures to protect women's human rights and are responsible for violating such obligations under international law. However, battering victims bear the burden of proving that the state was in violation and fostered "an environment allowing the serious injury and torture of battered women" (Culliton, 1993, p. 515). Therefore, victims of domestic violence must prove that the state was aware that domestic violence against women was occurring and negligently failed to take measures to protect women from this violence, allowing the batterer to act with impunity in violating women's rights as protected under CEDAW. "In cases where a woman has reported a case of domestic violence to the police or to other state agents, the failure of those agents to prosecute the victim's complaint can create state responsibility for the violation" (Culliton, 1993, p. 522).

See also: The United Nations and Domestic Abuse

Further Reading

Culliton, K. M. (1993). Finding a mechanism to enforce women's right to state protection from domestic violence in the Americas. *Harvard International Law Journal, 34*(2). Retrieved from http://www.heinonline.org.ezproxylocal.library.nova.edu/HOL/Page?handle=hein.journals/hilj34&id=513&collection=journals&index=journals/hilj

United Nations Department of Public Information. Report by the Committee on the Elimination of Discrimination against Women. Retrieved from http://www.un.org/womenwatch/daw/cedaw/reservations.htm

Kathryn Goesel

COURTS AND DOMESTIC ABUSE

Since the 1970s, one of the main rallying cries of domestic violence advocates was for the accountability of batterers. In the decades that followed, many changes occurred in regard to the apprehension, trial, and sentencing of batterers. In particular, Sherman and Berk's (1984) study on domestic violence arrests and recidivism in Minneapolis resulted in dramatic changes in police practice. With more people being arrested, there should have been a concomitant increase in the number of people being prosecuted for abuse. Yet several studies revealed that fewer than 10 percent of arrests resulted in prosecutions. In the 1980s and 1990s, some states adopted "no-drop" prosecution. Such policies account for the fact that many victims will refuse to go ahead with criminal charge when given the choice. Prosecutors were often reluctant to proceed without victims' help. Belknap, Fleury, Melton, Sullivan, and Leisenring (2001) interviewed battered women and found the main reason victims do not want to go to court is fear of retaliation by their abuser. Other commonly cited reasons for not wanting to appear in court include not wanting to miss work, a desire to work things out with the abuser, pressure from family or friends, bad experiences with the court, lack of child care and/or transportation, and fear of being arrested themselves.

Yet it is still not entirely clear whether criminal justice interventions are effective. Little empirical testing has been done regarding domestic violence court case processing and dispositions. Data is not clear whether prosecutions result in reduced recidivism or whether no-drop prosecutions are effective. Tolman and Weisz (1995) compared the recidivism of batterers who were not prosecuted with those who were and found a slight difference, but it was not statistically significant. Similarly, Murphy, Musser, and Maton (1998) found that batterers who were convicted and placed on probation had slightly (but not statistically significant) rates of recidivism. Thistlethwaite, Wooldredge and Gibbs (1998) found that sentence length was not related to recidivism, but a combination of jail sentence and probation was. They noted that, in general, sanctions were most effective for batterers who have the most stake in conformity to social norms. Ventura and Davis (2005) found that batterers whose cases were dismissed had more violent felonies in their history. They also found that the type of abuse matters in regard to whether a domestic abuse case will be dropped. Batterers who reportedly punched or threw their victims had higher rates of prosecution, while those who pushed or pulled were most likely to be dropped. In regard to recidivism, they found that batterers who were prosecuted were less likely to reoffend. Ford and Regoli (1992) found that, while the risk of reabuse is greatest when cases are dropped because the victim chose not to prosecute, they did not find that no-drop prosecutions reduced reabuse. Davis, Smith, and Nickles (1998) noted that no-drop prosecution results in case backloads and fewer convictions. Further, some advocates see no-drop prosecution as disempowering to victims. They argue that placing the decision making in the hands of the State instead of victims is simply another example of controlling behavior. Some states use evidence-based prosecutions for domestic abuse, which allows prosecutors to proceed with the case even when victims are unwilling to be involved because they have police officers' reports, photographs, witness testimony, and other forms of evidence.

Courts often mandate that abusers attend batterer intervention programs (BIP). Some research supports that batterers who were referred to BIP by courts had lower rates of reabuse than did those who entered the programs voluntarily. In all, however, data does not show significant positive impact from BIP.

Some jurisdictions have established specialized courts that only hear cases involving domestic violence. Advocates maintain that this sends a powerful message to the community about the importance of the issue and helps victims obtain justice by allocating judges who are most knowledgeable about the complexities of abuse. Critics maintain that such courts may be biased against offenders or victims, in particular when the individuals involved have appeared numerous times before the same judge.

New York introduced the first Integrated Domestic Court in the United States in 1996. It was intended to help streamline legal services related to abuse, locating them all in one courthouse. The Brooklyn Felony Domestic Violence Court, the very first to open, claims to have been successful given that no victims involved in open cases have been killed by abusers since the court started. Proponents of Integrated Courts feel that judges are better able to make informed decisions about domestic violence cases because they are more aware of the totality of issues and incidents involved.

Assigning child custody in cases involving domestic violence is one of the most challenging aspects for courts. It is estimated that, of the court cases for divorce, 75 percent involved substantiated claims of domestic violence. Research is clear about the detrimental effect of exposure to domestic violence, and in approximately half of all domestic violence cases child maltreatment is occurring as well. In divorce cases involving domestic violence, courts often turn to custody evaluators to assess the best options. Research has shown that custody evaluators tend to minimize the relevance of domestic violence allegations when they feel the abuse has no bearing on the individual's ability to be a good parent.

Some victims, in an attempt to flee abuse, take their children across international borders. The Convention on the Civil Aspects of Child Abduction was adopted at the Hague in 1980. To date, some 67 countries are party to what is generally called the Hague Convention. It was put into effect in the United States in July 1988 through the International Child Abduction Remedies Act. The Hague Convention set forth international guidelines on the handling of children who are abducted from one country to another. States party to the Hague Convention must work to quickly return abducted children to their habitual residence so that local authorities can resolve custody and other issues. The Hague Convention does specify certain exceptions where the best interests of the child can override the mandatory return of a child from one country to another. Weiner (2000) argued that the Hague Convention was drafted based on a stereotypical male abductor and thus does not adequately address female victims who may take their children across borders because they are fleeing abuse. Approximately one-third of Hague Convention cases involved some form of family violence, with 70 percent of those involving domestic violence. Shetty and Edleson (2005) tell the story of Karin Von Brenner, who fled Cyprus with her young son to escape brutal abuse. Shortly after fleeing to the United States, she was declared an international fugitive and forcibly removed from her home in Idaho by federal agents. When she tried to obtain counsel, no lawyer in Boise had heard of the Hague Convention. Article 13(b) of the Hague Convention provides an exception to the rule that a child must be returned to his or her habitual residence in cases where there "is a grave risk that his or her return would expose the child to physical or psychological harm or otherwise place the child in an intolerable situation." "Grave risk" defenses, as they are called, are most frequently used in cases where there is internal strife in the home country. Hilton (1997) argued that the concept of grave risk was not intended to apply to individual parents, a notion that has been incorporated into training for judges and lawyers. A review of the cases in which domestic violence was alleged to be the source of grave risk reveals a mixed bag. In some cases, judges ruled that the risk to the child identified by the victim was too vague to rise to the level of legal protection. The most successful claims were when the child was being abused as well as the victim.

See also: Batterer Intervention Programs; Child Abuse; Children, Impact of Domestic Abuse on; Mandatory Arrest Policies; Minneapolis Domestic Violence Experiment (MDVE)

Further Reading

Belknap, J., Fleury, R., Melton, H., Sullivan, C., & Leisenring, A. (2001). To go or not to go? Preliminary findings on battered women's decisions regarding court cases. In H. Eigenberg (Ed.), *Women battering in the United States: Til death do us part* (pp. 319–326). Prospect Heights, IL: Waveland Press.

Berk, R., Campbell, A, Klap, R., & Western, B. (1992). The deterrent effect of arrest in the incidence of domestic violence: A Bayesian analysis of four field experiments. *American Sociological Review, 57*, 698–708.

Cramer, E. (1999). Variables that predict verdicts in domestic violence cases. *Journal of Interpersonal Violence, 14*, 1137–1150.

Davis, R., Smith, B., & Nickles, L. (1998). The deterrent effect of prosecuting domestic violence misdemeanors. *Crime and Delinquency, 44*, 434–444.

Ford, D., & Regoli, M. (1992). The preventative impact of policies for prosecuting wife batterers. In E. Buzawa & C. Buzawa (Eds.), *Domestic violence: The changing criminal justice response* (pp. 181–207). Westport, CT: Greenwood.

Gross, M., Cramer, E., Forte, J., & Gordon, J. (2000). The impact of sentencing options on recidivism among domestic violence offenders: A case study. *American Journal of Criminal Justice, 24*, 301–312.

Hilton, W. (1997). Limitation on Article 13(b) of the Convention on the Civil Aspects of International Child Abduction. *American Journal of Family Law, 11*, 139–144.

Mills, L. (1999). Killing her softly: Intimate abuse and the violence of state intervention. *Harvard Law Review, 113*, 550.

Murphy, C., Musser, P., Maton, K. (1998). Coordinated community intervention for domestic abusers: Intervention system involvement and criminal recidivism. *Journal of Family Violence, 13*, 263–284.

Sherman, L. W, & Berk, R. (1984). The specific deterrent effects of arrest for domestic assault. *American Sociological Review, 49*, 261–272.

Shetty, S., & Edleson, J. (2005). Adult domestic violence in cases of international parental child abduction. *Violence Against Women, 11*(1), 115–138.

Specialized domestic violence court systems (2009, February). Retrieved March 29, 2012, from http://www.stopvaw.org/specialized_domestic_violence_court_systems.html

Thistlethwaite, A., Wooldredge, J., & Gibbs, D. (1998). Severity of dispositions and domestic violence recidivism. *Crime and Delinquency, 44*, 388–399.

Tolman, R, & Weisz, A. (1995). Coordinated community intervention for domestic violence: The effects of arrest and prosecution on recidivism of woman abuse perpetrators. *Crime and Delinquency, 41*, 481–495.

Ventura, L., & Davis, G. (2005). Domestic violence: Court case conviction and recidivism. *Violence Against Women, 11*(2), 255–277.

Weiner, M. (2000). International child abduction and the escape from domestic violence. *Fordham Law Review, 69*, 593.

Laura L. Finley

CRISIS LINES

Since the 1970s, crisis lines have been an invaluable service to victims of domestic abuse. Victims can call these numbers toll-free and speak to trained advocates, asking questions about abuse, obtaining referral information, and, when needed,

Joe Biden speaks during his visit to the National Domestic Violence Hotline Center in Austin Texas on April 28, 2009. During his speech, he pointed out that curbing violence against women also helps tens of thousands of American children who witness the violence and may become homeless because of it. (AP Photo/Harry Cabluck)

making arrangements to obtain safe shelter. Each year, the National Network to End Domestic Violence (NNEDV) coordinates a 24-hour census regarding utilization of domestic violence services. In 2011, 1,726 domestic violence programs participated, which is 89 percent of the identified domestic violence centers in the United States. The survey found that there were 22,508 calls made to crisis lines. Local and state hotlines answered 21,748 calls, and the National Domestic Violence Hotline answered 760 calls. This averages to more than 16 hotline calls every minute. The full report breaks down the number of crisis calls by state, as well as a variety of other services provided to victims.

Nationally, there are numerous crisis lines devoted to domestic violence in general as well as specific types of victimization. Below is a list of some of these crisis lines. It is far from exhaustive, however.

Created in 1996 after the enactment of the 1994 Violence Against Women Act (VAWA), the National Domestic Violence Hotline offers 24-hour support for victims, 365 days a year, in more than 170 different languages (via interpreter services) and through a TTY line available for the deaf, deaf-blind, and hard of hearing. Operating as a nonprofit organization, the hotline also provides crisis intervention, information and referral information, and coordinates advocacy to government officials, law enforcement, and the general public. The hotline provides access to more than 4,000 shelters and domestic violence service programs in the United States, Puerto Rico, Guam, and the U.S. Virgin Islands. It is the only nationwide hotline to do so. In addition to other information and links, NDVH also includes a listing of statewide coalitions for persons in need of more regional or localized help.

The Americans Overseas Domestic Violence Crisis Center is an international toll-free line designed to serve both civilian and military abused Americans overseas in more than 175 countries. It provides advocacy, safety planning, and case management, along with relocation assistance for victims, emergency housing funds, childcare assistance, and legal fees. In 2010, 5.25 million American civilians lived in other countries, according to the U.S. State Department. That same year, the

U.S. Department of Defense estimated there were approximately 500,000 military personnel and their families living overseas. More information is available at http://www.866uswomen.org/.

Teen victims can contact Love Is Respect, which offers numerous resources along with 24-hour, seven days a week peer advocacy via phone or live chat. The website http://www.loveisrespect.org/ provides a wealth of information about the issue of dating violence.

Runaway and homeless youth can contact the National Runaway Switchboard (NRS). NRS was established in 1971 as a source of comprehensive crisis intervention in 1971. According to its website, NRS "provides education and solution-focused interventions, offers non-sectarian, non-judgmental support, respects confidentiality, collaborates with volunteers, and responds to at-risk youth and their families 24 hours a day." Now expanded to address the needs of homeless and runaway youth nationwide, NRS serves as a clearinghouse of services. The 1-800-RUNAWAY hotline now handles more than 100,000 calls each year from throughout the United States as well as Puerto Rico, the U.S. Virgin Islands, and Guam. For more information, see http://www.1800runaway.org/

Lesbian, gay, bisexual, and transgendered persons can find help for domestic violence, among other things, at the GLBT National Help Center, a nonprofit, tax-exempt organization "dedicated to meeting the needs of the gay, lesbian, bisexual and transgender community and those questioning their sexual orientation and gender identity." The Help Center coordinates two national hotlines as well as helps organizations build their infrastructure to offer local support. Interested persons can find out more at http://www.glnh.org/index2.html

The National Human Trafficking Resource Center (NHTRC) is a program of the Polaris Project, a nongovernmental organization that works to end human trafficking, NHTRC offers a national, toll-free hotline available to answer calls 24 hours a day, 7 days a week, 365 days a year. More information is available at http://www.polarisproject.org/index.php

Hot Peach Pages is a great resource for an extensive list of global domestic violence crisis lines: http://www.hotpeachpages.net/

Crisis lines operated by domestic violence centers, as well as the nation-wide lines listed above, are operated by trained staff and volunteers. These people typically have received extensive training on domestic violence in general, on crisis intervention and suicide prevention, as well as on specific issues such as working with teen victims, addressing those with disabilities, the LGBT community, and more. Local domestic violence crisis line staff and volunteers need to also be trained on intake procedures for shelter space and on relevant state law related to confidentiality and privilege. All staff and volunteers working on local crisis lines should have access to a comprehensive list of referral information for victims, including but not limited to housing assistance, legal help, childcare needs, welfare and other social service agencies, and medical assistance.

It can be difficult work, and thus there is a fairly high turnover rate for staff and volunteers working on crisis lines.

See also: National Domestic Violence Hotline; National Network to End Domestic Violence; National Teen Dating Abuse Hotline; Shelters for Domestic Abuse Victims

Further Reading
Americans Overseas Domestic Violence Crisis Center: http://www.866uswomen.org/
Domestic Violence Counts. (2011). National Network to End Domestic Violence. Retrieved from http://nnedv.org/docs/Census/DVCounts2011/DVCounts11_NatlReport_BW.pdf
GLBT National Help Center: http://www.glnh.org/index2.html
Hot Peach Pages: http://www.hotpeachpages.net/
Love Is Respect: http://www.loveisrespect.org
National Domestic Violence Hotline: http://www.thehotline.org
National Human Trafficking Resource Center: http://www.hotpeachpages.net/
National Runaway Switchboard: http://www.1800runaway.org

Laura L. Finley

CULTURALLY COMPETENT SERVICES

People of all racial, ethnic, national, and religious groups experience abuse. As Sokoloff and Dupont (2005) explained, "Our definition of domestic violence is incomplete if it does not include the specific forms of abuse that are particular to women's cultural backgrounds" (p. 42). It is important to recognize that no culture is perfect when it comes to abuse. And, while abuse occurs among all groups, all cultures have histories of resilience and resistance to domestic violence as well. Sokoloff and Dupont (2005) caution against blaming an immigrant's cultures for abuse. They point out that "Domestic violence scholars struggling to achieve a balance between the role of culture and structure make it clear that culture should not be confused with patriarchy. Instead, we should look at how patriarchy operates differently in different cultures" (p. 47).

It is essential that domestic violence services accommodate the unique language, cultural, and other needs of victims. Warrier (2005) defined cultural competence as "a set of knowledge, skills and attitudes that can be developed over time in order to work with those who appear and may be different from us" (p. 9). According to the National Center for Cultural Competence, organizations must:

- have a defined set of values and principles, and demonstrate behaviors, attitudes, policies and structures that enable them to work effectively cross-culturally.
- have the capacity to (1) value diversity, (2) conduct self-assessment, (3) manage the dynamics of difference, (4) acquire and institutionalize cultural knowledge, and (5) adapt to diversity and the cultural contexts of the communities they serve.
- incorporate the above in all aspects of policy making, administration, practice, service delivery, and involve systematically consumers, key stakeholders, and communities.

One of the first steps in the pursuit of cultural competence is recognizing one's own biases and prejudices. There are a number of self-assessments available online to begin this process. One resource for self-assessments is the National Center for Cultural Competence (http://www11.georgetown.edu/research/gucchd/nccc/

resources/assessments.html). Staff should represent the people served as well. This entails continual examination of the changing demographics of a community.

Domestic violence service providers should assess all their policies and practices to ensure they are not unfair or discriminatory to any particular cultural group. Agencies must also ensure that survivors who are not English-speaking can communicate and can read necessary documents. It is essential to have translation or interpretation services, according to Warrier (2005), if there is any doubt about the effectiveness of the communication and if having such services would ensure a better process for the survivor. If it is not possible to use an interpreter, Warrier (2005, p. 22) recommends the following:

- Be polite.
- Pay attention.
- Avoid speaking loudly and using slang language.
- Be careful when pantomiming as certain actions, especially around physical violence, can trigger reactions.
- Use simple language.
- Give instructions in the sequence you want them to follow, e.g., look at the form, answer the questions, then take the form, and so on.
- Avoid using negatives—"He has been stalking you, hasn't he?" Replace with "Has John been stalking you?"
- Avoid asking leading questions; ask them to use their own words.
- Record things as they are said.
- Be patient.

Advocates should always listen to the survivor and not make assumptions based on some presumed understanding of that individual's culture. Each individual experiences his or her culture uniquely. It is critical to take care not to impose one's own cultural beliefs and values on survivors, such as judging decisions she or he may make about their sexuality or reproductive choices. Orloff, Little, and Spielwa (n.d.) provide the following examples:

> It is common for mothers from some Central American countries to feed their children their first meal of the day at one or two o'clock in the afternoon and the evening meal at eight or nine. During the day, they allow their children to snack whenever they like. Staff who are not aware of this may make the mistake of filing a child neglect report because the children are perceived to not be "properly" cared for.

In Southeast Asian cultures:

- It is considered rude to touch someone on the head because the head is considered the most sacred part of the body.
- A smile may mean many things—pleasure, scorn, shame, or indifference.
- Using waving or beckoning motions in some cultures may be considered rude as well (p. 17).

Domestic violence centers should always help survivors make safety plans. Orloff et al. (n.d., p. 50) recommend that immigrants' safety plans should:

- guarantee the victim the right to self-determination and allow her to choose the options that she feels most comfortable with.
- create a method for securing and making copies of documents and information that the client will need to prove her VAWA immigration case (including her green card, marriage certificate, wedding pictures, police reports, medical records, and copies of her husband's immigration papers.

Cultural competency training for all staff is imperative. Experts caution that one-time training on a specific racial, ethnic, national, or religious group is inadequate. Training to develop cultural competency should be ongoing for all staff involved in serving victims of domestic violence. Effective cultural competency training should also address privilege and oppression. Many state coalitions provide some type of manual and/or training on developing culturally competent practices that can be used by to train and guide staff and volunteers at domestic violence centers. Warrier (2005) prepared a *Culture Handbook for the Family Violence Prevention Fund* (now Futures Without Violence). It is available at http://www.vaw.umn.edu/documents/culturehandbook/culturehandbookpdf.pdf. Cultural competency training is also essential for others who interact with domestic violence victims, including police, courts, public services, and health-care professionals.

Collaboration between all cultural groups will be essential to ending abuse. Advocates must reach out actively to immigrant, faith-based, ethnic, and other organizations and groups to ensure their participation in community-wide programs. Many immigrant victims fear seeking help at a domestic violence center because they believe staff will call police and that they might be deported. No law requires domestic violence centers to report survivors' immigration status, however. Advocates should reach out to immigrant communities to let them know this, and should reassure immigrant victims immediately that authorities will not be contacted. Immigrant victims may not be aware of how the U.S. criminal justice system works, and thus advocates can help explain what to expect if they go to court or have other involvement. Similarly, many are unfamiliar with other help services they might need, such as Temporary Assistance to Needy Families (TANF) or Medicare. Advocates can accompany survivors to these welfare agencies to reduce their discomfort and help them should they need translation or other assistance.

There are many great resources about cultural competency. The U.S. Department of Health and Human Services Child Welfare Information Gateway provides links to numerous resources regarding cultural competence and working with specific populations at http://www.childwelfare.gov/systemwide/domviolence/casework_practice/cultural.cfm.

The National Center for Cultural Competence (NCCC) is another resource for information and strategies. Its mission is "to increase the capacity of health-care and mental health-care programs to design, implement, and evaluate culturally and linguistically competent service delivery systems to address growing diversity, persistent disparities, and to promote health and mental health equity."

See also: Crisis Lines; Immigrant Victims of Domestic Abuse; Shelters for Domestic Abuse Victims

Further Reading

Cultural Competence in Domestic Violence Services. (n.d.). U.S. Department of Health and Human Services Child Welfare Information Gateway. Retrieved June 27, 2012, from http://www.childwelfare.gov/systemwide/domviolence/casework_practice/cultural.cfm

Orloff, L., Little, R., & Spielwa, M. (n.d.). Cultural competence training. *Legal Momentum*. Retrieved June 27, 2012, from http://www.legalmomentum.org/assets/pdfs/wwwchapter_2-_cultural_competency.pdf

Sokoloff, N., & Dupont, I. (2005). Domestic violence at the intersections of race, class, and gender: Challenges and contributions to understanding violence against marginalized women in diverse communities. *Violence Against Women, 11*(1), 38–64.

Warrier, S. (2005). Culture handbook. Family Violence Prevention Fund. Retrieved June 27, 2012 from http://www.vaw.umn.edu/documents/culturehandbook/culturehandbook pdf.pdf

Laura L. Finley

CYCLE OF VIOLENCE

According to the U.S. Department of Health and Human Services, approximately 10 out of every 1,000 American children are subjected to physical abuse or neglect each year. In spite of child maltreatment occurring since the beginning of civilization, it is only recently that society has begun to recognize this problem. Research has focused on understanding this violence to prevent further child abuse and other types of violence. The cycle of abuse (also referred to as the cycle of violence or intergenerational transmission of violence) alleges that exposure to violence in a family of origin increases the risk of perpetuating or experiencing violence later in life. Curtis (1963) expressed that abused and neglected kids would "become tomorrow's murderers and perpetrators of other crimes of violence, if they survive" (p. 386). The cycle of abuse has been very controversial in the violence literature. Many researchers believe that abused children grow up to be abusing parents, while others question the validity of the hypothesis and if the cycle of violence is unfounded. Many of the studies that try to test the cycle of abuse hypothesis are based on case histories, agency records, clinical interviews, or self-report cases. Theories such as social learning and gene-environment correlations help to explain the case for the cycle of abuse, while many other researchers indicate that the types of methods and theories do not fully explain the cycle of abuse. Opponents of the cycle of abuse argue that it is individuals' resiliency and protective factors that are more important, and not the deterministic pathway that is often portrayed.

The cycle of abuse is generally explained by Bandura's social learning theory (1977). The violence that occurs in families is due to individuals being reinforced for their behaviors and additionally imitating their parents to further explain motivation toward violent behavior. Individuals who grew up in families where they were abused themselves or witnessed violence are more likely to become violent later in life. At the core of this theory is a process called modeling, in which people learn social and cognitive behaviors by observing and imitating others. Many studies have found that children raised in violent homes, where they either were abused or witnessed spousal abuse, are more likely to become abusers later in life. Individuals who are abused as children are more likely to abuse their own children later in life because they learned and modeled the behavior of their parents' actions, thus continuing the cycle of violence. To be more specific, individuals may learn violence through operant conditioning: when a person uses violence (actions) to coerce a child's compliance (consequences), then the child's compliance reinforces (rewards) the perpetrator's aggression. Thus, when abusive parents get what they want by mistreating the child, they are likely to become even more violent as time passes. Conversely, when parents are not punished for their behavior, violence is more likely to persist.

Research has found that the majority of individuals who reported abusing or neglecting their children reported a history of abuse as well. It is estimated that between 30 and 35 percent of parents abused as children will abuse their own children, in contrast to a population base of 4 percent. This relationship often remains after controlling for personality, emotional well-being, SES, and various aspects of parenting, such as the level of corporal punishment and parental warmth/involvement. Kaufman and Zigler (1987) found that harshly treated children were five times more likely to engage in abusive parenting than those not victims of severe corporal punishment. Another study reported that women who reported child abuse were five times more likely to have experienced severe partner violence, and that male partners with a history of childhood physical abuse were three times more likely to perpetrate severe partner violence (Cunradi, Caetano, & Schafer, 2002).

Individuals who witness parental violence indirectly, or are exposed directly, may be more likely to learn and model this behavior later in life. These children, as they grow into adults, learn maladaptive or violent methods of expressing anger, reacting to stressful situations, and coping with conflict. An example of this may be when these adults use violence as an acceptable form of controlling their own misbehaving child. In light of the intergenerational transmission, parenting styles may be passed from one generation to the next.

In addition, spanking has been discussed as another form of child abuse, but with much skepticism. Individuals who were spanked as children may be more likely to spank or become violent with their own children. These individuals learned through experiences with their parents that violence is acceptable and a morally correct method of child rearing. The more parents use corporal punishment as a method of discipline, the greater the odds the child will engage in many kinds of antisocial and violent behavior, including delinquency as a child, domestic violence as an adult, and possibly abusing one's own children. The more approval of violence and actual violent behavior that children experience in their childhood, the more likely the violence will continue in action and beliefs, such as approval of slapping a misbehaving partner. Thus, according to social learning theory, children simply model their parents' behaviors and beliefs of violence.

Along with social learning theory, gene-environment correlations are able to explain the influence of family abuse as a *passive genotype-environment correlation*. When assortatively paired (i.e., similar) parents produce children, they transmit both genes and environments to their offspring. This may produce a "double-whammy" effect. Thus, children are transmitted heritable vulnerabilities to violence and are also reared in a home where violence is learned. Children born to abusing parents may be at an increased risk of abusing as well. A genetic predisposition of abuse may make adolescents more vulnerable to the risks of an abusive environment. They are receiving a dose of genes and a dose of environment that contribute additively to abuse. If both parents abuse, then the children may receive a "double dose" of the genes of the parents. Thus, "each generation learns to be violent by being a participant in a violent family" (Straus, Gelles, & Steinmetz, 1980, p. 121).

Children may continue the cycle of violence by pairing up with future abusive partners, which in turn produces children who may have a genetic predisposition, and thus the cycle continues. Assortative pairing may be influenced by family background and genetic predispositions to violent behaviors. For example, adolescents may seek out romantic partners with similar habits because of a genetic predisposition. Adolescents may choose partners who reinforce their own genetic predispositions to violence. This may lead to partners becoming phenotypically similar because of the resemblance in violence.

Evidence for the cycle of violence does not include just one mechanism but multiple pathways, thus indicating a cumulative effect. It may be the combination of parental abuse, the genetic predisposition, as well as other factors including learned attitudes toward abuse or growing up in an alcohol/drug home that place individuals at risk for violence. Lastly, because individuals' violent acts may reflect the behavior of their parents and a genetic predisposition to abusing, adolescents may learn dysfunctional patterns of relating to others, which may later affect their intimate relationships.

The cycle of abuse is apparent in dating relationships as well, which has been called the training ground for marital violence. There seems to be a positive relationship between witnessing parental violence and later inflicting or experiencing violence in dating relationships. This relationship seems to be stronger for males than females in terms of experiencing childhood maltreatment and later inflicting or victimization of dating violence. For males, those who witnessed high levels of violence may find it acceptable or justifiable to use violence in future dating relationships. If males find it acceptable, the appropriate response to conflict may be violence against their female partners in a future dating and/or married relationship. For females, witnessing high levels of violence during childhood may make them susceptible to future dating violent relationships. The gender of the abuser and victim have been found to be important as well. For boys, witnessing their father hitting their mother may have a stronger relationship to domestic violence compared to if the family violence involved mother-to-father violence.

Researchers who find the cycle of violence to be unfounded cite methodological issues to be the sole reason. Many researchers feel that the alleged relationship between child and later domestic abuse does not really pass scientific muster, citing that social learning theory may be too overstated and narrow, with methodological shortcomings that cannot explain why some children do *not* become violent in the same circumstances. For example, 70 percent of those who were abused as children did not go on to become abusive adults (Barnett, Miller-Perrin, & Perrin, 2005).

Kaufman and Zigler (1987) found only one-third of individuals who are abused or neglected abuse their own children, whereas two-thirds do not. Thus, the majority of abused children do not become abusive parents or partners.

Many researchers highlight a wide variety of environmental factors that explain resiliency and protective factors. For example, dispositional attributes, environmental conditions, biological predispositions, and positive events can act to mitigate against early negative experiences. Resiliency within a person is a protective trait, as well as easy temperament, good self-esteem, good achievement in school, and a positive relationship with a parent. Other events, such as natural abilities, physiological predispositions, and social supports, may actually mediate the effects of child abuse/neglect and the long-term consequences. However, risk factors may include low SES, being in a minority group, coming from a large family, harsh parental discipline, and severe marital discord. Thus, according to some researchers, it is the multicomplex system that explains violence, rather than a cycle of violence.

Other problems with methodology include using only clinical case histories and few empirical investigations. Many studies have relied on retrospective accounts and case studies whereby people may distort reports of their childhood. There may be a retrospective recall bias that is a risk for distortion and loss of information that is unreliable. Social desirability factors may result in societal disapproval and redefining behaviors. Thus, an etiological error may result: by looking backward, antecedents of child abuse may seem apparent and inevitable, but looking prospectively, it becomes evident that multiple pathways are possible.

Although growing up in a violent family may put one at risk for using violence as an adult, the association is far from absolute. The fact remains that most adults who grow up in a violent homes do not become violent adults. Rather, researchers opposed to the cycle of violence often indicate that abuse may be a large risk factor, but it is not a direct or inevitable result. The cycle of violence is too complex and multidimensional. Thus, the majority of those who have observed or experienced violence do not later use violence against their dating partners.

See also: Child Abuse; Children, Impact of Domestic Abuse on

Further Reading

Bandura, A. (1977). *Social learning theory*. New York, NY: General Learning Press.
Barnett, O., Miller-Perrin, C. L., & Perrin, R. D. (2005). *Family violence across the lifespan: An introduction* (2nd ed.). Thousand Oaks, CA: Sage.
Cunradi, C. B., Caetano, R., & Schafer, J. (2002). Alcohol-related problems, drug use, and male intimate partner violence severity among US couples. *Alcohol Clinical Experimental Research, 26*(4), 493–500.
Curtis, G. (1963). Violence breeds violence—perhaps? *American Journal of Psychiatry, 120,* 386–387.
Kaufman, J. & Zigler, E. (1987). Do abused children become abusive parents? *American Journal of Orthopsychiatry, 57,* 186–192.
Straus, M., Gelles, R., & Steinmetz, S. (1980). *Behind closed doors: Violence in the American family*. Newbury Park, CA: Sage.

Jackie Wiersma

DEMOGRAPHIC AND HEALTH SURVEYS

Demographic and Health Surveys (DHS) are nationally representative household surveys conducted worldwide and intended to help provide information about numerous topics related to health, nutrition, and population. They are administered by the Demographic and Health Surveys Program (MEASURE DHS), which is funded by the United States Agency for International Development (USAID). There are two main types of DHS surveys: Standard and Interim. Standard DHS Surveys utilize large samples, typically between 5,000 and 30,000 households. They are generally conducted every five years and are thus useful in tracking changes over time. Interim Surveys are conducted between rounds of Standard Surveys and tend to be shorter. Although still nationally representative, they typically utilize smaller samples and may not include all the data that is on the Standard Survey.

The DHS program specific to gauging information about domestic violence was started in the early 1990s. In 1990, domestic violence data was collected in Colombia. In 1995, a set of domestic violence questions were fielded in Egypt, and violence was again measured in Colombia. Using these pilot attempts, a standard set of questions—developed in consultation with domestic violence, gender, and survey research experts and following World Health Organization recommendations for ethical data collection—was developed in the late 1990s. The objective is to capture demographic and health data from developing countries in particular, generally focusing on issues of fertility, family planning, infant and child mortality, reproductive health, children's health, and nutrition. Domestic violence is considered a significant health hazard. Data on domestic violence can also help scholars and practitioners understand the context in which it occurs. However, data is still limited about domestic violence, given that only 11 countries had implemented DHS surveys as of September 2003.

Data is collected from each household on the sex, age, education, head of household, relationship to the head of household for all members of the house, household possessions, and access to life necessities such as water, electricity, and toilets. A specific Women's Questionnaire collects data from women ages 15 to 49, including their age, marital status, use of contraceptives, educational attainment, and employment, as well as their husband's education, occupation, and rate of alcohol consumption. The combination of attributes from women and those reported of their husbands is called the characteristics of marital unions, which is used to describe who endures, who perpetrates, and the context of household violence. This information can help identify risk and protective factors.

One limitation is that not all the participating countries use the standardized domestic violence module of questions. Generally, two different approaches are used. One is a single-question threshold approach, which has been used in Egypt, India, Peru, and Zambia. In this approach, respondents are asked just one question to determine if they have ever experienced violence. If a woman responds affirmatively, she is then asked follow-up questions about the perpetrator and the frequency of the violence. The second approach, which is part of the DHS domestic violence module, combines the single question with a modified Conflict Tactics Scale (CTS). The modified CTS, which was originally developed by sociologist Murray Straus in the 1970s and included 19 questions, involves a series of approximately 15 questions about various forms of violence, such as kicking, slapping, and hitting. Next, a series of single questions are asked to identify whether the violence was perpetrated by a spouse or intimate partner and whether it occurred during pregnancy. The modified CTS approach has been used in Colombia, Dominican Republic, Haiti, and Nicaragua. This approach is considered preferable in that it provides more contextual information and is less subject to respondents' differing understandings of what constitutes violence. Additionally, respondents have multiple opportunities to disclose their experiences with violence, which might help those who are less comfortable speaking about the abuse. It is presumed that the modified CTS approach is more likely to accurately capture the incidence of domestic violence, whereas the single-question approach may underestimate it.

The CTS does have some critics, however. DeKeseredy and Schwartz (1998) for instance, argue that the questions situate abuse as part of a dispute or disagreement, rather than an independent form of conflict. Further, it does not include sexual forms of violence. Nonetheless, it is still the most commonly used quantitative measure of domestic violence, and the DHS-modified CTS does incorporate sexual violence along with a different setup for the questions that accounts for the many ways abuse occurs outside of disagreements. Additionally, the module addresses the consequences of abuse, as one set of questions asks about physical outcomes such as bruising and broken bones. Still, there are no questions that address the motives for the violence or that include the meaning an incident holds for the victim. Whichever of the approaches is used, the DHS report then provides two indicators of the prevalence of domestic violence: (1) having ever experienced it; and (2) having experienced it within the 12 months preceding the survey.

USAID has a complete set of the DHS domestic violence module questionnaires available at http://www.measuredhs.com/pubs/pdf/DHSQM/DHS6_Module_Domestic_Violence_3Jan2011.pdf.

Given that the information collected on the DHS Surveys is very personal, great efforts are made to ensure that international requirements regarding informed consent and privacy are followed. Names of respondents are never disclosed nor included in any data sets. Following the World Health Organization's (2001) ethical and safety recommendations for research on domestic violence, additional measures include:

- Instructions for interviewers to discontinue the interview and explain what happened in the event that privacy can no longer be ensured;

- The reading of a statement outlining the sensitive nature of the questions at the start of the module;
- Special training for supervisors and those conducting interviews that explains the dynamics of abusive relationships and addresses the challenges in collecting domestic violence data;
- Protocol to interview only one woman in a household about domestic violence to ensure there are no security breaches;
- Providing information on services and organizations to those who disclose abuse;
- Not including the domestic violence questions in interviews with men.

Translators are not recommended for the domestic violence questioning, as the questionnaires themselves are translated into major languages including Khmer for Cambodia; Spanish for the Dominican Republic, Colombia, and Peru; French and Creole for Haiti; as well as seven different languages for Zambia and 17 for India. Administrators also perform back-translations regularly to ensure the translations on the questionnaire are accurate.

Every effort is made to minimize underreporting. Recognizing that women may want to speak about abuse but are fearful or embarrassed, special attention is paid to training interviewers on how to build rapport, ensure privacy, ask questions in a nonjudgmental tone, and allow multiple opportunities for disclosure.

DHS reports from the 2004 study show that the proportions of ever-married women reporting spousal/intimate partner violence vary across countries. From highest to lowest, they are Zambia (48 percent), Colombia (44 percent), Peru (42 percent), Egypt (33 percent), Nicaragua (33 percent), Dominican Republic (22 percent), India (19 percent), and Cambodia (18 percent). The highest rates of abuse during pregnancy were found in Colombia and Nicaragua (11 percent), with the lowest in Cambodia (1 percent).

The most frequent type of abuse was physical violence, including pushing, being shaken, slapped, targeted with a thrown object, or having one's arm twisted. More than one in six of women in all the countries included had experienced these types of incidents. Sexual violence rates varied, with up to 17 percent reported in Haiti and a low of 4 percent reported in Cambodia. At least 10 percent of all female respondents cited being emotionally abused. In Colombia, over 50 percent of women reported experiencing physical signs of abuse, such as bruises and aches. In the other countries, between 5 and 13 percent of victims reported experiencing physical consequences of the abuse.

The data also show that relatively few women seek help for domestic violence. In Nicaragua, some 41 percent never sought help, while in Colombia, the rate was a shocking 78 percent. The most frequent source of support was family and friends.

Risk factors for abuse include being married more than once; being divorced or separated; marrying at a young age; having multiple children; being older than their husbands; living in an urban environment; living with a husband who is drunk frequently; and having grown up with parents who were abusive.

The DHS includes several indicators of gender roles and gender relations that are related to domestic violence. Rates of abuse were found to be lower among couples who share responsibility for household decisions and higher when women indicated that it was sometimes okay for a husband to hit his wife and when a husband uses one of six different controlling behaviors such as constantly accusing her of infidelity (and increasingly higher the more of those behaviors were reported).

The study also examined the relationship between domestic violence and other health outcomes. Consistent with other research, the study showed that domestic violence negatively impacts the health of both women and children. Women who had experienced violence were more likely to have discontinued use of contraception and to have unwanted pregnancies, as well as to report having had a sexually transmitted infection.

Children whose mothers experience domestic violence are less likely to receive care in the first trimester of the pregnancy, and women have a significantly higher rate of having a nonlive birth in most of the countries included in the study. In seven of the nine countries, rates of under-five mortality are higher among those whose mother experienced violence while rates of childhood vaccination are lower in six of the nine countries.

See also: Latin America and Domestic Abuse; World Health Organization (WHO)

Further Reading

DeKeseredy, W., & Schwartz, M. (1998). Measuring the extent of woman abuse in intimate heterosexual relationships: A critique of the conflict tactics scales. *VAWnet*. Retrieved June 19, 2012, from http://new.vawnet.org/assoc_files_vawnet/ar_ctscrit.pdf

Ellsberg, M., Heise, L., Pena, R., Agurto, S., & Winkvist, A. (2001). Researching domestic violence against women: Methodological and ethical considerations. *Studies in Family Planning 32*(1), 1–16.

Kishor, S., & Johnson, K. (2004). Profiling domestic violence: A multi-country study. *Measure DHS+*. Retrieved June 11, 2012, from http://www.measuredhs.com/pubs/pdf/od31/od31.pdf

Straus, M. (1979). Measuring intrafamily conflict and violence: The Conflict Tactics (CT) Scales. *Journal of Marriage and the Family 41*(1): 75–88.

World Health Organization. (2001). Putting women first: Ethical and safety recommendations for research on domestic violence against women. Department of Gender and Women's Health. Geneva, Switzerland.

Laura L. Finley

DESHANEY V. WINNEBAGO COUNTY DEPARTMENT OF SOCIAL SERVICES CASE

In *DeShaney v. Winnebago County Department of Social Services*, the U.S. Supreme Court determined that a child's right to liberty under the Fourteenth Amendment is not violated when a government entity fails to prevent the child from being abused by a custodial parent. The case was decided on February 22, 1989. The decision has generated much controversy over whether the government does too little to protect children from abuse. Each year in the United States, an estimated 1,100 children die from abuse and neglect, and some 12.5 percent of cases had been investigated by child protective services.

DESHANEY V. WINNEBAGO COUNTY DEPARTMENT OF SOCIAL SERVICES CASE

Randy DeShaney was given custody of his son Joshua (who was one year old at the time) in 1980, after Randy and Melody DeShaney divorced. Randy DeShaney moved to Winnebago County, Wisconsin, and Melody lived in Cheyenne, Wyoming. She saw Joshua very infrequently due to the distance between their homes. In January 1982, Joshua's stepmother reported abuse. In 1983, the county Department of Social Services (DSS) obtained a court order to hold Joshua at the hospital amid fear he was being abused. After a three-day review by a child protection team, which included a psychologist, pediatrician, a police detective, the county lawyer, some DSS caseworkers, and others on the hospital staff, Joshua was released to his father under an agreement that dictated his care. DSS visited the DeShaney home five times in 1983, concerned that Randy was not following the agreement, but took no action to remove Joshua. Even after another hospital visit in November 1983, where staff reported suspicions of abuse to DSS, no action was taken. In January and March 1984, Randy DeShaney told the DSS caseworker that Joshua was too ill to see her, and she left. Shortly thereafter, Randy DeShaney beat Joshua (now four years old) so badly that he suffered severe brain damage. At the hospital, surgeons found a series of hemorrhages caused by multiple traumatic injuries to the brain, and Joshua's body was covered with bruises. Although Joshua did not die, the assault was so brutal he is mentally retarded and confined to an institution. Randy DeShaney did not contest the child abuse charges, was tried and convicted, but served fewer than two years in jail.

Melody DeShaney considered suing the state of Wisconsin officials under state personal injury laws but was advised by her attorney not to do so, as the state would limit her damages at $50,000. Instead, she filed a federal lawsuit against Winnebago County, Winnebago County DSS, and DSS employees, maintaining that their failure to intervene when they knew or should have known that Joshua's life was at risk violated the due process clause of the Fourteenth Amendment. Title 42 of the United States Code, section 1983 provides for federal action in cases in which the state deprives citizens of constitutional rights. She sought $50 million. According to Glaberson (1988), "the authorities in Wisconsin had recorded Joshua's suffering with bureaucratic precision." There were frequent hospital reports in which doctors indicated they suspected Joshua was being abused. Ann Kemmeter, the main caseworker investigating the DeShaney case, told Melody DeShaney "I just knew the phone would ring someday and Joshua would be dead" (Glaberson, 1988). Before DeShaney, in *Estate of Bailey v. County of York*, the Third Circuit Court of Appeals recognized the duty to protect a child from abuse even when the child is not directly in state custody.

After a summary judgment by the U.S. District Court for the Eastern District of Wisconsin and an affirmation of the summary judgment by the Seventh Circuit Court of Appeals, the Supreme Court agreed to hear the case on March 21, 1988. The Supreme Court ruled 6–3 to uphold the summary judgment, meaning they did not find the actions of any of the respondents to have violated Joshua DeShaney's due process rights. The majority opinion was issued by Chief Justice William Rehnquist, who held that the due process clause only protects individuals against abusive actions of the state. In this case, it was not the state that abused Joshua but his father, a nonstate actor. Joshua was not in the care or custody of

DSS, the court determined. Although the court recognized that Joshua had briefly been under the care of the state, he was not in state custody at the time. In sum, the court ruled that there is no federal protection of children against their parents, and deferred to the state and local governments to intervene.

Two dissenting opinions were written. Associate Justice William Brennan asserted that Rehnquist used a flawed interpretation of precedent cases. Brennan also pointed out that because Wisconsin's child protection laws required individuals who suspected a child was being abused to report it to DSS, then DSS was, in effect, in a custodial situation and thus did indeed deprive Joshua of due process. Associate Justice Harry Blackmun, with Associate Justice Thurgood Marshall, concurred with Brennan that there had indeed been promised state action to protect Joshua. The fourth paragraph of Blackmun's dissent has become well known:

> Poor Joshua! Victim of repeated attacks by an irresponsible, bullying, cowardly, and intemperate father, and abandoned by respondents who placed him in a dangerous predicament and who knew or learned what was going on, and yet did essentially nothing except, as the Court revealingly observes, ante, at 193, "dutifully recorded these incidents in [their] files." It is a sad commentary upon American life, and constitutional principles—so full of late of patriotic fervor and proud proclamations about "liberty and justice for all"—that this child, Joshua DeShaney, now is assigned to live out the remainder of his life profoundly retarded. Joshua and his mother, as petitioners here, deserve—but now are denied by this Court—the opportunity to have the facts of their case considered in the light of the constitutional protection that 42 U.S.C. 1983 is meant to provide.

The DeShaney case is still considered controversial and has prompted numerous law review articles. One commentator noted that "now and again . . . an egregious case comes along epitomizing the Court's usual indifference so dramatically that one's blood boils anew. Such a case is that of Joshua DeShaney" (Peter Edelman, cited in Watts, 2012). In the 2005 case of *Castle Rock v. Gonzales*, Jessica Gonzales filed suit against the Castle Rock, Colorado, police for failing to protect her three daughters from her abusive ex-husband. Police failed to respond when her husband violated a restraining order, resulting in the death of all three girls. Gonzales's attorneys drew on DeShaney but framed it far more procedurally, rather than the more substantive focus used in the earlier case. The Supreme Court ruled against Gonzales, who then turned to the Inter-American Commission on Human Rights (IACHR). That court ruled in August 2011 that the Supreme Court had erred and that the state had deprived Gonzales's daughters of their fundamental human rights. Although the IACHR's is not binding, advocates are hopeful that it will prompt needed reform in the United States and help Jessica Lenahan obtain a sense of closure.

See also: Castle Rock v. Gonzales Case; Child Abuse; Children, Impact of Domestic Abuse on

Further Reading

Curry, L. (2007). *The DeShaney case: Child abuse, family rights, and the dilemma of state intervention.* Lawrence, KS: University Press of Kansas.

DeShaney v. Winnebago County. (1988). Retrieved from http://www.oyez.org/cases/1980-1989/1988/1988_87_154/

Glaberson, W. (1988, October 2). Determined to be heard. *New York Times.* Retrieved June 29, 2012, from http://www.nytimes.com/1988/10/02/magazine/determined-to-be-heard.html?pagewanted=all&src=pm

Grossman, J., & Friedman, L. (2011). *Inside the castle: Law and the family in 20th century America.* Princeton, NJ: Princeton University Press.

Watts, C. (2012, April 17). "Indifferent [towards] indifference:" Post-DeShaney accountability for social services agencies when a child is injured or killed under their protective watch. *Pepperdine Law Review, 30*(1), 125–160.

Laura L. Finley

DISABILITIES AND DOMESTIC ABUSE

Research has repeatedly shown that people with physical, mental, or emotional disabilities are at greater risk for abuse. In a survey of 200 women with disabilities, Powers and colleagues (2002) found that 67 percent had lifetime experiences of physical abuse and 53 percent had experienced sexual abuse in their lifetime. Compared with women without disabilities, Brownridge (2006) found that women with disabilities had a 40 percent greater chance of experiencing domestic violence, while Martin, Ray, Sotres-Alvarez, Kupper, Moracco, Dickens, Scandlin, et al. (2006) found that women with disabilities were four times more likely to have experienced sexual assault in the past year than were women without a disability. Risk of abuse differs by type of disability and type of abuse. Sobsey (1994) found that individuals with developmental disabilities are 10 times more likely to be sexually assaulted than are those with other disabilities. Johnson and Sigler (2000) found that 83 percent of females and 32 percent of males with developmental disabilities were victims of sexual assault. Persons with physical disabilities experience abuse at rates similar to or higher than those without physical disabilities. Schaller and Fieberg (1998) found that women with disabilities experience more severe victimization, experience it for a longer duration, are survivors of multiple episodes of abuse, and are likely to be victimized by a larger number of perpetrators. Nosek, Hughes, Taylor, and Taylor (2006) found that women with disabilities are most likely to experience abuse when they are younger, more educated, less mobile, and more isolated and depressed. Several studies have found that men with developmental disabilities are equally likely as women to endure abuse.

Abusers may use the same types of control against those with disabilities as with other victims. In addition, abusers may destroy medical equipment and communication devices, or withhold, steal, or make victims overdose on medications. Persons with disabilities may suffer from their partners but also from caretakers and personal assistants. The low pay and difficult conditions of this work seem to exacerbate the problem.

Several factors help explain why persons with disabilities experience abuse at higher rates than those without. They may be isolated; are often dependent on their partners, family, or caregivers; and may have limited ability to leave due to transportation difficulties. Abusers may take advantage of people they perceive are easy targets. Sometimes persons with disabilities are presumed to be less credible, and therefore their claims of abuse are less likely to be believed.

One important factor related to the issue of domestic violence and disabilities is the language used to describe those persons with various impairments. Advocates recommend using "people-first" language, so instead of saying "disabled woman," the appropriate language is "woman with a disability." Many times, domestic violence centers are unprepared to assist victims with disabilities. They may not have in place interpreters or others who can communicate with blind or deaf victims, may lack accessible accommodations, and may be unaware of the impact of abuse among those with mental, physical, or emotional problems.

Powers, Hughes, and Lund (2009) recommend the following for service providers:

- Provide every person with a disability and deaf persons with information about violence, safety promotion, and DV/SA advocacy and support groups, and help them screen for interpersonal violence and connect with resources, as they desire.
- Conduct cross-training activities and develop protocols, agreements, and funding strategies that enable victims' service organizations to increase their accessibility; that increase the capacities of community disability organizations to assist individuals to access resources; and that build linkages among violence, criminal justice, and disability organizations and agencies.
- Involve centers for independent living, self-advocacy organizations, psychiatric consumer/survivor groups, and other peer organizations in interpersonal violence education, screening, and support activities.
- Ensure that a survivor who discloses interpersonal violence will not be placed in a group home or institution nor have her children or companion animals taken away.
- Provide a 24-hour crisis line for survivors with disabilities/deaf survivors to talk with an advocate experienced in disability and victim services.
- Provide and fund emergency interpreter, personal assistance, child and pet care, and transportation services that survivors and the organizations that serve them can call upon.

Since 2006, the U.S. Department of Justice's Office on Violence against Women (OVW) has provided training and grants devoted to helping victims of elder abuse and victims with disabilities. OVW has also partnered with the Vera Institute of Justice to provide training and consultation on these issues.

The National Council on Independent Living has many useful resources related to abuse of persons with disabilities. CAVNET is also an important tool in disseminating information related to domestic violence and disabilities.

Police should also be trained on how to deal with victims and perpetrators who have disabilities. Protocols for communication and referrals should be established to ensure that victims' needs are met.

See also: Types of Domestic Abuse; Shelters for Domestic Abuse Victims

Further Reading

Brownridge, D. A. (2006). Partner violence against women with disabilities. *Violence Against Women, 12*(9), 805–822.

CAVNET: http://www.cavnet.org

Curry, M. A., Renker, P., Hughes, R. B., Robinson-Whelen, S., Oschwald, M. M., Swank, P., & Johnson, I., & Sigler, R. (1995). Community attitudes: A study of definitions and punishment of spouse abusers and child abusers. *Journal of Criminal Justice*, 23, 477–487.

Johnson, I., & Sigler, R. (2000). Forced Sexual Intercourse Among Intimates. *Journal of Interpersonal Violence*, 15 (1), 95–108.

Martin, S., Ray, N., Sotres-Alvarez, D., Kupper, L., Moracco, K., Dickens, P., Scandlin, D., et al. (2006). Physical and sexual assault of women with disabilities. *Violence Against Women*, 12, 823–837.

National Council on Independent Living: http://www.ncil.org

Nosek, M., Hughes, R., Taylor, H., & Taylor, P. (2006). Disability, psychosocial, and demographic characteristics of abused women with physical disabilities. *Violence Against Women*, 12 (9), 838–850.

Powers, L. E. (2009). Development of measures of abuse among women with disabilities and the characteristics of their perpetrators. *Violence Against Women*, 15(9), 1001–1025.

Powers, L., Hughes, R., & Lund, E. (2009). *Interpersonal violence and women with disabilities: A research update*. VAWnet. Retrieved June 29, 2012, from http://www.vawnet.org/applied-research-papers/print-document.php?doc_id=2077

Powers, L. E., Renker, P., Robinson-Whelen, S., Oschwald, M., Hughes, R. B., Swank, P., & Curry, M. A. (2009). Interpersonal violence and safety promoting behaviors of women with disabilities. *Violence Against Women*, 15(9), 1040–1069.

Schaller, J., & Fieberg, J. (1998). Issues of abuse for women with disabilities and implications for rehabilitation counseling. *Journal of Applied Rehabilitation Counseling*, 29(2), 9–17.

Smith, N., & Harrell, S. (2011, April). Forging new collaborations: A guide for rape crisis, domestic violence, and disability organizations. Vera Institute. Retrieved June 29, 2012, from http://www.vera.org/download?file=3242/Collaboration-pub-v4-corrected.pdf

Sobsey, J. (1994). *Violence and abuse in the lives of people with disabilities: The end of silent acceptance?* Baltimore, MD: Paul H. Brookes.

Laura L. Finley

DISASTERS AND DOMESTIC VIOLENCE

In the last four decades, a growing body of literature has documented the fact that disasters, both man-made and natural, tend to increase reports of domestic violence. Further, disasters often serve to weaken or even completely destroy needed services for victims of domestic abuse.

Disasters and Women

Natural disasters impact huge numbers of people across the globe in myriad ways. The World Health Organization (WHO) has noted that approximately two billion people were affected by natural or technological disasters between 1990 and 1999, with almost 600,000 fatalities. Of these, 86 percent were natural disasters. Technological or man-made disasters, however, also have a profound effect. Approximately five million people were impacted by the 1986 Chernobyl disaster, more than 500,000 of them children. More than two decades later, the legacy of Chernobyl persists, with affected persons suffering a slew of health-related problems. Similarly, persons impacted by the 1984 Bhopal disaster still suffer from respiratory damage or other infections.

Women may be uniquely vulnerable, suffering additional health problems related to menstruation and reproduction. In many cases, women represent a disproportionate number of victims. For instance, the powerful earthquake that hit Kobe, Japan, in 1995 killed 1.5 times more women than men. Three to four times more women than men were killed by the tsunami that hit the Indian Ocean in 2004. In addition to the physical impact, gender roles may result in certain types of disproportionate impact on women and girls. For instance, a study of the 1991 cyclone in Bangladesh found that many women and their children perished in their homes because they had to wait for their husbands to return home to make all evacuation decisions.

Gender roles also affect women's after-disaster options. "Although a disaster begins with or is triggered by a natural event, its effect upon society is grounded in the social system in which it takes place" (Fisher, 2010, p. 904). Women may not be able to access relief services in some cultures, as they are not allowed to mingle with men who are not their kin. In other cases, their childcare duties in the home prohibit them from being able to take advantage of available relief. Food or other household goods may be distributed to heads of household only, which in many cases excludes women. Women may be burdened with even more household duties after a disaster, especially in cases when men flee. The Pan American Health Organization Women, Health and Development Program noted in their Gender and Natural Disasters Fact Sheet (n.d.), "The majority of relief efforts are intended for the entire population of a disaster-affected area; however, when they rely on existing structures of resource distribution that reflect the patriarchal structure of society, women are marginalized in their access to relief resources." Studies in Miami, rural Bangladesh, the Caribbean, and Brazil have documented this "flight of men," who often use all relief aid for themselves. Females generally lower literacy levels and lower levels of land ownership result in greater difficulty finding work or providing for families. Another area in which women suffer disproportionately after a disaster is in rates of domestic and sexual violence.

Increases in Domestic Violence

Numerous studies have suggested an increase in domestic violence after natural disasters. The World Health Organization noted that increases in intimate partner violence levels have been reported in the Philippines after the Mt. Pinatubo eruption, in Nicaragua after Hurricane Mitch, in the United States after the Loma Prieta earthquake and the eruption of Mount St. Helens, and in several refugee camps worldwide. Lutheran Disaster Response of New York reported that after Hurricane Andrew in Miami, domestic violence calls to the local community helpline increased by 50 percent, and over one-third of 1,400 surveyed residents reported that someone in their home had lost verbal or physical control in the two months since the hurricane. In the six months after Hurricane Andrew, for instance, almost one-quarter (22 percent) of respondents reported a new conflict with someone living in their household. In the nine months after the 1993 Midwestern flood, 14 percent of respondents had experienced physical violence from their partners at least once. Seventy percent reported at least one instance of verbal abuse, 26 percent reported emotional abuse, and 86 percent reported increased anger from their partner ("The Impact of Disaster," n.d.). After the eruption of Mount St. Helens volcano, police reported a 46 percent increase in domestic violence calls (Adams & Adams, 1984).

Following the Red River floods in the United States in 1997 in North Dakota and Minnesota, local violence intervention centers recorded considerable increases in crisis calls and requests for protection orders while experiencing a reduction of resources. Enarson's (1999) study of domestic violence programs in the United States and Canada also found that those most severely hit by disaster faced increased service demand, from both new and existing users, yet fewer resources. According to executive director Pam Gonzales, calls to U Care, the domestic violence agency for Sampson County, North Carolina, and surrounding areas, tripled in the six months following Hurricane Floyd. A quarter (25 percent) of all community leaders responding to open-ended questions about the effects of the Exxon Valdez oil spill on family problems cited "increase in domestic violence" first, in contrast to increased child neglect (4 percent) and elder abuse (4 percent). Asked if the spouse abuse increased after the spill, 64 percent agreed; they also reported increased child physical abuse (39 percent), child sexual abuse (31 percent), elder abuse (11 percent), and rape (21 percent). Within the first week of the disaster, a group of Sri Lankan women's organizations, which went on to form the Coalition for Assisting Tsunami Affected Women (CATAW), set out to investigate reports of violence. They confirmed "incidents of rape, gang rape, molestation, and physical abuse of women and girls" and reported a "sense of insecurity and fear" and lack of security provision in camps (Vella, 2005). As is the case internationally, domestic violence is the most endemic form, affecting an estimated 60 percent of Sri Lankan women. The United Nations reported the case of Yashodhara, who was being abused prior to the 2004 tsunami off the coast of India that left 230,000 people dead. Women who were already experiencing abuse may find that it occurs more frequently or is more severe than prior to the disaster, as was the case with Yashodhara. South Asian relief policies generally distribute aid to heads of household, and Yashodhara's husband, Ghanshyam, spent virtually all of it on alcohol.

Hurricane Katrina offers additional evidence of the link between domestic violence and disasters. Since the storm occurred on a weekend, regularly scheduled visitations with noncustodial parents were interrupted. Victims were forced to reengage communication with abusive former partners to address custodial arrangements. Disasters may compel battered women to return to abusive partners when left with no other housing options and temporary emergency shelters afford batterers an opportunity abuse their partners.

Increased stress due to loss, and feelings of powerlessness due to loss of income and property, may help explain why domestic violence increases after a disaster, as do mental health problems like post-traumatic stress disorder (PTSD) and destruction of social networks of support. The already scanty resources for victims of domestic violence may be diminished or even decimated after a disaster. For example, a study by the Urban League and Louisiana Association of Nonprofit Organizations found that 95 percent of the 262 nonprofit respondents had been impacted by Hurricanes Katrina and/or Rita. In some cases, entire facilities were destroyed. At least seven domestic violence shelters, transitional housing programs, and outreach organizations were impacted by the storm's severity. Police services are also strapped after a disaster.

Impact

Domestic violence has been found to greatly influence women's postdisaster mental health. Thirty-nine percent of women in one study who experienced partner abuse developed PTSD after the disaster, compared to 17 percent of women who did not experience abuse. Fifty-seven percent of women who experienced partner abuse developed major depression, compared to 28 percent of nonabused women.

Resources

The National Coalition against Domestic Violence (NCADV) orchestrated a nationwide effort to relocate battered women and their children to shelters in other parts of the country with available space and resources. NCADV's website (http://www.ncadv.org) provided an opportunity for battered women's shelters to announce existing beds for battered women affected by hurricane Katrina. Programs from Alaska to Connecticut to Florida to Arizona provided a safe space for battered women, and many were able to assist with transportation.

Despite NCADV's best efforts to respond to the crisis of Hurricane Katrina, battered women's programs needed additional resources to rebuild and restructure. Restricted communication and relocation to mass evacuation sites isolated battered women from support systems. Battered women and their children will need domestic violence shelter and other social services for significantly longer periods of time following a disaster to keep them from danger. Unfortunately, little is known about the long-term effects of disaster on battered women, but current challenges exist involving an increase in demand for services and devastated resources.

The World Health Organization recommends predisaster activities like hazard mapping should integrate gender considerations. Disaster preparedness training and planning should include both men and women. Abused victims should be given special at-risk status for relief and recovery efforts. Emergency managers and health service providers should receive gender-based training and information about domestic violence.

See also: Asia and Domestic Abuse; Southeast Asia and Domestic Abuse; Shelters for Domestic Abuse Victims; World Health Organization (WHO)

Further Reading

Adams, P. R., & Adams, G. R. (1984). Mount Saint Helen's ashfall. *American Psychologist, 39,* 252–260.

Brooks, N., & McKinlay, W. (1992). Mental health consequences of the Lockerbie disaster. *Journal of Traumatic Stress, 5*, 527–543.

Enarson, E. (1999). Violence against women in disasters: A study of domestic violence programs in the US and Canada. *Violence Against Women, 5* (7), 742–768.

Fisher, S. (2010). Violence against women and natural disasters: Findings from post-tsunami Sri Lanka. *Violence Against Women, 16*(8), 902–918.

Fullerton, C. S., Ursano, R. J., Tzu-Cheg, K., & Bharitya, V. R. (1999). Disaster-related bereavement: Acute symptoms and subsequent depression. *Aviation, Space, and Environmental Medicine, 70*, 902–909.

Gender and natural disasters fact sheet. (n.d). Pan American Health Organization. Retrieved January 27, 2013 from http://www.paho.org/English/DPM/GPP/GH/genderdisasters.PDF

Gleser, G. C., Green, B. L., & Winget, C. N. (1981). *Prolonged psychological effects of disaster: A study of Buffalo Creek*. New York, NY: Academic Press.

The impact of disaster. (n.d.). *National Coalition against Domestic Violence*. Retrieved March 16, 2012, from http://www.ncadv.org/learn/TheImpactofDisaster.php

Norris, F. (2007). Disasters and domestic violence. U.S. Department of Veterans Affairs. Retrieved March 16, 2012, from http://www.ptsd.va.gov/professional/pages/disasters-domestic-violence.asp

Norris, F. H., Perilla, J. L., Riad, J. K., Kaniasty, K., & Lavizzo, E. A. (1999). Stability and change in stress, resources, and psychological distress following natural disaster: Findings from Hurricane Andrew. *Anxiety, Stress, and Coping, 12*, 363–396.

Norris, F. H., & Uhl, G. A. (1993). Chronic stress as a mediator of acute stress: The case of Hurricane Hugo. *Journal of Applied Social Psychology, 23*, 1263–1284.

Shariat, S., Mallonee, S., Kruger, E., Farmer, K., & North, C. (1999). A prospective study of long-term health outcomes among Oklahoma City bombing survivors. *Journal of the Oklahoma State Medical Association, 92*, 178–186.

Ursano, R. J., Fullerton, C. S., Kao, T. C., & Bhartiya, V. R. (1995). Longitudinal assessment of posttraumatic stress disorder and depression after exposure to traumatic death. *Journal of Nervous and Mental Disease, 183*, 36–42.

Vella, D. (2005, January 26). Violence against women continues after the tsunami. *Asia News*. Retrieved January 27, 2013 from http://www.asianews.it/index.php?l=en&art=2427

Wasserstein, S. B., & LaGreca, A. (1998). Hurricane Andrew: Parent conflict as a moderator of children's adjustment. *Hispanic Journal of Behavioral Science, 20*, 212–224.

Wave of domestic violence after tsunami. (n.d.). *The UN Works*. Retrieved March 16, 2012, from http://www.un.org/works/sub3.asp?lang=en&id=31

World Health Organization (2002). Gender and health in disasters. Retrieved March 17, 2012, from http://www.who.int/gender/other_health/en/genderdisasters.pdf

Laura L. Finley

DOMESTIC VIOLENCE PREVENTION ENHANCEMENT AND LEADERSHIP THROUGH ALLIANCES (DELTA) PROGRAM

Established and run by the Centers for Disease Control and Prevention (CDC), the DELTA program emerged from the Family Violence Prevention Services Act (FVPSA), which authorized the CDC to distribute federal funds to support coordinated community responses (CCRs) that address domestic and dating violence (often referred to by the CDC as intimate partner violence or IVP). In 2002, the DELTA program began focusing on primary prevention. Primary prevention refers to efforts to prevent abuse from ever occurring through changing social norms and the conditions that allow abuse to happen. The World Health Organization has also called for increased coordination of primary prevention programming to prevent domestic violence. Other international instruments and agencies also mandate prevention activities, including the United Nations Declaration on the Elimination of Violence against Women, the Beijing Declaration and Platform for Action, the United Nations General Assembly Resolution 61/143, and UN Women.

CCRs are key to the DELTA program model. A CCR is an organized, community collective that seeks to respond to and prevent IPV in a particular community. Each community selects their own members with the goal of involving key organizations, educators, faith leaders, politicians, criminal justice practitioners, and health professionals.

According to the DELTA Project webpage of the CDC website, prevention strategies are guided by a set of principles including:

- Preventing first-time perpetration and first-time victimization;
- Reducing risk factors associated with IPV;
- Promoting protective factors that reduce the likelihood of IPV;
- Implementing evidence-supported strategies that incorporate behavior and social change theories; and
- Evaluating prevention strategies and using results to form future plans

Primary prevention programs must address individual, relationship, community, and societal influences. Individual influences might include attitudes and beliefs that support domestic violence, personal history with abuse, and isolation. Activities at this level might include life skills training and other forms of education. At the relationship level, programs must address a person's closest social circle—their family and peers. Activities might include mentoring and peer programs that are based on trust and mutual respect. At the community level, primary prevention programs must address the climate, programs, and policies in schools, workplaces, and neighborhoods. Activities typically include social norms and social marketing campaigns. To address the larger societal factors that influence domestic violence, such as gender inequality, religion, cultural norms, and economic or social policies, requires a true community collaboration that can raise awareness and make needed legislative and other changes.

Currently, the CDC funds 14 state-level domestic violence coalitions. Funder coalitions are in Alaska, California, Delaware, Florida, Kansas, Michigan, Montana, North Carolina, North Dakota, New York, Ohio, Rhode Island, Virginia, and Wisconsin. These coalitions then provide financial support to CCRs, as well as offering training and technical support.

See also: Centers for Disease Control and Prevention (CDC); Educational Programs; Social Change Campaigns

Further Reading

Centers for Disease Control and Prevention (n.d.). The DELTA Program: Preventing intimate partner violence in the United States. Retrieved March 9, 2012, from http://www.cdc.gov/violenceprevention/pdf/DELTA_AAG-a.pdf

Harvey, A., Garcia-Moreno, C., & Butchart, A. (2007). Primary prevention of intimate partner violence and sexual violence: Background paper for WHO expert meeting, May 2–3, 2007. World Health Organization. Retrieved March 16, 2012, from http://www.who.int/violence_injury_prevention/publications/violence/IPV-SV.pdf

Laura L. Finley

DOWRY KILLINGS

Dowry killings are a type of domestic violence carried out against new brides, particularly within the countries of India and Pakistan. In these countries, a bride's dowry size is a reflection of the wealth of the bride's family. When dowry killings occur, they usually do so as a result of the groom's family having determined that the dowry was not as large as was promised; killing the bride thus punishes the bride's family and makes the groom eligible to remarry someone of the expected socioeconomic status.

Dowry killings are one of several types of related and often confused types of violence against women in South Asia. One related practice is *sati*, or the burning of a woman on her husband's funeral pyre, often in her wedding dress. Other related practices are acid attacks, in which acid is thrown at a woman, usually in order to disfigure her face and prevent marriage or to kill her. This practice usually occurs by a man whose advances have not been accepted by the bride or the bride's family. Another related aspect are the so-called honor killings, in which young women are killed often for perceived transgressions against sexual morality codes, or after cases of adultery, rape, or even when the wife receives unwanted male attention. And one last form of domestic violence against female children is the practice of selective infanticide or feticide against female babies and fetuses, in the belief that male children will be less expensive to raise and more worthwhile for the family.

Dowry has a long-standing tradition in the cultures of most of South Asia. Dowry means the clothing, money, belongings, household goods, property, appliances, and jewelry that a woman brings to a marriage or that are provided for the married couple by the bride's parents. Traditionally, this is separate and in addition to the expense of the wedding. Oldenburg (2002) makes the argument that this system became entrenched and reinforced with new European types of patriarchy under colonialism and that this has colluded to create the modern problem of dowry death. She further argues that this has increased lockstep with new diagnostic tools that allow pregnant women to learn the sex of fetuses and thus opened the possibility of female feticide.

An Indian woman marches in her undergarments to protest the constant harassment she endured for not providing enough dowry. (AP Photo)

Dowries were outlawed by the Dowry Prohibition Act in India in 1961. The law provided terms of jail for men or families overtly demanding or even suggesting that a dowry be paid. Additionally, those who provided a dowry could be punished under the act. Dowry is still allowed in countries other than India, notably in Pakistan, though occasional reports of dowry abuse in other countries such as China, North and South Korea, and Bangladesh exist. Although the most information is on India, the presence of legal dowries elsewhere in south Asia makes the practice potentially more widespread than currently documented. Because of the preponderance of information on India, and secondly on Pakistan, this article focuses on these two researched countries.

In countries such as India and Pakistan, when a bride marries, she becomes part of the groom's family and lives with her husband usually in the house of his parents. Although dowries have been outlawed since 1961, unofficially they still exist in a social system in which women's parents want to provide for the future couple. Aspects of this include providing an education, often focusing on an employable skillset, as well as monetary offers and gifts. By providing a dowry or expensive gifts, it is believed, the bride will be accepted into the family more easily, with less harassment from the mother-in-law. Dowry killings occur as a result of some breakdown in the negotiations between the provisions the bride's family will make, or by increased demands from the groom's family, or because of marital disputes between the bride and groom. Indian law declares that the death of a wife within the first seven years of marriage should be investigated as a potential dowry killing, giving a sense of the wide range of time in which dowry killings might occur.

Many dowry killings are disguised to look like "kitchen fires" or "stove fires." Other times, as *The Times* reported, women are tortured but kept alive as a means of extorting money out of the bride's parents, even long after the wedding. In the economic downturn of the mid-2000s, men saw extorting money from a possible bride as a way to gain economic status when jobs were hard to come by or weren't paying well.

In 1961, the government of India banned the practice of asking for a dowry in weddings. The practice of dowry killings was added as a listed form of domestic violence in 1986. Under the current penal code of India, section 304-B, a dowry death is defined as one that occurs within the first seven years of a woman's marriage; her death is determined to be a dowry killing if there is evidence of any type of abuse or harassment that occurred preceding her death by her husband or his relatives, or if such abuse mentions a dowry. As the *Times of India* has reported, dowry deaths are a convenient category that has some social acceptance, but that what gets classified as a dowry death might be generalized violence at the hands of the groom and his family that has built up for years. Often, by the time burned women make it to the burn wards at local hospitals—where women account for 90 percent of all patients—it is not clear where the woman's desire for suicide to rid herself of the pain inflicted on her and the daily violence against her begin and end.

Dowry killings have been on the rise in recent years, with *The Times* offering a figure of an estimated 7,000 or more occurring yearly in the last decade. Less than 30 percent result in prosecution and conviction. Those convicted face a minimum of seven years to as much as a death sentence in parts of India. According to the latest statistics in India, of the cases brought before the courts, one-third resulted in convictions and the other two-thirds in acquittals. Other countries such as Pakistan report a smaller number (the current figure for Pakistan is 300 per year).

In Bangladesh, the Asian Legal Resource Center reports that in that country there are roughly 22,500 cases of women's repression for the last data year (2003), and that there were 267 cases of dowry-related violence against women, including 165 deaths, 11 women led to suicide after repeated increases in dowry demands, and 77 acid attacks. Bangladesh forbad dowries in its 1980 law, imposing fines or imprisonment or both on those who offered or demanded a dowry. China, North and South Korea, Congo, and Uganda all have reports of bride killings, although little data and reporting in these countries yet exists.

Efforts to overcome dowry killings have begun to be implemented, particularly on the local level, where raising the level of women's education standards, educating them about safe alternatives, and community-level programs have diminished the importance of dowries. A number of organizations now work to provide aftercare for women who survive attempted dowry burnings and to provide them with both a means of independent economic support in the form of work and a community of doctors to attend to continuing medical care and reconstructive surgery.

Although the push to increase the prosecution of dowry killers is increasing, the law against dowry is seldom enforced, and is less likely to be enforced in rural areas.

Dowry or "honor" killings are also on the rise in Pakistan, with an estimated 300 or more killings suspected each year. Unlike the government of India, the government of Pakistan has so far refused to recognize dowry killings as either a form of domestic violence or as a crime. Dowry is also an accepted form of transaction, so killings that take place can only be tried as murder, which they rarely are.

The film *Silent Veil* investigates the prevalence of men burning women in rural outposts in Pakistan. The argument of the film is that the women who are burned in Pakistan are often very young—14 to 25—and the practice occurs in rural areas that are economically deprived. In these areas, men have little power except over the home, and the burning of women is one way to control the household in the absence of the men possessing other markers of power such as riches or education.

Efforts to protect women and to bring men to justice have been slower to roll out in rural areas. Education and publicity schemes seem to be reaching women, although in many cases, it is mothers-in-law that help perpetrate the crimes. As recent news stories indicate, women who resist dowry negotiations or who raise concerns with police over brutality from the groom and groom's family are slowly gaining the attention and respect of other women of marriageable age. Organizations such as Vimochana have worked to bring attention to the matter of violence against women and run hotlines that provide support for women who need it. They provide support for women who are first talking about domestic abuse, help find jobs for women wishing to leave home, and help find space in orphanages for women and children who leave abusive situations. They also help provide legal, social, and educational support for women who reach out to the organization and work as a network with various organizations to improve human rights conditions. The group has also sponsored nonviolent protests such as sit-outs as well as conferences to bring parties involved in different aspects of the fight for women's rights together.

See also: Acid Attacks; Forced Marriage and Domestic Abuse; Honor Killings; India and Domestic Abuse; Southeast Asia and Domestic Abuse

Further Reading

Alvarez, Milton. (2011). *Silent veil: Voices from the heart of Islam* [Film].
Ash, Lucy. (2003, July 21). Killing in the name of dowry. *The Times* (London).
Asian Legal Resource Center. (2005). *Dowries mean death and discrimination for Bangladesh Women: Written statement submitted by the Asian Legal Resource Centre (ALRC), a non-governmental organisation in general consultative status, 61st Sess., Item 12 (a) of the provisional agenda, Commission on Human Rights.* Retrieved from http://www.alrc.net/doc/mainfile.php/61written/300/function.mysql-connect
National Crime Records Bureau, India: http://ncrb.nic.in/CII2008/cii-2008/Table%204.9.pdf
Oldenburg, V. (2002). *Dowry murders: The imperial origins of a cultural crime.* Oxford, England: Oxford University Press.
Pope, N. (2011). *Honor killings in the twenty-first century.* New York, NY: Palgrave-Macmillan.
Ramanan, R. (2011, Feb. 21). Dowry deaths or suicides? *Times of India.* Retrieved from: http://articles.timesofindia.indiatimes.com/2011-02-21/chennai/28618274_1_dowry-deaths-burns-cases-burns-ward
Sen, M. (2002). *Death by fire: Sati, dowry, death, and female infanticide in modern India.* New Brunswick, NJ: Rutgers UP.
Vimochana Women's Rights Group, Bangalore, India: http://www.vimochana.in/home.html

Andrea J. Dickens

DRUGS AND DOMESTIC ABUSE

Although advocates are careful to point out that drug or alcohol use or abuse does not cause domestic violence, there is a significant correlation between the two.

According to the National Coalition Against Domestic Violence, regular abuse of alcohol is one of the most significant predictors of domestic violence. In 2002, the U.S. Department of Justice found that 61 percent of domestic violence offenders also have substance abuse problems. Further, the battering incidents that occur when an abuser is using drugs or alcohol tend to be more severe, often resulting in greater damage.

Batterers living with women who have alcohol abuse problems often try to justify their violence as a way to control their victims when they are drunk. Such men try to deny responsibility for their violence, blaming it on the effects of alcohol.

Not only are substance use and abuse correlated with the perpetration of abuse, but research has demonstrated a clear link between the two among victims. Studies have shown that alcoholic women are more likely to report having endured physical abuse than women who are not alcoholic. Compared to women who use drugs and alcohol sparingly or abstain, women who are being abused are 15 times more likely to abuse alcohol and 9 times more likely to abuse drugs.

Children of substance-abusing parents are more likely to experience physical, sexual, or emotional abuse than children in non-substance-abusing households. Children who have experienced family violence are at greater risk for alcohol and other drug problems later in life than children who do not experience family violence. Evidence suggests that children who run away from violent homes are at risk of substance abuse.

One problem is that courts still mandate attendance in substance abuse programs for abusers. While these programs may address the substance abuse problem, they have not been proven to reduce the incidence of domestic violence.

Although attention has been paid to the intersection of domestic violence and substance abuse, few domestic violence shelters have substance abuse treatment programs. This is for several reasons: (1) Domestic violence programs typically have limited resources and cannot afford to pay for the equipment, staff, and other resources needed to provide substance abuse programs; (2) Domestic violence programs primarily focus on providing safety and shelter and thus tend not to include other kinds of programming; and (3) There is a fear that focusing on the substance abuse problems of victims will encourage victim blaming. Women may fear seeking help for either issue because they think they will lose their children.

The Center for Substance Abuse Treatment recommends the following:

- More federal funding so that substance abuse services can be provided in shelters;
- Furthering efforts to link domestic violence and substance abuse treatment programs in human services systems;
- Providing counseling, child care, substance abuse and mental health treatment, among other services, in one program.
- Creating mechanisms for interagency cooperation at the state and local level; and
- Funding demonstration projects to test the feasibility and effectiveness of linking domestic violence and substance abuse treatment programs.

It is recommended that substance abuse providers screen participants for domestic violence. Staff should be trained to identify abuse, provide appropriate referral information, and help ensure victims in crisis receive appropriate intervention and safety planning.

See also: Alcohol and Domestic Abuse; Children, Impact of Domestic Abuse on; Effects of Domestic Abuse

Further Reading

Collins, J., & Spencer, D. (2002). Linkage of domestic violence and substance abuse services, research in brief, executive summary. U.S. Department of Justice.

Domestic violence and substance abuse. (n.d.). *National Coalition against Domestic Violence.* Retrieved June 8, 2012, from http://www.ncadv.org/files/SubstanceAbuse.pdf

Lawrence, S., Chau, M., & Lennon, M. (2004, June). Depression, substance abuse and domestic violence. National Center for Children in Poverty. Retrieved January 27, 2013, from http://nccp.org/publications/pdf/text_546.pdf

U.S. Department of Health and Human Services. *Substance abuse treatment and domestic violence: Quick guide for clinicians.* Retrieved June 8, 2012, from http://www.kap.samhsa.gov/products/tools/cl-guides/pdfs/QGC_25.pdf

Laura L. Finley

DULUTH MODEL

The Duluth Model has been the predominant approach to abuse intervention in the United States. Developed in the 1980s, the Duluth Model emerged from conversations with scholars and survivors. It focuses on holding batterers accountable and ensuring the safety of victims. The Duluth Model sees abuse as a pattern of behavior intended by abusers to obtain and maintain control and power over victims. Societal norms and institutions support men's violence against women, according to the Duluth Model, and must therefore be challenged. It emphasizes blaming offenders, not victims; prioritizes the voices of victims; focuses on accountability within the criminal justice system; and argues that batterers can change through participation in educational programs. According to the website http://www.theduluthmodel.org, the core elements of the Duluth Model are:

1. Written policies that centralize victim safety and offender accountability
2. Practices that link intervening practitioners and agencies together
3. An entity that tracks and monitors cases and assesses data
4. An interagency process that brings practitioners together to dialogue and resolve problems
5. A central role in the process for victim advocates, shelters, and battered women
6. A shared philosophy about domestic violence
7. A system that shifts responsibility for victim safety from the victim to the system

On the website, it is claimed that the approach is successful because it prompts innovation and collaboration between agencies. Because it is developed using the experiences of women who have been abused, the approach is said to be more effective at keeping victims safe. Given that some women want to stay with their partners but want them to change so they are not abusive, the model emphasizes intervention for batterers that helps them understand their behavior and change their thoughts and actions. The Duluth Domestic Abuse Intervention Project has developed and implemented the "Creating a Process of Change for Men Who Batter" curriculum for abusers. Some research has supported the Duluth model, while other studies have failed to find support for various reasons. A key element of the Duluth model is the development of Power and Control Wheels. These are tools used by advocates and educators to explain why abuse occurs and to highlight the many forms it takes.

Critics have expressed concern about the batterer intervention programs in particular. *Batterer Intervention Programs: Where Do We Go from Here?*, a report issued by the National Institute of Justice (NIJ) in 2003, suggested that batterer intervention programs are ineffective. Yet there were some limitations to that study. For instance, some of the sites evaluated were not using the Duluth Model's curriculum with all participants. Although the Duluth Model emphasizes swift, consistent consequences for those who fail to comply with program requirements, none of the sites included in the NIJ study included that. Thus test sites might not have been fully implementing the Duluth Model. Other research has shown that offenders who completed the Duluth Model curriculum were less likely to offend (Gondolf, 2007).

Another criticism of the Duluth Model is that is it based on shame. Advocates say it is not, arguing instead that it respectfully challenges men to think about their behaviors. Based on Paulo Freire's educational philosophy, the Duluth Model emphasizes dialogue, not confrontation. Another criticism is that the Duluth Model is too focused on men's violence against women and therefore doesn't adequately address women's violence against men. Since 2004, a separate curriculum has been developed for women who are violent toward their male partners. However, advocates maintain that the primary reason for women's violence is retaliation, and thus it does not require the same set of tools and practices that address gender roles and societal norms.

Some have maintained that, because Duluth, Minnesota is more than 90 percent white, the model cannot adequately address the experiences of marginalized groups. Yet Duluth Model advocates have repeatedly partnered with advocates representing other groups, in particular Native Americans, and thus have attempted to be responsive to victimization of all peoples. Critics assert that the Duluth Model is overly focused on criminal justice. Supporters maintain that criminal justice is one vehicle for redress, but they advocate alternative efforts and community responses that challenge gender-role norms and assist victims as well. Some scholars support restorative justice, a different model of criminal accountability that involves conferencing among victims, offenders, and community members to repair the harm done by a specific offense. Critics of the Duluth Model maintain it is not amenable to restorative justice. The Duluth Model in general does not support efforts like restorative justice, mediation, and couples counseling that bring victims and offenders together. The model does, however, incorporate some pieces of restorative justice in that victims are central to the process. More conservative critics argue that the Duluth Model encourages victims to leave or to divorce their partners. Advocates maintain that the focus is on empowering victims to make their own choices, and thus no one answer is promoted.

Many people want to believe that anger is the root cause of domestic violence. The Duluth Model acknowledges that anger may precede violence, but rejects the simplistic answer that batterers are simply acting out when they are angry. According to the Duluth Model, batterers do not suffer from "anger control" problems. They very much control their anger—they determine to whom they will direct it, under what circumstances, in what ways, and who will witness it. Batterers typically do not suffer from anger control issues with anyone but their partners, which suggests they are indeed able to control their responses. Some critics assert that the Duluth Model ignores or minimizes psychological problems among batterers. Although the model recognizes that some abusers suffer from psychological problems or mental health issues, it does not see these as the cause of abuse, as many abusers have no such diagnoses.

See also: Batterer Intervention Programs; Feminism and Domestic Abuse; History of Domestic Violence Developments, 1980s

Further Reading

The Duluth Model: http://www.theduluthmodel.org/about/index.html

The Duluth Model Wheel Gallery. (2011). Domestic abuse intervention programs. Retrieved from http://www.theduluthmodel.org/training/wheels.html

Gondolf, E. (2007). Theoretical and research support for the Duluth Model: A reply to Dutton and Corvo. *Aggression and Violent Behavior, 12,* 644–657.

Laura L. Finley

ECONOMIC RECESSION AND DOMESTIC ABUSE

The "Great Recession" of 2007–2009 significantly increased the focus of the impact of financial hardship on domestic abuse, not only in the United States, but also in other countries affected by the significant and long-term downturn in the global economy. While it is common knowledge that financial hardship has negative implications with regard to domestic abuse, it wasn't until the "Great Recession" that the impact of long-term severe financial hardship became such a significant topic in the domestic abuse dialogue. The ultimate question was whether recession *causes* domestic abuse. Available data or research is limited so most information relative to the subject is anecdotal. Given the available information, the short answer is that recession increases the severity of existing abusive situations but does not make individuals who were not previously abusive become abusive in domestic situations. The long answer is a bit more complex.

While one may think that the financial strain of a recession may cause more domestic abuse, it appears that, in general, it has not increased the rate of abuse but rather the severity of the abuse from those individuals who already commit domestic abuse. This isn't to say that recession has not caused previously nonviolent individuals to become violent to the point of committing domestic abuse but rather that the number of recession-related "new abusers" is limited.

Domestic abuse is often difficult to clearly define because it shows itself in so many different ways, including intimate partner violence, intergenerational abuse, and financial control. Trying to understand domestic abuse becomes even more complicated in the context of economic recession. Recession in and of itself is sometimes difficult to understand. Issues of when it started, when it ended, and whether it was local, regional, or even global are factors that complicate understanding of domestic abuse within the context of economic recession. While much of the focus of domestic abuse is related to intimate partner violence, domestic abuse can and does affect nonintimate partners within a "family system." Regardless of the specifics, domestic abuse is a serious problem that negatively affects individuals, families, communities, and the societies we live in.

The impact of recession on domestic violence is similar to the ways in which the economy and money influence domestic violence in nonrecession periods, from couples fighting over money to the societal manifestations of unemployment, foreclosures, and bankruptcy. At a more specific level, there are reports that due to victims' inability to afford to leave abusive situations, even given the likely increase in intensity of the abuse, that this may be increasing the level of not only domestic violence but also domestic violence homicides.

Even though there are differences in specific experiences and the research is limited, it is clear that there is a link between the financial hardship caused by recession and domestic abuse. However, relative to the Great Recession of 2007–2009, it wasn't just about financial hardship but rather about the pervasive "chronic stress" that individuals and societies experienced. The chronic stress basically "wore down" both individuals and societies to the point where individual and societal coping capacity and resources were all but exhausted. As a result, the "Great Recession," directly or indirectly, had significant impact on the expression of anger, aggression, and even violence. This was not only at a local or national level but also at a global level, as the recession has played a role in the increase in domestic violence in countries such as Australia, China, the United Kingdom, and Malaysia. The intensity and duration of stress related to financial hardship during the Great Recession was significantly greater than during other recent periods of economic recession or turmoil.

It got to the point where there was a "resetting" relative to financial matters, not only in the United States but throughout the globe. Severe financial troubles and hardships were experienced by individuals, communities, societies, and even countries. This affected the individual on a day-to-day work-related basis; a family's ability to maintain housing and access to existing support network and resources, as well as the interpersonal relationship troubles that come with prolonged stress.

These financial issues, in part, prompted social upheavals that often became extremely violent, including "overthrowing" the then-existing political power structure such as in Egypt and Italy. This upheaval occurred in the United States in the form of the Occupy or "Take Back Wall Street" movement. While the anger and violence displayed in the United States may not have been as intense as in other countries, the level of display and broad support for the movement had heretofore not been experienced within the United States.

At face value, it appears that the implications of economic recession on domestic abuse are primarily related to the financial hardship it causes for the individual, family, or community. However, this is only partially accurate. Recession, and more specifically the Great Recession, has had negative effects in many areas of the lives of individuals, families, and the communities they live in. It is not just the typical frustrations and problems that accompany trying to live on a budget or general financial hardship. Because of the extended time period of the Great Recession as well as the severity at local regional and even global levels, the stressors went beyond just financial hardship.

Thus, while recession-related variables do have negative implications on domestic abuse, many individuals, families, and communities have historically been able to make it through short periods of economic hardship. It wasn't until the Great Recession's intensity and duration that there was a marked change in domestic abuse as directly related to financial hardship. It is clear that prolonged severe financial hardship erodes individual's, families', and communities' support systems and ultimately the capacity to effectively cope. Individuals predisposed to perpetrating domestic abuse are likely to continue to maintain, if not increase, their abusive behaviors, while those without any domestic abuse intentions may fall prey to the chronic stressors and reactively engage in domestic abuse behaviors or attitudes.

The problem goes beyond the individual or family level to that of society. Whereas society used to have processes and resources to help mitigate problems faced by individuals and families, economic recession tends to limit or completely remove those resources. As a result, those who had once been able to effectively address or cope with domestic abuse were no longer able to muster the resources or energy to continue to do so. This had negative implications for individuals, families, communities, and society.

This situation causes a vicious cycle in that the coping capacity of an individual, family, or community is affected by the coping capacity of all those within the community or societal "system" they live in. When any of the components within the system becomes overstressed due to the implications of prolonged severe and chronic financial hardship, it negatively affects everyone within the given social system.

This was a consequence of the Great Recession. It weakened the entire social safety net which somewhat mitigated the negative impact of financial hardship because the pervasive and long-term chronic stress, including severe financial hardship, used up most individuals', families', and communities' coping resources. The complex constellation of the Great Recession–related factors did negatively impact the perpetation of domestic abuse. While there is significant room and need for focused research in this area, the implications of any recession would be similar to those experienced as part of the Great Recession, if only to a lesser extent.

Domestic abuse is an implication of economic recession. It appears that increased intensity or severity of existing abuse is related to pervasive and chronic stress, including severe financial hardship as manifested by recession and more specifically the Great Recession of 2007–2009.

See also: Financial Abuse; Housing and Domestic Abuse; Types of Domestic Abuse; Welfare and Domestic Abuse

Further Reading

Campbell, J., Glass, N., Sharps, P., Laughon, K., & Bloom, T. (2007). Intimate partner violence. *Trauma, Violence, & Abuse, 8*, 246–269.

Cohen, P. (2010, January 2). Recession begets family violence [Web log post]. Retrieved from http://www.huffingtonpost.com/philip-n-cohen/recession-begets-family-v_b_409502.html

Family Matters. (2010, March 31). Is the recession causing a rise in domestic violence? [Web log post]. Retrieved from http://blog.vision.org/FamilyMatters/bid/37505/Is-the-Recession-Causing-a-Rise-in-Domestic-Violence

Fontes, L., & McCloskey, K. (2011). Cultural issues in violence against women. In C. M. Renzetti, J. L. Edleson, & R. K. Bergen (Eds.), *Sourcebook on violence against women* (2nd ed., pp. 151–168). Thousand Oaks, CA: Sage.

Kilbane, T., & Spira, M. (2010). Domestic violence or elder abuse? Why it matters for older women. *Families in Society, 91*(2), 165–170.

Lamb, J. (2010, October 23). Merced County domestic violence worse during recession [Online News]. Retrieved from http://www.mercedsunstar.com/2010/10/23/1622273/merced-county-domestic-violence.html#ixzz1cI5ugNtd

National Domestic Violence Hotline: http://www.thehotline.org/2009/01/increased-financial-stress-affects-domestic-violence-victims/

Trotter, J., & Allen, N. (2009). The good, the bad, and the ugly: Domestic violence survivors' experiences with their informal social networks. *American Journal of Community Psychology, 43,* 221–231.

Walker, C. (2009, October 26). Domestic violence and the recession [Online News]. Retrieved from http://news.wfu.edu/2009/10/26/domestic-violence-and-the-recession/

Mark Marquez

EDUCATIONAL PROGRAMS

Most educational programs about abuse are targeted at teens and are implemented in a school setting. Programs can generally be separated into two categories: evidence-based promising practices and other curricula. Evidence-based promising practices have been identified by the Substance Abuse and Mental Health Administration (SAMHSA) or the Centers for Disease Control and Prevention (CDC) as evidence based, a promising program, and/or have been rigorously evaluated. Other curricula may have yet to be evaluated or have only been evaluated by less rigorous "in-house" approaches.

Expect Respect is an evidence-based program designed for middle and high school groups. CDC evaluations have indicated an immediate, positive effect on attendees. Other evaluations have found Expect Respect to increase healthy conflict resolution skills, increase ability to identify unhealthy relationships, and reduce perpetration among high-risk groups.

The Fourth R is a 21-lesson health education program for 9th–12th-grade students. Evaluations have found it to reduce physical dating violence in the subsequent year.

Ending Violence is a three-class-session prevention program developed by Break the Cycle. It focuses on legal issues, highlighting the legal rights of domestic violence victims and the legal responsibilities of perpetrators. It is taught by attorneys who are bicultural and bilingual and is aimed at changing attitudes and beliefs among Latino youth, many of whom may be unfamiliar with U.S. laws. An evaluation of the program, which involved 2,540 ninth-grade students from 10 schools and 110 classes in the Los Angeles Unified School District, found modest but significant increases in participants' knowledge of the laws related to dating violence. Participants retained this knowledge six months after the program. Participating teens were less accepting of female-on-male violence, but there was no change in attitudes toward male-on-female violence, perhaps because such attitudes were strongly negative from the outset of the program. Participants also reported increased likelihood of seeking help if they ever experienced abuse, although no change was found in the frequency of their violent or fearful dating experiences in the six months following the program.

The organization Break the Cycle provides educational programming specifically about dating violence. Their curricular programs are Safe Dates, Ending Violence, and Speak.Act.Change, a service-learning initiative. Another educational effort coordinated by Break the Cycle is their School Policy Kit, designed to train educators about abuse and help them craft appropriate policies and punishments for abuse occurring in school. The Safe Dates package includes five components: a 10-session dating violence curriculum, a play about dating violence, a poster contest, parent materials, and an evaluation questionnaire. Each of the 10 sessions is approximately 50 minutes long and can be used on a daily or weekly schedule. Ending Violence is intended for students in grades 8–12. It includes an interactive DVD that can be used in full or in part to educate students about abusive relationships, promote healthy ones, and teach them their legal rights and responsibilities. It also includes a video presentation for adults. The entire package is available in English and Spanish.

Kid & Teen SAFE is a program designed to educate youth with disabilities. Its aim is to reduce the risk of sexual, physical, and/or emotional abuse or exploitation of children and youth with disabilities and to increase the ability of that population to identify, prevent, and report abuse. Further, Kid & Teen SAFE aims to enhance awareness and strengthen the skills of family members, teachers, and other professionals to identify, prevent, and report abuse of children with disabilities. The program consists of three to four classroom presentations for children with disabilities in grades kindergarten through 12, training and workshops for special education teachers and professionals who work with children with disabilities as well as parents, and a National Resource Library of more than 350 items related to violence against people with disabilities. The classroom presentations focus on helping young people develop emotional and physical personal boundaries, identifying inappropriate touches, asserting your right to say no, escaping abuse, and identifying and reporting to trusted adults. An evaluation of the program showed that students gained knowledge on identifying inappropriate touches, saying no, and identifying trusted adults.

CDC's Choose Respect program is intended for middle school youth. Developed by the CDC in 2006, it is accompanied by a free online toolkit. CDC also developed the Dating Matters program, which it is piloting in four high-risk urban communities between 2011 and 2015. Upon evaluation of the pilot, CDC intends to make the entire curriculum widely available and free of charge. It also includes an educator training module.

Men Can Stop Rape has developed a program called MOST Clubs designed for high school–aged boys. Thirteen to 16 weeks long, this evidence-based program helps raise young men's awareness about their role in stopping sexual and dating violence and has been found by the CDC to increase the likelihood that young men will intervene.

Campuses are also ideal locations to host educational programs. Information about dating and domestic violence can be integrated into coursework in such fields as criminology, sociology, women's studies, social work, psychology, counseling, law, and political science. Medical-related programs like nursing can and should include such education as well, and medical schools and law schools are increasingly including domestic violence training as part of their required or elective curricula. Additionally, educational programming about domestic and dating violence can be coordinated outside of the classroom. This might include speakers, survivor panels, film screenings, and other types of efforts. The College Brides Walk is one effort designed to raise awareness about abuse on campus and beyond. Held since 2011 at Barry University in Miami Shores, the College Brides Walk is the collaborative effort of seven South Florida colleges and universities as well as area victim advocacy, law enforcement, and legal resources. Held in February on the Friday before Valentine's Day, the event includes specialized training on dating violence for teens, a variety of speakers, and exhibits by area agencies and resources, in addition to the actual walk. Students on campus can earn service-learning credit for helping before, during, and after the walk.

Many educational programs on campuses and in communities are held during the month of October, which has been designated as Domestic Violence Awareness Month. Communities often host panels, trainings, workshops, and other events to raise awareness about abuse. Many also sponsor fund-raisers as a way not only to educate but also to raise much-needed funds for services.

Many educational programs utilized a bystander intervention approach. Built on social norms theory, these approaches are based on the idea that people tend to overestimate the amount of negative and underestimate the positive or prosocial behaviors committed by their peers. Thus they may fail to engage in prosocial behaviors, believing themselves to be in the minority (a position that is uncomfortable for many), or they may conform to negative behaviors that they believe to be common among their peers. Bystander intervention programs help provide accurate information about social phenomena and challenge participants to speak up and to intervene when they see problem behaviors. Many campuses use the Mentors in Violence Prevention (MVP) program, although it can be used with students as young as middle school. It is an evidence-based bystander intervention program that has been found to increase knowledge about gender violence, improve attitudes toward the prevention of gender violence, and increase students' confidence that they can intervene to stop dangerous situations.

Most educational programs are universal in scope, meaning they are not tailored for specific groups. This can be problematic in that each group may have unique needs and experiences that must be addressed for educational programs to be effective. Ideal programs should be comprehensive, more than just one-time sessions, and incorporate multimedia and a diversity of learning methods. Further, the best programs are those that allow students a safe space and designated time for dialogue and reflection.

There is some question whether single-sex programs are more effective at preventing dating violence. Some maintain that it is easier for attendees to talk openly and honestly if they are with only people of their same sex. In particular, single-sex programs help men discuss their feelings about hegemonic masculinity and ways to challenge it. Further, given that statistics show the majority of offenders are male and victims are female, it can be considered inappropriate to mix the two in an educational setting as there might actually be offenders and victims in that group. Hickman, Jaycox, and Aronoff (2004) recommend more research to determine which type of programming is more effective.

See also: Break the Cycle; Brides Walk; Bystander Intervention Programs; Domestic Violence Prevention Enhancement and Leadership Through Alliances (DELTA) Program; Social Change Campaigns

Further Reading

Break the Cycle: http://www.breakthecycle.org
Choose Respect: http://www.chooserespect.org
Dating Matters Educator Training: http://www.vetoviolence.org
Hickman, L., Jaycox, L., & Aronoff, J. (2004, April). Dating violence among adolescents: Prevalence, gender distribution, and prevention program effectiveness. *Trauma, Violence & Abuse, 5*(2), 123–142.
Hoffman, J. (2010, June 3). Are single-sex groups better for preventing dating violence? *New York Times*. Retrieved June 19, 2012, from http://parenting.blogs.nytimes.com/2012/06/03/are-single-sex-groups-better-for-preventing-dating-violence/?ref=janhoffman
Safe Dates Curriculum: http://www.hazelden.org/web/go/safedates
Teen Dating Violence Awareness and Prevention Curricula and Comparison. (2010, April). *Violence against Women Network*. Retrieved June 19, 2012 from http://www.vawnet.org/Assoc_Files_VAWnet/ODVN_TeenDatingViolenceCurriculumComparison_April2010.pdf

Laura L. Finley

EFFECTS OF DOMESTIC VIOLENCE

Domestic violence involves one person, typically an intimate partner, using various forms of violence to obtain and maintain power and control over another person. It takes many forms, from physical abuse like kicking, punching, slapping, burning, and strangulation to destruction of property to abuse of pets. Domestic violence can also include emotional and verbal assaults as well as constant intimidation. Many abusers use threats to or actual abuse of children as a way of controlling their partners. However, abuse is more than bruises and broken bones. Some of the most devastating forms of abuse are verbal, emotional, psychological, sexual, and economic.

The statistics listed below highlight some of the ways abuse impacts victims but also the children who are witness to the abuse.

Statistics

- Medical providers have found that up to 30 percent of all pregnant women are battered at some point during their pregnancy (MNADV, 2001).
- The National Commission for the Prevention of Infant Mortality reports that there is a 25 percent greater likelihood that a baby will be born with a low birth weight if the mother is battered during pregnancy.
- Men who witnessed violence in their childhood homes are three times as likely to batter their wives and/or girlfriends (BJS, 1998).
- 75 percent of batterers witnessed violence in their childhood homes (BJS, 1998).
- 63 percent of males incarcerated between the ages of 12 and 20 were there for assaulting or killing the man who was abusing their mother (BJS, 1998).

- At least 3.3 million children between the ages of 3 and 19 are at risk of exposure to parental violence every year (Jaffe, Wolfe, & Wilson, 1990).
- In one study, 27 percent of domestic homicide victims were children (Florida Mortality Review Project, 1997).
- When children are killed during a domestic dispute, 90 percent are under the age of 10, and 56 percent are under the age of 2 (Florida Mortality Review Project, 1997).
- 26 percent of pregnant teens reported being physically abused by their boyfriends. And about half of them said the battering began or intensified after he learned of her pregnancy (Brustin, 1995).
- There is a strong correlation between individuals raised in violent homes and individuals who became perpetrators, and victims, of domestic violence in adulthood (Wexler, 2006).
- Based on research from other delinquent populations, Wexler (2006) estimates that between 20 and 40 percent of chronically violent adolescents had witnessed domestic violence (Wexler, 2006).

Victims suffer from numerous medical consequences of their abuse, including but not limited to lacerations, broken bones, bruises, head injuries, sexually transmitted diseases, vaginal and urinary tract infections, arthritis, hypertension, heart disease, chronic pelvic pain, and pregnancy-related problems. Because abusers sometimes deny victims access to medical care and/or needed medications, victims may suffer from problems like asthma and diabetes that went untreated. Psychologically, victims may experience depression, lack of trust, anger, and a host of other negative emotions.

People who have endured horrible events suffer predictable psychological harm. There is a spectrum of traumatic disorders, ranging from the effects of a single overwhelming event to the more complicated effects of prolonged repeated abuse (Herman, 1997). Those who endure trauma often suffer from post-traumatic stress disorder (PTSD). Repeated trauma in adult life erodes the structure of the personality already formed, but repeated trauma in childhood forms and deforms the personality (Herman, 1997). Children trapped in an abusive environment are faced with the formidable task of adaptation. In this dysfunctional environment they are forced to build their sense of trust with the untrustworthy. Their sense of safety is developed in an unsafe environment. Their sense of control is formed in a terrifying, unpredictable, uncontrollable setting. Unable to care for themselves, they must compensate for the failure of adult care and protection with the only means at their disposal, an immature system of psychological defenses. Research tells us that 40 percent to 60 percent of men who abuse women also physically abuse their children (APA, 1996). One thing we know for sure: 100 percent of those children are at the least victims of psychological abuse by simply being in that atmosphere. All of these children are trauma victims.

Although many times victims want to believe that children do not see or hear the abuse, they typically do. They are fearful for their own safety and that of their loved ones. Many also feel shame and are embarrassed by what is happening. Some children blame themselves for the violence occurring in their homes. Growing up in an abusive home increases the likelihood that children will be involved in abusive relationships when they are adults.

Infants are reactive to their environment; when distressed they cry, and refuse to feed. They may withdraw and are particularly susceptible to emotional deprivation. At infancy we are extremely limited in our cognitive abilities and our resources for adaptation. In a dysfunctional environment the results may manifest in poor health, poor sleeping habits, and excessive screaming. These babies are a product of their environment. They are aware of others' negative emotions, and they ultimately incorporate these emotions into their own responses. They are extremely vulnerable.

Language skill development actually begins very early, with words being understood in mid- to late infancy or early toddler. The latest research by early childhood development researchers tell us that the most affected area they see in children exposed to repetitive trauma is language development. According to these professionals, 67 percent of infants exposed to repetitive trauma develop expressive-recessive language delay. They are years behind their peers by the time they reach elementary school in the area of language development.

Exposure to trauma can cause behavioral problems such as frequent illness, severe shyness, and low self-esteem. Children may experience problems in day care, for instance, difficulty listening or following directions, or acting out against other children. By preschool, children tend to blame themselves for the abuse. Boys in particular may act aggressively. By primary school age, children growing up in abusive homes have learned that violence is a way to solve conflict. Children at this age often struggle academically. Girls are more prone to exhibit signs of depression. By adolescence, persons who grew up in abusive homes are likely to blame the victim for the abuse.

See also: Children, Impact of Domestic Abuse on; Psychological Effects of Domestic Abuse; Social and Societal Effects of Domestic Abuse

Further Reading

American Psychological Association (1996). *Violence in the family: Report of the American Psychological Association Presidential Task Force on Violence in the Family*. Washinton, D.C.

Brustin, S. (1995). Legal response to teen dating. *Violence Family Law Quarterly, 29*, 333–334.

Bureau of Justice Statistics (1998, March). *Violence by intimates: Analysis of data on crimes by current or former spouses, boyfriends, and girlfriends*. Washington, D.C.

Florida Mortality Review Project (1997). *Florida governor's task force on domestic and sexual violence*.

Garbarino, J. (2000). *Lost boys: Why our sons turn violent and how we can save them*. New York, NY: Anchor.

Herman, J. (1997). *Trauma and recovery: The aftermath of violence—from domestic abuse to political terror*. New York, NY: Basic.

Jaffe, P., Wolfe, D., & Wilson, S. (1990). *Children of battered women*. New York, NY: Sage.

Long-term effects of domestic violence. (2011, March 4). An Abuse, Rape, and Domestic Violence Aid and Resource Collection (AARDVARC). Retrieved June 28, 2012, http://www.aardvarc.org/dv/effects.shtml

Maryland Network Against Domestic Violence (2001). *The impact of domestic violence on children and teens.* Bowie, MD.

Wexler, D. (2006). *Stop domestic violence: Group leader's manual.* New York: W.W. Norton.

Sadé Brooks

ELDER ABUSE

Researchers agree that elder abuse occurs in all settings where older adults live. Nevertheless, elder abuse was only recognized as a social problem in the late 1970s when Congressman Claude Pepper brought the issue to the national level. Subsequent hearings and discussions led to the initial establishment of elder abuse legislation and amendments to the Social Security Act that mandated all states provide protective services to older adults in the United States. This law became the cornerstone of the 50 states' elder abuse regulations and adult protective services. Moreover, both the Select Committee on Aging of the United States House of Representative and pioneering research confirmed the existence of domestic neglect and abuse of the elderly between 1977 and 1981. Thereafter, states were mandated to develop procedures for receiving and investigating abuse reports, including conducting public education.

According to the National Research Council (2003), elder abuse or mistreatment is defined as intentional actions that cause harm or create a serious risk (whether or not harm is intended) to a vulnerable elder by a caregiver or other person who is in a trusting relationship with the elder, or failure by a caregiver to satisfy the elder's basic needs or to protect the elder from harm. According to the National Center on Elder Abuse (1996), elder abuse takes different forms including but not limited to: physical abuse, psychological/emotional and sexual abuse, financial exploitation, and neglect. Physical abuse refers to acts of violence including striking (with or without an object), hitting, pushing, kicking, slapping, or otherwise assaulting a person. Psychological abuse involves intimidation, humiliation, isolation, or verbally assaulting a person. Financial abuse occurs when individuals commit theft or fraud against a person. Sexual abuse is the least reported form of elder abuse, and it includes rape, exhibitionism, harmful touching, and involuntary deviate sexual behavior. Neglect, which is the most common form of elder abuse, is the refusal or failure to fulfill any part of a caretaker's obligations or duties to an elderly person.

Elder abuse occurs in many places including in the elderly individual's home, and the abuser may be the person's spouse or partner, adult children, other family and nonfamily members, or caregivers. Similarly, elder abuse is also widespread in institutional settings, such as hospitals, nursing homes, and long-term care and assisted-living facilities. Scholars argue that the actual incidence and prevalence of elder abuse in domestic and institutional settings is unknown and can only be estimated. For example, the National Center on Elder Abuse (2005) speculated that while many thousands of older Americans have been abused, there are no official national

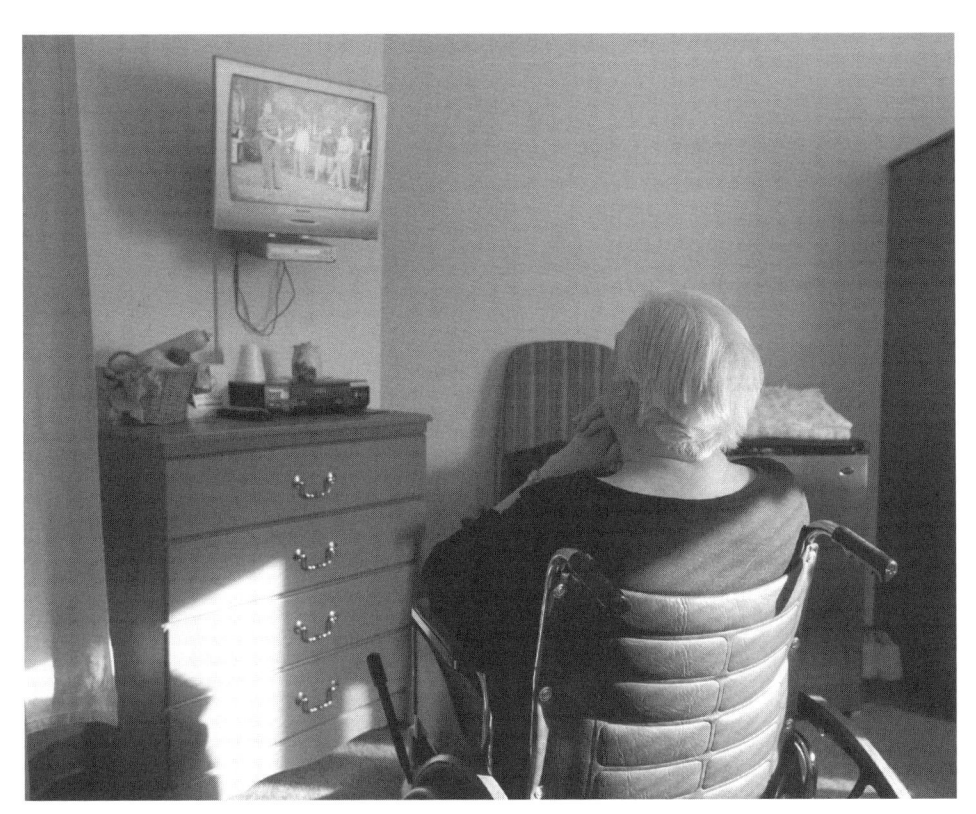

An elderly woman who has suffered abuse by a relative watches *I Love Lucy* on a television inside her room at a retirement community in Mason, Ohio on January 8, 2013. (AP Photo/Al Behrman)

statistics. Other researchers agree that in spite of the national mandatory reporting laws, most cases go unreported or underreported. For instance, Elder abuse is one of the most under-reported forms of violence in the United States, and research into the expanding problem of elder mistreatment has lagged behind other fields. Almost no research has been conducted on mistreatment prevalence in rural states. Furthermore, elder abuse was only criminalized in the 1990s. According to Bonnie and Wallace (2002) little is known about the characteristics, causes, or scope of the problem.

Existing data indicates that the rate of elder abuse has increased in the last three decades, becoming one of the most challenging social issues in the United States. Elder abuse is likely to gain in relevance as the population ages. The older adult population is growing faster than other groups. According to the U.S. Census Bureau (2007), individuals 65 years and older accounted for 12.5 percent of the U.S. population in 2000. The Bureau further projected that by 2020, the older adult population will increase by 5.5 percent, and by 2050, older adults will account for 20 percent (88.5 million individuals) of the total population. Moreover, it is estimated that between 2.5 and 5 million Americans ages 65 or older may be the victims of elder abuse at the rate of 3–6 percent in 2050. Similarly, Payne (2008) estimated that between 10 percent and 20 percent of older Americans have been victims of elder abuse. Like domestic violence, elder abuse that occurs in domestic settings is largely hidden and frequently overlooked; thus, this crime occurs often and goes unreported, underreported, and underpunished. The *National Center on Elder Abuse: Nursing Home Abuse Risk Prevention Profile and Checklist* (2005) noted that elder abuse in domestic settings in a person's home or in other noninstitutional facilities is a serious problem that affects hundreds of thousands of elderly nationwide. Yet information about domestic elderly mistreatment by relatives or caregivers was not published until 1978. Furthermore, only six investigations of elder abuse and neglect in an elderly person's home were conducted in the United States between 1978 and 1980. Equally disturbing, the National Center on Elder Abuse (1998) study that examined the national incidence of elder abuse estimated that 450,000 elderly individuals in domestic settings were abused and/or neglected in 1996. Similarly, Cornell and Gelles (1985) also estimated that 1 in 10 elderly individuals living with a family member was abused each year. Bonnie and Wallace (2002) reported that between one and two million Americans aged 65 or older were injured, exploited, or mistreated by someone on whom they depended for care or protection. Other researchers argued that victims of physical abuse who live with the abuser, particularly a spouse or a son, experienced more than one incident of abuse. A study by Teaster et al. (2006) found that 65.4 percent of abusers were family members ; adult children (32.6 percent); other family members (21.5 percent); and spouses or partner (11.3 percent). A nine-year observational cohort study by Lachs et al. (1998) discovered that, of the 182 victims of physical abuse aged 60 and over from New Haven, Connecticut, nearly 77 percent of abusers were family members, including adult sons (28.9 percent), spouses (26.8 percent), and daughters (21.6 percent), and 87 percent of the abusers cohabitated with the victim.

The forms of elder abuse found in nursing homes imitate those found in domestic settings and include physical and sexual assault, neglect, inappropriate restraint, financial abuse, isolation, verbal threats, and intimidation. Although researchers commonly agree that elder abuse and neglect in nursing homes, long-term care facilities, hospitals, and other institutional settings is widespread, the subject has received limited research attention. A review of the literature indicates that elder abuse is rampant in institutional settings; for instance, the Atlanta Long Term Care Ombudsman program (2000) revealed that 44 percent of the residents in nursing homes had been abused, 48 percent were treated roughly, 38 percent had witnessed other residents being abused, and 44 percent witnessed other residents treated roughly. Similarly, Pillemer and Moore (1989) surveyed 577 nursing home staff from 31 nursing homes in Massachusetts and reported that 10 percent knew attendees who had been abused during the past year and 40 percent knew those who had been psychologically abused. The results of the survey also identified the most common forms of physical abuse, including restraining patients (6 percent); pushing, grabbing, shoving, or punching (3 percent); hitting with an object (2 percent); and throwing something at a patient (1 percent). The most common forms of psychological abuse were yelling (swearing at or insulting residents), denying residents privileges, or threatening to hit or throw something at them. Of the staff interviewed, 36 percent had witnessed other employees physically abusing residents during the past year, and 81 percent had witnessed at least one incident of psychological abuse in the past year. A study by Cornell and Gelles (1985) revealed that 39 of 404 clients who were interviewed (ages 60 and older) were abused. The study speculates that if this rate was projected for the national population of elderly, nearly one million cases of elderly abuse would have occurred.

Research studies continue to consistently demonstrate that elderly victims with mental health and physical illnesses are potential victims of elder abuse. However, it is important to point out that even individuals without these risk factors can find themselves in abusive situations. Kolberg (2009) hypothesized that older individuals with physical or mental impairments were at greater risk of being abused than those of similar age who did not suffer from such impairments. Similarly, Godkin, Wolf, and Pillemer (1989) revealed that 61 percent of abused elders had suffered a recent decline in mental health preceding the abuse or neglect, but only 6.4 percent of the nonabused group had suffered mental health decline.

Studies are inconsistent regarding the sex of the perpetrator as a risk factor of elder abuse. For example, Pillemer and Finklehor's (1988) random survey of a community dwelling reported nearly equal numbers of men and women experienced abuse (52 percent to 48 percent). Moreover, the risk of abuse for elderly men was reported to be two times higher than for elderly women (51 per 1,000 vs. 23 per 1,000). Nevertheless, more recent studies have shown that sex is a strong risk predictor of elder abuse. Victims of elder abuse are primarily women as evidenced by the National Center on Elder Abuse (NCEA, 1998). Kolberg (2009) speculate that although abuse of older men is common worldwide, elder abuse affects mostly women. Furthermore, the NCEA (1998) study that identified patterns of male versus female abuse also reported the following findings: of substantiated cases of abuse and neglect, men were the most frequent abusers in abandonment (83.4 percent), physical abuse (62.6 percent), psychological/emotional abuse (60.1 percent), and financial exploitation (59 percent). Although a significant number of perpetrators were men, women were slightly more frequent perpetrators in neglect cases (52.4 percent) than men.

A review of the literature shows that lack of clear objectives and uniformly accepted definition of elder abuse has been a major barrier to the research, making it more difficult to compare the findings. There is a large reservoir of unreported and underreported cases of elder abuse; thus, these numbers underestimate the severity of the problem. To address these issues, uniformly accepted definitions of elder abuse should be identified and more methodology-based research studies conducted to ensure that accurate statistics are reported. More importantly, the federal government should coordinate with the states to create uniform policies and regulations to oversee the nation's institutions for older Americans. Furthermore, policies and inspections in elderly care facilities must be nationalized and enforced, and severe penalties should be applied, including jail time, in the most serious abusive situations. In addition, all institutions for older adults should develop a zero-tolerance response toward all elder abuse allegations to send a clear message that assaults on older people are unacceptable. Educating older Americans, health-care providers, and the general public on how to recognize elder abuse should always be a first approach. Despite immense challenges, efforts have been made to eradicate the problem, but a lot remains to be done. Finally, unless the federal government acts quickly, too many older Americans will continue to suffer the consequences of abuse and neglect in domestic and institutional settings.

See also: Disabilities and Domestic Abuse; Types of Domestic Abuse

Further Reading

Amstadter, A. B., Zajac, K., Strachan, M., Harnandez, M. A., Kilpatrick, G., Acierno, R., et al. (2011, November). Prevalence and correlates of elder mistreatment in South Carolina: The South Carolina elder abuse mistreatment study. *Journal of Interpersonal Violence, 26*(15), 2947–2972. doi:101177/0886260510390959. http://jiv.sagepub.com

Bonnie, R., & Wallace, R. (Eds.). (2002). *Elder mistreatment: Abuse, neglect, and exploitation in an aging America.* New York, NY: National Academies Press.

Cornell, C. P., & Gelles, R. J. (1985). Elder abuse: The status of current knowledge. *Family Relations, 31*(3), 457–465.

Douglass, R. L. (July 1983). Domestic neglect and abuse of the elderly: Implications for research and service. *Family Relations, 32*(3), 395–402.

Godkin, M., Wolf, R., and Pillemer, K. (1989). A case-comparison analysis of elder abuse and neglect. *International Journal of Aging and Human Development, 28*(3), 207–225.

Kolberg, J. I. (2009). The abuse of older men: Implications of social work. *Australian Social Work, 62* (2), 202–215.

Kosberg, J., & Garcia, L. (Eds). (1995). *Elder abuse: International and cross-cultural perspectives.* London: Routledge.

Lachs, M., Williams, C., O'Brien, S., Pillemer, K., & Charleson, M. (1998). The mortality of elder mistreatment. *Journal of the American Medical Association*, 280, 428–432.

National Center on Elder Abuse. (1996). National Elder Abuse Incident Study. Retrieved from http://aoa.gov/AoARoot/AoA_Programs/Elder_Rights/Elder_Abuse/docs/ABuseReport_Full.pdf

National Center on Elder Abuse. (2005). Nursing home abuse risk prevention profile checklist. http://www.ncea.aoa.gov/Main_Site/pdf/publication/NursingHomeRisk.pdf

National Research Council. (2003). Elder mistreatment,: Abuse, neglect, and exploitation in an aging America. Retrieved January 27, 2013 from http://www.nap.edu/openbook.php?isbn=0309084342

Payne, B. (2008). Training adult protective services workers about domestic violence. *Violence Against Women, 14,* 1199–1213

Pillemer, K., & Finkelhor, D. (1988). The prevalence of elder abuse: A random sample. survey. *Gerontologist, 28*(1), 51–57.

Pillemer, K., & Moore, D. W. (June 1989). Abuse of patients in nursing homes: Findings from a survey of staff. *Gerontological Society of America, 29*(3), 314–320.

Teaster, P., Dugar. D., Tyler A., Mendiondo, M., Abner, E., & Cecil, K. (2006). The 2004 Survey of State Adult Protective Services: Abuse of Adults 60 Years of Age and Older. The National Committee for the Prevention of Elder Abuse and The National Adult Protective Services Association, prepared for The National Center on Elder Abuse by the Graduate Center for Gerontology, University of Kentucky.

Njoki Kinyatti

END VIOLENCE AGAINST WOMEN (EVAW) INTERNATIONAL

End Violence Against Women (EVAW) International is an organization that provides expertise, resources and tools, offering numerous opportunities for collaborative learning for professionals who work in or in conjunction with the criminal justice response system. EVAW International's goal is to pursue a vigorous prosecution of perpetrators while providing a secure environment for victims and the communities they live in.

EVAW International was established in January 2003 as a nonprofit organization dedicated to providing affordable training for all disciplines with an emphasis on the law enforcement investigation and proper criminal justice responses to sexual assault and domestic violence. It also supports and conducts research on the sexual assault of women and adolescents. Its executive director, Joanne Archambault, who is also the president and training director of Sexual Assault Training and Investigations Inc, worked for the San Diego Police Department and used her almost 23 years of experience to found EVAW International.

The vision of the organization is a world where gender-based violence is unacceptable, where perpetrators are held accountable for their actions, and victims of domestic abuse receive the compassion, support, and justice they deserve to continue living as respected members of society. According to the organization's website, EVAW International has a mandate to "inspire and educate those who respond to gender-based violence, equipping them with the knowledge and tools they need to support victims and hold perpetrators accountable." It also promotes "victim-centered, multidisciplinary collaboration, which strengthens the response of the criminal justice system, other professionals, allies, and the general public, thus making communities safer" (http://www.evawintl.org).

In line with this mandate, the activities of the organization include providing education, training, technical assistance, and expert consultation; formulating policies and disseminating best practices to guide reform efforts; developing and disseminating original training curricula and resource materials; conducting and disseminating original research to guide reform efforts; evaluating, compiling, and disseminating findings from the research literature; planning, executing, and evaluating public education efforts (e.g., media campaigns); developing, implementing, and evaluating programs for prevention or risk reduction; promoting multidisciplinary collaboration; and coordinating with other organizations in pursuit of their shared vision.

As part of its quest to train professionals to properly advocate in their various capacities against domestic violence, EVAW International organizes annual training conferences and on-line training. The On-Line Training Institute (OLTI) offers 12 training modules that are available to professionals working in the criminal justice and community response to sexual assault. As of December 31, 2010, reports indicate that a total of 1,400 people had registered for the OLTI. The organization's mission is international in scope and has pursued this, for instance, by offering registration in the OLTI free to individuals in developing countries who are engaged in the field of domestic abuse/violence. In 2010 alone, 25 foreign registrations were received from Canada, Ghana, Kenya, Mexico, Nigeria, Pakistan, Sierra Leone, Somalia, Taiwan, and the United Kingdom.

In 2009, EVAW International began hosting webinars as an affordable way to reach a large number of professionals involved in criminal justice and community response to violence against women. A key activity is the annual conference. The international conference adopts a multidimensional framework with the aim of promoting innovative techniques, unique approaches, and promising practices in responding to crimes of violence against women. It engages with a variety of domestic violence professionals, including law enforcement personnel, prosecutors, victim advocates, judges, parole and probation officers, rape crisis workers, medical personnel, faith community members, and educators.

The most recent initiative that EVAW International is undertaking is the Making a Difference (MAD) project. It has become apparent through research that the criminal justice systems in the United States and Canada (as in other countries) are less likely to prosecute incidents of sexual assault if they do not resemble the stereotype of what is typically considered to be "real rape." This means that if they do not involve a stranger with a weapon, severe physical violence, and victim injuries, the perpetrator can escape punishment. Additionally, sexual assault cases receive less attention and are less likely to be prosecuted if the victim has consumed drugs or alcohol or otherwise engaged in behaviors that are viewed as high risk. The MAD Project, therefore, aims to challenge the status quo by facilitating reform in the legal processes of both the United States and Canada in order to more effectively prosecute sexual offenders. The MAD Project also collaborates with The Voices and Faces Project (TVFP), a national documentary project created to tell the stories of survivors of sexual violence.

The notion of violence against women or domestic abuse has certainly taken on international scope with several works being done in many countries (see theoretical and empirical surveys in Edwards, 2011; Johnson et al., 2008). EVAW International is one of the organizations committed to broadening this scope and training professionals to offer the requisite services to victims.

See also: Nongovernmental Organizations (NGOs) and Domestic Abuse

Further Reading

Edwards, A. (2011). *Violence against women under international human rights law.* Cambridge, New York, NY: Cambridge University Press.

EVAW International. 2010 annual report. Retrieved from http://www.evawintl.org/images/uploads/AnnualReport2010.pdf

EVAW International. The Making a Difference (MAD) project. Retrieved from http://www.evawintl.org/mad.aspx

Johnson, H., Ollus, N., & Nevala, S. (2008). *Violence against women: An international perspective.* New York, NY: Springer Science+Business Media.

United Nations (2007). Ending violence against women: From words to action: Study of the Secretary-General. UN Publications (Division for the Advancement of Women).

Nathan Andrews

EQUALITY NOW

Equality Now (EN) is a nongovernmental organization (NGO) focusing on protecting the human rights of women globally. It is a grassroots organization whose goals are to spread awareness and put pressure on governments to protect women. EN addresses many issues pertaining to women's rights but focuses on four main issues: (1) discrimination in law, (2) sexual violence, (3) female genital mutilation, and (4) trafficking. Through the Women's Action Network (WAN), it relies on over 35,000 individuals who work on actions that aim to raise awareness on individual cases of severe violations. The organization also provides support by building partnerships and coalitions with local women's rights groups to strengthen local and global advocacy by capacity building and raising funds for these groups.

Legal Discrimination

Laws discriminate against women in different countries around the world. EN calls for the repeal of such laws and ask governments to come into accordance with international and regional human rights standards. Some actions that EN and their members are working on now regarding discrimination in law are repealing Saudi Arabia's fatwa on women driving automobiles and giving Lebanese women equal citizenship rights.

Sexual Violence

Sexual violence happens in every culture, religion, class, and race. EN feels that sexual violence is both a cause and a consequence of the inequalities that women experience. EN focuses on ensuring that systems are in place for proper investigations, prosecutions, and punishments of perpetrators. A major focus is on adolescent girls and post-traumatic stress disorder after an unwanted sexual experience. EN feels that adolescent girls should live a life free of violence in their schools, communities, and homes. EN created the Adolescent Girls' Legal Defense Fund in order to help young women in these cases. Another focus is on the glamorization and promotion of sexual violence against women in the media including negative stereotypes that objectify them. Some actions being worked on currently are banning rape simulator games in Japan and stopping the rape of schoolgirls by their teachers in Zambia.

Female Genital Mutilation (FGM)

FGM is internationally recognized as a violation of women's health, security, and physical integrity. EN supports the work of grassroots groups to end this practice and focuses on the enactment of effective implementation of legislation against the procedure. Some actions against FGM are directed at encouraging Mali to enact an anti-FGM law. In Liberia, EN is calling for justice in the case of Ruth Berry Peal, who was forced to have the procedure against her will. EN has a fund in which (non)members can donate money that goes to different anti-FGM organizations.

Trafficking

Millions of women and children are victims of trafficking. EN feels that addressing the demand for prostitution is the most effective way to end trafficking. Their strategy includes putting pressure on governments to criminalize traffickers and buyers of sex while decriminalizing and rehabilitating the survivors. They support local grassroots groups with funds in which (non)members can donate money. Some actions that EN has available are ending exploitation and abuse of girls in domestic servitude in Pakistan and calling on the government of India to hold commercial sex buyers accountable.

Women's Action Network (WAN)

WAN is made up of 35,000 individuals and organizations who receive updates on different campaigns and actions to advocate for the advancement of women's rights. Actions are sent to members via e-mail and are posted on the EN website. This e-mail, or website page, includes a letter addressing the appropriate person(s) or department(s) within a government or company directly related to the issue. This letter can be modified or you can send it as is via e-mail, regular mail, or fax, with all appropriate numbers provided within the action. Other actions include calling an appropriate person with a prewritten script to discuss an issue; hosting a community event that brings attention to various issues; and campaigns to get as many people as possible to engage in letter-writing campaigns and petitions. The website and the actions are issued in Arabic, English, French, and Spanish to reach a large number of people.

Also on the EN website are fact sheets and resources that (non)members can utilize to self-educate or teach others about. Fact sheets focus on different issues such as child marriages, FGM, and trafficking. Each fact sheet describes the issue (how, what, where, when), the effects, some statistics, and ways that individuals can help through actions. The resources that are available are EN-researched guides, reports, and videos that provide in-depth information on topics and ways to help. Such resources include "A Guide to Using the Protocol on the Rights of Women in Africa for Legal Action," "Africa Rising," a video documenting the grassroots movement to end FGM, and "A Quick Guide to Reporting Human Rights Violations to the United Nations and the African Commission."

Annual reports are conducted highlighting the work that EN and their members do regarding their four main focuses. The report shows the Actions that were conducted and what the possible impact was on in the designated country or issue. The report documents new laws that were enacted, statistics, descriptions of new grassroots partners, different member activist profiles, and shows the financial statement for the year.

Finally, EN has launched a 100 Steps to Equality campaign, which is a compilation of facts and actions that individuals can carry out to reach equality for women. EN believes these Actions and government follow-up can help women live in a "better world." EN lists a problem and then an action to address it.

See also: Female Genital Mutilation (FGM); Human Trafficking; Nongovernmental Organizations; Types of Domestic Abuse

Further Reading

Charity Navigator Report on Equality Now: http://www.charitynavigator.org/index.cfm?bay=search.summary&orgid=6023
Equality Now: http://www.equalitynow.org/
Equality Now 2009 annual report: http://www.equalitynow.org/sites/default/files/annualreport_2009.pdf

Brandon Fryman

EUROPE AND DOMESTIC ABUSE

The European Union defines violence against women as "any act of gender-based violence that results in, or is likely to result in, physical, sexual, or psychological harm or suffering to women, including threats of such acts, coercion, or arbitrary deprivation of liberty, whether occurring in public or in private life." Domestic violence is considered the most common form of violence against women in the EU.

Statistics

In Europe, domestic violence constitutes between 16 and 25 percent of all recorded violent crime. The Regional Committee for Europe noted that across the World Health Organization's European Region, between 20 and 50 percent of women reported in 2001 having been subjected to one or more forms of gender-based violence. The Council of Europe says 6–10 percent of European women experience domestic violence each year. An incident is reported to police every minute, and 45 percent of women and 26 percent of men reported at least one incident during their lifetime.

Between February and March 2012, 26,800 female European citizens were interviewed about domestic violence against women, at the request of the European commission's directorate general for justice, freedom, and security. Respondents were from all 27 EU states. Since the previous survey in 1999 (which only included 15 member states), 25 percent of respondents said they knew someone who was experiencing abuse, up from 19 percent. Seventy-eight percent of Europeans see domestic violence as a common problem. Eighty-four percent of Europeans said that domestic violence is unacceptable and should always be punishable by law. While most respondents were knowledgeable that there are laws to address domestic violence in the European Union, only 14 percent knew any of the specifics of this legislation.

The Astra Network has reported that 29 percent of Romanian women, 22 percent of Russian women, 21 percent of Ukrainian women, and 42 percent of all married and cohabiting women in Lithuania have experienced either the threat of or actual physical or sexual violence by their present partner. A national survey of 4,750 women between 15 and 44 in Moldova found over 7 percent had been physically assaulted by an intimate partner in the previous 12 months and over 14 percent had been assaulted at some time in a relationship. A 2011 report found that 4 out of 10 women in Turkey are beaten by their husbands, yet almost 90 percent do not seek help from any organization. Rates of abuse doubled between 2008 and 2011. Rates of abuse are shockingly high in Kyrgyzstan, where the Network Women's Program reported that 89 percent of a survey of 1,000 women had been abused by husbands, intimate partners, children, or relatives.

An estimated 635,000 incidents of domestic violence occurred in England and Wales in 2001–2002, according to the British Crime Survey (BCS), which constituted 22 percent of all violent crime reported on the survey. Most respondents (57 percent) reported more than one incident of violent abuse, Of those reporting abuse, 81 percent were women. In England and Wales in 2000–2001, 42 percent of all homicides against females were perpetrated by a current or former partner, with an average of two women killed by domestic violence weekly.

Other data shows that police in the United Kingdom receive a domestic violence report every minute. This totals more than 570,000 per year, although experts suggest that because many victims do not call police, those figures represent only 35 percent of the true scope of domestic violence offenses.

Responses

In March 2012, European leaders from across the EU met, the result of which was the Cadiz Declaration. The Cadiz Declaration noted the need for continued work on domestic violence and reiterated the commitment to enforcing the gender equality provisions of the Convention on the Elimination of All Forms of Discrimination against Women (CEDAW), which was signed more than 30 years prior.

A 2006 USAID report found that despite rates between 20 and 30 percent in the Balkans (Albania, Bosnia and Herzegovina, Croatia, Kosovo, Macedonia, Serbia, and Montenegro), services for victims were noticeably absent. The report noted that services in other regions, in particular Russia, Belarus, Moldova, and Ukraine, were run by international NGOs and thus often under threat of closure due to insufficient funds. Further, the report recommended increased training for law enforcement across the EU, as victims often found officers to be nonresponsive. Also recommended were educational programs in schools, efforts to train health-care providers to recognize the signs of abuse, community-based programs, and social change campaigns to change attitudes about abuse.

Some countries in the EU have been slow to adopt specific legislation to address abuse. In 2004, Turkey took its most publicized step of introducing mandatory life sentences for those who carry out honor killings, a long-awaited action thought to be an effort to combat a crime that had marred its quest to join the EU. Most recently, on January 13, 2009, a Turkish court sentenced five members of the same Kurdish family to life imprisonment for the "honor killing" of Naile Erdas, 16, who got pregnant as a result of rape. Turkey has also instituted a widespread advocacy campaign, initiated by Ankara and supported by UNFPA. One of the most influential elements of the campaign was the involvement of the country's major league soccer players who spread the message—"Stop violence against women"—during half-time shows and in film spots across the country (Turkey sees rise in violence against women, 2012).

In the United Kingdom, long-established domestic violence centers help victims of domestic violence. The Women's Aid Federation of England helps 250,000 victims and children each year through their support of 500 domestic violence services across the country. Women against Violence Europe (http://www.wave-network.org) has a list of other providers, as does the Hot Peach Pages (http://www.hotpeachpeages.net/europe).

See also: Convention on the Elimination of All Forms of Discrimination Against Women (CEDAW); The United Nations and Domestic Abuse; Women's Aid Federation of England

Further Reading

The Advocates for Human Rights. (2006, February 1). Prevalence of domestic violence. Retrieved March 17, 2012 from http://www.stopvaw.org/prevalence_of_domestic_violence.html

Eurobarometer. (2010). Domestic violence against women report. Retrieved March 17, 2012, from http://ec.europa.eu/public_opinion/archives/ebs/ebs_344_en.pdf

Fabian, K. (2010). *Domestic violence in post-communist states: Local activism, national policies, and global forces.* Bloomington, IN: Indiana University Press.

Liverpool Women and Children's Center. (2002). Domestic violence statistical fact sheet, 2002. Retrieved March 17, 2012, from http://www.centre56.org.uk/facts_dom_stats_ver2.htm

Turkey sees rise in violence against women. (2012, March 14). UPI.com. Retrieved March 16, 2012, from http://www.upi.com/Top_News/World-News/2012/03/14/Turkey-sees-rise-in-violence-against-women/UPI-62861331730213/

USAID. (2006, July). Domestic violence in Europe and Eurasia. Retrieved March 16, 2012, from http://pdf.usaid.gov/pdf_docs/PNADG302.pdf

Women's Aid Federation: http://www.womensaid.org.uk/

Women against Violence Europe: http://www.wave-network.org/

Laura L. Finley

F

FAILURE TO PROTECT

Parents and legal guardians who intentionally abuse their children physically, sexually, or emotionally can be held criminally responsible. However, their duty of care extends beyond their own deliberate actions. If a parent or legal guardian fails to prevent their child from being abused by another individual, they can be charged with an appropriate criminal offense (e.g. manslaughter or assault) because of "failure to protect" legislation. Therefore "failure to protect" is a crime of omission. Some states even consider it a parent's "failure to protect" when they do not protect his or her children from the mere witnessing of intimate partner violence. In all these situations, the state has a statutory right to remove children from their homes, a right that has been heavily criticized. As it is mainly women who are charged under "failure to protect" legislation, the evident gender disparity is considered discriminatory. Some also deem it discrimination against battered women when the offender maltreats the mother; and children are removed from their homes based solely on the fact that they have witnessed intimate partner violence. Furthermore, it is argued that a child's separation from its nonabusive mother adds to the child's trauma and worsens detrimental effects on the child's development and well-being.

A Brief History

Palmer v. State (1960) was the first "failure to protect" case in U.S. legal history. The Supreme Court of Ohio convicted a mother of involuntary manslaughter because she did not remove her 20-month-old baby from her abusive intimate partner. The court found that a parent is burdened with the duty to prevent child abuse by any other person. Following this, "failure to protect" has been codified in federal and many states' legislation.

The Child Abuse Prevention and Treatment Act (Public Law 93-247) defines child abuse and neglect as a parent's act or failure to act that results in death, serious physical or emotional harm, sexual abuse or exploitation, or an act or failure to act that presents an imminent risk of serious harm. As is common with federal legislation, this definition is intentionally broad to set a minimum standard for state laws.

States have integrated regulations into their family laws that are designed to help protect children from maltreatment and safeguard their physical, mental, and emotional well-being. They provide a due process of law for determining when the state, through its authorized child service agencies and courts, may intervene against the wishes of a parent so that a child's needs are met. State regulations permit the removal of children from parents who commit child abuse or neglect and the child's placement into foster care. Under many "failure to protect" laws, a parent can be held accountable and be charged with a criminal offense if he or she does not stop the other parent (or any other person) from abusing his or her child.

Gender Disparity

Intimate partner violence predominantly victimizes women. Many of them are mothers, and their children live with them in the same household. Research indicates that child abuse is closely linked to intimate partner violence. It is estimated that child abuse and intimate partner violence overlap in 30 to 60 percent of cases. Findings based on the 1985 National Family Violence Survey revealed that if the mother is physically abused by her intimate partner on a weekly basis, physical child abuse is almost certain.

Although "failure to protect" legislation is formulated as gender-neutral and was first and foremost intended to be used against male batterers, mothers can be held accountable for either not stopping their intimate partner from physically abusing their children, or subjecting their children to witnessing intimate partner violence. In fact, the overwhelming majority of defendants charged under "failure to protect" legislation are women.

This gender disparity is explained through a combination of social reality and gender stereotyping. Women are more likely to have sole custody of their children and are therefore more frequently exposed to situations where they may fail to protect them. Also, women face higher expectations regarding nurturing and child care and are therefore subject to heightened expectations regarding their duty to protect. The fact that in many cases women are battered by the child abuser as well is often not considered a mitigating factor, but rather an aggravating one by the courts. A characteristic assertion can be found in *Phelps v. State* (1983), where the child's mother was charged with "failure to protect." The court argued that the intimate partner violence she suffered should have alerted her to the likelihood of child abuse and her duty to protect. She was blamed for failing to leave her violent spouse and was expected to sacrifice her own safety for her child's protection. Such decisions entirely ignore relevant research on why women fail to leave abusive partners (e.g., economic dependence, exhaustion, and low self-esteem) and the significantly heightened risk of homicide when battered women attempt to leave an abusive relationship.

Gender disparity in court decisions is also associated with the social reality that most judges, attorneys, and caseworkers are white, male, and middle-class, and therefore have difficulty empathizing with women who have abusive partners.

Witnessing Domestic Violence as "Failure to Protect"

Witnessing intimate partner abuse includes seeing or hearing an actual event, or observing the consequences of its impact—for example, bruises, tears, or broken household items. It is estimated that over 15 million children, aged between 3 and 17, witness an incident of intimate partner violence every year. In nearly half of these cases the observed violence is severe.

Studies indicate that the mere act of witnessing intimate partner violence has detrimental short- and long-term effects on a child's physical, emotional, and mental well-being. Research suggests that children who have witnessed intimate partner abuse are more likely to model that violent behavior in their adolescence and adulthood. Boys are more likely to condone violence in relationships and are 4 times more likely to become abusers and 25 times more likely to become rapists than boys who grew up in a nonviolent household. Girls are over six times more likely to become victims of intimate partner violence or sexual abuse in adult relationships compared to girls who grew up in a nonviolent family. They are also more prone to teenage pregnancy. Further empirical evidence reveals that children from abusive backgrounds are four times more likely to become juvenile criminal offenders, and suffer a higher mental illness and suicide rate.

These research results have been predominantly criticized because of the overlap effect between intimate partner violence and child abuse, as they blur cause-effect relationships. Researchers are not able to determine with certainty whether children are only witnessing intimate partner violence or are exposed to multiple forms of maltreatment. If children are witnesses of intimate partner violence, but are also victims of physical child abuse, a causal link of how the former affects the child's development and causes harm cannot be accurately established. Short- and long-term effects described by researchers may stem from the physical abuse alone, or a combination of both forms of maltreatment. Therefore, some argue that until further research identifies a threshold that determines how much exposure to intimate partner violence causes children serious harm, any protective intervention should be based on more certain factors. Others argue that the link between intimate partner violence and physical child abuse is so strong that child protective interventions are mandatory.

Despite substantial criticism, research results of children witnessing intimate partner violence have impacted on statutory child maltreatment definitions and child protection policies and practices since the late 1990s. Some U.S. states have included in the definition of "failure to protect" a parent's failure to protect children from witnessing intimate partner violence and classified the mere act of witnessing such events as child maltreatment. One of these states was New York. Subsequent to these legislative changes, the New York City Administration for Children's Services removed a number of children from families based solely on the fact that intimate partner violence had occurred in their homes. Affected mothers took legal action resulting in the divisive class-action lawsuit *Nicholson v. Williams* (2000). The District Court held that the City "may not penalize a mother not otherwise unfit, who is battered by her partner, by separating her from her children; nor may children be separated from their mother, in effect visiting upon them the sins of their mother's batterer." Later, the Court of Appeals found in agreement with the District Court's decision that a child witnessing intimate partner violence is not sufficient evidence to conclude that the child had been neglected by the child's parent.

Some reject the decision, arguing that the courts were more concerned with the rights of the abused mothers than with the rights of the children who had witnessed intimate partner violence and have to bear the long-term effects of its impact. Others argue that the judgment was a step in the right direction because "failure to protect" laws discriminate against battered women, and the long-term effects of separating children from their mothers are even more detrimental to the children's well-being than the effects of witnessing intimate partner violence.

Effects on Children

If the mother has been charged with "failure to protect" after her intimate partner has physically abused the child, the state can remove the child from her home and place it into foster care. It has been argued that removing abused children and breaking the mother-child bond unduly adds to a child's traumatic experience. It causes children fear and anxiety and diminishes their sense of stability and self. It is probable that children view their removal as a punishment. As a consequence, children will often blame themselves for either causing the abuse or for failing to prevent or stop it.

Moreover, "failure to protect" legislation assumes that abused children will receive better care in foster families. However, empirical evidence suggests that children in foster care are more likely to experience emotional or physical abuse than when left in sole custody of their mother. Therefore the majority of researchers suggest that child custody should remain with the mother, and adequate support services should be provided that enable her to leave the abusive relationship safely.

Some also argue that "failure to protect" legislation is detrimental to child safety as it provides male domestic abusers with another tool to intimidate and control their female partners. He can scare her with losing the child if she speaks out about his domestic abuse. Courts, he could threaten, would remove the child from her because she has failed to protect them from experiencing abuse or from witnessing intimate partner violence.

Mothers, and especially battered mothers, are disproportionately affected by "failure to protect" regulations, and current legislation is said to add insult to injury as it reinforces negative gender stereotypes. The criminalization of a parent's "failure to protect" is also considered detrimental to child safety as a mother's fear to be prosecuted for "failure to protect" is likely to reduce her readiness to report child or partner abuse, seek medical care in case of injury, or pursue other avenues to end the abuse.

See also: Child Abuse; Children, Impact of Domestic Abuse on; Courts and Domestic Abuse

Further Reading

Child Abuse Prevention and Treatment Act: http://www.acf.hhs.gov/programs/cb/laws_policies/cblaws/capta/

Fugate, J. (2001). Who's failing whom? A critical look at failure-to-protect laws. *New York University Law Review*, 76, 272–308.

Futures Without Violence: http://www.futureswithoutviolence.org/userfiles/file/Children_and_Families/Children.pdf

Kantor, G., & Little, L. (2003). Defining the boundaries of child neglect: When does domestic violence equate with parental failure to protect? *Journal of Interpersonal Violence* 18, 338–354.

Magen, R. (1999). In the best interests of battered women: Reconceptualizing allegations of failure to protect. *Child Maltreatment, 4,* 127–392.

Nicholson v. Williams: http://www.youthlaw.org/publications/fc_docket/alpha/nicholsonvwilliams/

Nowling, M. (2003). Protecting children who witness domestic violence: Is *Nicholson v. Williams* an adequate response? *Family Court Review, 41*(4), 517–526.

Ross, S. (1996). Risk of physical abuse to children of spouse abusing parents. *Child Abuse & Neglect, 20*(7), 589–598.

White, H. (2003). Refusing to blame the victim for the aftermath of domestic violence: *Nicholson v Williams* is a step in the right direction. *Family Court Review, 41*(4), 527–532.

Antje Deckert

FAMILY STRUCTURE AND DOMESTIC ABUSE

Family structure can certainly precipitate domestic violence or abuse. Family structure does not only refer to the size of a family but also to birth order and even socioeconomic status, ethnic background, and other factors. A family structure could be either nuclear or extended. A nuclear family structure is made up of parents and their immediate children, and extended family structure includes the parents, children and relatives.

The Heritage Foundation (2012) in *Family and Adolescent Well-Being* enumerates various ways that family structure could affect well-being and even precipitate violence. Family structure could impart emotional health problems, cause anti-social behavior, cause emotional distress, and result in juvenile delinquency, high-risk behavior, psychological disorder, and poor performance at school. Persons who grow up in abusive homes are more likely to later engage in abusive behavior or to be victimized in abusive relationships.

Family structure could precipitate domestic violence on the basis that the financial and economic pressures of taking care of members of the family could become so enormous that family members become agitated. In a family with a large number of children, there may be more conflicts, disagreements, and squabbling over scarce resources. This type of conflict is normal, but might lead to abuse in extreme cases (McCloskey & Eisler, 1999). Caring for elders living in the home is also stressful, and in some cases family members are abusive to those in their care.

In societies where patriarchy is still predominant, men are more likely to abuse women and children. A 2012 poll of G20 countries conducted by TrustLaw, a legal news service run by Thomson Reuters, shows that women fare the worst in the countries that are most patriarchal. At the bottom of the list were Saudi Arabia, India, Indonesia, Mexico, and South Africa (Baldwin, 2012).

In some cultures, arranged marriage is common. Families select spouses for their children, and, typically, the children give their consent. In other cases, forced marriage occurs. In forced marriages, the children do not consent but are made to marry the person their family chose. Activists say forced marriage is itself a form of abuse that occurs in the developing world but also in Western nations like the United

States and Great Britain. Domestic violence is more common among forced marriages, but there is no clear data on whether it occurs more frequently in arranged marriages (Goldberg, 2011). In cultures in which dowry is exchanged, family members have a vested interest in the success of the marriage. In some cases in which the groom's family believes the dowry to have been inadequate, family members abuse or even murder the new bride. Some do so by throwing acid at her, disfiguring her at best and perhaps killing her.

Family structure does not have to precipitate domestic violence or abuse. It could be avoided. This is where the role of education comes in. The basic rights of members of the family need to be made known to all family members. Family members, especially parents, should seek psychological counseling if they need assistance managing the pressures of family life.

See also: Family Violence, Risk Factors for; Feminism and Domestic Abuse; Patriarchy and Domestic Abuse

Further Reading

Baldwin, K. (2012, June 13). Canada best G20 country to be a woman, India worst. *Trustlaw*. Retrieved August 17, 2012, from http://www.trust.org/trustlaw/news/poll-canada-best-g20-country-to-be-a-woman-india-worst/

Goldberg, M. (2011, September 18). Marry—or else. *The Daily Beast*. Retrieved August 17, 2012, from http://www.thedailybeast.com/newsweek/2011/09/18/forced-marriage-and-honor-killings-happen-in-britain-u-s-too.html

The Heritage Foundation. (2012). *Family and adolescent well-being*. Accessed on January 10, 2012, from http://www.familyfacts.org/briefs/34/family-and-adolesent-well-being.

McCloskey, L. A., & Eisler, R. (1999). Family structure and family violence. In *Encyclopedia of Violence, Peace, and Conflict*. Retrieved January 10, 2012, from http://www.rianeeisler.com/documents/excerptsFAMILYSTRUCTUREANDFAMILYVIOLENCEANDNONVIOLCE.pdf

Mark Ikeke

FAMILY VIOLENCE, RISK FACTORS FOR

Family violence can take many forms including intimate partner violence (i.e., dating violence, domestic violence, and/or spousal violence), parent-to-child violence (i.e., child maltreatment), sibling violence, and elder violence. It also consists of various types of behaviors, such as physical (e.g., slapping, punching, beating, biting, kicking, shoving, strangling, suffocating, hitting with object, etc.), psychological (e.g., threats, verbal violence, manipulation, etc.), and sexual (e.g., rape, inappropriate touching of genitals, etc.) violence, exposure, and neglect (e.g., nutritional, educational, financial, etc.). A myriad of research has indicated that forms and types of family violence tend to co-occur; accordingly, many overlapping risk factors exist and have been identified. These factors have been recognized as predisposing one to aggression and contributing to the risk of violence within family units. This entry will examine those micro-, intermediate, and macro-level predictors of family violence. Intimate partner violence will be examined first, followed by a discussion of parent-to-child violence, sibling violence, and elder violence.

Macro-Level Predictors of Family Violence

Intimate partner violence is by far one of the most researched forms of family violence. At the macro level, the problem is viewed as a gendered issue. Patriarchal values, gender inequality, and men's sense of entitlement and power have been recognized as causes of intimate partner violence. According to the feminist view, the characteristics of perpetrators, victims, and interactions among perpetrators and victims are all influenced by gender and power. Nearly all cultures socialize males and females into specific gender roles based on ideologies. Males are taught to be aggressive, independent risk takers and tend to hold higher status in society. Conversely, females are taught to be passive and reserved and are considered to be of lesser value. This socialization has been seen as responsible for contributing to violence, particularly when the gender-role expectations are violated. For example, a man who is threatened by the abandonment of an intimate partner or even the loss of a job may seek to restore his status and redress the loss of power through the use of violence. Likewise, a female who speaks her mind and partakes in chancy behaviors may experience victimization as a result of being "un-ladylike" and failing to adhere to certain standards.

The superior status and value of males is evident across the world, not only reflected by violence against women who do not live up to expectations, but also evident by lethality in honor killings, bride burnings, and infanticide of newborn girls. Additionally, restrictions of female sexual behavior with practices like female genital mutilation reflect cultural beliefs about female behavior. Those who violate the double standard may be killed, victimized, or banished from the community. Cultural norms have also supported the use of violence against children in that parental rights are considered to supersede the rights of children. Thus, it is often considered normal and acceptable, for instance, for parents to discipline or punish children through the use of violence. A society tolerant of violence promotes the use of violence, and it is known that violence increases in frequency and severity over time.

Sibling violence has been noted as one of the most common yet overlooked forms of family violence commonly considered normal child's play. Societal norms tend to reflect that sibling violence is a natural phenomenon without any long-lasting consequences, although emerging research has indicated otherwise. Like sibling violence, elder violence is also a hidden form of family violence. Many times, victims of elder violence do not want to come forward because of embarrassment or fear, especially if they are dependent on their sons or daughters to take care of them. Once again, cultural values tend to play a role here in that adults are thought to be able to take care of themselves and have reign over their children.

Intermediate-Level Predictors

Family violence can be better understood when looking at the context of relationships. Relationships where violence occurs tend to have moderate to high levels of negative interactions and conflict. They are also characterized by aggression. Numerous factors at the family level relate to the use of violence. For instance, violence in the family of origin, whether experienced or witnessed, has been associated with later intimate partner violence perpetration, signifying that violence may provide a model in which individuals learn behavior and pass it on, as posited by social learning theory.

A copious amount of research has shown that those who batter their partners and/or children have witnessed violence between their parents while growing up or were abused themselves. This reflects that childhood family violence victimization increases the risk for family violence perpetration. Additionally, the mere presence of intimate partner violence in a home increases the risk for parent-to-child violence in that home as a result of opportunity and possible intervention. Many studies have found that children are disproportionately present in homes where violence between partners exists, which heightens the chance that they will experience, attempt to intervene in, or be exposed to violence.

Further, families that are characterized by intimate partner violence often have less capable parenting skills, which can contribute to abuse and neglect. Perpetrators of intimate partner violence are more likely to engage in violence against a child when compared to those who do not engage in such behavior, and victims have also been found to have an increased risk of doing so, which can be attributed to the stress experienced as a result of their victimization. Taken together, findings reveal a strong relationship between domestic violence and child abuse, regardless of whether the perpetrator of child abuse is the perpetrator or victim of intimate partner violence.

In addition, research on sibling violence has implied that it commonly takes place within a broader context of family violence and disorganization. Here, the children learn to behave from the actions they see others engage in. Thus, sibling aggression might imitate other forms of violence, like intimate partner violence and parent-to-child violence, which occur around children in a family.

Just as experiencing or witnessing violence early in life relates to an increased risk of violence perpetration, there has been increased recognition that it also leads to victimization. The intergenerational transmission of violence referred to as the "cycle of violence" states that a history of family violence victimization is associated with increased likelihood of becoming an abuser, or even victim, in adulthood. While some individuals may go on to offend, others may be revictimized.

Other correlates of family violence also exist at the intermediate level and include but are not limited to family size, family type, and family location. Specifically, having children increases marital conflict and violence, largely due to the dependency of the child on parents. Also, taking care of an elder parent increases the risk of violence attributable to the strain placed on caretakers to provide for another person, often accompanied by a change in lifestyle. Additionally, the more people there are present in the home, the greater the risk that violence will occur, especially when there are members not related by blood. For instance, single-parent homes and those with stepparents have been said to have higher rates of child abuse than homes with both biological parents living together with the child. Last, living in a transient neighborhood increases the risk of family violence, potentially due to lack of social support available in the community.

Micro-Level Predictors

Family violence varies among individual characteristics including sex, race/ethnicity, income, education, age, and marital status. While no group is immune from experiencing it, there have been some characteristics identified as increasing the risk. Males have been noted to perpetrate intimate partner violence, while females are more likely to fall victim. Males have also been noted to engage in more sibling violence. However, evidence regarding the parent-to-child violence and even elder violence is mixed, but in the latter, females are more likely to be victims.

Additionally, Asian/Pacific Islanders have been noted to have lower rates of family violence than do African Americans and American Indians/Alaska Natives. Also, those with low income and less education have higher rates of violence than their counterparts. Younger individuals have also been found to have higher rates of intimate partner violence, parent-to-child violence, and sibling violence in comparison to those older. Last, those who are separated or single experience more violence than those who are married, and those with children in the home experience higher rates of family violence.

Psychological characteristics and psychiatric disturbances have also been identified as correlates of family violence. For instance, stress, antisocial behavior, depression, learning disabilities, personality disorders, attachment issues, and substance dependency heighten the risk of family violence. These disturbances may inhibit the ability to form clear and healthy conflict-resolution strategies.

Putting It All Together

Family violence is a complex phenomenon involving numerous relationships and behaviors. While much research has been done on intimate partner violence and parent-to-child violence, less has been conducted on sibling violence and elder abuse, although research is emerging. The evidence that is present suggests there are many commonalities among the individual forms and types, insinuating that such violence may be part of a more complex family system rooted in cultural norms and shaped by individual characteristics. Macro-, intermediate-, and micro-level predictors of family violence have been identified and must be studied when determining factors that increase the risk of these negative behaviors.

See also: Children, Impact of Domestic Abuse on; Cycle of Violence; Family Structure and Domestic Abuse; Feminism and Domestic Abuse; Patriarchy and Domestic Abuse

Further Reading

Barnett, O., Miller-Perrin, C., & Perrin, R. (2011). *Family violence across the lifespan: An introduction* (3rd ed.). Thousand Oaks, CA: Sage.

Hines, D., & Malley-Morrison, K. (2005). *Family violence in the United States: Defining, understanding, and combating abuse*. Thousand Oaks, CA: Sage.

Morash, M. (2006). *Understanding gender, crime, and justice*. Thousand Oaks, CA: Sage.

Riggs, D., Caulfield, M., & Street, A. (2000). Risk for domestic violence: Factors associated with perpetration and victimization. *Journal of Clinical Psychology, 58*(10), 12.

Straus, M., Gelles, R., & Steinmetz, S. (2009). *Behind closed doors: Violence in the American family*. New Brunswick, NJ: Transaction.

Alison Marganski

FEMALE GENITAL MUTILATION (FGM)

It is tradition in many countries that women endure cutting of their genitals. In Somalia, female genital mutilation (FGM) is commonly done to girls at eight years of age, with the goal of reducing their sexual desire so that they are perceived to be more marriageable. In winter 1999, an African woman in France was sentenced to eight years in prison for the genital mutilation of 48 girls, ages one month to 10 years. In 2010, it was estimated that between 500 and 2,000 schoolgirls in Britain (primarily girls whose families are originally from non-British cultures) endured genital cutting (McVeigh & Sutton, 2010). Some would be taken abroad; others would be "cut" or circumcised and sewn closed in the United Kingdom by women already living here or who are flown in and brought to "cutting parties" for a few girls at a time in a cost-saving exercise. An estimated 66,000 girls have been illegally mutilated in the United Kingdom, but no one has yet been prosecuted for this practice. Until the 1950s, FGM was used in England and the United States as a "treatment" for lesbianism, masturbation, hysteria, epilepsy, and other so-called deviance (McVeigh & Sutton, 2010).

FGM is a term that describes all procedures that involve partial or total removal of the external female genitalia, or other injury to the female genital organs for non-medical reasons. Typically these procedures are conducted on young girls, sometime between infancy and age 15, although occasionally on adult women. Before the girl reaches puberty is recommended, but sometimes it is done just before marriage or during a woman's first pregnancy. In Egypt, about 90 percent of girls endure FGM between the ages of 5 and 14. In Yemen, more than 75 percent of girls are cut before they are two weeks old. A frightening trend is that the average age at which a girl undergoes FGM is decreasing in some countries (Burkina Faso, Côte d'Ivoire, Egypt, Kenya, and Mali). This may be so that it can be more easily hidden from authorities in countries where there may be laws against it, or because younger girls are less able to resist. Reports have shown that in Chad, girls have begun to seek FGM without pressure from their immediate family, believing this will prove they are clean and virginal. Those girls who are not cut are often labeled dirty or assumed to have had intercourse.

Typically the procedure is carried out by a traditional circumciser, someone who is well respected in the community and is involved in other traditions like attending childbirths. The trend of using health-care providers to perform FGM is increasing,

Masai and Kipsigis girls in Kenya participate in a run to eliminate Female Genital Mutilation. (AP Photo/Sayyid Azim)

however, and currently some 18 percent of all FGM is performed by those with some degree of medical training.

FGM is generally practiced in cultures in the Middle East, some parts of Southern Asia, and Africa, although immigrants from those regions have brought the practice elsewhere. According to the World Health Organization, about 140 million girls and women worldwide are living with the consequences of FGM, which has been documented in 28 African countries. The prevalence rate ranges from 98 percent of girls in Somalia to 5 percent in Zaire. Almost one-half of women who have experienced FGC live in Egypt or Ethiopia. It also takes place among ethnic groups in the Middle East, India, Pakistan, Malaysia, Indonesia, Australia, Canada, the United States, and New Zealand. In Africa alone, about 92 million girls age 10 and above are estimated to have undergone FGM, and about 3 million girls are at risk for FGM annually ("Female Genital Mutilation," 2012).

There are four major types of FGM.

- Clitoridectomy: partial or total removal of the clitoris or in very rare cases, only the prepuce (the fold of skin surrounding the clitoris).
- Excision: partial or total removal of the clitoris and the labia minora. This can occur with or without excision of the labia majora.
- Infibulation: Creation of a covering seal, made by cutting and refitting the inner or outer labia, to narrow the vaginal opening.

- Other: all other harmful procedures to the female genitalia for nonmedical purposes, such as painful and coerced pricking, piercing, incising, scraping, and cauterizing the genital area.

There are no known health benefits of FGM. Rather, the practice is harmful to women and girls. In the short term, FGM typically results in severe pain, hemorrhaging, tetanus or other bacterial infections, open sores in the genital region, urine retention, and shock.

As noted by the World Health Organization ("Female Genital Mutilation," 2012), long-term consequences can include recurrent bladder and urinary tract infections; cysts; infertility; an increased risk of childbirth complications and newborn deaths; the need for later surgeries. Infibulation, for example, must be cut open later in order for the woman to have sexual intercourse and to give birth. Many women endure the procedure repeatedly, leading to an increase in health risks.

A mix of cultural and social factors within families and communities cause FGM. There is tremendous pressure to conform in communities in which FGM is a tradition. Families believe it is part of the proper raising of a girl and see it as a way to transition her for adulthood and marriage. They fear being labeled bad parents if they do not have their daughters cut. Misconceptions about sexual behavior are also a factor. Some cultures believe FGM will reduce a woman's libido, thereby controlling her sexuality. The pain involved in opening a covered vaginal region is also said to deter women from engaging in illicit sexual behavior. Additionally, some cultures associate female genitalia as "unclean" and even "masculine" and therefore believe that removal of those parts helps purify and beautify a woman. Although no religious scripts endorse FGM, many mistakenly believe that religion supports it, and some religious leaders have been vocal supporters (just as others have been opponents).

Among the human rights world, FGM is recognized internationally as a major violation of the human rights of girls and women. Advocates maintain that it reflects deep-rooted inequality between the sexes. It violates women's right to health, safety, and not to be tortured. The practice, then, violates numerous international human rights treaties and agreements, including the Universal Declaration of Human Rights; the International Covenant on Civil and Political Rights (ICCPR); the International Covenant on Social, Cultural and Economic Rights (ICESCR); the Convention against Torture (CAT); the Convention on the Elimination of All Forms of Discrimination against Women (CEDAW); and more. Given that it is almost always carried out on minors, it can also be seen as a violation of the rights of children.

Much effort has been made since the later 1990s to end FGM. Currently, 22 African counties prohibit the practice, as do several states in 2 other countries and 12 industrialized countries with large migrant populations from countries that practice FGM. Research supports that these efforts have been effective, as the prevalence of FGM seems to be decreasing, and an increasing number of men and women no longer support it. For instance, a survey in Kenya found a fourfold drop in FGM rates among girls who had secondary education.

The World Health Organization (WHO) has been active in working to end FGM. In 1997, WHO issued a joint statement with the United Nations Children's Fund (UNICEF) and the United Nations Population Fund (UNFPA) opposing FGM. In February 2008, WHO issued another statement, this one with even greater support from the United Nations. The 2008 statement documented the evidence collected over the previous decade about the scope and frequency of FGM and highlighted the increased recognition of the human rights and legal dimensions of the problem. The report also detailed the causes of FGM, why it continues, its impact, and recommendations on how to stop it.

Currently, WHO efforts stress continued advocacy in the form of developing tools and publications for local, regional, and international activists' use in ending FGM, coordinating continued research about the causes and consequences as well as effective practices in ending it and responding to victims, and providing guidance to health-care professionals. WHO is particularly concerned about the increasing trend for medically trained personnel to perform FGM. WHO strongly urges health professionals not to perform such procedures. WHO is working on providing training materials and guidelines for professionals who work with FGM victims. In 2010, WHO published a "Global Strategy to Stop Health Care Providers from Performing Female Genital Mutilation" in collaboration with other key UN agencies and international organizations.

Many countries have outlawed the practice. Federal law in the United States prohibits FGM in anyone younger than 18, deeming it a felony that is punishable by fines or a prison term of up to five years. Australia, Belgium, Canada, Denmark, New Zealand, Norway, Spain, Sweden, and the United Kingdom also prohibit FGM. In Africa, Benin, Burkina Faso, Central African Republic, Chad, Cote d'Ivoire, Djibouti, Egypt (Ministerial decree), Ghana, Guinea, Kenya, Niger, Nigeria (multiple states), Senegal, Tanzania, and Togo, FGM is now prohibited. In Sudan, only the most severe form of FGM is forbidden by law.

The International Violence Against Women Act (IVAWA) would authorize funds to assist countries in eliminating female genital mutilation (FGM). In September 2001, the European Parliament adopted a resolution on FGM. It calls on the member states of the European Union to pursue and punish any resident who has committed the crime of FGM, even if committed outside the frontier ("extraterritoriality"). It further calls for the issuing of residence permits and protection for victims. The resolution also calls on the member states to recognize the right to asylum of women and girls at risk of being subject to FGM.

Amazing advocates have sponsored global grassroots campaigns that help raise awareness about FGM. Jane Roberts, a retired teacher in California, was so outraged that the Bush administration limited funds to UNFPA that she, and many others, called on the public to inspire wide-scale grassroots efforts to support UNFPA and its efforts to reduce FGM.

See also: Asia and Domestic Abuse; Convention on the Elimination of All Forms of Discrimination Against Women (CEDAW); International Violence Against Women

Act (I-VAWA); The Middle East and Domestic Abuse; World Health Organization (WHO)

Further Reading

Courtney, S. (2012, May 30). The horror of female genital mutilation. Al Jazeera. Retrieved June 5, 2012, from http://www.aljazeera.com/indepth/opinion/2012/05/2012528102139893735.html

The Female Genital Cutting Education and Networking Project: http://www.fgmnetwork.org/index.php

Female genital cutting fact sheet. (n.d.). Womenshealth.gov. Retrieved June 5, 2012 from http://www.womenshealth.gov/publications/our-publications/fact-sheet/female-genital-cutting.cfm

Female genital mutilation. (2012, February). World Health Organization. Retrieved June 5, 2012, from http://www.who.int/mediacentre/factsheets/fs241/en/

McVeigh, T., & Sutton, T. (2010, July 24). British girls undergo horror of genital mutilation despite tough laws. *The Guardian*. Retrieved June 5, 2012, from http://www.guardian.co.uk/society/2010/jul/25/female-circumcision-children-british-law

Laura L. Finley

FEMALE PERPETRATORS

It is often assumed that domestic violence is perpetuated almost exclusively by men toward women in an effort to control or dominate them, and that women arrested as batterers simply respond in self-defense to provocation from a male partner. Some researchers disagree, however. According to Hamel (2009) most domestic violence is mutual, with men and women emotionally abusing and controlling one another at approximately equal rates. He postulates that, "domestic violence is a human and relational problem, not a gender problem."

Background

Female-male domestic abuse can occur in many forms—physical, emotional, and psychological. In addition to the well-known types of abuse perpetrated by men and women in intimate relationships, female-male abuse can also include types of terror not usually perpetuated by men toward women. For example, men are often subjected to emotional terror such as being falsely accused of domestic abuse themselves, especially in divorce and custody cases. Another form of abuse, not often considered "traditional domestic abuse," is paternity fraud, in which a man is falsely accused of being a child's biological father.

Virtually nothing has been done to encourage men to report domestic abuse. The patriarchal view of society suggests the idea that men could be victims of domestic abuse and violence is so unthinkable that many will not even attempt to report the situation. It is often assumed that a man with a bruise was injured by another man or while playing sports. Underreporting of female-male domestic abuse is a huge issue due to societal stereotyping as well as the lack of investment in education, outreach, assessment, and treatment resources to address and understand the issues of domestic abuse and violence against men. Further, men and women experience victimization in very different ways.

First, when men do report domestic abuse and violence, most people are doubtful, suspicious, or downright shocked, leaving men feeling like nobody believes them and questioning their choice to report. Such negative and incredulous responses to the report often further injure the victim emotionally and psychologically. Men are often more susceptible to emotional and psychological abuse than physical abuse. In some cases, humiliating a man emotionally in front of other men can be more devastating than physical abuse. For example, for some men, being called a coward, impotent, or a failure can have a significantly negative psychological impact. Another impediment to accurate and timely reporting of female-male abuse is that at times, men incorrectly interpret the ability to tolerate and "brush off" a physical assault by a woman in front of other men as a sign that he is strong.

According to AARDVARC (An Abuse, Rape, and Domestic Violence Aid and Resource Collection), "Not considering a victim as a victim because of the gender of the abuser is the ultimate in victimization. Domestic violence, and the control, jealousy, emotional abuse, threats, and dangers associated with it cannot be predicted by gender, race, age, size, or other factors. A person 5 feet tall and 100 pounds soaking wet can still be an abuser."

Prevalence

As far back as 1974, Gelles reported that domestic violence occurs as frequently among both husbands and wives. Prevalence statistics are questionable due to underreporting. Underreporting is often due to men not wanting to suffer the stigma due to loss of "machismo"; men are often not believed by police or domestic violence crisis workers; misinterpretation of questions asked during phone surveys—not clearly identifying or defining issues as domestic abuse; as well as downright denial. In Hines and Malley-Morrison's (2001) description of the psychological effects of partner abuse against men, they describe data on the prevalence of violence directed at husbands by wives and the many different methodological issues surrounding existing data. Another study (Carrado, George, Lozam, Jones, & Templar, 1996) examining motives for domestic violence revealed that men and women assault their partners at the same rates and for the same reasons, most often "to get through to them," while self-defense was one of the least common motives.

Victim Characteristics

In a 2008 study of 302 men recruited via a domestic abuse helpline for men and women (Hines & Douglas, 2008), individuals seeking help were primarily white (87 percent), involved in a marriage (48 percent) or separated (18 percent), and employed full-time (69 percent). On average, the men were 41 years of age, well educated, professionally employed making $52,000 per year. All men reported minor psychological abuse during the past year, with an average incidence of 62.1 times. The next highest rates of physical, emotional, and psychological abuse included minor physical abuse (98.7 percent reporting; 31.6 times per year); severe psychological abuse (96.0 percent reporting; 27.8 times per year); controlling behaviors (93.4 percent reporting; 39.8 times per year); and severe physical abuse (90.4 percent reporting; 15.1 times per year). Minor injuries, very serious physical abuse, and insisting on sex were reported less, at a rate of 77.5 percent, 54.0 percent, and 41.1 percent respectively. After becoming involved in their relationships, these men reported developing depressive disorders (65 percent) and anxiety disorders (48 percent). Similar to women who have been abused, the 189 men who stayed in their abusive relationships reported staying due to concern for their children (89 percent); got married for life (80.5 percent); got married for love (71.3 percent); fear of not seeing children again (67.5 percent); thinks she will change (55.6 percent); not enough money (52.8 percent); nowhere to go (52.2 percent); embarrassed (52.2 percent); not wanting to take children from abuser (46.0 percent); abuser threatened to kill herself (27.5 percent); and fear abuser will kill him/someone he loves (24.2 percent).

In a 2012 review of the literature on domestic violence, Hoff reported that contrary to popular belief, more men than women are victims of intimate partner violence. Citing the National Intimate Partner and Sexual Violence Survey, released in December 2011, Hoff reported that within the last 12 months an estimated 5,365,000 men and 4,741,000 women were victims of intimate partner physical violence.

Abuser Characteristics

Some people attempt to downplay female violence by saying it is usually self-defense and that the prevailing research is not contextual enough. This is not supported by multiple studies and has been refuted many times (Archer, 2002; Straus, 2006).

In a 2002 *Equal Justice Foundation Newsletter*, Corry summarized a 2000 Report on Family Violence supporting the tenet that women are as violent as men. He stated that:

1. Women are three times more likely than men to use weapons in spousal violence.
2. Women *initiate* most incidents of spousal violence.
3. Women *commit* most child abuse and most elder abuse.
4. Women *hit* their male children more frequently and more severely than they hit their female children.
5. Women *commit* most child murders and 64 percent of their victims are male children.
6. When women murder adults, the majority of their victims are *men*.
7. Women *commit* 52 percent of spousal killings and are convicted of 41 percent of spousal murders.
8. Eighty-two percent of the general population had their first experience of violence at the hands of women.

See also: Male Victims of Domestic Abuse; Types of Domestic Abuse; Self-Defense, Homicides, and Domestic Abuse

Further Reading

Archer, J. (2002). Sex differences in physically aggressive acts between heterosexual partners: A meta-analytical review. *Aggression and Violent Behavior, 7*, 313–351.

Carrado, M., George, M. J., Lozam, E., Jones, L., & Templar, D. (1996). Aggression in British heterosexual relationships: A descriptive analysis. *Aggressive Behavior, 22*(6), 401–415.

Corry, C. (2002). Domestic violence against men. *Equal Justice Foundation Newsletter.* Retrieved from http://www.dvmen.org/dv-136.htm#pgfId-998197

Domestic Violence Works Both Ways: http://www.aardvarc.org/dv/malevictims.shtml

Gelles, R. (1974). *The violent home: A study of physical aggression between husbands and wives.* Beverly Hills, CA: Sage.

Hamel, J. (2009). Toward a gender-inclusive conception of intimate partner violence research and theory: Part 2—new directions. *International Journal of Men's Health, 8*(1), 41–59.

Hines, D., & Douglas, E. (2008). The Men's Experiences with Partner Aggression Project. Fact Sheet. Retrieved from http://wordpress.clarku.edu/dhines/files/2012/01/Men_closer_look_IT_factsheet_final.pdf

Hines, D. A., & Malley-Morrison, K. (2001). Psychological effects of partner abuse against men: A neglected research area. *Psychology of Men & Masculinity, 2*(2), 75–85.

Hoff, B. (2012). National study: More men than women victims of intimate partner physical violence, psychological aggression. Over 40% of victims of severe physical violence are men. *MenWeb On-line Journal.* Retrieved from http://www.batteredmen.com/NISVS.htm

Straus, M. (2006). Future research on gender symmetry in physical assaults on partners. *Violence Against Women, 12*(11), 1086–1097.

Stephanie A. Kolakowsky-Hayner and Kimberly Bellon

FEMINISM AND DOMESTIC ABUSE

The idea of a feminist or women's movement spread from Europe to North and South America in the late 1800s and early 1900s. Freedman (2002) defines feminism as "a belief that women and men are inherently of equal worth" (p. 7), while sociologist Michael Kimmel (2008) explains feminism more boldly, proclaiming that it "dares to imagine that women can be whole people, embracing and expressing ambition and kindness, competence and compassion. And feminism dares to expect more from men. Feminism expects a man to be ethical, emotionally present, and accountable to his values in his actions with women—as well as with other men" (p. 264). Although there are multiple types of feminists, most are critical of patriarchal societies.

In the United States, there have been three periods, or waves, of feminist activism. The first occurred roughly between the mid-1800s and the mid-1950s. Feminists of the first wave were most concerned with gaining suffrage, although many were active in the temperance movement and on other issues as well. Although domestic violence was not one of their main points of focus at this time, some first-wave activists did address the issue, often linking it to men's drinking and thus connecting domestic violence to the temperance movement and trying to prevent domestic abuse by curtailing access to alcoholic drinks. The second wave is what is widely referred to as the women's rights movement, which occurred between the mid-1950s and the later 1970s. Feminists in this era were responsible for initiating the domestic violence or battered women's movement. The third wave, which started in the 1980s, continues today. Many people today reject the label of feminist, however.

Feminists played an integral role in initiating the domestic violence movement in the 1970s. Concerned about inadequate legal attention to the abuse many women endured in their homes, feminists pushed for new laws criminalizing abuse, police protection, and holding abusers accountable via the courts. Additionally, feminists helped create the first shelters for victims of domestic abuse. Two main factions of feminists existed in the 1970s. Liberal feminists typically focused on legislation and the courts as a means of change. Radical feminists, on the other hand, argued that simply adding or revising laws would never be enough, and advocated more radical societal change that would destroy the patriarchal system. These feminists argued that abuse was a result of patriarchy. They maintained that men abused women because of rigid gender roles that teach men to control women or be viewed as too feminine. Many feminists still adhere to this belief, asserting that women are taught to be submissive and to see men's abuse as normal. Another category of feminists, known as socialist or Marxist feminists, see capitalism as the root cause of gender inequalities, asserting that the hierarchical economic system shapes gender roles in such a way that men are seen as the breadwinners and women are dependent on them for their literal survival. They advocate for replacing capitalism with a more egalitarian economic system.

Third-wave feminists are a more diverse group than previous iterations, which were critiqued for failing to include, or at least inadequately include, women of color, women from lower socioeconomic statuses, and men. Today there are many males who identify as feminists, including sociologist Michael Kimmel and activists Jackson Katz and Paul Kivel.

Feminist Solutions

In the 1980s, the Duluth Model was created by feminists to help explain abuse, protect victims, and hold batterers accountable. It has served as the template for numerous domestic violence shelters and services. The Duluth Model emphasizes that abuse is about power and control, and has formed the basis for many batterer intervention programs that teach men to accept responsibility for their actions and attempt to help them challenge their patriarchal beliefs and change their behaviors. In the event that a perpetrator refuses to give up his violent actions, the courts, police services, and other necessary institutions, which are parts of this solution model, are brought into action.

Feminists, both historically and today, also advocate for equal opportunities for women. They maintain that equal access to education, fair-paying work, and political advancements, among others things, will help ensure that women are independent and less subject to abuse. In earlier times, feminists challenged laws that prohibited women from owning or inheriting property, such as the British Marriage Act, which prohibited married women from owning property.

Critics maintain, however, that feminist theory fails to recognize abuse of men or abuse that occurs among same-sex couples. Some also argue that women are the perpetrators as often as are men, although research tends to support that women endure more frequent and more harmful abuse than do men. Others note that the feminist approach may alienate men who want to get involved in movements to end abuse, as they may feel defensive if they believe they are being labeled as would-be batterers.

See also: Duluth Model; Katz, Jackson; Kimmel, Michael; Kivel, Paul; Patriarchy and Domestic Abuse

Further Reading

Baumgardner, J., & Richards, A. (2005). *Grassroots: A field guide for feminist activism.* New York, NY: Farrar, Straus, & Giroux.
Collins, G. (2003). *America's women: 400 years of dolls, drudges, heroines and helpmates.* New York, NY: Harper Perennial.
The Duluth Model: http://www.theduluthmodel.org/about/index.html
Finley, L., & Stringer, E. (Eds.). *Beyond burning bras: Feminist activism for everyone.* Santa Barbara, CA: Praeger.
Freedman, E. (2002). *No turning back: The history of feminism and the future of women.* New York, NY: Ballantine.
Katz, J. (2006). *The macho paradox: Why some men hurt women and how all men can help.* New York, NY: Sourcebooks Trade.
Kimmel, M. (2008). *Guyland: The perilous world where boys become men.* New York, NY: HarperCollins.
McCue, M. (2008). *Domestic violence.* Santa Barbara, CA: ABC-CLIO.
Rowe-Finkbeiner, K. (2004). *The F word: Feminism in jeopardy.* Berkeley, CA: Seal Press.
Rowland, D. (2004). *The boundaries of her body: The troubling history of women's rights in America.* Naperville, IL: Sphinx.
Thatcher-Ulrich, L. (2007). *Well-behaved women seldom make history.* New York, NY: Alfred A. Knopf.

Mark Ikeke

FILMS AND DOMESTIC ABUSE

Given that popular culture is so pervasive in the United States and across the globe, it can be a great tool to help bring awareness about social issues. Films and documentaries have long included scenes depicting domestic abuse, albeit sometimes in erroneous ways. It is imperative that viewers critically examine the ways films depict victims as deserving, or as having no other choice but to physically fight and even kill their abusers. Below is a sampling of some American feature films that depict abuse, with a brief description of each. It is by no means an exhaustive list, and it does not include the many great documentaries about domestic abuse. A list of some of the best documentaries is available at the end of this book.

Raging Bull (1980) features Robert De Niro as prizefighter Jake LaMotta, who was the middleweight boxing champion from 1949 to 1951. A star in the ring, LaMotta also beats up his brother and his wife. De Niro won a Best Actor Award for his portrayal of LaMotta. Joe Pesci plays Joey, LaMotta's brother and manager. Cathy Moriarty is his abused wife.

Robert Greenwald's *The Burning Bed* (1984), a made-for-television movie, tells the true story of Francine Hughes, who sets fire to and kills her abusive husband Mickey (played by Paul Le Mat) one night in 1977 after he raped her. Farrah Fawcett stars as Francine Hughes. She was acquitted by reason of insanity, and the case as well as the movie were pivotal in raising awareness about abuse and ushered in the battered women defense.

Alice Walker's Pulitzer Prize–winning book *The Color Purple* was made into film in 1985 and features Whoopi Goldberg as Celie Johnson, who is abused and impregnated by her father in the early 1900s. She bears two children from the incest, and father Albert, played by Danny Glover, takes the second baby away from her. A local farmer called "Mister" wants to marry his prettier other daughter, Nettie, but Albert does not allow it, instead making Celie marry him. Mister is abusive to Celie, who finds some comfort from Sofia (played by Oprah Winfrey), the wife of one of Albert's sons from a previous marriage. Mister's mistress, Shug Avery (played by Margaret Avery), visits and befriends Celie, who eventually leaves him and is reunited with Nettie, who Albert had told her was dead, and her two children. The film was a blockbuster hit and was nominated for 11 Oscars.

A Cry for Help (1989) was a made-for-television movie that depicts the story of Tracey Thurman, played by Nancy McKeon, who eventually won a lawsuit against the Torrington, Connecticut, police who failed to respond to her repeated pleas for help from her abusive husband Buck (Dale Midkiff).

In *Shattered Dreams* (1990), based on a true story and also made for television, Lindsay Wagner plays Charlotte Fedders, who was the wife of a prominent Reagan-era official. The film shows Charlotte trying to get free and ends with a major court case against her husband John Fedders (Michael Nouri), which helped elevate the cause and raised awareness that abuse does not just occur in poor families.

Julia Roberts stars as Laura Burney in *Sleeping with the Enemy* (1991). Laura seems to be in a perfect, happy marriage with Martin (played by Patrick Bergin). Reality is far different, and seeing no other escape, Laura fakes her own death to be free of abuse. Martin finds out she has lied and will stop at nothing to find her.

Not without My Daughter (1991) is based on the true story of Betty Mahmoody, played by Sally Field, who is married to Iranian Sayed Mahmoody (Alfred Molina). The couple travel with their young daughter Mahtob to Iran, and Moody, as he is known, says he wants to stay. Betty wants to leave and Moody refuses, eventually becoming physically abusive to her. She realizes that under Iranian law he would get sole custody of Mahtob were the couple to divorce, so she makes a daring escape with her daughter to Turkey and then to the United States.

Fried Green Tomatoes (1991) tells the story of Evelyn Couch (Kathy Bates), who is upset in her marriage and befriends the elderly Ninny Threadgoode (Jessica Tandy).

Ninny tells Evelyn the story of the town, which features various instances of abusive relationships. Nominated for two Academy Awards, the film stars Mary Stuart-Masterson as Idgie Threadgoode and Mary-Louise Parker as Ruth Jamison.

Based on a true story, *When No One Would Listen* (1992) is a TV movie that stars Michelle Lee as an abused woman and James Farentino as her abuser.

The Joy Luck Club (1993) tells the stories of four Chinese women and their mothers. It features numerous challenges, including domestic violence.

This Boy's Life (1993), the memoirs of writer Tobias Wolff, was turned into a film that focuses on the rebellious teenager (played by Leonardo DiCaprio) and his abusive father (Robert De Niro).

What's Love Got to Do with It? (1993) tells the story of Anna Mae Bullock (better known as Tina Turner), who was abused by her husband Ike for years, even as the two had success as a musical duo. Tina is finally able to leave as she learns to defend herself and launches a successful solo career. Angela Bassett stars as Tina and Laurence Fishburne as Ike in this TV movie.

Dead by Sunset was a television mini-series based on the true-crime book by Ann Rule. Based on the 1986 murder of Cheryl Keeton, the miniseries aired in 1995. Brad Cunningham, played by Ken Olin, is the successful doctor with a hidden past. He had cheated on his first wife, raped her, abused her and the kids, then stabbed her to death when she attempted to leave him. Annette O'Toole plays Cheryl Keeton.

Donna Mills plays Beth Williams in *Dangerous Intentions* (1995), a woman whose husband Bill, played by Corbin Bernsen, abuses her. After he is released from prison, he comes after Beth.

Whoopi Goldberg, Mary-Louise Parker, and Drew Barrymore star in *Boys on the Side* (1995). Holly (Drew Barrymore) kills her abusive boyfriend, Nick, while defending herself from his attack. With Robin (Mary-Louise Parker) and Jane (Whoopi Goldberg), who had responded to an ad Holly placed seeking travel companions, the three women go on a road trip in which Holly meets and falls in love with a police officer named Abe Lincoln (Matthew McConaughey).

If Someone Had Known (1995) is a TV film that stars Kellie Martin as Katie Liner, who marries Jimmy Petit (Ivan Sergei). After the birth of their first son, Jimmy becomes jealous and begins beating Katie. When she finds out she is pregnant, things get worse, and Katie ends up killing Jimmy in self-defense. It is her father, a police officer played by Kevin Dobson, who must arrest her. She is put on trial and acquitted.

The 1996 drama/thriller *Fear* stars Reese Witherspoon as 16-year-old Nicole Walker. Nicole, from a nice family, meets David McCall, played by Mark Wahlberg, at a party and they begin dating. David is not so nice, however, and gets very jealous whenever she talks to other guys. David beats up one of Nicole's friends for walking her home, and Nicole breaks up with him. As is typical, that is not the end of the story, as David won't settle for a breakup and begins stalking Nicole, until the climactic end scene when Nicole's father Steven, played by William Peterson, throws David from a second-story window, killing him after David took Steven hostage and intended to kill Nicole.

Sling Blade (1996) features Billy Bob Thornton as a mentally disturbed man, Karl Childers, who has been released from a psychiatric hospital where he has been confined since he was 12 years old because he killed his mother and her lover. Karl befriends a young boy named Frank and is invited by Frank's mother, Linda, to move into their garage. This does not go over well with Linda's abusive boyfriend Doyle, played by Dwight Yoakam. In the end, Childers kills Doyle, thereby sparing Linda and Frank from further abuse. The film won Academy Awards for Best Writing and Best Adapted Screenplay. Thornton was nominated for Best Actor as well.

Sleeping with the Devil (1997) is a TV film based on a true story of the abusive marriage between a wealthy man and a poor woman. When she tries to leave, he attempts to murder her. She ends up wheelchair-bound but falls in love with a surgeon, and together they determine to help victims of domestic violence. Shannen Doherty stars as nurse Rebecca Dubrovich, and Tim Matheson is her abusive husband, Dick Strang.

Isabella Hoffman stars as Lisa in *The Promise* (1999). Based on a true story, Lisa and her three kids leave her abusive husband Bill (played by Neil Maffin), who stalks them, finds Lisa, and murders her despite an order of protection that is supposed to prohibit him from making contact. Lisa's dying wish is that her sister, who encouraged her to leave Bill, care for the kids. She does, but Bill remains an ever-present threat.

In *Affliction* (1999), Wade Whitehouse (Nick Nolte) is a policeman who suffered from abuse and struggles to cope as an adult. Sissy Spacek plays his love interest. The film focuses on the emotional toll that abuse leaves.

Enough (2002) stars singer and actress Jennifer Lopez as Slim, who marries Mitch Hiller, played by Billy Campbell, a customer at the diner where Slim had worked who intervened when she was being bothered by a male customer, and the two have a daughter, Gracie. Mitch turns out to be unfaithful, and when Slim threatens to leave him, he hits her. Slim begins to fear for Gracie's safety and eventually runs away with her. Despite Slim's efforts to stay underground, Mitch keeps tracking them. In the end, Slim decides she has to kill Mitch in order for her and Gracie to survive.

Keri Russell stars as Jenna Hunterson in *Waitress* (2007), a drama/comedy. She is stuck in an abusive relationship with Earl, played by Jeremy Sisto, and finds refuge in creating inventive pies at Joe's Pie Diner. Jenna is saving money to leave Earl, but things get complicated when a pregnant Jenna meets physician Jim Pommater (played by Nathan Fillion), who treats her well. The two begin an affair, but eventually Jenna ends up alone, raising her child and owning a diner she calls Lulu's Pies. The film was accepted to the 2007 Sundance Film Festival.

Precious (2009), based on the novel *Push* by Sapphire, is a disturbing portrayal of multiple forms of violence and abuse. Gabourey Sidibe, in her acting debut, stars as 16-year-old Claireece "Precious" Jones, who lives in a New York City ghetto with her abusive mother. Twice impregnated by her father, Precious suffers from the effects of all these abuses. Precious cannot read until, when it is discovered she is pregnant a second time, she is sent to an alternative school, where she gets help from her teacher, a social worker, and a nursing assistant. Music star Mo'Nique is mother Mary Jones and Lenny Kravitz is nursing assistant John McFadden. The film won the Audience Award and Grand Jury Prize at the 2009 Sundance Film Festival and received six Oscar nominations. Mo'Nique won for Best Supporting Actress and Geoffrey Fletcher won for Best Adapted Screenplay.

See also: Music and Domestic Abuse; News Media and Domestic Abuse

Further Reading

Berns, N. (2004). *Framing the victim: Domestic violence, media, and social problems*. New Brunswick, NJ: Transaction.
Lovell, J. (Ed.). (1998). *Insights from film into violence and oppression: Shattered dreams of the good life*. Westport, CT: Praeger.
O'Malley, M. (2011). Through a different lens: Using film to teach family law. *Family Court Review, 49*(4), 715–722.

Laura L. Finley

FINANCIAL ABUSE

Financial abuse is any act that affects the financial security of another person against that person's wishes or without that person's knowledge or reasoned consent. Financial abuse of vulnerable populations and economic abuse within intimate partner relationships are common forms of this abuse and manifest differently from each other. Though financial abuse is costly to victims and society, it generally goes unrecognized and underreported. Legislative efforts to curtail these crimes are relatively new or pending.

Financial Abuse of Vulnerable Persons

Financial abuse of vulnerable persons consists of the improper or illegal use of a vulnerable person's money, property, or assets against that person's wishes or without that person's knowledge or reasoned consent. Most often, vulnerable persons in these cases refer to older adults age 60 and above with or without disabilities, and adults age 18 and above with mental or physical disabilities. Children with monetary assets may encounter financial abuse as well; however, this phenomenon appears to be reported and studied less often.

Older persons are particularly vulnerable to financial abuse. As a whole, they possess a substantial share of the population's wealth in the form of property assets, investments, pensions, and/or monthly social security income. Furthermore, they are a conduit to Medicare or Medicaid funds. These resources, together with possible low social support, lower social competence, and/or decreased physical and mental abilities, make older adults a likely target for fraud and exploitation. It is estimated that American seniors lose more than $2.9 billion annually due to financial abuse by strangers (51 percent); family, friends, and neighbors (34 percent); the business sector (12 percent); and Medicare and Medicaid fraud (4 percent). Adults of any age with disabilities are at risk for similar abuse.

Financial abuse of vulnerable adults falls into three categories: opportunity, desperation, or predation. Crimes of opportunity are those crimes that have no planning; the predator stumbles upon an occasion to exploit the victim and does so. Conversely, crimes of desperation originate from extreme need such as poverty, debt, gambling, or drug addiction. Perpetrators of crimes of opportunity and desperation may use threats, intimidation, manipulation, misrepresentation, or fraud to obtain the victim's money or property. Such crimes include cashing the victim's checks without permission; forging the victim's signature; misusing or stealing the victim's money or possessions; coercing or deceiving the victim into signing documents (e.g., real estate, investment, bank accounts, wills, or other contracts); the improper use of conservatorship, guardianship, or power of attorney; obtaining access to bank accounts, credit cards, social security, and pension payments; and charging unreasonable and excessive fees for services such as cutting the lawn, transportation, and running errands. These types of crimes are more likely to be committed by family, friends, neighbors, and the business sector (e.g., caregivers, repair people, contractors, lawyers, insurance agents, bankers, and nursing home administrators).

Predatory crimes are those that are purposeful and planned. They are predominantly committed by strangers and include robbery and fraudulent schemes such as identity fraud, health-care/health insurance fraud (i.e., Medicare fraud, "rolling lab" fraud, services not performed, and medical equipment fraud); counterfeit prescription drugs; funeral and cemetery fraud; fraudulent "anti-aging" products; door-to-door, telemarketing, Internet and mail fraud; and investment and reverse mortgage scams.

Although addressed less often, financial abuse of children occurs when a parent or guardian takes or withholds financial assets rightfully belonging to the child; removes financial support when the child does not adhere to the parent's or guardian's wishes; or when the parent or guardian incurs debt under the child's name. These crimes very often go unnoticed outside the home.

While financial abuse of vulnerable persons is substantial, it remains underreported and underrecognized. Victims generally do not know where or how to report the crime, are ashamed or embarrassed of the crime, or are unaware that a crime has occurred. In some cases, victims may want to protect the abuser if the abuser is a family member or friend, or they may want to protect themselves if they feel intimated, fear reprisal, or fear placement in a facility outside the home.

Laws

Legislative action on financial abuse of vulnerable populations is relatively new. On the federal level, the Elder Just Act became law in March 2010, raising national awareness of elder abuse and elder financial abuse. Furthermore, the Elder Abuse Victims Act of 2011, S462, pending in congress, is a bill introduced to better protect, serve, and advance the rights of victims of elder abuse and exploitation and to establish an Office of Elder Justice in the Department of Justice. Each state has its own definition of financial abuse and legislative initiatives.

Economic Abuse in Intimate Partner Relationships

Economic abuse (or economic domination) within intimate partner relationships is another form of financial abuse. This abuse consists of one intimate partner (the abuser) willfully controlling the financial well-being of the other intimate partner (the victim) against the victim's wishes or better judgment. Economic abuse is not associated with a specific demographic group. Rather, it occurs within all socioeconomic and educational levels, racial and ethnic backgrounds, and sexual orientations. Though the abuser is more often male, females do perpetrate this abuse.

Economic abuse comes from a distinct patriarchal conceptualization of financial responsibility: those in power feel financially responsible for themselves alone, rather than providing for, or equitably sharing in, the financial well-being of the family unit. More often, the victim and children are treated as property instead of members of a cohesive unit that includes the abuser. Power imbalances in the relationship are used to exert control over financial decision making. Typically, economic abuse leads to poverty within the relationship despite overall family income or assets. Those who are abused are treated like a financial drain, which leads to diminished self-worth. Victims may feel guilty for spending on themselves and usually sacrifice their own needs for those of the children. When they do spend on themselves, they may hide their purchases. Some resort to begging their abuser for necessities; some may steal. Although economic abuse can have psychological and physical effects, this abuse usually remains unrecognized and unreported because discussion of money tends to be taboo in many cultures. Moreover, economic abuse is generally not an isolated event but a pattern that has been repeated in prior relationships.

Many variations of economic abuse exist. The abuser may withhold his income and assets, take the spouse's income and assets, prohibit or limit the spouse from generating income and assets, or any combination of these. Regardless of the scenario, the abuser actively coerces or deceives the victim into financial arrangements the victim normally would not consider.

The abuser may refuse to contribute to the upkeep of the house, forcing the spouse to take responsibility of family maintenance, even when the spouse has no income of her own. Should the spouse earn income and/or have assets, these are generally used for rent, food, clothing, medical and dental bills, and upkeep of the house and yard. In essence, the spouse's money is spent on items that have no monetary value once consumed. Conversely, the abuser's money is spent on tangible or appreciable assets, such as the house, car, certain furnishings, and electronic equipment—items that the abuser puts under his name, and takes possession of, should the relationship end. Moreover, the abuser may hide money and deliberately limit the victim's access to bank accounts and credit cards. In some cases, the abuser may withhold basic necessities such as food, clothing, sanitary products, and medications. In other cases, the abuser may give the victim a small allowance or pay the victim a salary. Some victims may feel forced to borrow or take out loans in order to provide adequate care for themselves and their children. Even though the victim may have her own income, the abuser exerts an extreme level of scrutiny and control over spending. The victim must receive the abuser's approval prior to any household purchase; then she must present receipts to account for every penny spent. However, for the abuser, spending on oneself may be unrestrained. In cases where food is scarce inside the home, the abuser will eat out of the house during the day where he can obtain a substantive meal. Although the abuser limits the victim's financial well-being, the abuser will claim the victim as a tax dependent.

In some cases, the abuser prevents the victim from working or choosing a career by sabotaging the victim's employment or expecting the victim to leave her job in order to take care of the children. The repercussions for the victim's future employability can be great and irreversible. Not only does the victim lose an income, along with possible retirement plans, bonuses, and promotions, but the victim's overall social security benefits may decrease. Furthermore, the gap in employment incurred during the relationship lessens the victim's value in the workforce, while the abuser's career and earnings remain intact.

Sometimes the financial abuse consists of thievery. The abuser may take possession of the assets and other financial resources brought into the marriage by the victim. He may coerce the victim into paying his debts and/or engage in unethical or deceptive practices by having the victim sign contracts and other legal agreements that are not in the victim's best interest.

Although the relationship may end, the economic abuse does not necessarily subside. A prenuptial or other legal agreement may have been particularly stringent and biased in favor of the abuser. The victim who used her money and assets to provide for the family during the relationship may leave with nothing while the abuser's assets, salary, and career remain intact. Moreover, the abuser may provide limited or no child support to the victim or may vie for sole custody of the children, forcing the victim to pay child support to him.

Legislation

At this time, there are no laws in the United States that specifically protect victims from economic abuse within intimate partner relationships. Legislation exists in Victoria, Australia, that recognizes economic abuse as a crime under the Family Violence Protection Act 2008.

Recommended Resources

The National Committee for the Prevention of Elder Abuse provides information on the key indicators of elder financial abuse at http://www.preventelderabuse.org/elderabuse/fin_abuse.html. The Elder Financial Protection Network website provides definitions, information on federal regulations, and resources for reporting suspected elder financial abuse at http://www.bewiseonline.org/what-is-financial-abuse/. The National Coalition against Domestic Violence provides information on current legislature and financial protection at http://www.uncfsp.org/projects/userfiles/File/DCE-STOP_NOW/NCADV_Economic_Abuse_Fact_Sheet.pdf

See also: Economic Recession and Domestic Abuse; Elder Abuse; Types of Domestic Abuse; Welfare and Domestic Abuse

Further Reading

Branigan, E. (2004). *His money or our money: Financial abuse of women in intimate partner relationships.* Coburg, Canada: The Coburg Brunswick Community Legal and Financial Counseling Centre.

Federal Bureau of Investigation (2011). Fraud target: Senior citizens. Retrieved October 25, 2011, from http://www.fbi.gov/scams-safety/fraud/seniors

MetLife Mature Market Institute (2011). *The MetLife study of elder financial abuse: Crimes of occasion, desperations, and predation against American elders.* New York, NY: Metropolitan Life Insurance Company.

University of Tennessee (2009). Chapter 16: Financial abuse. *Tennessee Victim Assistant Academy: Participant manual* (pp. 520–555). Chattanooga, TN: University of Tennessee.

AnneMarie Conlon

FORCED MARRIAGE AND DOMESTIC ABUSE

A marriage is considered "forced" when at least one party does not consent and is made to marry under some form of duress (Thomas, 2009, p. 2). It is recognized under international law as a human rights violation. Forced marriages often involve physical, sexual, and psychological abuse; denial of freedom of movement; denial of education and the right to work; and forced labor, among other forms of harm. Forced marriages occur throughout the world, including North America and Europe. Since the 1990s, government officials in many Western countries have begun responding to this fact, developing policies to address forced marriage among their own citizens and residents.

Forced marriage is distinguishable from arranged marriage, where family members may choose an individual's spouse, but the potential bride and groom ultimately consent to the marriage. The "duress" element present in a forced marriage may involve physical force, or may be some form of psychological or other coercion. A marriage involving a minor is often considered forced due to the minor's incapacity to consent.

Forced marriage can take numerous forms. In many cases, an individual's family forces him or her into a marriage. In other cases, a woman is kidnapped by a man who wishes to marry her or by traffickers who sell her to someone else as a bride. In communities where "widow inheritance" is practiced, a widow may be forced by her husband's relatives to marry her brother-in-law or another member of her husband's family. Under some national laws, a rapist may be acquitted of his crime if he marries his victim, and rape victims may face coercion from their rapists, or from law enforcement, judicial authorities, or family members who wish to avoid a criminal prosecution. These are just some examples.

Research from around the world indicates that most victims of forced marriage are women and girls, although male victims do exist. Compiling statistics on forced

A woman dressed in a wedding gown represents a child bride during a protest in Ankara, Turkey on November 27, 2011. She holds a placard that reads, "End Violence!" (AP Photo/Burhan Ozbilici)

marriage can prove difficult, as many of the marriages are unregistered, the practice is accepted in many communities, and victims are often reluctant to speak out against family members.

Effects

The experience of forced marriage is typically traumatic and can cause lasting physical and emotional effects. Social and legal constraints in victims' societies may make leaving a marriage difficult or impossible, so victims of forced marriage may face a lifetime of trauma.

Due to the nonconsensual nature of forced marriage, rape is an inherent element. For female victims, sexual violence may also be utilized to force them to agree to a marriage. In many societies, an unmarried woman who loses her virginity is considered shamed and may face severe social ostracism if she does not marry her sexual partner, even in cases of rape. This scenario is common in cases of "bride kidnapping"—where a man abducts a woman he wishes to marry. Once in a forced marriage, women face repeated rape, as well as forced pregnancy and childbearing. Conversely, a woman may face forced abortion if her husband does not want children at that time.

Physical and psychological violence are common in forced marriages. Domestic violence tends to be inherent in nonconsensual relationships; violence may also be employed as a means to coerce people into marriage or keep them from leaving. Victims of forced marriage may face violence at the hands of their in-laws as well, and are commonly forced to perform domestic labor for the family. Further, in societies that practice female circumcision, an uncircumcised woman will likely be forced to undergo the procedure.

Victims of forced marriage are commonly withdrawn from school and prohibited from attaining further education. This in turn limits available economic opportunities, and particularly for women, may render a victim financially dependent on the spouse or in-laws. Many women in forced marriages are prohibited from working, or their earnings are taken, creating complete financial dependence. This dependence compounds the cultural or legal impediments to leaving the marriage.

Victims of forced marriage also typically face restrictions on their freedom of movement and association. Social interaction may be limited to the family, and female victims may be forbidden to leave the home unaccompanied, or at all. The resulting social isolation increases the difficulty of leaving the relationship and can result in impaired social development for young victims. Removal to another country for marriage is another common means of coercion, and those taken abroad for marriage may face extreme isolation, especially where the country and/or language are unknown.

As a result of all these forms of harm, victims of forced marriage commonly suffer depression and may develop other psychological disorders. Many become suicidal.

People who leave the marriage, or attempt to leave, face additional harm. In some societies, leaving a marriage is considered shameful, particularly for women. Women who leave their husbands may be ostracized by their community and even family. Severe ostracism can make economic survival impossible. Furthermore, women who leave their husbands may face physical harm, including honor-based violence. In a society where "honor" is carefully guarded, a woman's own family may punish or murder her as a result of the shame believed to have been brought on the family. Even absent family violence, a woman who is considered "shamed" may be a target for violence from other men in her community.

Factors That Drive Forced Marriage

Though the forces fueling forced marriage vary in different communities, and can be driven by cultural, economic, or other factors, there are commonalities shared by many societies where the practice flourishes. These factors will not necessarily exist in every community, nor will the cultural beliefs discussed below necessarily be held by everyone in a community where forced marriage occurs.

Women subjected to forced marriage often come from communities with historically patriarchal social structures, where women are expected to obey and be cared for by their fathers until marriage. Upon marriage they owe absolute obedience to their husbands or husbands' families. Particularly in societies where a husband pays a bride price, a wife may be thought of as her husband's or in-laws' property upon payment. This payment may be understood to make the marriage agreement irrevocable, even if the bride-to-be has not been consulted. In many highly patriarchal societies, women are strongly discouraged from living alone and remaining unmarried, even after being widowed. All of these factors can make it difficult for a woman to oppose a marriage that her parents want to arrange. In some communities, these ideas may be thought to justify using physical force against a woman who has managed to resist psychological coercion.

Deeply held beliefs about sexual purity, honor, and appropriate gender roles may drive families to force sons or daughters into marriage. For example, parents seek to prevent premarital sex, to break up an ongoing relationship or other behavior the family disapproves of, to mitigate the shame of rape, or to hide or "cure" homosexuality.

Economic motivations may also fuel a forced marriage. Parents may feel a marriage is the best way to ensure their son or daughter has future financial support. Families may also be motivated by potential gain. In some societies marriage will mean a bride price payment to the bride's family, while in others the husband's family may receive a dowry from the bride's family. For a family suffering economic hardship, marriage can be a means to gain income and potentially to lessen their burden by removing one person from the household. Marriage may also ensure that land or other wealth remains within a family, or it may strengthen a family's standing by tying it to an influential family.

Of course, forced marriages can occur without any family involvement, or without the bride's family's involvement. Many female victims of forced marriage are kidnapped, and their families never know what becomes of them, or only find out after the marriage. In China, for instance, the one-child policy and resulting high levels of selective abortion and female infanticide have created a significant gender imbalance, with men greatly outnumbering women. As a result, bride trafficking has flourished, and many women are abducted within and outside of China and sold to Chinese men as wives. In other countries, particularly several former Soviet republics, bride kidnapping has become common. While consensual staged abductions have a long history in this region as a means for couples and their families to avoid the cost of a traditional marriage, true abductions followed by forced marriages have reportedly been increasing since the end of the Soviet era.

It is important to note that while these various practices may be especially pervasive in certain areas, they occur all over the world. Over the last two decades, many Western governments have begun to recognize and investigate the existence of forced marriage among their own citizens and residents. Statistics from Britain alone indicate that at least 1,000 women are taken abroad from Britain by their families every year and forced into marriages overseas. The families involved are not of exclusively any one ethnicity.

Legal Responses

Governments around the world are increasingly developing strategies to combat forced marriage, particularly in the West. Several European countries have already instituted policies, while other Western governments have begun investigating the problem. Governments differ over whether to take a criminal or civil law approach.

Supporters of criminalization suggest that a law specifically criminalizing forced marriage would be a strong deterrent, would empower victims, and would make prosecuting offenders easier than by relying on related criminal offenses. Many advocates have cautioned against a criminal approach, however. They argue that a criminalization focus would make many victims reluctant to seek help, as victims of forced marriage may wish to avoid charging family members with crimes. Advocates have also expressed concern that criminal laws would make some families more likely to remove their children to other countries to be married, rendering government assistance difficult if not impossible.

Numerous countries have passed laws specifically criminalizing forced marriage, regardless of the victim's age or gender, including Norway, Germany, Belgium, Bulgaria, and Macedonia. Other countries have criminal laws against forcing women into marriage, including New Zealand, Pakistan, and Uzbekistan. Even where not criminalized, in many countries forced marriages violate civil marriage laws and can be annulled or voided.

In 2008, the British government instituted an extensive legal scheme to combat forced marriage. The Forced Marriage (Civil Protection) Act utilizes civil legal remedies, although the British government encourages prosecutions in appropriate cases using related criminal provisions, such as rape or abduction. Any individual who has suffered or faces a threat of forced marriage can seek a "forced marriage protection order," which empowers courts or law enforcement to intervene to protect the beneficiary. If a protection order is violated, the perpetrators can be imprisoned for up to two years. The new law also established a Forced Marriage Unit to assist British nationals dealing with forced marriage in other countries.

European nations have also responded to the issue of forced marriage within their borders by amending immigration laws and/or marriage laws. For instance, Denmark has tightened immigration restrictions governing the immigration of spouses or fiancés, and France has increased the minimum age of marriage and requires public officials to interview couples applying to marry in order to determine the relationship's validity. Advocates and politicians in other countries have been watching the various European developments in policies on forced marriage to determine whether and how to respond to the issue.

See also: Dowry Killings; Honor Killings; India and Domestic Abuse; The Middle East and Domestic Abuse; Southeast Asia and Domestic Abuse

Further Reading

Clark, B., & Richards, C. (2008). The prevention and prohibition of forced marriages: A comparative approach. *International and Comparative Law Quarterly*, 57, 501–528.

Dostrovsky, N., Cook, R. J., & Gagnon, M. (2007). *Annotated bibliography on comparative and international law relating to forced marriage*. Ottawa, ON: Department of Justice Canada.

Thomas, C. (2009). *Forced and early marriage: A focus on Central and Eastern Europe and Former Soviet Union Countries with selected laws from other countries* (U.N. Doc. EGM/GPLHP/2009/EP.08). Geneva, Switzerland: United Nations Division for the Advancement of Women.

U.K. Foreign and Commonwealth Office (2008). *The right to choose: Multi-agency statutory guidance for dealing with forced marriage.* London, England: Author.

Lynsay Gott

FUNDING FOR DOMESTIC VIOLENCE SERVICES

In the United States, nonprofit domestic violence centers often rely largely on grants to fund their work. There are many entities that provide grants to address domestic violence.

The U.S. Department of Justice's (DOJ) Office on Violence against Women (OVW) funds 21 programs. These include the Children and Youth Exposed to Violence Program; Grant to Encourage Arrest Policies and Enforcement of Protection Orders Program; Court Training and Improvements Program; Culturally and Linguistically Specific Services for Victims of Domestic Violence, Dating Violence, Sexual Assault and Stalking; Education, Training, and Enhanced Services to End Violence Against and Abuse of Women with Disabilities Grant Program; Engaging Men and Youth Program; Enhanced Training and Services to End Violence Against and Abuse of Women Later in Life Program; Grants to Reduce Sexual Assault, Domestic Violence, and Stalking on Campus Program; Legal Assistance for Victims Grant Program; Rural Domestic Violence, Dating Violence, Sexual Assault and Stalking Assistance Program; Services to Advocate for and Respond to Youth Program; Sexual assault Service Program; Tribal Sexual Assault Service Program; State Sexual Assault and Domestic Violence Coalitions Program; Services, Training, Education and Policies (STEP) to Reduce Domestic Violence, Dating Violence, Sexual Assault and Stalking in Secondary Schools Grant Program; STOP Violence Against Women Formula Grant Program; Transitional Housing Assistance Grants for Victims of Domestic Violence, Dating Violence, Stalking or Sexual Assault Program; Tribal Governments Program; and the Tribal Domestic Violence and Sexual Assault Coalitions Grant Program.

The DOJ's Office for Victims of Crime (OVC) also offers grants for services for domestic violence victims. The U.S. Department of Health and Human Services Office on Women's Health funds work to address victims and prevent abuse as well. Numerous state and local grants are available, too. Private foundations like the Robert Wood Johnson Foundation also provide grants for domestic violence.

Several resources compile grant requests for proposals (RFPs) for domestic violence work. Violence against Women Network (VAWNet) provides a link to funding sources and updated requests for proposals, as well as tools for writing grants. The National Network to End Domestic Violence (NNEDV) also provides a listing of funding sources.

Many corporate foundations also offer grants to assist victims of domestic violence. Some of the most well known include Verizon Foundation, Liz Claiborne, Mary Kay, Allstate Foundation, and Avon Foundation. The Mary Kay Foundation's shelter grant program supports at least one domestic violence shelter in every state. In 2011, the foundation awarded $20,000 grants to more than 150 women's domestic violence shelters across the nation for a total of $3 million. Shelters use the funds to hire staff, expand services, and make improvements to shelter spaces. The Liz Claiborne Foundation was established in 1981 to support initiatives related to domestic violence, transitioning from poverty, and women's empowerment. The Verizon Foundation is committed to using technology, financial resources, employees, and partnerships to solve critical social issues, including domestic violence. In 2012, the Avon Foundation provided grants for the financial empowerment for DV Survivors, dating abuse prevention programs implemented on college and university campuses, and direct services provided by DV shelters and programs in the United States and globally. The Allstate Foundation recognizes that "financial factors are the strongest predictors in a survivor's decision to stay, leave, or return to an abusive relationship." The Allstate Foundation's grant program focuses on helping survivors through:

- Financial education using the Allstate Foundation's *Moving Ahead through Financial Management* Curriculum
- Matched saving programs including individual development accounts
- Job readiness and job training
- Microloans and microenterprise

For global efforts, the UN Trust Fund to end violence against women, established in 1996 by the UN General Assembly, is managed by UN Women. According to the organization's website: "The only multilateral grant-making mechanism exclusively devoted to supporting local and national efforts to end violence against women and girls, the UN Trust Fund works with partners across the world to secure much-needed services for women and girls affected by violence. Through its partners, the Fund also invests in long-term solutions for a world free of violence." The Global Fund for Women supports women's groups outside of the United States that seek to advance the human rights of women and girls.

One concern is that grant funding is not always a sustainable way to operate services. Competition for grants is steep, and funding sometimes runs out. Further, critics maintain that domestic violence services sometimes tailor their work to fit a grant RFP, rather than doing what is most needed.

See also: Avon Corporation; Global Fund for Women; Liz Claiborne Company; Mary Kay Corporation; The United Nations and Domestic Abuse; U.S. Government Responses to Domestic Violence; Verizon Foundation

Further Reading

All State Foundation: http://www.allstatefoundation.org
Avon Foundation: http://www.avonfoundation.org
Global Fund for Women: http://www.globalfundforwomen.org/index.php
Mary Kay Foundation: http://www.marykayfoundation.org
National Network to End Domestic Violence: http://www.nnedv.org
U.S. Department of Justice Violence against Women: http://www.ovw.usdoj.gov/
Verizon Foundation: http://www.foundation.verizon.com
Violence Against Women network: http://www.vaw-net.org

Laura L. Finley

FUTURES WITHOUT VIOLENCE

Futures Without Violence, formerly known as the Family Violence Prevention Fund, was founded more than 30 years ago with the mission of helping create futures without violence for all families. The organization works on child abuse, sexual assault, domestic and dating violence by promoting legislation, providing training and resources, and challenging social norms. Between 2006 and 2010, Futures Without Violence received a four-star rating by Charity Navigator, the nation's top independent charity evaluator. It has won the Community Leadership Award from the San Francisco Office of the FBI, was a finalist in 2011 for the Y-Pulse GennY award, which recognizes initiatives that use new and innovative techniques to connect with teens, tweens, and college students, was rated one of America's top 100 charities by *Worth* magazine two years in a row (2002 and 2003), among many other awards.

Futures Without Violence broke ground on a new location in the Presidio area of San Francisco, which will be open to the public in 2013. It features a large conference facility, an exhibit hall, and three galleries for exhibits. It also has offices in Boston and Washington D.C.

The organization's work is focused on the following: (1) 16 Days of Activism; (2) Women & Girls; (3) Boys & Men; (4) Tweens & Teens; (5) Child Well-Being; (6) Health; (7) Judges; (8) Employers & Employees; (9) Leadership Training Programs; (10) Policy & Advocacy; and (11) International.

Activists hold hands to form a human chain at the closing ceremony of the "16 days of activism to end violence against women 2010" campaign held by Kafa (enough) organization in front of UNESCO in Beirut, Lebanon on December 10, 2010. (AP Photo/Bilal Hussein)

The 16 Days of Activism is a campaign aimed to rally and coordinate efforts to end gender violence. It occurs between November 25, the International Day Against Violence Against Women, and December 10, International Human Rights Day.

Futures Without Violence's work on women and girls involves multiple pieces. It addresses efforts on college campuses, reproductive or sexual coercion among teens, and stopping violence against women globally. The organization has compiled a compendium for those working on campuses called *Beyond Title IX: Guidelines for prevention and responding to gender based violence in higher education*. It outlines how to create a campus that is free of gender-based violence as well as model policies and procedures. Knowmoresaymore.org is the organization's new website devoted to educate youth about reproductive coercion and the health consequences of violence and sexual coercion. Regarding international gender violence, Futures Without Violence has a fact sheet about these issues and supports passage of the International Violence Against Women Act (I-VAWA), which would coordinate funding, resources, and educational programs globally. Additionally, the link on the organization's website for Women & Girls features information for working with immigrant victims, including fact sheets, relevant laws, and toolkits for making services culturally competent. A toolkit for understanding maternal health kits is also available.

Men & Boys initiatives include an Engaging Men program and the highly acclaimed Coaching Boys Into Men program. The Engaging Men program involves a collaboration with the Office on Violence Against Women, Men Stopping Violence, A Call to Men, and the Texas Association Against Sexual Assault. Emerging from the 2005 Violence Against Women Act reauthorization, the program provides support to 23 projects across the country that create public education campaigns and community organizing to encourage men and boys to work with women and girls on prevention efforts. Coaching Boys Into Men was launched in 2001 to inspire men to serve as role models and teach young boys to be strong but respectful men. Used by various men's groups, specialized training and toolkits are available for use by coaches with athletes.

Futures Without Violence offers a wealth of information relevant to abuse involving tweens or teens. The website includes fact sheets, information about the link between dating violence and other unhealthy behaviors, emerging issues (such as the use of various technologies by abusers as a tool of power and control), creating safety plans, and more. In 2012, Futures Without Violence won a Communicator Award from the International Academy of Visual Arts for its *That's Not Cool* educational website.

Childhood well-being efforts are diverse, focusing on everything from understanding the impact of childhood exposure to domestic violence to promoting legislation to stop child marriage to collaborating with the U.S. Department of Justice on the Defending Childhood Initiative. The Defending Childhood Initiative, a project of U.S. Attorney General Eric Holder, is intended to engage six cities and two tribes in comprehensive solutions to address all forms of violence against children, including domestic violence, child abuse, sexual assault, incest, and more.

Futures Without Violence is perhaps the strongest leader on training for health-care professionals regarding screening of and responding to domestic violence. The organization offers fact sheets, materials that can be ordered, sponsors regular webinars, and sponsors the e-journal *Family Violence Prevention and Health Practice*. The website features tutorials and toolkits for various health-care professionals, including pediatricians, ob-gyns, dentists, and others, regarding screening and protocol when abuse is identified. Additionally, Futures Without Violence sponsors an annual Health Cares About Domestic Violence Day, which takes place the second Wednesday of October.

It is imperative that judges are adequately trained about the dynamics of abuse. Futures Without Violence provides tools for the continuing legal education of judges, including a toolkit for creating a domestic violence court. It also sponsors three intensive training programs: the Enhancing Judicial Skills in Domestic Violence Cases Workshop (EJS), the Continuing Judicial Skills in Domestic Violence Cases Program (CJS), and the Enhancing Judicial Skills in Elder Abuse Cases Workshop.

For employers and employees, Futures Without Violence offers numerous fact sheets and resources. It also provides a link to Workplaces Respond to Domestic and Sexual Violence: A National Resource Center. This resource center emerged when on April 18, 2012 "President Obama signed a memorandum that requires federal agencies to develop policies to address the workplace effects of domestic violence and provide assistance to employees who are victims of domestic violence" (http://www.workplacesrespond.org/). The site is a wealth of information for employees and supervisors regarding laws, policies, and recommended protocols.

The Leadership Training Program includes the Supporting Organizations Sustainability Institute (SOS Institute), the National Institute on Fatherhood and Domestic Violence, and the Institute for Leadership in Education Development (I-LED) program. Started in 2010, SOS "offers an interactive training and technical assistance to assist U.S. Department of Justice Office on Violence Against Women (OVW) grantees to enhance their organizational infrastructure" (http://www.futureswithoutviolence.org/content/features/detail/1975/). The National Institute on Fatherhood and Domestic Violence provides support for those working with abusive fathers, while I-LED "offers hands-on workshops and technical assistance to help US Department of Justice Office on Violence against Women (OVW) grantees to improve the organization, quality, and consistency of education and training programs" (http://www.futureswithoutviolence.org/content/features/detail/1735/).

Futures Without Violence offers up-to-date information about bills under consideration and provides recommendations and action plans through its Policy & Advocacy efforts. The website provides useful information about the Violence Against Women Act reauthorization efforts, I-VAWA, and other global efforts.

International efforts focus on providing facts and resources relevant to global gender violence. A list of Futures Without Violence's international achievements is available at http://www.futureswithoutviolence.org/userfiles/file/PublicCommunications/Futures%20International%20Policy%20Accomplishments.pdf.

Futures Without Violence encourages people to get involved by using their materials to sponsor local trainings, workshops, and events; to learn more by reading their fact sheets and resources; and to donate, if possible, to support their efforts.

See also: Educational Programs; Immigrant Victims of Domestic Abuse; International Violence Against Women Act (I-VAWA); Physicians, Health Care Providers, and Domestic Abuse; Teen Victims; Violence Against Women Act (VAWA); Workplace Violence and Domestic Abuse

Further Reading

Coaching Boys into Men: http://www.coachescorner.org
Futures Without Violence: http://www.futureswithoutviolence.org
That's Not Cool: http://www.thatsnotcool.com/
Workplaces Respond to Domestic and Sexual Violence: http://www.workplacesrespond.org/

Laura L. Finley

GENDER-RELATED THEORIES
Theories and Gender

While the field of criminology has offered numerous theories to help explain crime, for much of history the discipline suffered from androcentrism—being male identified, male centered, and male focused. That is, criminology was dominated by male academics, studying male subjects, and devising theories to explain males' criminality and even males' victimization. The little attention paid to females tended to stress their pathology, as in Sigmund Freud's theorizing that female deviants suffer from hysteria.

This androcentrism began to be challenged in the 1970s, with the rise of the second wave of the women's rights movement. In 1973, Rita Simon proposed what is called the liberation hypothesis. As women gained greater rights—most notably, in the workplace—they would subsequently become more involved in certain types of crime. According to Simon, greater opportunities in the workplace would lead more women to commit white-collar offenses. Support for the liberation hypothesis seemed to come from Freda Adler, who that same year published data showing large increases in the number of women arrested for property crimes (Adler & Simon, 1979). Critics noted that Adler's data could have been misconstrued. The number of female arrests for property crimes was still quite low, so any increase seemed like a large one. Additionally, male crime rates rose over the same time period, suggesting it was not liberation but some other factor that explained the increase. Finally, it could have been that the increase was not due to females committing more property crimes but instead to police paying more attention to them, thus making more arrests.

The 1990s again saw increased attention to female criminality, as academics, politicians, and pundits noted increased arrest rates for certain crimes, in particular, assault. Deborah Prothrow-Stith (1991) argued that, because the United States equates violence with power, women too must resort to violence to acquire the power they still lack in other realms. Yet again, data about increased arrest rates for females may well have been a function of changing police practices. It was in the 1980s and 1990s that many police agencies shifted to dual arrest practices when investigating a domestic violence call. Thus instead of it being just one arrest—typically, the male, as data show it is more often males who perpetrate domestic violence—now both parties were being arrested (although not necessarily charged with an offense). The result might have been a fairly stable arrest rate for men but a much higher arrest rate for females.

Explaining Domestic Violence

Several theories were developed in the 1980s and 1990s to explain female criminality and, in particular, why it is generally far less than that of men. John Hagan's power-control theory explained that both macro- and micro-level forces constrained women from crime. Family structures typically mirror those of the broader patriarchal society, according to Hagan, and thus feature strict gender-role divisions. In patriarchal families, there is much greater control over the behavior of girls than of boys, who are often encouraged to take risks and show leadership. Hagan speculated that as families become more egalitarian, girls' delinquency would become more like that of boys (Hagan, Simpson, & Gillis, 1987). This theory would seem to suggest that men perpetrate far more domestic violence due to the combination of societal norms and parenting practices that reinforce the idea that men are to be in control.

Other theories posit that it is hormones that result in males perpetrating the bulk of crime in general and, particularly, violent crime. Higher rates of testosterone have been linked to more aggressive behavior among males in animal studies. Researchers have proposed that higher testosterone levels might cause someone to react aggressively when challenged or when they feel threatened.

Many theorists have noted the relationship between violent crime and gender-role socialization. As males continue to be socialized to be stereotypically masculine—to need to be in control, to appear tough and not emotional, for instance—they will continue to perpetrate crimes like domestic violence. Jackson Katz (2006), for example, has repeatedly maintained that in sports and popular culture, young men receive extensive messaging that they are supposed to dominate young women and that these women either "asked for it" or "like it." These theories come from the social learning tradition, arguing that crime, like other behavior, is learned.

Another theory that has been used to explain domestic violence is Sykes and Matza's techniques of neutralization. Sykes and Matza (1957) proposed that offenders use a series of mental techniques to rationalize or neutralize their actions, both before they commit them and afterwards. These include denying the victim, denying injury, denying responsibility, condemning the condemners, and appealing to higher loyalty. Abusers often deny responsibility, instead maintaining that it was the victim's actions (or in some cases, inactions) that "made" them offend.

Rational choice theory maintains that offenders choose to commit a crime after weighing the perceived costs and benefits. In the case of domestic violence, for instance, offenders might see little cost, as often their actions go unreported and unpunished. Similarly, routine activities theory sees crime occurring when motivated offenders see the right opportunity—one in which they find a suitable target and a lack of capable guardians. Domestic violence offenders carefully select both the victim and the tactics they use so as to obtain and maintain control. They generally perpetrate in the home, thus there are no "guardians."

See also: Biological and Psychological Theories about Domestic Abuse; Katz, Jackson; Patriarchy and Domestic Abuse; Sociological Theories about Domestic Abuse; Women's Rights Movement

Further Reading

Adler, F., & Simon, R. (1979). *The criminology of deviant women*. New York, NY: Houghton Mifflin.
Barak, G. (2006). Theories of violence. Retrieved March 17, 2012, from http://www.greggbarak.com/custom3_2.html
Garbarino, J. (1998). *Lost boys*. New York, NY: Free Press.
Hagan, J., Simpson, J., & Gillis, R. (1987). Class in the household: A power-control theory of gender and delinquency. *American Journal of Sociology, 92*(4), 788–816.
Katz, J. (2006). *The macho paradox: Why some men hurt women and how all men can help*. Naperville, IL: Sourcebooks.
Kimmel, M., & Mahler, M. (2003). Adolescent masculinity, homophobia, and violence. *American Behavioral Scientist, 46*(10), 1439–1458.
Prothrow-Stith, D. (1991). *Deadly consequences: How violence is destroying our teenage population and a plan to begin solving the problem*. New York, NY: HarperCollins.
Sykes, G., & Matza, D. (1957). Techniques of neutralization: A theory of delinquency. *American Sociological Review, 22*(6), 664–670.

Laura L. Finley

GLOBAL FUND FOR WOMEN

Introduction

The Global Fund for Women (GFW) is the largest nonprofit grant-making foundation focusing on women's human rights around the world. Their mission is to advance "women's rights by making grants that support and strengthen women's groups around the world . . . that promotes women's action for social change, equality, peace, and justice worldwide." Founded in 1987 by Anne Firth Murray, Frances Kissling, and Laura Lederer, it first awarded grants in 1988 to eight grantees totaling US$31,000 and continue to give more each year. The organization's vision is "a just, compassionate and equitable world in which all people, regardless of their gender, class, age, ethnicity, race, religion, sexual orientation or physical ability may live free from poverty, violence, and all forms of discrimination." Not only does it provide funds, the organization also produce newsletters and other resources about civil, cultural, economic, political, and social issues.

Funding

GFW relies on contributions from over 20,000 people and institution in a network that pools resources and shares a passion for advancing women's rights, rather than relying on a single funding source or government entity. The organization believes that in order to realize a vision of a better world, everyone has the responsibility to give. Each year, between 30 and 40 percent of the group's funds come from individuals, while remainder come from various foundations, businesses, religious groups, and community organizations.

Grants

GWF believes that by putting resources into the hands of grassroots women leaders, women can change the world. Since 1987, it has awarded over US$85 million in grants to 4,200 organizations in over 171 countries. In 2010, GWF's efforts reached 125,000 women and girls, which in turn benefited countless other families and communities. The majority of grants rage between US$500 to a maximum annual grant of US$20,000. GFW accepts and supports a little over 500 grants a year. Former and current grantees play a vital role in helping identify, refer, and recommend new and emerging groups that are eligible for grants. These grants are informed by over 100 women and men on an international advisory board and then approved by the board of directors. Many of the grantees have gone on to become internationally recognized for their work.

Newsletter and Resources

Creating a newsletter helps members keep up with current grantees and the work they are doing. These newsletters highlight individual projects by giving a short history of the issue, the amount of the award, and how the project is helping the community. They also print interviews with different people in the media around the globe who help advance women's rights such as Abby Disney, who directed *Pray the Devil Back to Hell*. Throughout the newsletter are ways that individuals can help different grantees and causes. The resources they offer on the website are reports, books, fact sheets, annual reports, and handbooks.

Focuses

Currently, GWF is focused on health and sexual rights, peace and gender violence, economic and environmental justice, civic and political participation, access to education, and social change philanthropy.

Health and Sexual Rights

In many parts of the world, women are denied control over their bodies. According to GFW, women are controlled by men, governments, and religious institutions. Countries have introduced laws that restrict women in this regard, including their sexual preference and antiabortion laws. GFW feels that women have the right to bodily integrity and access to quality health services. The organization provides grants to women's right activists working to preserve and expand women's rights to health and the freedom to fully express their sexual and reproductive choices, including the number and spacing of their children.

Peace and Gender Violence

During active conflicts and postconflicts, violence against women escalates. Money going to militarize the state is diverted from social services, education, and hospitals, which decreases women's participation in education and employment. GFW supports women-led efforts to build peace through peace negotiations, reconciliation, gender-sensitivity training, and rehabilitating women survivors of violence.

Economic and Environmental Justice

In most parts of the world, poverty rates for women are much higher than men. Women are faced with unforeseen challenges caused by climate change and natural disasters. They have difficulty accessing water and food, sometimes having to spend up to eight hours a day collecting and carrying water. GFW feels that everyone has the right to food, economic security, clean water and air, natural resources for survival, and a life of dignity. The organization supports women-led efforts to preserve biodiversity; conserve energy, water, and natural resources; and ensure women's representation in global negotiations.

Civic and Political Participation

According to GFW, women account for only a fraction of business, university, and NGO leaders, nor are they allowed to vote, inherit land, or challenge certain laws in some countries. The organization feels that when women become more involved, civically and politically, they improve their lives, their families, and society overall. GFW supports women's organizations that are working to advance women's leadership roles domestically and publicly including women with disabilities, the young and the elderly, widows, and women from ethnic minorities and from lower socioeconomic levels.

Access to Education

It has been shown that when women are more educated, their families, communities, and countries become stronger and healthier; child mortality drops 10 percent; and the risk of contracting HIV/AIDS drops by half. GWF believes that education should be offered to everyone equally, either formally or informally, in religious or secular setting, and can be practical or academic. The organization supports women's movements that are investing in education as a way to reduce gender inequalities and discrimination, including training programs that develop confidence, leadership, and self-sufficiency.

Social Change Philanthropy

GFW believes that putting money directly in the hands of women's groups working on gender equality and social change will have a dramatic effect on transforming systems, institutions, and cultures that are the root of injustice. Unrestricted funding goes toward operational costs, programmatic work, or urgent campaigns, which allows groups autonomy in decision making; space to strategize, plan, and network; and the flexibility to respond to emerging operational needs. GFW supports groups that have difficulty accessing resources such as indigenous women, rural and poor women, lesbians, young women, and women with disabilities.

See also: Funding for Domestic Violence Services

Further Reading

Gianturco, P., & Ramdas, K. (2007). Women who light the dark. Brooklyn, NY: Powerhouse
Global Fund for Women: http://www.globalfundforwomen.org/

Brandon Fryman

GRASSROOTS MOVEMENTS

Much of the attention given to domestic violence in liberal democracies like the United States, and the emergence of efforts to raise awareness to stop domestic violence, has come from grassroots movements of women, typically involving those who have been subjected to domestic violence themselves.

Historically, liberal democratic states have shown little interest in responding to or preventing domestic violence. Governments at all levels have generally overlooked domestic violence, in policy and in practice, or treated it as a matter not for the public realm. Domestic violence was viewed as a private trouble and not an affair of society, government, or the law.

The relationship between gender and violence, socially and domestically, only came under greater public scrutiny as a result of the grassroots activism of the women's movements of the 1960s and 1970s. Efforts were geared toward not only stopping domestic violence but ending the subordinate positions of women in society more broadly. During the 1980s and since, gay and lesbian activists have turned attention to domestic violence within GBLTQ (gay/bisexual/lesbian/transgender/queer) communities. Policy shifts over the last four decades have been impelled by the activities of grassroots movements and community advocacy groups.

Early grassroots projects included practices of meeting and participating in consciousness-raising circles. In these participatory sessions, women were encouraged, in a supportive environment, to share their experiences and explore positive responses and solutions drawn from women's own needs. These revealed the extent of abuse suffered by women and led to efforts to create more durable projects and resources to end domestic violence and support victims.

The most significant grassroots projects involved the development and maintenance of shelters for women and children. Rape crisis centers were also initiated. These made evident the broad occurrence of sexual assault within domestic environments and led to efforts to change sexual assault laws and perceptions of assault within domestic contexts.

Grassroots movements also challenged the silencing of women within academic circles. They noted that victimization surveys in criminology did not accurately or reliably measure women's experiences of victimization, particularly in domestic contexts.

Grassroots movements have played important parts in the development of women's centers on university and college campuses. These centers have provided space for work raising awareness and striving to end domestic violence among students and youth and in the community more broadly.

Some grassroots approaches have focused on legislative and legal approaches to prohibit domestic violence. Efforts in this direction focused on changes to laws and criminal justice system practices as a means to educate the public about issues of domestic violence and to penalize abusers in order to reduce incidents of domestic violence.

This has also included lobbying for changes in policing practices. Through the late twentieth century, domestic violence was not consistently pursued as a criminal offense. Police regularly used their own discretion in assessing cases of domestic violence, often failing to pursue domestic violence calls or arrest accused abusers. In Canada, for example, it was not illegal for a man to rape his wife until as recently as 1983. Up to the 1980s, it was very rare for police to lay charges, particularly assault charges, against abusive men. Those charges that were laid were typically for drunk and disorderly conduct or causing a disturbance (if a neighbor called police).

Movements have led to zero tolerance policies and mandatory charging—in which police have to bring a charge against anyone accused (male or female) in a domestic violence call, regardless of evidence or witnesses. Police incident reports have only recently included documentation of domestic violence and not in all jurisdictions consistently. In response to public efforts, a Family Violence Court was established in Winnipeg in 1990 to provide greater attention and resources to address issues.

Other approaches have focused on the social costs of domestic violence in terms of criminal justice systems, health, employment, education, and social services. One such study estimated $4,225,954,322 per year in related social costs (O'Grady, 2007). The study concluded that 87.5 percent of the costs were borne by the state with 11.5 percent borne by the individual.

Another key grassroots innovation, particularly within indigenous communities, has been the development of restorative justice practices to address issues of violence. These efforts have included addressing the historic violence inflicted on indigenous communities by ongoing state practices of colonialism and cultural genocide that have left legacies of poverty, cultural erasure, and disempowerment with effects on abuse and violence within communities. For the restorative justice movements, there is recognition that the continued involvement of the state to address issues of violence both overlooks the role of the state in creating and perpetuating violence within indigenous communities and furthers the breakdown of community and cultural, as well as familial, bonds, which has generational impacts. There is, as importantly, recognition that victims also need access to resources and support services that respect the specific cultural and community practices of their own communities.

In more radical approaches, anarchist women have taken to collectively confronting and shaming abusers who are active within radical movements. Contemporary anarchists have continued earlier practices of support circles and collective solidarity along with provision of shelter and child care. At the same time, they have challenged governments over the persistence of policies and practices that reinforce patriarchal relations broadly and contribute to the economic and social exploitation and marginalization of women. This includes campaigns against cuts to welfare, health care, child care, and shelter services. Contemporary activists also target capital. Campaigns are directed against business practices that disadvantage women in the workplace and contribute to economic vulnerability.

See also: Nongovernmental Organizations; Nonprofit Organizations

Further Reading

Allen, P. (1970). *Free space: A perspective on the small group in women's liberation.* New York, NY: Times Change Press.

Baumgardner, J., & Richards. A. (2004). *Grassroots: A field guide for feminist activism.* New York, NY: Farrar, Straus, & Giroux.

Comack, E., Chopyk, V., & Wood, L. (2008). Aren't women violent too? The gendered nature of violence. In *Marginality and condemnation: An introduction to criminology* (pp. 330–349). Halifax, NS: Fernwood.

Janovicek, N. (2008). *No place to go: Local histories of the battered women's shelter movement.* Vancouver, BC: University of British Columbia Press.

Johnson, H. (1996). *Dangerous domains: Violence against women in Canada.* Toronto, ON: University of Toronto Press.

O'Grady, W. (2007). *Crime in Canadian context: Debates and controversies.* Toronto, ON: Oxford University Press.

Shantz, J. (2010). *Constructive anarchy: Building infrastructures of resistance.* Surrey, England: Ashgate.

Jeff Shantz

HEALTH EFFECTS OF DOMESTIC ABUSE

Exposure to violence and abuse has been repeatedly and significantly associated with negative health-related outcomes. Violence and abuse impact multiple dimensions of health, with long-reaching consequences for physical and emotional health in particular. Violence and abuse exert their adverse influence on health through multiple pathways including direct tissue injury, chronic stress and problems associated with it, and increased engagement in health-related risk behaviors (such as smoking) that are commonly used as coping mechanisms.

Health Effects of Violence and Abuse

The health effects of intimate partner violence (IPV), child maltreatment, and elder abuse are generally studied separately in different empirical studies. However, all forms of violence and abuse appear to increase the risk of poor health, and the conditions to which people with violence histories are susceptible are similar regardless of the specific type of violence exposure. In addition, when people experience multiple forms of violence victimization, the risk of poor health increases. Most health-related violence and abuse research has focused on women as victims. However, increasing evidence suggests that male victims are subject to the same adverse outcomes.

Physical Health

Many common illnesses that deleteriously affect long-term physical functioning have been found to be significantly associated with violence and abuse, specifically fibromyalgia and other chronic pain syndromes; irritable bowel syndrome; asthma; chronic obstructive pulmonary disease; and cardiovascular disease. In addition, in a nationally representative sample, Bonomi et al. (2007) found lower self-reported measures of overall health and dimensions of health-related quality of life, including vitality, mental health, and social functioning among women reporting exposures to sexual or physical IPV.

Emotional Health

Psychological effects include increased rates of depression, anxiety, cognitive disturbance, dissociation, somatization; sexual problems, post-traumatic stress disorder (PTSD), and suicidality (Bonomi et al., 2007).

Childhood Exposure to Violence and Adult Health Consequences

Foundational work by Felitti and Anda has improved understanding of the association between childhood exposure to violence and health-related outcomes. Their body of work known as the ACEs (Adverse Childhood Experiences) Study continues to assess associations of health-related outcomes with childhood adversity, characterized as abuse (emotional, physical, or sexual), neglect (emotional or physical), or household dysfunction (including exposure to domestic violence directed at one's mother). The ACEs Study has repeatedly demonstrated a strong, dose-dependent association between childhood adversity and myriad outcomes ranging from health-related quality of life to cancer, ischemic heart disease, and depression (Centers for Disease Control and Prevention—ACEs Study; Centers for Disease Control and Prevention—ACEs Study—Major Findings; Centers for Disease Control and Prevention—ACEs Study-Pyramid).

Health Impact of IPV Perpetration

Few studies have examined the health effects of IPV perpetration, and the clarity of cause and effect remain ill-defined. Higher rates of traumatic brain injury are one of the few medical conditions that has repeatedly been proposed as a causal mediator of IPV perpetration (Murphy, 1994).

Risky Behaviors

Women with a history of abuse were twice as likely as those without to smoke cigarettes (Lemon, Verhoek-Oftedahl, et al., 2002). Heavy alcohol use has been reported from two to three times the rate among men and women reporting abuse exposures compared to controls (Lemon et al., 2002). Childhood sexual abuse has repeatedly been associated with the development of childhood and adult obesity (Gunstad et al., 2006).

We are only just beginning to uncover the true depth and magnitude of the impact of experiencing violence and abuse. Identifying people affected by violence and abuse and connecting them with appropriate services provides the opportunity for healing and potentially reverses the harmful health impact. Thus, health care providers must be vigilant about screening for violence and abuse and supporting patients in their pursuit of treatment.

See also: Children, Impact of Domestic Abuse on; Effects of Domestic Abuse; Physicians, Health Care Providers, and Domestic Abuse; Psychological Effects of Domestic Abuse

Further Reading

Adverse health conditions and health risk behaviors associated with intimate partner violence—United States, 2005. (2008). *Journal of the American Medical Association, 300*(6), 646–649.

Bonomi, A. E., M. L. Anderson, et al. (2007). Health outcomes in women with physical and sexual intimate partner violence exposure. *Journal of Women's Health, 16*(7), 987–997.

Briere, J., & Jordan, C. (2004). Violence against women: Outcome complexity and implications for assessment and treatment. *Journal of Interpersonal Violence, 19*(11), 1252–1276.

Campbell, J. C. (2002). Health consequences of intimate partner violence. *Lancet, 359* (9314), 1331–1336.

Centers for Disease Control and Prevention. Adverse Childhood Experiences (ACEs) Study—Retrieved August 29, 2011, from http://www.cdc.gov/ace/index.htm

Centers for Disease Control and Prevention. Adverse Childhood Experiences (ACEs) Study—Major Findings. Retrieved April 26, 2011, from http://www.cdc.gov/ace/findings.htm

Centers for Disease Control and Prevention. Adverse Childhood Experiences (ACEs) Study—Pyramid. Retrieved April 26, 2011, from http://www.cdc.gov/ace/pyramid.htm

Futures without Violence. (2002). *National consensus guidelines: On identifying and responding to domestic violence victimization in health care settings.* San Francisco, CA, Futures.

Gunstad, J., Paul, R., et al. (2006). Exposure to early life trauma is associated with adult obesity. *Psychiatry Research, 142*(1), 31–37.

Lemon, S. Verhoek-Oftedahl, W., et al. (2002). Preventive healthcare use, smoking, and alcohol use among Rhode Island women experiencing intimate partner violence. *Journal of Women's Health & Gender-Based Medicine, 11*(6), 555–562.

Murphy, C. (1994). Treating perpetrators of adult domestic violence. *Maryland Medical Journal, 43*(10), 877–883.

Peter F. Cronholm and Megan Bair-Merritt

HISTORY OF U.S. DOMESTIC VIOLENCE BEFORE 1970
Before the Women's Rights Movement

Despite its prevalence, little has been written about family violence in American history before second-wave feminism helped catapult it into a pressing national issue in the 1970s. According to historian Elizabeth Pleck (1987), there were two epochs of abuse reform before the women's liberation movement: between 1640 and 1680 in colonial Massachusetts, and from 1874 to 1890 in larger urban areas. The third and final reform movement, which she argues began in 1962, would grow to become the battered women's movement. Rather than indicating spikes in domestic violence throughout American history, the sparse occurrence of reform movements throughout American history reflects changing social and cultural norms about family privacy, conjugal and parental rights, and family stability. Until the second wave, these reform efforts were squashed by countermovements that sacrificed women and children in order to protect the mythic American family ideal—the (white) married, two-parent household with children. Although the 1970s battered women's movement was coupled with strong criticism from the family-focused New Right, it survived and over time grew into a transnational, multicultural, and coalitional human rights movement.

The two most consistent barriers to reform against domestic violence have been the gendered boundaries between public and private and the preservation of the "family ideal." Until the battered women's movement there was little legal repercussion for abusers because domestic violence was perceived as a private family matter.

Until second-wave feminists and sociologists began repoliticizing domestic violence and presenting it as an urgent national issue, violence against women and children had consistently been considered nonexistent (in the case of white upper-class women), a reoccurring problem (in the case of working-class families or immigrants), or ignored altogether (as in the case of African Americans and other racial and ethnic minorities). Domestic violence has most often been viewed as an exclusively heterosexual male crime—most often attributed to lower-class male depravity.

Seventeenth Century

Traditionally, men have always had control and, therefore, the right to discipline wives, children, servants, and slaves. Historian Linda Gordon (1988) argues that laws such as the often-cited "rule of thumb"—a measurement indicating the largest width of an object a man could use to hit his wife—not only demonstrate limits to excessive violence, but are also evidence of a degree of women's power rather than their powerlessness and humiliation. Other historians have noted that though this rule of thumb is often discussed, there is no evidence that it existed. Nonetheless, it was certainly true that men had dominion over their wives and daughters. Throughout the seventeenth and eighteenth centuries, however, most communities had laws limiting the excessiveness of violence against women and children. Pleck (1987) argues that the first criminal codes restricting types of family violence—called the *Body of Liberties*—were instituted in the Massachusetts Bay and Plymouth colonies in 1641. These statutes declared, "Everie marryed woeman shall be free from bodily correction or stripes by her husband, unlesse it be in his owne defence upon her assault" (qtd. in Pleck, 1987, p. 22). These laws were created in order to preserve the Christian moral foundation of the "city upon a hill" rather than to protect the rights of women and children. Neighborly surveillance was utilized to monitor sexual deviance, drunkenness, thievery, Sabbath breakers, and female independence in addition to excessive violence. The Puritans believed that bringing abuse to light through public ridicule or scorn would ultimately bring salvation rather than women's safety, as divorces were strongly discouraged and shelters and orphanages were nonexistent. Pleck (1987) argues that by the end of the seventeenth century, however, church courts were no longer used to legislate morality. Despite this effort to curb family violence, men would continue to have the right to physically discipline women and children—the most excessive violence often sanctioned by social and cultural norms.

Early Nineteenth Century

While no significant public reform movement against family violence began to coalesce until the 1870s, the nineteenth century witnessed a dramatic restructuring of power relations within the American family. By the 1830s, the boundaries between public and private became more solidified, separating women's private domestic space from men's public domain. Women's magazines and advice manuals began to preach a new ideology of separate spheres, in which women would have greater maternal authority in the home and men would control political, social, and economic matters. Playing on gender stereotypes of (white) women as weaker and purer, the ideology argued that a True Woman judged herself by four virtues: piety, purity, submissiveness (to both men and morality), and domesticity. The "Cult of Domesticity" was both confining and uplifting, as it offered white middle-class women a distinct identity through women's work and the camaraderie of other True Women, while offering the home as their sphere of influence (despite ultimate male authority). However, in placing pressure on the distinctions between public and private, these changing social and cultural norms relegated women to the home with limited access to work, education, political authority, economic rights, and a social presence.

Although the cult offered "membership" to very few middle class white women, the ideology pervaded the whole of society, leaving poorer working women and nonwhites without a sense of self and belonging. As Deborah Gray White (1985) argues, the virtues of middle-class white mothers were preserved on the backs of enslaved and free African American women. White argues that proponents of slavery created and fueled the negative racial stereotypes of African American women as jezebels and mammies in order to boost white women's own social standing: "Black and white womanhood were interdependent. They played off one another. The white woman's sense of herself as a woman—her self-esteem and perceived superiority—depended on the racism that debased black women" (p. 6). Enslaved women were physically and psychologically abused, often raped by enslaved and white men, bred like cattle to produce more slaves, and forced to work as mothers, caregivers, wet nurses, and sexual partners in addition to their normal work. More so, this cycle of violence was so psychologically detrimental that it was sometimes replicated within the relationships of enslaved peoples—mothers beating children and men raping women. This enslavement and abuse was not only sanctioned for centuries in American history, but was excused as part of white men's paternal responsibility to morally guide the African race.

Over time, many upper-class white women began to negotiate a public sphere of influence by creating social policies and institutions that reinforced the four tenets of the Cult of True Womanhood. During the first-wave feminist movement of the 1850s, movement leaders Elizabeth Cady Stanton and Susan B. Anthony protested against the cultural norms regarding privacy that silently condoned family violence. Utilizing rhetoric that emphasized women's moral high ground and maternalism, white women expanded their domestic authority to the public domain, fighting against alcoholism, prostitution, gambling, and domestic abuse.

Late Nineteenth Century

Pleck (1987) argues that the second reform epoch occurred between 1874 and 1890, when the punitive approach to family violence reached its height as reformers helped to define domestic violence as a serious crime. The movement to prevent and end child abuse grew during the late nineteenth century with help from the temperance movement. By the 1870s, many women organized social services for family violence victims across the nation, including settlement houses, SPCCs (Societies for the Prevention of Cruelty to Children), orphanages, shelters, and support centers, most often organized and staffed by women. According to Pleck, male lawyers, district attorneys, and other law enforcement officials believed that fines and imprisonment had failed to reduce wife beating, and began to call for corporal punishment of batterers.

Twentieth Century

In light of the Progressive Era's emphasis on state regulation, from 1910 to 1930 family violence intervention and prevention became institutionalized as a state-sponsored social welfare movement. However, during this time, specialized tribunals for children and families were utilized in cases of domestic violence. Influenced by Freud's theories of psychoanalysis, courts utilized mental health and child guidance clinics to provide individual or marital therapy as a new, noncriminal approach to family violence. These social, political, and economic factors were used to excuse family violence, rather than to understand its roots. Reconciliation and economic aid became the most common treatments for family violence (Gordon, 1988). In light of the economic hardship experienced by families during the Great Depression, violence was interpreted as a product of a male breadwinner's frustration. Gordon argues that during this time, violence was deemphasized as courts focused more on "child neglect, primarily in terms of economic neglect, such as malnutrition or inadequate medical care" (p. 21).

Until the women's liberation movement, "pro-family" values hindered the progression of abuse reform movements. One of the major criticisms by feminist activists was lack of police assistance. According to Women's Advocates, one of the first women's shelters in America, police referred to domestic violence calls as "domestic disturbances" and told victims that their job was to maintain the family. Police also refused to take women to hospitals or other safer locations and "often relied on a 'stitch rule'—arresting an abusing husband only if his wife had been injured badly enough to require a specific number of surgical sutures" (Pleck, 1987, p. 186). Without public support, victims of domestic abuse dealt with the issues privately. In proclaiming "the personal is political," women's shelters and support organizations in the battered women's movement argued that the notion of dichotomous public and private spheres isolated women and children and privileged white, middle- and upper-class, heterosexual men.

Pleck (1987) argues that the third era of reform began in 1962, when five physicians published an article about "the Battered Women Syndrome" in the *Journal of the American Medical Association*. However, many scholars agree that the modern domestic violence movement began around 1970 when feminists began to discuss the prevalence of domestic violence in feminist consciousness-raising sessions. During these group conversations, women began to critique the separate-spheres ideology that not only restricted women's rights but forced families to hide abuse in order to fulfill the family ideal. Shelters, service organizations, and feminist groups helped propel wife beating and marital rape to national headlines. This reform movement opened up public discussion of many other types of family violence, including elderly abuse, sibling violence, incest, child molestation, and dating violence.

See also: Feminism and Domestic Abuse; Women's Rights Movement

Further Reading

Brief history of the movement to address domestic violence. *CBA: Colorado Bar Association.* Retrieved August 30, 2011, from http://www.cobar.org/index.cfm/ID/0/subID/161/Brief-History-of-the-Movement-to-Address-Domestic-Violence/

Enke, A. (2003). Taking over domestic space: The battered women's movement and public protest. In V. Gosse & R. Moser (Eds.), *The world the sixties made: Politics and culture in recent America* (pp. 162–190). Philadelphia, PA: Temple University Press.

Gordon, Linda. (1988). *Heroes of their own lives: The politics and history of family violence, Boston 1880–1960.* New York, NY: Viking Penguin Group.

Harrison, R. K. (2009). *Enslaved women and the art of resistance in antebellum America.* New York, NY: Palgrave Macmillan.

Howard, A., & Lewis, S. (1999). Herstory of domestic violence: A timeline of the battered women's movement. SafeNetwork: California's Domestic Violence Resource, Minnesota Center *Against Violence* and Abuse (MINCAVA) electronic clearinghouse, http://www.mincava.umn.edu/documents/herstory/herstory.html

Pleck, E. (1987). *Domestic tyranny.* New York, NY: Oxford University Press.

Reinelt, C. (1995). Moving onto the terrain of the state: The battered women's movement and the politics of engagement. In M. M. Ferree & P. Y. Martin (Eds.), *Feminist organizations: Harvest of the new women's movement* (pp. 84–104). Philadelphia, PA: Temple University Press.

Schechter, S. (1982). *Women and male violence.* Boston, MA: South End Press.

Women's Advocates. (1980). *The story of a shelter.* St. Paul, MN: Women's Advocates.

White, D. G. (1985). *Ar'n't I a woman? Female slaves in the plantation South.* New York, NY: W. W. Norton.

Kera Lovell

HISTORY OF U.S. DOMESTIC VIOLENCE DEVELOPMENTS, 1970s

Many scholars agree that the modern domestic violence movement, initially termed the "battered women's movement," began around 1970 when women started to discuss the prevalence of domestic violence in feminist consciousness-raising sessions. Nationally, the movement was begun and sustained largely by feminist leadership, yet in other places former battered women, neighborhood women, or professionals led the movement. While several women's shelters had sprouted across the country by 1972, Minnesota-based Women's Advocates is considered the first emergency shelter for women in America, after which more than 300 shelters and 48 state coalitions of service providers were formed by 1982. Women's shelters, support groups, and feminist organizations worked with police and political leaders to help provide funding for shelters, improve reporting procedures, and establish more effective criminal court procedures. Many advocacy groups and shelters also participated in national women's rights commissions and conferences that helped the movement gain legitimacy and unity. Alliances between radical feminists and liberal feminists, feminists and nonfeminists, enabled the problem of violence against women to reach national levels through movement organizations, public education, and crisis centers. Women from different ages, races, classes, occupations, incomes levels, and political affiliations merged to transform domestic violence into a pressing national issue with a national movement behind it. Despite substantial budget cuts to shelters and organizations during the 1980s, domestic violence prevention and activism would persevere through the beginning of the twenty-first century.

Haven House in Pasadena, California, was the first shelter to receive a government contract in 1972. Another women's shelter, Rainbow Retreat, opened in Phoenix, Arizona, the same year. However, Women's Advocates in St. Paul, Minnesota, is remembered as the first women's shelter, made popular by their self-published book *The Story of a Shelter* (1980), which detailed their foray into assisting domestic violence victims. Although there were 37 emergency shelters for men in the Twin Cities, women with children only had one alternative—they could receive emergency housing for one night in a motel booked through Emergency Social Services. Women's Advocates members began taking callers into their homes before they eventually purchased a house in 1974. Within shelters, women crossed boundaries of race, class, age, and feminist ideology to facilitate a more inclusive and supportive emergency refuge. These early collective experiences prepared advocacy groups and shelters to deal with more laborious efforts to reform police and court procedures and ally with nonfeminist and antifeminist organizations. While mainly middle-class white women initially led the movement in many communities, shelters immediately served a diverse group of women. Women's Advocates and some other shelters were organized around a radical feminist ideology of creating a separatist and egalitarian space for women with a communal structure. By modeling a shelter after a home, collectives showed how the private sphere was both public and political. At first, Women's Advocates mandated few rules within the shelter and utilized an egalitarian structure in order to eliminate hierarchical power in both the public and private spheres.

Shelters increasingly addressed the needs of their residents by offering various forms of support: procuring income assistance, legal counsel, and protection orders; finding job training, employment, and education; apartment search, apartment furnishings, and very limited transitional housing. These organizations also recognized their responsibility in educating their communities about domestic violence and the need for emergency housing for women in crisis. Representative of other organizations and shelters in the battered women's movement, Women's Advocates' educational strategies included a community newsletter, speaking engagements, workshops, a college-level course, relationships with local schools, and minority community outreach, in addition to organizing training sessions with police, medical personnel, and social workers.

The two major battlegrounds for the movement were police and court reform. Advocacy groups helped battered women sue police departments who would not assist them. In 1976, two major lawsuits, *Scott v. Hart* and *Bruno v. Codd*, were filed against police departments. Settled in 1979, *Scott v. Hart* required police to "stop training officers to avoid arrest in domestic violence cases, to treat each case on its own merits, to allow the plaintiff's attorneys to do weekly squad trainings with the officers, to hand out resource cards to victims, and to donate money to local battered women's shelters" (Howard & Lewis, 1999). Settled out of court, *Bruno v. Codd* mandated that New York City police "1. arrest men who commit felonious assaults; 2. send out officers for every call from a battered woman; 3. arrest in misdemeanor cases unless there is justification not to arrest; 4. arrest where a husband has violated a ... protection order; 5. assist the women in receiving medical help; and 6. search for a husband who has fled the scene of the crime ..." (Schechter, 1982, p. 160). These cases inspired battered women to file lawsuits nationwide against police departments, as well as departments of probation and the Family Court. Family Court probation employees repeatedly denied women access to protection orders and coerced women out of court and into private family counseling. Unmarried women often had no recourse for legal action. By 1980, 44 states had enacted laws requiring automatic arrests in domestic violence cases. In both police and court reform, advocacy groups continued to fight to legitimize domestic violence as a crime and pass laws to provide more social services for battered women.

Although many domestic violence shelters were initially organized as separatist institutions operating outside of the legal framework, radical feminists quickly realized that these utopian alternative communities could not grow to support the thousands of women in need of services. Shelters, advocacy groups, and organizations would need to form coalitions with organizations acting within the hegemonically masculine organizational structure. Advocacy organizations began to relocate the private issue of domestic violence outside of shelters in order to challenge sexually discriminating police and court procedures. As in the case of the Texas Council on Family Violence, shelter activists practiced what Claire Reinelt (1995) calls "a politics of engagement," or the combination of liberal and radical feminism, in order to challenge sexually discriminating police and court procedures (85). In her study on Women's Advocates, Enke (2003) states, "Far from cutting themselves off from people who did not share their feminist or leftist analyses, leaders in the battered-women's movement engaged state agencies and capitalist funding sources to create a lasting network of institutions" (p. 164).

In search of funding, advocacy groups forged bonds with governmental agencies and commissions. At national and international women's rights conferences, shelters and service organizations worked together to testify at commission hearings and assist in creating a national agenda on domestic violence. On January 9, 1975, in response to the United Nations' declaration of International Women's Year (IWY), President Gerald Ford established the National Commission on the Observance of International Women's Year. In 1976, *Ms.* became the first national magazine to put a battered woman on the cover and catapulted the issue of domestic violence into a national movement. Legislation was eventually passed in that same year to fund national and international women's conferences, which provided opportunities for advocacy groups to form extensive networks within and beyond the feminist movement. The U.S. Civil Rights Commission held hearings on domestic violence in 1978. Organized by Carole Bonasarro, head of the Women's Rights Project in the Civil Rights Commission, the domestic violence hearings enabled shelters to forge a comprehensive national network. In her book *Tidal Wave* (2004), Sara Evans describes the mood of the commission hearings according to Bonasarro: "Accustomed to dignified and professional meetings, she was stunned that so many of the shelter staff came—with sleeping bags. Shelter staff shared battle stories, institutional struggles, and strategies, and sensed not only their need for a continuing network but also the potential power of a national voice" (p. 130). The hearings proved instrumental in the formation of the National Coalition Against Domestic Violence (NCADV).

In 1979, President Carter established the Office on Domestic Violence, which "was seen as a central locus for policy planning, information dissemination, and interagency coordination" (Schechter, 1982, p. 193). The movement was unable to fully utilize the Office of Domestic Violence, however, as it was closed in 1981 shortly after President Reagan took office. Although many radical feminist domestic violence shelters had initially organized around the concept of gender as structure, feminist organizations were forced to utilize more amiable rhetoric when providing solutions for a growing antifeminist public. A bipartisan bill providing extensive funding for domestic violence shelters was quickly quashed under the New Right. In their efforts to strengthen the American family and preserve the "family ideal," which had stiffened activism against domestic violence for centuries, the New Right cut substantial portions of funding to feminist emergency shelters. In avoiding radical rhetoric and packaging the issue of domestic violence in less structurally threatening terms, organizations gained political capital and legitimacy during a period of profound antifeminist backlash.

Many antifeminist activists such as Phyllis Schlafly argued that, in removing women from the home, shelters promoted an antimotherhood, antifamily, and anti-Christ ideology. These criticisms from the New Right and the subsequent depoliticization of the movement were the impetus for Schechter's *Women and Male Violence* (1982) and subsequent third-wave scholarship. In anchoring the battered women's movement to radical feminism, Schechter called feminists to act against the separate-spheres ideology that the second wave had worked so hard to defeat. Many women's rights advocacy groups dissolved under the weight of the New Right, the media's antifeminist backlash, and severe budget cuts. Organizations that did survive eliminated their rhetoric of radicalism, including their focus on gender as structure, to maintain political power and funding. In light of massive budget cuts, the battered women's movement agreed to a cross-political coalition by tacking shelter funding onto the Child Abuse and Prevention Treatment Act (1982). The bill, which allocated $6 million for emergency women's shelters, marked an end to the long 1970s in domestic violence intervention and prevention.

See also: Feminism and Domestic Abuse; U.S. Government Responses to Domestic Violence; Legislation and Policies, Domestic Abuse; National Coalition Against Domestic Violence (NCADV); Schechter, Susan; Women's Rights Movement

Further Reading

Brief history of the movement to address domestic violence. *CBA: Colorado Bar Association*. Retrieved August 30, 2011, from http://www.cobar.org/index.cfm/ID/0/subID/161/Brief-History-of-the-Movement-to-Address-Domestic-Violence/

Enke, A. (2003). Taking over domestic space: The battered women's movement and public protest. In V. Gosse & R. Moser (Eds.), *The world the sixties made: Politics and culture in recent America* (162–190). Philadelphia, PA: Temple University Press.

Evans, S. (2004). *Tidal wave: How women changed America at century's end*. New York, NY: Free Press.

Howard, A., & Lewis, S. (1999). Herstory of domestic violence: A timeline of the battered women's movement. SafeNetwork: California's Domestic Violence Resource, Minnesota Center Against Violence and Abuse (MINCAVA) electronic clearinghouse, http://www.mincava.umn.edu/documents/herstory/herstory.html

Our history—1970s. *Women's Aid*. Retrieved August 30, 2011, from http://www.womensaid.org.uk/landing_page.asp?section=00010001001900040004

Pleck, E. (1987). *Domestic tyranny*. New York, NY: Oxford University Press.

Reinelt, C. (1995). Moving onto the terrain of the state: The battered women's movement and the politics of engagement. In M. M. Ferree & P. Y. Martin (Eds.), *Feminist organizations: Harvest of the new women's movement* (pp. 84–104). Philadelphia, PA: Temple University Press.

Rosen, R. (2000). *The world split open: How the modern women's movement changed America*. New York, NY: Penguin Books.

Schechter, S. (1982). *Women and male violence*. Boston, MA: South End Press.

Spalter-Roth, R., & Schrieber, R. (1995). Outsider issues and insider tactics: Strategic tensions in the women's policy network during the 1980s. In M. M. Ferree & P. Y. Martin (Eds.), *Feminist organizations: Harvest of the new women's movement* (pp. 105–127). Philadelphia, PA: Temple University Press.

Women's Advocates. (1980). *The story of a shelter*. St. Paul, MN: Women's Advocates.

Kera Lovell

HISTORY OF U.S. DOMESTIC VIOLENCE DEVELOPMENTS, 1980s

The primary focus of the 1980s in terms of domestic violence was on enhancing the criminal justice response. Great efforts were made to increase police response to domestic violence and to hold batterers accountable via legal action. Prompted by lawsuits against law enforcement for failure to respond in the later 1970s, the effort to improve police responses to domestic violence gained steam when the results of the Minnesota Domestic Violence Experiment (MDVE) were released in 1984. MDVE, coordinated by researchers Lawrence Sherman and Richard Berk, with funding from the National Institute of Justice, was the first scientific study to find out which police responses were most effective at reducing repeated incidents of violence. Sherman and Berk found that arresting the perpetrator was the most effective response. These findings, along with the 1985 federal lawsuit won by Tracey Thurman against the City of Torrington police for failing to protect her from her husband's violence, ushered in the trend for mandatory arrest policies for domestic violence. Thurman's story was made into an NBC drama called *A Cry for Help: The Tracey Thurman Story*, which aired in 1989. By 1986, almost half of urban police departments had enacted mandatory arrest policies, and by 1989, 12 states had enshrined these policies into law. The policies require that police arrest abusers where there is probable cause, and led to a dramatic increase in arrests for domestic violence. For instance, after the mandatory arrest policy was enacted in Denver, arrests rose from 1,700 in 1984 to 5,000 three years later. This effort to increase police response occurred outside the United States as well. For example, between 1985 and 1995, 100 special police stations for women were opened in Brazil. Throughout the 1980s, the United Kingdom continued to be a global leader on the issue of domestic violence.

The 1980s also built on the momentum of the 1970s movement to continue efforts to provide safety for victims. Moving away from the movement's earlier feminist lens, however, the discourse utilized in the movement and in the shelters in the 1980s shifted to a more individualistic focus. In the early 1980s, state governments began to allocate state revenues and discretionary federal funds—for example, Title XX of the Social Security Act and Emergency Assistance funds—to services for domestic violence victims. Between 1979 and 1989, the number of shelters in the United States quadrupled due to these new funding sources. Few of these shelters were started by feminist groups, which had been the impetus behind the shelter movement of the 1970s. Instead, it was religious groups, YMCAs, and other civic organizations that obtained the state and federal funding to operate domestic violence shelters. Yet there was still not enough shelter space for all the victims in need: Park, Schindehette and Speidel (1989) pointed out in 1989 that some 40 percent of victims were turned away because there was not enough shelter space, and Philadelphia had three animal shelters but just one domestic violence shelter. In 1987, the National Coalition Against Domestic Violence established the first national toll-free domestic violence hotline, an important move in allowing victims in any part of the country to obtain crisis assistance.

The availability of state and federal funds prompted changes in the way that shelters operated. To be eligible for such funding, shelters were to avoid radical feminist activism, for instance. As Casa de Esperanza (2005) noted in "Where Did the Movement Go?": "As more and more domestic violence programs received public revenue, subtle shifts began to occur in the organizations. Because federal funds were designated for services and not community education, more attention was focused on individual counseling for women and less on peer support and advocacy. To receive public contracts, shelters felt the pressure to employ credentialed staff and move toward more widely recognized social service models. To maintain these government contracts, they needed to provide evidence that their interventions were having the desired effect. Slowly, staff began talking about *treatment* for *clients*, rather than *empowerment* for battered *women*."

In 1982, sociologist Kathleen Tierney predicted that domestic violence would be medicalized and individualized, a trend that did indeed occur throughout the decade and, some assert, continues today.

It was in the 1980s that the general public began to put a "face" or identity to domestic violence victims. Events like the first National Day of Unity, held in October 1980 (which later became a week and is now Domestic Violence Awareness Month), and national conferences held by the National Coalition Against Domestic Violence, as well as media attention, helped bring increased attention to the plight of victims. When *60 Minutes* in 1982 aired "A Place to Go," which focused on the work of domestic violence shelters in Austin, Texas, more people watched the program than any other that season.

A major improvement over times in which the discourse about abuse was held only in whispers, this identity was constructed as largely white. This served to minimize the abuse that is experienced by women of color.

> Hedda Nussbaum, Nicole Brown Simpson, Sheila Hollabaugh, for example—constructs the identity of the battered woman, which helps construct the process and the practice of the law. Each of these particular faces is that of a white woman who only gained notoriety because of her association with domestic violence and the legal system, which helps to construct the face in the public eye. The white battered woman identity, the white-focused empowerment continuum and the white-dominated legal practice are the elements that construct a legal discourse. This legal discourse renders women of color invisible, and subjects victims of domestic violence who are not white to further abuse within a system purporting to exist to help them. Legal discourse includes language written in statutes and spoken in courtrooms, visual images and iconography, and the behavior of those involved with the system. Domestic violence legal discourse has all of these integrants contained within the three essential elements of identity, process and practice. (Morrison, 2006, pp. 1075–1076)

In 1985, Evelyn White published *Chain, Chain Change: For Black Women Dealing with Physical and Emotional Abuse*, the first book about African American women and abuse. Although the book was tremendously important in giving voice to women of color who endured abuse, the dominant frame of white victims remained largely the focus of public attention. As a result, women of color began to organize separate movements and efforts designed to address their unique needs, which come from living in not just a patriarchal but also a racist society.

Berns (2004) explained that the dominant ideology about domestic violence remained victim focused, now urging him or her to "take back the power." She commented, "This focus may help build support for programs that help victims of domestic violence. However, it does little to develop public understanding of the social context of violence and may impede social change that could prevent violence" (p. 3). The result of this framing of victims and the movement is that the "critique of women's position within the family and the larger culture has been silenced by the rhetoric of 'family values.' As the battered women's movement has become institutionalized and bureaucratized, individual family pathology has been substituted for radical critiques of the status quo" (Ferraro, 1996, p. 80).

Adding to the shift in the 1980s domestic violence movement away from the previous feminist perspective was what Susan Faludi (1991) called a "backlash" against women's rights. Economic recession and a conservative government resulted in backlash against the gains made toward gender equality in the 1970s. Women's rights activism was even blamed for many of the social problems of the decade.

The federal government both helped and hurt the movement in the 1980s. In 1984, the U.S. Attorney General established a task force that included public testimony in six cities by nearly 300 witnesses. The final report issued from the task force included a variety of recommendations related to training, legislation, data collection, and education. In 1985, Surgeon General C. Everett Koop issued a report in which he called domestic violence a major health problem. Thus began an important line of research and training directed at medical professionals, who are, aside from police, most likely to be the first responders in abuse cases. In 1988, the surgeon general called domestic violence the leading health hazard for women.

At the same time, citing budget problems, President Ronald Reagan dismantled the Office on Domestic Violence that his predecessor, President Jimmy Carter, had created.

See also: Feminism and Domestic Abuse; Funding for Domestic Violence Services; Shelters for Domestic Abuse Victims; Mandatory Arrest Policies; Minnesota Domestic Violence Experiment; U.S. Government Responses to Domestic Violence; Women's Rights Movement

Further Reading

Berns, N. (2004). *Framing the victim: Domestic violence, media, and social problems.* New York: Aldine de Gruyter.

Faludi, S. (1991). *Backlash: The undeclared war against American women.* New York, NY: Doubleday.

Ferraro, K. (1996, fall). The dance of dependency: A genealogy of domestic violence discourse. *Hypatia, 11*(4), 77–92.

Freedman, E. (2002). *No turning back: The history of feminism and the future of women.* New York, NY: Ballantine.

McGregor, H. (1989). *Working for change: Movement against domestic violence.* Concord, MA: Paul and Co.

Morrison, A. (2006). Changing the domestic violence (dis)course: Moving from white victim to multicultural survivor. *UC Davis Law Review.* Retrieved June 11, 2012, from http://lawreview.law.ucdavis.edu/issues/39/3/deconstructing-image-repertoire-women-of-color/DavisVol39No3_MORRISON.pdf

Park, J., Schindehette, S., & Speidel, M. (1989, October 9). Thousands of women, fearing for their lives, hear a scary echo in Tracey Thurman's cry for help. *People.* Retrieved June 15, 2012, from http://www.people.com/people/archive/article/0,,20121378,00.html

Pleck, E. (1989). *Domestic tyranny: The making of American social policy against family violence from colonial times to the present.* New York, NY: Oxford.

Tierney, K. (1982). The battered women movement and the creation of the wife beating problem, *Social Problems, 29,* 207–220.

Weissman, D. (2007). The personal is political—and economic: Rethinking domestic violence. *BYU Law Review.* Retrieved June 11, 2012, from http://lawreview.byu.edu/archives/2007/2/3WEISSMAN.FIN.pdf

Where did the movement go? (2005). Casa de Esperanza. Retrieved June 15, 2012, from http://www.casadeesperanza.org/pdfs/WhereDidMovementGo%20ENG.pdf

Laura L. Finley

HISTORY OF U.S. DOMESTIC VIOLENCE DEVELOPMENTS, 1990s

During the 1990s, domestic violence (DV) was acknowledged as an unacceptable social challenge. Since then, society has achieved significant strides to address DV, including service delivery to DV survivors. DV was once considered one of the most under-estimated crimes since it often went unreported by the victims themselves, and the legal-judicial system did not regard it as criminal behavior. This era demonstrated a remarkable response to DV and the tremendous growth in the literature on partner violence. Identifiable benchmarks of DV events in the 1990s included enacted legislation, literature publications, programs, and services.

One of the most overwhelming and insidious issues in the 1990s that threatened families and society, the 1990s saw significant changes in the nation's response to DV. During this era, the third wave of feminism emerged with a focus on inequality at different levels and combatting sexism. To address violence against women institutionally, the Violence Against Women Act (VAWA) (1994) and the antistalking law (1997) were enacted. Accordingly, supportive services for victims such as emergency shelters and aggressive batterer interventions that included pro-arrest policies were created. In the United States, DV became more widely recognized in state institutions and the criminal justice system. As a result, the civil court began to increase significantly the legal response to DV. This provided greater victim safety, increased offender accountability, decreed pro-arrest polices for law enforcement and mandatory rehabilitation programs for batterers. Options were also made available to DV survivors to strengthen their involvement in their cases.

Protection from abuse changed radically. The lack of serious attention paid to DV was dramatically exposed in 1994 when the mass media aired the contentious trial of O. J. Simpson for the murder of former wife Nicole Brown Simpson and her friend Ronald Goldman. During this trial, the press revealed her ex-husband, former football star, O. J. Simpson, was a batterer. Consequently, outspoken advocates all over America intensified the thrust toward reforming the government's response to DV against women. The unheeded cries of family violence victims could no longer be ignored. Thus, the National Council of Juvenile and Family Court Judges drafted and introduced the model DV Code to the National Conference of State Legislatures. Specifically, it sought to upgrade interventions and limit discretion of individuals within the criminal justice system to be more responsive to DV victims' safety needs. The code imposed mandatory arrest, mandatory no-contact orders, and restrictions on home detention and deferred prosecutions for batterers, restrictions on plea bargaining in DV cases, and standards for certification of DV treatment programs.

The government's aggressive move to tackle DV reached its peak when the federal government passed the Violence Against Women Act (VAWA). Under the Victims of Crime Act, President Clinton signed the VAWA into law in September 1994. This act stated that a gender-motivated crime is considered a violation of women's civil rights, and the victim has a legal right to sue the perpetrator. The act also makes restraining orders valid across state lines and therefore prohibits interstate abuse or stalking of a victim. The passage of VAWA secured additional federal funding for DV programs. This was designed to improve interstate criminal justice enforcement and provide adequate funding for criminal justice interventions and social services for victims (Cho & Wilke, 2005). VAWA supported the creation of the National Domestic Violence Hotline in 1996. The hotline provided crisis intervention information and assistance to DV victims. In its first year of operation, the hotline responded to more than 73,000 calls for assistance from around the United States (Richie & Menard, 2011). People's opinions are divided about the VAWA. While many view it as a milestone in the nation's efforts to treat DV as a serious issue, some feel that it does not address the DV survivors' needs. With the passage of the law, women got a legal escape and choice. By passing the VAWA of 1994, the government toughened its stance against DV perpetrators. In 1995, under VAWA, Christopher Bailey became the first batterer convicted of a felony for crossing state lines from West Virginia to Kentucky to assault his wife, Sonya Bailey, in the 1990s.

Another significant development concerned the passage of the antistalking law. Legal reforms at the state level led to federal DV legislation. Before 1990, no states had antistalking laws. California was the first to enact an antistalking law in 1990. Since then every other state has created a similar statute. In 1993, the U.S. Department of Justice's National Institute of Justice under the U.S. Congress directives developed a model antistalking code. It intended to provide a constitutional and enforceable legal framework for states to use to formulate their antistalking laws. This was followed with President Clinton's signing of an antistalking law in 1997. For the first time in U.S. history, stalking, or a repeated harassment and threatening behavior, was recognized as a serious crime. Stalking behaviors may include following the victim, waiting for and watching the victim, showering the victim with unwanted attention or gifts, threatening to hurt the victim, and using technology such as hidden cameras to track the victim's whereabouts. The purpose for making stalking illegal was to intervene before the victim sustained an injury or was killed. Until the passage of this law, police officers and prosecutors felt restricted in assisting victims threatened by a stalker. This law made interstate stalking and harassment a federal offense.

In the 1990s, DV research also evolved. Scholarly research on DV distinguished types of partner violence and explored feminist allegations that men use violence to control their partners in intimate relationships. From the feminist perspective, DV is directly related to the inequality of power upheld in a patriarchal society. In their view, violence is the most obvious and efficient means of social control used by men to uphold dominance over women. Some of the momentous publications that emerged in the 1990s include the *Journal of Family Violence*, developed for improving court practices in family violence cases. At the annual meeting, July 1990, the National Council of Juvenile and Family Court Judges adopted as official policy recommendations from dedicated advocates for battered women to view family violence as criminal conduct, to improve judicial leadership and the training for court-related agencies encompassing law enforcement, prosecutors, court administration, probation, victim advocates, child protective services, and treatment providers. "Femicide: The Politics of Women Killing" was also published in 1992.

Research indicates that criminal justice agents' approach to DV in the 1990s emphasized victim's choices. Hoyle and Sanders (2000) found that police response to DV was based on women's conveyed desires. This approach allows an individual victim to decide what may be best for her. Critics argued that this victim choice approach could be a mantle to cover police reluctance to treat DV as other crimes. In addition, they contended that the victim choice approach was shortsighted about the impact of nonprosecution on both the perpetrators and victims of DV. Further, they maintained that the victim choice approach exposes women to the manipulation of their abuser, police officers, as well as family members who may want the criminal prosecution dropped. Furthermore, they viewed police acting only on the women's choices as sending the message that women could achieve the right choice without legal intervention.

Another milestone in 1990 was the founding of the National Network to End Domestic Violence (NNEDV). The NNEDV mission ensured that national public policy attend to the concerns and interests of battered women and their children as well as educate the general public about issues concerning DV. NNEDV was also developed to strengthen the growth of relationships among DV coalitions that were designed to provide services, provide community education, offer technical assistance to programs, and establish shelter and related services to battered women and their children. One other essential 1990s development was creating the DV Coalition on Public Policy. The DV coalition was developed by state coalitions in 1991 to scrutinize Native American public policy issues. Accordingly, in 1993, the family violence and intimate violence team emerged within the division of Violence Prevention at the National Center for Injury Prevention and Control. In the same year, the U.S. Centers for Disease Control and Prevention began to fund community-based prevention efforts, studies on causality and consequences of DV, evaluation programs, public education, and training. Furthermore, the DV coalition on public policy was amalgamated as the National Network to End DV. Donna Edwards became the director and the first woman of color to head a national DV organization. Through funding from the U.S. Department of Health and Human Services, the Domestic Violence Resource Network was also created. This includes the National Resource Center on DV, the Battered Women's Justice Project, the Resource Center on DV: Child Protection and Custody, and the Health Resource Center on DV.

Other developments in the 1990s include the first joint meeting of the U. S. Department of Justice and Health and Human Services Advisory Council on Violence Against Women in 1995 co-chaired by then-Attorney General Janet Reno and Secretary of Health and Human Services Donna Shalala. Also, the Institute on Domestic Violence in the African American Community under the leadership of Dr. Oliver J. Williams held its first forum to discuss DV in the African American community. Further, in 1996, under the leadership of Dr. Robert McAfee, the American Medical Association launched a campaign against family violence and formed the National Coalition of Physicians Against Family Violence. This association also created diagnostic and treatment guidelines on DV and the mental health effects of family violence. To address the issue of DV in the Latino community, in

1997, the National Latino Alliance for the abolition of DV was formed by a group of 40 Latin American activists, clinicians, and researchers from the United States and Puerto Rico. In 1998, the U.S. Department of Justice announced grants totaling $53.8 million to help investigate and prosecute DV, and the Asian Institute on DV held its first national forum on DV. Also, in 1999, Vice President Gore announced the federal government disposition to provide $233 million to help states and communities detect and stop violence against women and provide shelter for victims of DV. Lastly, in 1999, VAWA II was introduced on the floor of the U.S. Senate and called for the reauthorization of funding.

In conclusion, the 1990s recorded momentous changes in the nation's response to DV. DV became more widely recognized in the U.S. state institutions and criminal justice system, and the civil courts began to administer more severe responses to it. This provided supportive services for victims, increased offender accountability, and decreed pro-arrest polices for law enforcement and mandatory rehabilitation programs for batterers. The drive toward change in the government response to DV reached its height with the federal government passing of the Violence Against Women Act (VAWA) 1994 and the antistalking law in 1997.

See also: Feminism and Domestic Abuse; Funding for Domestic Violence Services; National Network to End Domestic Violence (NNEDV); U.S. Government Responses to Domestic Violence; Violence Against Women Act (VAWA)

Further Reading

Cho, H., & Wilke, D. J. (2005). How has the violence against women act affected the response of the criminal justice system to domestic violence? *Journal of Sociology & Social Welfare, 32*(4), 125–139.

Hoyle, C., & Sanders, A. (2000). Police response to domestic violence: From victim choice to victim empowerment. *British Journal of Criminology, 40*(1), 14–36.

Johnson, M. P., & Ferraro, K. J. (2000). Research on domestic violence in the 1990s: Making distinctions. *Journal of Marriage and the Family, 62,* 948–963.

Richie, B., & Menard, A. (2011). *Time of milestones*. Retrieved from http://www.dvmillennium.org/Timeline.htm

Yllo, K. A. (1993). Through a feminist lens: Gender, power, and violence. In R. J. Gelles & D. R. Loseke (Eds.), *Current controversies on family violence* (pp. 47–62). Newbury Park, CA: Sage.

Wasserman, C. (2004). Dating violence on campus: A fact of life. *National Center for Victims of Crime Networks,* 16–21.

Catherine Ekwe (Kate) Ngozi

HISTORY OF U.S. DOMESTIC VIOLENCE DEVELOPMENTS, 2000s

In the 2000s in the United States, legislation continued to emerge at the federal and state levels. The Violence Against Women Act (VAWA) was reauthorized twice during the decade. In 2000, a bipartisan coalition helped enact the Trafficking Victims Protection Act (TVPA) to enhance prevention efforts and enable swifter and more appropriate responses to human trafficking. The 2009 Tribal Law and Justice Act helps address abuse on Native American lands. Advocates saw the Supreme Court's decision in *Castle Rock v. Gonzales* as a huge setback. Jessica Gonzales contacted the Castle Rock, Colorado, police numerous times to report that her husband, Simon Gonzales, had kidnapped their three daughters, in violation of a restraining order. Police failed to respond, and Simon Gonzales killed the three girls. Jessica sued the police, maintaining that their failure to protect her daughters resulted in the murders. The Supreme Court ruled in 2005 that victims are not entitled to the enforcement of their restraining orders, a decision that advocates called "a serious blow." Gonzales, now Jessica Lenahan, and her team of lawyers appealed to the Inter-American Commission on Human Rights, which issued a decision in August 2011. That court found the U.S. Supreme Court had erred and that the enforcement of restraining orders is a fundamental human right.

Outside the United States, many nations added their first legislation related to domestic abuse in the decade between 2000 and 2010. For instance, Nepal outlawed marital rape in 2002, and by April 2011, at least 52 countries have explicitly prohibited the practice. In 2009, Uganda passed a law criminalizing domestic violence and outlawing female genital mutilation. After two Austrian women were murdered by their abusive husbands despite having protection orders, the Austrian government enacted an amendment to the Code of Criminal Procedure providing new protection measures, creating specialized domestic violence prosecutors, and increasing funding to implement the law. Throughout the decade, international tribunals in Rwanda and the former Yugoslavia addressed, among other things, the use of rape and other gender violence as part of war or violent conflict.

The International Violence Against Women Act (IVAWA) was introduced in the House and the Senate during the 111th Congress. According to Women Thrive Worldwide, a group that helped write the bill, IVAWA

> would for the first time comprehensively incorporate solutions into all U.S. foreign assistance programs—solutions such as promoting women's economic opportunity, addressing violence against girls in school, and working to change public attitudes. Among other things, the IVAWA would make ending violence against women a diplomatic priority for the first time in U.S. history. It would require the U.S. government to respond to critical outbreaks of gender-based violence in armed conflict—such as the mass rapes now occurring in the Democratic Republic of Congo and Haiti—in a timely manner. And by investing in local women's organizations overseas that are successfully working to reduce violence in their communities, the IVAWA would have a huge impact on reducing poverty—empowering millions of women in poor countries to lift themselves, their families, and their communities out of poverty.

In the United States, following the movement to increased criminal justice intervention and responses to domestic abuse, the time between 2000 and the present has seen some signs of a return to the more grassroots, victim-centered focus of the origin of the movement. Some nonprofit organizations have renounced their 501c3 status in the belief that they are better able to meet the unique needs of all victims when their efforts are coordinated by volunteers instead of paid staff and through community-based coalitions. In 2000, Incite! Women of Color Against Violence was formed to address all forms of violence against women. It received most of its funding from individual donations and from foundations, but organizers became troubled when the Ford Foundation retracted a grant because the group's work was too radical. Incite! then returned to a more grassroots form of soliciting funds, hosting bake sales, house parties, and making individual calls.

Additionally, the 2000s has seen increased attention to social change and prevention campaigns. Male feminist activists like Jackson Katz, Paul Kivel, and Ben Atherton-Zeman have developed programs to inspire men to get involved in prevention efforts. In 2002, the Centers for Disease Control (CDC's) Domestic Violence Prevention Enhancement and Leadership Through Alliances (DELTA) program began focusing on primary prevention of domestic abuse. Primary prevention involves efforts to change the conditions and social norms that lead to abuse, thereby preventing it from occurring. The DELTA program provides funding and support for the development of coordinated community responses (CCRs) that integrate key community leaders from law enforcement, the courts, service providers, education, health care, clergy, and others to challenge gender norm socialization, address social issues like poverty and inequality, and develop programs and practices that encourage young people to live healthy, nonviolent lifestyles.

Additionally, the decade saw increased and enhanced efforts to train groups and individuals most likely to interact with domestic violence victims. Programs have been developed for health-care providers, educators, law enforcement, prosecutors, and faith leaders so that they can be trained to identify and respond to victims appropriately.

The United Nations has also promoted several social change campaigns. In 2008, Secretary General Ban Ki Moon launched UNiTE, a campaign intended to integrate efforts to address violence against women and girls. UNiTE aims to achieve the following by 2015: adopt and enforce national laws to address and punish all forms of violence against women and girls; adopt and implement multisectoral national action plans; strengthen data collection on the prevalence of violence against women and girls; increase public awareness and social mobilization; and address sexual violence in conflict

In July 2010, the United Nations merged several groups to announce the creation of UN Women, devoted to addressing global gender inequalities. UN Women supports and funds numerous social change campaigns across the globe addressing such topics as human trafficking, female genital mutilation, domestic and dating abuse, rape during conflict, and others. UN Women's first Progress of the World's Women, 2011–12 report highlighted the many initiatives occurring globally as well as the remaining challenges involving such things as the gender wage gap, inadequate or underenforced legislation addressing marital rape, and recommending ways that countries can continue to work toward achieving the Millennium Development Goals (MDGs). In 2000, 189 countries agreed to work toward eight goals: (1) ending poverty and hunger; (2) universal education; (3) promoting gender equality; (4) ensuring child health and (5) maternal health; (6) combating HIV/AIDS; (7) promoting environmental sustainability; and (8) developing global partnerships.

Further, the United States has also seen far more attention to the unique experiences of specific demographic groups, including teen victims, male victims, immigrant victims, abuse in same-sex relationships, and victims with disabilities. Some of those same trends can be seen globally, although issues related to homosexuality in particular remain highly political. Global studies, such as the 2005 World Health Organization multi-nation comparison, helped focus additional attention on abuse worldwide.

As noted, much of the legislation enacted in the decade addressed teen dating violence, and numerous scholarly research articles as well as practitioner-driven materials became available to address the scope, extent, forms, and impact of dating abuse. As of May 2012, 18 states had legislation related to dating violence, and 6 states had new legislation proposed. Organizations like Break the Cycle and Love Is Not Abuse are raising awareness about dating violence, and studies like the Tween and Teen Dating Violence and Abuse Study of 2008 (available at http://www.loveisrespect.org/wp-content/uploads/2008/07/tru-tween-teen-study-feb-081.pdf) helped address the issue as well. High-profile cases—like that of pop singer Rihanna, whose eye was blackened by her boyfriend and fellow pop star Chris Brown—also brought attention to dating violence. Rihanna publicly spoke about the abuse, and with rapper Eminem wrote and performed "Love the Way You Lie," a song that focused on the "stormy" relationship she had with Brown. Advocates applauded the attention but expressed mixed feelings about the song and video, which in many ways made abuse look mutual.

Fueled in part by the men's rights and fatherhood movements, increased attention has been paid to male victims. Authors like Michael Kimmel highlighted that while men's violence against women tends to be more severe, it is imperative that activists consider all forms of domestic abuse unacceptable and offer resources for male victims, be they in heterosexual or same-sex relationships. Advocacy groups addressing LGBT rights have increasingly included domestic violence in their campaigns, and shelters across the country have trained domestic violence advocates on how to work with LGBT victims.

Immigrant victims face tremendous barriers in escaping abuse. Improvements have been made, however, through greater attention to the issue. For instance, the Violence Against Women Act (originally enacted in 1994, then reauthorized in 2000 and 2005) includes provisions for immigrant victims to self-petition for residency status. Conversely, the decade saw the issue of immigration become politically charged, in particular after the September 11, 2011, terrorist attacks in the United States. Laws and practices allowing law enforcement greater involvement in addressing immigration issues resulted, according to advocates, in fear that contacting police about abuse might result in unwanted attention, even deportation. Erez, Adelman, and Gregory (2008) noted, "The rise in anti-immigrant public sentiment has resulted both in the exclusion of some immigrants from access to education and medical care and in increased local law enforcement of immigration law. When coupled with post-9/11 delays in processing visa applications, the consequences of anti-immigrant sentiment further complicate the implementation of legal reforms for immigrant battered women" (p. 37).

The 2000s also saw greater use of the Internet and social networking sites as a way to draw attention to the issue of domestic abuse and to share information and resources. This technology has also been used by abusers, however. From constant calling, e-mailing, and text messaging victims to the installation of tracking devices on victims' cars, abusers have used new technologies to obtain and maintain power and control over victims. The National Network to End Domestic Violence (NNEDV) has a page devoted to technology safety. It highlights the many ways abusers can spy on or stalk their victims via computers, how to be safe using social networking sites, and much more. It is available at http://nnedv.org/resources/safetynetdocs.html.

In October 2011, *Forbes* magazine announced the creation of a new computer app that allows victims to document abuse and threats through video. The U.S. Department of Health and Human Services (HHS) launched an app challenge in 2012, calling on developers to create apps that can help prevent abuse.

See also: Immigrant Victims of Domestic Abuse; Lesbian, Gay, Bisexual, and Transgendered (LGBT) Victims; Male Victims of Domestic Abuse; Technology and Domestic Abuse; Teen Victims; Trafficking Victims Protection Act (TVPA); Violence Against Women Act (VAWA)

Further Reading

Apps against abuse. (2012). Available at http://appsagainstabuse.challenge.gov/

Erez, E., Adelman, M., & Gregory, C. (2008). Intersections of immigration and domestic violence: Voices of battered women. *Feminist Criminology, 14*(12), 1397–1412.

Finn, J. (2000). Domestic violence organizations on the web. *Violence Against Women, 6*(1), 80–102.

The International Violence Against Women Act 2010. (n.d.). Women Thrive Worldwide. Retrieved June 4, 2012, from http://www.womenthrive.org/index.php?option=com_content&task=view&id=366&Item id=115

Kimmel, M. (2001). Male victims of domestic violence: A substantive and methodological research review. *VAWnet.* Retrieved June 5, 2012, from http://new.vawnet.org/Assoc_Files_VAWnet/GenderSymmetry.pdf

Millennium Development Goals: http://www.un.org/millenniumgoals/

Scott, C. (2011, October 30). New technology for domestic violence and stalking victims. *Forbes.* Retrieved June 4, 2012, from http://www.forbes.com/sites/crime/2011/10/30/new-technology-for-domestic-violence-and-stalking-victims/

Teen dating violence. (2012). National Conference of State Legislatures. Retrieved June 4, 2012, from http://www.ncsl.org/issues-research/health/teen-dating-violence.aspx#2010

UN Women. (2012). 2011–12 *Progress of the world's women: In pursuit of justice.* Retrieved June 1, 2012, from http://progress.unwomen.org/pdfs/EN-Report-Progress.pdf

Laura L. Finley

HONOR KILLINGS

Introduction

Honor killings are acts of retribution, usually perpetrated by a male family member against a female family member who has brought dishonor upon the family or community through actual or perceived immoral behavior. This perceived dishonor,

Mother of Pakistani woman murdered in an honor killing holds her daughter's picture. (AP Photo/Shakil Adil)

against the family or community, is customarily the result of one of the four following behaviors: (1) going against cultural norms of dress or attitude; (2) wanting to terminate or thwart an arranged marriage or wishing to marry one's own choice; (3) engaging in sexual acts outside marriage; and (4) involvement in a nonsexual relationship perceived as inappropriate.

Honor

Honor-based violence (HBV), such as acid throwing and honor killings, occurs in cultures where the concepts of honor and shame are prevalent. Honor, as a social concept, has different meanings from society to society, and the "justification" of HBV is for the protection of honor as a norm or custom. These concepts, honor and shame, are often linked with the expected behaviors of families and individuals, specifically those of women. Honor in this sense revolves around the public perception of the individuals more than their actual behavior. Causing a scandal or gossip within the community is often the most significant aspect of an offense against honor. Ultimately, it is those with power within the family and the community who decide what acts are honorable or shameful.

Male honor is increased or decreased through their and their family's actions within the community. By contrast, a female's honor, is static; it can neither be increased nor regained, and once lost, is lost forever. Female chastity and modesty are considered to be essential components of the family's honor. By being perceived as having entered into an inappropriate relationship, a woman is seen as having defiled her guardian's and family's honor. The family loses their honor because either they failed to protect her or they failed to bring her up correctly. Therefore, the man of the family must publicly demonstrate his power to safeguard his honor by killing those who have damaged it and thereby restoring it.

Honor Cultures

Honor killings cut across ethnic, class, and religious lines. Many families in honor societies are based around the extended family. If these families are not organized within a single household, they are spread across smaller nuclear households within the community. As HBV is a method of enforcing compliance to community norms, it is often considered licit, and even demanded by the community. Community pressure is an important part of HBV. Oftentimes, the community sees honor-related violence as a private matter and is hesitant to intervene. Additionally, community members may put pressure on individuals or families to clear their name, according to Stophonourkillings.com. Once the killing has happened, the community members will erase the existence of an individual in order to release the family from the dishonor that was brought upon them.

Honor societies tend to have tightly knit communities, even among immigrant communities. They usually cluster together within a city. Younger immigrants often adopt the culture of the majority, which is seen as unacceptable by the family. In immigrant communities, this creates a network of constant gossip and surveillance, where women's moral behavior is the subject of constant scrutiny comparable to how it was in their ancestral land. Once again the family or community takes an active role in suppressing female autonomy by supporting and encouraging violence against individuals who go against traditional customs. Women usually play a role in regulating and monitoring the behavior of other women and have the possibility to participate in the killings.

According to Sikhs, Hindus, and Muslims in South Asia, maintaining the reputation of oneself and one's family is part of the concept of honor (*izzat*), as is the obligatory taking of revenge when one's izzat has been violated. The notion of izzat is both singular and collective in Northern India and Pakistan. There are two words for honor in Arabic, which are gender specific: *namus*, the masculine form, and *sharaf*, the feminine form. Both derive from patriarchal systems relating to familial duties relating to honor, respectability, and modesty. The man has to provide financially for his family and to defend the namus of his house—such as the sexual integrity of women and their chastity—from the outer world.

Honor-Based Killing versus Domestic Violence

There are many factors that distinguish killings motivated by honor from other forms of domestic violence murders. Human Rights Watch defines honor killings as "acts of vengeance, usually death, committed by male family members against female family members, who are held to have brought dishonor upon the family."

Honor killings diverge significantly from domestic violence in four basic ways. First of all, most domestic violence murders result from escalating episodes of abuse accompanied by alcohol and/or drugs, while honor killings are perpetrated within a relatively peaceful family unit. Secondly, honor killings are aggregated acts in which at least one other family member approves of or is active in the killing, while the majority of domestic violence cases involve a single person, normally a husband or a boyfriend, who acts alone. The third reason is based on men's putative right to control women's sexual and social choices, with the perception that women are seen as the property of men. The fourth difference is the valorizing or not condemning the perpetrators of the honor killing. Cultures where HBV is practiced also tend to find other forms of violence against women socially acceptable. Domestic violence and violence against children may also be widespread and characterized as a rightful chastisement.

Statistics

According to the *Extrajudicial, Summary and Arbitrary Executions* report conducted by the United Nations in 2000, killings have been reported in Bangladesh, Brazil, Ecuador, Egypt, India, Iran, Israel, Italy, Jordan, Lebanon, Morocco, Pakistan, Sweden, Syria, Turkey, Uganda, and Yemen. These killings also happen in refugee hosting countries such as Australia, France, Germany, the United States, and the United Kingdom. Most instances are concentrated in Pakistan and Jordan. The United Nations Population Fund estimates that as many as 5,000 women and girls a year are killed by members of their own families, while many NGOs working in the Middle East and Southwest Asia suspect that the numbers are at least four times higher. As honor killings largely remain a private family affair, it is hard to obtain reliable official statistical data, and thus it is difficult to collect accurate data on the occurrence in a given country. Many victims are never reported as having been killed and are often just reported missing or abducted.

According to the website Stophonourkillings.com, women and girls (77.8 percent) are killed at a much higher rate than men (22.2 percent). These reports also show women under the age of 19 have the highest incidents rates at 51.8 percent; the figure drops to 30.4 percent between the 20 and 29 age range. Almost half (44.7 percent) of all reported female honor killings happen among married individuals. Analyses of press clippings on honor killings in Egypt from 1998 to 2001 found that 79 percent of women were killed for being suspected of adultery, 9 percent for actual adultery, 6 percent for acts of incest, and 6 percent for miscellaneous reasons. The perpetrator was the husband 41 percent of the time, the father 34 percent of the time, the brother 18 percent, the mother 4 percent, and other relatives 3 percent.

Perpetrators

In honor-based societies, men are defined as the head of the family, specifically the eldest man within the household. The man is the protector of his and the family's honor. It is his duty to defend it against any behavior that might be seen as shameful or dishonoring toward the family or the community. Men usually are the perpetrators of these killings but usually do not work alone. In most cases, honor killings are an intrafamily collective decision, the family not only determining whether a woman's actions merits death, but perhaps also planning how the murder will be committed and who will carry it out. The chances of the family pardoning the dishonorable offense are small. If the intended victim survives, she will need protection for the rest of her life from her family's extended network of relatives, friends, and associates that might help them.

The woman's natal family bears the responsibility for carrying out an honor killing until she becomes married; then the responsibility passes to her husband. Honor killings may be committed by fathers, husbands, uncles, brothers, cousins, sisters, mothers, aunts, paid killers, or other members of the family or community. According to Stophonourkillings.com, honor killings are most often carried out by strangling (11 percent), poisoning (7 percent), stabbing (34 percent), shooting (4 percent), decapitating/cutting of throat (25 percent), drowning (13 percent), immolation (3 percent), and burning (2 percent).

Where

Honor killings may occur in public, for all to see, in order to display honor reclaimed by the family. In the past, they were public events for all to see and celebrate. However, most happen at home in the privacy of the family since honor killings were outlawed in the Convention on the Elimination of All Forms of Discrimination Against Women (CEDAW). Either way, honor killings have a threefold communal objective: (1) they reproduce a collective pressure and the motivation to police women's behavior, (2) demonstrate their commitment to a patriarchal society, and (3) have a deterrent effect on other girls and women who may also be rebelling against the rules of the community or family.

Male Victims

Men may also occasionally fall victim to honor killings for not obliging an arranged marriage. They are rarely killed by their own families, but instead by the relatives of a woman who is believed to have been dishonored by the victim. For the males involved in alleged affairs with women, killings are often not carried out because women are typically killed first, giving men a chance to flee retribution. Men also have greater bargaining power and may sometimes avoid death by paying the other family off with money, or because of their tribal or community connections. Men who participate, or are perceived to have participated, in homosexual acts may also become victims to honor killings by their own family members.

Reasons

A woman can be targeted for a variety of reasons. It does not matter if accusations are real; the perception that a woman has dishonored her family is enough for some. Honor killings are often the result of perceptions of lost virginity outside of marriage, premarital pregnancy, infidelity by the woman (not the man), refusal of an arranged marriage, seeking a divorce or child custody, leaving the marital or familial home without permission, or somehow causing gossip in the community. Even minor things, such as a woman laughing too loudly, using a public toilet, or receiving a gift from a man, have reportedly been the cause of honor-based violence.

Patriarchy helps explain why HBV occurs. In some cultures, men generally get to control women's sexuality, and virginity is the only approved sexual status. A whitesheet test is sometimes used during a marriage ceremony. This is where women must show that they bleed upon their wedding night. If the woman does not bleed, her family is dishonored. She may be deemed "unmarriageable" and thus returned to her parents. Her parents may feel dishonored and perpetrate an honor killing as a way to restore their status.

Appellation

Some argue against calling these murders honor killing, in order to delink the term "honor" from violence. Some argue that there is no honor involved in these murders and that calling them honor killings belittles the victims and plays down the severity of the crimes. Some NGOs have suggested *femicide, shame killings,* and *so-called honor killings* as alternatives but without luck, because honor is a very complex concept and no one kills in the name of shame.

See also: Acid Attacks; Asia and Domestic Abuse; Dowry Killings; Forced Marriage and Domestic Abuse; India and Domestic Abuse; The Middle East and Domestic Abuse; Southeast Asia and Domestic Abuse

Further Reading

Council of Europe. (2002). *Crimes of honour*. Stockholm, Sweden: Council of Europe Publications.
Human Rights Watch. (2004, April). Jordan: Honoring the killers, justice denied for "honor" crimes in Jordan, *16*(1).
Iranian and Kurdish Women's Rights Organisation: http://www.ikwro.org.uk/index.php?option=com_content&view=article&id=369 &Itemid=54
Kressel, Gideon. (1981). Sororicide/filiacide: Homicide for family honour. *Current Anthropology, 22,* 141–158.
Kurdish Women's Rights Watch: http://www.kwrw.org/
Madre: http://www.madre.org/index/press-room-4/news/honor-crimes-44.html
Welchman, L., & Houssain, S. (Eds.). (2005). *Honour: Crimes, paradigms, and violence against women*. London, England: Zed Press.

Brandon Fryman

HOSPITAL AND MEDICAL RECORDS AND DOMESTIC ABUSE

Domestic violence (DV) is a public health concern as well as a criminal justice concern. Consequently, there has been a concerted effort to improve record gathering in emergency rooms and other health care facilities, for assessment purposes, treatment, prevention, and to help substantiate criminal charges of domestic violence. Both public health and criminal justice approaches stress proactive rather than reactive responses, emphasize reduction in harm to victims, and focus on the prevention of violence through the identification of and response to risk factors. Both perspectives seek to conserve valuable but limited public resources.

Hospital records (both clinical records and interviews with patients who present with certain injuries/symptoms) are important to the study of DV, since victims may visit emergency rooms or other health-care providers but seek no nonmedical assistance. Early identification and intervention may save victims' lives. Records are useful in assessing danger and immediate threats, preventing violence through referrals to specialized non–health care services, and aiding victims in the prosecution of criminal cases. Records are also useful for measuring the extent of the problem, estimating the health care burden, efficiently allocating limited health-care resources, evaluating program effectiveness, informing community education efforts, and assessing social costs (such as victims' missed days of work each year).

Many hospitals have protocols for handling DV cases. Protocols may include definitions, guidelines for patient care, training of medical personnel to deal with domestic violence (e.g., screening a victim in private to avoid further danger), response, referrals, intervention services, and education of the public. Many problems associated with hospital records may be addressed, in part, by hospital protocols.

One problem is the low rate of screening for DV. Screening (either universal or high risk) may be done by physicians, medical social workers, nurses, psychologists, physician assistants, counselors, family practitioners, or obstetrician-gynecologists, since DV often manifests in gynecological problems, breast pain, miscarriage, neonatal death, and other physical ailments such as gastrointestinal problems, chest pains, and more. But studies indicate that only one in five practitioners regularly screen for DV. Barriers to screening include societal beliefs about gender roles, including blaming of the victim; lack of time; lack of training; privacy issues, including fear of offending the patient; safety issues; and patients' reluctance to talk if they feel they will be judged or encounter a negative response.

It is important to educate practitioners. One study indicated that practitioners who were educated in DV screening were more likely to screen and more likely to discover DV victims. To increase compliance in screening among staff members, some suggest the use of administrative interventions, specifically hospital disciplinary actions, from discussion of noncompliance to job termination for continued refusal to screen.

One recommendation is to ask emergency room patients if they are victims; though they may not volunteer the information on their own, they are quite likely to answer when asked. One study found women were more likely to report domestic violence on self-administered questionnaires than in face-to-face interviews at clinics, so questionnaires could be used. Because of health problems associated with pregnant DV victims and their babies, it is important to screen for DV during various stages of pregnancy.

Another concern is the need for more complete records; emergency room records typically lack pertinent information such as the circumstances surrounding an incident, and even the victim-perpetrator relationship. Hospital protocols can address this shortcoming in a number of ways. Structured charting, wherein certain questions are asked and the answers are accurately coded, would improve data gathering. Some advocate a universal coding system. Some believe that information on high-risk cases should be entered into an electronic database, to facilitate future risk prediction.

Hospital protocols may address screening techniques (how to frame questions, the use of direct and indirect questions) and documentation guidelines (the inclusion of details such as date and time, account of incident, physical findings, photographs, body maps). Protocols may require the taking of photos, exactly how to do so and what to include, and where the equipment is to be found.

Medical records may be used to supplement police records in substantiating incidents of violence. Records may also help victims get social services benefits and victim's compensation. Since medical records, such as emergency room reports, may be used as legal evidence in cases of domestic violence, it is important to collect this data and make it available for use. The many barriers to good documentation include liability issues, a concern with the confidentiality of medical records, the reluctance of medical personnel to testify in legal proceedings, and a fear of harming rather than helping the victim through the wording of the account.

Well-written reports can be used by the prosecution even when a woman is afraid to testify in court. Some practitioners drop inadvertently use language that may harm a victim's legal case. Derogatory statements about victims (patients) should be omitted from reports, as should statements that cast doubt on the patient's account, such as "patient alleges" or "patient claims." Reports should not include statements such as "the patient denies abuse" or "patient was hysterical."

While courts in all states prohibit hearsay evidence, all states have exceptions, such as "information related to diagnosis and treatment," "medical record exception," or the "excited utterance" exception, which allows statements that may have been made in a state of agitation, rather than premeditated. Certain criteria must be met for a statement to be considered "excited utterance," and it is essential that practitioners adhere to those conditions when writing their reports, if the statements are to be used effectively in court.

Medical notes must be legible. It is helpful if photographs are included in the medical reports, though they seldom are. Injuries should be described in detail. Finally, EMS personnel responding shortly after an incident takes place may be especially useful sources of information on details of violent incidents.

See also: Courts and Domestic Abuse; Health Effects of Domestic Abuse; Physicians, Health Care Providers and Domestic Abuse

Further Reading

California Medical Training Center, Office of Family Planning, California Department of Health Services. (2002). *Family PACT Guidelines for developing office policies and procedures for victims of intimate partner violence at Family PACT sites*. Retrieved from http://www.familypact.org/_Resources/Documents/DV_Manual.pdf

Isaac, N. E., & Enos, P. (2000). *Medical records as legal evidence of domestic violence, summary report*. Document Number 184528. Retrieved January 28, 2013 from https://www.ncjrs.gov/pdffiles1/nij/grants/184528.pdf

Larkin, G. L., Rolniak, S., Hyman, K. B., MacLeod, B. A., & Savage, R. (2000). Effects of an administrative intervention on rates of screening for domestic violence in an urban emergency department. *American Journal of Public Health, 90*(9), 1444–1448.

Saltzman, L. E., Mahendra, R. R., Ikeda, R. M., & Ingram, E. M. (2005). Utility of hospital emergency department data for studying intimate partner violence. *Journal of Marriage and Family, 67*(November), 960–970.

Tower, L. E. (2006). Barriers in screening women for domestic violence: A survey of social workers, family practitioners, and obstetrician-gynecologists. *Journal of Family Violence, 21*, 245–257. doi: 10.1007/s10896-006-9024-4

Carol Lenhart

HOUSING AND DOMESTIC ABUSE

Once a victim of domestic abuse has escaped his or her abusive situation, he or she is still subject to a host of other problems, most notably, the problem of housing and homelessness. A study by the National Law Center on Homelessness and Poverty indicated that domestic violence is the number one cause of homelessness in the nation (Domestic violence and housing, 2006). Many domestic violence victims end up homeless after they are forcibly evicted from or denied housing because of the violence they have survived. According to the National Coalition Against Domestic Violence, about 1.3 million women are victims of some type of physical assault by an intimate partner every year. Several of these victims are inevitably required to either stay with—or in some cases, return to—their abusers because they cannot afford housing on their own. In 2000, more than half of the U.S. cities surveyed in the U.S. Conference of Mayors reported that domestic violence was a primary source of homelessness. The Wilder Research Center says in some areas of the country, about one-third of all homeless women lack housing due to domestic violence. In fact, one study reports that nearly half of homeless women, 46 percent, say they stayed in an abusive relationship because they simply had nowhere else to go. The Temporary Assistance to Needy Families (TANF) program has indicated that about half of the women receiving funds from them have said domestic violence is a leading factor in their need of financial help.

Indeed, there are many shelters for battered women across the country, but these are only temporary. The Women's Institute for Housing and Economic Development explains that the majority of battered women's shelters do not permit victims to reside there any longer than three months because the need for beds in such places is so great. This presents an enormous problem for the abuse victim because it takes an average of 6 to 10 months for a homeless woman to secure housing for herself and her family. The National Resource Center on Domestic Violence reports that most victims staying at battered women's shelters are between the ages of 18 and 34 years old, and they have one or more children under the age of 18. While shelters are a vital part of a victim's survival plan, staying at one is often very hard on the abused and her children. It is difficult for a survivor to have much privacy in a shelter, and many victims struggle with abiding by all of the shelter's rules and structure, according to the Meeting Survivor's Needs study (2008).

If a victim is fortunate enough to obtain housing help from federal housing programs and move out of a homeless shelter, she or he and the children can still experience stress and other problems. One of these is the potential that the abuser will re-appear. In this case, a victim may select to obtain a restraining order. Enacted in 1994, the Violence Against Women Act (VAWA) urges survivors to file restraining orders against their abusers and to call police if there are further instances of abuse.

Additionally, there are rigid rules for tenants of federal housing programs. These rules may pose challenges to victims of domestic violence. These programs are mostly administered on a local level through public housing authorities (PHAs). PHAs are public organizations run by individual municipalities and/or counties. The U.S. Department of Housing and Urban Development (HUD) has set up guidelines based on laws passed by the U.S. Congress. The most popular kind of housing program is called tenant-based subsidy. These subsidies allow a tenant to choose her own apartment. Once accepted, the tenant puts a certain percentage of her total income toward rent payments, and the remainder is paid directly to the landlord or owner. Section 8 is this type of subsidy. Section 8 will cover rent for specific units in an apartment building or for privately owned homes. However, according to a study by Hammeal-Urban and Davies (1999), "the number of people in need of federal rent subsidies ... far outweighs the number of units available." In many states, people have been on housing waiting lists for years. In May 1999, HUD proposed a rule that urges PHAs to give preference to victims of domestic violence. When a battered man or woman is finally approved for such housing, she is issued Section 8 vouchers for a specific number of bedrooms based on how many children—and the gender of each child—a tenant has. When a tenant chooses a home that is privately owned, the landlord or owner decides what the monthly rent payment will be. The PHA decides the amount they will pay for each tenant. HUD has set up income eligibility standards for federal housing programs, and the tenant must meet these standards. The income standards typically work in a victim's favor, as a woman is less likely to have much money after separating from her partner. However, it is required that the tenant be able to pay her portion of monthly rent expenses on time, as well as other household bills such as public utilities, in order to be granted housing. Applicants must also not have any outstanding debt to any other PHA, or a history of disturbing the neighbors or destruction of property. Applicants for public housing also cannot have a criminal record or a history of eviction from any housing programs. Any history of violence is deemed criminal activity, so oftentimes, even if housing is available, the applicant is unable to obtain a lease due to a history of past violent incidents. Even if a victim engaged in violence due to self-defense, a landlord can use this as an excuse to not rent a unit to her.

Victims of domestic abuse are greatly benefitted by federal housing programs, mostly because the results afford the victim and her family a better chance of survival. Benefits include, but are not limited to: lower rent payments, allowing, for example, a mother to provide much-needed clothes and other supplies for her dependent children; and mobility, which allows a victim to move to a certain area in which she has an established support system, or to move to a different location if her abuser continues the threat of violence.

Tenants must also submit to regular reexaminations by the PHA in regard to income and the residents of the rental home. A subsidized tenant must also report any changes in income or other people living in her household. Tenants are expected to allow only those people listed on the lease to live in the subsidized housing. Obviously, the tenant must obey all other rules and regulations specified in the lease agreement. These regulations stipulate that tenants and their guests must not disturb neighbors or create any disturbances, and must not engage in any criminal activity, including violence or drug-related activity. If a tenant does not abide by these obligations, she can be permanently removed from federal housing programs.

Currently, HUD enforces a "zero tolerance" policy for any criminal activity on the premises of subsidized housing. This poses a dire predicament for thousands of blameless abuse victims. As reported in the Federal Housing and Domestic Violence study cited earlier, a family can be evicted from subsidized housing the very first time any family member engages in criminal activity. HUD defines "criminal activity" as "any crime that threatens the health, safety, or peaceful enjoyment of apartments by other tenants," and also incorporates any and all illegal drug activity on or even near the premises. The Stop Violence Against Women organization argues that these no-tolerance policies "have caused landlords to evict battered women along with their abusers if the police make too many visits to their housing unit." Unfortunately, however, it is not even necessary for a tenant to have any police contact in order to be evicted—engaging in criminal activity is enough grounds for a landlord to evict a tenant. Neighbors may see or hear violent outbursts and report incidents to the landlord or owner. Such zero tolerance policies can have a profound negative impact on a victim who is trying to rebuild her life and provide safety and stability for her children.

Take the fictional examples of Roy and Jennifer. Jennifer lives in a small Section 8 apartment with her three daughters. Her boyfriend and father of the children, Roy, lives with them but is not listed on the lease. Jennifer was afforded her Section 8 housing on the basis that she was the sole parent. Both parents' drug addictions often connect to domestic violence issues. Although the neighbors have called the police only a couple of times, Jennifer's landlord has threatened her with eviction due to the outbursts and disturbance to the neighbors in her building. After the last incident when a neighbor did call the police, Roy was ordered to never return to the apartment. If he is seen on or near the property, Jennifer and her daughters will be immediately evicted. To compound the issue, due to her drug addiction, Jennifer cannot work, and Roy's job was the family's main source of income. Sometimes Roy will sneak into the apartment under cover of night. While he is never violent toward the children, Jennifer is less inclined to call the police when she suffers abuse by his hand—she knows that even though she is the victim of said violence, not the perpetrator, if the police are called to the home, she and her girls will be evicted and out on the streets.

If a victim is evicted from subsidized housing, it is likely to cause even worse suffering for her and her children. As we all know, children need and crave stability. If a victim and her children are forced to vacate their home due to these no-tolerance policies, the stability they were just starting to experience is ripped from them, and their lives are thrown into upheaval once more. Children may be forced to change schools, and their mother may be unable to find work without a legal residence. If a shelter is incapable of providing them with temporary housing, child protective services is likely to get involved and may even seize the children. Some families who are evicted from federal housing programs are forced to live with relatives or friends—often in apartments that are much too small. The greatest negative impact of a battered woman being evicted from federal housing is that once it happens, she is no longer eligible for any other federal housing program assistance. For this reason, it is not uncommon for a victim to return to her abuser just so she and her children have a roof over their head. And of course, once a victim returns to the home of her abuser, it is just that much harder for her to leave again.

See also: Economic Recession and Domestic Abuse; Welfare and Domestic Abuse

Further Reading

Author Unknown. Domestic violence & fair housing. Retrieved from http://www.fairhousingrights.org/Housing_Laws/Domestic_Violence.htm

Barata, P., & Stewart, D. (2010). Searching for housing as a battered woman: Does discrimination affect reported availability of a rental unit? *Psychology of Women Quarterly, 34*, 43–55.

Domestic violence and housing (2006, February 1). Stop Violence Against Women—A Project of the Advocates for Human Rights. Retrieved from http://stopvaw.org/Domestic_Violence_and_Housing.html

Domestic violence shelters are meeting needs of most victims, comprehensive federally-funded study finds. (2009, February 18). National Resource Center on Domestic Violence. News Release. Retrieved from http://snow.vawnet.org/Assoc_Files_VAWnet/MeetingSurvivorsNeeds-NewsRelease.pdf

Hammeal-Urban, R., & Davis, J. (1999, October). Federal housing and domestic violence: Introduction to programs, policy, and advocacy opportunities. Retrieved from http://www.mincava.umn.edu/documents/fedhouse/fedhouse.html#id471802

Meeting survivors' needs: A multi-state study of domestic violence shelter experiences (2008, October). Retrieved January 26, 2013 from http://new.vawnet.org/Assoc_Files_VAWnet/MeetingSurvivorsNeeds-FullReport.pdf

National Coalition Against Domestic Violence. Domestic violence and housing. Retrieved from http://www.ncadv.org/files/DomesticViolenceFactSheet(National).pdf

National Law Center on Homelessness & Poverty (2007, February). Lost housing, lost safety: Survivors of domestic violence experience housing denials and evictions across the country.

Weiser, W. R., & Boehm, G. (2002, March-April). Clearinghouse review: Housing discrimination against victims of domestic violence. Retrieved from https://www.idaholegalaid.org/files/HousingDiscrimination_DomVioVict.pdf.pdf

Kristin Franklin

HUGHES, FRANCINE

Francine Hughes, a Michigan housewife, set her husband James "Mickey" Hughes on fire in their home on March 9, 1977. By that time, Hughes had endured 13 years of emotional and physical abuse that began when the couple married in November 1963. For years she tried to get help from family, friends, police, and social workers in Ingham County, Michigan, but was unsuccessful. The abuse and neglect were unrelenting. Mickey was rarely employed. In need of food for her children, Hughes applied for welfare and was told she had to divorce Mickey in order to receive benefits. Even after the divorce, he refused to move out of her home.

Hughes was abused during a time when support for battered women and their children was virtually nonexistent; laws to protect her were few; shelters and safe houses for battered women were sparse; and the general public response to abuse seemed to suggest that the battered woman was somehow responsible. It was in this climate that Hughes was arrested and charged with first-degree murder for the killing of her husband. Women around the country supported Hughes and argued that laws and public consciousness needed to change so battered women could have a safe space to thrive and support their families. After the jury deliberated for hours, Hughes was acquitted on the grounds of temporary insanity.

Author Faith McNulty used records of the trial, Hughes's written version of the events, and interviews with people involved in the case to tell Francine Hughes's story in a best-selling book in 1980 titled *The Burning Bed*. Four years later, McNulty's book was used as the basis for the movie *The Burning Bed*, starring Farrah Fawcett and Paul Le Mat. The movie was viewed by over 75 million people, making it one of the highest-rated television movies at that time. The trial, the book, and the movie helped publicize Francine Hughes's story and call attention to the plight of other battered women. This attention helped fuel the battered women's movement, which changed police, court, and the general public's response to battered women.

Francine Hughes was born in Stockbridge, Michigan, in 1947, the third of Walter and Hazel Moran's six children. The family was poor. Her mother was a waitress and her father was a factory worker, prone to drinking too much, gambling, and abusing his wife. Hughes was 15 when she met 18-year-old Mickey Hughes. The following year, she quit Jackson High School in the 10th grade and married Mickey two months later on November 4, 1963. The couple moved into Mickey's parents' home in Dansville, and a few weeks later, he beat Hughes because he said her outfit was too revealing. While Mickey had trouble remaining employed, Hughes secured a job at a restaurant but soon lost it when Mickey demanded she leave work before her shift ended. Once at home, he ripped off her clothes and beat her. After one particularly brutal beating in the spring of 1964, Hughes left Mickey and tried to find refuge at her parents' home, but her mother encouraged her to reconcile with Mickey, especially since she suspected that Hughes was pregnant with the couple's first child, Christy. Hughes's father was abusing her mother as well, suggesting that such behavior might have been a negative, but inevitable, aspect of married life.

Hughes and Mickey went on to have three more children, Jimmy, Dana, and Nicole, but Mickey's abuse remained constant. With Mickey either unemployed or spending his earnings irresponsibly, in 1971, Hughes was forced to file for divorce so she could get welfare benefits. Once the divorce on the grounds of extreme cruelty was final, Mickey refused to leave the family residence. He continued to abuse Hughes and neglect the children.

By March 9, 1977, when Hughes poured gasoline around the bed where her former husband lay drunk, Hughes had experienced 13 years of abuse and believed Mickey was going to kill her. Earlier that day he had locked the children outside and refused to allow Hughes to feed them. While the children were outside, he beat her, ripped up her school books from classes she was taking at Lansing Business College, and demanded that she burn the books. Hughes remembers, "he was pulling my hair and he was hitting me with his fist and he had hit me on the mouth and my lip was bleeding."

When the police arrived, they were not helpful. Hughes says, "What [the police] could do, they did. Their hands were tied." Mickey continued verbally, physically, and sexually abusing Hughes long after the police were gone. At one point he threatened her with a knife in front of the children. When he finally went to sleep, she recalls, "I was thinking about all the things that had happened to me . . . all the times he had hurt me . . . how he had hurt the kids. . . . " Hughes decided to take the children and leave Mickey, but she feared he would find her. Once the children were in the car, she says, "I walked into the bedroom with the gas can and I started pouring it around on the floor. There was an urgent whisper saying, 'Do it! Do it! Do it!' over and over, and I just kept on . . . I stuck my hand out with the match . . . there was a swish . . . I looked back and saw the flames." Emotionally distraught, Hughes drove to the county jail and confessed to officers that she poured gasoline around the bed where Mickey lay and threw a lit match on it. The police called the fire department, but by the time they arrived at the home, Mickey had died.

During the trial, a clinical psychologist, Dr. Berkman, testified that Hughes had repressed her anger for years and was terrified that if she left Mickey, he would kill her. He also suggested that Hughes's longing for approval and desire to be a good wife allowed her to repress anger toward Mickey. Dr. Berkman explained, "She was overwhelmed by the massive onslaughts of her primitive emotions. Emotions she had suppressed. . . . She experienced a breakdown of her psychological processes so that she was no longer able to utilize judgment . . . no longer able to control her impulses . . . unable to prevent herself from acting in the way she did." A psychiatrist, Dr. Anne Seiden, took the stand and corroborated Dr. Berkman's findings. One doctor, Dr. Blunt, disagreed with this finding. Michigan defined insanity as "a substantial disorder of thought or mood which significantly impairs judgment, behavior, capacity to recognize reality, or ability to cope with ordinary demands of life." Dr. Blunt wrote in his report that Hughes did not show evidence of being mentally ill, but he did agree with the other doctors on one point: Hughes was not capable of premeditated murder. Dr. Blount's finding was an important turning point in Hughes's case.

In the closing argument of *The People v. Francine Hughes*, the prosecutor asked the jury to find Hughes guilty of first-degree murder. Hughes's lawyer argued for a not guilty plea: "Francine Hughes was temporarily insane ... she was acting against an evil force that was threatening her life. She was acting in self-defense, protecting herself." After five hours of deliberation, the jury foreman, Jeffery Hill, announced the verdict, not guilty by reason of temporary insanity. According to Michigan state law, Hughes was acquitted, and on November 4, 1977, she was released. Hughes returned to her home in Jackson, Michigan, enrolled in nursing school, and eventually remarried.

The verdict in Hughes's landmark case was attacked from several perspectives. When Hughes stood trial, there were few, if any, nonconfrontational murder cases where self-defense was used as a legal defense. Some still claimed Hughes got away with murder by killing her husband while he slept defenseless. Attorneys continue to debate the issue of nonconfrontational homicide by battered women. Joshua Dressler maintains, "the proposition that a battered woman is justified in killing her sleeping abuser, although well-meaning, is wrong." Dressler also says this led defense lawyers to abandon the temporary insanity approach when defending battered women in nonconfrontational murder cases for a self-defense argument. Similarly, Brenda L. Russell says the law of self-defense was expanded after Hughes's case, but there are still those who believe battering is used as an excuse for murder. Women's rights groups felt the not guilty by reason of temporary insanity plea suggested Hughes was mentally disturbed and wrong for killing her husband. Some disagree with this assessment. Instead, they believe her act was courageous and done in self-defense of her right to live free of abuse.

Hughes's experiences helped the country understand the complexity of battered women's lives. Francine Hughes's story revealed that she was not alone. There are other women and children experiencing domestic violence who need laws and policies to protect them.

See also: Battered Woman Syndrome; Self-Defense, Legal Issues; Self-Defense, Homicides and Domestic Abuse; Walker, Lenore

Further Reading

Diliberto, G. (1984, October 8). A violent death, a haunted life. *People*. Retrieved March 17, 2012, from http://www.people.com/people/archive/article/0,,20088845,00.html

Dowd, M. (1991). Dispelling the myths about the "battered woman's defense": Towards a new understanding. *Fordham Urban Law Journal, 19*(3), 567–583.

Dressler, J. (2005). Battered women and sleeping abusers: Some reflections. *Ohio State Journal of Criminal Law, 3*, 457–471.

McNulty, F. (1980). *The burning bed*. New York, NY: Harcourt Brace Jovanovich.

Russell, B. (2010). *Battered woman syndrome as a legal defense: History, effectiveness and implications*. Jefferson, NC: McFarland.

Yahoo Contributor Network. (2007, June 29). Domestic violence pre-Francine Hughes: How did the *Burning Bed* help bring light to the issue? Retrieved March 17, 2012, from http://voices.yahoo.com/domestic-violence-pre-francine-hughes-did-the-408575.html

Kaavonia Hinton-Johnson

HUMAN TRAFFICKING

Pulitzer Prize–winning authors Nicholas Kristof and Sheryl WuDunn (2009) have called the struggle for gender inequality in the developing world the most important moral challenge of the twenty-first century. Among the many issues related to gender inequality is the trafficking of women. Trafficking is typically defined as taking someone by force or deception, and it has been called "modern-day slavery." It is distinct from human smuggling, which involves illegally transporting someone across a border. While trafficking of men occurs as well, typically for labor purposes, the primary victims of human trafficking are women and girls.

It is difficult to get accurate estimates of the number of people who are trafficked annually. The International Labour Organization, a UN agency, estimates that as many as 12.3 million people may be engaged in some form of forced labor at any given time. The U.S. State Department estimates that between 600,000 and 800,000 people are trafficked across international borders each year. Eighty percent of those are estimated to be women and girls, with 70 percent of them trafficked for commercial sexual exploitation. The largest number of trafficked persons come from East Asia and the Pacific, followed by Latin America, Europe, and Eurasia. Millions are estimated to be trafficked within domestic borders as well. This number dwarfs that of the transatlantic slave trade, which at its peak involved somewhat less than 80,000 slaves being shipped from Africa to the Americas.

One reason for the expansion of trafficking is the collapse of Communism in Eastern Europe and Indochina, which resulted in severe economic hardships and gave rise to criminal gangs that capitalized on the new market: people. The Russian Mafia, for instance, is heavily involved in human trafficking. Globalization has also contributed, as it has made travel easier, for both good and bad purposes. Kristof and WuDunn argue that AIDS has also contributed in the sense that customers seeking prostitutes often prefer younger girls who they do not believe are infected. In Asia in particular, the sale of virgins is highly valued, and thus very young girls are the targets of traffickers. Another factor is the gender-role norms for women and girls. Girls worldwide often are raised to be quiet and submissive, which makes it easier for traffickers to prey on them.

In developing countries, girls may be kidnapped or sold into modern-day slavery. One estimate suggests that at least 1 million children are forced into prostitution each year, but the number could be as high as 10 million. Antitrafficking organizations tend to put the numbers even higher, suggesting that there are currently as many as 27 million slaves worldwide. There are an estimated 2 to 3 million prostitutes in India. It is not clear how many are doing so willingly, but most experts believe a vast number have been trafficked. China has even more prostitutes than

India, with some estimates higher than 10 million, although fewer are victims of trafficking. Kristof and WuDunn estimate there are 3 million women and girls, as well as some boys, who are sex slaves. Human traffickers prey on the most vulnerable, so often lure young girls through promises of modeling or acting careers or other lucrative work. Homeless youth are particularly at risk. Globally, child sex tourism (CST) is a significant problem. CST involves people traveling from their own country to another in which they engage in commercial sex acts with children. In addition to the terrible impact on young people's self-esteem, mental, and physical health, CST also spreads HIV and other sexually transmitted diseases.

Meena, for instance, was just eight or nine when she was kidnapped from her poor family on the border of Nepal and sold to a clan, who took her to a brothel where prepubescent girls were held until they were mature enough to attract paying customers. Meena fought her first client and the brothel owner's returned his money, then beat her with a belt, sticks, and iron rods. She resisted even when they brought in four or five more clients and threatened to kill her. The owners finally drugged her, and one of them raped her. She believed, as so many do, that she was so sullied by the rape that she gave in and stopped fighting the customers. Meena was beaten if she so much as cried. Such beatings and rapes are common in brothels, as a means of breaking the spirit of the girls, making it less likely they will try to escape. She and the other girls in the brothel were never paid nor allowed to leave. Each was expected to service at least 10 customers each day, and none of the clients used a condom. Police officers were regular customers. Often, these young girls, like Meena, become pregnant. Virtually as soon as she gave birth, the brothel owner took her baby as a way to force Meena to stop lactating and as yet another means of keeping her there. Essentially, generations of girls are raised to be prostitutes in these brothels. Many brothel operators get the girls hooked on dangerous drugs like methamphetamines. Such addictions keep them quiet and compliant and make eradicating trafficking more difficult than simply rescuing girls. Kristof and WuDunn recount the story of Srey Momm, who returned to her brothel in Poipet because she was so addicted to meth.

A study of women who had been trafficked into the European Union for prostitution found that 95 percent had been violently assaulted, either physically or sexually, and 60 percent reported feeling fatigue, neurological difficulties, gastrointestinal problems, back pain, and increased gynecological infections. Victims of sex trafficking are far more likely to suffer from pelvic inflammatory disease, as well as endure ectopic pregnancies, chronic pelvic pain, and are at increased risk of having to undergo a hysterectomy.

Kristof and WuDunn argue that westerners tend to lack the political will to truly invest in a modern-day abolition movement. Westerners should care, they assert, because it is essential if slavery is to be stopped. Although a variety of bipartisan groups in the United States worked together to enact the historic Trafficking Victims Protection Act (TVPA) of 2000 (described below), partisan politics have impeded other efforts. One of the problems lies in how westerners view the issue of prostitution. The left has often criticized the right for its judgment of "sex workers," while the right—joined, interestingly, by some feminists—argues that prostitution is inherently demeaning. Feminists maintain that prostitution is rarely consensual in the true meaning of the word, as women who elect to sell themselves tend to lack other viable opportunities. Many have advocated for a harm reduction approach, maintaining that prohibition of global prostitution is unrealistic and thus efforts should be focused on helping prostitutes remain safe and healthy. In countries like India and Cambodia, brothels are technically illegal already, but such legislation is rarely enforced. Kristof and WuDunn disagree, maintaining that such efforts rarely work where governments are poor and ineffective. Instead, crackdowns on brothels can be successful, especially when combined with services for those housed in them. They point to the different approaches taken in the Netherlands and Sweden. The former legalized prostitution in 2000, while Sweden took the opposite approach in 1999, criminalizing prostitution in a way that punishes the purchaser, not the prostitute. Sweden's approach seems to have been effective, in that the number of prostitutes dropped 41 percent in the first five years, resulting in Sweden becoming a less attractive destination for sex tourism, while Amsterdam is an epicenter of it.

In 2000, the United States passed the TVPA, which helps to punish traffickers, help victims, and prevent trafficking through educational and outreach efforts. The TVPA distinguishes between sex trafficking—defined as a commercial sex act that is induced by force, fraud, or coercion or in which the person induced to perform the act is under the age of 18—and trafficking for labor purposes. The latter refers to the recruitment, harboring, transportation, provision, or obtaining of a person for labor or services through the use of force, fraud, or coercion, for the purpose of subjection to involuntary servitudes, peonage, debt bondage, or slavery. In addition to addressing sexual and labor-related trafficking, the 2011 report addresses child soldiers, the vulnerability of migrant laborers, and other specific issues such as the connection between child trafficking and food. Tier One countries are those that fully comply with TVPA's standards for the elimination of trafficking. Tier Two countries are not in full compliance but are making efforts to eliminate trafficking, while those on the Tier Two watch list are of greater concern. Tier Three countries are those that are neither complying fully with TVPA nor attempting to do so. Governments of Tier Three countries are subject to sanctions, including the withholding of nonhumanitarian aid. Tier Three countries in 2011 included Myanmar (formerly Burma), Central African Republic, the Democratic Republic of Congo, Cuba, Equatorial Guinea, Eritrea, Micronesia, Mauritania, Madagascar, Libya, Lebanon, Kuwait, North Korea, Guinea Bissau, Iran, Papua New Guinea, Saudi Arabia, Sudan, Turkmenistan, Venezuela, Yemen, and Zimbabwe. In 2010, there were 6,017 prosecutions of traffickers, resulting in 3,619 convictions. One of the important elements of the TVPA is that it required the State Department to publish an annual Trafficking in Persons (TIP) report, which ranks countries in terms of how they are working to reduce trafficking. This provision prompted discussion about the topic and elevated the issue among governments.

The United Nations Palermo Protocol was adopted by the General Assembly in 2000. It is designed to guide countries in preventing trafficking of persons and to provide assistance to victims. It requires signatories to adopt specific legislation criminalizing trafficking; adopt measures designed to assist victims, such as provision of shelter and residency status; coordinate training, educational, and mass media campaigns; and adopt appropriate measures for border control. The Palermo Protocol has been ratified by 142 countries.

In 2008, the United States passed the Child Soldiers Prevention Act (CSPA) as part of its efforts to end human trafficking. The act requires annual publication of governments or government-supported armed groups that used child soldiers in the previous year. Such governments are subject to a number of restrictions, including military training and aid. The countries listed on the 2011 CSPA include Burma, Chad, the Democratic Republic of Congo, Somalia, Sudan, and Yemen.

Many nonprofits and nongovernmental organizations are also helping to raise awareness and to provide services to victims. A list of some of these organizations is available at http://humantrafficking.org/countries/united_states_of_america/ngos. Even small efforts can make a big difference. Zach Hunter was just 12 years old when he heard about trafficking. He formed a group called Loose Change to Loosen Chains (LC2LC) and raised $8,500 in his first year. In 2007, he presented a petition to the White House with more than 100,000 signatures demanding more attention to trafficking. He authored a book called *Be the Change: Your Guide to Ending Slavery and Changing the World.* There are many international nongovernmental organizations (NGOs) working on the issues of human trafficking and sexual slavery. In Kolkata, India, the Apne Aap Women Worldwide organization provides help to victims. Other organizations focus on preventing trafficking via increased emphasis on education for girls. The American Assistance for Cambodia organization helps provide funds for schools in Cambodia, with the goal of keeping girls in school and thus reducing the risk that they will be trafficked. It started an innovative program called Girls Be Ambitious, which offered bribes to families who would keep their girls in school. The families of girls with perfect attendance for a month earn $10. The idea is that families who are financially strapped cannot afford to keep their girls in school, so providing them with financial incentives allows them to make the important investment in their daughters' education.

The U.S. Department of Homeland Security provides resources related to trafficking, including posters, brochures, and training information (see http://www.dhs.gov/files/programs/gc_1298391518163.shtm). Persons who suspect that they have identified a trafficker or trafficking victims can call 866-347-2423.

See also: Kristof, Nicholas and Sheryl WuDunn; Mam, Somaly; Trafficking Victims Protection Act (TVPA); U.S. Government Responses to Domestic Violence

Further Reading

Bales. K. (2007). *Ending slavery: How we free today's slaves.* Berkeley, CA: University of California Press.
Bales, K., & Soodalter, R. (2010). *The slave next door: Human trafficking and slavery in America today.* Berkeley, CA: University of California Press.
Batstone, D. (2007). *Not for sale.* New York, NY: Harper Collins.
Brown, L. (2000). *Sex slaves: The trafficking of women in Asia.* New York, NY: Vintage.

Gaon, I., & Forbord, N. (2005). *For sale: Women and children*. Victoria, BC: Trafford.
Kristof, N., & WuDunn, S. (2009). *Half the sky: Turning oppression into opportunity for women worldwide*. New York, NY: Alfred A. Knopf.
Protocol to Prevent, Suppress, and Punish Trafficking in Persons ... (n.d.). Office of the United Nations High Commissioner for Human Rights. Retrieved May 31, 2012, from http://www2.ohchr.org/english/law/protocoltraffic.htm
Sage, J., & Kasten, L. (Eds.). (2006). *Enslaved: True stories of modern day slavery*. New York, NY: Palgrave Macmillan.
Shelley, L. (2010). *Human trafficking: A global perspective*. New York, NY: Cambridge University Press.
Trafficking in Persons Report 2011. (2011). U.S. Department of State. Retrieved May 31, 2012, from http://www.state.gov/j/tip/rls/tiprpt/2011/index.htm
U.S. Laws on Trafficking in Persons. (n.d.). U.S. Department of State. Retrieved May 31, 2012, from http://www.state.gov/j/tip/laws/

Laura L. Finley

1

IMMIGRANT VICTIMS OF DOMESTIC ABUSE

When addressing the problem of domestic abuse, it is important to consider immigrant victims in advocacy, research, and policy-making to ensure victims receive help and are able to cooperate with law enforcement. Immigrant victims face unique challenges in accessing legal, medical, and other services to escape abuse. "The challenges include cultural beliefs and practices that provide rationalizations used to excuse and deny the existence of domestic violence in immigrant and refugee communities and barriers that confront battered immigrant and refugee women when accessing the services provided by public and private social service programs" (Shetty & Kaguyutan, 2002). Immigrant victims may be documented (have legal documents for having entered and remained in a country) and undocumented (lacking legal documents of entry or have overstayed their legal entry period).

Whether documented or undocumented, immigrant victims face various barriers to seeking help and obtaining safety. Language and cultural barriers make it difficult for some immigrant victims to understand their rights, access services, and work with law enforcement. Furthermore, abusers of immigrant victims often have additional power over their victims through deliberate attempts to misrepresent the law and by controlling immigration documents and threatening deportation or losing custody of their children if they report violence (NNEDV, 2007–2011). For example, an abuser may threaten that if she reports the violence, then he (the abuser) will receive full custody of the children because of her immigrant status. If the abuser is an immigrant, he may threaten to kidnap the children and bring them to his homeland if she seeks help in the new country.

An immigrant victim may believe that the police will return her to the abuser if she flees, or that the police will abuse her if she goes to the police station. If police in her native country are corrupt and/or abusive toward victims who report domestic abuse, she may not trust any police officer until she has more time and the opportunity to learn that police in her new country can be trusted to help victims of abuse. The abuser may deny her language and driving lessons to prevent her from learning about her safety options and seeking refuge in her new country. Abusers often take an immigrant victim's identification documents (e.g., passport), and this creates a barrier for immigrants who fear reaching out for help without identification documents. Depending on the country or state where the immigrant victim resides, she may fear being (temporarily) placed into an immigration detention center or being deported for reporting abuse.

Each victim's situation is unique and complex. If an abuser is not an immigrant, other problems may arise. For instance, mail-order brides facing abuse may learn that an abusive husband has never filed the proper paperwork with immigration authorities; the abuser may threaten to have her deported or refuse sponsorship if she reports the abuse. Some immigrant women feel trapped in domestic abuse, because (1) her native culture may not accept her back (e.g., as a divorced woman) and she would be deemed unmarriageable or shameful if she returns to her homeland; (2) she fears returning to poverty in her native country (especially if she has a child); (3) she is expected to support her family back home by sending money, and if she returns, she would be viewed as an economic burden; and (4) her native culture may "accept domestic violence," thus making her less likely to be aware that domestic violence is a crime in the new country.

Immigrant women may feel trapped in abusive relationships due to immigration laws, isolation, language barriers, and lack of financial resources. Further, for "most immigrant women their only means of support is an abusive husband and they may lack alternative support networks, such as extended families, in their new country. Leaving her husband for a safer environment may alternately mean losing not only his financial support and her possessions, but also the extended family or community that can provide her with the support needed to obtain work" (Shetty & Kaguyutan, 2002).

Immigration policies overlap with public policies to protect crime victims. In the case of spousal abuse involving documented immigrants within a country, a victim will likely have less economic opportunities than the abuser, not simply due to the economic abuse often found in abusive relationships, but also based on their immigrant work status in the country. For instance, a married man from Asia may be recruited to work for a U.S.-based tech company. The company assists him in receiving legal entry for himself and his immediate family to the United States, but only the husband receives a work permit. In this case, while she was capable of contributing to the household income in Asia, the wife is placed in a position of great economic dependence on her spouse. The allowance for the recruited worker to bring his wife to the United States, but to not allow her to work legally in the United States, puts her in a precarious situation that can increase the risk of domestic abuse in the household due to the stress on the family and her increased dependence. Should she need to escape domestic abuse, it decreases the economic opportunities for her to flee and the opportunities for her to learn about safe options (like shelter), because she is more isolated since she cannot work legally outside of the home.

Controversy arises in legislative debates as immigration policies overlap with violent crime prevention, as evidenced by those who focus on deportation of undocumented immigrants and those who focus on assisting all immigrant victims of abuse. When considering immigrant victims, law enforcement officials face pressures from both sides of the issue. Advocates for immigrant victims "monitor ongoing immigration reform debate for proposals that could "expose victims to even greater danger," and they "support immigration reform provisions that ensure immigrant victims of violence have access to law enforcement and services to escape violence" (NNEDV, 2007–2011).

The controversy over how to best regulate immigration while helping immigrant victims is discussed in many countries, and here is one example from the United States:

> In 2007, following the lead of the National Network to End Violence Against Immigrant Women, NNEDV [National Network to End Domestic Violence] organized in support of the Senate Comprehensive Immigration Reform bill and in opposition of several amendments ... , particularly the Coleman Amendment to deputize local police to enforce federal immigration law and the Vitter Amendment that would have denied Community Oriented Policing Services (COPS) grants to cities that do not ask about immigrant status when people report crimes. [According to advocates, these amendments would have had a devastating effect on immigrant victims of domestic and sexual violence, who would have likely become extremely reluctant to call the police.] (NNEDV, 2007–2011)

Advocates for immigrant victims across the United States asked their senators to oppose the amendments. These amendments did not pass, and advocates viewed this as a "victory for immigrants in abusive relationships" (NNEDV, 2007–2011).

Legislation against domestic abuse for all victims is important to maintain law and order, decrease the harmful effects of abuse on individuals and communities, and send a message to all people—including immigrants—that abuse is not condoned within a country. Futures Without Violence (formerly Family Violence Prevention Fund) reports: "Despite recent federal legislation that has opened new and safe routes to immigration status for some immigrant women who are victims of domestic violence, abuse is still a significant problem for immigrant women, as it is for all women in the United States."

- A recent study in New York City found that 51 percent of intimate partner homicide victims were foreign-born, while 45 percent were born in the United States (Femicide in New York City, 2004).
- Forty-eight percent of Latinas in one study reported that their partner's violence against them had increased since they immigrated to the United States (Dutton, Orloff, & Hass, 2000).
- A survey of immigrant Korean women found that 60 percent had been battered by their husbands (Tjaden and Thoennes, 2000).
- Married immigrant women experience higher levels of physical and sexual abuse than unmarried immigrant women, 59.5 percent compared to 49.8 percent, respectively (Dutton, Orloff, & Hass, 2000).
- Battered immigrant women who attempt to flee may not have access to bilingual shelters, financial assistance, or food. It is also unlikely that they will have the assistance of a certified interpreter in court, when reporting complaints to the police or a 911 operator, or even in acquiring information about their rights and the legal system (Orloff et al., 1995) (Futures Without Violence, p. 1).

To maintain and improve law and order within a country, law enforcement officials seek to improve the likelihood that all crime victims—including undocumented and documented immigrants—report crimes and cooperate with police and the judicial system. Yet immigrant victims are "less likely to report crimes or seek police assistance because they fear they will be reported to federal immigration authorities and deported" (NNEDV, 2007–2011). A "variety of barriers present themselves as immigrant victims seek assistance, including family and community resistance, fear of official institutions, inability to communicate in a common language, and program design features that inhibit help seeking"—for example, some social service programs fail "to adequately integrate race and ethnicity into an understanding of and response to domestic violence" (Shetty & Kaguyutan, 2002). Further, some interpreters do not remain professional, judge the immigrant victim, and/or inadequately interpret dialects.

To combat domestic abuse and its negative effects in communities, improved advocacy and legislation are important to ensure immigrant victims' access to protection and services. "Since [the U.S.] Congress first passed the Violence Against Women Act (VAWA) in 1994, federal legislation has addressed the additional challenges facing immigrant victims of domestic and sexual violence. In 2005, Congress took significant steps in the VAWA reauthorization to increase protections for immigrant victims of violence" (NNEDV, 2007–2011). Such U.S. protections include the right to receive police protection, access social services, and receive restraining orders.

See also: Culturally Competent Services; Forced Marriage and Domestic Abuse; International Violence Against Women Act (I-VAWA); Violence Against Women Act (VAWA)

Further Reading

Battered Women's Justice Project: http://www.vaw.umn.edu/documents/assistingimmigrantdv/assistingimmigrantdv.pdf

Dutton, M., Orloff, L., & Hass, G. (2000). Characteristics of help-seeking behaviors, resources, and services needs of battered immigrant Latinas: Legal and policy implications. *Georgetown Journal on Poverty Law and Policy, 7*(2).

Femicide in New York City: 1995–2002. (2004, October). New York City Department of Health and Mental Hygiene. Retrieved January 28, 2013 from http://www.nyc.gov/html/doh/downloads/pdf/ip/ -2002_report.pdf

Futures Without Violence. (n.d.) The Facts on Immigrant Women and Domestic Violence. Retrieved from http://www.futureswithoutviolence.org/userfiles/file/Children_and_Families/Immigrant.pdf

National Network to End Domestic Violence (NNEDV). (2007–2011). Immigration section. Retrieved from http://www.nnedv.org/policy/issues/immigration.html

Orloff, L., Jang, D., & Klein, C. (1995). With no place to turn: Improving advocacy for battered immigrant women. *Family Law Quarterly, 29*(2), 313.

Shetty, S., & J. Kaguyutan. (2002, February). Immigrant victims of domestic violence: Cultural challenges and available legal protections. Harrisburg, PA: VAWnet. Retrieved from http://www.vawnet.org/applied-research-papers/print-document.php?doc_id=384

Tjaden, P., & Thoennes, N. (2000). Full report of the prevalence, incidence, and consequence of violence against women. Washington, D.C: U.S. Department of Justice. Retrieved January 28, 2013 from https://www.ncjrs.gov/pdffiles1/nij/183781.pdf

Cheryl O'Brien

INCITE!

Incite! Women of Color Against Violence is a grassroots activist network of self-identified radical feminists of color who mobilize to end violence against women and against racialized communities more broadly. In addition to local organizing and critical awareness raising about issues of violence against women, Incite! advocates direct action to address concerns rather than relying on political elites or government representatives to solve community issues. Indeed, Incite! recognizes the role played by governments at all levels in perpetrating and legitimizing violence against people and communities of color in the United States.

Consisting of local chapters and affiliates, Incite! is a national network with groups throughout the United States. Specific collectives work on local campaigns around issues including police violence, media representations, and reproductive justice issues. A national collective helps to support and coordinate local campaigns in order to provide a national and international platform for addressing issues and advancing group concerns. Incite! claims thousands of members and supporters nationally.

Incite! identifies violence against women of color at social-structural as well as individual and interpersonal levels. Violence against women includes violence against communities, including police violence. It also involves global manifestations of violence such as war and colonialism that disproportionately impact women of color worldwide. At the same time, Incite! confronts violence within communities including sexual assault and domestic violence. The group asserts, in public statements and organizing, the intersection of issues of class, gender, sexuality, and racialization in practices of oppression and domination within stratified societies. Incite! openly mobilized opposition to the U.S. war and occupation against Iraq. They have also opposed the expansion of the military-industrial complex and the diversion of public funds to support militarism.

Strategies to address domestic violence must intersect with strategies for addressing the violence that shapes specific communities historically and currently. As one example, the history of colonialism against indigenous communities has diminished the role of women within some communities, erasing the role of women as leaders and/or elders involved centrally in community decision making and governance. Colonial governance regimes and government agencies have rendered women as dependents or social subordinates within some communities. These factors cannot be excluded from discussions of community or domestic violence. Similarly, state practices that criminalize members of communities of color often leave women with extra burdens around child care, elder care, or community service.

Local groups within the Incite! network thus develop projects that oppose state violence as well as interpersonal violence. Among the ongoing Incite! projects are a radio program produced by women of color in issues impacting their lives, self-defense training, the establishment and operation of a grassroots health clinic, and the open critique of the professionalization of antiviolence movements and the domination of social justice projects in poor and oppressed communities by non-governmental or nonprofit institutions. Other projects include street protests against street harassment of women and organizing mothers receiving social assistance. Incite! also distributes a biweekly e-newsletter with almost 3,000 subscribers. In addition to protests and community organizing, Incite! hosts conferences and gatherings to share strategies, tactics, and political perspectives while building connections of solidarity. In 2006, Incite! released the groundbreaking anthology *Color of Violence*, which brings together essays by 33 activist feminists to address interlinked concerns of violence and class, gender, sexuality, and racism.

See also: Grassroots Movements; Nonprofit Organizations; Social Change Campaigns

Further Reading

Incite! (2006). *Color of violence: The Incite! anthology*. Boston, MA: South End Press.
Incite! (2007). *The revolution will not be funded: Beyond the non-profit industrial complex*. Boston, MA: South End Press.
Smith A. (2005). *Conquest: Sexual violence and American Indian genocide*. Boston, MA: South End Press.

Jeff Shantz

INDIA AND DOMESTIC ABUSE

India suffers from high rates of domestic abuse. The Center for Research on Women reported in 2002 that 45 percent of Indian women are slapped, kicked, or beaten by their husbands. Of the women reporting violence, 50 percent were kicked, beaten, or hit when pregnant. About 74.8 percent of the women who reported violence have attempted to commit suicide. The National Family Health Survey found that a low of 16 percent of women in Maharashtra and a high of 31 percent in Tamil Nadu had experienced physical abuse by a partner during their lifetime, while a low of 9 percent in Maharashtra and high of 23 percent in Bihar had experienced physical abuse in the previous 12 months. Another study using national data from the 29 member states of India indicated 14 percent of women had experienced emotional abuse, and 8 percent had endured sexual violence by an intimate partner. The highest-risk women were those whose husbands exhibited controlling behaviors, who were practicing Muslims, and who were of scheduled castes. Importantly, however, abuse was found among women of all regions, all religious groups, and all social classes. Research has shown that the abuse of women also has tremendous impact on children. Studies have shown that children of women who have been abused in India are more likely to die in their first year than those born to nonabused women.

As in some other third world countries, there are numerous economic, political, and social factors that contribute to rates of domestic abuse. In addition to limited economic, political, and social resources, women in India experience institutional oppression in the form of traditional, patriarchal family structures; the caste system; and in their religious freedom. According to the third-century BCE lawyer Manu, girls are to obey their fathers, youth their husbands, and once the husband passes, women are to obey their sons. Males are privileged even before they are born. Although the practice is prohibited, sex-selective abortion is still not uncommon, as families who learn they are having daughters see them as little but an economic drain. Girls are less likely to be vaccinated or taken for medical treatment; thus, more Indian girls die when they are young than do boys. Boys are far more likely to be sent to school or to advance in schooling than are girls. Daughters are trained to serve their families and their future families. Their behaviors are tightly controlled. As girls get older, many times they become subject to harassment and sexual advances by male family members, while male siblings express their power over their sisters by demanding their services, sometimes even sexually. Boys, then, can easily develop the mindset that men are to dominate and women are objects who serve men. Not having a girl means not having to worry about paying a dowry, either.

Advocates say that the dowry system in India is a major reason for harassment and abuse. The dowry system, which involves gift giving by the bride's family to the groom's family, emerged in the second century BCE. It was originally set up as a father's gift to his daughter, a way for a woman to share her father's property and to maintain control over it, but over time it changed to a system that involved negotiation and bargaining, rather than a voluntary gift. As the stakes got higher, a woman became vulnerable because the groom's family might perceive her father's dowry as inadequate and punish her for it.

In 1961, the Dowry Prohibition Act was passed, but implementation was a failure. Amendments to the act were passed in 1984 and 1986, but their impact has also been negligible. Critics say that rising economic pressures and increased consumerism, coupled with the decreasing status of women, resulted in a lack of political will to end the dowry system.

Dowry is the leading cause of death among young brides. A 2000 report found that a young married woman is beaten, burned to death, or pushed to kill herself every six hours in India. In 1997, some 64 percent of unnatural deaths for women were because they were burned, although most were recorded as kitchen accidents. Because families of daughters want them to marry into wealthier families, they may agree to a dowry that is too high for them to pay. If the daughter then tells the economically struggling family that she is being abused, she typically receives little support. It would be considered shameful if a married daughter left her husband and returned to the family. This would also threaten the chances for marriage for any younger sisters. In the new family, the bride is often not seen as a welcome addition personally but rather as an economic asset and hopefully a bearer of sons. Oftentimes, not just her new husband but the entire family, with whom the couple may live, abuses the new wife. Virtually the only way to elevate her status in the new family is to produce sons.

In a patriarchal system such as that in India, it is little wonder that women, too, believe domestic violence is often justified. In a 2001 survey, 56 percent of the women interviewed felt that it was valid for a man to beat his wife if she neglected the house or children. Many women also agreed that abuse was justified if she did not cook her husband's food on time or well, if she spoke disrespectfully to her husband or in-laws, if she complained about either, if she socialized excessively, if her dowry was inadequate, and if she failed to bear sons. Girls as young as 15, socialized into this patriarchal culture, expressed the same sentiments.

Many studies have found that most women who are abused never tell anyone. Of those women who remained silent about their abuse, 75 percent expressed that they did not want to dishonor their husband. The primary reason for not discussing the abuse, however, was their children. Abraham (2000) explained, "South Asian women are expected to sacrifice their individual identity to the priorities of their fathers, husbands, in-laws, children and community" (p. 20).

A growing number of educated women are enduring abusive relationships. Experts assert that men find it troubling when women obtain more education than they do, as it is a challenge to the patriarchal norm. Some respond violently, trying to put women "back in their place." Research also shows that it is more educated men who are the most abusive.

India first criminalized domestic violence in 1983 under Section 498A of the Indian Penal Code, which covered physical and mental violence inflicted by a man against his wife. The Indian Penal Code was amended twice, first in 1983 and then in 1986. A man found guilty of violating the Section 498A could be imprisoned for up to three years as well as fined.

As Mitra (2000) pointed out, however, "there is a wide divergence between the legal provision and the perception of those associated with its implementation. The legal system gives pre-eminence to the notion of homogeneous family, thus disregarding the subordinate status of women within the family, and of her experiences of violence that this entails" (p. 11).

Police officers still emphasize family preservation, and counselors and courts often encourage women to reconcile with abusive men so as to keep the family together. Police often see abuse as a way of disciplining wives or blame it on men's drunkenness. If a woman persists and takes an abuse case to court, she must provide evidence or witnesses. Sometimes doctors refuse to write reports documenting physical abuse. Family members and family friends or in-laws are the most likely witnesses to the abuse and are typically not eager to testify. Servants fear for their jobs, and neighbors still may see abuse as a family affair and not their business. Women who are sexually abused are considered to have dishonored or dirtied the family, and thus victims of sexual abuse are particularly hesitant to discuss it.

In 1980, a group of women lawyers in New Delhi and Bombay formed the Lawyers Collective. Composed today of lawyers and law students, the group promotes legal education and research and runs free legal aid centers for poor women. It also campaigns for legal reform and spearheaded the 2000 effort to enact new clauses to the legislation prohibiting domestic violence. The bill promoted by the Lawyers Collective expanded the range of abuse covered, as the law only defined abuse as occurring in a marital household. The new bill included violence in "shared households," that is, against elderly parents, abuse of female children, and violence against domestic servants. Abuse was defined as sexual physical, verbal, mental, or economic in nature. Further, the bill expanded domestic violence into the realm of civil law, authorized protection orders, and included the right to reside in shared households and the right to access service providers. The parliament generally ignored these recommendations, leaving out violence not perpetrated by anyone but a relative. Parliament offered a new definition of domestic violence, saying it occurs when any male "habitually assaults or makes the life of the aggrieved person miserable by cruelty of conduct even if such conduct does not amount to physical ill-treatment" (Protection From Domestic Violence Act, 2002, chap. 2). Further, it allows for no penalty if the respondent was reasonably acting for his own protection or the protection of his or another's property. Given the patriarchal society in which a man's word is almost always believed over a woman's, such a defense makes it easy for male abusers to perpetrate with impunity. The suggested provision to allow women to remain in their homes was essential, given that one of the main reasons women do not report abuse is because they fear being homeless. The law enacted by parliament did not contain this provision.

Women can file for divorce, although it is still very much stigmatized. Many times, abusive men will agree to the divorce on the conditions that all domestic violence charges are dropped. If the divorce is granted before the criminal hearing, this automatically occurs. Thus, laws often encourage husbands accused of abuse to file for divorce first.

Some women have taken matters into their own hands. In India's northern Uttar Pradesh state's Banda area, several hundred women have banded together to form a group called the gulabi gang, or pink gang. Adorned in pink saris, they are making public the abuse and political corruption they see. They coordinate marches on the homes of abusers, publicly shaming them for their actions.

A list of services for victims in India is available at Hot Peach Pages: http://www.hotpeachpages.net/asia/asia1.html#India.

See also: Acid Throwing; Dowry Killings; Forced Marriage and Domestic Abuse; Honor Killings; South and Southeast Asian Victims

Further Reading

Abraham, M. (2000). *Speaking the unspeakable: Marital violence among South Asian immigrants in the United States.* New Brunswick, NJ: Rutgers University Press.

Ahmed-Ghosh, H. (2004). Chattels of society: Domestic violence in India. *Violence Against Women, 10*(1), 94–118.

Bhattacharya, R. (2004). *Behind closed doors: Domestic violence in India.* Thousand Oaks, CA: Sage.

Biswas, S. (2007, November 26). India's "pink" vigilante women. *BBC News.* Retrieved June 26, 2012, from http://news.bbc.co.uk/2/hi/7068875.stm

Dalal, K., & Lindqvist, K. (2012). A national study of the prevalence and correlates of domestic violence among women in India. *Asia Pacific Journal of Public Health, 24,* 265–277.

Koenig M. et al. (2010). Domestic violence and early childhood mortality in rural India: Evidence from prospective data. *International Journal of Epidemiology, 39*(3), 825–833.

Majumdar, S. (2003, November 6). In India, domestic violence rises with education. *Women's Enews.* Retrieved June 25, 2012, from http://womensenews.org/story/domestic-violence/031106/india-domestic-violence-rises-education

Mitra, N. (2000). *Domestic violence as a public issue: A review of responses* (Unit for women's studies). Mumbai, India: Tata Institute of Social Sciences.

Protection From Domestic Violence Act. (2001). Lok Sabha, Government of India Publication.

Rosenberg, J. (2010). Intimate partner violence and infant death in India. *International Perspectives on Sexual and Reproductive Health, 36*(3), 121.

Laura L. Finley

INTERNATIONAL VIOLENCE AGAINST WOMEN ACT (I-VAWA)

"The International Violence Against Women Act (I-VAWA) is a historic and unprecedented effort by the United States to address violence against women and girls globally" (Futures Without Violence, 2011b). This effort was proposed because of the scope of the problem. The United Nations estimates that one-third of the world's women will endure physical, sexual, or some other form of abuse during her lifetime, while rates of abuse have been found as high as 70 percent in some countries. Abuse takes many forms, from rape to domestic violence and acid burnings to dowry deaths and so-called honor killings. "Violence against women and girls is an extreme human rights violation, a public health epidemic and a barrier to solving global challenges such as extreme poverty, HIV/AIDS, and conflict. It devastates the lives of millions of women and girls—in peacetime and in conflict—and knows no national or cultural barriers" (I-VAWA, n.d.a.). A bill in the U.S. Congress, the I-VAWA "would, for the first time, systematically integrate efforts to end gender-based violence (GBV) into foreign assistance programs, applying the force of U.S. diplomacy and foreign aid to prevent the abuse and exploitation that affects up to one in three women worldwide" (Futures Without Violence, 2011a).

History

Futures Without Violence spearheaded the campaign behind I-VAWA, working with partners Amnesty International and Women Thrive. The aim of the campaign was "to engage concerned Americans on U.S. foreign policies, activities and resources that have the potential to end and prevent violence against women and girls worldwide. Futures Without Violence envisions this campaign as a vehicle to underscore the importance of eliminating violence as a key strategy toward promoting the economic, social, and political status of women and girls worldwide; thereby, advancing efforts toward building civil and stable societies" (Futures Without Violence, 2011a).

Futures Without Violence utilized the support of more than 150 U.S.-based entities, as well as 40 global women's rights organizations, to help then-U.S. Senator (now Vice President) Joe Biden D-DE), Senator Richard Lugar (R-IN), and Representative Howard Berman (D-CA) draft the International Violence Against Women Act (I-VAWA). I-VAWA was initially introduced to the 110th Congress, but did not make it deep into consideration.

I-VAWA was reintroduced in February 2010 to the 111th Congress. This time it had more bipartisan support in both the House and Senate. In the Senate, lead sponsors were John Kerry (D-MA), Barbara Boxer (D-CA), Olympia Snowe (R-ME), and Susan Collins (R-ME), while in the House I-VAWA was sponsored by

Representatives Bill Delahunt (D-MA), Red Poe (R-TX), and Jan Schakowsky (D-IL). The bill made it to the Senate Foreign Relations Committee, where on December 14, 2010, I-VAWA passed without any amendments. Senate Foreign Relations Committee Chairman John Kerry, who introduced the bill in February, said, "This bill tells women and girls that that they are valued, respected members of society who do not have to suffer in silence. I-VAWA will use U.S. assistance wisely, bring greater transparency, and improve coordination inside the government and with key stakeholders in civil society," and Futures Without Violence (formerly Family Violence Prevention Fund) President Esta Soler stated, "We thank Senators John Kerry, Barbara Boxer, Olympia Snowe and Susan Collins for their continuing work to pass this critical legislation. There is too much at stake, for our country and the world, to wait" (Futures Without Violence 2010).

The 111th Congress recessed shortly after the approval of the Senate Foreign Relations Committee, and no time was allotted in either chamber to bring the bill to the floor. Futures Without Violence and its partners expressed disappointment that I-VAWA did not come up for a direct vote, but were pleased that it moved farther along in the legislative process than ever before. They noted a "groundswell of congressional support in Congress and in the Administration for ending violence against women and girls, both at home and abroad." "The Administration and congressional allies in the 112th Congress are committed to ending violence against women and girls and planning to re-introduce the bill" (Futures Without Violence, 2011a).

Public Support

Futures Without Violence and Women Thrive Worldwide attempted to gauge public support for I-VAWA. Their research indicated that 61 percent of voters, crossing party lines, thought global violence against women should be a major U.S. priority. Some 80 percent supported I-VAWA, and 62 percent expressed intense support. Further, more than 200 violence prevention, humanitarian, faith-based, human rights, refugee, and women's organizations have acknowledged their support of I-VAWA.

Overview

I-VAWA will allow the United States government to help coordinate a 5-year international strategy to reduce violence against women and girls. I-VAWA authorizes more than $1 billion dollars in U.S. assistance to international organizations and programs that are already working to prevent and respond to violence, including survivor services, health care, legal programs, economic projects, and educational initiatives. Additionally, I-VAWA includes provisions for the training of foreign security forces on various forms of gender-based violence. It also encourages U.S. collaboration and funding of institutions like the UN's special Trust Fund on Violence Against Women, and emphasizes support and capacity building for overseas women's organizations working to stop violence against women and girls.

The I-VAWA also makes ending violence against women and girls a top diplomatic priority. It creates the Office of Global Women's Issues at the State

Department to coordinate all efforts to combat violence against women and girls, and the Office of Global Women's Development at the U.S. Agency for International Development (USAID), which will be responsible for integrating violence prevention programming into current foreign assistance activities.

I-VAWA Details

I-VAWA is the first legislation specifically devoted to ensuring that stopping violence against women and girls is a priority for American diplomats and for the dissemination of foreign aid. I-VAWA would help end violence against women through: (1) prevention programs that establish or improve educational opportunities for women and girls; (2) improving economic opportunities for women and girls; (3) supporting men and boys' efforts to partner to end abuse; (4) health and support programs for survivors; (5) legal and judicial training programs to hold perpetrators accountable; (6) investing in community organizations and foreign governments; and (7) funding and training for addressing violence against women in humanitarian crises.

A major focus of I-VAWA is the promotion and support of laws and legal structures that can both prevent and respond to various forms of violence against women, including rape, abuse, honor killings, and child marriage. I-VAWA promotes political, legal, and institutional reforms, including training for police, prosecutors, and judges such that women and girls can feel a sense of justice, not revictimization. The unique needs of female refugees are also included in the provisions of I-VAWA. Given that disasters, both man-made and natural, increase the likelihood of violence against women and girls, I-VAWA would expand funding for disaster assistance and humanitarian programs. I-VAWA would also authorize the U.S. Secretary of State to develop emergency measures to address violence against women and girls during violent conflicts, including both services for victims and accountability for offenders. Training on abuse, assault, and stalking for militaries and police working overseas, as well as for humanitarian aid workers, is included as well.

Improving the economic and educational status is key to reducing the vulnerability of women and girls. I-VAWA promotes job and employment training as well as opportunities for women to own land and property. Further, recognizing that sexual harassment and assault are barriers to girls' school attendance globally, I-VAWA is aimed at reducing these problems and thereby increasing girls' educational status.

I-VAWA is crafted to be holistic and to address both criminal justice and the health care industry. It promotes training of health care providers so they can recognize abuse and support victims.

Finally, the goal of I-VAWA is to prevent abuse by changing social norms. The legislation will support public awareness programs and community-based solutions to abuse.

See also: Futures Without Violence; U.S. Government Responses to Domestic Violence; Women Thrive Worldwide

Further Reading

Futures Without Violence. (2010, December 14). Key Senate Committee Passes I-VAWA. Retrieved from http://www.futureswithoutviolence.org/content/features/detail/1635/

Futures Without Violence. (2011a). International Violence Against Women Act (I-VAWA) section. Retrieved from http://www.futureswithoutviolence.org/content/features/detail/1766/

Futures Without Violence. (2011b). I-VAWA: International Violence Against Women Act. Retrieved from: http://www.futureswithoutviolence.org/content/features/detail/1765/

IVAWA (International Violence Against Women Act). (n.d.). Homepage. Retrieved from http://www.PassIVAWA.org/

Cheryl O'Brien

ISLAM AND DOMESTIC ABUSE

Islam is the world's second-largest religion, behind Christianity. The phenomenon of domestic violence among Muslims has just recently begun to be studied. Victims' voices amplified by advocates and some Islamic leaders are just beginning to shatter the silence that had allowed domestic violence to continue unrestrained in the Muslim community. However, as with any social construction, the continuum of religious adherence and interpretation is heterogeneous. Among the contentious issues are whether domestic violence exists in Muslim homes; whether it should be a public or private issue; the scope, severity, and foundation of domestic violence; and how best to deal with it. In addition, underreporting, patriarchal beliefs and traditions, and the focus on ensuring family purity are further impediments for adequately dealing with domestic violence in Muslim communities. In short, domestic violence in Islamic households is a very contentious issue within Islamic communities and the larger public arena.

Perpetrators of domestic violence are not always extremists who lock their wives in their homes. They can also be charismatic community leaders and professionals. Approximately 10 percent of Muslim families in the United States experience domestic violence (Alkhateeb, 1999). However, emotional and verbal abuse may be as high as 50 percent (Alkhateeb, 1999). In another study, 34 percent of women and 33 percent of men supported a man hitting his spouse if she offends or insults him when they are alone (Kulwicki & Miller, 1999). Moreover, 17 percent of women and 43 percent of men are supportive of the husband hitting the woman if she publicly insults him, and 59 percent of both men and women approve of domestic violence if she hits him first (Kulwicki & Miller, 1999).

What makes domestic violence in Muslim communities in the United States more difficult to ascertain is the criticism of Islam in the larger U.S. public. Even though, domestic violence occurs in every religious group and socioeconomic class, examples of domestic violence in the Muslim community further solidify the negative perception that some Americans have of Islam in general. For example, the murder of Aasiya Zubair Hassan by her husband in 2009 led many in the media to view domestic violence as a purely religious issue rather than an issue of power and control that affects all communities regardless of race, class, or worldview (Weiner, 2009). In addition, Aasiya and her husband cofounded Bridges TV with the hope of giving Islam a positive public face in the United States and unfortunately ended up becoming the face of domestic violence in the Muslim American community.

While this tragic case added to some Americans' negative perception of Islam, it also demonstrated the extent of the Muslim communities' response to and fight against domestic violence. For example, activists from Turning Point for Women and Families and Peaceful Families Project, along with the founder of House of Peace, Shaykh Bashir, decried the murder and urged Muslims and their leaders to fight against the scourge of domestic violence (Weiner, 2009).

The plethora of interpretations of the Islamic moral and religious teachings and laws leads some to argue that Islam is supportive of domestic violence and others to argue that Islam liberates victims from the abusive cycles of domestic violence (Finigan, 2010). In chapter 4, verse 34 of the Quran, two different interpretations demonstrate the extent to which diverse readings affect the social and cultural life of family relationships. "Good women are obedient; and as to those on whose part you fear desertion, admonish them, and leave them alone in their sleeping places and beat them" (Faizi, 2001; Tindale, 2006).

However, another interpretation of the same verse reads, "As for women you feel are averse, talk to them persuasively; then leave them alone in bed; and go to bed with them when they are willing. If they open out to you, do not seek an excuse for blaming them" (Tindale, 2006). The conflicting interpretations of the above verse are just one example of how some in the Islamic community diverge on the status of women. Some argue that women are equal to men and should be held in high esteem and therefore never beaten. Others argue that men are by nature superior to women and therefore have the inherent right to control and dominate women by instructing them on how to live, and abusing them if necessary (Finigan, 2010).

Some Muslims and even some imams and mullahs condone domestic violence, and others condemn it (Faizi, 2001; Tindale, 2006). Furthermore, while too many Muslims are perpetrators of domestic violence, they are still a minority and negatively affect public opinion of all Muslims (Tindale, 2006). Universalism and cultural relativism complicate the issue, with some arguing that western conceptions of right and wrong in regard to violence against women cannot and should not be implemented in nonwestern societies. However, others (Hajjar, 2004) argue that women's rights should not be viewed as a western conception, but rather as a necessity for all women in all cultures. Domestic violence is further complicated in Muslim societies due to the private lives and closed nature of many abusive homes. Moreover, strict interpretations of Sharia law and other Islamic texts sanctify some husbands' views of their wives as inferior beings in need of domination. However, others argue that the Quran views men and women as equals.

Moreover, the power structure, the view of domestic violence, and the fear of retribution affect how victims view seeking help and how perpetrators view committing intimate partner violence (IPV). However, now that many in the Muslim community have accepted that domestic violence is a reality in their communities, educating Islamic religious and community leaders on how to counsel victims and deal with perpetrators must become a priority. Moreover, educating victims on available resources, such as shelters and their legal rights, is imperative (Finigan, 2010). A lot of work has been done in the last decade to illuminate the scourge of domestic violence. Hopefully, in the next decade, victims will begin to feel confident to report all cases of domestic violence and stand up to their perpetrators.

The Faith Trust Institute has a variety of resources aimed at understanding abuse among Muslims. Founded in 2000, the Peaceful Families Project coordinates awareness campaigns and provides training and resources for victims and advocates. The Muslim Women's League also provides information and resources about abuse among followers of Islam.

See also: Christianity and Domestic Abuse; Judaism and Domestic Abuse; Spiritual Abuse

Further Reading

Alkhateeb, S. (1999). Ending domestic violence in Muslim families. *Journal of Religion and Abuse*, 1(44), 49–59.

Alkhateeb, M., & Abugideiri, S. (Eds.). (2007). *Change from within: Diverse perspectives on domestic violence in Muslim communities*. Great Falls, VA: Peaceful Families Project.

Alkhateeb, M. (2009). DV organizations serving Muslim women: Preliminary results of a 2009 quantitative survey. *Peaceful Families Project*. Retrieved from http://www.peacefulfamilies.org/DVOrgsSurvey.pdf

Ammar, N. H. (2007). Wife battery in Islam: A comprehensive understanding of interpretations. *Violence Against Women, 13*(5), 516–526.

Boy, A., & Kulczycki, A. (2008). What we know about intimate partner violence in the Middle East and North Africa. *Violence Against Women, (14)*1, 53–70.

Chavis, A. Z., & Hill, M. S. (2009). Integrating multiple intersecting identities: A multicultural conceptualization of the power and the control wheel. *Women and Therapy, 32*(1), 121–149.

Domestic violence and Muslim women FAQs. (n.d.). Faith Trust Institute. Retrieved June 29, 2012, from http://www.faithtrustinstitute.org/resources/learn-the-basics/dv-muslim-women-faqs

Douki, S., Nacef, F., Belhadj, A., Bouasker, A., & Ghachem, R. (2003). Violence against women in Arab and Islamic countries. *Archives of Women's Mental Health, 6*, 165–171.

Ellison, C. G., Bartkowski, J. P., & Anderson, K. L. (1999). Are there religious variations in domestic violence? *Journal of Family Issues, 20*(1), 87–113. Retrieved from http://jfi.sagepub.com/content/20/1/87.abstract

Faizi, N. (2001). Comment: Domestic violence in the Muslim community. *Texas Journal of Women & the Law*, 10, p. 209.

Finigan, M. (2010). Intimate violence, foreign solutions: Domestic violence policy and Muslim-American women. *Duke Forum for Law and Social Change, 2*, 141–154.

Hajjar, L. (2004). Religions, state power and domestic violence in Muslim societies: A framework for comparative analysis. *Law & Social Inquiry, 29*(1), 1–38.

Haj-yahia, M. M. (1998). Beliefs about wife beating among Palestinian women: The influence of the patriarchal ideology. *Violence Against Women, 4*(5), 533–558.

Hassouneh-Phillips, D. S. (2001). Marriage is half of faith and the rest is fear of Allah: Marriage and spousal abuse among American Muslims. *Violence Against Women, 7*(8), 927–946.

House of Peace. (2009). *House of Peace*. Retrieved from http://houseofpeace.com/

Jayasuriya, V., Wijewardena, K., & Axemo, P. (2011). Intimate partner violence against women in the capital province of Sri Lanka: Prevalence, risk factors, and help seeking. *Violence Against Women, 17*(8), 1086–1102.

Kulczycki, A., & Windle, S. (2011). Honor killings in the Middle East and North Africa: A systematic review of the literature. *Violence Against Women, 17*(11), 1442–1464.

Kulwicki, A. D. (2002). The practice of honor crimes: A glimpse of domestic violence in the Arab world. *Issues in Mental Health Nursing, 23*, 77–87.

Kulwicki, A., & Miller, J. (1999). Domestic violence in the Arab American population. Transforming environmental conditions through community education. *Issues in Mental Health Nursing, 20*, 199–215

Lambert, N. M., & Dollahite, D. C. (2006). How religiosity helps couples prevent, resolve, and overcome marital conflict. *Family Relation, 55*(4), 439–449.

Muslim Women's League: http://www.mwlusa.org

Peaceful Families Project: http://ww.peacefulfamilies.org

Stotland, N. L. (2000). Tug-of-war: Domestic abuse and the misuse of religion. *American Journal of Psychiatry, 157*, 696–702.

Tindale, R. (2006). Board's eye view. *Emergency Nurse, 14*(7), 37–57.

Weiner, M. (2009). Domestic violence, Islam, and the unexpected response. *Huffington Post.* Retrieved from http://www.huffingtonpost.com/matthew-weiner/domestic-violence-islam-a_b_171278.html

Chuck Goesel

JUDAISM AND DOMESTIC ABUSE

The Jewish community has just recently begun to acknowledge the existence of domestic violence in Jewish homes and therefore has just started to fight against it. Consequently, important facts regarding the scope and degree of intimate partner violence (IPV) within Jewish homes is just beginning to emerge. The correlation between Judaism and domestic violence is believed to be contingent on one's interpretation of scripture and ancient writings, segregation of the sexes, closed and secretive communities, subjugation of the individual identity for the perceived greater good of the community, and the close relationship between adherents and their rabbis.

Religion, like other social constructions, occurs on a continuum, with degrees of liberalism and extremism. The three monotheistic religions; Judaism, Christianity, and Islam share many of the same scriptural stories found in the Jewish Torah, the Christian Old Testament, and the Islamic Tawrat (Torah) and the Zabar (Psalms). It has been argued that these stories and traditions aid in the propulsion of the past patriarchal system into modernity. Some (See for example Stein, 2005) believe that scripture has set the patriarchic tone for the domination of women, which has resulted in the prevalence of domestic violence in religious homes. Some perpetrators view the male domination inherent in religious dogma as a free pass to commit emotional, physical, financial, and psychological abuse.

Stein (2005) argues against the often-cited Maimonides proclamation that perpetrators often use to justify beating your wife if she fails to do her housework. Stein (2005) contends that the words were taken out of context and that in all actuality Maimonides was arguing *against* beating one's wife. Judaism, like all religions and other social constructions, comprises a diverse set of interpretations of scripture, laws, and ancient writings. Those interpretations affect how adherents of the Jewish faith live their lives. Within those interpretations lies the debate of whether Judaism leads to the perpetration of domestic violence, assists in the recovery from it, or is a combination of both.

The social stigma concerning divorce within many Jewish communities is another impediment for victims seeking help. Many view divorce as sacrilegious and therefore that they must live with the abuse and hope it will diminish. In addition, "lashon hara" or "the evil tongue" (Ringel & Bina, 2007), derived from the Ten Commandments, is another impediment to seeking help. The "evil tongue" is the religious idea that community members must not talk poorly of others.

While some (Sisselman, 2011) argue that the Jewish community views domestic violence differently from other religious or secular communities, others, like the

Jewish Women International, agree but argue that the gap is closing. Jewish Women International (JWI) offers a wide range of resources on perpetrators, victims, and advocates. In the 2004 Needs Assessment report, JWI outlined many key findings of their research as well as a call to action.

JWI (2004) explains that intimate partner violence can affect all communities, all relationships, all classes and ages, and all aspects of one's religious and culture life. The Jewish community is not immune from the scourge of domestic violence. Furthermore, the perpetuation of the myth that domestic violence does not affect Jewish families keeps those in positions to help victims from seeing the signs of violence (JWI, 2004). Moreover, JWI argues that domestic violence is not just physical, but can also be sexual, verbal, psychological, and financial. In addition, many Jewish women fail to seek help because of shame, fear of being separated from their children, lack of financial or legal resources, and housing needs (JWI, 2004).

The continuum of beliefs within Judaism stretches from secular beliefs about Judaism to a strict orthodox view of Jewish scripture. Ringel and Bina (2007) explain that within the orthodox tradition are the Hasidic faction, which has the most conservative view of religious traditions and laws; the more modern, Ultra Orthodox; and the Modern Orthodox, who are more liberal. Some studies (Yehuda, Friedman, Rosenbaum, Labinsky, and Schmeidler, 2007) have shown that domestic violence is more prevalent in more Ultra Orthodox families than in Modern Orthodox homes. However, more abuse occurred in those who became more religious in later life than those who were raised observant (Yehuda et al., 2007).

In most Ultra Orthodox communities, gender roles are nonnegotiable, education is segregated between the sexes, and contact between men and women is denied until marriage (Ringel & Bina, 2007). In addition, the habit of rabbis holding joint counseling sessions with the victim and the perpetrator prevents the victim from fully being able to explain the abuse and express his or her feelings openly without fear of reprisal when victim and perpetrator meet alone behind closed doors (Twerski, 1996).

Moreover, members of the Ultra Orthodox community allow the male rabbi to regulate a couple's sex life. For example, Ringel and Bina (2007) explain that the rabbi "approves the end of the wife's monthly menstrual cycle and thus [gives] the couple permission to resume sexual relations" (277). In sum, the religious structure typically subsumes one's personal identity. This leads some (Ringel & Bina, 2007) to conclude that the causes of intimate partner violence are getting married at an early age, the segregation of men and women, and the formation of identity based on religious morals and traditions. In addition, not only did victims cite these as causes of domestic violence, but they also argued that the causes kept victims from looking for a way out of their violent relationships.

Some rabbis view domestic violence as isolated occurrences, arguing that it is caused by personality deficiencies rather than religious regulations and principles (Ringel & Bina, 2007). However, others (Ringel & Bina, 2007; Stein, 2005) argue those adherents and rabbis distort the "true" meaning of religious writings and scripture when they deny that domestic violence occurs in the Jewish community and therefore refuse to talk about it or teach it to their congregants. The denial of the existence of IPV in Jewish communities keeps women from seeking help (Ringel & Bina, 2007). In addition, rabbis' attitudes toward non-Jewish resources such as secular courts, advocates, and counselors keeps domestic violence confined behind the walls of abuse.

Many argue that a majority of Jewish communities have existed in such secrecy from the outside world that perpetrators of domestic violence could operate free from punishment for their crimes, leaving victims feeling helpless and shameful (See for example Ringel & Bina, 2007). However, the recent acknowledgment that domestic violence does in fact occur in Jewish households has been an important advance in the struggle against it. This acknowledgment has empowered victims to seek help, led rabbis to learn more about domestic violence, and given communities the knowledge needed to fight the problem (Kaufman, 2010). Furthermore, others (JWI, 2004) contend that rabbis are an integral component in fighting against domestic violence because victims are more likely to seek help if a rabbi has previously addressed the issue of intimate partner violence. In addition, others (Lambert & Dollahite, 2006) argue that religiousness aids couples in preventing relationship problems, resolving conflicts, and working toward meaningful solutions when conflicts arise.

Some (Levitt & Ware, 2006) contend that domestic violence is caused by inequitable relationships, and therefore equality should be taught in all communities in order to end spousal abuse. Moreover, temple leaders should manage inequality by promoting compassion as a way to lessen misinterpretations (Levitt & Ware, 2006). In addition, religious leaders in general and rabbis specifically are caught between fighting to save women from domestic violence and upholding traditional views and ideals (Levitt & Ware, 2006).

The Jewish Coalition Against Domestic Abuse (JCADA) describes the following issues among Jewish victims of domestic abuse on their website, http://www.jcada.org:

- **Secretiveness:** It was not discussed in public forums, not mentioned by rabbis until recently, and not written about in synagogue bulletins. As a result, Jewish women never felt that the community was ready to listen and may have stayed in their abusive marriage too long. Jewish women tend to stay in abusive relationships 2 to 3 times longer than those in the general population. Non-Jewish women stay from 3 to 5 years, Jewish women from 7 to 13 years.
- **Socioeconomic:** This situation speaks to the entrapment that many middle- to upper-middle-class Jewish women face around lifestyle issues. They feel stuck in their abusive situation because they cannot support their standard of living on their own. They cannot replicate their lifestyle, so they remain in a lovely home that may feel like a prison. Many have no knowledge of the family finances, limited access to money, or may be threatened with financial ruin.
- **Shanda (shame):** Women experience shame as members of the Jewish community because they know that Jews are not supposed to be victims of abuse. These women feel that they are alone, that no one else in the Jewish community is living with abuse, and that no one will understand or believe them. There are those whose husbands are

community or business leaders, and they fear that no one will believe that a pillar of the community can also be abusive.
- **Shalom Bayit**: *Shalom Bayit* is one of the few *mitzvot* (commandments) given primarily to women; it is the pride and joy of the observant Jewish woman to create "peace in her home" . . . a home that is a source of family identity, education, and affection. If a woman admits to others that she has been abused in any way, she loses her pride in her home and in her family. She feels intense guilt, shame, and stigma for shattering the myth of *Shalom Bayit* that many women work so hard to maintain. In some cases, this admission may cause a backlash, and the woman may be blamed and ostracized for coming forward.
- Observant women's concerns about leaving the home include the need to have kosher food at a shelter, to keep the Shabbat and other observances, and to be close to their children's school.

Jewish Women International offers a wealth of resources and assistance for victims. It is aimed at "empowering women and girls—through economic literacy; community training; healthy relationship education; and the proliferation of women's leadership." Since 1987, JWI has provided information and resources for Jewish women and for rabbis seeking to address the issue of domestic violence. The JCADA also provides information and resources.

See also: Christianity and Domestic Abuse; Islam and Domestic Abuse; Spiritual Abuse

Further Reading

Butler, S. (2000). A covenant of salt: Violence against women in Jewish life. *Journal of Religion and Abuse, 2*(2), 49–65.

Cwik, M. (1997). Peace in the home? The response of rabbis to wife abuse within American Jewish congregations. *Journal of Psychology and Judaism, 21*(1), 5–81.

Ellison, C. G., Bartkowski, J. P., & Anderson, K. L., (1999). Are there religious variations in domestic violence? *Journal of Family Issues, 20*(1), 87–113. Retrieved from http://jfi.sagepub.com/content/20/1/87.abstract

Faith Trust Institute. (n.d.). Domestic violence and Jewish women FAQs. *Faith Trust Institute*. Retrieved from http://www.faithtrustinstitute.org/resources/learn-the-basics/dv-jewish-women-faqs

Frishtik, M. (1990). Violence against women in Judaism. *Journal of Psychology and Judaism, 14*(3), 131–153.

Graetz, N. (n.d.). Domestic violence in Jewish law: How Judaism views wifebeating. *My Jewish Learning*. Retrieved from http://www.myjewishlearning.com/life/Relationships/Spouses_and_Partners/Domestic_Violence.shtml

Graetz, N. (2009). Wife beating in Jewish tradition. *Jewish women: A comprehensive historical encyclopedia*. Jewish Women's Archive. Retrieved from http://jwa.org/encyclopedia/article/wifebeating-in-jewish-tradition

Grodner, E., & Sweifach, J. (2004). Domestic violence in the Orthodox Jewish home: A value sensitive approach to recovery. *Affilia, 19*, 305–316.

Jewish Coalition Against Domestic Abuse: http://www.jcada.org

Jewish Women International. (2004). A portrait of form of domestic abuse in the Jewish community: Key findings from the national and Chicagoland needs assessment. Washington, D.C: JWI.

Jewish Women International. (2011). Embracing justice: A guide for Jewish clergy on domestic abuse. *Jewish Women International*. Retrieved from http://www.jwi.org/document.doc?id=307

Kaufman, C. (2010). Domestic violence and the Jewish community: The literature expands. *Nashim: A Journal of Jewish Women's Studies and Gender Issues, 20*, 172–175.

Lambert, N. M., & Dollahite, D. C. (2006). How religiosity helps couples prevent, resolve and overcome marital conflict. *Family Relation, 55*(4), 439–449.

Lev, R. (2002). *Shine the light: Sexual abuse and healing in the Jewish community*. Boston, MA: Northeastern University Press.

Levitt, H. M., & Ware, K. (2006). "Anything with two heads is a monster": Religious leaders' perspectives on marital equality and domestic violence. *Violence Against Women, 12*(12), 1169–1190.

Ringel, S., & Bina, R. (2007). Understanding causes of and response to intimate partner violence in a Jewish Orthodox community: Survivors' and leaders' perspectives. *Research on Social Work Practice, 17*(2), 277–286.

Rosen, R. (2011). One in four Jewish women suffer abuse in the home. *Jewish Chronicle Online*. Retrieved from http://www.thejc.com/news/uk-news/46410/one-four-jewish-women-suffer-abuse-home

Sisselman, A. (2011). *Domestic violence and faith communities: An exploratory study examining beliefs and experiences of Jews, non-Jews, and Rabbis*. ProQuest Dissertation Publishing.

Stein, D. E. S. (2005). Did Maimonides really say that? The widespread claim that he condoned wife-battering may be mistaken. *Journal of Religion and Abuse, 6*, 1–17.

Steinmetz, S., & Haj-Yahia, M. (2006). Definitions of and beliefs about wife abuse among Ultra-Orthodox Jewish men from Israel. *Journal of Interpersonal Violence, 21*, 525–554.

Twerski, A. (1996). *The shame borne in silence: Spouse abuse in the Jewish community*. Pittsburgh, PA: Mirkov.

Yehuda, R., Friedman, M., Rosenbaum, T. Y., Labinsky, E., & Schmeidler, J. (2007). History of past sexual abuse in married observant Jewish women. *American Journal of Psychiatry, 164*(11), 1700–1706.

Chuck Goesel

KATZ, JACKSON

Jackson Katz, PhD, is a long-recognized and award-winning educator, filmmaker, social critic, and activist who specializes in the study of contemporary U.S. masculinity, most notably the social construction and persistence of male aggression and violence. Katz has made a unique contribution to the movement against domestic violence by situating it not as a "women's issue" but as a distinctly male problem that must be addressed actively by all, including men. Katz's work focuses on images of violent masculinity in U.S. culture, paying close attention to complex dimensions of identity, privilege, and social power such as race, social class, and sexuality. In addition to editing several scholarly collections, Katz publishes academic articles in journals and books, as well as contributes regularly to the *Huffington Post*. His book *The Macho Paradox: Why Men Hurt Women and How All Men Can Help* (2006) identifies violent masculine norms in the United States and strategies for creating safer, more equitable relations between men and women. Katz has created and been featured in several educational films and is perhaps best known for the film *Tough Guise: Violence, Media, and the Crisis in Masculinity* (2000). In addition to other film projects, he envisioned and cofounded the multiracial Mentors in Violence Prevention (MVP) training program at Northeastern University's Center for the Study of Sport in Society in 1993. MVP is the most widely used gender violence prevention program in college and professional athletics. He and his staff implement training in the U.S. military, law enforcement agencies, colleges, high schools, community organizations, and small and large corporations. Katz speaks to national and international audiences.

Born in the Boston area, Katz was the first man to earn a minor in women's studies from the University of Massachusetts, Amherst. He earned his master's degree from the Harvard School of Education and his PhD in cultural studies and education from University of California, Los Angeles. Katz's early scholarly work revealed violent images of male heterosexuality in pornography. Examining the impact of these images on the masculine consciousness, Katz argued that pornographic films promote male aggression and sexual abuse against women.

A former all-star football player, Katz is well known for conducting antisexist training in traditionally masculine arenas such as sports and the military. His films and training curricula are popular in high schools and colleges in the United States and abroad. His philosophy and practice teach men to identify aggressive norms and behavior. Trainees challenge each other to be "better men" who support the cessation of violence and the promotion of safer and more equitable relations despite gender, race, sexuality, social class, and other differences.

Jackson Katz is an author, filmmaker, social critic, and activist whose work studies male agression and violence. (Jackson Katz)

Katz's films have been instrumental in the field of masculinity studies. Katz has worked on several projects with award-winning filmmaker Sut Jhally. In their first film, *Tough Guise*, which was named among the Top Ten Young Adult Videos for 2000 by the American Library Association, Katz and Jhally focus on masculine standards in popular U.S. media. Previous to Katz and his contemporaries, scholars in women's studies and related fields had established the role of the media in shaping cultural standards for women. The ideal woman is white-skinned, extremely thin, and submissive. *Tough Guise* reveals the U.S. cultural standards that construct the ideal male as tough, aggressive, and violent. Violent men are featured as heroes; demonstrations of vulnerability and emotional sensitivity are taboo, while the heavily muscled man is rewarded with status, wealth, and fame. Racist depictions of men of color as poor and hypersexual heterosexuals fuel an understanding of these men as thugs. All men are encouraged to treat women as accessories. Women are objectified for male pleasure, and, as Katz points out, "real men" gain status through sexual conquest. Popular films, music, and advertising portray emotional, physical, and sexual abuse of women as in line with masculine norms and when enacted help men earn each other's respect. Thus, tough guys wear a "tough guise," a mask that renders them devoid of emotion and full of aggression. These strict gender roles harm both men and women, Katz and Jhally point out. Men's violence harms women, but men also hurt other men.

Featured in Jhally's *Dreamworlds* video series (1991, 1995, 2007), Katz charts the continuing portrayal of women as sexualized objects in music and other cultural forms. The media continues to define sexuality and gender for young men and women in very narrow ways, again with men as the aggressors and women as the objects.

In *Wrestling with Manhood: Boys, Bullying, and Battering* (2002), Katz and Jhally identify professional wrestling culture and the massive popularity of this staged performance-sport that glorifies homophobia and violence. Katz highlights young men's obsession with this industry and its relationship to bullying in school environments, sexual assault, and relationship violence. The film shows how professional wrestling demeans and degrades women, spinning storylines that say "she deserved it." Disturbing scenes show male athletes/performers sexually harassing female characters, verbally assaulting them, and pretending to physically assault them. *Wrestling with Manhood* notes the difficulty these athlete/performers have in separating their work from their personal lives, as many have been arrested for domestic violence.

In *Spin the Bottle: Sex, Lies, and Alcohol* (2004), Katz and cultural critic Jean Kilbourne highlight the U.S. media's portrayals of binge drinking and other risky behaviors, focusing on the real-world effects these portrayals have on the choices young men and women make with alcohol and sex. The relationship between masculinity and violence is fueled by alcohol and the pressure youth exert on each other to engage in dangerous behaviors.

Katz's Mentors in Violence Program was founded in 1993 with support from the U.S. Department of Education. Utilizing his Mentors in Violence Strategies (MVS), Katz has directed the multiracial MVP-MVS since 1997. MVP-MVS has been implemented by a quarter of the teams in the NFL, a number of Major League Baseball clubs, NASCAR, and many other sports organizations. The program is the first worldwide gender violence prevention program implemented in the history of the U.S. Marine Corps. U.S. Army personnel in Iraq have received MVP training, which is also being piloted in four sites around the world. Katz has also served as a subject matter expert and consultant for the U.S. Air Force.

The philosophy behind the program involves understanding the potential of "empowered bystanders." A bystander is defined as "a family member, friend, classmate, teammate, coworker—anyone who is embedded in a family, school, social, or professional relationship with someone who might in some way be abusive, or experiencing abuse" (Katz, 2011). Many believe that witnesses to violence or potential violence have only two options: to intervene or remain silent. But there are other options. Through active dialogues the training helps individuals find the choices that make sense for them. Ultimately they develop a host of strategies for delivering strong messages against rape, battering, sexual harassment, gay-bashing, and all forms of sexist abuse and violence.

Katz's *Huffington Post* commentaries educate readers about racist, sexist, classist, and heteronormative discourse in the realms of media and politics. For example, he urges an acknowledgment of the power that conservative radio talk show hosts wield as millions of listeners tune in daily. Critics should not dismiss these hugely popular media personalities as radical; instead, Katz encourages his readers to tune in and analyze the arguments that the hosts and their guests articulate.

Expanding his cultural critique to men in U.S. politics, Katz focuses on the exclusively male presidential scene. Presidents and high-powered political figures gain and maintain popularity by presenting themselves as international powerhouses. Negotiations are considered weak (i.e., feminine), and status is gained through espousing aggressive interventionist militaristic policies. Going to war helps male leaders win points and thus votes.

Katz has also authored important commentary about the ways perpetrators and victims of sexual assault are discussed in media. In February 2011, he wrote about Pittsburgh Steelers quarterback Ben Roethlisberger, who was facing multiple allegations of sexual assault (none of which had resulted in criminal charges) as the team contended for the Super Bowl win. Recognizing that the allegations represented a "teachable moment," Katz called on coaches, parents, and others to discuss with young people the mixed messages they receive about treating people with respect and dignity, the fact that "Big Ben" made choices that led to the controversy, that true athletes are leaders both on and off the field, that men who mistreat women are never "manly" or "masculine," and that friends and teammates have an important role to play in interrupting various forms of harassment and abuse.

Similarly, when the allegations that Penn State football Assistant Coach Jerry Sandusky had sexually assaulted young boys emerged, Katz called out the media for referring to the boys as "accusers" rather than "victims." He noted similar coverage of the sexual assault allegations against former International Monetary Fund (IMF) head Dominique Strauss-Kahn and former Republican presidential candidate Herman Cain. The term "accusers" is a not-so-subtle way to suggest their stories are untrue—a form of victim-blaming that is insidious.

His journalistic coverage of contemporary scholars allows wider audiences access to his academic work. Note, for example, his recent two-part interview with USC sociologist Michael Messner that explores the issues of men's emotional connection with guns.

Katz's professional service has included membership in the U.S. Secretary of Defense's Task Force on Domestic Violence in the military from 2000 to 2003. From 1998 to 2000, he served on the American Bar Association's Commission on Domestic Violence. He also consulted for nearly a decade with the Liz Claiborne Company's award-winning Women's Work campaign (Jackson). He was the chief organizer for Real Men, the Boston-based antisexist men's group.

See also: Athletes and Domestic Abuse; Bystander Intervention Programs; Educational Programs; Films and Domestic Abuse; Men's Efforts against Domestic Abuse; Social Change Campaigns

Further Reading

Jackson Katz: http://www.jacksonkatz.com

Jackson Katz's blog in the *Huffington Post:* http://www.huffingtonpost.com/jackson-katz

Jhally, S. (Producer). (1999). *Tough guise: Violence, media, and the crisis in masculinity* [Film]. Media Education Foundation.

Jhally, S. (Producer). (2003). *Wrestling with manhood: Boys, bullying, and battering* [Film]. Media Education Foundation.

Jhally, S. (Producer) (2007). *Dreamworlds* [Film]. Media Education Foundation.

Katz, J. (2011, February 2). What to say to boys and young men about Big Ben. *Huffington Post*. Retrieved March 19, 2012, from http://www.huffingtonpost.com/jackson-katz/what-to-say-to-boys-and-y_b_817291.html

Katz, J. (2011, November 18). There are victims in the Penn State tragedy, not "accusers." *Huffington Post*. Retrieved March 19, 2012, from http://www.huffingtonpost.com/jackson-katz/penn-state-victims_b_1098571.html

Ridberg, R. (Producer). (2004). *Spin the bottle: Sex, lies, and alcohol* [Film]. Media Education Foundation.

Allison Brimmer

KIMMEL, MICHAEL

Michael Kimmel is an American sociologist whose expertise is in the field of gender studies, and masculinity in particular. After receiving his bachelor's degree at Vassar College (1972), he completed a PhD at Columbia (1981). He is the author of numerous books and is a highly sought-after speaker on issues concerning manhood in America. A devout feminist, believing that the eradication of sexism benefits all, Kimmel's work reflects active deconstructions of gender categories, including violence. His book *Guyland: The Perilous World Where Boys Become Men* (2008) paints a stark portrait of young American men who occupy a new social world—an extended youth—avoiding traditional adult responsibility and at risk for various problems, including potential abuse of each other and of women.

Kimmel's most significant argument about domestic abuse, titled " 'Gender Symmetry' in Domestic Violence: A Substantive and Methodological Research Review" (2002), countered the vocal claims in several studies that men and women committed domestic abuse in equal numbers. Kimmel argues that the political use of these studies made them particularly problematic since some people insisted gender symmetry should negate the funding for women's shelters, as compassion should be extended to neither abuser (1334). He created a complex analysis of the other studies' evidence, placing the neglected category of gender at the center.

Kimmel demonstrates that problems with the original studies are numerous: some only questioned cohabitating couples about the abuse in their homes, omitting the thousands of abusive situations involving separated couples; most studies involved only heterosexuals; some framed questions so that violent incidents could only be reported as a result of a particular issue (such as a foul mood or a fight) and only in a single-year window, rather than as part of a long-term, systematic effort by one partner to control the other person. Kimmel took special issue with the omission of variations in kinds of violence; studies discounted the physical difference between most men and women, and a punch by a man, typically larger and stronger, was equated with a (smaller) woman's slap. He also notes that studies assumed men rarely reported violence despite experiencing it because of shame (it's not manly to be beaten by a woman) and that women were too embarrassed to report using violence.

Kimmel's refutation examines all of these issues through a gendered lens. He notes, "What is missing, oddly, from these claims of gender symmetry is an analysis of gender. By this, I mean more than simply a tallying up of which biological sex is more likely to be perpetrator or victim. I mean an analysis that explicitly underscores the ways in which gender identities and gender ideologies are embodied and enacted by women and men" (Kimmel, 2002, p. 1344). Socialization, for example, impacts how people see and report violence. Kimmel argues that women are socialized not to use violence and thus remember and report every incident that they commit, as they see themselves transgressing norms and feel guilty. Men, on the other hand, are socialized to be in control and thus may not report their behaviors to those conducting surveys because of fears of appearing to have no control over women and thus having to resort to violence to do so. Women also tend,

Kimmel writes, to justify the violence of men as something they deserved and thus do not report all of what actually occurs. He then points to statistics that demonstrate how males are, contrary to assumptions, the more frequent pressers of domestic violence charges and often go the hospital for resulting wounds; Kimmel understands this phenomenon as a function of men seeing themselves as wronged and women seeing abusers as people who hit out of love and are thus worthy of forgiveness.

Kimmel offers a substantial argument for contextualizing domestic abuse. In contrast, the studies he discusses offer little context—little sense of patterns of "causes and consequences"—which hinders their usefulness and weakens any claims to gender symmetry in such violence (p. 1346). Women's violence, he explains, is often in self-defense and performed when women fear for their lives or the lives of their children. It is often a result of years of growing intensity in forms of abuse. Women's violence is thus very different from that used by men to control their relationship partners. Women are often far more injured than men in domestic violence cases: Kimmel argues that gender symmetry exists at the low end of the violence spectrum, with minor injuries, but shifts dramatically at the higher end. Women need medical care more often and for more serious injuries. So while both sexes may be actively hostile toward each other, only one can be said to wield violence as a weapon (p. 1348).

Significantly, Kimmel argues, many women are stalked and harmed by former partners, who use violence as a means of controlling women who have left them; this violence surely needs to be included in various studies. Furthermore, he notes, ex-spouse violence tends to be much more intensive, resulting in death more often. While substantial numbers of female homicide victims are killed at the hands of intimate partners, the number of men killed by women in domestic relationships has dropped. Kimmel explains that the reason for this is the vast array of programs now open to women who are abused. Women have places to go and services to use when they are beaten; places like shelters give them opportunities to be free of the men's grasp, and as a result, fewer women kill men in self-defense.

Kimmel's point here is not to dismiss women's acts of violence, but to argue for compassion and services for all victims, regardless of sex, and to understand what women's violence can reveal about men's. In "family conflict" situations, Kimmel posits a 4:1 ratio of men to women, closer to symmetry; in violence as a result of efforts to control, he suggests a 9:1 ratio, with men the overwhelming number of aggressors and prone to use more intensive violence (p. 1358). Thus Kimmel dispatches the claims of gender symmetry in domestic abuse as well as the politicians who seek reduced funding for shelters, and also seeks greater efforts for both women and men who find themselves in abusive situations.

Kimmel's *Guyland: The Perilous World Where Boys Become Men* (2008) explores the culture of young men in American society during the last several years and concludes that such men now embody a life stage ("Guyland") previous generations did not pass through; this life stage is one where young men are mainly with and influenced by other young men, behave with a sense of entitlement, and care little for the critiques of female peers, parents, teachers, or other figures.

One key element of *Guyland* is violence. From boyhood, males engage in violence with each other, a tendency that has its roots deep in American history. Then as now, "its use, its legitimacy, and its effectiveness are all well understood by most adolescent guys. They use violence when necessary to test and prove their manhood, and when others don't measure up, they make them pay" (p. 57). Though this use of violence and acceptance of it starts early, Kimmel argues, in their college/early adult years it grows, particularly in the homosocial environments of fraternities. Hazing is a key form of ritualized violence against other men in order to establish manliness; so is using sexual violence against women.

Many men embedded in the culture of *Guyland* understand sex as something they, as men, are entitled to, and they often feel pressured by the other young men in their peer group to "hook up" with women, particularly at fraternity parties. Furthermore, young men feel they are the abused ones in the pursuit of intercourse—as one student said, girls "have all the power ... I want sex with them ... and some bitch decides whether or not I get laid. It's not fair" (p. 227). This bitterness produces the sense that sex is something men deserve and that other men are getting far more often (a myth, in most cases, perpetrated by the male peer group), and such men often feel disempowered in social situations, particularly if young women dress provocatively. Such a mindset, which Kimmel argues is common in *Guyland*, leads to frequent incidents of predatory sex on college campuses. Perpetrators do not see themselves as rapists, but will often commit various forms of sexual assault in order to live up to the "Guy Code" that governs *Guyland*. Kimmel's own students admitted that they thought, " 'girls have to say no' to protect their reputations, they 'mean yes, even if they say no,' and 'if she's drunk and semi-conscious, she's willing' " (p. 218). Thus violence is perpetrated against women as they are actively encouraged to overconsume alcohol by *Guyland's* residents, who will occasionally resort to giving the women drugs as well; women who are on the verge of passing out and who are clearly incapable of giving informed consent are understood to be particularly fair game. A code of silence prevails in *Guyland*, which further condones the behavior.

Ultimately, many young men emerge from college extremely confused about women, sex, and violence, and some who might be perfectly well adjusted and respectful of women elsewhere end up prosecuted for attempted (and committed) rape. In the minds of many young men, having sex with nearly unconscious women is perfectly okay; *Guyland* is marked by a pursuit of sexual conquest, where women's actions—or lack of actions, because of alcohol—matter very little.

Michael Kimmel is a major American sociologist and a prolific writer who has spent much of his career examining concepts of gender and, in particular, manhood. Because of that focus, he frequently explores domestic and sexual violence—its construction, its meaning, its uses. His work is key reading for anyone interested in the intersection of masculinity, violence, and sex.

See also: Feminism and Domestic Abuse; Men's Efforts against Domestic Abuse; Sociological Theories About Domestic Abuse

Further Reading

Kimmel, M. (2002). Gender symmetry. In domestic violence: A substantive and methodological research review. *Violence Against Women*, Special Issue: Women's Use of Violence in Intimate Relationships, Part 1. 8(11), 1332–1363.

Kimmel, M. (2008). *Guyland: The perilous world where boys become men*. New York, NY: Harper.

Kimmel, M. (2011). *Manhood in America: A cultural history* (3rd ed.). London, England: Oxford University Press.

Jennifer Cote

KIVEL, PAUL

Paul Kivel is a social justice educator, activist, writer and cofounder of the Oakland Men's Project, a community education center and prevention organization devoted to stopping male violence. He has been an innovative leader in violence prevention for more than 35 years. Kivel speaks throughout the United States on issues such as racism and diversity, challenges of youth, teen dating and family violence, raising boys to manhood and the impact of class and power on daily life.

According to his website (http://www.paulkivel.com), the vision Kivel carries through his work is a society where each person is valued regardless of gender, race, cultural background, sexual identity, ability or disability, or access to wealth. This society, according to Kivel, would provide adequate shelter, food, education, recreation, health care, security, and well-paying jobs for all. He goes on to say that the land would be respected and sustained, and justice and equal opportunity would prevail. Lastly, Kivel states on his website (www.paulkivel.com) that "this society would value cooperation over competition, community development over individual achievement, democratic participation over hierarchy and control, and interdependence over either dependence or independence." Through his writing and presentations, Kivel emphasizes the importance of cooperation and interdependence.

Kivel offers workshops, training, keynotes, and consultation on eradicating racism, preventing male violence, averting youth violence, promoting progressive parenting, halting homophobia, uprooting class and gender discrimination, and promoting social justice by helping people come together to form productive alliances. His workshops are founded on books and curricula developed specifically for grassroots activists and others working for social justice. A central theme to Kivel's message regarding social justice is that we have to take into account the experiences of all individuals. For example, we cannot discuss women's issues without taking into account women of color, women of marginalized classes, or lesbian women. Kivel's workshops, books, and interactive curricula work to help individuals understand intersecting forms of oppression.

Kivel has authored numerous book and curricula including *Uprooting Racism: How White People Can Work for Racial Justice*, *Men's Work*, *Making the Peace*, *Young Women's Lives*, *Helping Teens Stop Violence*, *Boys Will Be Men*, *I Can Make My World a Safer Place*, and *You Call This a Democracy?: Who Benefits, Who Pays, and Who*

Really Decides. He also authors a newsletter, *Getting Together*, sharing his latest information, at no cost, with the public. Curricula developed by Kivel include participatory, interactive methodologies for training youth and adults in a variety of settings. He incorporates the concept of being allies in community struggles to end oppression and injustice to transform organizations and institutions into each of his curricula.

Paul Kivel recently expanded his repertoire to include writings and teachings geared toward challenging Christian hegemony. He defines Christian hegemony as the everyday, pervasive, and systematic set of Christian values and beliefs, individuals and institutions that dominate aspects of our society through the social, political, economic, and cultural power they wield. Kivel explains that Christian hegemony is a system of domination that is complex, shifting, and operates through the agency of individuals, families, church communities, denominations, parachurch organizations, civil institutions, and through decisions made by members of the ruling class and power elite. Kivel is not critiquing individual Christians or their beliefs through this project but merely shining a light on the Christian hegemony that has shaped our lives here in the West. Kivel's Challenging Christian Hegemony project includes booklets, articles, videos, a website, blog, exercises, resources, workshops, trainings, and consultations. He anticipates a book forthcoming on the subject as well.

Paul Kivel is a respected member of the domestic violence field, especially on the subject of violence prevention. His notable contributions relate to engaging men and boys and to the importance of inclusivity and activism in the movement.

See also: Feminism and Domestic Abuse; Men's Efforts against Domestic Abuse

Further Reading
Paul Kivel: http://www.paulkivel.com
Paul Kivel's Challenging Christian Hegemony project: http://www.christianhegemony.org

Jennifer Rey

KRISTOF, NICHOLAS AND SHERYL WUDUNN

Nicholas Kristof is an author and award-winning columnist for the *New York Times*. Among other topics, he writes regularly about global human rights issues, in particular those impacting women. Kristof has been a regular columnist with the *Times* since 2001. He has won the Pulitzer Prize twice, in 1990 and 2006.

Kristof grew up on a farm in Oregon. He worked in France after high school and traveled around Africa and Asia as a college student, writing about what he saw. Kristof attended Harvard College, where he graduated Phi Beta Kappa, then studied law at Oxford University on a Rhodes Scholarship. He graduated from Oxford with first-class honors. Kristof later studied Arabic in Cairo and Chinese in Taipei.

Kristof's 1990 Pulitzer Prize, with his wife Sheryl WuDunn, also a *Times* journalist at the time, was for their coverage of China's Tiananmen Square democracy movement. They were the first married couple to win a Pulitzer for journalism. Kristof's second Pulitzer, in 2006, was for his commentary on the genocide in

Darfur, Sudan. Kristof is also the recipient of the George Polk Award, the Overseas Press Club Award, the Michael Kelly Award, the Online News Association Award, and the American Society of Newspaper Editors Award. He was also the first blogger for the *Times*. A 1997 article he wrote about child deaths in the developing world resulted in Bill and Melinda Gates focusing their philanthropy on global health.

Not shy about expressing his opinions, Kristof was an early opponent of the war in Iraq and the first person to report that President Bush had contradicted his administration's own investigation when he claimed in the State of the Union address that Iraq was seeking uranium from Africa. He has also been criticized for critiquing the anti-sweatshop movement. Kristof helped make the case of Mukhtar Mai, a Pakistani woman who was gang-raped, an international cause.

In 2006, the *New York Times* launched the Win a Trip with Nick Kristof contest. The college student who best describes what s/he would like to accomplish on a trip to Africa can win a reporting trip accompanied by Kristof. A total of 3,800 students submitted entries, and Kristof chose Casey Parks. They traveled to three countries: Equatorial Guinea, Cameroon, and the Central African Republic, where they reported on AIDS, poverty, and maternal mortality. During the trip, Kristof published his *New York Times* columns while Parks wrote about her observations in her blog. The contest was held again in 2007, and Kristof selected Leana Wen, a medical student, and Will Okun, a teacher from Chicago. The three traveled to Rwanda, Burundi, and eastern Congo, accompanied by filmmaker Eric Daniel Metzgar, who documented the trip and created the documentary *Reporter*, which premiered at the 2009 Sundance Film Festival and was aired on *HBO* in February 2010. In 2008, Kristof selected Paul Bowers, with whom he traveled to Senegal, Guinea Bissau, Guinea, Sierra Leone, and Liberia. In 2010, Kristof traveled with student Mitch Smith to Gabon, Republic of Congo, and the Democratic Republic of Congo, and in 2011, he took Saumya Dave, a medical student, and Noreen Connolly, a teacher, to Morocco, Mauritania, Senegal, Niger, and Burkina Faso. In December 2011, Kristof described the many interesting women they encountered, and they ways they have suffered, during a talk at the TedxWomen Conference.

Kristof married Sheryl WuDunn in 1988. WuDunn is a graduate of Cornell University. She earned an MBA from Harvard Business School and an MPA from Princeton University's Woodrow Wilson School. She has worked for the *Wall Street Journal* and later joined the *New York Times* as the Beijing Bureau correspondent. WuDunn was the *Times*' first Asian American reporter. WuDunn has also been a senior lecturer at Yale University's Jackson Institute for Global Affairs and has received honorary doctorates from the University of Pennsylvania and Middlebury College. She regularly commentates on China, global affairs, and gender issues on *National Public Radio*, *The Colbert Report*, and *Charlie Rose*. In 2010, WuDunn spoke about global gender inequalities at the Ted Global Conference. Currently, she is a senior managing director with Mid-Market Securities, an investment banking firm, where she raises capital for a variety of clients. WuDunn has also been vice president in the investment management division at Goldman, Sachs & Co. and a commercial loan officer at Bankers Trust. In addition to the Pulitzer, she has also won other journalism prizes, including the George Polk Award and Overseas Press Club

Awards. Ms. WuDunn has also won a White House Project EPIC Award, the Asia Women in Business Corporate Leadership Award, the Pearl S. Buck Woman of the Year Award, the Harriet Beecher Stowe Prize, among others (*Half the Sky* website 2012). In 2011, *Newsweek* called WuDunn one of the "150 Women Who Shake the World." WuDunn and Kristof have three children.

Kristof and WuDunn have coauthored *China Wakes: The Struggle for the Soul of a Rising Power*, *Thunder from the East: Portrait of a Rising Asia*, and, most recently, *Half the Sky: Turning Oppression into Opportunity for Women Worldwide*.

Half the Sky informs readers about the many injustices facing women globally, including sex-selective abortion, inadequate medical attention, rape and sexual assault, poverty, acid attacks, domestic violence, human trafficking, and inadequate education. In the book, Kristof and WuDunn tell the horrifying stories of women who have been raped, endured traumatic fistulas, suffered from forced prostitution, and more. Yet they also leave readers hopeful, noting that women are not the problem but instead should be seen as the solution. They advocate for the economic and educational empowerment of women and girls worldwide, which will not only address the many social problems cited above but will, importantly, better utilize half of humanity. When educated, financially supported, and empowered, women and girls help the economy and raise their children differently, thereby resulting in a world less plagued with violence. Rather than simply a catalog of horrors, *Half the Sky* is inspirational in that it relays the stories of women's resilience and activists all over the globe who are working to end these inequalities.

The book has drawn great praise and has now been expanded into a movement. The Half the Sky movement includes a website that features short videos recorded by dozens of celebrities, additional information about various gender-related issues, links to additional resources, and opportunities to get involved. Partners for the movement are extensive and listed on the website.

A four-hour *PBS* television series has been filmed and will air in October 2012. The series was shot in 10 countries (Cambodia, Kenya, India, Sierra Leone, Somaliland, Vietnam, Afghanistan, Pakistan, Liberia, and the United States) and features women's stories coupled with commentary from celebrities like Eva Mendes, Meg Ryan. America Ferrera, and Gabrielle Union. Additionally, a Facebook game and mobile phone game addressing gender and human rights issues are being developed.

See also: Human Trafficking; Mai, Mukhtar

Further Reading

Half the Sky: http://www.halftheskymovement.org

Kristof, N., & WuDunn, S. (2009). *Half the sky: Turning oppression into opportunity for women worldwide*. New York, NY: Alfred A. Knopf.

Sheryl WuDunn: Our century's greatest injustice. (2010). TED Talks. Retrieved June 22, 2012, from http://www.ted.com/talks/sheryl_wudunn_our_century_s_greatest_injustice.html

TedxWomen—Nicholas Kristof. (2011). Retrieved June 22, 2012, from http://tedxtalks.ted.com/video/TEDxWomen-Nicholas-Kristof-2

Laura L. Finley

LATIN AMERICA AND DOMESTIC ABUSE
Introduction

Domestic abuse has begun to be recognized in Latin America as a family and social problem, which does not distinguish social class, age, or any other demographic characteristic. Most countries in the region have created legislation against physical violence, and nongovernmental organizations have helped develop awareness campaigns and a small number of shelters for survivors. However, victims in Latin America continue to face numerous obstacles including poverty, lack of knowledge of the law, difficulty finding available shelter, insufficient legislation to protect them from sexual and psychological violence, lack of education, lack of institutional support, lack of treatment and prevention networks, and abusers' disregard for the law. Moreover, strong cultural beliefs are often used to maintain the type of gender inequality that leaves women vulnerable to suffer from abuse.

Studies conducted in Latin America indicate that between 33 and 40 percent of women are victims of physical violence and that between 60 and 68 percent suffer psychological violence. According to a study by UN Women in 2011 in 11 Latin American and Caribbean countries, sexual violence on average reaches 16 percent, and in some countries, like Costa Rica and Paraguay, it reaches 20 percent.

Other data from the United Nations emphasized that physical violence rates during the past 10 years differ significantly among countries. For instance, victims of physical violence in Chile make up 15 percent of the population, victims in Costa Rica and Colombia 33 percent, and victims in Peru represent 31 percent of the general population. The same study indicates that psychological violence is more prevalent than physical and sexual violence. For example, Peru's figures are 68 percent of psychological violence as opposed to 31 percent physical and 20 percent sexual violence.

Furthermore, 25 percent of women in Latin America report having experienced some form of control by their partner. However, in countries like Colombia and Peru, the rates exceed 65 percent. Also 25 percent of women in Bolivia, Dominican Republic, Colombia, Peru, Honduras, and Haiti report that they do not make decisions at home because such decisions are made by the man.

In order to learn more about the reality of the prevalence of domestic violence in Latin America, it is important to carry out public awareness campaigns and for researchers to take into account issues regarding the use of assessment tools designed for Latin American participants. Experts have noticed that a lack of consensus regarding what constitutes physical, psychological, and sexual violence compromises the effectiveness of assessment tools used to measure domestic violence in the region. Garcia-Moreno, Jansen, Ellsberg, Heise, and Watts (2006) indicated that

Table 1 International Studies on Domestic Violence and Violence against Women.

STUDY	Country(ies)	Prevalence
World Sage Study	Chile	Physical violence 25%
The International Violence Against Women Survey	Costa Rica Intimate partner violence (IPV)	**Sexual Violence** 15%
Demographic and Health Surveys	Colombia, Haiti, Dominican Republic, Nicaragua IPV. Women ages 15 to 49 years.	Physical violence Colombia 40% Haiti 17% Dominican Republic 18% Nicaragua 28% **Sexual violence in couples** Haiti 17% Nicaragua 10% Colombia 11.5% Dominican Republic 6%

many women found it difficult to identify the meaning of sexual abuse and did not understand questions that included terms such as abuse, rape, and violence. Nevertheless, they did indeed understand when specific words were used, such as hitting, yelling, or humiliating.

Characteristics

Some of the characteristics of domestic violence in several Latin American countries, according to Cáceres (2011), include:

- Most victims suffer violence on more than one occasion and by the same perpetrator.
- Violence is chronic, meaning that women tolerate violence for a long period of time. For example, a study conducted in Colombia found that 57 percent of battered women stayed with their abusers for more than 10 years.
- Domestic violence often occurs on weekends, a situation associated with alcohol consumption by the abuser.
- Physical violence is usually directed toward the woman's face and leaves scars.
- Victims are often both women and children, who may be direct victims or witnesses of violence.

Femicide

The death of women by an intimate partner or former partner has received increased attention in recent years. The Centro Reina Sofia (CRS) conducted an international study on the prevalence of femicide (number of women murdered per million inhabitants) in 44 countries in seven regions (Africa, North America, South America, Central America, Asia, Europe, and Oceania). The highest rates were for Latin American countries. The following countries rank in the top five list reported in 2010: El Salvador (129.43), Guatemala (92.74), Colombia (49.62), and Honduras (44.64).

The perpetrators of femicide in Latin America are characterized by the use of firearms or weapons, with some exceptions. For example, in Costa Rica, perpetrators use their hands (manual homicide). Victims tend to be younger than age 30. The batterer's use of alcohol and a victim's attempt to leave the abuser are two risk factors found to be associated with femicide.

Risk Factors

Several risk factors that facilitate and maintain domestic violence in Latin America have been identified. These risk factors include poverty, lack of education, lack of knowledge of the law, lack of treatment and prevention networks, abusers' disregard for the law, use of alcohol, tolerance of violence, and strong cultural beliefs regarding unequal gender roles.

According to the Economic Commission for Latin America and the Caribbean (ECLAC), in 2010 Latin America was the world's most unequal region with a poverty rate of 33.1 percent including 13.3 percent living in extreme poverty. This social inequality leaves victims of domestic abuse even more vulnerable. Poverty is reflected in the lack of institutional resources for protection and care such as sufficient number of secure shelters for victims. These factors must be taken into account when studying domestic violence because they facilitate and maintain the problem by leading women to confront the situation with few if any resources.

ECLAC noted in 2009 that the women who suffer greater physical and sexual violence in Latin America are those with less education. It has been estimated that over 39 million people in Latin America are illiterate, 55 percent of whom are women. ECLAC's report on the social situation of women advocates for the role of education, social, and economic development of women to halt dependence on men and violence.

Overall, 97 percent of Latin American countries have laws that criminalize domestic violence. The passing of legislation has been attributed to the work of human rights and women's rights organizations. It was a lengthy process even for the outlawing of honor killings in Brazil, which came after a 10-year legal battle. Until 1991, men were allowed to justify murdering their wives in Brazil using the "defense of honor." Despite the fact that such defense was not part of the country's legal code, it was used by thousands of men who were acquitted after murdering their wives.

A significant amount of legislative work remains to be done in Latin America, particularly regarding sexual violence. Indeed, only 50 percent of countries in the region have laws that criminalize sexual violence within the couple. In addition, there are problems in different countries in accessing the justice system and law enforcement.

Fortunately, people in Latin America are beginning to recognize domestic violence as a problem. The results of a study on tolerance of violence indicates that 85 percent of men in seven Latin American and Caribbean countries do not justify under any circumstances beating their wives. However, certain cultural norms continue to make attitude changes toward domestic violence very difficult—for instance, the belief that women should be submissive and men should maintain control and authority. This idea leads to gender roles sustaining inequality in which women are unlikely to achieve autonomy.

Gender roles in Latin America are similar to the roles in the Iberian Peninsula (Spain, Portugal, and Andorra). Both regions share roots derived from colonization, transmission of cultural values, religious institutions, and patriarchal dynamics. Social beliefs that are a product of the Catholic religion such as *marianismo* support the traditional role that women should be submissive, selfless, and virgin until marriage. The attitude deriving from patriarchy known as *machismo* emphasizes the idea that men are the strongest individuals in the home and the ones who should protect and provide for their families. Although this belief leads many men to be supportive husbands and fathers, it can become negative when men use it to exercise control and domination over their families. This form of socialization facilitates the reproduction of inadequate models of conflict resolution and tolerance of violence.

Indigenous Groups

It is important to recognize that in Latin America and the Caribbean, approximately 10 percent of the population is indigenous and have different ethnicities, languages, and customs. Most are women (59 percent) — in numbers approximately 26.5 million as of 2005. Although most countries in Latin America still preserve ethnic groups, this situation is more noticeable in countries such as Bolivia, Guatemala, Mexico, and Peru. Different issues prevent indigenous victims of domestic violence from seeking help. First, a large number of them do not speak Spanish fluently. Second, they are often discriminated against by others and victimized by the police or the military. Third, lack of education, different cultural beliefs, and lack of understanding of the justice system prevent indigenous people in Latin America from reporting domestic abuse.

Achievements and Initiatives

In addition to the achievements regarding legislation, the United Nations continues to lead projects to end domestic violence in Latin America. For example, the ECLAC Division of Gender Affairs was created to promote gender equality and ensure compliance with agreements made in Latin America to prevent violence against women.

In Latin America, the implementation of a program led by the secretary general of the United Nations has begun. The Unite to End Violence Against Women program focuses on five pillars: the creation and strengthening of national legislation, implementation of a multisector action plan, development of national capacities for social awareness, and the prevention of the systematic use of sexual violence as a tactic of war in armed conflicts. Former Chilean President Michelle Bachelet was selected as the first executive director of UN Women, which helped elevate consideration of the treatment of women in Latin America.

In the majority of Latin American countries, hotlines have been set up to treat crimes of violence as well as shelters for female victims and their children. There is progress on the level of work conducted by governments, NGOs, and the civilian population. For example, in Chile a total of 59 battered women shelters were created in 2009. Brazil and Nicaragua now have police units specifically formed to respond to crimes against women, and some of those police units are comprised by female officers only. In Mexico and Argentina, women victims of domestic violence who report that they are being abused can receive medical and psychological care, legal advice, and financial assistance. Ecuador has been considered the region's leader in addressing domestic violence. It drafted legislation in 1995 to prohibit domestic violence and began establishing female-operated police stations as early as 1981 (Knarr, 2011).

Despite the progress in the fight against domestic abuse in Latin America, a significant amount of work remains to be done. It is necessary to increase research, improve reporting, and raise awareness to combat the tolerance of violence and the attitudes favoring gender roles that promote inequality.

See also: Demographic and Health Surveys; South America and Domestic Abuse; The United Nations and Domestic Abuse

Further Reading

Cáceres, E. (2011). Tratamiento psicológico centrado en el trauma en mujeres víctima de violencia de pareja. Tesis doctoral. Universidad Complutense de Madrid.

Calfio & Velasco, (2005). Mujeres indígenas en América Latina: Brechas de género o de etnia? In *International seminar Pueblos indígenas y afrodescendientes de América Latina y el Caribe: relevancia y pertinencia de la información sociodemográfica para políticas y programas*. Santiago, Chile: CEPAL

Centro Reina Sofía. (2010). Informe Mujeres asesinadas por su pareja España (2000–2009). Valencia, España. Retrieved from http://www.observatorioviolencia.org/documentos.php?id=

Garcia-Moreno, C. G., Jansen, H., Ellsberg, M., Heise, L., & Watts, C. H. (2006). On behalf of the WHO Multi-country Study on Women's Health and Domestic Violence Against Women Study Team. Prevalence of intimate partner violence: Findings from the WHO multi-country study on women's health and domestic violence. *The Lancet, 368* (9543), 1260–1269. doi: 10.1016/S0140-6736(06)69523-8

Knarr, A. (2011). Ecuador leads the battle against domestic violence in Latin America. *Council on Hemispheric Affairs*. Retrieved August 17, 2012, from http://www.coha.org/ecuador-leads-the-battle-against-domestic-violence-in-latin-america/

Lary, H., & Garcia-Moreno, C. (2009) Partner aggression across cultures. In O. Daniel & M. W. Erica (Eds.), *Psychological and physical aggression in couples: Causes and interventions* (pp. 59–75). Washington, DC: American Psychological Association Press.

UNESCO (2004). *EFA Global Monitoring Report 2005: Education for All, the Quality Imperative* . Paris, France: UNESCO.

United Nations (2009). La violencia contra las mujeres en América Latina y el Caribe. Ni una más! Del dicho al hecho: ¿Cuánto falta por recorrer? Retrieved from http://www.eclac.org/mujer/noticias/noticias/2/37892/Niunamas2009.pdf

UN Women (2011). Progress of the world's women. In pursuit of justice. Retrieved from http://progress.unwomen.org/pdfs/EN-Report-Progress.pdf

Eduin Caceres-Ortiz and Maria F. Espinola

LEGISLATION AND POLICIES, DATING VIOLENCE

Approximately one in three adolescent girls in the United States is a victim of physical, emotional, or verbal abuse from a dating partner, a figure that far exceeds victimization rates for other types of violence affecting youth. Like domestic violence, the abuse in dating violence can be physical, emotional, or sexual in nature. Dating violence knows no boundaries: it is experienced by all races, ages, cultures, sexualities, incomes, and education levels. The violence can occur within a serious or casual, monogamous or nonmonogamous, and sexual or nonsexual relationship.

Currently in the United States there are a few policies that address dating violence. Such policies vary state to state, and other forms of legislation are mandated at the federal level. This entry explores the definition of dating violence, civil and criminal law options for legal protection, personal protection orders (PPOs), dating violence policies in schools, the Office of Violence Against Women's contributions to dating violence policy, and future policies to be implemented. Some scholars discuss a cycle of dating violence that many victims will experience. Dating violence typically involves a series of abusive behaviors over a course of time. It is necessary that policies be written to clearly describe the many forms of dating violence and how, over time, the violence tends to escalate in abusive relationships. Physical violence includes the intentional use of physical force with the intent to cause fear or injury, like hitting, shoving, biting, strangling, kicking, or using a weapon. It also can involve emotionally violent behaviors such as threats, insults, constant monitoring, humiliation, intimidation, isolation, or stalking. Finally, the violence may include a sexual violation. Sexual abuse is any action that impacts a person's ability to control her or his sexual activity or the circumstances in which sexual activity occurs, including rape, coercion, and restricting access to birth control.

Civil and criminal law offer different legal options. Criminal law is when a guilty defendant is punishable by one of the following options: incarceration, fines paid to the government, or execution. Conversely, under civil law the defendant is never incarcerated or executed. The defendant reimburses the plaintiff for losses caused by the defendant's behavior. Once a plaintiff has officially filed charges against the abusive partner, the case is in the hands of the county prosecutor. The prosecutor has the power to decide whether or not to move forward with the case or to dismiss the charges. If the abuser is found guilty, the individual can be jailed or put on probation.

Another legal option involves obtaining a PPO or restraining order. A PPO is issued by the court. It can protect individuals from harassment, assault, beating, molestation, wounding, or stalking by another person. A PPO has the authority to order the abuser not to do the following; enter the victims property; assault, attack, or wound the victim; threaten to kill or physically harm; remove one's children from the victim; interfere at the victim's place of employment; interfere with the victim's efforts to remove his/her children or their personal property; contact the victim by telephone, mail, or e-mail, and purchase or possess a firearm. The cost of a PPO is minimal, and individuals have the option to waive the fee. If a person is in immediate danger they have the option of an *ex parte* order (without hearing). Also, if you are filing a PPO, you do not need the assistance and representation of an attorney. A PPO goes into effect right when the judge signs off on it. Also, for the order to be effective, the respondent needs to be notified of the PPO. At this point, the PPO is in full effect. Each state has its own specific sanctions for violating a PPO. For example, the maximum penalty in Michigan is 93 days in jail or a minimum $500 fine.

Although PPOs or restraining orders are widely available in every state, teens who face dating violence may still encounter difficulties seeking to obtain one. The Break the Cycle website addresses three items in need of improvement when it comes to retraining orders. Break the Cycle strongly believes teen victims of dating violence deserve the same level of protection that adults receive in domestic violence legislation. For instance, currently there are eight states that define a legal relationship as those who live together, have a child together, or are married. Therefore, those in a dating relationship have little legal protection from their abusers. A second item that requires modification is that of age. Many laws do not specify the age at which to obtain a restraining order. As a result, each court has discretion regarding whether teens can apply. This leaves young victims with unpredictability and limited access to the courts for legal protection. A final recommendation by Break the Cycle is to revise the parental consent and notification requirements for teens in need of protection. States like Florida require a parent or guardian to be present when a teen applies for a restraining order. Given that many teens do not tell their parents or guardians about the abuse, this requirement may prohibit them from seeking the protection of the restraining order. The progress of each state is measured annually by how well they meet the modifications and alterations to the three items addressed above. The State-by-State Teen Dating Violence Report can be found on the Break the Cycle web page. Here each state is given a grade on their progress in terms of teen dating violence. Surprisingly, the report shows only six states and Washington, D.C., with a grade A for the year 2010. Those states include California, Illinois, New Hampshire, Oklahoma, Rhode Island, and Washington. Those states received A grades due to the access they allow minors to legal protections like restraining orders and schools' responses and implementation of prevention programming. The fact that only six states have a "grade A" shows that there is still a dire need for change when it comes to dealing with teen dating violence policies. The organization's website states, however, that they did not assign grades for 2011 and are rethinking whether grading is useful.

Some schools have addressed teen dating violence by implementing their own policies. For instance, some schools have recently begun practicing the "Stay Away Agreements" for those individuals who are affected by dating violence in schools. Over 40 percent of young people who report they are victims of dating violence say that the incidents occurred in a school building or on school grounds. The intent of such an approach is to provide safety for students who are targets of bullying, harassment, and dating violence. The common process is to have a student, legal parent or guardian, or school staff member file a student complaint form on behalf of the victim. Following the complaint is a meeting with a school official and the offender and his or her parent or legal guardian. The "Stay Away Agreement" restricts the individual from coming into any contact with the targeted student on school property. This includes not talking to, sitting by, or having any contact with the individual on school property as well as at any school events. Violation of such an agreement results in disciplinary actions that may vary from school to school and under different circumstances.

The Office on Violence Against Women is a federal organization that supports policies and programs on dating violence in the United States. The mission of the Office on Violence Against Women (OVW), a component of the U.S. Department of Justice, is to provide federal leadership in developing the nation's capacity to reduce violence against women. They also aim to administer justice for victims of domestic violence, dating violence, sexual assault, and stalking. The OVW was created in response to the Violence Against Women Act of 1994 (VAWA). The act is a landmark piece of legislation that sought to improve criminal justice and community-based responses to domestic violence, dating violence, sexual assault, and stalking in the United States. The OVW offers funding to local, state, and tribal governments. Additional funding is available but not limited to, nonprofit organizations, community-based organizations, and schools. Funding allows these institutions to provide an assortment of services to work toward effective responses to violence against women, such as providing needed shelter, financial support, child day care, legal advocacy, and counseling to heal. Funding for these organizations also provides safety to victims of violence and mandates that violent offenders be held accountable for their actions.

Another federal initiative to address teen dating violence is the declaration of February as Teen Dating Violence Awareness Month. In 2006, Congress followed the lead of dozens of national, state, and local organizations in declaring the first full week in February "National Teen Dating Violence Prevention and Awareness Week." Then in 2010, Congress began dedicating the entire month of February to teen dating violence awareness and prevention.

Another aspect of dating violence that policies need to address is regarding public health. Besides the physical injuries left by dating violence, it is known that these victims face negative mental health consequences. Due to these troubling consequences, political officials have suggested new legislation to reduce teen dating violence. The Stop Abuse for Every Teen Act, or SAFE Teen Act, has recently been introduced. This act addresses dating violence in schools based on findings that a large portion of dating violence occurs on school property and on the consequences of health issues in the future. The SAFE Teen Act urges school boards to develop curricula on teen dating violence. The bill would do the following: expressly authorize schools to use existing grant funding for teen dating violence prevention; highlight teen dating violence prevention as part of the comprehensive, community prevention program; and support better teen dating violence data to understand the scope of the problem as well as having a means of measuring the impact of prevention programs and policies. Some states already require that dating violence be addressed academically. Twelve states require teen dating violence be covered in school curricula. Five other states do not require it but urge schools to include it. Legislation is pending in five other states.

Much is being done outside the courts to help combat dating violence. Today, an array of programs, services, nonprofit organizations, and community-based programs exist to help put an end to this violence. Break the Cycle, Choose Respect, Futures Without Violence, and Love Is Not Abuse are just a few major organizations out there that are devoted to the cause. The work done by these influential groups would not be possible without the funding provided to them from the OVW.

Much can be done to help prevent this emerging issue of dating violence. Expanding awareness and legislation will aid in the fight. Support for community programs and nonprofit organizations are needed with this sensitive issue. For instance, although the SAFE Teen Act is gaining support across the country, it is still in need of cosponsors.

See also: Break the Cycle; Restraining Orders/Personal Protection Orders; Teen Victims; U.S. Government Responses to Domestic Violence

Further Reading

Break the Cycle. (2009). School dating violence policy. Retrieved from http://www.breakthecycle.org/content/school-policy

Break the Cycle. (2011). Dating violence 101. Retrieved from http://www.breakthecycle.org/dating-violence-101

Centers for Disease Control and Prevention. (2011). Understanding dating violence. Retrieved from http://www.cdc.gov/violenceprevention/intimatepartnerviolence/teen_dating_violence.html

Family Violence Prevention Fund. (2009). The facts on teens and dating violence. Retrieved from http://www.futureswithoutviolence.org/userfiles/file/Teens/teens_facts.pdf

Love Is Not Abuse. (2011). A list of warning signs. Retrieved from http://loveisnotabuse.com/web/guest/a-list-of-warning-signs

Michigan State University Safe Place (2010). What is a personal protection order? Retrieved from: https://www.msu.edu/~safe/facts/ppo.htm

Open Congress for the 112th United States Congress (n.d.). Representatives. Retrieved from http://www.opencongress.org/bill/all

Teen Dating Violence Awareness Month: http://www.teendvmonth.org/

Teen dating violence. (2009). National Conference of State Legislatures. Retrieved March 16, 2012, from http://www.ncsl.org/issues-research/health/teen-dating-violence.aspx

Ashley Wiegand

LEGISLATION AND POLICIES, DOMESTIC ABUSE
United States

At the federal level, the 1994 Violence Against Women Act (VAWA) was the first legislation to create programs for victims and to provide funding and support for domestic violence services. Reauthorizations in 2000 and 2005 extended provisions to ensure immigrant victims who are not documented due to abuse be allowed to self-petition for residency status, expand prevention programs, protection against eviction in cases of domestic violence, accommodations for victims with disabilities, and services for children and teens. The Family Violence Prevention and Services Act (FVPSA) is the main federal funding source for housing for victims and their children. FVPSA provides formula grants to states, territories, and tribes; established the National Domestic Violence Hotline; and supports the Domestic Violence Prevention Enhancement and Leadership Through Alliances (DELTA) Program. Other relevant federal legislation includes the 2000 Trafficking Victims Protection Act and the Tribal Law and Order Act, which was signed in 2009 by President Barack Obama to help provide resources and support for reducing domestic violence among tribal communities.

Every state in the United States as well as Washington, D.C., prohibits domestic violence, although each statute reads differently. For instance, Florida's statute 741.28 defines domestic violence as "any assault, aggravated assault, battery, aggravated battery, sexual assault, sexual battery, stalking, aggravated stalking, kidnapping, false imprisonment, or any criminal offense resulting in physical injury or death of one family or household member by another family or household member." Family or household members is defined as "spouses, former spouses, persons related by blood or marriage, persons who are presently residing together as if a family or who have resided together in the past as if a family, and persons who are parents of a child in common regardless of whether they have been married. With the exception of persons who have a child in common, the family or household members must be currently residing or have in the past resided together in the same single dwelling unit." Indiana's C 35-42-2-1.3 defines domestic battery as "A person who knowingly or intentionally touches an individual who: (1) is or was a spouse of the other person; (2) is or was living as if a spouse of the other person as provided in subsection (c); or (3) has a child in common with the other person; in a rude, insolent, or angry manner that results in bodily injury to the person described in subdivision (1), (2), or (3) commits domestic battery, a Class A misdemeanor. A commonality among most state definitions of domestic violence is that they tend to utilize largely if not exclusively physical descriptors of abuse. Thus victims experiencing emotional abuse or other forms that do not result in physical injuries may find it difficult to utilize the criminal justice system for help.

All states plus Washington, D.C., also offer some type of restraining order or protection order for victims. Valid restraining orders are applicable in other states and tribal courts, per the full faith and credit extension of the 1994 Violence Against Women Act. In 39 states, victims of dating violence can apply for restraining orders as well.

Because dangerous abusers often take any means necessary to track down victims who have escaped, including whatever public information they can find, 32 states have enacted address confidentiality programs. Beginning with Washington in 1991, these programs give victims substitute, government-managed addresses (often a post office box) to use in place of their physical address. All the victim's first-class mail is routed to the substitute address and then forwarded to the victim's actual address, decreasing the victim's vulnerability to stalkers and other offenders who attempt to locate them.

Some states also prohibit dating violence. Thirteen states even mandate dating violence education be incorporated into school curricula. For instance, Connecticut's legislation 2010 Conn. Acts, P.A. 91 (2010 HB 5315) includes teen dating violence and domestic violence education as part of the in-service training program for certified teachers, administrators, and pupil personnel. Florida's 2010 Fla. Laws, Chap. 217 (2010 SB 642/HB 467) requires a comprehensive health education taught in the public schools to include a component on teen dating violence and abuse for students in grades 7 through 12 and compels district school boards to adopt and implement a dating violence and abuse policy. It also requires the Department of Education to develop a model policy that includes school personnel training. Similar legislation is pending in several other states.

Fifteen states require domestic violence training for physicians and other health-care providers, and some require such persons to report abuse to specific authorities (which is required in every state when child abuse or elder abuse are suspected). The specific instances under which a health-care provider is obligated to report vary but can generally be classified into three types: (1) states that require mandatory reporting of injuries caused by weapons; (2) states that mandate reporting for injuries caused in violation of criminal laws, as a result of violence, or through nonaccidental means; and (3) states that specifically address reporting in domestic violence cases.

Until passage of the Patient Protection and Affordable Healthcare Act in 2010, no federal legislation prohibited insurance companies from discriminating against victims of domestic violence. Investigations found that in many cases, victims were denied insurance coverage because domestic violence was considered a preexisting condition.

The Convention on the Elimination of All Forms of Discrimination Against Women (CEDAW) requires signatories to enact legislation that protects women from various forms of discrimination. To date, 189 countries have signed on to CEDAW.

A total of 125 countries have enacted domestic violence laws, yet 603 million women live in the countries that have no such legislation. As in the U.S. states, what specifically is covered by these laws varies. For instance, in Afghanistan, the Law on Elimination of Violence Against Women was enacted in 2009. The following are considered violence against women and are punishable by law:

1. Rape
2. Forcing into prostitution
3. Recording the identity of victim and publicizing it in a manner that damages the personality of victim.
4. Setting into flames, using chemicals or other dangerous substances
5. Forcing into self-immolation or suicide or using poisonous or other dangerous substances
6. Causing injury or disability
7. Battery and laceration

8. Selling and buying women for the purpose or under pretext of marriage
9. *Baad* (retribution of a woman for a murder, to restore peace)
10. Forced marriage
11. Prohibiting from right of marriage or choosing husband
12. Marriage before the legal age
13. Abusing, humiliating, intimidating
14. Harassment/persecution
15. Forced isolation
16. Forced labor
17. Marrying more than one wife without observing the provision of Article 86 of Civil Code

In 1999, Trinidad and Tobago passed its Domestic Violence Act, which, among other things, provides a protocol for police and outlines how to obtain a protection order. Japan has 12 different laws that address domestic violence, addressing guidelines for police, housing needs, criminal penalties, and more.

The laws in Spain, the Philippines, and Austria are considered model legislation by the United Nations. The Austrian law, enacted in 1997, is considered exemplary due largely to the way it mandated protection orders. It has now been replicated in other European countries, including Germany. It was evaluated in 1999 and 2002 and results show it increases victims' sense of support and helps interrupt the cycle of violence. The Philippines' law is considered a model statute to provide legal protection for rape victims. Spain's Integrated Protection Measures against Gender Violence, enacted in 2004, is considered exemplary because "The Act includes numerous provisions on education and training. The sphere of prevention, awareness-raising and detection is given significant attention through a clear focus on education, advertising, and health care. The law requests actions by educational centres to influence the contents of the curricula in order to offer education that stresses the values of tolerance, respect, peace, and equality. The actions are also directed at different professional groups to improve the training of those who handle problems arising from ill-treatment" (http://sgdatabase.unwomen.org/searchDetail.action?measureId=3204&baseHREF=goodpractices).

In addition to lauding the Duluth Model for victim safety in the United States, UN Women also refer to the Australian Capital Territory Family Violence Intervention Programme, the London Domestic Violence Forum, and the Indian Andhra Pradesh Public Model as best practices in interagency cooperation. All three integrate survivor safety with accountability and rehabilitation for offenders and work both inside and outside of criminal justice systems to do so. The U.S. VAWA is praised for service to victims, as is "the Indian "Dilassa" Model, which is a model of health service delivery ... based on a preventive approach and aims to integrate violence against women in intimate relationships within health care services" (UN Women, 2011, p. 14).

UN Women (2011) has also issued a list of recommendations for domestic violence legislation. These include:

- Domestic violence laws should address specific cultural manifestations of violence.
- All relationships in the shared residence should be included within the ambit of the domestic violence law with a clear listing of the nature of relationships covered,

especially all relationships of dependency, including domestic workers, as well as a definition of the "shared residence.
- Complaints mechanisms should be easily accessible, provide immediate protection to the complainant, and ensure access to support services. Prelitigation measures should aim to immediately stop violence.
- Emergency orders should be available prior to the issuance of a court order to immediately prevent future acts of violence.
- Access to information on rights and assistance to initiate legal processes are essential to facilitating access to justice.
- Assisted alternative dispute resolutions at the pre- and postlitigation stages should be attempted only if there is a guarantee of nonviolence.
- Prelitigation mediation should not impede access to the courts or court-ordered remedies and, to avoid bias in the event of a settlement, should not be conducted by courts. Postlitigation mediation should be conducted by authorized professional bodies or individuals.
- In court proceedings, it is advisable to elaborate on reliefs available under the law to aid to judges in deciding the nature of orders to be granted.
- Providing timelines for disposing complaints and applications filed under the laws will ensure speedy processes.
- Making the violation of court orders a punishable offense will aid their enforcement.
- Laws should mandate institutionalized, regular training and education of police officers, prosecutors, judiciary, social workers, and public officials in protecting survivors of domestic violence and preventing further acts of violence.
- Public awareness campaigns on violence against women are an important measure to eliminate violence and change social attitudes.
- Monitoring the implementation of domestic violence laws is essential to ensuring effective implementation. It is advisable for states to incorporate such provisions into the law.

The U.N. Secretary General's Database on Violence Against Women, created after a General Assembly mandate in 2006, offers a wealth of information on laws, statistics, and resources.

See also: Convention on the Elimination of All Forms of Violence Against Women (CEDAW); Duluth Model; Legislation and Policies, Dating Violence; The United Nations and Domestic Abuse; U.S. Government Responses to Domestic Violence; Violence Against Women Act (VAWA)

Further Reading

Compilation of Gender Equality & Domestic Violence Laws from around the World. (2012). Wellesley Centers for Women. Retrieved June 23, 2012, from http://www.wcwonline.org/People-Extra-Information/compilation-of-gender-equality-a-domestic-violence-laws-from-around-the-world

Domestic violence laws of the world. (2010, February 2). Retrieved June 23, 2012, from http://www.hsph.harvard.edu/population/domesticviolence/domesticviolence.htm

Durborow, N., Lizdas, K., O'Flaherty, O., & Marjavi, A. (2010). Compendium of state statutes and policies on domestic violence and healthcare. Retrieved January 31, 2013, from http://www.futureswithoutviolence.org/userfiles/file/HealthCare/Compendium%20Final.pdf

Hot Peach Pages: www.hotpeachpages.net

Restraining orders. (2008). WomensLaw.org. Retrieved June 23, 2012, from http://www.womenslaw.org/laws.php?reset=1

State law overview. (2008). WomensLaw.org. Retrieved January 31, 2013, from http://www.womenslaw.org/laws_state_type.php?id=51&state_code=WA

Teen Dating Violence. (2012, May). National Conference of State Legislatures. Retrieved June 23, 2012 from http://www.ncsl.org/issues-research/health/teen-dating-violence.aspx

UN Women. (2011). Domestic violence legislation and its implementation. Retrieved June 23, 2012, from http://cedaw-seasia.org/docs/DomesticViolenceLegislation.pdf

Laura L. Finley

LESBIAN, GAY, BISEXUAL, AND TRANSGENDERED (LGBT) VICTIMS

Studies vary as to how frequently abuse occurs in lesbian, gay, bisexual, or transgender relationships. Kelly and Warshafsky (1987) found 47 percent of gays and lesbians had been victims of domestic abuse, while a number of studies put the rate of abuse between 25 percent and 50 percent. The most common figure is that domestic abuse occurs in approximately 30 to 40 percent of LGBT relationships, which is generally the same percentage as in straight relationships. Despite the prevalence of abuse in same-sex relationships, the topic has only received scholarly attention in the United States in the last few decades. Very little scholarly work addresses international comparisons of LGBT domestic violence. In Venezuela, while the Penal Code of 1999 does not make homosexuality illegal, case law has interpreted it as such, according to Burke, Owen, and Jordan (2001). Because of widespread homophobia in Venezuela, police often ignore LGBT victims. Burke, Jordan, and Owen (2002) found domestic violence to be widespread in Venezuela. Approximately two-thirds of the sample of 74 they studied had experienced some form of abuse. Yet few were aware of resources for victims. In Scotland, approximately 1,000 incidents of same-sex domestic violence were reported to authorities in 2008, but experts estimate the true number may be four times higher.

There are many myths or misconceptions about abuse in same-sex relationships. Some people mistakenly believe that lesbian relationships cannot be abusive as they view women as naturally nurturing and nonviolent. Others claim that same-sex couples are just fighting or that abuse is mutual, rather than the result of the same power dynamics seen in heterosexual relationships. Another misconception is that LGBT persons like "kinky" or violent sex, and thus it is not really abuse.

Like same-sex domestic abuse, LGBT partner abuse takes many forms, ranging from physical and sexual assault to verbal and emotional abuse, as well as failure to provide medication, property damage, threatening to "out" the victim, and prohibiting contact with family and friends. Abusers may make harmful accusations against their victims, including accusing them of really being bisexual or calling them sluts. Victims may be hesitant to report abuse because they fear that doing so will reinforce stereotypes about same-sex relationships being dysfunctional.

While rates of abuse may vary little from those experienced by people in heterosexual relationships, the legal protections afforded LGBT persons vary dramatically. The lack of legal support is likely a major factor in why few instances of LGBT domestic abuse are reported to police. In the United States, seven states explicitly prohibit LGBT victims from applying for protection orders. Only four states have legislation explicitly providing protection to gay and lesbian couples.

Similarly, LGBT victims may receive little help from police. Law enforcement may be nonresponsive or even abusive when reporting to a domestic abuse incident among LGBT persons. Reports show that victims have been arrested, transported, and housed in the same jail cells as their abusers. In their 2005 report called *Stonewalled: Police. Abuse and Misconduct against Lesbian, Gay, Bisexual and Transgender People in the U.S.*, Amnesty International documented horrifying examples of how LGBT domestic violence cases were mishandled by police. The report also noted that abuse was generally worse when the parties involved held multiple subordinated identities, for instance, a black transgendered woman. Transgendered interviewees told of police verbally harassing them, demanding to know if they were "he's" or "she's." Transgendered persons also told of being stereotyped by police as sex workers, with innocent people being arrested by police while doing such benign activities as walking their dogs. Because transgendered people often change their names to fit their gender identity but may find it difficult to obtain new identification, many reported that police harassed them because the name on their identification did not match the name they gave. Of the 29 police departments included in the research, 72 percent had no policy that guided interactions with transgendered persons. More than 40 years after the original Stonewall raid that prompted the gay rights movement in the United States, law enforcement in major cities were still reported to target gay bars, clubs, and other meeting places. Additionally, the Amnesty International report found widespread targeting of LGBT activists. Reports of verbal, physical, and sexual abuse by police were common. Police often use demeaning slurs, such as "faggot" and "dyke" to refer to LGBT persons. A significant portion of reports of verbal, physical, and sexual abuse were of LGBT people of color. Interviewees reported police telling them that they would be arrested for prostitution unless they had sexual relations with the officer, with one person stating "The police are not here to serve . . . they are here to get served. Every night I'm taken into an alley and given the choice between having sex or going to jail" (Amnesty International, 2005, p. 61). One LAPD officer explained why physical abuse occurs, saying "It's easier to thump a faggot than an average Joe. Who cares?" (Amnesty International, 2005, p. 66). More masculine-looking lesbians frequently reported physical abuse. In Washington, D.C., in 2001, police were found to have been sending derogatory and homophobic messages through their patrol car computer systems. LGBT persons were called "disgusting" and "freaks" with some regularity. The cruel and degrading treatment continued during invasive and often unnecessary searches as well as within the corrections system. Although the United Nations recommends that body searches be conducted by someone of the same gender, police agencies all over were not adhering to that recommendation. The same kinds of verbal, physical, and sexual abuse perpetrated by police was also perpetrated by corrections officers.

In addition to outright mistreatment, the Amnesty International report documented that police often fail to respond with due diligence in cases when LGBT persons are involved. Police were found not responding or responding inappropriately in hate crimes and domestic violence incidents particularly. Victims said that because police seemed uncomfortable with them, interviews and investigations were often cursory, at best. The result is that many LGBT persons are fearful of reporting crimes to law enforcement, which may help foster a climate of impunity for perpetrators. Only 17 percent of reporting police departments had policies specifically addressing same-sex domestic violence. Some police said they handle all domestic violence situations the same. This is problematic, however, as the issues that arise may be different in same-sex relationships than in heterosexual relationships. Police have been reported to tell gay partners that both will be arrested, failing to investigate and identify who is the primary aggressor. Interviewees reported police saying that "real men can fight their own battles" (Amnesty International, 2005, p. 127). Advocates say it is common for both abuser and victim to be arrested. This clearly revictimizes those who have already suffered. When police do try to determine who is the primary aggressor, they often assume it to be the larger or more masculine-appearing person, which can be incorrect.

Amnesty International argues that the failure to adequately protect LGBT persons is a human rights violation. Police mistreatment and institutionalized discrimination are violations of the International Covenant on Civil and Political Rights (ICCPR), the Convention Against Torture (CAT), and the International Convention on the Elimination of All Forms of Racial Discrimination (CERD). The United States is party to all of these. UN Declarations on policing require that law enforcement treat all victims with compassion and respect their dignity. These declarations recommend that police receive training specifically to sensitize them to the unique needs of various victim groups and that agencies establish mechanisms and procedures to ensure that the rights of all persons are guaranteed.

Some have even criticized academics for neglecting the issue of LGBT abuse. Perhaps not intentionally, those who hew to a feminist perspective on abuse, which has historically emphasized that abuse is male violence against female, derived from a patriarchal culture, may have failed to draw needed attention to situations where it is two men or two women in an abusive relationship.

Victims may find a scarcity of shelter space, or may find that existing shelters are not accommodating. In particular, gay men face huge challenges in obtaining safe shelter, as many domestic violence shelters do not accept males. Consequently, these victims may end up staying with family or friends, homeless, or in homeless shelters that are not secure or confidential. Shelter staff, like the general public, may suffer from homophobia or simply be ill equipped to help LGBT victims heal.

Whether provisions to protect LGBT, undocumented immigrant, and Native American victims should be included has been a major point of contention in the 2012 debate over the reauthorization of the Violence Against Women Act (VAWA).

Outside the United States, the situation may be much worse, as homosexuality itself is sometimes viewed as a crime. The *International Herald Tribune* reported in 2011 about a gruesome series of gang rapes of lesbians and lesbian activists in South Africa that some were calling "corrective rapes" because perpetrators told their victims they were being raped to "cure" them of their "unnatural" sexual orientation. May 2012 saw a series of violent attacks on activists in Armenia, the republic of Georgia, and Azerbaijan, including a firebomb attack at a gay-friendly bar in Armenia's capital. In 2009, Ugandan legislators promoted a bill that would have made homosexuality punishable with a death sentence. The bill has yet to pass, although supporters vow to continue to push. Yet some nations have passed legislation guaranteeing protection for LGBT victims of domestic violence. For instance, Hong Kong did so in 2009.

Although much more is needed, there are some resources available for LGBT victims of domestic violence. The Network/LA Red provides a list of helpful resources for survivors and service providers at their website, http://tnlr.org/resources/for-survivors/#national. An Abuse, Rape, and Domestic Violence Aid and Resource Collection (AARDVARC) also provides a wealth of information and resources at http://www.aardvarc.org/dv/gay.shtml.

See also: Amnesty International; Female Perpetrators; Male Victims of Domestic Abuse; Violence Against Women Act (VAWA)

Further Reading

An Abuse, Rape, and Domestic Violence Aid and Resource Collection (AARDVARC). (2011, March 3). Domestic violence in gay and lesbian relationships.

Amnesty International. (2005). Stonewalled: Police abuse and misconduct against lesbian, gay, bisexual and transgender people in the U.S. Retrieved May 30, 2012, from http://www.amnesty.org/en/library/info/AMR51/122/2005

Burke, T., Jordan, M., & Owen, S. (2002). A cross-national comparison of gay and lesbian domestic violence. *Journal of Contemporary Criminal Justice, 18*(3), 231–257.

Burke, T., Owen, S., & Jordan, M. (2001, May/June). Law enforcement and gay domestic violence in the US and Venezuela. *ACJS Today, 24*, pp. 1, 4–6.

Gay domestic abuse "suffered in silence." (2009, October 24). *The Scotsman*. Retrieved May 30, 2012, from http://www.scotsman.com/news/health/gay-domestic-abuse-suffered-in-silence-1-1362439

Gay, Lesbian, Bisexual and Transgendered Domestic Violence. (n.d.). Retrieved May 30, 2012, from http://www.rainbowdomesticviolence.itgo.com/

International Gay and Lesbian Human Rights Commission. (2009, December 22). Hong Kong: Same-sex coupled included in the amended domestic violence law. Retrieved May 30, 2012, from http://www.iglhrc.org/cgi-bin/iowa/article/takeaction/resourcecenter/1056.html

Kelly, E., & Warshafsky, L. (1987). Partner abuse in gay male and lesbian couples. Paper presented at the Third National Conference of Family Violence Researchers, Durham, NH, July 1987.

Kron, J. (2012, February 28). Resentment toward the West bolsters Uganda's new anti-gay bill. *New York Times*. Retrieved May 30, 2012, from http://www.nytimes.com/2012/02/29/world/africa/ugandan-lawmakers-push-anti-homosexuality-bill-again.html?pagewanted=all

McKeiser, E. (2011, November 9). Gay rights, homophobic wrongs. *International Herald Tribune*. Retrieved May 30, 2012, from http://latitude.blogs.nytimes.com/2011/11/09/gay-rights-homophobic-wrongs-in-south-africa/

Virulent homophobic attacks put South Caucasus activists at risk. (2012, May 18). Amnesty International. Retrieved May 30, 2012, from http://www.amnesty.org/en/news/virulent-homophobic-attacks-put-south-caucasus-activists-risk-2012-05-18

Laura L. Finley

LINGUISTIC ANALYSIS OF VERBAL ABUSE

Verbal abuse is a systematic pattern of emotional and intellectual battering by means of language. Verbal abuse has often been difficult to demonstrate because (1) it is easy for an abuser to abuse a person only in private; (2) the abused person does not have obvious, physical wounds that prove the damage; and (3) what makes verbal abuse a pattern of battering and not simply another set of words has not been well understood.

Linguistic analysis of verbal abuse can identify how verbal abuse is a technique for emotional abuse. Verbal abuse presents on the surface as merely another instance of unkind verbal communication, and linguistic analyses of the sounds, structures, and meanings of the words and sentences used to perpetrate verbal abuse might lead observers to think that there is nothing distinctive about it. However, an examination of the pragmatics of verbal abuse demonstrates that there are significant abnormalities at work in verbal abuse that can have the devastating effects on abused people that are known to exist.

Linguistic pragmatics is the study of the contexts of language and the assumptions that allow communication to work or cause communication to fail. Effective communication depends on the assumption that all participants in a communicative context are starting from the same set of assumptions and are working toward the shared goal of rational and efficient communication. The assumptions that communicants are all working to understand and be understood are used cross-linguistically even though specific ways of instantiating the assumptions might occur.

When communicants fail to share these assumptions about cooperation, communication fails. When one communicant uses these assumptions and another communicant systematically and repeatedly changes them, communication not only fails, but verbal abuse has taken place. It is possible to imagine that communicants could change their assumptions and communicate successfully based on a different set of assumptions. Such an agreed-upon set of assumptions would still be cooperative because the assumptions are shared between or among all of the participants in the communicative situation. Verbal abuse does not comprise a possible set of agreed-upon assumptions unless communicants are mutually abusive, because it includes the idea that the conversation partners are both working toward their own goals without the cooperation or agreement of the other participants in the communicative situation.

The assumptions that are known as the "cooperative principle" and its subprinciples were delineated by H. Paul Grice (1975, 1978, 1989):

- The cooperative principle: make your contribution such as is required, at the stage at which it occurs, by the accepted purpose or direction of the talk or exchange in which you are engaged.
- The maxim of quality: try to make your contribution one that is true, specifically: (i) do not say what you believe to be false; (ii) do not say that for which you lack adequate evidence.
- The maxim of quantity: (i) make your contribution as informative as is required for the current purposes of the exchange; (ii) do not make your contribution more informative than is required.
- The maxim of relevance: make your contributions relevant.
- The maxim of manner: be perspicuous, and specifically: (i) avoid obscurity; (ii) avoid ambiguity; (iii) be brief; (iv) be orderly.

In contrast, verbal abuse relies on an "abusive principle," as delineated below:

- The abusive principle: make your contribution such as is required to get what you want, prioritizing unpredictability, by the purpose or direction that you have determined without informing or consulting your partner, by use of the talk or exchange in which you are engaged.
- The maxim of falsehood: try to make your contribution one that is only as true as is convenient, specifically: (i) say anything, especially if false; (ii) say as little as possible for which you have adequate evidence.
- The maxim of disinformation: (i) do not make your contribution informative relative to the current purposes of the exchange; (ii) make your contribution less informative than is expected.
- The maxim of irrelevance: make your contributions irrelevant.
- The maxim of discourtesy: be incomprehensible, and specifically: (i) be obscuring; (ii) include ambiguity; (iii) be verbose; (iv) be random.

Verbal abuse is devastating because the cooperative principle and its subprinciples are such basic assumptions for communicants around the world that when an abuser chooses to ignore them, the abused person is left without an intellectual and emotional foundation. The cooperative principle is strong enough that, even if a person tries to work with what has been identified as a noncooperative assumption, the fact that the person is trying to accommodate the new assumption shows that the overall assumption of cooperation remains in effect. The cycle of trying to work with abusers who are systematically uncooperative can lead to a mental learned helplessness in which abused people become unwilling or unable to think independently because they doubt everything about the ways in which they have been accustomed to thinking and thus lack a starting point for generating thoughts.

The techniques of verbal abuse as listed by Patricia Evans (1996) and expanded here to include monopolizing and propagandizing violate the cooperative principle and accord with the abusive principle.

Threatening and name-calling are the components of verbal abuse that are most readily recognized. They violate the entire cooperative principle because they rely on the idea that one person has more power or importance than another and is therefore entitled to decide on the identity and fate of another person. They follow the abusive principle in that they avoid including all communicants in the goals of the communication.

Withholding is a choice not to communicate, which violates the cooperative principle as a whole because withholding does not acknowledge the requirements of a communicative situation. Withholding follows the abusive principle because communication can be given or withheld unpredictably.

Countering is disagreement as a matter of principle. It violates the maxim of relevance in that it derails a communicative situation because it indicates an insistence that the situation proceed in directions that the person who initiated the communication does not intend the situation to go or does not expect it to go. Countering works with the abusive principle (discourtesy) because it is random, relative to the communicative situation, and because it is irrelevant to the real issue that is being discussed.

Discounting, denial, and forgetting deny the reality of another person, particularly when a person is making claims about emotions or intellectual states. Discounting, denial, and forgetting violate the second segment of the maxim of quality because challenges to personal information inherently lack adequate support. Short of significant advances in the neurosciences, only the people making the claims about themselves have access to what might be considered adequate evidence. These techniques follow the abusive principle (falsehood) because the abuser makes claims about what cannot currently be addressed by anyone other than the person who has the experiences and because, in the case of forgetting, it denies the competence of the other person.

Mean jokes are disparagement or criticism disguised as humor. They violate the second part of the maxim of manner because they rely on ambiguity: humor and seriousness are not well defined from the perspective of the person at whose expense the jokes and disparagement are being made. Because of the lack of definitive distinctions, mean jokes and disparagement follow the abusive principle (discourtesy) in obscuring intentions and being ambiguous.

Blocking and diverting are means for controlling topics, content within topics, and duration of any given communicative situation. It violates the maxim of relevance because it is not orderly and the cooperative principle as a whole because control of this kind is not required in communicative situations that are cooperative. Blocking and diverting work with the abusive principle as a whole because they rely on not consulting with or informing the conversation partner about the controls.

Accusing and blaming are strategies for putting someone on the defensive. These strategies violate the maxim of quality by being false or not being adequately supported by evidence in many cases. It follows the abusive principle (falsehood and discourtesy) by being false or unsupported and by being seemingly random with regard to the communicative theme at work.

Judging and criticizing are pointless or unhelpful corrections. They violate the second part of quantity in that they are more informative than required because they interrupt the communication in order to clarify a point that is already understood.

The apparent help is intended as a distraction or diversion rather than as help. It follows the principle of disinformation because it provides more information than is required and because it raises the expectation, never met, that help is being offered.

Trivializing and undermining denigrate real achievements, priorities, skills, interests, and so on. They violate the principle of relevance because the abuser knows what is intended or important and avoids acknowledging those intentions and priorities. This implies a violation of the first part of quality as well, because the abuser knows what the other communicant is good at and values but denies them and thereby denies the separate personhood of the communicant. Trivializing and undermining work with falsehood and irrelevance because they imply a denial of what the abuser knows and because another person's characteristics are rarely the main focus of a conversation.

Ordering is an abuser commanding someone else to do something. It violates the cooperative principle as a whole because, like threatening and name-calling, it denies the equality of both participants in a communication situation. It works with the abusive principle because ordering inherently lacks consultation with another person involved in the communication.

Monopolizing is the act of communicating incessantly so that another participant cannot contribute. This monopolizes time, energy, and thought, as well as the communication. Because there is no time or energy for a partner to be or construct a self, it violates the cooperative principle as a whole. Monopolizing also violates the second maxim of quantity in being more informative than required and the third maxim of manner in not being brief. It works with the abusive principle as a whole and especially with the third maxim of discourtesy in being verbose.

Propaganda and denial are related phenomena: denial tries to ignore what is the case, and propaganda tries to convince someone that what is not the case is an ideal scenario. They violate both parts of quality in being false or lacking evidence. It also violates relevance because an equal who is in a situation would not need to have the situation interpreted. Propaganda and denial work with falsehood and irrelevance because they are false or unsupported and because the communicative contribution is at best unnecessary.

Pragmatic analyses of the various strategies for verbal abuse clarify what is truly abusive about verbal abuse. The violation of assumptions that are basic to communication around the world systematically and repeatedly imbalances abused people intellectually, emotionally, and linguistically. The abusive principle gives abusers leverage and removes personal resources from the abused.

See also: Types of Domestic Abuse

Further Reading

Evans, P. (1996). *The verbally abusive relationship: How to recognize it and how to respond* (2nd ed.). Avon, MA: Avon Media Corporation.

Grice, H. P. (1975). Logic and conversation. In P. Cole & J. Morgan (Eds.), *Syntax and semantics* (Vol. 3) (pp. 41–58). New York, NY: Academic Press.

Grice, H. P. (1978). Further notes on logic and conversation. In P. Cole (Ed.), *Syntax and semantics, vol. 9: Pragmatics* (pp. 113–128). New York, NY: Academic Press.

Grice, H. P. (1989). Presupposition and conversational implicature. In P. Cole (Ed.), *Radical pragmatics* (pp. 183–198). New York, NY: Academic Press.

Marla Perkins

LIZ CLAIBORNE INC.

Violence against women is an ongoing problem in the world and has far-reaching consequences. Domestic violence is a leading cause of injury to women in the United States. It occurs across many different ages, ethnicities, religions, economic backgrounds, or sexual preferences; domestic violence sees no boundaries. Corporations, nonprofit organizations, as well as government agencies have been joining forces to battle domestic violence. One of the first major corporations in the United States to take an active stand against it was Liz Claiborne Inc. Since 1991, the company has been striving to end domestic violence by bringing awareness and educating the public on this important issue.

More than 10 years ago, in an effort to bring awareness to the public at a local and national level, Liz Claiborne Inc. launched Women's Work. Women's Work is a program created to bring about awareness and educate women and their families about the extent of domestic violence. The overall goal of the program is to establish a society that does not tolerate abuse, and Liz Claiborne feels it is her duty to give back to the individuals who have helped the corporation thrive, the consumers and employees. The Women's Work campaign has reached the public sphere through television, radio, and even educational handbooks. In 1998, when the program decided to focus on the importance of education, a series of handbooks was created. The first was titled A *Parent's Handbook: How to Talk to Your Children about Developing Healthy Relationships*," focusing on teaching parents how to steer their children onto the path of positive and healthy relationships.

Another success for Liz Claiborne Inc. in the fight against domestic violence is the Love Is Not Abuse Curriculum. In the past six years, the company has worked hard to address violence in relationships, and focusing primarily on teens. This curriculum was originally a three-day course geared toward 8th, 9th, and 10th graders, designed to enhance students' and teachers' understanding about teen dating abuse. This curriculum has expanded and changed over time and now includes a college edition. In February 2007, the National Teen Dating Abuse Helpline was established as a direct consequence of the curriculum This helpline provides support to those involved in abusive relationships and to the people concerned for them. In 2008, Liz Claiborne Inc. created the Love Is Not Abuse Coalition, consisting of parents, teachers, and concerned citizens, that encourages schools to adopt education on teen dating abuse. Many parents who joined this coalition had children who were victims of dating abuse or violence, and they wanted to make sure it would not happen to anyone else's child.

Liz Claiborne Inc. is equally committed to providing public awareness and to offering support and creating a safe workplace environment for the employees who are domestic violence victims or have concerns about the issue. The Employee Assistance Program offers resources to employees in abusive relationships, such as counseling and referrals to trained professionals available 24 hours a day via phone. Other ways they help are by assigning special parking spots, escorting people to and from their mode of transportation, and working with local law enforcement to exercise restraining orders. Liz Claiborne Inc. also provides contact information for community agencies that are available 24 hours a day, 7 days a week, and can offer support and services to victims.

The company commissioned a study in March 2006, conducted by Teenage Research Unlimited (TRU). The purpose of the study was to research physical, verbal, and sexual abuse among teenagers. Results of the study showed that an alarming 80 percent of females reported having experienced at least one incident of physical or sexual aggression by the end of college. Perhaps more alarming is the finding that 81 percent of parents either believe teen dating violence is not an issue or don't know if it is an issue. This demonstrates parents' lack of knowledge and understanding on this matter, which results in a failure to support the child being victimized.

In January 2007, Liz Claiborne Inc. commissioned another study conducted by TRU focusing on teen dating behaviors that involve the use of technology devices such as cell phones and computers. According to the study, one in four teens in a relationship say they have been called names, harassed, or put down by their partner through cell phones and texting. More than 8 in 10, or 82 percent, did not tell their parents they'd been asked to engage in unwanted sexual activity (Picard, 2007). In the study, teens often minimized the seriousness of such behaviors. Technology has made teen dating abuse pervasive and hidden.

Through campaigns, internal policies, and educational efforts, Liz Claiborne Inc. has helped raise a certain level of consciousness in the public sphere. The company has also provided assistance and support for women who have been victims of abusive relationships. The company has made it their mission to promote antiabuse and to construct a society that does not stand for such violence.

See also: Technology and Domestic Abuse; Teen Victims

Further Reading

Love Is Not Abuse: http://loveisnotabuse.com/web/guest/for-adults
Love Is Respect: http://www.loveisrespect.org/is-this-abuse/dating-violence-statistics
Picard, Peter. (2007, January). *Tech abuse in teen relationships Study*, 1–19. Retrieved January 31, 2013 from http://www.loveisrespect.org/wp-content/uploads/2009/03/liz-claiborne-2007-tech-relationship-abuse.pdf
Safe@Work Coalition. (n.d.). Success stories: Liz Claiborne Inc. Retrieved from http://www.safeatworkcoalition.org/successstories/lizclaiborne.htm
Safe@Work Coalition. (2002, November 14). Liz Claiborne, Inc.: Associate handbook. Retrieved from http://www.safeatworkcoalition.org/workplacepolicy/lciwpdvpolicy.htm

Vanessa Marquez

M

MAI, MUKHTAR

Mukhtar Mai grew up in a peasant family in southern Punjab, in a village called Meerwala. Like so many rural Pakistanis, and particularly girls, Mukhtar never attended school. In fact, there was no school for girls in Meerwala, so Mukhtar Mai grew up knowing nothing but household chores. Her simple life changed in July 2002, when her younger brother, Shakur, who was 12 or 13 at the time, was kidnapped and gang-raped by a group of men from the Mastoi, a higher-status class. The Mastoi became nervous that they would face punishment for their offenses and dreamed up a story to cover it up. They claimed Shakur had had sex with a Mastoi girl, Salma, which required a tribal assembly because of the status difference between the two. The village assembly was dominated by the Mastoi. Mukhtar attended on behalf of her family, and despite there being no truth to the accusation against her brother, she apologized and tried to bring peace to the situation, as was typical in this kind of case. At some point a crowd of armed Mastoi men gathered around Mukhtar, and the tribal council decided her apology was not enough. They proceeded to punish Shakur by gang-raping his sister. Four men dragged the kicking, screaming Mukhtar Mai into an empty stable near the meeting place, stripped her naked, and raped her on the dirt floor, one by one, as the crowd waited outside. The rapists pushed Mukhtar out of the stable and forced her to stagger home, near naked, as the crowd jeered.

Women who have been humiliated in this way are expected to commit suicide as a way to cleanse themselves and their family from the shame. Mukhtar's mother and father watched over her, however, so she could not. At Friday prayers, a local Muslim leader spoke out about the rape, calling it an outrage against Islam. With this unusual outpouring of support, Mukhtar began to feel outrage instead of shame, courage instead of humiliation. Mukhtar went to the police to report the rape, an almost unprecedented move for someone of her social standing. Even more surprising was that the police actually arrested the attackers. Pakistani President Pervez Musharraf heard about the case and even sent the equivalent of $8,300 in compensation to Mukhtar Mai and her family. Mukhtar decided to use the money in another way, though—to build a school for girls in Meerwala.

Mukhtar Mai has repeatedly expressed her belief that it is education that will change the way men behave toward women. The best way to respond to what happened to her, she believed, was to educate young people so it wouldn't happen to anyone else. Mukhtar enrolled to attend her own school so that she could learn to read and write, but soon the school was struggling for funds and remained unfinished. U.S. journalist and author Nicholas Kristof began covering Mukhtar Mai's case, and his work helped garner $430,000 for the school, largely through Mercy Corps, an NGO that operates in Pakistan. The attention irked President Musharraf, who disliked that international scrutiny was focused on the gender violence so common to Pakistan. Mukhtar's public comments denouncing the attack and pronouncing it a systemic problem for poor women that received virtually no attention prompted the Pakistani intelligence service to pressure her to keep quiet. She refused. The government responded by releasing her attackers from prison.

Although she was fearful for her life, Mukhtar Mai refused to back down. She continued her plans to travel to the United States to speak at a women's rights conference. President Musharraf put her on the exit control list, a blacklist that banned her from leaving the country. Again, Mukhtar refused to be intimidated and, despite the government cutting of her telephone land line, she snuck onto the roof of her building and used her weak cell phone connection to continue to report to Kristof and others that the police who were supposed to be "protecting" her were now aiming their weapons her way. Musharraf next ordered that Mukhtar be brought to the capital. Intelligence agents whisked her away to Islamabad, where she was berated for betraying her country. Mukhtar was taken to a safe house where it was alleged that she could be kept quiet.

President George Bush had praised President Musharraf for his leadership, but Musharraf's handling of Mukhtar Mai became an embarrassment. Secretary of State Condoleezza Rice called the Pakistani foreign minister and asked him to stop the mistreatment of Mukhtar Mai, and President Musharraf proposed that a team of his aides accompany Mai to the United States. She refused, asserting that she would only go on her free will. Her continued courage paid off, and Musharraf returned her passport.

Because the case had risen to the level of foreign government involvement, Mukhtar Mai was invited to the White House and the State Department. She was flown to New York courtesy of *Glamour* magazine so that she could be honored as "woman of the year," introduced by actress Brooke Shields, and given a video tribute by First Lady Laura Bush. Mukhtar Mai remained stubborn on that trip, telling reporters and aid groups that they were wrong for focusing their attention on Lahore, Islamabad, and Karachi. Instead, she told them, they need to go to the villages like Meerwala.

Remarkably, some of the children of Mai's rapists attended her school. After successfully operating her school for several years, she expanded her efforts, building a high school and a school for boys that she operated through donations and from funds obtained through profits from the herd of cows she purchased. Mukhtar Mai also bought a school van that serves as an ambulance to take pregnant women to the hospital when they are ready to deliver. She then built a school in a gang-ridden area where even the government wouldn't operate a school. Miraculously, she even persuaded the province to build a women's college. Women from around the country began to show up in need of help. She operates her own aid group, the Mukhtar Mai Women's Welfare Organization, which includes a 24-hour crisis line for abused women, a shelter, a free legal clinic, and a library. Personally, Mukhtar became fluent in Urdu.

The pressure from the government, however, continued. Pakistani intelligence continued to harass Mukhtar Mai and her family, even issuing an arrest warrant for one of her brothers on false charges. Even reporter Kristof and his wife Sheryl WuDunn were temporarily denied visas for their support of Mai. Inaccurate articles were placed in Urdu-language newspapers calling Mai a stooge for the Indian government and referring to her as an uneducated peasant who was eager for her 15 minutes of fame. She felt that the government wanted her either in prison or dead, and she was told by a senior police official that if she remained uncooperative she would be imprisoned for her "fornication." Amna Buttar, a Pakistani American who had agreed to accompany Mukhtar Mai to New York, even felt threatened, telling Kristof and WuDunn, "I want you to know that no matter how we are killed, even if it looks like an accident, it isn't. So if we die in a train accident, a bus accident, or a fire—then tell the world that it was not actually an accident" (Kristof & WuDunn, 2009, p. 77). Mukhtar Mai, however, has prevailed and is still operating her school.

Although rapes of young women have not stopped completely, Mukhtar Mai has been an inspiration for women worldwide and is indeed making an impact in Pakistan. In 2007, a case similar to hers occurred in the village of Habib Labano. Because a young man of a lower caste eloped with his high-caste girlfriend, the village council decided to seek revenge on a 16-year-old girl, Saima, a cousin of the young man. Eleven men kidnapped her, then paraded her naked through the village. Two men then raped her, on the order of the council. But, like her inspiration, Mukhtar Mai, Saima refused to kill herself, seeking prosecution instead. Aid groups helped her, eventually leading to the arrest of the suspects. A police chief, Farooq Leghari, was sent to Meerwala.

In March 2009, Mukhtar Mai married a police constable who was assigned to guard her in the wake of the attack. She is his second wife. Her marriage challenged yet another stigma against rape victims in conservative Pakistani society.

In 2011, the Pakistani Supreme Court upheld the acquittals of five of the six men who attacked Mukhtar Mai. The sixth attacker, Abdul Khaliq, is completing a life sentence. She expressed her deep sadness at the injustice, noting that there was ample medical and other types of evidence to convict the attackers. She referred to the judgment as "humiliating to every Pakistani woman" (True Survivor, 2011). She also expressed concern about her own safety and the safety of her family in light of the decision, yet she again continues to refuse to leave her home in Pakistan.

In 2006, former Bollywood actress and model Somy Ali, who now runs the nonprofit No More Tears, which assists victims of domestic violence, made a short documentary film about Mukhtar Mai's case after having served as a translator for Mai when she was in the United States.

See also: Ali, Somy; Kristof, Nicholas and Sheryl WuDunn; The Middle East and Domestic Abuse

Further Reading

Kristof, N., & WuDunn, S. (2009). *Half the sky: Turning oppression into opportunity for women worldwide*. New York, NY: Alfred A. Knopf.

Masood, S. (2011, April 21). Pakistani top court upholds acquittals in notorious rape case. *New York Times*. Retrieved May 31, 2012, from http://www.nytimes.com/2011/04/22/world/asia/22pakistan.html?_r=1&ref=mukhtarmai

Mukhtar Mai. (2009, March 18). *New York Times*. Retrieved May 31, 2012, from http://topics.nytimes.com/topics/reference/timestopics/people/m/mukhtar_mai/index.html

True Survivor. (2011, May 1). *Daily Beast*. Retrieved May 31, 2012, from http://www.thedailybeast.com/newsweek/2011/05/01/true-survivor.html

Laura L. Finley

MALE VICTIMS OF DOMESTIC ABUSE

The majority of victims in domestic violence cases involve women. According to the CDC, citing the National Violence Against Women Survey in 2000, each year approximately 4.8 million women experience intimate partner physical assaults and rapes. Men are the victims of about 2.9 million intimate partner–related physical assaults. While many studies have focused on female victimization in domestic violence, little is known about violence committed by women against men. Male victims tend to be African American, younger, single, and uninsured; these characteristics are parallel to female victims. Men are likely to suffer minor consequences that are similar to female victims. In some cases, male victims also suffer more severe physical harm, although research shows this occurs less frequently than for female victims.

Research on male victimization is quite new. Since the 1970s, the feminist perspective has dominated the research literature, which has tended to present the issue as men's violence against women. Before the 1980s, it was unacceptable to even consider studying female aggression, due to battered women advocates working extensively to bring the topic of domestic violence to attention and to involve the criminal justice system in protecting women. Early researchers who tried studying female aggression were denied grant funding for their work, and some even received death threats.

One of the first researchers to study the topic of male victimization was Gelles (1974), who reported that there was an equal amount of perpetration of domestic violence among husband and wives. A few years later, using the National Family Violence Survey, Straus and Gelles (1986) found that 12 percent of both husbands and wives were victims of spousal violence in the past year, indicating equal amounts of victimization. The U.S. National Youth Survey (Elliott, Huizinga, & Morse, 1985) results indicated that females reported higher rates of minor perpetration (i.e., kicking, biting), while men scored higher on severe types of violence—for example, beating up, choking, or strangling. The same data indicated little or no change over the years, other than slightly more female-initiated violence as compared to men.

Continuing to examine the rates of male victimization, Straus (1993) reported that 53 percent of women reported hitting their male partner first compared to 43 percent who reported their male partner initiated the aggression. This study rejected the self-defense approach that many studies allude to. In another study using the U.S. Department of Justice data, approximately 167,000 men were the victims of assault that year. In one of the largest studies conducted, women appeared as likely or slightly more likely to use physical aggression during conflicts compared to men (Archer, 2000). The U.S. National Comorbidity Survey (NCS) had mixed differences, indicating no gender difference in minor victimization. With the increasing number of studies reporting on male victimization, domestic violence reports were indicating that between 25 and 50 percent of victims of domestic violence are men.

Many of the studies through the early 1990s only included married couples' domestic violence. New research began studying young adult samples with dating partner violence. Studies began finding that the prevalence of perpetrating dating violence is much higher for females as compared to males. In one of the largest dating violence studies, Douglas and Straus (2003) found that girls were 1.15 times more likely to assault their male partner.

Chuck Finley, seen here while he was a free agent pitcher answering questions during a news conference in 1999, became a victim of domestic violence when his wife, actress Tawny Kitaen (left) allegedly kicked him repeatedly and hit him with her shoe during an argument in 2002. (AP Photo/Tony Dejak)

This study collected data of dating violence reports in other countries as well: in Scotland, girls were 5.52 times more likely to initiate severe violence; in Singapore, females were 4.57 times more likely to be perpetrators of violence; in New Zealand, females were 2.96 times more likely to be perpetrators.

With the abundance of mixed research on domestic violence, Johnson (1995) was the first to describe two types of violence that may be occurring within domestic assault cases. Minor acts of violence appear more often in relationships and are equally likely to be perpetrated by both men and women, a situation referred to as *common couple violence*. This is in contrast to *intimate terrorism*, which occurs less often and is predominately perpetrated by men. Common couple violence is characterized by both male and female becoming aggressive, with little or no escalation. Conflict is often less frequent, situational, and not solely about control. In contrast, intimate terrorism is characterized by males being the perpetrator of violence against females, where violence most often escalates, is more frequent, and more severe with men controlling and abusing their female partners. Intimate terrorism explains violence primarily against women, and the central theme of this is male domination leading to the subordination of women. It involves patriarchy, male dominance, and control and becomes most prevalent when women threaten to leave or assert their rights in the relationship. This is as seen from a feminist perspective, in which domestic violence is highly gendered and should thus be approached as a social problem for women.

There has been mixed research about male victimization, often noting that it only reflects female self-defense. Self-defense is often noted as the main motivation for women attacking men; however, little research has been able to test this assumption. Most research concludes that women are showing anger to retaliate for emotional hurt, to express feelings, or to gain control. Other reasons include jealousy, anger, confusion, dominance and control, and the need for affiliation. In many ways, both men and women report similar reasons for domestic violence.

Male victims also suffer in many similar ways as compared to female victimization. The most common abuse involves unarmed physical assaults and throwing objects. The use of weapons is very rare. The majority of male victims report being kicked, bitten, or choked, while some were threatened with a knife by their female partner. In general, male victims tend to experience more verbal aggression than physical violence. Even though male victims tend to not have as many severe consequences as do female victims, male victims still suffer emotionally and psychologically, enduring the same fear, helplessness, anger, depression, and other effects suffered by female victims (Hines & Malley-Morrison, 2001). Men also are at risk of emotional hurt, fear, helplessness, anger, revenge-seeking, sadness, shame, humiliation, depression, stress, psychological distress, and psychosomatic symptoms.

With both men and women obviously reporting domestic abuse, why is it that male victimization receives so little attention? One reason may be the stigma associated with male victimization: the embarrassment of a man being beaten by a woman—it is considered emasculating for a man to report abuse. Thus, few male victims report seeking help of any type, whether it be legal action, medical attention, or counseling. Injuries against males tend to be less severe and less visible, which could affect a man's likelihood to report the abuse. No one will believe him. And there is little or no attention in the media to encourage men to report abuse. Thus, male victimization does not exist. And what happens to these men who are abused? Few shelter houses exist for them. The problem is neither recognized nor sympathized with, with many people believing that violence is brought upon the man himself.

Other reasons for males not reporting domestic abuse include the assumption that women are more credible in their reports. There is a cultural belief that men should be able to defend themselves, thus a disbelief in females perpetrating any types of violence. In addition, other studies report that law enforcement is lax when men are injured. In the case of John Wayne Bobbit's penis that was cut off by his wife in 1993, it became material for late-night comedy routines. The wife was found not guilty by reason of temporary insanity, which would be unthinkable if the sexes had been reversed. Police rarely arrest a female perpetrator, and male self-defense is not believed in today's society. Male victimization cases are usually rejected by prosecutors or dismissed by a judge. With this very apparent gender paradigm, it is no wonder that men refuse to report domestic abuse.

In addition to the various reasons why male victimization is ignored, research has failed to fully capture the nuances of male victimization. First, there is a lack of clear definitions and terms for domestic abuse, whether it concerns female or male victimization. There is no universally accepted definition of what characterizes domestic violence against men. Second, there is the concern that acknowledgment of violent women will be used to defend male violence. Few studies have addressed the issue of female perpetration of violence, resulting in mixed findings. In addition, the types of outcomes studied do not access gender roles and social norms of abuse, or the consequences of abuse on men. One of the biggest concerns about domestic abuse is, is it self-defense? Who initiates the violence? Few studies, if any, have been able to address this issue. Last, there is a lack of clarity about who is being studied. Domestic violence rates of perpetration and victimization should be asked by both men and women in all relationships, regardless of gender. Grouping acts committed by women and men may be a disservice to men and women victims of domestic violence. For example, women's claims may be downplayed. Research suggests that there needs to be a uniform definition to distinguish female victimization from male victimization.

Research concludes that the most common abuse is common couple violence, in which both men and women can become victims of abuse. As Moffitt, Caspi, Rutter, and Silva (2001) report: "the argument that women's abuse perpetration in the community is too trivial to research could prove to be tantamount to arguing that smoking in the community is too trivial to research and scientists should focus on the cases of lung cancer" (p. 69).

It is also important to note that males may be victimized by other males in intimate relationships. Estimates are that abuse is as common in same-sex relationships as it is in heterosexual relationships.

See also: Female Perpetrators; Lesbian, Gay, Bisexual, and Transgendered (LGBT) Victims; Self-Defense, Homicides, and Domestic Abuse; Self-Defense, Legal Issues;

Further Reading

Archer, J. (2000). Sex differences in aggression between heterosexual partners: A meta-analytic review. *Psychological Bulletin, 126*(5), 651–680.

CDC. Preventing intimate partner and sexual violence. http://www.cdc.gov/violenceprevention/pdf/IPV-SV_Program_Activities_Guide-a.pdf

Douglas, E. M., & Straus, M. A. (2003). *Corporal punishment experienced by university students in 17 countries and its relation to assault and injury of dating partners.* Helsinki, Finland: European Society of Criminology.

Elliott, F., Huizinga, D., & Morse, B. J. (1985). *The dynamics of delinquent behavior: A national survey progress report.* Boulder, CO: Institute of Behavioral Sciences.

Gelles, R. J. (1974). *The violent home: A study of physical aggression between husbands and wives,* Beverly Hills, CA: Sage.

Hines, D., & Malley-Morrison. K. (2001). Psychological effects of partner abuse against men: A neglected research area. *Psychology of Men and Masculinity, 2*(2), 75–85.

Johnson, M. P. (1995). Patriarchal terrorism and common couple violence: Two forms of violence against women. *Journal of Marriage and the Family, 57,* 283–294.

Moffitt, T. E., Caspi, A., Rutter, M., & Silva, P. A. (2001). *Sex differences in antisocial behavior.* Cambridge, England: Cambridge University Press.

Straus, M. (1993). Physical assaults by wives: A major social problem. In R. Gelles & D. Loseky (Eds.), *Current controversies on family violence* (pp. 67–87). Newbury Park, CA: Sage.

Straus, M. A., & Gelles, R. J. (1986). Societal change and change in family violence from 1975 to l985 as revealed by two national surveys. *Journal of Marriage and the Family, 48,* 465–479.

U.S. Department of Justice: http://bjs.ojp.usdoj.gov/

U.S. National Comorbidity Survey (NCS): http://www.hcp.med.harvard.edu/ncs/

Jackie Wiersma

MAM, SOMALY

A victim of human trafficking, Cambodian-born Somaly Mam has become a leader in the fight against trafficking. Mam was honored in 2007 as a CNN hero and in 2008 and 2009 by *Time* magazine (as one of its 100 Most Influential People). She has received numerous other awards, including the Prince of Asturias Award for International Cooperation, the World's Children's Prize for the Rights of the Child, *Glamour* magazine's 2006 Woman of the Year award, as well as recognition from the U.S. Department of State.

Mam was born in the Mondulkiri province of Cambodia. She was a small girl when brutal dictator Pol Pot took over the country, torturing and killing some 1.5 million people. Her family was a tribal minority and was desperately poor, thus did what many in that situation must do to survive: they sold their daughter into sexual slavery. Mam is unsure exactly how old she was when she was forced to work for a man (who posed as her grandfather) as a prostitute in a brothel with other children. She and the others were routinely raped and tortured, and Mam was forced to watch the murder of her best friend. Mam described her time at the brothel: "I was dead. I had no affection for anyone" (Jolie, 2009). Fearing that she would suffer the same fate as her friend, Mam was able to escape the brothel in 1993. She determined to do everything she could to help other victims and to end human slavery. Some 1 in 40 Cambodian girls are sold into sex slavery, some as young as five.

Her first effort was to establish a nongovernmental organization in Cambodia in 1996. Called Agir Pour les Femmes en Situation Precaire (AFESIP), the organization helps victims escape trafficking and emotionally and economically heal. In 2007, Mam started the Somaly Mam Foundation as a funding entity that supports various antitrafficking organizations globally. Her goal is to allow the voices of survivors to be heard and to encourage collaboration to end trafficking. Mam and her family have endured death threats and attacks for her work. In 2006, brothel owners kidnapped, drugged, and raped Mam's then 14-year-old daughter. Yet she carries on. A humble woman, Mam still works at the Cambodian centers and lives with the women and children she assists.

The New York–based Somaly Mam Foundation operates on a three-step approach: Action, Advocacy, and Awareness. Efforts are focused on Southeast Asia but address other regions as well. Programs supported by the foundation include those that use a holistic approach to support victims of human trafficking and sex slavery. AFESIP still coordinates much of the actual rescue and reintegration process. AFESIP operates a free clinic open to women who need a shower, clean clothes, food, or medical services. It also coordinates outreach in the red-light districts of Cambodia to supply condoms and hygiene supplies to sex workers and victims. Its investigative team utilizes undercover members to visit sex establishments to gain information about the number of women and girls there and the conditions under which they are working. The team then issues a report to the legal team, who contact appropriate agencies and law enforcement. Victims are then rescued and taken to one of AFESIP's recovery centers, where they are provided medical, psychological, and legal help. AFESIP centers all employ a psychologist and some have a trauma care specialist. In addition, the centers provide art therapy, meditation, traditional dance, and yoga to aid in the healing process. Education and job skills training programs are offered at the centers as well. Residents choose from sewing, weaving, and hairdressing and receive training as well as classes in English, Khmer, computers, agriculture, small business management, and life skills. Job placement officers then help victims find internships, apprenticeships, and paid work. As part of their reintegration, AFESIP supports victims' ongoing medical and psychological needs for a minimum of three years. In all, Mam's organization is credited with having saved at least 6,000 Cambodian girls. AFESIP also works in Thailand, Vietnam, and Laos.

The Voices for Change (VFC) provides a platform for survivors to speak out, which can also assist them in healing as well as help others understand what these victims endure. According to the foundation's website, VFC "is designed to give survivors an opportunity to help themselves by helping others, to have their voices heard in the courts of law and public perception, and to have influence and impact on effectuating change. It is our vision that from those who have struggled through the pain of slavery will arise a new generation of leaders who stand for justice and free will." Those who elect to participate in VFC help with the intake of new women, teach classes at the centers, and share their stories in public venues. The foundation's website highlights the stories of several VFC members. Pheap is an intern with AFESIP's Outreach/HIV Prevention team who is studying computers, English, and Khmer. Sina is leader of the VFC team. She helps coordinate with other NGOs and works tirelessly with reintegrated victims. Sok also works with other Cambodian NGOs, while Mey assists largely with administrative tasks. Srey Pov works with the Outreach/HIV Prevention team, visiting brothels to encourage use of condoms and to provide sex education. The Somaly Mam Foundation also works through social media, with celebrities, and through collaborations with other NGOs to help eradicate human slavery.

In 2008, Mam wrote a book about her life called *The Road to Lost Innocence*. Emily Cook of *Booklist* applauded the work, saying "The story of Mam, nearly a twenty-first-century Mother Teresa, both inspires and calls to action." In 2009, author and *New York Times* journalist Nicholas Kristof and his wife Sheryl WuDunn shared Mam's and other victims' stories in their book *Half the Sky: Turning Oppression into Opportunity for Women Worldwide*. In 2011, Kristof accompanied Mam on a brothel raid. He described his experience, saying, "In the abstract, the 21st-century abolitionist movement sounds uplifting and even glamorous. But riding beside Somaly in her car toward a brothel bristling with AK-47 assault rifles, it was scary" (Kristof, 2011).

See also: Human Trafficking; Kristof, Nicholas and Sheryl WuDunn; Nonprofit Organizations and Domestic Abuse; Southeast Asia and Domestic Abuse

Further Reading

AFESIP Cambodia: http://www.afesip.org

Jolie, A. (2009). Somaly Mam. *Time*. Retrieved June 22, 2012, from http://www.time.com/time/specials/packages/article/0,28804,1894410_1894289_1894268,00.html

Kristof, N. (2011). Fighting back, one brothel raid at a time. *New York Times*. Retrieved January 30, 2013, from http://www.nytimes.com/2011/11/13/opinion/sunday/kristof-fighting-back-one-brothel-raid-at-a-time.html

Kristof, N., & WuDunn, S. (2009). *Half the sky: Turning oppression into opportunity for women worldwide*. New York, NY: Alfred A. Knopf.

Mam, Somaly. (2011). Top 100 Women. http://www.guardian.co.uk/world/2011/mar/08/somaly-mam-100-women

Mam, Somaly. (2012). Somaly Mam Foundation. Retrieved June 11, 2012, from http://www.somaly.org/about-smf/somaly-mam

Mam, S., & Marshall, R. (2008). *The road to lost innocence*. New York: Spiegel and Grau.

Laura L. Finley

MANDATORY ARREST POLICIES

Concerns that police responded lackadaisically to calls involving domestic violence, along with high-profile cases, prompted changes in police practice in the 1980s and 1990s.

In 1976, *Scott v. Hart* was a class-action lawsuit filed against the Oakland, California, city police. Two months later, in *Bruno v. Codd*, activists filed suit, on behalf of 12 women who said that police refused to arrest their husbands despite repeated incidents of abuse, against the New York City Police for failure to comply with state laws. The lawsuits were settled when both police departments agreed to change their practices in domestic violence cases.

The 1980s saw the first scientific study testing the effects of arrest in misdemeanor cases of domestic violence. The Minneapolis Domestic Violence Experiment (MDVE) was implemented over an 18-month period in 1981–1982 by the Minneapolis Police Department and the Police Foundation. Researchers Lawrence Sherman and Richard Berk, with National Institute of Justice funding, tested which police response to domestic violence was most effective in reducing repeat incidents of violence: arrest, separation, and mediation. The research found that arrest was the most effective strategy, and the results, when released in 1984, helped fuel the call for mandatory arrest policies.

By the mid-1990s, 15 states plus Washington, D.C., had adopted mandatory arrest laws for domestic violence. By 2007, 22 states had mandatory arrest laws. Such laws require officers to arrest someone when there is probable cause, regardless of whether the victim wants an arrest made. Before such laws, victims might be asked whether they wanted their perpetrator arrested, and out of fear, lack of interest in being involved in the criminal justice system, or other factors, they might say "no." New York passed its mandatory arrest law in 1994, and it was widely heralded by feminists and women's rights advocates as a step toward greater accountability for abusers. Yet, after some time living with these laws, some advocates see them as disempowering to victims, who now do not get any say in whether they want their batterer arrested. And, although mandatory arrest laws were intended largely to protect women, they have been used against women as well. When police respond to a domestic violence call, both parties may have injuries, although one person's may have been the result of the other's self-defense. Some officers, however, will arrest both parties, leaving it to the courts to figure out. The result has been a fairly dramatic increase in the arrest of women, with not nearly as large an increase in the arrest of men. Vermont saw an 8 percent increase in the number of women arrested for domestic violence between 1997 and 1999, for instance, largely attributed to the imposition of mandatory arrest laws. The *New York Times* reported in 2007 that the number of domestic violence homicides is significantly higher in states with mandatory arrest laws, on average, 50 percent higher. This is due to a confluence of factors. Victims may be delaying calling police because they fear retaliation from their abuser or fear they will be arrested as well. In particular, victims with children fear that they will be arrested and are unsure what will happen to their kids. Canadian police forces have also adopted mandatory arrest policies.

Many studies have shown that, when police have discretion regarding domestic violence incidents, they tend not to make arrests. Buel (1988) cites three different studies in which arrest rates for domestic violence were 10, 7, and 3 percent.

Pros of Mandatory Arrest Policies

For some, there is a symbolic benefit to these policies, in that they demonstrate that law enforcement is taking the issue of domestic violence seriously. Psychologically, mandatory arrest may make victims feel as though abuse will not be tolerated. Such policies may also be helpful to police in terms of clarifying their roles and duties. Some evaluations have found that mandatory arrest policies help keep police safer during domestic violence responses. Further, shifting the onus of arrest to the police prevents victims from being in the difficult position of desiring their perpetrator's arrest while knowing that it may result in retaliatory violence. Victims may perceive mandatory arrest policies as more fair, believing that they help ensure that race, class, and other characteristics will not impact an officer's decision to arrest a batterer. It is hoped that mandatory arrest leads to other action within the criminal justice system as well as helps victims find appropriate help.

Cons or Concerns

Studies seeking to replicate MDVE tended to find that arrest was less significant a factor or, in some cases, actually increased the likelihood of reoffense. These studies generally concluded that arrest worked in specific cases. That is, when offenders who have a stake in conformity (typically, married and employed) are arrested, it seems to dissuade them from future offending. Those who are single and unemployed—who lack a stake in conformity—are less likely to be impacted by arrest. Even one of the primary MDVE researchers, Lawrence Sherman, has since argued against mandatory arrest policies. Some research shows that even with mandatory arrest laws or policies, officers are relocated to respond quickly to domestic violence calls, either out of concern for their own safety (as these calls can be dangerous for police) or because they believe the victim won't want them to make an arrest and will consequently be upset.

Some have expressed concern that police have used mandatory arrest policies improperly. Instead of determining who was the aggressor, in some cases, police simply arrest both parties. The result of this, of course, is that victims feel revictimized.

Incite! Women of Color Against Violence, opposes mandatory arrest policies. In its Statement on Gender Violence and the Prison Industrial Complex, Incite! explains: "Under mandatory arrest laws, there have been numerous incidents where police officers called to domestic incidents have arrested the woman who is being battered. Many undocumented women have reported cases of sexual and domestic violence, only to find themselves deported. A tough law-and-order agenda also leads to long punitive sentences for women convicted of killing their batterers. Finally, when public funding is channeled into policing and prisons, budget cuts for social programs, including women's shelters, welfare and public housing are the inevitable side effect. These cutbacks leave women less able to escape violent relationships."

Pro-arrest policies are slightly different from mandatory arrests. Pro-arrest means that, in cases involving simple or minor injuries, police officers can make arrests based on the presence of evidence (such as damaged property, visible injuries, or a frightened woman) that would lead to the conclusion that an assault occurred, without having witnessed the crime. Essentially, such policies are based on the probable cause standard.

The problem of police inattention or inadequate attention to domestic violence calls remains, both in the United States and in other countries. Court cases sometimes favor victims who assert the police did not respond appropriately, while other times the courts rule on the side of law enforcement. Below is a sample of cases showing the complexity of the decisions.

In 1984 in *Cellini v. Sterling Heights* (Michigan), the "court ruled that the estate of a woman killed by her husband after she had reported the husband's abusive acts to police five times could sue the city on allegations that it had a policy of treating domestic violence assaults differently than other assaults" ("Civil Liability and Domestic Violence Calls—Part Two," 2008, p. 3).

In contrast, in *White v. Beasley* in 1996, the Michigan Supreme Court ruled that the "police officer who arrived on scene of domestic disturbance in response to neighbors' 911 phone calls, but allegedly did not attempt to contact a woman who neighbors stated had been attacked by her husband, was not liable for woman's death three hours later; no special relationship, imposing a duty of protection, existed between decedent and officer, as there was no direct contact between them" ("Civil Liability and Domestic Violence Calls—Part Three," 2008, p. 6).

Today, police organizations continue to work on how best to handle domestic violence calls. Townsend, Hunt, Kuck, and Baxter (2006) authored a report on police response to domestic violence calls based on research conducted in 2002 with funding from the National Institute of Justice. The research involved a survey regarding policies and procedures related to domestic violence obtained from a nationally representative sample of the more than 14,000 law enforcement agencies across the country. Additionally, the researchers conducted nine interviews with community-based domestic violence victim advocate groups and focus studies with three law enforcement agencies. Results indicated that 77 percent of respondents had written policies and procedures for domestic violence calls. Most had updated those policies based on changes in state law, while few had made changes based on recommendations from community advocacy organizations. Most (95 percent) of the departments included procedures for making arrests. Most police departments require some, if not significant, documentation of actions taken by officers on domestic violence calls. The study found 88 percent of departments require officers to complete an incident report for all domestic violence calls they are dispatched to, regardless of what occurs on scene, 63 percent of departments require officers to complete a supplemental form for documenting domestic violence calls, 68 percent of departments require officers to provide a written justification when no arrest is made for domestic violence, and 86 percent of departments require a written justification when both parties are arrested. However, only 11 percent of departments have a specialized domestic violence unit, which has been shown to help in the handling of domestic violence calls. These were found in the larger police departments.

Puerto Rico is struggling with the same problem today. The ACLU reports that Puerto Rico has the highest per capita rate in the world of women over the age of 14 being killed by their partners, with 107 women murdered between 2007 and 2011. Thirty women were killed by their partners in 2011, a rate six times higher than that of Los Angeles, which has about the same population (3.7 million). Many of these women went to the Puerto Rico Police (PRPD) numerous times seeking help and were denied assistance. In 2007, 25 percent of the women killed by their partners had previously reported incidents of domestic violence to the PRPD. There have also been numerous complaints of domestic violence by PRPD officers. Between 2005 and 2010, the PRPD recorded nearly 1,500 domestic violence complaints against police officers. According to the ACLU, at least 84 still-active officers have been arrested two or more times for domestic violence.

See also: History of U.S. Domestic Violence Developments, 1980s; Incite!; Minnesota Domestic Violence Experiment (MDVE)

Further Reading

Buel, S. (1988). Mandatory arrest for domestic violence. *Harvard Women's Law Journal*, 11, 213–226.

Civil liability and domestic violence calls—Part two. (2008, June). *AELE Monthly Law Journal*. Retrieved June 22, 2012, from http://www.aele.org/law/2008LRJUN/2008-6MLJ101.pdf

Civil liability and domestic violence calls—Part three. (2008, July). *AELE Monthly Law Journal*. Retrieved June 22, 2012, from http://www.aele.org/law/2008LRJUL/2008-7MLJ101.pdf

Failure to police crimes of domestic violence and sexual assault in Puerto Rico. (2012, June 19). *ACLU*. Retrieved June 22, 2012, from http://www.aclu.org/human-rights/failure-police-crimes-domestic-violence-and-sexual-assault-puerto-rico

Hoyle, C. (2000). *Negotiating domestic violence: Police, criminal justice, and victims*. New York: Oxford University Press.

Incite! Women of Color Against Violence and Critical Resistance: Statement on gender violence and the prison industrial complex. (n.d.). Retrieved June 22, 2012, from http://www.incite-national.org/media/docs/5848_incite-cr-statement.pdf

Iyengar, R. (2007, August 7). The protection battered spouses don't need. *New York Times*. Retrieved June 4, 2012, from http://www.nytimes.com/2007/08/07/opinion/07iyengar.html

Prah, P. (2006, January 6). Domestic violence. *CQ Researcher, 16*, 1–24. Retrieved from http://library.cqpress.com/cqresearcher/

States with mandatory arrest provisions: http://www.nij.gov/publications/dv-dual-arrest-222679/exhibits/table1.htm

Townsend, M., Hunt, D., Kuck, S., & Baxter, C. (2006). Law enforcement response to domestic violence calls for service. *National Institute of Justice*. Retrieved June 22, 2012, from https://www.ncjrs.gov/pdffiles1/nij/grants/215915.pdf

Laura L. Finley

MARY KAY CORPORATION

Over the years a number of corporations have stepped up to speak out for domestic abuse victims, educate victims and the general public, and fund programs for victims of abuse. In 1996, Mary Kay Inc. established The Mary Kay Foundation. Its purpose, in part, is to "end the epidemic of violence against women."

The foundation supports a number of activities and programs to assist victims of domestic violence. These efforts, either directly or indirectly, address a number of needs pointed out by scholars in the field: hotlines, temporary shelters with adequate staffing, legal issues, health and mental health issues, safety planning, and special needs of children. The Better Business Bureau recommends that charities spend 65 percent of contributions on programs and research; the foundation spends over 97 percent on programs and research, and less than 3 percent on administrative costs.

For three years, the "Mary Kay Truth About Abuse" survey of domestic violence shelters has been conducted online, with well over 600 respondents representing all areas of the country. The survey covers changes in shelters, clients, funding,

Mary Kay Corporation supports victims and advocates for legislation like the Violence Against Women Act. (PRNewsFoto/Mary Kay)

and circumstances since the economic downturn in 2008. These surveys reveal an increased need for shelters at a time when funding is being cut; an increase in the amount and severity of domestic violence incidents; victims' decreased ability to find employment; an increased length of time women must stay in abusive relationships; and shelters' decreased ability to provide services, maintain staffing, or provide for the transitional housing needs of potential clients. Scholars agree that an economic downturn does not cause domestic violence; it is an added stressor, contributing to the frequency and severity of abuse.

The Beauty That Counts campaign, started in 2008, donates a dollar for each of certain products sold to help fight domestic abuse in the United States and other countries worldwide. Almost $4 million has been given thus far. This year Mary Kay Inc. will donate up to $1 million (at a dollar apiece) for new Facebook friends. A company website offers posters, books, pins, DVDs, and checkbooks for sale, with a portion donated to women's charitable causes.

Customers may use the reward cards from various grocery stores to direct a portion of their purchases to the foundation, and Internet searches through Goodsearch.com generate a penny a search. Free postage-paid mailing envelopes for recycling laptops, phones, and printer cartridges result in monetary donations to the foundation. At the annual Leadership Conference (2011), attendees were encouraged to bring "lightly worn" women's business suits for donation to local women's shelters. Mary Kay donates money to Amy's Courage Fund, which provides money for victims of domestic abuse who leave their abusers; money can be used for travel, legal fees, car repairs, or other expenses necessary for escape.

Each of the past 10 years, the foundation has provided $3 million ($20,000 to each of 150 shelters each year), totaling almost $28 million to shelters in every state. These funds provide basic daily needs such as food and clothing, purchase transportation vehicles, provide counseling and other rehabilitation, or keep the shelters open or more fully staffed. One shelter used grant money to drive clients to job interviews and other appointments. Another shelter was made handicap-accessible through grant funds.

The foundation encourages individuals to donate money and time to community members and organizations in need. It not only encourages people to hold fundraisers but offers ideas, guidelines, agreement forms, and examples of recent fundraising activities. Their "How to Host a Fundraiser" website features sample letters, fliers, postcards, e-mails, public service announcements, event checklists, sample tickets, and other valuable aids. Fund-raising events include auctions, drawings, fashion shows, retreats, and sporting events.

In 2011, Mary Kay sponsored its first "Global Month of Service," encouraging employees, sales reps, their families and friends to donate time to help women and children worldwide. Activities related to domestic abuse included working in women's shelters and providing basic care products for shelter women and children.

The website provides a hotline number for victims of domestic abuse. The documentary video *Breaking the Silence: Journeys of Hope* is made available for educational purposes. Downloadable referral cards and brochures may be printed for distribution to those in need. Brochures offer helpful suggestions on how to protect oneself and one's children, how to plan an escape, how to use the law and criminal proceedings for protection, how to spot signs of an abusive person, and how to document abuse.

Nature Explore Classrooms provide outdoor spaces that aid in the healing process of children victims and observers of abuse. By the end of 2011, the foundation had placed 13 of these classrooms in women's shelters in Texas, Georgia, California, Illinois, New Jersey, Colorado, and Massachusetts.

The foundation encourages people to become advocates. In Massachusetts, Mary Kay Inc. and its independent sales representatives joined with other women's advocacy groups to lobby for funding for domestic abuse programs. For more than 15 years, Mary Kay Inc. has lobbied federal and state lawmakers across the country on behalf of domestic abuse victims and their need for crucial services. They have lobbied in Pennsylvania and Oklahoma for teen violence prevention education in the schools.

Online, the foundation publishes stories of Mary Kay women who are inspiring survivors of domestic abuse. These women have not only freed themselves from abusive situations, but in some cases have worked on behalf of other victims of abuse. Linda Johnson Thomas, for example, began a domestic violence ministry, testified before the Maryland House Judiciary Committee to encourage passage of domestic violence laws, and helped raise money for beds for a domestic violence shelter.

See also: Shelters for Domestic Abuse Victims

Further Reading

Mary Kay Foundation: http://www.marykayfoundation.org/Pages/Home.aspx
Mary Kay Shelter Grant Program: http://www.marykayfoundation.org/pages/sheltergrantprogram.aspx

Carol Lenhart

MEDIATION AND DOMESTIC ABUSE

Mediation in the United States is the process in which a neutral third party attempts to guide conflict partners in the search for a mutually agreeable and beneficial solution through open and honest communication. As mediation continues to grow in popularity, its use in cases where domestic violence has occurred has been contentious. Some academics, lawyers, judges, advocates, and mediators argue that mediation should never be used in cases where domestic violence has occurred. They argue that the use of mediation in such cases is a step backward to a time when domestic violence was accepted as a private matter, which the public sphere should stay out of. In addition, some argue that at times mediation is not only inappropriate, but can also be dangerous to victims of domestic violence. In contrast, others argue that the process of mediation gives both parties the ability to reach an equitable solution and can give a voice to the powerless by empowering the parties to reach a mutually agreeable decision without the impediment of the courts.

The hope of mediation is that the parties become empowered by finding a mutually agreeable solution that strengthens respect and trust and that either transforms their relationship or dissolves their relationship. At the same time, mediation is intended to reduce mental and emotional harm (Moore, 2003). However, some domestic violence advocates, academics, and concerned parties argue that mediation, court orders, and restraining orders all fail when one of the parties seeks to cause emotional, physical, or mentally harm to the other party. The face the parties are showing in mediation or the courtroom might not be the same face that leaves the watchful eye of police, lawyers, judges, mediators, and victim advocates.

Many advocates further argue that mediation can put the victim in danger because often the victim and the abuser are in the same building and in many cases the same room. Some argue that mediation should never be used in cases where domestic violence has occurred, citing the safety of the victim before, during, and after mediation. Those in this camp argue that the victim might be made to feel empowered and hence talk openly and honestly about her/his experiences as the victim of domestic violence. The victim might be making quick calculations that ensure her long-term safety over her current short-term interests. However, when the victim leaves the safety of the courthouse, her/his safety can never be ensured. Others argue that this is the case with a courtroom, a police station, and a mediated session. They cite the problems of restraining orders as evidence of the courts' failure to address safety and not necessarily a fault of mediation.

Moreover, it has been argued that leaving the abuser is the most dangerous time for a victim of domestic violence. Therefore, the mediation might prove to be more dangerous without the use of shuttle mediation, where the mediator shuttles from one party to the other while they are in separate rooms. One of the tenets of mediation is that the parties work together equally to resolve their disputes or conflicts. Therefore, if the mediator can get the abusers to see their victims in a different light, it is suggested that mediation can be safer than the traditional courtroom.

However, some argue that victims of domestic violence by its very nature cannot work equally with their abuser. Mediation requires the parties to work together to find a mutually agreeable solution that encompasses all the needs and interests of the parties; however, others worry that victims of domestic violence are unable or unwilling to adequately express their interests, increasing the likelihood of an inequitable solution. Others argue that the process of mediation subsumes the power dynamic that might inhibit an equitable resolution because the role of the mediator is to ensure that one party does not have more control than another does. However, a system that ensures all abusers and all victims are identified is necessary, and all mediators are not as astute at seeing the signs of domestic violence. Yet others argue that because all people, including the abuser, the victim, the mediator, and any screener, are all different individuals, a policy that seeks to say all cases or no cases where domestic violence has occurred is faulty. They argue that each case should be reviewed case by case to determine if mediation is appropriate.

There are three main mediation styles; evaluative, facilitative, and transformative. Evaluative mediators are often lawyers and focus on the legal rights of the parties. An evaluative mediator will often speculate on what will occur if the case goes to court. Some argue that an evaluative approach to mediating a case where domestic violence has occurred opens the possibility of ignoring the effects of the past and/or current abuse in order to focus on legal issues such as custody or separation of assets. Those that take this view argue that victims of abuse are often unable to fight adequately for their legal rights when attaining those rights might take something away from the perpetrator of abuse.

Rather than focusing on the legal rights of the parties, facilitative mediation focuses on the interests of the parties. The facilitative mediator assists the parties in uncovering their interests and finding mutually beneficial solutions. The facilitative mediator will often not give opinions on the case or offer solutions. Typically, the facilitative mediator will attempt to control the conversation while giving parties the ability to control the process and the outcome. Those who argue against the use of mediation in cases where domestic violence has occurred might argue that a victim of domestic abuse is unable to adequately express his or her interests in front of the abuser.

Transformative mediation focuses on transforming the negative relationship and the conflict. The parties are given greater control over the process and the outcome, while the mediator assists the parties in understanding each other's interests, values, and perspectives. Those who argue against the use of mediation in cases where domestic violence has occurred argue that a transformation of the relationship gives credence to the legitimacy of the abuse.

It is necessary to know what type of mediator one is getting and to know the style they practice and the experience they have had in dealing with domestic violence. However, because not all cases of domestic violence are reported, ensuring that all victims are given the best opportunity for the best outcome while remaining physically, mentally, emotionally, and financially safe becomes problematic. In addition, to understanding the style of mediation and the experience of the mediator, it is also important to know the standards the mediator follows.

The Model Standards of Practice for Family and Divorce Mediation are an attempt by the mediation community to establish a combined set of standards in order to increase public confidence and guide mediators. In 1984, the Association of Family and Conciliation Courts (AFCC) drafted a set of model standards with over 30 interested organizations. Also in 1984, the American Bar Association (ABA) drafted the Standards of Practice for Lawyer Mediators in Family Law Disputes. However, many organizations and states used the model standards as guides but drafted their own standards.

In 1996, the Family Law Section of the ABA concluded that the 1984 standards should be reviewed. After an assessment of the original standards, which included the AFCC and other interested organizations, many critical issues were identified. One of the major criticisms was that the original standards failed to deal with domestic violence. In fact, the 1984 standards did not specify the need for expertise and training for mediators dealing with domestic violence. In order to resolve this issue, a committee was formed to conduct research and consult with family mediators, lawyers, and domestic violence experts.

In 1998, the AFCC led a symposium in order to draft model standards for family mediation. The American Bar Association and the National Council of Dispute Resolution Organizations joined with the Academy of Family Mediators, Conflict Resolution Education Network, the National Association for Community Mediation, the National Conference on Peacemaking and Conflict Resolution, and the Society of Professionals in Dispute Resolution. The proposed changes were sent out to over 90 groups for review, and over 80 proposals were received.

The Symposium on Standards of Practice changes included the need to "have knowledge of and training in the impact of family conflict on parents, children and other participants, including knowledge of child development, domestic abuse and child abuse and neglect." In addition, "A family mediator shall recognize a family situation involving domestic abuse and take appropriate steps to shape the mediation process accordingly." Moreover, the new changes stated that without proper training, a mediator should not mediate a case involving domestic violence. Furthermore, due to threats and coercion, safety, and control issues, mediators must screen domestic violence prior to beginning mediation and throughout mediation. If the screening reveals that domestic violence occurred or is occurring, the mediator must ensure the security of the parties by making security arrangements; caucusing or holding separate sessions; allowing and even encouraging advocates, lawyers, or friends to be present and to give advice; referring parties to community resources; and/or ending the mediation safely (Symposium on Standards of Practice, 2000).

However, some argue that while the model standards are a step in the right direction, they are simply a set of good practices. They are not legal rules and therefore fail to ensure the safety and security of domestic violence victims. Moreover, some argue that a power imbalance will result in a one-sided outcome. Moreover, those against the use of mediation argue that a lack of reporting domestic violence negates the possibility of ensuring that all victims and perpetrators are identified and properly dealt with in the mediation session.

In addition, many argue that the screening processes for identifying perpetrators and victims of domestic violence are underused, nonexistent, or faulty. Moreover, they argue that mediators lack the training and knowledge concerning domestic violence. Furthermore, those against the use of mediation in any case where domestic violence has occurred cite the long fight that has been waged to bring domestic violence out of the private home and into the public eye.

On the other side of the argument are those who do not believe in mediating violence but rather argue that the process of mediation has been set up in order to empower and give voice to those who decide to take part in mediation. Moreover, they argue that safety precautions can be undertaken to ensure the safety of all involved and that screening processes can and should be used in an attempt to identify victims and perpetrators of domestic violence. While some might admit that more training can be done regarding domestic violence, others argue that training and education further the positive role of mediation in transforming the conflict and the relationship. In addition, some argue that mediation offers a better alternative than the cold judicial system. Finally, there are those who argue that each case is different and should be judged on the merits of those involved in the conflict.

The root cause of the problem concerning domestic violence and mediation appears to be the difficulty of applying agreed-upon definitions to domestic violence and mediation. While the exact definition of domestic violence is widely known, the challenges arise in determining who the victims and perpetrators of domestic violence are. It is fairly easy to observe physical symptoms, but the emotional, psychological, and financial scars that victims often hide from the public are often much more difficult to decipher.

If victims and perpetrators are not properly identified, then the arguments concerning the use of mediation becomes nothing more than an intellectual exercise where arguments are tossed back and forth while the victims continue to suffer in silence. Furthermore, just as all domestic violence victims deal with their abuse in distinct ways and present a unique set of circumstances for the court system, mediators also approach mediation in various ways and bring different talents and setbacks to the mediation session.

Those who argue in favor of the use of mediation in cases involving domestic violence contend that through open and honest dialogue, the parties can find a mutually beneficial long-term solution to the dispute. Nonetheless, most agree that at the very minimum, cases involving domestic violence should be given special treatment in litigation and mediation. However, the exact nature of current and proposed special treatments remains elusive in some courts and nonexistent in others. Regardless of one's view on the use of mediation in cases involving domestic violence, most agree that obtaining accurate reports on those that have fallen victim to domestic abuse poses the greatest challenge.

Those who argue that mediation should never be used in cases where domestic violence has occurred contend that there is a power imbalance between the abuser and the victim and that current and future safety concerns for the victim should surmount any agreed-upon settlement. Many domestic violence advocates argue that domestic abuse has taken away the ability of victims to stand up for themselves. Because mediation requires that the parties work together to reach an agreement, the victims enter mediation with little or no power. Without equal power, many maintain that the outcome will favor the abuser. Moreover, some say that mediation fails to adequately punish the abuser.

In contrast, many of those in favor of mediation also argue that one should never mediate violence, yet they contend that mediation could be used to resolve custody battles or divide assets in divorce. In these cases, they would say that mediation is not being used to resolve domestic violence. However, they stress that the process of mediation and the mediator can equalize a power imbalance.

Recommendations

- Know your mediator and his or her style of mediation.
- Ensure open communication and honesty with your mediator. If the mediator does not know that you have experienced domestic violence, he or she cannot help balance power.
- Have a victim's advocate, friend, or lawyer attend mediation sessions with you.
- Be informed on your community resources and the court's view and screening process for domestic violence.

See also: Courts and Domestic Abuse

Further Reading

Bush, R. A. B., & Folger, J. P. (2005). *The promise of mediation: The transformative approach to conflict.* San Francisco, CA: Jossey-Bass.

Cobb, S. (1997). The domestication of violence in mediation. *Law & Society Review, 31*(3), 397–440.

Coker, D. (2006). Restorative justice, Navajo peacemaking and domestic violence. *Theoretical Criminology, 10*(1), 67–85.

Garrity, R. (1998). Mediation and domestic violence: What domestic violence looks like. Retrieved from http://www.biscmi.org/documents/MEDIATION_AND_DOMESTIC_VIOLENCE.html

The Green Book. (n.d.). Mediating when domestic violence/control exists. Retrieved from http://www.thegreenbook.info/documents/EPC_Mediate_DV.pdf

Imbrogno, A. R., & Imbrogno, S. (2000). Mediation in court cases of domestic violence. *Families in Society, 81*(4), 392–401.

Maxwell, J. P. (1999). Mandatory mediation of custody in the face of domestic violence: Suggestions for courts and mediators. *Family Court Review, 37*(3), 335–355.

Moore, C. W. (2003). *The mediation process: Practical strategies for resolving conflict.* San Francisco, CA: Jossey-Bass.

Murphy, J. C., & Rubinson, R. (2005). Domestic violence and mediation: Responding to the challenges of crafting effective screens. *Family Law Quarterly, 39*(1), 53–85.

Phillips, B. A. (2001). *The mediation field guide: Transcending litigation and resolving conflicts in your business or organization.* San Francisco, CA: Jossey-Bass.

Rimelspach, R. (2001). Mediating family disputes in a world with domestic violence: How to devise a safe and effective court-connected mediation program. *Mediate.com.* Retrieved from http://www.mediate.com/articles/rimelspach.cfm

The Symposium on Standards of Practice. (2000). Model standards of practice for family and divorce mediation. Retrieved January 30, 2013 from http://www.afccnet.org/Portals/0/PublicDocuments/CEFCP/ModelStandardsOfPracticeForFamilyAndDivorceMediation.pdf

Thompson, M. G. (2007). Mandatory mediation and domestic violence: Reformulating the good-faith standard. *Oregon Law Review, 86,* 599–633. Retrieved from http://www.law.uoregon.edu/org/olr/archives/86/thompson.pdf

Vestal, A. (2007). Domestic violence and mediation: Concerns and recommendations. *Mediate.com.* Retrieved from http://www.mediate.com/articles/vestala3.cfm

Winslade, J., & Monk, G. (2000). *Narrative mediation: A new approach to conflict resolution.* San Francisco, CA: Jossey-Bass.

Chuck Goessel

MEN'S EFFORTS AGAINST DOMESTIC ABUSE

During the era of the women's rights movement, a common critique was that women blamed men for abuse as well as a host of other problems. This attitude persisted among some feminist groups and had the effect of alienating men, who became defensive at being called would-be batterers. Today, most advocates recognize that men must be involved if abuse is to be ended. Further, there is growing recognition that men, too, are victims of abuse and that abuse against anyone hurts the whole community.

Increasingly, advocates are noting that it is rigid gender roles that create the attitudes and beliefs that lead to abuse, and that these attitudes and beliefs are harmful not just to women but to men as well. Many male scholars and activists have taken leading roles in raising awareness about these gender roles and in helping to educate and inspire young people to take action to challenge them.

In recent years, a number of authors have asserted the need for men to help lead movements to prevent men's violence against women, both inside the United States and globally. Activists like Jackson Katz and Paul Kivel and scholars and authors like Jeff Benedict, Michael Kimmel, and Nicholas Kristof are among the leaders in making this argument. Additionally, male athletes and coaches have spoken out and gotten involved to help end abuse.

Key Figures in the Movement

Jeff Benedict has authored numerous books about athletes and crime, largely focusing on violence against women. *Public Heroes, Private Felons, Pros and Cons: The Criminals Who Play in the NFL, Out of Bounds: Inside the NBA's Culture of Rape, Violence & Crime,* and *Athletes and Acquaintance Rape,* as well as the many journal articles Benedict has authored or coauthored, have helped call much-needed attention to the overrepresentation of athletes as abusers and assailants.

Through his regular blog in the *Huffington Post*, his book *The Macho Paradox*, his numerous films from the Media Education Foundation, and his activism, Jackson Katz, PhD has been one of the United States' strongest advocates for men's work to end violence against women.

Paul Kivel is an educator, author, and activist who cofounded the Oakland Men's Project. His efforts are also intended to bring communities together to prevent violence. In particular, Kivel's work emphasizes the need to be culturally sensitive. His programs incorporate multimedia and interactive methods.

Michael Kimmel is an American sociologist whose work focuses on critiquing traditional gender roles and promoting gender equality. He actively counters claims of "gender symmetry" in abuse—that is, the idea that males and females experience abuse at similar rates.

Nicholas Kristof is a Pulitzer Prize–winning journalist with the *New York Times* and coauthor, with his wife, Sheryl WuDunn, of the 2009 book *Half the Sky*, which focuses on global gender inequalities. His writing has raised awareness about rape, human trafficking, maternal mortality, and more.

Sample Programs for Men

In 1993, Jackson Katz formed Mentors in Violence Program (MVP), which utilizes a bystander empowerment focus to encourage men to take action to end abuse. MVP is tailored for use with male groups, such as athletes, fraternities, and the military. To date, it has been implemented by a quarter of the teams in the NFL, a number of Major League Baseball clubs, NASCAR, and many other sports organizations. It was also the first gender violence prevention program implemented in the history of the U.S. Marine Corps.

Coaching Boys Into Men (CBIM) is designed for adult males to use with boys. Men are trained to be mentors who role model for boys how to treat others with respect and honor. A version of CBIM has been implemented in India as well.

Dads & Daughters helps fathers learn how to communicate with their daughters and to discuss and critique the cultural messages that subordinate and oppress women.

Founded in 1982, Men Stopping Violence works with female domestic violence advocates to provide interventions for individual batterers and to promote a shift in the cultural norms that condone violence.

National Compadres Network empowers Latino males to challenge the patriarchal family to become strong yet respectful, nonviolent leaders.

National Organization for Men Against Sexism (NOMAS) was founded in 1975 as a profeminist men's group. It promotes gender equality through an annual conference, training and educational opportunities, scholarship and more.

In 2002, New York Yankees Manager Joe Torre founded the Joe Torre Safe at Home Foundation. The organization provides educational programs to help end the cycle of domestic violence.

The National Coalition Against Violent Athletes (NCAVA) has a program called INTERCEPT, which utilizes athletes, coaches, and administrators to raise awareness about abuse.

In Europe, EuroPRO-Fem is a male profeminist organization that tries to counter the homophobic, sexist social norms in society.

In Canada, Men for Change started after the Montreal Massacre of 1989. It is based in Halifax, Nova Scotia, and works to promote gender equality and to end violence. The White Ribbon Campaign is another Canada-based movement. Founded in 1991, it coordinates educational campaigns in schools and via media, asking participants to wear a white ribbon as a pledge not to commit or condone violence against women and to speak out about violence against women and girls.

Evaluations of programs for men are somewhat limited. Most assessments measure changes in attitudes rather than actual violent behavior. Literature suggests that the most effective prevention programs involve peer-led initiatives that engage small, all-male groups. Such programs can provide space for honest, open dialogue. Adult male role models who can demonstrate positive attitudes toward women and engage in healthy relationships are also important. Although women can successfully lead prevention programs for males, they must be cautious so as to ensure that their leadership does not reinforce the conception that prevention of domestic violence primarily involves women and that all men are being accused of abuse. Further, programs should be culturally relevant and tailored to the specific demographics of the participants. That is, programs targeting male athletes can focus on sports, for instance. Research has shown that generic programs targeting white men may work with those of European heritage, but are often not effective with men of color. In contrast, programs for men of color that use a presenter of color and integrate statistics about abuse in ethnic communities have been found to be far more effective with that population. The most effective programs are ongoing, rather than one-time speakers or presentations, and are comprehensive in that they involve community members and local domestic violence leaders. Further, those that provide only information, not strategies for behavior change, have generally not proven to be effective. Data shows that men are more receptive to positive messages than to negative messages that promote fear or blame or fail to empower them to take action.

See also: Educational Programs; Katz, Jackson; Kimmel, Michael; Kivel, Paul; Kristof, Nicholas and Sheryl WuDunn; Social Change Campaigns

Further Reading

Benedict, J. (1997). *Public heroes, private felons*. Boston, MA: Northeastern University Press.
Benedict, J. (1998). *Athletes and acquaintance rape*. Thousand Oaks, CA: Sage.
Benedict, J. (1998). *Pros and cons: The criminals who play in the NFL*. Santa Ana, CA: Grand Central Press.
Benedict, J. (2004). *Out of bounds: Inside the NBA's culture of rape, violence & crime*. New York, NY: HarperCollins.
Cissner, A. (2009). Evaluating the Mentors in Violence Prevention Program. Retrieved March 16, 2012, from http://www.courtinnovation.org/sites/default/files/MVP_evaluation.pdf

Coaching Boys into Men: http://www.futureswithoutviolence.org/content/features/detail/811/
Dads & Daughters: http://www.thedadman.com
EuroPRO-Fem: http://www.europrofem.org
Jackson Katz.: http://www.jacksonkatz.com
Joe Torre Safe at Home Foundation: http://www.joetorre.org/
Katz, J. (2006). *The macho paradox*. Naperville, IL: Sourcebooks.
Kaufman, M., & Kimmel, M. (2011). *The guy's guide to feminism*. Berkeley, CA: Seal Press.
Kimmel, M., & Messner, M. (Eds.). (2001). *Men's lives*. Boston, MA: Allyn & Bacon.
Kristof, Nicholas: http://topics.nytimes.com/top/opinion/editorialsandoped/oped/columnists/nicholasdkristof/index.html
Men for Change: http://www.m4c.ns.ca/index.html
Men Stopping Violence: http://www.menstoppingviolence.org
Michael Kimmel: http://www.michaelkimmel.com
Moynihan, N., Banyard, V., Arnold, J., Eckstein, R., & Stapleton, J. (2010). Engaging intercollegiate athletes in preventing and intervening in sexual and intimate partner violence *Journal of American College Health, 59*(3), 197–204.
National Coalition Against Violent Athletes: http://www.ncava.org/Prevention.html
National Compadres Network: www.nationalcompadresnetwork.com
O'Neil, D. (2010, October 14). Athletes part of problem, solution, *ESPN*. Retrieved March 16, 2012, from http://sports.espn.go.com/ncaa/columns/story?columnist=oneil_dana&id=5680182
Paul Kivel: http://www.paulkivel.com
White Ribbon Campaign: http://www.whiteribbon.ca

Laura L. Finley

MIDDLE AND UPPER CLASSES AND DOMESTIC ABUSE

Many people mistakenly believe that domestic abuse happens only to poor women. That belief perhaps comes from news and popular culture, which often presents economically struggling victims. It is also true that official data does show an overrepresentation of poor women as victims of domestic violence. The reason for that, however, may not be that middle- and upper-class women are free from abuse. Rather, it might be that they simply are more hesitant to report it to authorities or to call crisis lines or other support services.

Middle- and upper-class victims may not seek help for a variety of reasons. Many victims feel a degree of embarrassment or shame, but middle- and upper-class victims may feel this more acutely given that they are presumed to be intelligent, capable, and with ample resources to leave abusive situations. While the family may have higher incomes and more assets, the victim may not actually be able to access those resources to leave. Others remain with abusers because they believe it would be better for their children or because they want to maintain the same level of status in the community for the kids. In her book *Not to People Like Us*, psychotherapist Susan Weitzman (2001) explained that many more affluent women tell their therapists about the abuse but never report it elsewhere. Unfortunately, therapists are not always helpful. One affluent victim whose identity is not revealed here explained that her therapist told her she could end the abuse by simply doing something nice for her husband. Her husband controlled all access to the family finances and aggressively demanded regular sexual intercourse. Although he was routinely unfaithful to her, he constantly accused her of infidelity and threatened to make these accusations public, thereby discrediting her in the community, if she were ever to tell anyone about the abuse or to leave him.

Evan Stark, codirector of the Domestic Violence Training Project in New Haven, Connecticut, has stated that 40 percent of the victims they work with are from the middle and upper classes. Kameri Christy-McMullin, professor of social work at the University of Arkansas, analyzed data from the National Crime Victimization Survey and found more-educated African American women suffer from greater levels of abuse. Specifically, black women with a college degree or higher were 145 times more likely to experience abuse than women with less than a high school diploma.

In 1985, Charlotte Fedders's divorce after suffering 16 years of abuse drew some attention to the fact that affluent women also endure abuse. Charlotte Fedders was abused by her husband, John Fedders, Chief of the Enforcement Division of the Securities and Exchange Commission for the Reagan Administration. In 1999, *Time* magazine profiled the abuse of Charlotte Fedders this way: "Over the years, the 6'10" John Fedders, a former Marquette University basketball center who was highly regarded as a vigorous prosecutor of fraud and insider trading, terrorized Charlotte. He punched her in the abdomen in 1968 while she was pregnant with their first son, Luke; gave her a black eye when she allowed the boys to stop shoveling snow; instituted military-like house rules—no shoes on the carpets, no laughing at mealtime—which, if broken, sometimes resulted in punishment and humiliation."

In 1987, America was riveted by the case of Hedda Nussbaum and Joel Steinberg, two affluent Manhattan professionals, who were accused of beating their adoptive 6-year-old daughter Lisa Steinberg until she died. When police entered their apartment, they found Lisa, dying; Mitchell, a bloodied toddler soaked in urine; and Hedda, who was battered almost beyond recognition. Initially, charges were filed against both Nussbaum and Steinberg, but all charges were dropped against Hedda. Steinberg went on trial in 1988, and Hedda agreed to testify against him; he was found guilty of first-degree manslaughter in the death of Lisa and sentenced to 8 to 25 years in prison. When O. J. Simpson was on trial for murdering his ex-wife Nicole Brown Simpson and her friend Ronald Goldman, it was increasingly clear that women of all social classes endure abuse.

Given the global economic recession that started in 2008, once-middle-class women are now struggling to make it, resulting in an increase in reports of abuse. This increase has been documented in the United States as well as in the United Kingdom. In Argentina, the Gender Policy Office of the Province of Buenos Aires reported that 70 percent of female domestic violence victims who lodged a complaint at special police stations for women and families are from a middle- or upper-class background.

In the Middle East, Asia, and South Asia, women who obtain higher levels of education than their husbands are particularly vulnerable to abuse. In India, 16 percent of women with either secondary or postsecondary education reported enduring domestic violence on the 2008 National Family Health Survey. Kamlesh, an advocate with the Centre for Social Research (CSR) in India believes middle- and upper-class women constitute approximately half of the victims she sees, but they are far less vocal about it than the poorer women. Williams (2009) explained, "India's economic boom has brought a rise in affluent women, often with careers, who enjoy greater freedom than their parents' generation. They dress in Western clothes and visit restaurants, bars and night clubs . . . The battered wives of Delhi's rich say husbands use their wealth and influence to delay court cases and muddy proceedings." Majumdar (2003) echoed those sentiments:

> Domestic violence experts say the problem in India stems from a cultural bias against women who challenge their husband's right to control their behavior. Women who do this—even by asking for household money or stepping out of the house without their permission—are seen as punishable. This process leads men to believe their notion of masculinity and manhood is reflected to the degree to which they control their wives. Bribery is a common trick, they say, another is to hire private detectives to follow wives around and get false evidence of the wife's "adultery" by photographing them near random men.
>
> These changes sometimes clash with hard line elements of what remains a largely conservative society. Even among India's upper crust, women's freedom can be superficial.

The International Violence Against Women Survey (IVAWS) demonstrated that in Singapore between February and May 2009, 30 percent of the women who reported experiencing domestic violence had university and postgraduate education.

The Economist reported UNICEF data in 2012 showing that more educated and affluent women in many countries support abuse in certain circumstances. In Jordan, for instance, almost 80 percent of the richest quintile believe abuse is sometimes justified, and 50 percent of more of women respondents in Cote d' Ivoire, Algeria, Somalia, Congo and Ethiopia agree.

American Autumn Whitefield-Madrano shared her story with *Feministe* in 2011. She described the time when her boyfriend hit her, landing her a visit to the emergency room, bleeding profusely. "The receptionist says words to me that make no sense. The only words that make sense are the ones that spill out of my mouth over and over again, the only words that will let the receptionist and the nurses and my friends and my parents know that this isn't what it looks like, that I'm not one of *those* women, those women in abusive relationships, those women who can't help themselves enough to get out: *I went to college, I went to college, I went to college.*"

See also: Asia and Domestic Abuse; The Middle East and Domestic Abuse; Simpson, O. J. Case

Further Reading

Chitlangia, R. (2010, July 18). Victim of domestic abuse, she tells them how to fight. *The Times of India*. Retrieved January 30, 2013, from http://articles.timesofindia.indiatimes.com/2010-07-18/delhi/28277244_1_domestic-violence-middle-class-counselling

Domestic violence among middle class grows. (2011, October 3). *UK Telegraph*. Retrieved June 23, 2012, from http://www.telegraph.co.uk/news/uknews/crime/8803777/ Domestic- violence-among-middle-classes-grows.html

Fedders, C., & Elliott, L. (1987). *Shattered dreams: The story of Charlotte Fedders*. New York, NY: Harper & Row.

Hitting women. (2012, March 8). *The Economist*. Retrieved June 23, 2012, from http://www.economist.com/blogs/graphicdetail/2012/03/daily-chart-6

Immigration and Refugee Board of Canada. (2008, January 17). *Argentina: Women victims of domestic violence; state protection and resources available to victims (2005–2007)*, ARG102689.E, Retrieved June 25, 2012, from http://www.unhcr.org/refworld/docid/47ce6d7ca.html

Majumdar, S. (2003, November 6). In India, domestic violence rises with education. Womens-e-news. Retrieved June 23, 2012 from http://womensenews.org/story/domestic-violence/031106/india-domestic-violence-rises-education

National Public Radio. (2007, August 20). Ethnicity, education linked to domestic violence, part 11. Retrieved June 23, 2012, from http://www.npr.org/templates/story/story.php?storyId=13744347

Profiles in courage. (1999, March 15). *Time*. Retrieved June 23, 2012, from http://www.people.com/people/archive/article/0,,20063609,00.html

Russo, F. (1997, March 30). The faces of Hedda Nussbaum. *New York Times*. Retrieved June 23, 2012, http://www.nytimes.com/1997/03/30/magazine/the-faces-of-hedda-nussbaum.html?pagewanted=all&src=pm

Weitzman, S. (2001). *Not to people like us: Hidden abuse in upscale marriages*. New York, NY: Basic.

Whitefield-Madrano, A. (2011, August 8). "I can handle it": On relationship violence, independence, and capability. *Feministe*. Retrieved January 30, 2013 from http://www.feministe.us/blog/archives/2011/08/08/i-can-handle-it-on-relationship-violence-independence-and-capability/

Williams, M. (2009, June 7). Domestic abuse plagues India's upper crust. *Reuters*. Retrieved June 23, 2012, from http://www.reuters.com/article/2009/06/08/us-india-violence-women-idUSTRE55707G20090608

Laura L. Finley

THE MIDDLE EAST AND DOMESTIC ABUSE

The Middle East/North Africa (MENA) region (Algeria, Bahrain, Egypt, Iran, Israel, Jordan, Kuwait, Lebanon, Libya, Morocco, Oman, Palestine, Qatar, Saudi Arabia, Syria, Tunisia, Turkey, the United Arab Emirates, and Yemen) encompasses a great degree of religious, ethnolinguistic, and cultural diversity. In the region, domestic abuse is increasingly being recognized as a legal and social problem. Yet few statistics on the prevalence of domestic abuse and limited legal reforms indicate that much more needs to be done. This is complicated by widespread acceptance and justification of domestic abuse against female family members, as well as the belief that females are responsible for the abuse directed at them. Furthermore, deeply ingrained societal views about abuse have made it difficult for survivors to receive assistance. Many survivors of abuse do not seek help from formal institutions for a variety of reasons; lack of resources, mistrust of service providers and law enforcement, ineffective legal frameworks, and/or harmful cultural attitudes and traditions. Perceptions of honor and shame make discussing domestic abuse, let alone seeking help, very difficult. Domestic abuse in the MENA region covers intimate partner violence as well as the nuclear and extended family, given the central role this institution plays in a female's life.

Forms and Rates of Domestic Abuse

Domestic abuse can take on many forms in the Middle East and North Africa region, yet there are limited statistics documenting the full scope of abuse. Many countries in the MENA region have not documented domestic abuse thoroughly. The earliest documentation in the MENA region was in 1996 when El-Zanaty, et al. recorded that 12.5 percent of Egyptian women had been beaten at least once during the year of the survey (Boy & Kulczycki, 2008, p. 56). Subsequent quantitative documentation in the region has varied. Elsewhere in North Africa, a 2006 survey in Algeria found that 10 percent of females endured "daily" or "often" physical abuse, and 31.4 percent were regularly threatened with violence (Kelly & Breslin, 2010, p. 40). In Tunisia, 25 percent of females experienced violence within the family, and a similar number of males divulged abusing their wives, sisters, or daughters (Kelly & Breslin, 2010, p. 497).

In the eastern Mediterranean, a 2005 domestic abuse survey in Palestine revealed that 61.7 percent of married women were exposed to psychological violence, 23.3 percent to physical violence, and 10.9 percent to sexual violence (Kelly & Breslin, 2010, p. 371). In Israel, 5.7 percent of females were exposed to some form of physical violence in 2004 (Boy & Kulczycki, 2008, p. 56). A 2005 survey revealed that 67 percent of Syrian females had been abused in their families through verbal abuse, denial of money, or physical abuse. Additionally, 21.8 percent of females had been exposed to violence. The majority of abusers were husbands and fathers (Kelly & Breslin, 2010, p. 469). In Lebanon, almost 80 percent of female survivors of domestic abuse have been subjected to marital rape (Kelly & Breslin, 2010, p. 263).

In the Gulf, specifically Bahrain, studies indicate that about 30 percent of women face some type of domestic abuse, and between 2007 and 2008 an anti–domestic abuse center noted that the number of females seeking assistance doubled (Kelly & Breslin, 2010, p. 69–70). Domestic abuse is not talked about openly in Saudi Arabia. However, in 2004, Rania Al Baz, a television personality, went public with her own experience of domestic abuse.

Domestic abuse of young or unmarried female family members is a significant problem. Family members may treat young females as subordinate to brothers, who, in turn, are likely to exercise potentially abusive control. This may include, but is not limited to, restrictions on freedom of movement, control over clothing and makeup, and physical violence. In Palestine, 25 percent of unmarried females (aged 18 and over) who lived at home reported physical violence, and 52.7 percent reported psychological violence from a household member during the year 2005. Sexual violence and incest may occur, with the survivor unable to go to the police to file a complaint due to the need for a male guardian to accompany her.

In adulthood, restrictions may be placed on unwed females regarding their choice of marriage partner. While it is common that all family members weigh in on a marriage, lack of choice constitutes a breach of human rights. In Palestine and Yemen, 54.3 percent and 52.1 percent (Ouis & Myhrman, 2007, pp. 76 and 119) of females, respectively, reported early marriages. In recent years, a number of high-profile cases have come out of Yemen garnering international attention. In 2008, eight-year-old Nojoud Mohammed Ali was forced to marry a man in his twenties; she was subsequently granted a divorce.

Murder in the name of family honor, as known as honor-based killings or sometimes more generally femicide, has received much attention in the MENA region. An estimated 200 women are murdered each year in Syria despite government intervention (Kelly & Breslin, 2010). In Palestine, women's and human rights organizations have noted anecdotally that murder in the name of honor has increased since the start of the Second Intifada in 2000. A report published by a coalition of women's organizations in 2007 found that 32 females had been murdered between 2004 and 2006, and the Palestinian Central Bureau for Statistics documented 10 females killed in 2007 (Kelly & Breslin, 2010). In Lebanon, between 1999 and 2007, 82 crimes of honor were documented (Kelly & Breslin, 2010). Save the Children-Sweden reports an average of 20 murders per year in Jordan (Ouis & Myhrman, 2007, p. 29).

Legal Frameworks Addressing Domestic Abuse

Legal frameworks addressing domestic abuse in the MENA region vary considerably; in the vast majority of countries there are no laws specifically addressing domestic abuse. Domestic abuse may also not be viewed as a crime because a wife is considered under the authority of her husband or a female under the authority of her male family members.

Israel and Turkey were the first countries to pass domestic abuse legislation in the region. In 1991, Israel passed the Israeli Law for Prevention of Family Violence that allows for protection orders for physical, sexual, or psychological abuse; the law was further amended in 1998. During the same decade, Turkey adopted Law No. 4320 (1998) allowing for domestic violence protection orders; the law was further amended in 2007. Later, in 2004, the Turkish Penal Code redefined sex-based crimes, including criminalizing marital rape and increasing sentences for crimes of honor.

Jordan is the first Arab country to pass legislation on domestic abuse. The Protection from Family Violence Law (2008) outlines procedures for reporting domestic violence, including sexual violence and harassment, and allows for victim compensation in cases of physical or psychological abuse. Protection orders may also be issued. In 2009, a special court was created to hear cases concerning crimes of honor.

Lebanon has a Draft Law on the Protection of Women from Family Violence (first drafted in 2008) under parliamentary consideration as of 2011. The draft law criminalizes all forms of domestic abuse, including spousal rape and crimes of honor.

Included in the draft law is a stipulation of the death penalty for premeditated homicide against female family members. The creation of specialized family courts operating under a civil law is required, and domestic abuse cases can be heard privately before judges. A draft law is also under consideration in Palestine, entitled the Family Protection Law. Drafted by a coalition of women's organizations, civil society, legal specialists, and government representatives, the law calls for the criminalization of domestic abuse and requires that a perpetrator be removed from the home, that counseling be provided to the survivor, and the issuance of protection orders.

Elsewhere in the Middle East and North Africa region, some states have reformed their family codes to varying effect; yet reform does not outlaw abuse. While reform has taken place in Morocco and Egypt, victims of domestic abuse are not protected and there are no laws specifically prohibiting domestic abuse. In 2008, Egypt adopted a law banning female genital mutilation. Tunisia criminalized acts of violence that occur within the family, yet legislation only acknowledges physical violence. Likewise, while the penal code punishes rape, marital rape is not acknowledged.

In Iraq, while the constitution speaks out against violence in the family, the penal code allows for husbands to discipline their wives. In Syria, there are no laws prohibiting domestic abuse, though the penal code was amended to penalize crimes of honor. In Bahrain, while the penal code criminalizes violence against citizens, there are no laws prohibiting domestic abuse. The same is true in the United Arab Emirates (UAE), where physical abuse is prohibited under the law but domestic abuse is not penalized.

Response to Domestic Abuse and Support Systems

The strength and status of the family within the MENA region make it difficult for females to turn to institutional support systems and report abuse or seek assistance. This is often true whether a female is assaulted by a relative or by an intimate partner. For the most part, females do not report abuse due to fear of isolation or retribution.

According to Freedom House (Kelly & Breslin, 2010), the number of shelters and hotlines assisting survivors of domestic abuse in the MENA region has increased in recent years. In Bahrain, a women's society provides legal advice to abused females and also has a hotline; and, as of 2007, only one private shelter is functioning. The UAE has two shelters in Dubai, one private and the other public. The Ministry of Social Development in Jordan is responsible for the Family Reconciliation House in Amman (founded in 2007), where women and their children can stay up to six months; there are a number of temporary shelters elsewhere in the country. Jordan also has hotlines and legal assistance offered by various women's organizations. Egypt has seven shelters, but they are not confidential and are more commonly regarded as rehabilitation and mediation centers. In Palestine, two long-term shelters and one temporary shelter function in the West Bank; there are no shelters in Gaza, and Jerusalem shelters fall under Israeli jurisdiction. Qatar has a hotline at the Family Consultation Centre. In Algeria, there is a shelter run by a governmental ministry, in addition to others runs by nongovernmental organizations. In 2005, Israel listed 49 centers to address domestic abuse.

Survivors' access to medical care and psychological services is limited in many countries. In Algeria, a women's network provides assistance to victims of domestic abuse through judicial and psychological counseling. In Jordan, the Family Protection Law specifies how medical workers and law enforcement should handle domestic abuse cases.

Many women find it difficult to turn to law enforcement or the criminal justice system for assistance. Often these institutions lack the ability to respond appropriately to domestic abuse. Police may consider mediation and reconciliation over penalization, and judicial systems may sympathize with the abuser. Women may feel compelled to return to the household for lack of services and to preserve the family's honor. In Bahrain, the government has initiated training for judges who deal with domestic abuse and has increased the number of policewomen. In Jordan, changes have occurred in law enforcement and the judiciary resulting in the murder of females being taken more seriously and prosecutors prosecuting more crimes. In the UAE, mediation services are provided at police centers.

See also: Acid Attacks; Asia and Domestic Abuse; Dowry Killings; Forced Marriage and Domestic Abuse; Honor Killings; Southeast Asia and Domestic Abuse

Further Reading

Boy, A., & Kulczycki, A. (2008). What we know about intimate partner violence in the Middle East and North Africa. *Violence Against Women, 14*(1), 53–70.

Kelly, S., & Breslin, J. (Eds.). (2010). *Women's rights in the Middle East and North Africa: Progress amid resistance.* New York, NY: Freedom House.

Ouis, P., & Myhrman, T. (Eds.). (2007). *Gender-based sexual violence against teenage girls in the Middle East: A comparative situation analysis of honour violence, early marriages and sexual abuse in Lebanon, the Occupied Palestinian Territories and Yemen.* Beirut: Save the Children-Sweden.

Stephanie Chaban

THE MILITARY AND DOMESTIC VIOLENCE

Although abuse can happen anywhere to anyone, some groups are overrepresented as abusers. One of these groups is members of the military. Studies have repeatedly found higher rates of abuse among active-duty personnel as well as veterans.

In 1998, much attention was focused on domestic violence in the military when a spike of homicides occurred at the army post Fort Campbell, Kentucky. In 2001, more than 18,000 incidents of domestic violence were reported to U.S. military authorities, a rate more than five times that among the civilian marital community. Shortly thereafter, *60 Minutes* aired a scathing critique of the military's inadequate prevention and response efforts, prompting a congressional investigation of the issue. In June and July 2002, five domestic violence homicides again drew scrutiny to the issue. Reports showed an increase in incidents between 2009 and 2011, although it is not clear whether that was due to more incidents occurring or more people reporting. In fiscal year 2010, six domestic abuse deaths were reported to the Family Advocacy Program. In 81 percent of the cases, the alleged perpetrator was in an active-duty troop. Including nonfatal incidents, army figures showed there were 832 victims of domestic violence between 2002 and 2004 at Fort Bragg alone. The typical victim is a female, civilian spouse of an active-duty member. The Army has consistently reported more incidents than the Marines, Navy, and Air Force. Victims are often hesitant to report abuse out of concerns about confidentiality and privacy as well as a lack of victim services.

In the 1990s, domestic violence rates shot up from 19 per 1,000 soldiers in 1990 to 26 per 1,000 soldiers in 1996. Critics said the military did little to address this increase. In 2004, according to Department of Defense figures, there were 16,400 cases of domestic violence reported, with 9,450 of them substantiated. That is a rate of 14 cases for every 1,000 couples, almost five times higher than the 3 per 1,000 rate among civilians. Domestic violence advocates claim that the rates are much higher than the Department of Defense reports. For instance, if military spouses live off-post, and 60 percent of them do, they might not show up in the military's statistics. An examination by the *New York Times* (Alvarez & Sontag 2008) found more than 150 cases of fatal domestic violence or child abuse in the United States involving service members and new veterans during the wartime period that began in October 2001 with the invasion of Afghanistan through 2004. In more than a third of the cases, the *Times* determined that the offenders had deployed to Afghanistan or Iraq or to the regions in support of those missions.

One suggestion is that veterans are suffering from post-traumatic stress disorder (PTSD), which might lead them to act violently in their relationships. A 2006 study addressing veterans who sought marital counseling at a Veterans Affairs medical center in the Midwest between 1997 and 2003 found that those given a diagnosis of PTSD were significantly more likely to perpetrate violence toward their partners, with more than 80 percent committing at least one act of violence in the previous year, and almost half at least one severe act (The Facts on Military and Violence Against Women, n.d.).

Military members use a variety of tactics to obtain and maintain power and control over victims. In addition to the same emotional, verbal, financial, physical, and sexual means used by civilian batterers, they may attempt to intimidate their partners by claiming they were trained to kill or playing with/cleaning weapons. They may isolate victims by controlling access to their military ID cards. The military life itself, which often requires multiple moves, makes isolation easier. Financially, military members may control victims by refusing to leave allotments when they are deployed, for instance.

Historically, the military was accused of paying too little attention to claims of domestic and sexual violence. After the spate of domestic violence homicides at Fort Bragg in June and July 2002, Congress enacted the Armed Forces Domestic Security Act in 2002. The act specifies that a civilian protection order is applicable on military bases, closing a major loophole that prevented victims from being protected. The National Defense Authorization Act prompted the convening of the Defense Task Force on Domestic Violence by the Secretary of Defense in 2000. The task force worked for three years to study the prevalence of domestic and sexual violence in the military, to analyze services for victims and responses on bases, and to make recommendations for improvement. The 168 recommendations included:

- Shifting the culture such that it is the system, not the victim, that holds abusers accountable;
- Establishing a victim advocate program with provisions for confidentiality and nondisclosure;
- Including a fatality-review process;
- Strengthening collaborations between military and local programs;
- Evaluating the results of intervention and prevention efforts;
- Enhancing training for military law enforcement.

A number of websites and tools have been created to help guide military personnel on crafting coordinated responses to domestic and sexual violence. A compendium of some of these resources is available at http://www.bwjp.org/articles/article-list.aspx?id=30.

See also: Biological and Psychological Theories About Domestic Abuse; Traumatic Brain Injury and Domestic Abuse; War and Domestic Violence

Further Reading

Alvarez, L., & Sontag, D. (2008, February 15). When strains on military families turn deadly. *New York Times*. Retrieved May 31, 2012, from http://www.nytimes.com/2008/02/15/us/15vets.html?pagewanted=all

The facts on military and violence against women. (n.d.). Futures Without Violence. Retrieved May 31, 2012, from http://www.futureswithoutviolence.org/userfiles/file/Children_and_Families/Military.pdf

Hickman, L., Davis, L., & Steinberg, P. (2003). Approaches to making military-civilian domestic violence collaborations work. *RAND*. Retrieved May 31, 2012, from http://www.ncdsv.org/images/ApproachesMakingMilitary.pdf

Houppart, K. (2005, July/August). Base crimes. *Mother Jones*. Retrieved May 31, 2012, from http://www.motherjones.com/politics/2005/07/base-crimes

MacDonald, P., & Tucker, D. (2003). The war on violence: Improving the response to domestic violence in the military. *Juvenile and Family Court Journal* 54(4), 121–132. Retrieved May 31, 2012, from http://www.ncdsv.org/images/War_Violence_NCJFCJ.pdf

The military's response to domestic and sexual violence. (2012, May 3). National Center on Domestic and Sexual Violence. Retrieved May 31, 2012, from http://www.ncdsv.org/ncd_militaryresponse.html

Montgomery, N. (2011, July 11). Reports of family violence, abuse within military rise. *Stars and Stripes*. Retrieved January 30, 2013, from http://www.stripes.com/reports-of-family-violence-abuse-within-military-rise-1.148815

Tucker, D. (2003). As military addresses domestic violence, sheriffs and deputies have role to play. Retrieved May 31, 2012, from http://www.ncdsv.org/images/sheriffs.pdf

Laura L. Finley

MINNEAPOLIS DOMESTIC VIOLENCE EXPERIMENT

Recognized as a landmark study in the field of criminal justice, the Minneapolis Domestic Violence Experiment (MDVE) was the first scientific, controlled study to test the effects of arrest on any crime; in this case, it tested police responses to misdemeanor cases of domestic violence in the city of Minneapolis, Minnesota. The study was implemented over an 18-month period in 1981–1982 by the Minneapolis Police Department and the Police Foundation under a grant from the National Institute of Justice. Guided by Lawrence Sherman and Richard Berk, the study sought to test three different police responses to domestic violence to determine what works best in reducing repeat episodes of violence: arrest, separation, and mediation. The results, released in 1984, revealed that arrest was the most effective strategy. However, replications cast doubt on these findings. This entry will examine the MDVE. Specifically, it will touch upon the historical context in which the study emerged followed by the study's purpose, design, implementation, and findings. It will then discuss the implications of the study, replications, and a conclusion.

Context

Examining social and political trends facilitates an understanding of the context in which the MDVE brewed. Historically, violence against a significant other or family member was not treated as a serious matter; it was commonly regarded as acceptable if done with the intent to discipline or correct one's behavior. Slowly, recognition of the serious nature and extent of domestic violence began to emerge, and restrictions were placed on violence against women and children over time. Yet the actual enforcement was limited, if applied at all. Victims were commonly left without legal protection and support. It was not until the 1960s and 1970s that interest in protecting victims of domestic violence was rekindled.

Police response to domestic violence calls traditionally involved the presumption that such incidents were private matters. They were considered personal events that would work themselves out and thus deemed unworthy of arrest. It was customary for police to ignore complaints by victims, even for those who had court orders of protection; arrest was a method of last resort, while "peacemaking" or mediation was considered a better option. Victims as well as members of society began voicing their outrage regarding police operations pertaining to domestic violence situations and challenged traditional practices. It was believed that such practices that based action on the victim-offender relationship rather than the offense itself were unconstitutional.

At this time, women's groups began to advocate for victims of domestic abuse Together, bureaucratic and collective activists pushed for reform in legislation and policing practices. They argued that domestic violence is not a private matter but rather a larger societal problem. The efforts of these groups helped to raise awareness among the public. This led to what known as the "battered women's movement," also referred to as the "domestic violence movement," which challenged the way the criminal justice system handled domestic violence and sought to address the issue. Advocates then pushed for redress in domestic violence laws so that it would be treated the same as any other assault—as a criminal offense. This centered on the protection of victims and establishment of services (e.g., hotlines, shelters, etc.) to help those in need.

Police increasingly began to face lawsuits for failure to arrest and protect citizens. Some of the first and best-known class-action suits were brought by victims of domestic violence against the Oakland Police Department and the New York City Police Department, declaring their practices as violations of one's constitutional rights. Other police departments were also threatened. This stemmed from the fact that victims of domestic violence were treated differently because of the victim-offender relationship, thereby constituting a violation of the equal protection clause of the 14th amendment. Changes in policies and procedures followed.

Additionally, some cases like *Thurman v. City of Torrington* and *Sorichetti v. City of New York* became highly publicized and illustrated inadequate police protection for those victimized by intimate partners. The courts deemed the treatment of victims to be a violation of their rights, and victims were awarded compensation for the egregious suffering they endured. Protection was expected to be equal under the laws.

Various Perspectives

Debate among practitioners, public administrators, women's groups, researchers, and others reached a peak in regard to policies and police practices implemented at the time. As a result, the timing for an experiment to test what the best strategy is was at its prime. The experiment was grounded in three perspectives: the women's rights approach, traditional policing, and a psychologically oriented perspective. The women's rights approach pushed to treat domestic violence the same as other assaults. This approach advocated for the arrest of offenders and criminalization of the act. The traditional policing method dealt with using the least intrusive tactic: separation. In this approach, it was thought best to remove the perpetrator from the household for a period of time, usually a few hours, to "cool off." Last, the psychological perspective, developed from a clinical standpoint, called for mediation by officers arriving to domestic disputes. The belief was that listening to both sides would help in understanding the situation inciting the violence, and the officers would be able to offer advice or counsel couples through the episode.

The Study

The MDVE was the first large-scale experiment conducted to analyze police response to domestic violence situations. This is important given that experimental designs are often considered the gold standard in research in their ability to infer cause and effect. The MDVE tested three different responses, each emerging from one of the perspectives, to see which method of policing was the most effective in stopping repeat domestic violence within that household. Arrest was one of the treatment options, whereby an offender would be taken into custody and spend one night in jail. Separation was another, where the perpetrator would be sent away from the scene for eight hours. The last was mediation, which involved officers providing advice to the couple at his/her discretion. The experimental nature of the study would permit researchers to determine which one of the three responses was the most effective in reducing violence.

The MDVE was conducted in two precincts of the city by officers who volunteered to carry it out. The study relied on misdemeanor cases of domestic assault where victims and perpetrators were both present at the time officers arrived. It also used a lottery selection of the responses where police officers used color-coded notepads to deliver one of the three treatments; the color that appeared on the page when the officer arrived determined which policing strategy was to be employed. The officers were to follow the order presented in the pad. The only exception was in life-threatening situations. In these cases, different action, usually arrest, was warranted and occurred in some instances. After police responded to the incident, they would complete a report about it and submit it to researchers.

Two additional sources of data were gathered for purposes of this study: official police reports and victim interviews. The offenders were tracked for a six-month period of time via official records to determine whether they engaged in any other domestic violence offenses. Additionally, victims were interviewed starting at the initial intervention and then followed up with for a period of 12 weeks. However, rates of attrition interfered with obtaining data from the complete sample and therefore limited generalizability of the victim interviews.

Results of the study using the mentioned data found that arrest was the most effective method in reducing repeat domestic violence. Separation and mediation were less effective. While the results showed that arrest was the response that best prevented repeat offenses, limitations and mistakes were evident in this experiment, including that it was conducted in one city alone and not all the participants could be tracked down for a follow-up after the initial findings were recorded. Further, some of the victims refused to give initial interviews with the researchers and/or could not be found after six months for the follow-up interview.

Policy Implications

The results of the MDVE revealed that arresting suspects was the best method in reducing repeat episodes of domestic violence. Those who were arrested were less likely to engage in subsequent violence when compared to their counterparts. Over the six-month follow-up, the number of repeat episodes of violence was cut in half. Thus, the experiment concluded that arrest served as a powerful deterrent of future violence.

Sherman and Berk (1984) offered recommendations favoring mandatory arrest policies, although they cautioned that it might not be appropriate in all cases and that replications were necessary prior to implementing such a policy. As a result of the findings, along with media attention to cases of violence and the push by various groups, new arrest policies were developed in departments across the United States. By the late 1980s, the vast majority of police departments had revised strategies for dealing with domestic violence cases, including warrantless arrests as well as mandatory arrest and pro-arrest policies, which extended into later years and eventually set forth probable cause as a standard to arrest in DV cases when the offense was not committed in the officer's presence. Training programs were also developed that emphasized the effectiveness of arrest in reducing repeat violence.

Replications and Discussion

Given the need for replication in research to validate findings, the National Institute of Justice funded additional research in six participating cities (Omaha, Nebraska; Milwaukee, Wisconsin; Metro Dade County, Miami, Florida; Charlotte, North Carolina; Colorado Springs, Colorado; and Atlanta, Georgia) in what is referred to as the Spousal Assault Replication Program (SARP). The studies were conducted in line with the purpose underlying the MDVE: to determine whether arrest is the best method of reducing violence. Each city, however, had alterations in police responses to domestic violence. Nevertheless, the replication sites concluded that arrest might not be as powerful a deterrent as assumed. In fact, two of the sites concluded that arrest may actually increase repeat violence due to a retaliation effect. Other cities found that arrest was no better than no arrest.

Further analyses concluded that arrest only worked for certain groups of people, typically those with a "stake in conformity." This includes those who are married and employed. However, those without something to lose (i.e., the unemployed and single-status offenders) were not deterred by arrest. The findings also revealed that a small percentage of offenders are responsible for the majority of calls for service where police respond, indicating that certain people may not be deterred by any action. Nonetheless, arrest was still considered the best method, as differential treatment of offenders by job status and marital status would raise issues of equal and fair treatment.

Conclusion

While current police strategies in handling domestic violence have improved, the MDVE is largely credited with promoting change in police policy and practices to respond to the matter as a criminal offense rather than a private matter. Other groups, as mentioned, have also helped to do so. Since the MDVE, laws have been enacted across the country to help victims of domestic violence, and many police departments have begun to collaborate with mental health and medical practitioners to treat it as a serious matter.

See also: History of U.S. Domestic Violence Developments, 1980s; Mandatory Arrest Policies

Further Reading

Buzawa, E., & Buzawa, C. (2003). *Domestic violence: The criminal justice response*. Thousand Oaks, CA: Sage.

Sherman, L. (1992). Introduction: The influence of criminology on criminal law: Evaluating arrests for misdemeanor domestic violence. *Journal of Criminal Law and Criminology*, 83(1), 1–45.

Sherman, L., & Berk, R. (1984). *The Minneapolis Domestic Violence Experiment*. Police Foundation Reports. Retrieved January 30, 2013 from http://www.policefoundation.org/content/minneapolis-domestic-violence-experiment

Sherman, L. Schmidt, J., & Rogan, D. (1992). *Policing domestic violence: Experiments and dilemmas*. New York, NY: Free Press.

Sherman, L., Smith, D., Schmidt, J., & Rogan, D. (1992). Crime, punishment, and stake in conformity: Legal and informal control of domestic violence. *American Sociological Review*, 57(5), 680–690.

Alison Marganski

MORTALITY REVIEW BOARDS AND DOMESTIC ABUSE

Mortality review boards (MRBs) have existed in various cities, counties, and states since the early 1990s for the dual purposes of determining cause of death (how and why) and prevention of certain types of death in the future. Some boards, such as Child Death Review Teams (CDRTs), are specialized with regard to age of victims. MRBs attempt to identify deaths (including homicides and abuse-related suicides) related to domestic violence (DV), compile statistical data, perhaps analyze a small sampling of cases in-depth, track agency response, and make recommendations on how to improve future interventions. Because DV deaths are considered "preventable," the goal is to prevent these deaths in the future by facilitating changes in the responses to DV without casting blame on any group or agency. Frederick County, Maryland, not only seeks to prevent these deaths but to "humanize those who have died." Some teams attempt to discover abuse-related deaths that were not previously identified as such, and determine why not, with a goal of better reporting. In many jurisdictions, these goals are facilitated by team access to otherwise private and confidential information (such as hospital records), though teams are not typically allowed to view private information on cases that are still ongoing in the criminal justice system.

Some MRBs are created by state statute, while others are teams without legislative backing. Boards may consist of few or many individual and agency representatives. Possible members include police officers, coroners, counselors, hospital and other health-care providers, school officials, district attorneys, family/social services workers, family court judges, probation and parole officers, victim/witness advocates, psychologists, corrections personnel, forensics experts, criminologists, and public defenders.

A number of MRBs publish extensive reports. Reports may include the team members by name and agency, the operating philosophies/purposes and goals of the teams, definitions, a summary of the homicide/suicide data collected, recommendations, responses to previous recommendations, and specific case review information. Case reviews include demographic characteristics of perpetrator and victim, situational details such as the lethal incident itself, time, place, season, witnesses, police reports, prosecution records, domestic shelter records, medical records, serious threats, escalation of violence, criminal histories, access to weapons, mental health problems, or substance abuse. They include risk factors that preceded the death, such as a history of abuse, stalking, orders of protection, or the impending or completed termination of the relationship by separation, divorce, or estrangement. Many reports examine strengths and weaknesses in the responses of assisting agencies, from counseling and mental health services to emergency rooms. The Georgia Annual Report includes case analysis and recommendations for prevention of dating violence, and domestic violence in the workplace. Among Georgia's findings: domestic violence perpetrators are not only likely to stalk victims at their places of employment, but in many cases may cause victims to lose their jobs, and thus their source of economic survival. The Frederick County, Maryland, report points out the DV perpetrator's use of multiple child support court appearances to adversely affect the victim's employment and finances. Some reports contain resources such as agencies and hotlines, and tip sheets for domestic abuse victims. While some states include spouses, ex-spouses, boy/girlfriends, and ex-boy/girlfriends in their statistics, some states do not include intimate-but-nonfamily incidents.

Team recommendations range from better inter- and intra-agency communication (information sharing), to better training for professionals dealing with abuse cases, public education and outreach, autopsy protocol, and better treatment and follow-up procedures. There were recommendations (in various reports) for mandated reporting legislation; better identification and assessment of risk factors; better data gathering; and adequate funding of government programs such as public health-care and child-care subsidies, which would serve to decrease a victim's dependence on the perpetrator.

Across the United States, in a typical year, there are over 1,000,000 reported DV incidents and over 1,300 DV deaths. Victims and perpetrators span all walks of life, all racial and ethnic groups, all ages, all socioeconomic classes, and all educational levels. They include students, the unemployed, retirees, blue- and white-collar workers, police officers, lawyers, secretaries, homemakers, and those from urban, suburban, and rural areas.

Recent available MRB reports (Virginia, Georgia, Arizona, Vermont, New Jersey, West Virginia, and Frederick County, Maryland) indicate that over the past 20 years, intimate partner homicide has increased from 14 to 36 percent. Most statistics indicate that the ratio of men who murder their wives is much, much higher than women who murder their husbands. In Virginia, for example, in 2007, female victims outnumbered male victims four to one. And some studies indicate that many of the male homicide victims may have precipitated their own demise with abusive and threatening behavior. In fact, a West Virginia report (2003) points out that none of the female perpetrators had a history of domestic violence, whereas their male victims did. Conversely, over 65 percent of the West Virginia male perpetrators that year had a history of domestic violence. West Virginia, in 2003, reported 18 female and 21 male fatalities; however, the report pointed out that the men were more likely to be suicides (in cases of homicide/suicide), while women were more likely to be homicides. Interestingly, the Georgia report noted that in cases where a victim sustained a serious injury, while law enforcement was made aware in only 57 percent of the cases, family and friends knew in every case.

MRBs have been useful in unearthing and compiling information on previously known and unknown DV deaths. They have been instrumental in gathering and analyzing data, and in making recommendations on how to prevent future deaths by improving various agencies and agency responses, and educating victims and the public on DV and available resources. MRBs have been instrumental in involving individual employers, and various agencies in measures that would be helpful to DV victims.

Further Reading

Domestic Violence Fatalities and Homicides: http://www.ncdsv.org/publications_domhomicide.html
National Domestic Violence Fatality Review Initiative: http://www.ndvfri.org

Carol Lenhart

MUSIC AND DOMESTIC ABUSE

The intersection of domestic abuse/violence and music is an area almost entirely without any credible research. Much research has been done on domestic abuse/violence, but very little on the impact of music on domestic violence. What has been done has mostly focused on children or college students. Most of the research exists within the discipline of psychology. This entry will mention a few studies that have investigated the intersection of violence and music. To strike a balance, it will also offer the positive side of music, its usefulness as a component of rehabilitative services for the domestically abused.

Two studies have suggested that music with violent themes or lyrics does have an impact on aggression or aggressive thoughts and feelings. One of these studies, conducted by Barongan and Hall (1995), was designed to gauge the influence of misogynistic rap music on sexual aggression against women. Its starting premises were that misogynistic messages are frequently conveyed in the media, that there are many musical lyrics that convey negative and sexist attitudes about women, and that such messages may have a negative attitudinal and behavioral impact toward women. In previous studies, men who were shown violent rock videos demonstrated more negative attitudes toward women than men who were exposed to nonviolent rock videos; the limitation with these studies is that the lyrical content of heavy-metal music was excessively difficult for the research participants to recognize. It is a genre where the lyrical content is often emphasized and easier to discern than perhaps the lyrical content in heavy metal. As a result of this difference, rap music may play a more influential role with its listeners. Barongan and Hall's (1995) study was conducted under experimental conditions (in a laboratory) where direct observation of aggressive behavior could be done.

The study focused on whether or not listening to misogynistic rap music would have a negative impact in terms of perceived sexual aggression of the male participants toward a female confederate (someone who is actually a member of the

Eminem performs at the Grammy Awards in Los Angeles on January 31, 2010. (AP Photo/Matt Sayles)

research team but feigns equal participant status with the other participants). For the purposes of this study, sexual aggression was defined in a very broad way "ranging from sexually impositional acts such as telling a sexually oriented joke to someone who finds such jokes offensive, to extreme forms of sexual aggression like rape" (Barongan & Hall, 1995, p. 198). The sexual aggression in this study was considered to be of the milder sort. The prediction of the study was that male participants who listened to misogynistic rap music would be more likely to show the female confederate a misogynistic vignette that featured either physical aggression or rape than those male participants who listened to rap music of a neutral nature. The researchers deemed that showing the female confederate a misogynistic vignette was considered sexually aggressive because of its content and because male participants perceived the women as being upset and uncomfortable.

For this study, 54 college male participants volunteered, of which 27 were exposed to the control condition (the rap music of a neutral nature) and the rest listened to the misogynistic rap music. The male participants in the control group first listened to four rap songs and were asked to rate each on a five-point Likert Scale (from strongly dislike to strongly like). These songs did not feature any references to sex or violence. The other group listened to four rap songs in which there were many references to sex and violence. After each group listened to their respective rap songs, they were shown three two-minute vignettes: a neutral vignette of a man and woman conversing, a sexually violent vignette where a man was ripping off a woman's clothes and raped her with the assistance of other men, and a third vignette that featured assault, where a man was physically being aggressive to a seminude woman. After viewing these vignettes, participants had to choose one of the three to show to the female confederate. Confederates were instructed in advance not to react to the vignettes.

The results from Barongan and Hall's (1995) study indicated several interesting findings. The extent to which participants rated their own level of liking of the music did not influence, in any significant way, which vignette they showed the confederate. The number of participants who listened to the misogynistic rap music who showed either a sexually violent or assaultive vignette was much higher than those who listened to the neutral rap music (i.e., 30 percent compared to 7 percent).

This finding affirmed the study's hypothesis, which suggested that "misogynous music facilitates sexually aggressive behavior in the laboratory and lends support to the relationship between cognitive distortions and sexually aggressive behavior" (Barongan & Hall, 1995, p. 203). A self-critique of this study was its exclusively college-student sample, and that it only studied the effects of music on men. However, the authors did note that most common forms of sexual aggression occur in college populations, and that most aggressors in domestic violence cases are usually men. The researchers did explicitly state that it is an unknown whether sexually aggressive behavior is predictive of the same behavior outside the experimental parameters of a laboratory.

In a more recent study conducted, researchers ran five experiments to investigate the effects of songs with violent lyrical content on aggressive thoughts and hostile feelings. They acknowledged that most of the past research on media and violence focused on television and movies, and reminded the reader that although the populist belief in the catharsis hypothesis—"the belief that experiencing and expressing aggressive emotions and thoughts will decrease subsequent aggressive thoughts, feelings, and emotions" (Anderson & Carnagey, 2003, p. 960)—had been thoroughly debunked, little research had been conducted on the effects of violent songs on aggressive thoughts and feelings.

Anderson and Carnagey (2003) reiterated the differences between violent television and listening to violent music: the absence of the video component, and the potential inattentiveness of the listener to the lyrical content in music. Despite this, they posited that there were legitimate concerns about the influence of violent music because listeners are capable of recognizing violent themes within music even when the specificity of the lyrical content is difficult to discern. They documented past research involving music without lyrics, which showed that tense music without lyrics had a negative impact on the stories that participants wrote, and that only a few studies were conducted looking at the impact of violent songs on "aggression-related variables." In the first of their five experiments, they found that a violent rock music song effectuated higher levels of hostility than did the nonviolent songs. In their second experiment, they found that listening to a violent rock song influenced the way participants interpreted the meanings of ambiguous words such as "rock" and "stick"; they viewed these in an aggressive way. The aggregate findings from these experiments "provide strong evidence that songs with violent lyrics increase aggression-related cognition and affect and that this effect is the result of the violence in the lyrics. It is not an artifact of confounded musical style, specific performing artist or arousal" (Anderson & Carnagey, 2003, p. 968).

It should be noted that this study focused on the "precursors of aggression" and not on aggressive behavior itself. The 1995 study by Barongan and Hall is therefore quite complementary to the 2003 study by Anderson and Carnagey. Nonetheless, the findings here are valuable in that they indicate how exposure to violent lyrics augments "the accessibility of aggressive thoughts and affect" (p. 969). The researchers posited that repeated exposure to violent lyrics may be influential in the development of an aggressive personality. However, despite these two groundbreaking studies and others, research on the effects of violent lyrics is in its nascent stages.

The above section has explored the negative nexus of music and violence. The subsequent section will focus on the positive effects of music in the therapeutic recovery of women who have been domestically abused.

Researchers note that many abused women stay with their abuser or return to him, even after staying at a shelter. However, one factor that is linked to the woman's decision to leave the batterer is a longer shelter stay; the qualitative caliber of the shelter the woman stays in can have an impact on her decision to leave a violent home. Therapies that the women find beneficial at the shelters do contribute to their perception of the shelters as offering a quality environment.

Many domestically abused women have been diagnosed with post-traumatic stress disorder (PTSD). PTSD is intensified with the presence of anxiety, all of which tend to produce sleep disturbances for abused women. Hernandez-Ruiz (2005) noted the dearth of research about the impact of music therapy interventions on domestically abused women. Therefore, Hernandez-Ruiz (2005) sought to investigate the positive effect of music therapy on the sleep quality of women in shelters.

In this study, 28 women volunteered as participants. Their anxiety levels were assessed before and after the music therapy. This therapy involved music that the participants selected paired with progressive muscle relaxation (PMR). PMR was employed in this study because previous researchers found that women used varied relaxation techniques while listening to music, even when this was not a required aspect of the study.

The results of Hernandez-Ruiz's (2005) study indicated that there was a statistically significant reduction of anxiety among the women who experienced the music therapy as opposed to the group that had no music therapy. Of note in this study was the significance of the impact of the intervention as relates to the length of time the experiment ran for. Hernandez-Ruiz (2005) noted that studies usually take one month to investigate persistent sleep disorders, and over a period of two days significant changes were observed in this scenario. Additionally, many of the participants reported using the music therapies independently even beyond the termination of the study.

The studies mentioned here represent some of the best and most recent research on the intersection of music and violence. None of them infer causality of actual domestic violence, which is quite difficult to ascertain with any sort of academic rigor. It is important, however, to present both sides of the coin, so that readers can see that music can be utilized for myriad reasons: for ill and for healing.

There are some areas that have been definitely omitted in the research agendas for music and domestic violence. Perhaps a study can be conducted that involves more ethnographic approaches, where domestically abused persons are asked about the musical tastes of their partners (i.e., the abusers). Studies can also be conducted where actual abusers are participants. In summary, one should acknowledge that the dearth of research on music and domestic violence indicates the complexity of this research area. Domestic violence is usually not caused by a single factor, and music may be but one slice of the overall pie. It is encouraging, however, that domestically abused persons find many recuperative benefits in music.

See also: Celebrities and Domestic Abuse; Films and Domestic Abuse; News Media and Domestic Abuse

Further Reading

Anderson, C. A., & Carnagey, N. L. (2003). Exposure to violent media: The effects of songs with violent lyrics on aggressive thoughts and feelings. *Journal of Personality and Social Psychology, 84*(5), 960–971.

Barongan, C., & Hall, G. C. N. (1995). The influence of misogynous rap music on sexual aggression against women. *Psychology of Women Quarterly, 19*, 195–207.

Hernandez-Ruiz, E. (2005). Effect of music therapy on the anxiety levels and sleep patterns of abused women in shelters. *Journal of Music Therapy, XLII*(2), 140–158.

Music therapy for the domestically abused: http://www.enterthefreudianslip.com/music_therapy_and_domestic_violence.htm

National Coalition Against Domestic Violence: http://www.ncadv.org/aboutus.php

Songs about domestic abuse: The hits keep coming: 30 songs inspired by domestic violence. The AV Club. http://www.avclub.com/articles/the-hits-keep-coming-30-songs-inspired-by-domestic,57741/

Hakim Mohandas Amani Williams

NATIONAL COALITION AGAINST DOMESTIC VIOLENCE (NCADV)

In January 1978, the U.S. Commission on Civil Rights held a national conference to discuss policy approaches concerning the problem of domestic violence. The National Coalition Against Domestic Violence (NCADV) emerged as one product of this meeting. The NCADV represents the interests of state and local coalitions and shelters in the ongoing battle to eliminate violence against women and children. The organization is comprised of individuals hailing from a variety of personal and professional backgrounds, including attorneys, medical professionals, lobbyists, and self-indentified victims of abuse.

The NCADV was created in the midst of a wave of late 1970s coalition building, and fostering connections among abuse advocates at the local, state, and national levels continues to be one of its primary goals. The coalition serves as an information clearinghouse, providing valuable statistics and resource guides on various types of domestic conflict. It also supports the efforts of community-based programs and shelters and pursues a wide variety of public education initiatives. In addition, to foster systemic change, the NCADV has a public policy office in Washington, D.C., that promotes legislative and policy reforms.

The NCADV is governed by a Board of Directors comprised of caucus representatives and community members. The caucuses provide underrepresented individuals with a space where they can meet and contemplate issues of mutual concern. A few of the current NCADV caucuses are Rural Women, Jewish Women, and Women of Color. In addition, the NCADV allows individuals to petition for a position on the Board of Directors, a process outlined on the coalition's website. Although the caucus system is designed to provide representation for all, some scholarly critics allege that the NCADV ignores the needs posed by male victims of domestic abuse.

The public policy office of the NCADV aims to alleviate various social and cultural conditions that encourage the development of patterns of violence within American homes. Poor housing options, weak government assistance programs, and cultural understandings of violence can all lead to women being trapped in abusive situations. The NCADV's public policy office monitors legislative reforms at the state and federal levels. Based on these observations, it crafts an agenda of legislative priorities, a list of which is posted on the coalition's official website. As the lobbying arm of the NCADV and a member of the National Taskforce to End Domestic and Sexual Violence, the public policy office can claim partial credit for the passage (1994) and subsequent reauthorizations (2000, 2005) of the Violence Against

Women Act. The NCADV also provides policy assistance and advice aimed at promoting legislative change at the grassroots level. It disseminates a "Legislative Action Guide" that gives step-by-step instructions for those individuals interested in becoming a domestic violence advocate. Through the guide and other educational materials, the public policy office attempts to demystify otherwise complicated legislative processes and procedures.

In addition to lobbying, the NCADV promotes a wide variety of programs aimed at improving the quality of life for victims of domestic abuse. The Cosmetic and Reconstructive Support Program (CRS) aims to lessen the scars of physical violence by providing free cosmetic and reconstructive surgery of victims. The dental portion of this program sponsors procedures to repair damage to the front teeth, a common site of injury in domestic violence situations. The Financial Education Project educates women on how to become financially independent. By holding meetings on budgeting and other related issues, the project encourages women to view money as a tool and not an obstacle.

To promote its various programs, the NCADV uses national publicity campaigns, corporate sponsorships, and celebrity advocates. Numerous corporate entities, including Johnson Products Inc., give part of their proceeds to support NCADV initiatives. One of the most controversial, and highly visible, media campaigns launched by the coalition is the "Remember My Name" Project. This campaign began in conjunction with *Ms.* magazine in October 1994.

It involves the coalition collecting the names of women and family members killed as a result of domestic violence. These names are then listed on a series of posters and other materials promoting domestic violence awareness. Another initiative, Voices Against Violence, launched in 1999 and features celebrities and other public personalities speaking out against domestic abuse. The purple ribbon, representing domestic violence advocacy, is a constant presence within NCADV media campaigns, and the coalition has expressed the hope that one day this symbol will be recognized internationally. Similarly, the NCADV has worked to secure the recognition of October as Domestic Violence Awareness Month (DVAM).

Although it maintains its policy of direct interaction with local organizations, the NCADV is also utilizing technology to assist potential, or current, victims of domestic abuse. The coalition uses its official website, Facebook, and Twitter to keep the public informed. Through these venues, the NCADV provides information on how to navigate the Internet safely as well as tips on avoiding identity theft. On the official NCADV website a user can also access guide sheets describing how to obtain a lawyer for child custody and divorce proceedings. For those victims seeking immediate assistance, the NCADV makes available a list of local coalition and shelter contact information.

See also: History of U.S. Domestic Violence Developments, 1970s

Further Reading

Bureau of Justice Statistics Clearinghouse: http://bjs.ojp.usdoj.gov/
Davis, R. L. (2008). *Domestic violence: Intervention, prevention, policies, and solutions.* New York, NY: CRC Press.

National Coalition Against Domestic Violence: http://www.ncadv.org/
National Domestic Violence Hotline: http://www.thehotline.org/
Renzetti, C., & Bergen, R. K. (Eds.). (2005). *Violence against women*. New York, NY: Rowman and Littlefield.
Roberts, A. R. (Ed.). (2002). *Handbook of domestic violence intervention strategies: Policies, programs, and legal remedies*. New York, NY: Oxford University Press.

Robin C. Sager

NATIONAL CRIME VICTIMIZATION SURVEY (NCVS)

The National Crime Victimization Survey (NCVS) is a nationally representative sample and the main source of statistical information on the persons who have been victimized by crime and the characteristics of violent offenders. The NCVS establishes the incidence, characteristics, and consequences of criminal victimization from two categories of property and personal crimes. Property crimes include theft, motor vehicle theft, vandalism, and burglary. Personal crimes include robbery, simple and aggravated assault, rape and sexual attack, and larceny. Because it is a representative sample, it covers all segments of the U.S. population, including all ethnic groups, the elderly, rural and urban inhabitants, and so on. The NCVS is based on surveying a household every six months for three years. It was established in 1972 and at the time called the National Crime Survey; in 1992 it become known as the NCVS. It is administered by the U.S. Census Bureau for the U.S. Department of Justice: Bureau of Justice Statistics.

History

The origin of the NCVS dates back to President L. B. Johnson's administration. In 1965, President Johnson created a Commission on Crime in order to better understand crime characteristics and develop policies that would create crime reduction programs. During this time, the only national crime-reporting database was the Federal Bureau of Investigation (FBI) Uniform Crime Report (UCR). President Johnson's Commission on Crime noted several limitations of the UCR. First, UCR's data was based on crimes reported and recorded by law enforcement agencies. Next, the UCR did not collect statistical data on victim or offender characteristics nor on the cost of crimes and criminal activity. Lastly, the UCR's official figures were limited in determining crime trends because the reporting and recording were not methodologically rigorous or standardized. Based on these findings, President Johnson's Commission on Crime recommended pilot studies to determine if a national survey could collect additional crime data not reported to law enforcement agencies. The goal of these pilot studies was not to replace the UCR but to complement it. The studies were considered successful, and it was determined that a regular and continuous national survey was viable and necessary to understand crime characteristics in the United States. Out of these initial pilot studies the National Crime Survey (NCS) evolved. The NCS was officially launched in 1972 and was the largest survey of its kind, with a sample of 60,000 to 70,000 households surveyed every six month. The NCS cost approximately $15 million a year. The original survey consisted of three parts: (1) a survey of businesses; (2). household survey of major cities; and (3) a national household survey. The first two were dropped in the initial stages and the national household survey remained.

From its inception, critics noted that it was difficult to confirm the self-reported data and that the survey questions lacked precision in gathering information on certain crimes, such as domestic violence and sexual assaults. In response to the criticisms, an advisory group of social scientists, statisticians, and policy makers in the late 1980s were formed to improve the survey procedures. They also made the sexual victimization questions more direct and added questions that improved the respondents' recall on certain types of victimization. The redesigned survey was pilot tested and evaluated for several years prior to being implemented in 1992–1993. The new survey was called the NCVS. Even though the instrument was changed in 1992, much of the redesigned survey data is comparable to the 1973–1992 NCS data. The differences between the NCS and NCVS data were attributed to the survey procedures and not the victimization experiences.

Methodology/Data

The NCVS survey is a stratified multistage cluster sample consisting of more than 70,000 households and 130,000 persons. The households are randomly selected and interviewed every six months for three and a half years. The household's first interview contact is in person and the successive interviews typically conducted over the telephone. The response rate has consistently remained around 95 percent. When participants do not answer a question, the data is weighted and adjusted for statistical analysis.

The NCVS collects a wide range of data, including the basic demographic information (sex, age, income, and ethnicity), which is used to compare and contrast subgroup victimizations. Information on the type of crime, property lost (if any), the location, and whether it was reported to the police is collected. Data is also collected on the reasons for reporting and not reporting the crime as collected. Data on the relationship between the victim and offender, the protection activities of the victim and their results, the consequences of the victimization, the characteristics of the offender, and the offender's use of alcohol/drugs or a weapon are also gathered. Periodically, supplemental questions are asked on topics ranging from attitudes toward police, particular crimes like hate crimes, and school violence.

Limitations of NCVS

There are a number of limitations of the NCVS. First, there are certain groups excluded from the sample, including but not limited to those who are in an institution such as prisons, hospitals, mental health facilities, nursing homes, or in segregated schools. Other excluded groups are the homeless, military personal in barracks, crew members of ships, and persons under the age of 11. Thus, the NCVS data cannot be used to generalize or inform the public about these groups.

Next, the NCVS data is limited to national and, as of 1996, four broad regional level (Midwest, South, West, and Northeast) estimates. Thus, the NCVS has small domain estimation problems in that the data cannot be used to estimate crime at the local, county, or state level. Third, many crimes—such as identity theft, embezzlement, arson, violence directed at and involving immigrants, kidnapping, stalking, vagrancy, and homicide—are either excluded or only periodically included in the survey. Fourth, some common methodological criticisms of the NCVS are the telescoping (people tend to remember events as being more recent than they actually occurred) and recall (people forget the event occurring) errors, and underestimation of those repeatedly victimized. Lastly, because the NCVS utilizes a complex survey design, the data is not independent, and as a result, standard statistical tests that rely on independence will not be accurate.

See also: Uniform Crime Reports

Further Reading

Karmen, A. (2009). *Crime victims: An introduction to victimology* (7th ed.). Belmont, CA: Wadsworth.

Lynch, J., & Addington, L. (Eds.) (2007). *Understanding crime statistics: Revisiting the divergence of the NCVS and UCR.* New York, NY: Cambridge University Press.

National Archive of Criminal Justice Data. (2011). *National Crime Victimization Survey Resource Guide.* Retrieved from http://www.icpsr.umich.edu/icpsrweb/NACJD/NCVS/

Office of Justice Programs: Bureau of Justice Statistics. (2011). *National Crime Victimization Survey (NCVS).* Retrieved from http://bjs.ojp.usdoj.gov/index.cfm?ty=dcdetail&iid=245

Andrew Hund

NATIONAL DOMESTIC VIOLENCE HOTLINE

In 1994, the Violent Crime Control and Law Enforcement Act, a part of which was the Violence Against Women Act (VAWA), was signed into law by President Bill Clinton. VAWA was a legislative package designed to protect victims of domestic violence, dating violence, sexual assault, and stalking. It was comprised of multiple federal laws and grant programs, including an appropriation of $3 million over three years to establish and maintain a national domestic violence hotline. The National Domestic Violence Hotline (NDVH), also known as The Hotline, was created in order to provide a 24-hour lifeline to any individual impacted by domestic conflict. The telephone number is 1-800-799-SAFE (7233), and the organization's hotline is at http://www.thehotline.org/.

Offering a hotline for victims of abuse was not a new idea, as mental health organizations had been providing various services of this nature since the 1970s. However, early crisis call lines suffered from serious inconsistencies in terms of professional service and levels of assistance. Not all states possessed hotlines, making it nearly impossible for some women to reach out for help. The passage of VAWA and its subsequent reauthorization in 2000 and 2005 ensured that all grant programs, including the NDVH, would fall under federal standards for accessibility and professionalization.

The organization of the hotline follows a standard business managerial model with a chief executive officer (CEO) and president at the helm. In 2003, the NDVH added an advisory board of 17 professionals hailing from the business, legal, nonprofit, and education sectors to assist and advise the CEO.

The call center of the NDVH, located in Austin, Texas, serves all 50 states and operates every day, and every hour, of the year. Since 1996, the hotline has received over two million calls. It averages over 21,000 calls each month. The NDVH operates on the belief that a person calling a crisis hotline should have the call answered immediately by a professional. Placing a call on hold or requiring a caller to leave a message is not effective in curbing violence. The domestic violence advocates who volunteer for, or are employed by, the NDVH receive in-depth training in crisis assistance. They must remain calm, speak in a steady voice, and hold back personal judgments. Each call requires that they ask a series of questions to determine the extent of danger. Many times a caller is simply seeking information, but a crisis call is one occurring in the midst of imminent danger. After determining a caller's needs, an advocate can provide a referral to a local shelter or domestic violence coalition. As a clearinghouse for information on domestic abuse, the NDVH has a comprehensive directory detailing the unique facilities and services available across the country.

In order to help the widest variety of individuals possible, the hotline offers a variety of accessibility options. Advocates are immediately available for assistance in English and Spanish, and more than 170 languages are possible through interpreter services. The NDVH also has a program in place to service hearing-impaired or deaf men and women in need of support. The organization contends that deaf individuals are too often overlooked as possible victims of domestic abuse. In addition, the NDVH website has a special section devoted to the unique needs of immigrant and refugee women who fear the consequences of speaking out for help. The NDVH counsels these women on legal ways to seek assistance and protection from violence. Technological advances have made it possible for advocates to reach even more victims via the Internet as it is now possible for individuals to e-mail the NDVH anonymously to request information or advice.

To further its message and enhance its public exposure, the NDVH has employed numerous publicity tactics. It has welcomed the support of corporate America and currently benefits from domestic violence awareness programs operated by Polaroid, Liz Claiborne, Aetna, and others. In addition, the NDVH publishes a biannual newsletter, "Hotlines," containing news on the organization as well on the national movement to oppose violence. On the NDVH website, the hotline also sells t-shirts and other items embossed with the phrase "Love. Dignity. Respect." The goal is to have this message about healthy relationships reach as many people as possible. To achieve this aim, the NDVH has used celebrities as the centerpieces of many media campaigns. For example, in a series of public service announcements, various personalities, including Marlee Matlin, told the public exactly what "Love Is" to them. The celebrity influence even impacts the NDVH on an organizational level as a celebrity board, created in 2008, offers advice on combating domestic violence.

See also: Crisis Lines

Further Reading

Davis, R. L. (2008). *Domestic violence: Intervention, prevention, policies, and solutions*. New York, NY: CRC Press.

Henderson, H. (Ed.). (2000). *Domestic violence and child abuse sourcebook*. Detroit, MI: Omnigraphics.

National Coalition Against Domestic Violence: http://www.ncadv.org/

National Domestic Violence Hotline: http://www.thehotline.org/

Renzetti, C., & Bergen, R. K. (Eds.). (2005). *Violence against women*. New York, NY: Rowman and Littlefield.

Renzetti, C., Edleson, J. L., & Bergen, R. K. (2001). *Sourcebook on violence against women*. London, England: Sage.

Roberts, A. R. (Ed.). (2002). *Handbook of domestic violence intervention strategies: Policies, programs, and legal remedies*. New York, NY: Oxford University Press.

Robin C. Sager

NATIONAL FAMILY VIOLENCE SURVEY

The National Family Violence Survey was originally conducted by Murray A. Straus and Richard J. Gelles, in the Family Research Laboratory at the University of New Hampshire, in 1975 and repeated in 1985, to detect any changes in the amount of family violence over that 10-year period. The 1975 survey included 2,143 families; the 1985 survey included 3,520. Both the public concern with the issue of intimate violence and the interconnectedness of various types of family violence and other negative behaviors are demonstrated in part by the number and range of organizations providing funding for the research, including the National Institute of Mental Health, National Science Foundation, Office of Child Abuse and Neglect, Office of Juvenile Justice and Delinquency Prevention, National Center on Child Abuse and Neglect, National Institute of Justice, National Institute on Aging, National Institute on Alcohol Abuse and Alcoholism, National Center for Missing and Exploited Children, Boy Scouts of America, and the Graduate School of the University of New Hampshire.

These surveys, as well as hundreds of similar studies, utilized the Conflict Tactics Scales (CTS, created by Straus in 1979), the Revised Conflict Tactics Scales (CTS2), or more recently, the time-saving Short Form Conflict Tactics Scales (CTS2S), designed to measure violence, verbal/psychological aggression, reasoning/negotiation in dealing with conflict, and mutuality in dating, married, and cohabiting relationships. Mutuality refers to whether partner violence is carried out by one or both people in the relationship. Two additional scales, which measure sexual coercion and injuries from assault, were added to CTS2. Child-report, adult-recall, and sibling versions have been created to measure a child's view of parental violent or neglectful behavior and other disciplinary techniques, or violent behavior between siblings or friends. Differences between CTS and CTS2 include wording changes, additional items, new scales, and "better differentiation between minor and severe" incidents. The revised scale is arguably the most widely used measure of domestic violence, with more than 600 papers written as of 2005, and 1 to 5 more papers written each month. The CTS2 contains 39 items, applied to the respondent and the partner ("I used a knife or gun on my partner" and "My partner did this to me." "I choked my partner" and "My partner did this to me."), for a total of 78 responses. The CTS2S contains only 10 items, asked about the respondent and the partner, for a total of 20 responses. Items include pain or injury from a fight; pushing, shoving, or slapping; destruction of property; threats of injury; doctor visits as a result of fighting; unwanted sex; and more. Respondents may answer "never"; "yes, but not in the past year"; or indicate, from 1 to more than 20, the number of incidents in the past year. The scales differentiate between less severe and more severe intimate violence, distinctions that, according to Straus (2007), roughly correspond to the legal categories of "simple assault" and "aggravated assault." The surveys include demographics, such as income, race, religion, employment, marital history, and more.

While rates of domestic violence against both children and adults were disturbingly high in both years, the rates were significantly lower in 1985 than in the previous study. In good research, it is important to consider all likely explanations for the results (in this case, for the significantly lower numbers in the second survey). When Straus and Gelles (1986) compared the 1985 results with the 1975 results, they addressed a number of factors, or possible explanations, that could account for the decreased numbers. The first possible explanation had to do with the surveys themselves, or "differences in the methods of studies." This is an important factor because design effects and interviewer effects—which could manifest in a number of different ways such as sampling problems, wording of questions, respondent's desire to please the interviewer, or many other possible manifestations—could greatly alter the survey results and/or affect the generalizability of the survey findings. In this case, the 1975 study was conducted in person, whereas the 1985 study was conducted over the phone. The authors theorized that the greater anonymity of phone interviews, if it had any effect, should have increased, not decreased, the reporting of domestic violence.

When analyzing results, it is equally important to examine outside societal factors that could have an impact on the behavior being studied. Thus, Straus and Gelles (1986) also considered "changes in American society and family patterns" over the 10-year period, to ascertain whether changes such as the economy, the influence of feminist ideology, shifts in cultural attitudes, and/or family structure caused the decrease in domestic violence, independent from prevention and treatment strategies. Straus and Gelles (1986) also considered an "increased reluctance to report," as well as the effects of a decade of "prevention and treatment effort."

The consideration of the above factors is essential, not only to ascertain whether domestic violence really is decreasing, but because research often informs policy making, funding for programs, and lawmaking. Poor research could lead to bad policy making, which could mean a waste of funding, or conversely, inadequate programming to address societal needs. Straus and Gelles (1986) believe there has likely been a decrease in violent behavior, related to changes in attitude and increased treatment options. They support the continued treatment efforts.

One of the most interesting criticisms of the CTS comes from feminists who believe that family violence is a predominantly male-perpetrated crime. Results of surveys using the CTS indicate that the percentage of male and female perpetrators is roughly the same, thus (according to the feminist view) calling the validity of the CTS into question. This criticism, as Straus (2007) points out, is based on ideological differences rather than on sound empirical evidence. Others praise Straus for creating the tool (CTS) that caused scholars to examine behavior previously considered to be a private family matter.

See also: Female Perpetrators; Male Victims of Domestic Abuse; Straus, Murray

Further Reading

Family Research Laboratory, University of New Hampshire. (n.d.) Family violence research program. http://www.unh.edu/frl/frlbroch.htm

Straus, M. A. (2007). Conflict tactics scales. In N. A. Jackson (Ed.), *Encyclopedia of domestic violence*. New York, NY: Routledge, Taylor and Francis Group, 190–197.

Straus, M. A., & Douglas, E. M. (2004). A short form of the revised conflict tactics scales, and typologies for severity and mutuality. *Violence and victims, 19*(5), 507–520, including the CTS2S Short Form, copyright 2004 by Western Psychological Services. Retrieved January 30, 2013 from http://pubpages.unh.edu/~mas2/CTS37-%20Short%20Form%20of%20CTS2%20Oct%202004.pdf

Straus, M. A., & Gelles, R. J. (1986). Societal change and change in family violence from 1975 to 1985 as revealed by two national surveys. *Journal of Marriage and the Family, 48*(August), 465–479.

Straus, M. A., Hamby, S. L., Boney-McCoy, S., & Sugarman, D. B. (1996). The revised conflict tactics scales (CTS2): Development and preliminary psychometric data. *Journal of Family Issues, 17*(3), 283–316.

Carol Lenhart

NATIONAL NETWORK TO END DOMESTIC VIOLENCE (NNEDV)

NNEDV was initially known as the Domestic Violence Coalition on Public Policy. Formed in 1990, it was started by a small group of domestic violence victim advocates with the goal of promoting federal legislation related to domestic violence. Over the next four years, it became an alliance of domestic violence shelter programs and statewide groups and coalitions against domestic and sexual violence across the country. It became NNEDV in 1995.

NNEDV helped lead efforts to pass the Violence Against Women Act (VAWA) in 1994. VAWA was the first federal legislation to strengthen the government's response to domestic violence, sexual assault, dating violence, and stalking.

Today, NNEDV helps raise awareness about abuse, supports the 56 statewide and territorial domestic violence coalitions, works to advance the economic empowerment and financial literacy of survivors so they can lead lives free of abuse, provides education and information about the ways batterers use technology and how to use it safely, promotes federal legislation to hold abuses accountable and to provide services and protection for victims and their children, and provides up-to-date information on domestic violence cases.

Since 2006, NNEDV has coordinated the U.S. National Census of Domestic Violence Services, a 24-hours survey of domestic violence shelters regarding how many people were served, in what ways, and what more is needed. The 2011 census included participation from 1,726 out of 1,944, or 89 percent, of identified local domestic violence programs in the United States and territories. The report showed that these agencies served 67,399 in just one day, with 36,332 housed in shelters or transitional facilities and another 31,007 adults and children receiving nonresidential assistance and services, including counseling, legal advocacy, and children's support groups. More than 10,000 requests for shelter, counseling, transportation, child care, or legal help went unmet, as the agencies lacked staff, did not have specialized services, were already at capacity, or had limited funding

NNEDV also sponsors the Coalition Capacity Project, which provides technical assistance and training to state and territorial domestic violence coalitions. This training helps them develop greater understanding of the problem and identifies ways to build communities' abilities to address the systemic barriers facing victims and their children, challenge social norms that result in abuse, and strengthen services.

The Economic Justice Project is focused on strengthening the economic resources available to victim advocates so that they can better assist survivors. It is the result of collaboration between the Allstate Foundation and NNEDV. The program also provides small grants to survivors to achieve their educational and job-related goals.

NNEDV's housing project supports coalitions, local domestic violence programs, state and local agencies, and other nonprofit organizations that are helping provide housing, transitional housing, and other related services to victims and their children.

Through its Media Advocacy Project, NNEDV helps to improve media coverage of domestic violence. It also provides resources for advocates so that they can better communicate with media.

Given that the use of various technologies as a tool of power and control have increased, NNEDV's Safety Net: National Safe & Strategic Technology Project is a critical program to educate victims and advocates about the ways technology is being used by abusers. It also helps provide information and tools for safe usage of technology, including ideas and recommendations for how technology can aid in prevention campaigns and other efforts to create safe homes and communities.

NNEDV also sponsors the Women's Law Project, which is designed to provide legal information and resources to victims in a way that is simple to understand. Founded in February 2000, WomensLaw.org became an NNEDV project in 2010 and has since provided countless women with accessible legal information.

In 2010, NNEDV initiated its HIV/AIDS & Domestic Violence Project to help address the intersection of domestic abuse and HIV/AIDS and to provide tools for advocates working with HIV-positive victims. NNEDV also sponsors the Women of Color Leadership Project, which provide leadership training to women of color in terms of program development, project management, and policy advocacy.

NNEDV continues to lobby for federal and state legislation related to domestic violence, sexual assault, and stalking. For the 112th Congress, NNEDV was lobbying for reauthorization of the Violence Against Women Act, and funding and appropriations for VAWA, the Family Violence Prevention and Services Act (FVPSA), and the Victims of Crime Act (VOCA).

In February 2012, NNEDV helped sponsor the 2nd World Conference of Women's Shelters, which included representatives from 96 countries.

NNEDV's website also features a calendar of events related to domestic violence, sexual violence, and stalking. Additionally, the website offers links to state and local coalitions and other resources, as well as a listing of employment opportunities in the field.

See also: AIDS and Domestic Violence News Media and Domestic Abuse; Shelters for Domestic Abuse Victims; Technology and Domestic Abuse

Further Reading

Domestic Violence Counts National Summary. (2012). Retrieved June 21, 2012, from http://nnedv.org/docs/Census/DVCounts2011/DVCounts11_NatlSummary_BW.pdf
National Network to End Domestic Violence: http://www.nnedv.org/WomensLaw: http://www.womenslaw.org

Laura L. Finley

NATIONAL ORGANIZATION FOR MEN AGAINST SEXISM (NOMAS)

The National Organization for Men Against Sexism (NOMAS) is an activist non-profit organization comprising men and women who support positive changes for men. According to the organization's all-encompassing mission, "NOMAS advocates a perspective that is pro-feminist, gay affirmative, anti-racist, dedicated to enhancing men's lives, and committed to justice on a broad range of social issues including class, age, religion, and physical abilities" ("Statement of Principles," 2008). As NOMAS has expanded to include national conferences, local chapters, newsletters, and other events, the organization has remained a strong advocate of ending men's violence. "Today with its history of more than 35 years, it remains the oldest and the most politically progressive network of men who share a hopeful perspective about men and masculinity" ("36 Years," 2008).

While the organization was formally founded in 1982, NOMAS was inspired by men's consciousness-raising groups during the 1970s profeminist men's movement. In 1975, a group of men enrolled in a women's studies course at the University of Tennessee formed "The First National Conference on Men and Masculinity" in Knoxville, Tennessee. At the third Men & Masculinity Conference in 1977, some participants began to discuss the idea of a national profeminist organization, and by 1983 participants elected an 18-person council to collectively lead the National Organization for Men. In 1983 the retitled National Organization for Changing Men (NOCM) was officially announced at a press conference. NOCM held its first annual meeting at the eighth Men & Masculinity Conference in August 1983. In 1990, the organization voted to change its name to the National Organization for Men Against Sexism.

Throughout its existence, NOMAS has facilitated several journals and newsletters including the *Men's Studies Review* and *Changing Men*. The quarterly newsletter *Brother* has been its official publication since 1999. In addition to organizing and facilitating the Men & Masculinity Conferences, NOMAS also has 17 specialized task groups on the following topics: child custody, classism, eliminating racism, ending men's violence, fathering, GLBT affirmative, globalization, homophobia and heterosexism, men's health and mental health, men and prisons, men and spirituality, men's culture and art, men's studies, pornography and prostitution, profeminism, reproductive rights, and sexual harassment.

Ending Men's Violence—the organization's task force on domestic violence—facilitates a network of activism, information, and discussion analyzing men's violence as an intersection of social justice issues. Linking the three tenets of the organization's mission, NOMAS most importantly fosters discussion and activism around their core belief that all oppressions are linked through the institution of patriarchy. Reflecting that philosophy, NOMAS has staged its own "Campaign to End Homophobia" and has supported many antirape projects and efforts to end domestic violence, such as "Brother Peace: An International Day of Men Taking Action to End Men's Violence." The organization's alliance with feminism and its dedication to the cause of ending men's violence remains strong. The 37th National Conference on Men & Masculinity was presented in partnership with the National Coalition Against Domestic Violence, NCADV's 15th National Conference on Domestic Violence in Denver, Colorado, in July 2012.

Reflective of the rhetoric and ideology of the profeminist men's movement, NOMAS has always been an organization in which gay, bisexual, and heterosexually identified men have worked together toward the common goals of ending homophobia and building masculine brotherhood. However, both NOMAS and many other profeminist organizations and men's groups have always suffered critiques due to their participation from predominantly white, middle-class, educated men. By the late 1980s, NOMAS began to reposition race as an integral component to its critique of hegemonic masculinity. In 1992, antiracism was added as a major commitment of NOMAS, along with profeminism, gay-affirmation, and enhancing men's lives. Since then, more men of color have begun to participate as active members and leaders. The organization, however, continues to suffer criticism due to its void in scholarship and activism regarding economic oppression, as well as its lack of participation from working-class men and women.

During the 1970s and 1980s, many radical feminists criticized the profeminist men's movement's predominantly white, heterosexual, middle-class male composition, fearing that such a male-centered organization would reinforce hegemonic masculinity rather than challenge it. Likewise, other second-wave feminist critics believed that a men's movement focused on men's personal growth and healing would detract attention away from the critical issues presented by the women's liberation movement. While some feminists like Gloria Steinem have supported profeminism since the 1970s, other feminists like bell hooks began to show their support in the 1990s as NOMAS became more vociferous in its profeminist politics during the 1990s.

See also: Feminism and Domestic Abuse; History of U.S. Domestic Violence Developments, 1990s; Men's Efforts against Domestic Abuse

Further Reading

A brief history of NOMAS. (2008). NOMAS: National Organization for Men Against Sexism. Retrieved August 28, 2011, from http://www.nomas.org/history
Clatterbaugh, K. (1997). *Contemporary perspectives on masculinity: Men, women, and politics in modern society* (2nd ed.). Boulder, CO: Westview.
Doyle, J., & Femiano, S. (1999). The early history of the American Men's Studies Association and the evolution of men's studies. *American Men's Studies Association.* Retrieved August 28, 2011, from http://mensstudies.org/?page_id=5
Goldrick-Jones, A. (2011, April 30). Pessimism, paralysis, and possibility: Crisis-points in profeminism. *Journal of Men's Studies,* 9(3), 323–339.
Messner, M. A. (2000). *Politics of masculinities: Men in movements.* Walnut Creek, CA: AltaMira Press.
Newton, J. (2005). *From panthers to promise keepers: Rethinking the men's movement.* Lanham, MD: Rowman and Littlefield.
Statement of principles. (2008). NOMAS: National Organization for Men Against Sexism. Retrieved August 28, 2011, from http://www.nomas.org/principles
Steinem, G. (1992). Foreword. In K. L. Hagan (Ed.), *Women respond to the men's movement: A feminist collection* (pp. v–ix). San Francisco: Pandora.
36 years of NOMAS. (2008). NOMAS: National Organization for Men Against Sexism. Retrieved August 28, 2011, from http://www.nomas.org/node/35

Kera Lovell

NATIONAL ORGANIZATION FOR WOMEN (NOW)

NOW is an organization based in the United States that works to promote the equality of women through education, political action, and support programs. Among the many problems that NOW has worked to end are domestic violence, discrimination, and limited opportunities for women. NOW works through grassroots involvement, legislative lobbying, development of educational programming, and in collaboration with other groups that seek to eliminate other types of oppression.

NOW is the largest feminist organization in the United States, with an estimated contributing membership of a half million as of 2011. It was founded in 1966 by 28 women and men who were attendees of the Third National Conference of the Commission on the Status of Women. Among its founders were Betty Friedan, Shirley Chisholm, and Rev. Pauli Murray. The purpose of the organization is to secure political, professional, and educational equality for women. Identifying itself as a multi-issue progressive organization, NOW works in solidarity with other groups to end oppression of other sorts besides sexism, such as ageism, homophobia, and racism.

Through its 1966 Statement of Purpose, NOW laid out the early work of the organization. Written by Betty Friedan, the statement declared that the group saw that their purpose was to move from discussion and thinking about women's issues to taking concrete action. It also stated that the group saw their work as being a continuation of the strides that women had made in the last half-century, and that it was spurred on by a commitment to more fully realizing the equality of women in social, political, economic, and educational arenas. Other ambitions that the statement delineated included a commitment to changing social, religious, and media perceptions of women that denigrated women or denied them opportunities. Finally, NOW is committed to keep itself free of any political party affiliation.

A year after its founding, the 1967 NOW Bill of Rights addressed three particular political goals: the repeal of all abortion laws, the passage of the Equal Rights Amendment (ERA), and publicly funded child care.

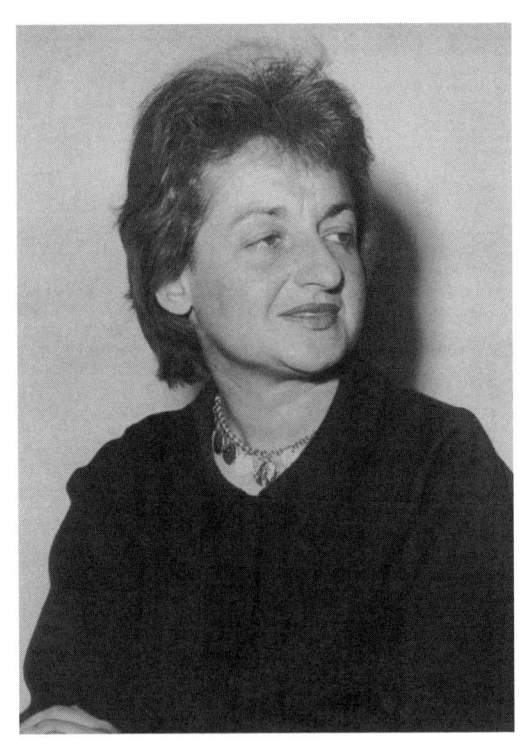

Betty Friedan, cofounder of the National Organization for Women. (Library of Congress)

Betty Friedan served as the organization's first president, from 1966 to 1970. From its beginning, NOW worked tirelessly to focus on legislative changes that would protect women's rights in the workplace. Among its early campaigns were a campaign to lobby the Equal Employment Opportunity Commission to enforce laws against discrimination in hiring ads and in listing jobs as segregated by sex; pressuring airlines to end practices that only allowed young, single female flight attendants and made them retire either at marriage or at age 32; and working with President Johnson, encouraging him to sign an Executive Order that banned federal contractors from sexual discrimination in the workplace.

The second president, Aileen Hernandez, helped extend NOW's focus beyond just middle-class women, and in particular she worked to include women of color as well. Under her leadership, NOW promoted campaigns that supported the role of women under affirmative action, such as during the summer of 1970 when the organization filed a blanket sex discrimination complaint with the Office of Federal Contract Compliance, which objected to 1,300 federal contractors not having yet filed affirmative action plans detailing plans for the hiring of women under affirmative action. The next month, NOW supported protests in 14 states in support of affirmative action mandates for the hiring of women, something the Secretary of Labor then went on to draft.

Other significant women in the women's movement that have a long history with NOW include Pauli Murray and Gloria Steinem.

In 1988, NOW drafted a Declaration of Sentiments that draws on the past 75 years of women working toward their equality and places this within the goals the organization has for equality within all of society. As the statement declares, "In 1923, on the seventy-fifth anniversary of the historic Seneca Falls convention, feminists led the demand for constitutional equality for women to win full justice under the law in order to end economic, educational, and political inequality." As the declaration states, women's justice is one part of a larger societal justice and part of a larger vision of a place where all have equal opportunities, rights, and are free of harm and violence. Another of the goals of NOW is to recognize the economic and social power that homemakers have had.

NOW aims for a grassroots leadership, and the membership meets once a year to determine its leadership. Made up of a large number of local chapters and organizations, the organization achieves its goals both through concerted focus on legislative lobbying and through grassroots group efforts to talk to voters and hold protests in support of issues and causes.

Currently, NOW identifies six core issues that it aims to address: reproductive rights and access to abortion, violence against women, constitutional equality, promoting diversity, lesbian rights, and economic justice. NOW also deals with partner issues including immigration reform, educational reform, Title IX, promoting woman-friendly workplaces, and women in the military.

Today there are 550 NOW chapters in all 50 states and the District of Columbia.

See also: Feminism and Domestic Abuse; Nonprofit Organizations; Women's Rights Movement

Further Reading

Banaszak, L. (2005). *The U.S. women's movement in global perspective*. Lanham, MD: Rowman and Littlefield.
Basrakso, M. (2004). *Governing NOW: Grassroots activism in the National Organization for Women*. Ithaca, NY: Cornell University Press.
Laughlin, K., &. Castledine, J. (2010). *Breaking the wave: Women, their organizations, and feminism 1945–1985.* New York, NY: Routledge.
NOW website: http://www.now.org

Andrea J. Dickens

NATIONAL TEEN DATING ABUSE HELPLINE

The National Teen Dating Abuse Helpline is a free, confidential service provided by the National Council on Family Violence and sponsored by the U.S. Department of Justice, Liz Claiborne Inc., Verizon, and others. The National Council on Family Violence collaborates with the leading national teen dating violence organization Break the Cycle for the most current information on teen dating violence.

The Helpline is the direct service provider behind Loveisrespect.org, launched in February 2007. The helpline is a 24-hour resource designed for teens and young adults to discuss their concerns with their dating relationships, abuse, safety planning, and access to resources for dating violence. Youth can access The Helpline by phone, text, or online chat offering real-time, one-on-one support, information, and advocacy to those experiencing dating violence. The Helpline is also a resource for friends, family, teachers, clergy, law enforcement, and service providers to discuss their questions about teen dating violence or learn how to support a young adult dealing with dating violence.

Loveisrespect.org is the access point to the live chat feature of the National Teen Dating Abuse Helpline. The site carefully explains that this feature is not a public chat room but a private one-on-one session with a peer advocate that is confidential. This is an important message now that the dating violence helpline offers more technologically advanced ways of accessing support. Loveisrespect.org also conveys to youth that no question is too crazy or embarrassing—nothing is off limits.

Loveisrespect.org offers educational information about the basics of dating violence, definitions of abuse, how to help young adults dealing with relationship abuse, and how they can take action to bring dating violence information to their peer groups and politicians. Lesbian, gay, bisexual, transgender, and queer/questioning youth experience dating violence at the same frequency as heterosexual youth. Loveisrespect.org honors and respects this fact by educating youth on LGBTQ relationship violence on the website. The website discusses the additional challenges that LGBTQ youth may face in dealing with relationship abuse and that The Helpline is a supportive and understanding resource for LGBTQ youth needing to discuss concerns about their relationship.

In addition to the basic information, Loveisrespect.org has interactive quizzes for youth to assess their overall relationship. Once the relationship quiz is over, the website offers some information regarding the results of the quiz and what steps the individual may want to explore next. Quizzes available are "Am I a Good Boy/Girlfriend?," "Healthy Relationship Quiz," and "Do Abusers Change?" This tool allows a young person to gather direct information about his or her relationship without the fear of contacting someone directly. Resources like the quizzes are important for youth as they serve as another alternative to access information. The more alternatives available for them to gather information, the more likely they are to continue to assess their relationship and eventually reach out for help.

Break the Cycle has compiled detailed information pertaining to the legal protections per state in the United States for youth experiencing dating violence. Youth and adults can access this information at loveisrespect.org. The Legal Help section details the differences between the civil and criminal justice systems and the process for obtaining an order of protection, information teens have historically had little access to. Since youth are typically concerned about the support they would receive from police interventions, Loveisrespect.org outlines the types of support law enforcement can offer to them and gives practical tips about what their role can be in working with law enforcement. The site encourages youth to take the officers' name and badge number, ask them to take pictures of injuries, show any threatening text messages, let the officers listen to violent messages on voice mail, and other details that are helpful when law enforcement intervention is necessary. The Legal Help section also teaches youth how to document the abuse, which is helpful if they move forward with an application for a restraining order.

The National Teen Dating Abuse Helpline is an amazing resource for youth and their supporters in dealing with relationship abuse and serves as the central point of information for domestic violence providers working with youth. Loveisrespect.org encourages action steps to educate about and prevent dating violence in our society.

See also: Break the Cycle; Crisis Lines; Teen Victims

Further Reading

Love Is Not Abuse: http://loveisnotabuse.com
Love Is Respect: http://www.loveisrespect.org
The Hotline: http://www.thehotline.org/is-this-abuse/teens-and-dating-abuse/

Kera Lovell

NATIVE AMERICANS AND DOMESTIC ABUSE
Introduction

The lack of representative statistical data and the legacy of governmental policies that deterred justice from taking place are the present reality for Native American women. Domestic violence is a long-standing and pervasive issue in the Native American populations. Native American women experience purposeful coercive behaviors of emotional/mental and psychological abuse, sexual assault as well as social isolation, intimidation, and deprivation at a rate equal to or greater than all other race or ethnic groups in the United States. The persistence of domestic violence in the Native American population is generational and unduly burdened with bureaucratic, institutional, and political inadequacies, which highlights a continued lack of social and political will to address the issue.

Defining Native American

Native Americans are the indigenous people of what is presently known as the United States. The term "Native Americans" incorporates hundreds of culturally distinct nations into one category, and this disguises the distinctiveness of the groups. There are approximately 330 federally recognized nations in the continuous 48 states. There are numerous nations that lack federal recognition and 23 that are only recognized by the state in which they live.

As of the 2000 U.S. Census, the Native American and Alaskan Native population was a little over 4.3 million. Of this total, approximately 2.4 million self-identified as being only Native American or Alaska Native, while 1.6 million self-identified as Native American and Alaska Native and one or more additional racial/ethnic group. Native American populations are unevenly distributed across the United States.

Over half of Native Americans live on reservations, and a little over 50 percent of the Native American populations are made up of five nations: (1) Cherokee (370,000); (2) Navajo (225,000); (3) Sioux (107,000); (4) Chippewa (105,000); and (5) Choctaw (86,000). States with high concentrations of Native Americans are New Mexico, South Dakota, Oklahoma, and Montana.

Native Americans and Alaska Natives are frequently aggregated into one group. However, these groups have very different lived experiences because Alaska Natives are organized as a shareholder in a regional and village corporation, while Native Americans are commonly located on or near a reservation system. Native Americans and Alaska Native women as a group experience some of the highest rates of violence as well as sexual, physical, and emotional/mental abuse in the United States.

Domestic Violence Statistics

In a national sample, Tjaden and Thoennes (2000) found that Native Americans' (n = 88) lifetime prevalence rates for physical assault was 30.7 percent, for rape 15.9 percent, and stalking 10.2 percent. These rates were double that of the white population (n = 6,452), which had experienced lifetime rape (7.7 percent) and stalking (4.7 percent) rates. The lifetime rate of physical assault for whites was about a third less (21.3 vs. 30.7 percent) when compared to Native Americans. In 2006, Tjaden and Thoennes found that lifetime rate of rape for Native American (n=88) was highest of all race/ethnic groups at 34.1 percent or almost double that of whites' (n = 6,217) rate of 17.9 percent. Native American women described the rape/sexual assault offender 34 percent of time as an acquaintance and 25 percent of the time as an intimate partner or family member (Southwest Center for Law and Policy Statistics, 2005).

Characteristics of the Native American domestic violence victim, who is predominately female, have been noted. The most common of any age category of race/ethnic group are Native American victims aged 18–24. This group accounts for approximately one-third of all Native American violent crime victims. Violent victimization of this teen and young adult group is about one in four. There is a rural and urban difference in violent Native American violent crime rates. Even though about 40 percent of the Native American population lives in rural areas, the highest rates of violent crime occur in urban areas. The difference is 207 per 1,000 for urban areas and 89 per 1,000 for rural areas. The perpetrator is different compared to all other race/ethnic groups, because the offender is more likely to be a member of a different race/ethnic group. In addition, the violent and nondomestic violent perpetrator being under the influence of alcohol is common. Based on data from 1992 to 2001, Native American victims of nondomestic violence crime reported alcohol being a factor 60 percent of the time, and alcohol was a factor 61 percent of the time in domestic violence incidents.

Intimate Partner Violence

Native American estimated rates of intimate and family violence are similar to all other race/ethnic groups (i.e., 9 percent). Other research conducted by the Centers for Disease Control (2008) suggests that Native Americans/Alaska Natives have the highest rates of intimate partner victimization at 11.1 per 1,000, which is double the rates of black women (5/1,000) and white women (4/1,000). However, it should be noted that Native American researchers as well as the Centers for Disease Control claim there is no reliable data in regard to intimate partner violence in Native American/Alaska Native populations.

The data presented above is mostly at the population level and does not include subgroup differences within Native American nations. There have been a limited number of national studies examining domestic violence that include Native Americans as a group. The sample sizes of the Native Americans in domestic violence research are small and commonly lack statistical rigor. All of these domestic violence estimates for Native Americans should be viewed critically and with caution. It is held by many advocates and researchers that the official statistics are substantially low estimates. Collectively, the nonrepresentative small sample of such a vast and distinct population necessitates a study specific to Native American domestic violence that collects data across the hundreds of Native American nations.

Problems with the Data

There are two main problems with data on Native Americans. The first is that aggregating 330 distinct groups is potentially misleading because of subgroup differences. It is plausible that there is considerable variation in domestic violence rates due to demographic, social, cultural, and/or environmental factors as well as considerable intertribal differences among the hundreds of Native American nations. Tribal, nation-specific, or even community-level data is presently lacking, making it difficult to determine the domestic violence rates among nations. Further, basic information or data is lacking on individual nations. Also, the lack of data specific to Native Americans does not allow for an understanding of the magnitude of the domestic violence problem, and it impedes policy decisions as well as the allocation of state and federal funds to address the issue.

Federal Policies over Jurisdiction

Federal policies have a long history of hindering the investigation and prosecution of domestic violence directed at Native Americans. There are five policies that have resulted in federal, state, and criminal courts disregarding cases of domestic violence involving Native American women: (1) Major Crimes Act of 1885; (2) Public Law 83-280 of 1953; (3) Indian Civil Rights Act of 1968; (4) the 1978 court case *Oliphant v. Suquamish Indian Tribe*; and (5) the Violence Against Women Act of 1994 (Title IX, Section 904(a)(1)(2) (2000; 2006).

Federal intervention into tribal law dates back to 1883 in the court case *Ex parte Crow Dog* (109 US 556). Crow Dog was alleged to have killed another Native on reservation land and was tried in Tribal Court. He was found guilty and under traditional Sioux tribal punishment was required to pay restitution. The U.S. government, however, tried Crow Dog for murder, found him guilty, and sentenced him to death by hanging. Crow Dog appealed his case to the Supreme Court, which held that unless authorized by Congress, the U.S. government had no jurisdiction over the case. Following this, in 1885, Congress passed the Major Crimes Act, 18 U.S.C. § 1153, which mandated that seven major crimes (murder, manslaughter, rape, assault with intent to commit murder, arson, burglary, and larceny) committed in Indian Country be adjudicated in the federal judicial system. This act placed the responsibility for investigating and prosecuting major crimes under the domain of the federal government and deterred tribes from prosecuting and punishing tribal members for these crimes.

In 1953, Congress enacted Public Law 83-280. This law transferred jurisdiction from the federal to state governments (California, Minnesota, Nebraska, Oregon, Wisconsin, and Alaska) in Indian Country. Under Public Law 83-820, the Native American nations in the states listed above had limited recourse for gaining control over creating their own judicial systems. There were several exceptions when the nation successfully demonstrated that they already had reasonable law enforcement capabilities. Public Law 83-280 was an unfunded mandate. Like the Major Crimes Act, tribal governments under P.L. 83-280 states were deterred from prosecuting and punishing tribal members for major crimes. The difference was that jurisdiction switched from the federal government to the state governments and the states lacked the resources to investigate and prosecute major crimes such as sexual assault and others.

In 1968, the Indian Civil Rights Act (ICRA—25 U.S.C. 1302) was enacted. The goal of this legislation was to have the Bill of Rights integrated into tribal governments. The ICRA allowed for tribal governments to investigate, prosecute, and sentence major crimes offenders. However, tribal court sentencing was limited to incarceration for no more than six months and a fine of no more than $500. The ICRA did not alter the federal or states' jurisdiction over major crimes. These provisions made it less likely for tribes to prosecute major crimes.

Another jurisdictional barrier was handed down through the U.S. Supreme Court in 1978 with the court case *Oliphant v. Suquamish Indian Tribe* (435 U.S. 191, 98 S.Ct. 1011, 55 L.Ed.2d 209). Mark Oliphant, a non-Native who was living on the Port Madison Indian Reservation of the Suquamish Tribe, was arrested for allegedly assaulting a tribal officer and resisting arrest. Mark, through his lawyers, claimed he was not under tribal jurisdiction because he was not Native American. In a 6-2 decision, the Supreme Court ruled in his favor, and this court case limited tribal jurisdiction to only Native members who have allegedly committed a crime on a reservation.

In 1994, the Congress passed the Violence Against Women Act (VAWA) of 1994. It was part of the Violent Crime Control and Law Enforcement Act of 1994. The goal of the VAWA was to end violence against women, and it has been reauthorized twice, in 2000 and 2005. The act authorized the National Institute of Justice in partnership with the Department of Justice to conduct research on identifying the factors that result in victimizations, improving response, and the types of violence (e.g., domestic violence, sexual assault, stalking, murder, etc.) directed at American Indian and Alaska Native women in Indian Country. Collectively, these five policies have resulted in federal, state, and criminal courts disregarding cases of domestic violence involving Native American women.

The lack of representative statistical data and the legacy of governmental policies have deterred justice from taking place, and this is the present reality for Native American women. Compounding the problem are a lack of resources and the bureaucratic obstacles of determining federal, state, and tribal jurisdiction. The complicated jurisdiction issues are a considerable deterrent to law enforcement and to attorneys pursuing a domestic violence case on behalf of Native American women and maintaining their basic human rights. As a result, domestic violence is a long-standing and pervasive issue in the Native American populations, and without the social and political will to address it will continue to be so.

See also: Alaska Natives and Domestic Abuse; Tribal Law and Justice Act; U.S. Government Responses to Domestic Violence; Violence Against Women Act (VAWA)

Further Reading

Bureau of Justice Statistics. (1999). American Indians and crime. Washington, DC: BJS, http://bjs.ojp.usdoj.gov/content/pub/pdf/aic.pdf

Chester, B., Robin, R., Koss, M., Lopez, J., & Goldman, D. (1994). Grandmother dishonored: Violence against women by male partners in American Indian communities. *Violence and Victims, 9*(3), 249–258.

Mending the Sacred Hoop: http://www.mshoop.org/

Murphy, S. B., Risley-Curtiss, C., & Gerdes, K. (2003). American Indian women and domestic violence: The lived experience. *Journal of Human Behavior in the Social Environment, 7,* 159–181.

National Sexual Violence Resource Center: http://www.nsvrc.org/

Native American Circle: http://www.nativeamericancircle.org/

Perry, S. (2004). American Indians and Crime, Bureau of Justice Statistics. Washington, DC: U.S. Department of Justice.

Smith, Andrea (2005). *Conquest: Sexual violence and American Indian genocide.* Cambridge, MA: South End Press.

Southwest Center for Law and Policy: http://www.swclap.org/

Southwest Center for Law and Policy. (2005). Statistics. Available at http://www.swclap.org/statistics.htm

Tjaden, P., & Thoennes, N. (2000). *Extent, nature, and consequences of rape victimization: Findings from the National Violence Against Women Survey*, Rep. No. NCJ181867. Rockville, MD: Office of Justice Programs, National Institute of Justice.

Tjaden, P., & Thoennes, N. (2006). *Extent, nature, and consequences of rape victimization: Findings from the National Violence Against Women Survey*, Rep. No. NCJ 210346. Rockville, MD: Office of Justice Programs, National Institute of Justice.

Wahab, S., & Olson, L. (2004). Intimate partner violence and sexual assault in Native American communities. *Trauma Violence Abuse, 5,* 353–366.

Andrew Hund

NEWS MEDIA AND DOMESTIC ABUSE

News media plays an essential role in shaping public opinion. They not only provide information but also influence peoples' attitudes when interpreting social events. Before the 1980s, few news media reports dealt with domestic violence, as the topic was long considered a personal affair. Since then, feminists have campaigned against patriarchal attitudes and have helped engage the news media to turn domestic violence from a private to a public matter. They have been partially successful in their endeavor. News media was criticized for inaccurately reflecting on the topic, for reinforcing stereotypes, and for misleading the public by distorting facts through under- or overrepresentation. It has been suggested that media-led reinforcement of gender-based stereotypes may even be a contributing factor to why the problem persists. Much improvement has been made in these areas.

Studies have shown that the wider public continues to perceive domestic violence as being generated by individuals within the context of their specific relationship. It is regarded as an isolated conflict that victim and perpetrator are responsible to solve. Its epidemic sociocultural character is largely ignored, and therefore domestic violence is not identified as a problem requiring a public policy response. Berns (2004) maintains that news media and other forms of media (such as popular magazines, television, and music) all reinforce this perception.

Under- and Overreporting

Crime stories form a substantial portion of our daily news. In fact, Kappeler and Potter (2004) maintain that 95 percent of Americans receive all of their information about crime and criminal justice from the daily news media. However, the media create a distorted image of crime, and particularly violent crime, because it is considered newsworthy. Hence, violent crimes account for over 60 percent of crime stories, although they account for less than 10 percent of crime statistics. Studies repeatedly find that crimes consumers read the most about are crimes they are least likely to experience (Kappeler & Potter, 2004). This is referred to as "the law of opposites." News media reporting on domestic violence adheres to this law; it is both under- and overreported.

Standard cases of domestic violence are rarely deemed newsworthy and remain underreported because they are such a common occurrence. Domestic violence accounts for 25 percent of all violent crime; however, only 8 percent of newspaper articles that relate to violent crimes cover incidences of domestic violence (Carlyle, Slater, & Chakroff, 2008).

On the other hand, domestic abuse cases receive excessive media attention if the extent of physical injuries is significant or the incident is fatal. Almost 60 percent of domestic violence stories presented in the news media are cases of fatal violence, although statistically they account for less than 1 percent of cases reported to the police. In over 95 percent of newspaper articles on domestic violence, the type of domestic violence described is physical. Verbal, emotional, sexual, and passive abuse through neglect or economic deprivation go largely uncovered by the news media (Carlyle et al., 2008).

This under- and overrepresentation of different forms of domestic violence may shape news media consumers' opinion in a number of ways. It may create the impression that only severe physical abuse constitutes domestic violence. Victims of nonphysical abuse may be led to believe that they are not being victimized and that protection is therefore not available. Perpetrators of nonphysical abuse may continue their behavior falsely convinced that it is appropriate.

The overrepresentation of fatal cases may, however, be beneficial to victims. It may alert them to the significantly heightened homicide risk when leaving an abusive relationship and may therefore result in victims seeking help to create a safety plan. News coverage of the O. J. Simpson case, for instance, resulted in an increase in calls to domestic violence crisis lines, thus potentially providing for greater assistance to victimized persons.

Female Victims and Male Perpetrators

According to Carll (2005), women are more likely to be victims of domestic violence than men. Ninety-two percent of domestic abuse is committed by men against women. This is fairly consistent with news media reporting, where in 80 percent of news items the victim is female and the perpetrator male. What can be considered problematic, however, is that women are often not portrayed as innocent victims. Subtle language techniques may be used to convey the message that victims are at least partially to blame for what has happened to them.

Passive language is often used to describe an incident—"she was beaten" rather than "he beat her," which portrays the incident as if it had no perpetrator. Additionally, news media items regularly contain reasons for why women have become victims. Excuses are made for male violence by referring to the victim's infidelity, disobedience, or otherwise irritating behavior (e.g., nagging). Extenuating circumstances are often mentioned in the story headline. If domestic abuse was ongoing, the news media question why the victim had not left the relationship. Unaddressed, however, are the most common factors that compel women to continue an abusive relationship and are often a result of the abuse—economic dependence, exhaustion, and low self-esteem (Berns, 2004).

White males (especially celebrities) who admit to domestic abuse are often framed by news media in a "sin and redemption" narrative. They are portrayed as victims of obsessive affection who need counseling rather than as perpetrators of criminal activity. By presenting offenders as victims, their culpability is diminished and the victim is blamed for the violence. It also enhances the public's perception of domestic violence as isolated incidences of individual pathology (Berns, 2004).

The amount of personal information provided about victim and offender influences how cases of male violence against women are perceived by the consumer. The more an individual is personalized, the more newspaper readers express empathy and the less they tend to assign blame. Generally, female victims are less personalized than male victims, which reduces empathy for female victims and increases the tendency to blame them. Tolerating and participating in domestic violence is easier when victims are depersonalized (Anastasio & Costa, 2004). If the news media do not provide personal information about victims of domestic abuse, they aid in normalizing the behavior and in exacerbating gender inequality. On the other hand, news media find it difficult to personalize victims, in particular those who have suffered from domestic abuse, as they are often unwilling to share the details of their experience with reporters due to fear, shame, or other emotions.

Overall, it is the female's behavior that may be scrutinized by the media, not the actions of the male perpetrator. Focusing on the victim shifts culpability away from the offender, and the victim is presented as being at least partially responsible for what happened. The common preconception that it is the victim's responsibility to stop the violence by ending the relationship is reinforced. The news media may then allow the wider public to blame the victim. Such a perspective may permit perpetrators to justify and continue their abusive behavior.

Male Victims and Female Perpetrators

In the past decade, the news media discourse has partly shifted to emphasize that males are not only perpetrators but also victims of domestic violence. Some argue that male overrepresentation in offender statistics of domestic violence persists because the criminal justice system discriminates against men. Females are believed to be just as violent as men but seldom held accountable. Others dismiss this "iceberg theory" as an antifeminist sentiment attempting to sustain male dominance by clouding the reality of domestic abuse. Although men are victims of domestic violence too, research has revealed that many men have been perpetrators before they were victimized. Compared to women, male victims are less likely to suffer serious injury or to be victimized repeatedly. Spousal homicide is usually a rare female response to long-term male abuse and markedly overrepresented in the news media. Between 1976 and 2005, intimate partners were responsible for 30 percent of fatal attacks on female victims and 5 percent on male victims. According to the "law of opposites," female-perpetrated domestic violence receives disproportionately more news coverage than male domestic violence because it is a rare occurrence and thus considered of interest. Especially, female spousal homicide receives front-page exposure. Such overreporting leaves the public with the impression that female domestic abuse, and in particular spousal homicide, occurs more often than it actually does.

When the news media portray women as perpetrators of domestic violence, females are often demonized and depicted as evil, mad, and incomprehensible. Corresponding rhetoric may be used in the headline—for example, "Wife Blasted Spouse with Shotgun." Excuses may not be made for female offenders as is often done for male perpetrators of domestic abuse. Instead it is stressed that the female offender is breaking not only legal norms but also gender norms by emphasizing her femininity. Labels like "black widow" or "femme fatale" are used. News media discuss in great detail female offenders' appearance, demeanor, and conduct as wives. The more feminine and adjusted the perpetrator, the more empathy is expressed. Conversely, a less feminine appearance, as in the case of Aileen Wuornos, renders little empathy from the news media. Stressing unfeminine appearances is one way of dealing with the challenge that female violence presents for conventional thoughts about gendered behavior (Meyers, 1997; Carll, 2005). It is important to note, however, that improvements have been made. News media are constantly improving, and the wealth of more feminist-friendly media outlets, like the *Huffington Post*, have helped address these issues.

Framing Domestic Abuse

News media do not only provide information; they influence public perceptions of a subject matter by providing analysis of causes and effects presented within episodic or thematic frames. Episodic frames are often used by the news media when presenting crime stories. They concentrate on individual incidents and specific characters, motivations, and dispositions of offender and victim. Thematic frames, on the other hand, include social context and provide explanations that point to situational forces behind individual incidents. For example, official statistics on victimization rates are presented or wider societal consequences of certain behaviors are explained. If an issue is repeatedly presented through episodic frames, public opinion is shaped in a way that attributes responsibility for the matter to the individual and not to the community, whereas thematic framing has the opposite effect (Berns, 2004).

Anastasio and Costa (2004) found that in almost 90 percent of newspaper reports on domestic violence, cases are presented using episodic framing focusing on isolated incidences without addressing social dynamics that perpetuate the problem. For example, in 75 percent of domestic violence cases, the perpetrator is under the influence of alcohol and/or drugs. However, alcohol or drugs are mentioned as a factor in only 8 percent of newspaper articles (Anastasio & Costa, 2004). It is argued by some that alcohol and drug abuse is underreported because it may be perceived as excusing violent behavior. However, it does constitute major underreporting of a significant contributing cause to domestic violence and neglects that alcohol and drug abuse may amplify the brutality of an incident. If the news media minimize the role alcohol and drugs play, they also avoid discussing domestic violence from a public health perspective and subsequently a thematic frame.

The few articles that use thematic framing most commonly refer to public policy responses and laws in place to address domestic violence. A study by Anastasio and Costa (2004) found that only 5 percent of newspaper articles on domestic violence provide information for victims by referring to phone hotlines, websites, women's shelters or refuges, and counseling services. Generally, ignoring these services reinforces the stereotype that domestic abuse is not widespread and rather an isolated incident than an epidemic sociocultural issue.

Summary

Although feminist movements benefit from news media exposure of domestic violence in turning domestic abuse from a private into a public matter, the way news media portray female victims and offenders may cause problematic public perceptions. A number of media techniques may still convey the erroneous message that domestic violence is not a serious crime, not widespread, and that female victims are to a degree responsible for their victimization.

Although advocates have long critiqued news media for its coverage of domestic abuse, in the 1990s and 2000s some began to work with media to help address their concerns more proactively. Some created toolkits for media in how to address victims and offenders (see Weller, n.d.). The National Center on Domestic and Sexual Violence features a number of articles and guides on the topic as well, available at http://www.ncdsv.org/publications_media.html.

See also: Female Perpetrators; Films and Domestic Abuse; Male Victims of Domestic Abuse; Music and Domestic Abuse

Further Reading

Anastasio, P., & Costa, D. (2004). Twice hurt: How newspaper coverage may reduce empathy and engender blame for female victims of crime. *Sex Roles, 51*, 535–542.

Berns, N. (2004). *Framing the victim: Domestic violence, media, and social problems.* New York: Aldine de Gruyter.

Boyle, K. (2005). *Media violence: Gendering the debates.* London, England: Sage.

Carll, E. K. (2005). Violence and women: News coverage of victims and perpetrators. In E. Cole & J. H. Daniel (Eds.), *Featuring females: Feminist analyses of media.* Washington, D.C: American Psychological Association.

Carlyle, K. E., Slater, M. D., & Chakroff, J. L. (2008). Newspaper coverage of intimate partner violence: Skewing representation of risk. *Journal of Communication, 58*, 168–186.

Jewkes, Y. (2011). *Media and crime.* London, UK: Sage.

Kappeler, V., & Potter, G. (2004). *The mythology of crime and criminal justice* (4th ed.). Long Grove, IL: Waveland Press.

Meyers, M. (1994). News of battering. *Journal of Communication, 44*(2), 47–63.

Meyers, M. (1997). *News coverage of violence against women: Engendering blame.* Thousand Oaks, CA: Sage.

Taylor, C. A., & Sorenson, S. B. (2005). Community-based norms about intimate partner violence: Putting attributions of fault and responsibility into context. *Sex Roles, 53*, 573–589.

Weller, C. (n.d.). Covering domestic violence: A guide for informed media reporting in Nevada. Retrieved August 18, 2012, from http://www.nnadv.org/pdfs/Press_Room/Covering%20Domestic%20Violence-Media%20Guide.pdf

Antje Deckert

NONGOVERNMENTAL ORGANIZATIONS (NGOs) AND DOMESTIC ABUSE

Nongovernmental Organizations (NGOs) have been immersed in global and domestic politics for quite a long time. With the wide variety of NGOs that currently exist and the enormity of issues they cover, these organizations have become formidable forces to reckon with in terms of agent- and grassroots-oriented programs and initiatives. Domestic abuse is one of the issues that has captured the attention of many NGOs, especially when considered both as a human rights and health issue. Regardless of issues of performance, representation, accountability, and legitimacy that they are have to deal with internally, NGOs in general (and those taking on issues of domestic abuse in particular) have been effective in their campaigns because they possess "the power to persuade," which makes it easy for governments, international organizations, and global leaders to listen to and act on their concerns. This is because they have the expertise and potential to represent the diverse interests of society. The power NGOs possess is enhanced by the fact that they are mostly nonprofit organizations advocating crucial policy changes. This is why the NGO position on domestic abuse remains useful.

The term "nongovernmental organization" was coined around the time the United Nations (UN) was formed in 1945. The main rationale was to distinguish private from intergovernmental organizations (IGOs) such as the UN itself. NGOs are thought to have been in existence centuries ago. For instance, in 1910, 130 international groups formed a body called the Union of International Associations that was an umbrella body meant to coordinate all the affairs of the member groups.

While it is difficult to pin down precisely due to the term's ambiguous usage, a definition of NGO popularized by the United Nations is "any international organization which is not established by intergovernmental agreement" (Ahmed & Potter, 2006, p. 9). Simply put, they are NGOs when they do not receive the backing or endorsement of any particular government or (inter)governmental institution, and are nonprofit in most cases. The United Nations in particular has ensured that NGOs continually play an effective role in international politics. Article 71 of the 1945 UN Charter formalized this engagement. The UN Non-Governmental Liaison Service (UN-NGLS), for instance, is an interagency program of the United Nations mandated to promote and develop constructive relations between the United Nations and civil society organizations. This relationship empowers these organizations to play instrumental roles in their specific issue areas. NGOs are sometimes used synonymously with interest and pressure groups, especially when their operations and activism are mostly focused on domestic rather than international issues.

NGO work related to the United Nations comprises a number of activities including information dissemination, awareness raising, development education, policy advocacy, joint operational projects, and providing services and technical expertise. The usual critique is that most of the NGOs that work closely with the United Nations are often Western (those in the global North) that already have broad-based support and resources at their disposal. But the Committee on Non-Governmental Organizations, which is a standing committee of the Economic and Social Council (ECOSOC). was established by the council in 1946 to ensure equitable geographical representation of the organizations the United Nations works closely with. Representatives on this committee are mostly chosen from all the continents of the world—five members from African states; four members from Asian states; two members from Eastern European states; four members from Latin American and Caribbean states; and four members from Western European and other states.

The issues that NGOs deal with include human rights, environmental, social justice, empowerment, poverty alleviation, and social development, among others. The issues tackled by NGOs are wide-ranging, but their role can be categorized into three main components: implementer, catalyst, and partner. In the implementer role, NGOs are concerned with gathering resources to provide needed goods and services aimed at addressing a particular need. Some of these organizations can be contracted by governments to do this work. The catalyst role is where NGOs inform, direct, and/or instigate a particular course of action. The catalyst role ensures that the issues deemed pertinent by the organization maintain the attention of all relevant stakeholders. In their role as partners, NGOs engage in "mutually beneficial" relationships with a combination of governments, corporations, donors, and private individuals to deliver needed programs and initiatives. In view of these roles, NGOs can be service driven, empowerment driven, participation oriented, or charitable in nature.

There are a plethora of NGOs acronyms that have emerged due to changes to the nature, scope, and goals of these organizations. The names include Nongovernmental Development Organization (NGDO); Government-Operated NGOs (GONGOs); Social Change Organizations (SCOs); Transnational NGO (TNGO); Technical Assistance NGO (TANGO); Quasi-Autonomous Non-Governmental Organizations (QUANGOs); Business-Friendly International NGO (BINGO); Civil Society Organization (CSO); Donor Organized NGO (DONGO); International NGO (INGO); and Environmental NGO (ENGO), among others. These acronyms symbolize both the heterogeneity and ambiguity embedded in the term "nongovernmental organization."

NGOs that specifically deal with domestic abuse issues are many, ranging from domestic-based to international organizations. Some of them include End Violence Against Women International, National Coalition Against Domestic Violence, Amnesty International, Incite!, Women Thrive, Vital Voices, Equality Now, and Break the Cycle, among many others. Like every other organization, NGOs do have challenges—most of which can make one question their legitimacy and ability to succeed at their diverse mandates. Particularly, the notion that NGOs possess the "magic bullet" to deal with diverse societal issues (including domestic abuse) has waned over time. However, these organizations contain the administrative machinery and capability necessary to address grassroots issues that are usually overlooked in the official governmental and intergovernmental relations.

See also: Amnesty International; End Violence Against Women International; Equality Now; Nonprofit Organizations; The United Nations and Domestic Abuse; Vital Voices; Women Thrive Worldwide

Further Reading

Ahmed, S., & Potter D. (2006). *NGOs in international politics.* West Hartford, CT: Kumarian Press.

Brinkerhoff, J. M., Smith, S. C., & Teegen, H. (Eds.). (2007). *NGOs and the millennium development goals: Citizen action to reduce poverty.* New York, NY: Palgrave Macmillan.

Karns, M. P. (2012). Nongovernmental organization (NGO). *Encyclopædia Britannica Online Academic Edition.* Encyclopædia Britannica Inc. Retrieved January 6, 2012, from http://www.britannica.com/EBchecked/topic/759090/nongovernmental-organization

Lewis, D. (2007). *The management of non-governmental development organizations* (2nd ed.). London, England: Routledge.

NGO Branch, Department of Economic and Social Affairs, http://csonet.org/
UN Non-Governmental Liaison Service (UN-NGLS), http://www.un-ngls.org/spip.php?page=article_s&id_article=796

Nathan Andrews

NONPROFIT ORGANIZATIONS AND DOMESTIC ABUSE

Nonprofit organizations are tax-exempt. There are more than two million nonprofits or nongovernmental organizations (NGOs) in the United States today, most of which were formed in the last three decades. Other countries have seen a similar rapid growth of nonprofits/NGOs. For instance, before the fall of communism in Russia, there were only a few NGOs; now, there are at least 65,000 in the country. In Kenya, approximately 240 new NGOs are created each year.

Today, it is nonprofit organizations that provide the bulk of direct services to domestic violence victims in the United States. Nonprofits operate virtually all of the domestic violence centers in which crisis lines, shelters, and outreach services are located. Likewise, most of the prevention and social change work in the field is coming out of nonprofits.

Some critics have maintained that there is a glut of nonprofits/NGOs. Instead of helping victims, these groups compete against one another for scarce resources—namely, funding. Another criticism, made largely by those on the political left, is that nonprofits and NGOs are doing the work the government should be doing. On the political right, a frequent criticism is that nonprofits or NGOs experience "mission creep"; that is, they do work that strays from the stated mission.

Some have gone so far as to argue that there is a nonprofit-industrial complex, like the military-industrial complex first described by President Dwight D. Eisenhower. The nonprofit-industrial complex has been defined as "a set of symbiotic relationships that link political and financial technologies of state and owning class control with surveillance over public political ideology, including and especially emergent progressive and leftist social movements" (Rodriguez, 2007, p. 8).

Critics refer to nonprofits as a "shadow state" that performs the functions that government should be doing. This absolves the government from those tasks, thereby allowing them to spend funding on other things. Those other things, according to critics, often involve expanding the military and have little to do with helping people. Further, nonprofits are not required to disclose their actions publicly in the same way that government entities are expected to. This lack of transparency may result in victims not knowing what type of help is available and where to acquire it, and it may result in the public having little knowledge of these issues.

Additionally, the result of the move away from government services and into the nonprofit realm has served to professionalize nonprofit social service entities. Although professionalization can be good, it can also result in more bureaucratized services. One particular concern is that laws often prohibit nonprofit employees from politically lobbying, or even from taking stances on political issues. Thus, as Gilmore (2007) explained, "the shadow state, then, is real but without significant political clout, forbidden by law to advocate for systemic change, and bound by public rules and nonprofit charters to stick to its mission or get out of business and suffer legal consequences if it strays along the way" (pp. 45–46). Some have gone so far as to argue that nonprofits run like factories, with the same hierarchies and focus on efficiency.

As nonprofits do not generally obtain all of their funding from government sources (some may receive none at all), there is stiff competition to acquire financial backing. Thus, nonprofits seek to cultivate donors, for which they must compete with other nonprofits doing similar work and/or work in their geographic region. Many nonprofits rely largely on grants to finance their work. Yet grants are not a stable source of funding, given that they are only for specific work during a designated time period and often are not renewable. Funders often place constraints on the kind of work a nonprofit can do with their monies, which sometimes results in inadequate service to victims. Major endowments are increasingly conservative, such that many are not looking for creative or innovative practices but instead for "best practices." Most funders discourage even semiradical activism that would call attention to broader systems of inequality that result in abuse.

Because they are unable to be politically active, scholars have argued that employees at domestic violence services do not look at broader issues of inequalities, nor at the role of feminism in challenging them. Durazo (2007) explained, "the nonprofit system ... supports the professionalization of activism rather than a model of everyday activism" (p. 205). Further, funders "are not interested in funding the much slower work of base building, which takes years and years to do. Consequently, nonprofits become short-term-goal oriented, even if they did not begin that way. Many also become focused on 'smoke and mirrors' organizing, in which you do something that looks good for a photo op but has no real power behind it" (Durazo, 2007).

Nonprofits devoted to assisting domestic violence victims run the risk of becoming so bureaucratized and cold that they reproduce the very violence they are intending to address. Employees working at domestic violence centers report being disillusioned with their lack of voice and the hierarchical, overcontrolling atmosphere. Work environments may be frustrating as well due to the long hours and low pay. Many times victims have to be shuffled to various agencies, as shelters do not provide the full scope of services an individual victim requires.

In recent years, some nonprofit victim-serving groups have renounced their 501(c)3 status in favor of a more grassroots, community organizing approach. For instance, Incite! and Women of All Red Nations no longer operate under nonprofit status. Although not devoted specifically to domestic violence, the Occupy movements of 2011–12 show the power of organizing masses about critical issues. In Latin America, large, nonhierarchical social change movements have proven to be very successful by using consensus to drive the groups' agenda.

There are some nonprofits that still operate under a more grassroots structure. No More Tears, a nonprofit in South Florida, utilizes no paid staff but instead relies on volunteers to come together to address each victim's needs. No More Tears currently relies on small fund-raisers and donations to support its work. Although this makes it challenging to acquire sustainable funding, it ensures that the organization is not beholden to any funding source and not restricted from assisting victims that might fall slightly outside of its mission.

See also: Feminism and Domestic Abuse; Funding for Domestic Violence Services; Incite!; Nongovernmental Organizations

Further Reading

Baumgardner, J., & Richards, A. (2005). *Grassroots: A field guide for feminist activism.* New York, NY: Farrar, Straus, & Giroux.
Chen, C., Dulani, J., & Piepzna-Samarasinha, L. (Eds.). (2011). *The revolution starts at home: Confronting intimate violence within activist communities.* Boston, MA: South End Press.
Durazo, A. (2007). "We were never meant to survive": Fighting violence against women and the fourth world war. In INCITE! Women of Color Against Violence (Ed.), *The revolution will not be funded: Beyond the non-profit industrial complex* (pp. 113–128). Boston: South End.
Finley, L. (2010, March). Where's the peace in this movement? A domestic violence advocate's reflections on the movement. *Contemporary Justice Review, 13*(1).
Finley, L., & Stringer, E. (Eds.). (2010). *Beyond burning bras: Feminist activism for everyone.* Santa Barbara, CA: Praeger.
Gilmore, R. (2007). In the shadow of the shadow state. In INCITE! Women of Color Against Violence (Ed.), *The revolution will not be funded: Beyond the non-profit industrial complex* (pp. 41–52). Boston: South End.
Incite! (2007). *The revolution will not be funded: Beyond the non-profit industrial complex.* Boston, MA: South End Press.
Incite! Women of Color Against Violence: http://www.incite-national.org
No More Tears: http://www.nmtproject.org
Rodriguez, D. (2007). The political logic of the non-profit industrial complex. In INCITE! Women of Color Against Violence (Ed.), *The revolution will not be funded: Beyond the non-profit industrial complex* (pp. 21–40). Boston: South End.

Laura L. Finley

NONVIOLENCE THEORIES AND DOMESTIC ABUSE

The concept of nonviolence is not limited to political intervention: it can be developed and employed in all relationships. On the individual level, it is a positive force emerging from the transformation of a negative impulse. The cultivation of this force generates a unique form of power, with which we can create a healthier, and more nurturing, culture.

While almost all work on domestic abuse falls within an antiviolence rubric, the possibility of a nonviolent response to abuse has been passed over, probably due to misconceptions regarding the normal field of engagement of nonviolent direct action, namely in the larger social world, and ultimately, a misconception regarding the nature of that kind of power that Gandhi said was "the law of the humans." More than simply not-being-violent, nonviolence implies an expanded concept of security based on healthy human relationships, thus making it an ideal candidate for application to the domestic arena. This possibility is usually not addressed by those who strictly relegate nonviolence to the field of settling political disagreements without the necessary cultural change in which to house the settlement, or by those who believe that using nonviolence is akin to being passive or fearful. There is no reason, however, not to introduce nonviolence, properly understood in the context of personal abuse, that is, expanding it to include the arena of individual relationship: dictators do not only lead countries, they lead families; they dominate in the private as well as the public spheres. Similarly, Gandhi upheld that there is a concentric relationship extending from first the individual to the family, from the family to the state, from the state to the world. From that angle, there are hidden principles of nonviolence we can explore in order to learn how it actually works. This learning, when applied to our personal relationships, can help to build a strong foundation, not just for personal healing, but also for a world with fewer victims of abuse.

Michael Nagler (2004) tells the story of a woman in rural, sub-Saharan West Africa whose husband used to beat her often. One day the woman no longer felt afraid and instead of begging him to stop, stood up, looked him in the eye, and said, "Why don't you go ahead and kill me and get it over with." He stopped beating her and never did so again. Another story comes from a young man whose father, a veteran of Vietnam, used to beat his older siblings after he came home from his military service. His brother would offer his father the tools with which to beat him, and the father backed down every time. These two stories are only a small sample among thousands attesting to one very basic principle of nonviolence: it is not passive. Standing up to a threat with the willingness to risk punishment or even one's life if necessary, without offering threats in return, requires strength and courage. When we stand up to a bully and deny the power of his or her threat of force, we deny that person the power to bruise us spiritually. It is the force of our own dignity that propels us from passive acceptance of violence and abuse into a course of action. That action becomes nonviolent when the disrespect offered to us is not returned, but actively transformed. How do we do this?

Consider this statement from Gandhi, "I have learned through bitter experience the one supreme lesson to conserve my anger, and as heat conserved is transmuted into energy, even so our anger controlled can be transmuted into a power that can move the world." This is another basic principle of nonviolence: it draws its energy from the transformation of a negative impulse into a positive, conscious drive. Anger, for example, is an emotion, a form of energy. It can be expressed in constructive or destructive ways. When we express anger with discipline, directing it toward constructive ends, then we have used that energy in such a way that we are not left with bitterness or resentment. We can find deeper contentment and satisfaction with ourselves in the process, because in directing anger toward a constructive goal, we have participated actively in resolving the issue that frustrated us in the first place. This does not in any way mean suppressing the negative emotions. Suppression is the ground for violence to emerge, because we frustrate our strong emotional drives in patterns of behavior that sink us deeper into difficulties. Transformation does entail the cultivation of self-knowledge and emotional awareness that allows us to understand and recognize what causes the onset of negative emotions, what spurs us to choose (consciously or unconsciously) negative means for emotional expression and the daring to stake out a new direction of conscious, creative, and constructive action.

That kind of risk taking is very demanding. As a stage between passive acceptance of one's own abuse (which Gandhi would actually consider a form of violence) and the kind of dangerous, dramatic conversion just described, there is at least the option—difficult enough in most cases—of ending a toxic relationship in order to chart a new course for oneself and sometimes one's dependents. For example, a friend was in a situation of abuse where her partner would insult and demean her on a daily basis. Sometimes the abuse would happen in front of their toddler, who was also beginning to show signs of suffering negative emotional effects from living with an abusive parent. My friend could have directed her anger and sadness toward her child; instead, she transformed her anger into constructive action by gathering the courage to move away from the person issuing abuse and working to ensure that her boy would grow up feeling unconditionally loved and emotionally healthy so that he might end the cycle of abuse that started in his childhood.

In a less dramatic form, every time we refuse to hate someone who has done harm to us, we are transforming a negative drive, ever so slowly. Another friend's story illustrates this very well: after an instance of verbal abuse by her husband, this friend prepared him a cup of tea just the way he liked it. She said that it was the hardest thing that she had ever done; and her husband was entirely taken by surprise and much softened by the gesture. She watched how her anger became transformed; that she could control it and it was not controlling her. This takes discipline, and nonviolence requires more than mere outward discipline: we not only refuse to hate a person, but we use our love for them as our motivation for action. This is a third principle of nonviolence: it is an expression of love. This definition of nonviolence comes directly from the Sanskrit *ahimsa*, literally meaning "extinguishing the desire or intent to harm or kill," which was the basis of the translation of the concept into English. What is missing for English speakers was the deeper understanding embedded therein that in order to extinguish desire to harm, we have to replace it with something positive (otherwise we are indeed just repressing). This is where love comes in, because only love, as the wisdom traditions uphold, can overcome hatred and harm. This sentiment was echoed by Martin Luther King Jr. when he said, "Darkness cannot drive out darkness, only light can do that; hate cannot drive out hate, only love can do that." Nonviolent loving, however, is very different from the kind of emotional love portrayed by popular culture: it means the willingness to encourage someone when she or he is doing good, *and* to be prepared to prevent that person from doing harm without hatred in our hearts.

Nonviolent love is closely related to nonviolent power. King succinctly draws out the interrelated nature of these two concepts, stating, "power without love is reckless and abusive, and love without power is sentimental and anemic." In a general definition, power means the ability to get what one wants. What does this look like in terms of nonviolence? Political scientist Gene Sharp of the Albert Einstein Institute defines nonviolent power strategically: a ruler cannot rule without the consent of the ruled. The power, therefore, lies with the people's willingness to support and give consent to being ruled over. When a person realizes that she or he is in a position to withdraw consent, she or he becomes aware internally of this power and is able to remove the moral authority that the ruler has previously enjoyed.

In large numbers, this phenomenon is known as "people power." Sharp's conception of power, however, seems to be missing a key component that someone in a situation of personal abuse will find necessary because it begs the question: what next? Others want an understanding of power that allows us to generate it at any time, to find empowerment to create what we want without depending on others to give it to us. For these reasons, the Metta Center for Nonviolence suggests a different approach to power that is rooted in the integral meaning of human responsibility and security: we call this "person power." This kind of power draws from the model presented by Kenneth Boulding's "three faces of power" (Boulding, 1989). According to Boulding, power has three faces: political (threat power), economic (exchange power), and social (integrative power). Where political power offers a threat to coerce what it wants, and economic power offers an exchange of some kind for what it wants, social or integrative power offers dignity and love to get what both parties not only want but arguably need to reaffirm their humanity. Integrative power maintains a dynamic where one party might say to the other, "I'll do what I think is right, and it will eventually bring us closer." It does not require masses of people coming together, only one person doing what is right and generating the kind of energy that can compel the person inflicting violence to realize the ineffectiveness of violence to obtain what he or she wants and especially needs.

For most people to engage this higher order of empowerment, the kind based in authenticity and detachment, we need to build institutions that support and reinforce the power of nonviolent as opposed to passive or romantic love. These include restorative justice and victim-offender mediation and counseling, as well as education within families and schools about alternatives to violence. Some even believe, however, that these new institutions in turn require that we uphold, and eventually embody, a higher image of the human being. In other words, domestic abuse is a symptom of a deeper current in human culture to degrade, manipulate, and violate others because we believe at some level that we are separate from one another, and how we treat each other does not matter. The problem is, as a situation of abuse clearly demonstrates, it does matter. If it is true for families, how much more for nations? There is a little-explored principle of nonviolence that it is not only about having power, but that it matters what we do with that power once we have it. Embodying nonviolent love brings this principle to light. If we can express our love by renouncing our fear and hatred while responding to a situation of abuse, on any level, we can begin to generate the kind of nonviolent energy that can be used to empower us on a daily basis to create and sustain the rewarding human relationships we need to thrive both individually and collectively.

See also: Social and Societal Effects of Domestic Abuse

Further Reading

Albert Einstein Institute: http://www.aeinstein.org
Bondurant, J. (1988). *Conquest of violence*. Princeton, NJ: Princeton University Press.
Boulding, K. (1989). *Three faces of power*. Newbury Park, CA: Sage.
Gandhi Serve Foundation: http://www.gandhiserve.org
Martin Luther King Institute, Stanford University: http://mlk-kpp01.stanford.edu/

Metta Center for Nonviolence: http://www.mettacenter.org

Nagler, M. (2004). *The search for a nonviolent future: A promise of peace for ourselves, our families, and our world.* Novato, CA: New World Library.

Sharp, G. (1973). *Methods of nonviolent action.* Boston, MA: Porter Sargent.

Stephanie Van Hook

NORTH AMERICA AND DOMESTIC ABUSE

Compared to some other regions of the world, North America has lower rates of domestic violence. However, far too many people still suffer from abuse in the United States and Canada.

Statistics in Canada

A 1999 report from the Center for Health and Gender Equity found 29 percent of Canadian women had endured physical assault by a partner. Each year, the Canadian Centre for Justice Statistics publishes a report on Family Violence in Canada. The last report, from 2009, was focused on self-reported incidents drawn from the 2009 General Social Survey on Victimization. The report also utilized police data to detail the amount of violence against children and youth, seniors, and family-related homicides. The study found that 6 percent of Canadians with a current or former spouse reported being physically or sexually victimized in the five years preceding the survey, while 17 percent reported experiencing some form of

Native American women endure high rates of abuse in North America. (AP Photo/Navajo Nation, Rick Abasta)

emotional or financial abuse. Rates were similar across all of the provinces, although Labrador, Newfoundland, and Quebec had slightly lower rates. Persons aged 25–34 reported three times more abuse than did those aged 45 and older. Less than one-quarter of victims stated that they reported the abuse to police, and only 10 percent reported obtaining a restraining order. One-third of victims who obtained a restraining order reported that the abuser violated the order. Almost 55,000 children and youth were victims of sexual or physical violence, with 30 percent of those perpetrated by a family member. Family violence represented approximately one-third of the 2,400 incidents of violence against senior citizens reported to police. Between 2000 and 2009, Canada saw 738 spousal homicides, representing 16 percent of all solved homicides and almost half of all family-related homicides. Women were three times more likely to be murdered by their spouses. Eighty-four percent of homicides against children were family related. As in the United States, immigrants are less likely to report abuse. The annual costs of direct expenditures related to domestic violence have been estimated at close to $1 billion Canadian, with almost $700 million Canadian spent on the criminal justice system, close to $200 million for police, and nearly $300 million for counseling and training.

Statistics in the United States

According to the National Coalition Against Domestic Violence, in the United States, an estimated 37 percent of women seeking attention at emergency rooms in the United States had been injured by an intimate partner, according to a 2000 study. Domestic violence is often lethal. An estimated 1,300 women in the United States are killed from domestic violence annually. More women in the United States are injured from domestic violence than from car accidents, rapes, and muggings combined. African American women endure 35 percent more abuse than do Caucasian women, according to the National Coalition Against Domestic Violence. These women face additional barriers in getting help, including racially discriminatory criminal justice and social service systems. Numerous studies have shown that Native American women experience the highest rates of violence of any group in the United States, enduring rates three and a half times greater than the national average (Perry, 2004). According to the Centers for Disease Control (CDC), 1 in 11 teens have experienced dating violence. Domestic violence is estimated to cost more than $5.8 billion per year: $4.1 billion is for direct medical and health-care services, and nearly $1.8 billion in productivity costs.

Canadian Resources and Policies

The Public Health Agency of Canada features a National Clearinghouse on Family Violence, started in 1982, which includes research and best practices, news updates, and resources. The Family Violence Initiative involves 15 departments, agencies, and Crown corporations. The Canadian government funds the initiative. According to the Public Health Agency of Canada, "The FVI promotes public awareness of the risk and protective factors associated with family violence; works with government, research and community partners to strengthen the capacity of criminal justice, housing and health systems to respond; and supports data collection, research and evaluation efforts to identify innovative/promising practices and a range of effective interventions" (http://www.phac-aspc.gc.ca/ncfv-cnivf/initiative-eng.php).

Most forms of family violence are crimes in Canada. Although the Criminal Code does not refer to any specific "family violence offence," an abuser can be charged with an applicable offense. Criminal charges could include sexual offenses against children and youth; trespassing at night; child pornography; failure to provide life necessities to children; abandonment of a child; criminal negligence; homicide (murder, attempted murder, infanticide, and manslaughter); criminal harassment, also known as stalking; uttering threats; assault (causing bodily harm, with a weapon, and aggravated); sexual assault (causing bodily harm, with a weapon and aggravated sexual assault); kidnapping and forcible confinement; abduction of a young person; making indecent and harassing phone calls; mischief; intimidation; and breach of a court order, recognizance (peace bond), and probation order.

The sentencing provisions of the Criminal Code provide that where an offender abuses his spouse or child or any position of trust or authority while committing another offense, it will be considered an aggravating factor.

Many substantive and procedural changes to the Criminal Code have been made in recent years that have increased the safety of victims of family violence. These include improving availability of testimonial aids for vulnerable adult victims/witnesses, including victims of family violence (January 2006); ending the use of "house arrest" for offences involving serious personal injury (December 2007); strengthening the peace bond provisions concerning those previously convicted of sexual offenses against children (May 2008); and increasing mandatory minimum penalties for serious offenses where a firearm is used (May 2008).

Given the size of the country and the structure of its government, provincial and territorial governments make laws in areas of their own jurisdiction, including providing victims' services. To date, six provinces (Alberta; Manitoba; Nova Scotia; Prince Edward Island; Newfoundland and Labrador; and Saskatchewan) and three territories (Northwest Territories, Yukon, and Nunavut) have proclaimed specific legislation on family violence. Alberta's Protection Against Family Violence Act has been in effect since 1999, Manitoba's Domestic Violence and Stalking Act since 2009, Nova Scotia's Domestic Violence Intervention Act since 2003, Prince Edward Island's Victims of Family Violence Act since 1996, Newfoundland and Labrador's Family Violence Protection Act since 2006, and Saskatchewan's Victims of Domestic Violence Act since 1995, The Protection Against Family Violence Act has been in force since 2005 in Northwest Territories, the Yukon Territories Family Violence Prevention Act since 1999, and the Nunavut Family Abuse Intervention since 2008. These statutes complement protections enacted in the Criminal Code.

On December 6, 1989, 15-year-old Marc Lepine shot and killed 14 women and wounded 14 more at l'Ecole Polytechnique, an engineering school in Montreal.

Lepine wanted to attend the school but was denied admission. He clearly targeted women, having asked the men to leave the room before starting the massacre. He left a suicide note explaining that he believed the university's policies gave preferential treatment to women. He also noted his hatred for feminists. In 1991, the Canadian Parliament established December 6 as the National Day of Remembrance and Action on Violence Against Women. Also in 1991, a small group of feminist men created the White Ribbon campaign as a way to inspire men to help end domestic abuse.

U.S. Resources and Policies

Every state in the United States has legislation prohibiting domestic violence, and most have dating violence legislation as well. Several states require that dating violence be included in school curricula. Each state also has some provision for obtaining restraining orders or protection orders.

The federal Violence Against Women Act (VAWA) was first enacted in 1994, then reauthorized in 2000 and 2005. It is being considered for reauthorization again in 2013 VAWA provides funding for domestic violence training, prevention programs, and victim assistance. It also offers assistance to immigrant victims who are undocumented due to domestic violence, allowing them to self-petition for residency. Support is building for the International Violence Against Women Act (I-VAWA) as well.

In 2000, the United States passed the Trafficking Victims Protection Act to provide assistance and education about human trafficking. The Tribal Law and Justice Act, signed into law by President Barack Obama in 2010, helps provide assistance to Native American victims. It also helps ensure that tribes are prepared to investigate and prosecute offenders.

Despite the passage of significant legislation, there is still much room for improvement in addressing dating and domestic violence. Research shows that U.S. police officers still may not treat domestic violence seriously. In some cases, police have failed to enforce restraining orders, leading to fatalities. In 2005, the U.S. Supreme Court ruled that domestic violence victims are not entitled to enforcement of their restraining orders. The case involved an appeal by Jessica Gonzales, whose husband kidnapped and murdered her three daughters in violation of a restraining order in Castle Rock, Colorado. Although Gonzales (now Lenahan) contacted police numerous times, they failed to respond. In 2011, the Inter-American Commission on Human Rights ruled that the Supreme Court was in error and that enforcement of a protection order is part of a fundamental human right to safety. Approximately 60 percent of restraining orders are violated within one year, with one-third of those resulting in severe violence.

Research clearly supports that less serious attacks occur when restraining orders are enforced. One study found that enforcement of restraining orders resulted in a 38 percent decrease in the proportional rate of domestic violence homicides in Orange County, Florida. The United States has never ratified the Convention on the Elimination of All Forms of Discrimination Against Women (CEDAW), despite the fact that former President Jimmy Carter was instrumental in getting it passed by the UN General Assembly.

There are numerous resources for victims of domestic violence in the United States. Nationally, the National Coalition Against Domestic Violence (NCADV), the National Network to End Domestic Violence (NNEDV), the Teen Dating Violence Hotline, and other organizations provide a wealth of information. State coalitions provide resources to shelters and service centers in each state. A listing of these coalitions is available at http://www.ncadv.org.

October is Domestic Violence Awareness Month in the United States, and February is Teen Dating Violence Awareness Month.

See also: Castle Rock v. Gonzales Case; Legislation and Policies, Dating Violence; Legislation and Policies, Domestic Abuse; U.S. Government Responses to Domestic Violence: Violence Against Women Act; White Ribbon Campaign

Further Reading

Family violence in Canada: A statistical profile. (2011). Retrieved May 31, 2012, from http://www.statcan.gc.ca/pub/85-224-x/85-224-x2010000-eng.pdf

Family Violence Initiative. (2011). Canadian Department of Justice. Retrieved May 31, 2012, from http://www.justice.gc.ca/eng/pi/fv-vf/laws-lois.html

Jessica Gonzales v. USA. (2011, October 24). ACLU. Retrieved May 31, 2012, from http://www.aclu.org/human-rights-womens-rights/jessica-gonzales-v-usa

Malette, L., & Chalouh, M. (1991). The Montreal massacre. Charlottetown, PE: Gynergy.

National Coalition Against Domestic Violence: www.ncadv.org

Perry, S. (2004). A Bureau of Justice Statistics Statistical Profile, 1992–2002: American Indians and Crime. Retrieved January 30, 2013 from http://bjs.ojp.usdoj.gov/content/pub/pdf/aic02.pdf

Rosenberg, S. (2006). Neither forgotten nor fully remembered: Tracing an ambivalent public memory on the tenth anniversary of the Montreal massacre. In A. Burfoot & S. Lord (Eds.), *Killing women: The visual culture of gender and violence* (pp. 21–45). Waterloo, ON: Wilfrid Laurier University Press.

State Domestic Violence Statutes: http://www.womenslaw.org/statutes_states.php

Laura L. Finley

0

OUTREACH SERVICES

While shelter programs throughout the United States provide a safe refuge for thousands of victims of domestic violence each year, the vast majority of victims never enter a shelter. For those victims and survivors, answers are found in a multitude of outreach programs. Those outreach efforts include activities such as safety planning, education, counseling, advocacy, training initiatives, and more. Service providers often hear victims say they did not recognize the beginning signs of abuse in their intimate partner relationships because they had grown up in a toxic environment of family violence, making them immune to the early pains of domestic violence. Outreach efforts strive to balance both education and service provision to inform victims and empower them to make positive change, with the goal of ending what is often a cycle of family violence. A parallel goal of outreach work is to raise awareness in the general public and ensure that the voice of the domestic violence movement roars. Most if not all outreach services are accessed through domestic violence organizations' 24-hour crisis hotlines.

The Outreach Worker Defined

The outreach worker is both the fierce advocate and the soulful counselor. They understand the services available to victims throughout the community and understand the gaps and how to navigate them. They inform and empower clients, guiding them along a journey of self-determination and autonomy. They have privileged access to the clients' passage from victim to survivor, and affirm each client along the way. They guard their confidentiality, and they give them voices. Outreach workers engage the broad and dynamic public within which they work. They acknowledge and overcome barriers to advancing the message that domestic violence is a crime and help is available to victims tangled in its web.

The Safety Plan

The most dangerous time for a victim of domestic violence is the moment it becomes clear to the abuser that the victim is permanently leaving the relationship. At that moment physical violence often escalates, as does the risk for homicide. Experience has shown us clearly that domestic homicide is predictable and therefore preventable. These well-known facts have informed the safety planning process—the first step in keeping victims safe. Most often this happens on a hotline call when an outreach worker asks questions to assess the needs of the caller, find a match for services available, and ultimately educate her about the risk she is in. At that moment it becomes incumbent on the outreach worker to connect with the caller in a way that she is able to understand and guide her to a path of safety. This, for some, can mean the difference between life and death.

The educational component of the safety planning process has emerged within the domestic violence movement as a key strategy for helping victims make informed decisions for their safety and the safety of their children. The Danger Assessment tool developed by Dr. Jacquelyn Campbell of Johns Hopkins University School of Nursing in 1986 is intended to be an objective instrument to measure the level of risk an abused woman has of being killed by her intimate partner (http://www.dangerassessment.org). The Danger Assessment tool has also been modified into a four-item version for law enforcement professionals responding to domestic violence calls so that they can quickly identify the risk of lethality. Most recently the tool has been revised to predict reassault in same-sex female intimate relationships. Providers can become certified in the use of the Danger Assessment tool so that they can employ them effectively. The opportunity to measure risk in this way has changed the landscape of safety planning practices and advanced the practice of outreach work beyond reflective listening and moved it into the realm of assertive education and active protection for callers.

Legal Services and Immigration Outreach

Victims of domestic violence are in need of support, advice, and expert representation when navigating the tangled web of the legal system. In cases when victims cannot afford legal representation, they can access either a court-appointed attorney or an attorney through a publicly supported legal services organization. These free or low-cost legal services are intended to assist clients with orders of protection, child and spousal support, child custody and visitation, divorce, immigration, and criminal court issues. In theory, legal services offer advice and expert representation in the judicial system. In practice, attorneys can be difficult to reach, with little time available to spend with victims to understand their individual concerns and explain the process and outcome. In these situations the role of the outreach worker is heightened, and active advocacy becomes essential so that the victim receives the representation she is entitled to. The outreach worker may also need to assist with an intake appointment, help the victim tell her story in a succinct manner that highlights key legal issues, and define expectations for the client.

Immigrant and undocumented women face unique challenges when they are in a domestic violence relationship and can find it more difficult to escape because of immigration laws, language barriers, social isolation, and economic deprivation. Abusive partners often use immigration status as a tool to further control the victim, making escape feel impossible especially if the couple have children, espousing fears about the loss of custody. Immigrant women may also come from cultures that tolerate abuse, and they may have a false sense that the laws in the United States that are intended to protect victims of abuse do not apply to them. The unique role of the outreach worker in these cases is to focus on accessibility and education, as well as facilitating the flow of information to the victim. This may require advocating for a certified language interpreter in court, when filing reports with police, and when inquiring about their legal rights. For immigrant victims of domestic violence the isolation, threats of deportation and loss of custody of children, and a false sense of the protection they are entitled to in the United States make escaping from abuse an almost insurmountable challenge. The outreach worker debunks these notions and helps victims overcome their fears and access services to free themselves from abuse.

Counseling and Support Groups

Isolation from family and friends, and victim blaming are hallmarks of an abusive relationship. Healing begins with supportive counseling from skilled professionals and from peers who share the experience of living in and leaving a domestic violence relationship. Through individual sessions and support groups, clients benefit from the opportunity to understand the cycle of domestic violence while receiving support to break free. Support groups break down the overwhelming sense of isolation that has plagued victims in their abusive relationship, empowering them along their journey as a survivor. Together, survivors mourn the death of their dreams, comfort one another through the pains of the process of separations, take solace in their solidarity, and become emboldened in their pursuit to rebuild their lives free from violence. The outreach worker identifies opportunities to work with clients individually and facilitates support groups so that they are productive and empowering.

Advocacy

Outreach advocates are prepared to walk beside a victim of domestic violence as she encounters roadblocks in her process of leaving an abusive relationship and rebuilding a life for herself. This can include applying for public assistance, obtaining legal services, communicating with child protective services, completing petitions for family court, working with law enforcement, and more. An outreach advocate is dedicated to empowering the client to engage the systems that are designed to protect her by accompanying her, and in some cases speaking for her when she is unable to.

Children's advocates offer a special opportunity to connect with the voices of youth exposed to family violence and create programs to heal their invisible wounds while advocating for their rights. So often, adult victims of domestic violence tell us stories of childhood abuse and families plagued with fighting and violence. Children's advocates work not only to improve conditions for children existing in families entrenched in violence and abuse, but also to increase the public's awareness of the high rate of occurrence of childhood exposure to family violence and the devastating lifelong effects.

Cross Systems Collaboration

Effective outreach requires a true collaboration with partners in law enforcement, service provision, housing, public assistance, the judicial system, medical services, child welfare, and other systems that potentially impact the outcome for the client. Our experience is that this close relationship is necessary to ensure that each sector is able to fully engage around the needs of the client. The outreach worker participates in these collaborative efforts both proactively by designing strategies that remove barriers to different services, and reactively by engaging systems that have not met the clients' needs or expectations. The needs of victims are sometimes vast and complicated. A collaborative response is necessary to effectively rise to the challenge.

Economics

Economic control and deprivation are pervading factors of domestic violence relationships. When victims consider leaving their relationship, regardless of whether they come from wealth or poverty, the separation will force an economic strain. Outreach advocates work with clients to secure whatever resources they might have, apply for public assistance if needed, maintain or gain employment, and pursue financial stability. This can be a long, scary road particularly if the imbalance in resources means that an abusive partner is able to leverage more legal and support services against the victim with the goal of an unfair outcome in divorce and custody proceedings. The role of the outreach worker is to connect the victim with adequate support services and representation while empowering her along the way.

Accessibility to a Diverse Population

Outreach efforts are ineffective if they are not accessible to the full range of victims who need them. From hotline screening questions to language translations, outreach workers strive to increase their capacity to connect with as many victims and children as possible. Strategies to increase accessibility include being mindful of the questions being asked, times and locations of services being offered, the capacity to produce multilingual brochures, and an awareness of ethnic and religious difference. One way to work toward ensuring services are available to the entire population is to establish a coalition that addresses accessibility issues. Coalitions should be representative of the population being served (or sought to be served), and practices can emerge from the dialogue that takes place.

The Unexpected Outreach Worker

Looking beyond the typical outreach worker at domestic violence programs, we find potential to vastly expand the capacity to make a vital connection with victims who may not be aware of the danger they are in and the help that is available. Health-care providers, therapists, employers, educators, clubs, and other collections of active people can be educated and inspired to advance the mission to end domestic violence by sharing information with the people they are routinely in contact with. By opening the conversation to domestic violence and creating a safe place for the dialogue, the concept of an "outreach worker" can be expanded exponentially.

The Movement—A Public Awareness Campaign

Beyond service provision to clients, outreach efforts include the implementation of a public awareness campaign aimed at educating the broad community about the issue and dangers of domestic violence so that victims no longer suffer in silence. Brochures, poster campaigns, billboards, public service announcements, press releases, public speaking, training programs, and social media are all tools available for launching these initiatives. Public awareness campaign materials are widely available for replication and distribution.

Where Do We Go from Here?

In order to be effective, outreach services must be accessible and providers must understand the community in which they are offering services. Barriers of cultural perspective, language, socioeconomics, geography, and more must be acknowledged and mitigated so that providers connect with the people they intend to serve. Providers also need to understand the gaps that exist within the system they are working. The outreach worker empowers clients to reach safety.

See also: Culturally Competent Services; Shelters for Domestic Abuse Victims; Therapy and Counseling for Domestic Abuse

Further Reading

Danger assessment (Johns Hopkins School of Nursing). http://www.dangerassessment.org
Violence Against Women Network (VAWnet): http://www.vawnet.org

Renee Fillette

P

PATRIARCHY AND DOMESTIC ABUSE

Some believe that the root cause of domestic abuse is patriarchy. The argument is that, in societies in which males dominate and men and boys are socialized to see women as inferior, it should not be surprising that some utilize emotional, verbal, physical, sexual and other means of control to continue to maintain their superior status.

Defining Patriarchy

According to Johnson (2003), patriarchy is a term that refers to societies that are male dominated, male identified, and male centered (p. 165). He explains, "Patriarchy is male-dominated in that positions of authority—political, economic, legal, religious, educational, military, domestic—are generally reserved for men. Heads of state, corporate CEOs and board members, religious leaders, school principals, members of legislatures at all levels of government, senior law partners, tenured full professors, generals and admirals, and even those identified as 'head of household' all tend to be male under patriarchy" (p. 165). This all results in a society that oppresses women.

Male-dominated societies exhibit numerous gender inequalities. Men earn more than women for comparable work, are able to control the passage of laws, the enforcement of those laws, and the content of popular culture, for instance, all in ways that benefit men. "Male dominance also promotes the idea that men are superior to women. In part this occurs because we don't distinguish between the superiority of *positions* in a hierarchy and the kinds of people who usually occupy them. This means that if superior positions are occupied by men, it is a short leap to the idea that *men* must be superior" (Johnson, 2003, p. 166). That is, if every president, and most generals, lawmakers, judges, faith leaders and corporate CEOs are men, men as a group are identified as superior, even if individually not all men feel superior to women. Johnson (2003) explained, "in this sense, every man's standing in relation to women is enhanced by the male monopoly over authority in patriarchal societies" (p. 166).

Further, in patriarchal societies, the core ideas about "what is considered good, desirable, preferable or normal are associated with how we think about men and masculinity" (Johnson, 2003, p. 166). Highly valued characteristics in patriarchal cultures include strength, control, efficiency, rationality, competitiveness, decisiveness, self-sufficiency, and forcefulness—all qualities generally associated with men. These characteristics are valued in the workplace, in politics, in the military, in criminal justice, in medicine—in virtually every field. As Johnson (2003) explains,

"Of course, femaleness isn't devalued entirely. Women are often prized for their beauty as objects of male sexual desire, for example, but as such they are often possessed and controlled in ways that ultimately devalue them" (p. 167). Thus the ways that patriarchal societies define and encourage adherence to rigid gender roles provides the macro setting for micro problems of power and control by those who are viewed as superior over those who are seen as inferior.

In a male-identified society, women see few leadership role models. Referring to famous female leaders like Margaret Thatcher, Queen Elizabeth 1, Catherine the Great, Indira Gandhi, and Golda Meir, Johnson (2003) explains,

> patriarchy can accommodate a limited number of powerful women so long as the society retains its essential patriarchal character, especially in being male-identified. Although some individual women have wielded great power, it has always been in societies organized on a patriarchal model. Each woman was surrounded by powerful men—generals, cabinet ministers, bishops, and wealthy aristocrats or businessmen—whose collective interests she supported and without whom she could not have ruled as she did. And not one of these women could have achieved and held her position without embracing core patriarchal values. Indeed, part of what makes these women stand out as so exceptional is their ability to embody values culturally defined as masculine: they've been tougher, more decisive, more aggressive, more calculating, and more emotionally controlled than most men around them. (pp. 167–68)

Patriarchy is also male-centered, "which means that the focus of attention is primarily on men and what they do ... A male center of focus is everywhere. Research makes clear, for example, what women probably already know: that men dominate conversations by talking more, interrupting more, and controlling content" (p. 168).

Patriarchal systems manifest in the macro and micro levels. Macro-level systems include schools, law, politics, criminal justice, religion, and medicine. At the micro level, family interactions tend also to be patriarchal, with men still viewed as head of the household and those households led by single females the most demonized.

Many fail to see that the United States is a patriarchal culture. One reason for this is that some women enjoy class or race privilege, and thus their oppression as women is masked. Further, as Johnson (2003) explained, "along with not seeing women as oppressed, we resist seeing men as a privileged oppressor group" (p. 171) because to do so means that men might have to find ways to reduce their privilege and increase the standing of women—a threat to the collective power they hold in a patriarchal society. And it is true that, individually, men do not all feel privilege in their daily lives. The concept of patriarchy is not intended to focus on individual men, however, but on men as a whole and gender relations contextually.

More than just hurting women, patriarchy hurts men, too. Rigid gender roles, referred to by some as hegemonic masculinity, result in men feeling unable to express emotion and feeling pressure to conform. This is emotionally dangerous. It prevents many men from developing and enjoying healthy relationships. A study in England found that the most patriarchal societies were also those that the life expectancy for men was much lower than for women. *Newsweek* magazine annually ranks the best and worst places to be a woman. In general, the best places are those in which there is greater gender equality, and these are the same countries that tend to have lower rates of domestic abuse. Similarly, the annual Global Peace Index results show that the most peaceful societies—in terms of violent crime as well as war and militarism—tend also to be those with greater gender equality.

In the 1970s, socialist and Marxist feminists pointed to the capitalist economic system as the root cause of patriarchy. They maintained that capitalism is a hierarchical system built on competition, which inevitably means there are winners and losers. Gender roles are built around the economic system whereby men are perceived as the breadwinners. When they feel they cannot be successful as providers, the result might be violence against women as a means of reasserting feelings of power and control. Research does bear out that women are at highest risk for lethal abuse when they are employed and their abuser is unemployed, suggesting this situation is perceived as a threat to the man.

Although not all feminists adhere to the socialist or Marxist ideas, most agree that it is males' perceived superiority that leads some to obtain and maintain power and control over women. This feminist view has been widely offered as an explanation for domestic violence, and is integrated into the educational materials provided via the Duluth Model, including the many Power and Control Wheels that help identify the forms or types of abuse. Advocates generally present this perspective in the community and work with survivors to "take their power back." The feminists who started the advocacy group for the battered women's movement, however, recognized that patriarchy is a system and thus must be addressed in that way. Empowering individual women does little to change the broader inequalities that result in abuse, such as poverty, gender roles, and lesser political influence. Some advocates today are suggesting a need to return to this macro-level understanding so as to better highlight the interlocking systems of oppression women experience and to identify possibilities for systemic change.

Not all people believe that patriarchy explains domestic violence. Some reject that explanation, pointing to cases in which a man is abusing another man, a woman is abusing a man, or a woman is abusing another woman. They maintain that it is more individual, psychological variables that better explain abuse. In the 1980s and 1990s, some men's rights and father's rights groups challenged feminists on the patriarchal explanation, arguing that any kind of violence, whether the victim be male or female, is damaging and that advocates must work equally to end it all.

See also: Duluth Model; Feminism and Domestic Abuse; History of U.S. Domestic Violence Developments, 1970s; Women's Rights Movement

Further Reading

Douglas, C., et al. (2005, November/December). Patriarchy sucks for men too? *Off Our backs*, 5.
Freedman, E. (2002). *No turning back: The history of feminism and the future of women.* New York, NY: Ballantine.
Hunnicutt, G. (2009). Varieties of patriarchy and violence against women: Resurrecting "patriarchy" as a theoretical tool. *Violence Against Women, 15*(5), 553–573.

Johnson, A. (2003). Patriarchy, the system: An it, not a he, a them, or an us. In Kirk, G., & Okazawa-Rey, M. (Eds.), *Women's lives, multicultural perspectives* (pp. 25–32). New York: McGraw-Hill.

Kimmel, M. (2006). *Manhood in America* (2nd ed.). New York, NY: Oxford University Press.

Pleck, E. (1989). *Domestic tyranny: The making of American social policy against family violence from colonial times to the present.* New York, NY: Oxford.

Laura L. Finley

PERSONAL NARRATIVE: KRISTIN FRANKLIN

I am 35 years old and I have had five abusive relationships. Five. Think about that for a moment. One abusive relationship is certainly bad enough. But five? It's actually really embarrassing to admit that I have been a victim that many times. My first abusive boyfriend was also my first real relationship. His name was John (not his real name), he was a year older than I, and I was simply caught up in the excitement that an older guy was interested in me at all. I was young—only 14 years old. I was insecure. I was stupid. I was unprepared for the monumental impact this first relationship would have on the next two decades of my life.

Things with John were really great for a while. I had a boyfriend. A high school boyfriend at that. It was like a fairy tale. And then he hit me. I don't even remember why he did it. All I remember, after all these years, is that it was definitely my fault. That's what he said, anyway. I don't remember being mad (or sad, for that matter) that he hit me. I was just confused. I confided in one of my good friends from my church's youth group for advice. I braced myself for the possibility that she would urge me to break up with him and be done with it. But she didn't. She merely told me that most men acted that way from time to time, and that it was my job, as a good girlfriend, to anticipate his needs and moods and just not make him mad. Members of my own family also fought quite regularly, and although they never resorted to physical violence, I began to think that fighting was just a natural part of any relationship. So I stuck it out. For two years, John and I did the break-up/make-up thing that is so popular in teenage relationships. When things were good between us, they were really good. When they were bad, however ... well, let's just say the staff at the local urgent care was on a first-name basis with me. I even tried to get a restraining order once, but because I was a minor, I was told that I would need one of my parents to file it on my behalf.

It turned out that I didn't need a restraining order after all. I was safe after my father moved us across the country during my junior year of high school. At the start of the second semester of my freshman year of college, I met Don (not his real name), the man I would end up marrying two years later. At first, Don was only verbally and mentally abusive. It seemed only natural that since I had always provoked John to violence, I was the cause of Don's anger as well. I didn't conform to what he thought a wife should be like, so he spent the first few years of our relationship "grooming" me into a woman he could bring home to his family. After my first year of college concluded, Don pressured me to move down to his parents' house in the southwest corner of the state. He forced me to join his religion, about which I had serious misgivings. When I told him I didn't want to join his church, he threatened to kick me out of his home.

Years later, after being married for only four years, he began to get physically abusive. It wasn't nearly as bad as it was with John, but it was abuse just the same.

He used to like to push or throw me into walls, and when he was really angry, he would strangle me (in retrospect, I suppose it wasn't the best of ideas to tell him how much John used to strangle me to shut me up), and he constantly threatened to leave me. This increasingly bad abuse led to the return of my night terrors and flashbacks. Drenched in sweat, heart pounding, I would wake up in the middle of the night in panic and dread. Sick of being woken up by my thrashing and screaming on an almost nightly basis, Don forced me to go to counseling (the third time he enrolled me in therapy since I'd met him), where, this time, I was diagnosed with post-traumatic stress disorder along with an anxiety disorder and lots of medication. The medication did not help—in fact, it actually made things worse for me. My insecurities increased exponentially. Don finally began cheating on me and subsequently threw me out of our home.

My rebound relationship after my marriage crumbled ended up lasting three and a half years. His name was Oliver (not his real name) and I thought he was the smartest, funniest, cleverest man in the world. And I really thought he loved me. It turns out that what Oliver loved about me was that since he supported me financially, I was indebted to him, meaning he had a built-in maid and servant at his disposal. His abuse was sporadic enough that every time an attack occurred, I thought it was a fluke. He, too, convinced me that I caused his brutality—I picked fights constantly and had trust issues that drove him to his breaking point. After he punched me in the chest and then threw me into my five-foot-tall, solid-brick mailbox, I ended up checking myself into a mental health facility for 72 hours. I was then paired with a fabulous therapist who helped me to change my life, and I finally left Oliver for good.

To anyone who suffers in an abusive relationship, I say: if you persevere, you will be compensated. I was fortunate enough to fall in love with the man who had become my best friend after I cut all the bad people out of my life. I firmly believe he is my reward from God. Happiness and real, unconditional love are finally mine. I guess I wouldn't truly appreciate what I have now were it not for what I endured.

PERSONAL NARRATIVE: LAUREN PILNICK
I Am Not the Perpetual Victim

I write this piece as I approach the date that marks 14 years since a relationship with a man I'll call Mitch began. I was 16 years old, unsure of myself, and I desperately wanted to be in love. We had such good times together. I remember how we'd let our smiles fade as we came close enough to share our breath. Once, he came to a date carrying this single, red rose. It gave him so much joy to give it to me. That was the real gift; not the rose. He'd always wear this big, expensive watch on his right wrist, and it would always flip around his wrist under its own weight. Flipping it back around was one of my favorite things to do while he drove us to our destination. I'd do it slowly, watching his skin rotate and release, as I was careful not to pull any of the hair that lay perfectly on his wrist. One time we went to this festival, and we played those carnival games. He won this "Honey Bear" stuffed animal for me. It had a jar of honey and everything. He was so proud to win that for me, and I was beyond happy to receive it.

A defining memory from the relationship with Mitch is from when we'd go to diners, which are just everywhere in my hometown, he'd take his straw wrapper off as delicately as he could so that it would remain in one long piece. Then he'd tie it around my left ring finger and tell me, "That's going to be real one day." I remember tying a straw wrapper around his finger too, kissing him on the cheek, and receiving that contagious smile in return. I dreamt of a happily ever after with Mitch.

I didn't get that happily ever after. For me, it began slowly with, "Oh, do you have to hang out with Jess tonight? I kind of want you all to myself." I was in a place where I was deeply seeking Mitch's approval, attention, and love. So when Mitch asked to have a night alone with me instead of my going to a friend's house, I gladly and eagerly obliged. I was giddy to receive his attention. It was a flattering, seemingly healthy form of jealousy. It did not stay healthy for very long. He even got jealous towards the time I dedicated to sports. To punish me, he never came to any of my games.

I choose to give you background to my experience because while I've worked hard to starve power from those memories, I know that I've taken back the power over my mind, my thinking, and what memories shape me. The dating violence I experienced was primarily emotional, verbal, and mental abuse mixed with fairly constant sexual abuse. Physical violence was a rarity and was never as clear and obvious as punching, slapping, or hitting would have been. A couple of times, I was grabbed by the upper arms and shaken—hard—when I "wasn't listening." If I ever defied him by not looking at him when he was screaming at me, he would put his hand on my shoulder with his thumb in the front of my neck. His thumb had power. That one finger's pressure ... on my throat ... sent such a clear message.

Ultimately, we fought several times every day. It often happened while he was driving us somewhere and it was usually at night. He was in control of the car, and he was in control of the argument. Everything was, without fail and without exception, my fault. He'd go on these rants. Yelling. His voice boomed inside his SUV. It was a prison cell on wheels. I found my own way to cope and get through those outbursts by finding my own reflection in my car window, illuminated by the dashboard lights. I found refuge in my own face. While staring at my reflection, I'd rebel against the man I couldn't face and put my middle finger up against my cheek or stick my tongue out in such a way that he could not see from his seat while driving. Immature? Sure. Did it get me through those fights? Sure did.

I was forced into his backseat with the threat of walking myself home 30 miles if I didn't comply with his sexual demands in that backseat. Once, he'd thrown his phone against the wall during a fight and I watched it, as if in slow motion, break apart into hundreds of black plastic pieces exposing brightly colored wires.

Eventually, I was told nearly every day that I was stupid, fat, ugly, wouldn't get into college without his help on my entrance essays, I was selfish, no good at anything, would never find another partner if I left him ... the list went on. Remember, this did not happen on our first date. Surely if these behaviors surfaced on first dates, we could all engage in a much more successful screening process of potential partners. Rather, this starts subtly, gradually, and escalates over the course of time. People who abuse in relationships will typically wait until they know that they have their victim invested enough in them and the relationship that an incident will not send them packing. Mitch waited until I told him I loved him and lost my virginity to him to begin exerting power and control in more extreme ways. I can even recall receiving crisis line calls while working at a rape and domestic violence crisis center (long after leaving my relationship with Mitch) where women told me they weren't hit until their wedding night. It's typical abuser behavior.

After three years, I found the strength to leave for good. I estimate that I attempted to break up with Mitch between 40 and 50 times over the course of those three years. All but ONE was unsuccessful. While my feelings for and attachment to him existed, I got glimpses of a better life—without him—while I was away at college. With the support and urging of some close friends, I was finally able to break up with Mitch for good. He stalked me for nine months following our breakup, and once that dissipated, he was finally out of my life. The real recovery process could begin.

I started the very hard work of surviving. I engaged in countless therapy sessions (with countless therapists as I searched for "the right one"), took sleep aids, got massages to release tension that was manifesting into raging headaches, was prescribed antidepressants and antianxiety medications, went to group counseling, had appointments with advocates, wrote poetry, got pissed off (really, really pissed off!), even spoke out about my experiences publicly at awareness events even though it was one of the hardest things I'd ever done (next to finally leaving Mitch)—the list of things that I did for myself to survive and recover from dating abuse is lengthy. Getting back to my baseline was a daily goal that involved daily effort.

I even began to see a pattern emerge in my life. I was stuck in a pattern of abusive situations. I was the perpetual victim. I accepted that things were happening to me. That I was out of control. That I was passive. So the pattern resurfaced in almost every future romantic relationship I pursued, several career relationships, and if I'm really going to look "big picture" at this, even in minute details of my personal life ("How could such-and-such phone company do this to me?").

So I found myself at 28 years old, finally in a healthy romantic relationship, but now in a dream-job-turned-waking-nightmare because of an abusive boss. I had been applying for new jobs practically upon this new boss's arrival with no luck after 14 painful months. Finally, I made an appointment with Human Resources (HR) to file a formal complaint. I did it not only for myself, but for all of the other people I saw suffering at the hands of this woman. I returned from the meeting with HR, sat down, took a deep breath, and got back to work. Then I opened my e-mail and there it was. An invitation for an interview for the job I really, really wanted (and was later hired for).

It dawned on me then that it was as if greater forces were at work. They were telling me, "Lauren, you need to accomplish the lesson here before we'll let you move on." I never faced Mitch during those fights in the car. But I had grown since then. And I learned. This boss I would face. When I made my report to HR, those greater forces instantly responded and set me free. The lesson I speak of was not relevant to just this one, very specific work situation. It was finally breaking the pattern . . . the cycle. This larger pattern of accepting victimhood as my reality and allowing (to the point of not doing anything to change it) *abuse to happen to me in my life, was crumbling all around me. It was beautiful. I felt set free. I did that.*

As I mentally and emotionally prepared to write this chapter, I kept realizing that I don't think of Mitch regularly anymore. Please pause with me for a moment and listen. I cannot even begin to describe to you how monumentally huge it is that I do not think of Mitch regularly anymore. I had to deliberately and purposefully revisit the memory of this relationship with him in order to write. Once all of this dawned on me, I had no clue what to write. To bear witness to myself realizing that this past experience is fully and completely in the past was almost startling. It was so subtle that I cannot even tell you when exactly this occurred. Then another revelation. That's what I write about. Mitch has got nothing on me. What a story to share!

And here I am, 11 years free from Mitch and feeling pretty amazing knowing I've finally broken this cycle that started nearly half my life ago. I never thought I would ever achieve residency in a place of such freedom. And peace. And self-assuredness. Today, I am 30 years old, hold two bachelor's degrees and a master's degree, created a 10-year (and still counting) career of serving as an advocate in the field of domestic violence and sexual assault, and most importantly—I know, love, and honor the person that I am right now and here.

What I want you to know . . . is that it actually does get better. They aren't just all saying so. You can believe it. It's true. I'm here to tell you that. Because writing this chapter wasn't the hardest thing I've ever done.

PERSONAL NARRATIVE: PATRICIA

My name is Patricia. I have been a victim of domestic violence and extreme emotional cruelty from a man I will call Leroy.

I came to Ft. Lauderdale, Florida, at age 16 from Montego Bay, Jamaica, with my two brothers and with my uncle's girlfriend. It was November 5, 2001. We arrived at night. I was so happy. It was my dream to go to America. We thought moving to America was the best thing in the world. My mom was so happy to see us. Everything in America, including the airport, was so big.

My younger sister had moved to America to live with my mom two years ago, and my cousin lived near my mom's apartment as well. I met Leroy right away, as he was in a crowd of guys that hung out at the complex and who my cousin knew. Leroy introduced himself and said he had heard about me. He was very nice.

The following week my mom took my brother to go to Lauderhill Middle School and my older brother and I to go to Boyd Anderson High. At school I saw Leroy at lunch time, we would talk a lot. He was nice and polite. He always called me sexy and "fresh."

At some point he stopped coming to school. Leroy would wait for me and walk me to the building. He said he liked me. I liked him too. He was tall, skinny, nice, and he had nice hair. He asked how old I was, and I told him I was 16, he said he was 18. I asked why he wasn't at school, and he said he had got in trouble. He would call my mom's house phone. He would borrow my cousin's car, because they were good friends. He would come over a lot while my mom was at work.

In February, my aunt was having a party and I invited him. My whole family was there. Everyone seemed to like him, and we had a good time. We danced and had fun. That was our first time really going out.

We continued to see each other. On early release days at school we would go to a party and I would see him there. My mom wouldn't let me go out on dates with him, but we saw each other at events like this, and he would still hang out at the complex. Leroy told me that his dad's wife kicked him out so he was staying with his best friend.

The first time we had an altercation was at an early release party. I was talking to someone, and he thought I was too close. He pulled me away. Everyone was looking. He said I was disrespecting him and accused me of wanting to sleep with them. It was the first time I realized he was jealous. He was pushing me against the wall and grabbing my shirt. You could see in his face he was getting really upset. One of his friends pulled him away because he was saying and doing all this in front of everyone there. I left and didn't talk to him for about a week. Another time I was talking to some friends, and he didn't like it. He came up and pushed me away, and then slapped me in the face in front of this guy. My cousin heard it and came out and asked why he was always embarrassing and hitting me. I left with my cousin, crying.

In 2003, we moved to a bigger apartment. One of my brothers was giving my mom a lot of trouble. She was working hard and was gone a lot. My mom sent him back to Jamaica. So it was me, my sister, my other brother, and my uncle.

I still talked on the phone with Leroy. One time there was a knock on the door, and it was the FBI. I think I was 17. My mom was talking to them. I didn't know what they wanted at that time. When I went downstairs, they had handcuffed my mom and put her in the van. I called my aunt and told her. I called my cousin, too. I found out later that my mom had helped some relatives come here illegally. One of my other relatives was also taking others illegally here and got caught and had told about my mom to get a better deal. We didn't sleep at the house that night. They put my mom in the detention center in Pompano Beach. After she went to court she was deported back to Jamaica. My cousin took in my sister and my aunt took in me, my brother, and my uncle. My brother and uncle bounced around, sleeping different places every night because my aunt kicks them out.

Leroy would borrow a car to come see me there. He would call me, too. We were now going to Plantation High School. He said he was sorry that he had hit me, that he was just jealous because he loved me so much. He said he would never do it again. It was hard because my mom was gone and my aunt made me do a lot of work, cleaning the house every day. My aunt wanted me to stay home all the time. She wouldn't let us bathe in the morning when we wanted to. I had to get to school really early because they needed to go to work. I was depressed. I wrote letters to my mom about it all, and she gave me a friend's number to contact her to see if I could stay with her. I went to live with her, but it was a long way away. Because it was so far away I had to take lots of buses to get anywhere. I liked going to school because I could see my brother and uncle there. My mom's friend was nice. She treated me well, but I was by myself. Leroy would call and borrow a car and bring me food.

A lot of Jamaican adults don't tell kids things, so I never knew I was illegal. I had a nine-digit number at school, and I thought that was my social security number; also I had my school ID card. I even flew once to D.C. with this ID so I didn't realize this wasn't a real ID, it was only for school. I was so excited to be in America, and I trusted everyone in my family.

When I talked to my mom, who had been deported to Jamaica, she said she wanted us all to be together, so we all got a one-bedroom apartment not far from where my mom used to live. Leroy would come there and give us a ride to school sometimes. One time I saw him with another girl, and she told me that they were boyfriend/girlfriend. I told her to let him know I was looking for him. He tried to convince me it was no big deal, but I broke up with him. I was really upset he was with someone else. It broke my heart. I would see him at the early release parties and was still upset at him. But he would come over and tell me that he was still in love with me.

I didn't see Leroy in 2005. I dated other people. Then we got evicted because my mom couldn't pay the bills up here and in Jamaica together; it got too hard for her. My brother and uncle moved into their girlfriends' houses. I moved in with some friends. I still wasn't seeing Leroy. I was happy even though things were hard. I went to New York (Long Island) to stay with some of my friends who had moved there after leaving school.

I came back home now in 2006; my school ID was the only ID I had, still. I began having a sexual relationship with one of the guys I had dated. I got pregnant, even though he used a condom. I was almost 21. I was really surprised. I told the boy and he said it wasn't his, that I must have been pregnant before he met me, but that was not true. He stopped taking my calls and I stopped calling him. I was living with my cousin. One day I was home alone, and there was a knock on the door, and it was Leroy. I was really surprised. My belly was huge from the pregnancy. He was there with his little cute baby boy. We talked for a while. He said how much he missed me so much. I told him how much he had hurt me. Leroy and I started dating again, and so I moved in with him. It was like September of 2006. He worked in security.

I had my baby Danique on New Year's Day, 2007. Leroy kicked me out when my baby was just six days old. I didn't know where to go. I stayed a bit with my cousin, and then I called Danique's dad to tell him I needed help. He said if it is his kid he'd help, but he wanted me to do a DNA test. I knew it was his, so I agreed. The DNA test showed Danique was his son.

Leroy called and said he was sorry for kicking me out. I eventually when back home to live with him. He cooked for me to show me that he was sorry and he would never kick us out again or hurt me in any way. At first he said It was ok for Danique's dad to pick him up that the house, but after a while he told me that he can't pick up our son at our home anymore and he don't want to see me talking with him. One day when he was at work, Danique's dad came to get our son. Leroy came home and saw us outside talking. Leroy got mad, and when I went inside he walked up to me and hit me in my belly with his hand and said "This is the last time I am telling you, next time I will show again more." I held my belly and just cried; it hurt a lot. I called my cousin, and she said I could stay with her. I didn't go back for a while. I would only go there when I know he was at work to get some of my stuff.

I gave birth to Dominique in October 2008. Dominique was born with a kidney problem, so I had to stay in the hospital longer. Leroy didn't even come there. My cousin invited me to stay with her, and she would help me with the babies. My stuff was still at Leroy's, and when we went to get my stuff he was mad because I was there. I did go back to him, though. He always made it a big deal that I had two kids with two different fathers. We were back together again, and he was not abusive for about a month. Then one night he wanted me to do something for him and when I did not do it right away, he began insulting me by saying that I am good for nothing and I am just existing and living a worthless life. I went in the bathroom and was crying for a long time.

The abuse did not stop there, and the last incident took place [when] I was driving to the bank with him and my son. I asked him a question, and he started to get upset and called me names. He said I am disgusting and he can't stand me and that I am worthless. I asked him why he is always insulting me and making me feel bad about myself. I told that I was always encouraging him and he did the complete opposite to me. Then out of nowhere, he punched me extremely hard in my left eye. My son, Dominique, was in the backseat. I did not even have the strength to look back and check on him because I was in such severe pain. I was embarrassed in front of my son and afraid that he saw his mother being punched. I put my face in my hands and cried. Leroy kept on driving like nothing happened and told me to shut up.

I called No More Tears, a nonprofit to help victims of domestic violence; I got their number from a crisis call hotline. They immediately told me to come to their office and helped me move out with my kids into a safe place. I am currently under the organization's care, and they have put me in therapy. They took me to an eye doctor and then an eye specialist as I have been in severe pain and have trouble seeing from light to dark.

I am somewhat comforted by the fact I no longer have to see him and my kids are not around him. But it is still hurtful to think of all I went through and all my children were exposed to.
I wish I had never met him. I am trying to make a better life for me and my children.

PERSONAL NARRATIVE: SABRINA

My name is Sabrina. I am 30 years old. I have a two year and five-month-old daughter. I have been married for four years to a man I will Ted. I came to the U.S. when I was 19 years old from Recife Pernambuco, Brazil. I came with my family to meet with my brother who lived in the U.S. I fell in love with the country and I told my family I wanted to stay here.

I met Ted in 2006 when I was working in an import Brazilian company. I had a car accident at that time and was looking to get my car fixed. I called a man (Barren) who worked for Ted. Barren told Ted to come meet me. Ted called me every day for a few days and came to my work to fix my car. He was very persistent about fixing my car, so I let him look at the car with me. Ted asked me if I was married, and I said no and he asked me to dinner. I told him I didn't have time.

PERSONAL NARRATIVE: SABRINA

Ted asked for my business card, so I gave him the card for my business. He kept calling me to go out to lunch. After a week of persistence, he brought me a large bouquet of roses to work. He said nothing when he set them down and left. After this, he asked me to breakfast, and I decided to go. Then he began buying me gifts such as bottles of wine.

A month later, he asked me to breakfast again, and he told me he was separated with two kids. He seemed very nice. Three months later, we went out for dinner, which we considered our first date. After another month we went on a second date, and he gave me a diamond necklace. No one had ever given me such a nice gift, and I was impressed. Over time, he continued to give me a lot of expensive gifts. It was always diamonds or expensive clothing.

I went on vacation to Texas, and when I came back he asked me to go with him and a well-known celebrity on vacation to Orlando. We had a great week together. He was always super nice to me. He took me shopping and spent over $4,000 on clothes for me. After six months, he took me to a salon to get my hair done, and then he asked me to marry him. I told him I had to speak with my family and ask them first.

A little while later, he gave me a two-and-a-half-carat diamond ring, and we were engaged. He always bought everything for me. After this, my lease ran out so he found me another apartment and paid for everything. We began preparing for our wedding over the next year. He continued with his hospitality, taking me on vacation, buying me expensive gifts, and constantly sending flowers.

Before we got married, he got upset with me for seeing a picture of my ex-boyfriend and I, and he broke up with me. I kept seeing pictures of this one woman around him, and we broke up again and again. He wanted to know how many men I have had sex with, and he didn't believe my answers. He kept disappearing to Aruba, but I saw his passport and that he'd been to Colombia.

Next, I moved in with him. He continued to ask me if I had sex with my ex-boyfriend. I told him I did, and he kicked me out of his apartment. My mom was with me, and she began picking my things up. So he kicked my mother out of the apartment. I gave him the ring back, and then he disappeared again. I tried to leave the apartment he rented for me, and he called, crying and begging me not to leave.

One day, I went to his house, and we were playing pool. He got angry at me, and I didn't know why. He threw the pool stick over my head and told me to get out. Later, he called and asked for forgiveness. I forgave him because I thought he was just stressed out.

We got back together, and we went to a wedding together, where he also kept disappearing. We got re-engaged, and he planned all the details: where, when, and how it would be. One night before the wedding I went and got food for myself, and when he came home he was angry that I hadn't brought him food. I apologized to him, and he threw the food all over the floor and called me selfish. I also found out that his daughter didn't know that he was married twice. He got mad at me because I asked his daughter about it. He asked me who I thought I was, and I told him I didn't mean it and I was sorry. He came to my apartment and threw a binder of mine against the wall. I thought he was just upset. Everything that ever happened was my fault, and I always felt bad.

He made me promise to cut everyone out of my life for him. So I stopped talking to my friends. Then he and I, along with our immediate families and his celebrity friend, went to Las Vegas and we got married.

When we arrived in Vegas, Ted began yelling in the airport because we forgot a suitcase. My family was very embarrassed. Then we got in a limousine, and we went into a fancy hotel. When we got back to the hotel, Ted kept yelling at me. I tried to please him and kiss him, and he kept complaining and calling me names. I kept crying and asking him to forgive me. That night we had dinner in the hotel, and he had a bachelor party.

On Saturday, we were supposed to get married. Before we got married, I saw something about his celebrity friend on television. I had not seen it before. When I got to the wedding chapel, there were hundreds of people, so they rushed me inside to get the ceremony done.

We hurried back to the hotel to have our after party. We had a nice dinner. After, we were going to a club, but his daughter couldn't get in. So Ted told me to go upstairs with the guests. Then when I went back to the club I became very drunk. We went back to the hotel room, and I fell asleep because I was drunk. Not exactly how I imagined my wedding night.

The next morning the phone wouldn't stop ringing, so Ted kicked me. This was the first time he physically hurt me.

The next day we were supposed to go on our honeymoon to Hawaii. As soon as we got to Hawaii, Ted's ex-wife kept calling to see if he was okay. The ex-wife was constantly calling. It seemed crazy to me. We arrived in the hotel, and I brought flowers. I was trying to make him happy. While we were on our honeymoon, his ex-wife kept calling. I was upset. He was still mad at me for drinking too much on our wedding night. He kept telling me everything was my fault and it was my job to make him happy and make it up to him.

I remember he was always cranky, never happy. Nothing I did was ever good enough. After the honeymoon, his ex-wife called again. I told him I didn't like her calling all the time, and he left the house. So I tried to work things out anyways.

We had sex one night, and he got mad at me because I left the room and went to the kitchen to make us food. He threw juice in my face and the sandwich against the wall. I left for my friends. When I came back, he asked me to sit down, and then he slapped me in my face.

I had some revealing photos I had taken for modeling in the past. When he found them, he was very upset. He said he was going to get the pictures for me because he was embarrassed. He beat me up for this. He hit me so hard my earrings fell out. He pushed me into the bathroom and kicked me with his feet. Then he took me in the bedroom, pushed me against the dresser and threw me against the wall. I kept apologizing and told him I didn't want to hurt my husband.

The next morning I couldn't move. He came home in the morning and had sex with me even though I couldn't move. I remember looking in the mirror and having bruises all over my body. I called a friend and told her about the pictures and how mad he was about them. She tried to talk to him, and he kept telling me this woman isn't my friend. At this time, I believed it was my fault. I thought I deserved to get beat up for these photos.

One time when we were at dinner, he told me I needed to tell him everything about the pictures: whether the photographer had touched me, and so on. He beat me up again. He called me awful names I cannot print here. Again, he hit me so badly my earrings all came out.

I called the same friend again and told her I wanted to go home. She thought he was beating me, but I lied and said he wasn't. I went back to my husband, and he told me he had a reason to beat me up and it was embarrassing. I kept apologizing.

We were supposed to travel to New York, and when we were on the airplane for two hours he again kept berating me for the pictures. I kept saying how sorry I was. The whole plane ride he said horrible things to me, and I was embarrassed because we were around other people. I thought it was my fault, and I felt horrible.

Ted didn't want me to talk to my family sometimes. If I did complain, he'd go ballistic. He spit in my face and called me names. He said "You have to defend me! How do you not do that?" I hid in the bathroom and cried and apologized.

One time my sister spoke with him on the phone and told him he can't treat me this way. He got mad at my sister and told her not to get involved. I went into the room, and he smacked my hand and asked me again how can I not defend him. I went outside and told him I couldn't handle this so I was leaving. He got in the car and started driving crazy and saying he was going to commit suicide. When I got home, I saw a gun with pills, and I spoke with him and told him not to kill himself.

For some reason, Ted believed that I had slept with his celebrity friend. Even though I agreed to take, and passed, a lie detector test, he still kept accusing me of having slept with his friend. A week after I passed the test, he put a gun in my face and kept asking me. I kept begging him to believe me. I couldn't handle it anymore. He had narcotics in his room, so I took some Percocet and Vicodin because I couldn't take it. Then he took me to the hospital.

I woke up in the ICU. I woke up crying and asking for forgiveness for complaining about his ex-wife. He then explained to me that I had stopped breathing and had been in the ICU for a week. I called my mom, and he hung up the phone on me and wouldn't let me talk to her.

When I went home I remember him constantly complaining. He always felt sick, nothing was ever right. He always blamed me and said I caused all the problems.

Once, when we went to Las Vegas, he threatened me again, and I told him I was scared of him. He slapped me and split my lip open, and he threw me against the sink. I hit my head and locked myself in the bathroom crying all day. I kept crying and saying sorry.

Many times when we went on vacations and stayed in the guest houses, he beat me up. He knew I was embarrassed and didn't want people to know. I thought I deserved it.

Another incident happened in California. Ted kept badgering me about how many men I had slept with and that he didn't believe me when I answered. That day I was using the bathroom at a friend's house when he broke in and started beating me. I didn't want to make noise because I didn't want anyone to hear. He took me outside; he pulled my hair and continued to beat me up.

The next day, we went to another friend's house. When we arrived, he began saying that my ex-boyfriend had make a pornography video of me. I spoke with my ex-boyfriend, who said that had never happened. My husband kept saying I was lying and kept bringing up the pictures. Again, he beat me up in the bathroom. I got a black eye, and his hands were bleeding. I lost my earrings again and had to clean up all the blood. I had to wear a hat and makeup to hide my black eyes.

He kept begging me not to call the police because he didn't want to go to jail. He kept going to buy me jewelry and clothing.

After a year of marriage, we went to Hawaii to celebrate our anniversary. We rented a car to drive around the island, and he kept calling me names and verbally abusing me. I started to block out what he was saying, but I continued to try to make him happy. One night I said something he didn't like, and he slapped me in the face so I apologized again.

One time we went out to a nightclub, and he wanted to have intercourse with me in the nightclub. He forced me to have sex with him. I was crying and begging him to stop. He told me if I told anyone, he would call someone to kill my family in Brazil. He said he has connections that could make it happen. He always threatened me with showing my family my pictures.

Another time, we went to the house of a friend, and I told the woman how my husband thought I slept around. Ted found out, so I began taking out my earrings, knowing what was about to happen. When we were alone, he grabbed my hair, threw me into the chair. He picked me up and pushed my head into the bed. He kept asking me how many men I slept with and what they did to me. He kept pulling out chunks of my hair and questioning me about everything. He kept hitting me for hours. I called my mom in Brazil and told her I needed help. I called my sister and told her where I was and asked for help. Security came to my door, and there was a towel with blood on, so I hid it. My mouth and nose were bleeding. My husband said we were just fighting. They asked me if I was okay, so I shook my head yes. Then my husband apologized and asked me to go for a walk. He kept crying and apologizing. I was trying to comfort him and was embarrassed because he was crying in the streets. We went back to the hotel, and he had sex with me. He told me he'd never do it again, and he bought me gifts.

One day I was going to the gym, and another man and a driver came with me. My husband called me, and I told him I was with them. He got very mad and said I shouldn't be alone with two men, and he beat me up. He kept begging me to have children and saying things would change when I had a baby.

I got pregnant. One time I told him how I want to be buried in Brazil, and he pushed me against a wall because I didn't want to be buried next to him. One night while watching television he got really angry, and he called me to come to him. The neighbor called the cops, and the police came to the door. I was three months pregnant at this time. I told the cops my husband got mad while watching the movie.

When I was seven months pregnant, his sister asked me to have dinner with her. I said no because Ted didn't want to, and she began yelling at me and calling me a spoiled brat and disrespectful. They kept screaming at me, so I grabbed my bag and went to a hotel. The next day I got paperwork to leave the country. So I flew back to Brazil.

My husband called my family, asking for me to come back. Because my family is religious, after a week they told me to go back to my husband. They believed he was upset and stressed and I should be with him.

When I was eight months pregnant, he was jealous because my friend was over and she whispered in my ear. He threw food on the wall, so I told him I was going to call the police. He called the cops before I could, and he told me he lied to them saying that I beat him up. I was so upset and had to hide from the cops because he had lied to them. I felt betrayed because I never called the cops, and he had beaten me up so many times.

When I was with him, I had to wait until he was home to eat. I wasn't able to read if he wasn't home, I couldn't be on the computer or the phone. When he was home, he would force me to hold his genitals while he watched television. He would call me bad names for hours and hours.

I was looking for a new apartment for us. He wanted a three bedroom, but they only had two bedrooms so I looked at the two bedroom. He told me how stupid I was, in no uncertain terms. He picked up a knife and threw it, and it almost hit my dog.

He asked me to do a second lie detector test about having an e-mail he didn't know about. The lie detector test worker said I was lying. So we went to a man who did it for over 40 years. He asked me if I ever tried to kill myself, and I said yes, and Ted pulled me out of the chair and took me home. He took me to the bathroom, and he was throwing things. He broke the toilet seat and was calling me names. He was angry that I told the man that he beat me up, but I told him I was trying to prove to him that I'm not lying. He made me write a letter saying that I lied to this man, and Ted used this against me in a restraining order case in Miami. So the judge issued a two-year injunction against me.

Right after I had my baby, he was trying to force me to have sex with him. When my baby was four months old, I called the cops again, and they told me because of the open case against me from my husband I had to go to jail and leave my baby. I knew then that I needed to get out.

One night, he went through my phone and got angry and said I was cheating on him. He kept accusing me, and I asked him to stop. He went outside, and I asked him to please stop, I'm tired of this. He called the cops, and they came to the house. He scratched himself on the door and the cops blamed it on me. They thought it was me since I had been previously in jail. They told me I needed to leave since they had come so many times. So I packed and left and went to a woman's refuge in Miami.

I felt better, more secure. I had no one here.

PHYSICIANS, HEALTH-CARE PROVIDERS, AND DOMESTIC ABUSE
Prevalence of IPV in Health-Care Settings

Victims of domestic violence often require medical care. As such, healthcare providers are ideally suited to help identify abuse, document its' impact, and put victims in contact with local resources.

Intimate partner violence (IPV) is a prevalent public health issue affecting 25–33 percent of women in the United States during their lifetime, and annually, approximately 1.5 million women and 834,700 men are raped and/or physically assaulted in other ways by an intimate partner in the United States (Tjaden & Thoennes, 2000). In addition, nearly half (48 percent) of all U.S. women and men have experienced psychological aggression by an intimate partner in their lifetime (Black et al., 2011).

Prevalence of IPV in patients presenting to health-care settings is similarly high. For example, approximately 14–35 percent of women visiting an Emergency Department and 12–23 percent of women in Family Medicine settings reported having been physically abused or threatened by their partner within the previous year (Bradley et al., 2002). Similar, if not higher, prevalence rates have been noted in obstetrics-gynecology and pediatric offices, with pediatric offices offering an opportunity to discuss IPV with women who may seek medical attention for their children but lack their own insurance or primary care provider.

Few studies have explored the prevalence of IPV perpetrators seeking care in primary care settings. Oriel and Fleming (1998) documented 13.5 percent of male patients in a primary care setting disclosed perpetration of minor violence (throwing, pushing, or slapping) over the past 12 months, and 4.2 percent reported at least one episode of severe violence (kicking, beating, threatening to use or using a knife or gun). Two samples of IPV perpetrators reported high rates (42–63 percent) of health-care access within the six months previous to being sentenced to mandatory treatment programs (Coben & Friedman, 2002).

IPV survivors have increased rates of health-care utilization compared to controls. About half of incidents of IPV reported in national surveys result in physical injury to the survivor (i.e., a partner in an intimate relationship who has been or is currently subjected to violence or abuse), with some 552,000 women requiring medical treatment for IPV-related injury annually (Tjaden & Thoennes, 2000). However, women experiencing IPV most commonly present to health-care providers with myriad concerns not related to direct injury. IPV perpetrators described seeking care for injury, medical illness, and "check-ups." Costs of IPV are estimated to exceed $5.8 billion annually, of which $4.1 billion are for direct medical and mental health services (Coker, Davis, et al., 2002).

Association between IPV and Health Outcomes

Experiencing IPV has well-documented associations with negative health outcomes, with IPV impacting the physical, emotional, social, and financial dimensions of health. IPV survivors suffer direct physical injury resulting in bruising, lacerations, broken bones, damage to internal organs, and potentially death. In addition, experiencing IPV places women at higher risk of physical health problems, including (but not limited to) sexually transmitted infections, pelvic inflammatory disease, chronic pain syndromes, gastrointestinal and genitourinary syndromes, obesity, and neurological sequelae (neurological problems as a result of IPV experiences). Higher rates of depression, anxiety, substance abuse, and post-traumatic stress disorder have been frequently associated to past and present IPV exposures. IPV may limit social networks and support systems through isolation mechanisms used by the perpetrator to control the survivor. IPV may limit access to employment or be associated with higher rates of lost days at work due to IPV-related social isolation or injury.

Identification

Although patients state that they would like to and feel comfortable discussing IPV with a trusted health-care provider, they often do not bring it up unless asked in an appropriately sensitive and empathetic manner. Patients and providers may miss that the root cause of the patient's presentation is IPV unless providers systematically assess for the presence of IPV in symptomatic and asymptomatic patients.

Data suggest that few primary care providers screen for IPV. Rates of screening tend to range between 10 and 25 percent of providers. Providers cite a variety of barriers to screening related to a perceived lack of time, training, comfort, and access to effective resources (Lapidus, Cooke, et al., 2002). Providers have also raised concerns over the possibility of harm related to screening that might include fear of offending the patient, possible retaliation, and police involvement as well as cultural differences.

Asking about IPV in the setting of patients presenting with obvious physical injury is less of a clinical challenge than helping providers understand their role in identifying the linkages between IPV exposures and rates of chronic medical conditions such as chronic pelvic pain, abdominal pain, headaches, depression, anxiety, post-traumatic stress disorder, and other Screening for IPV includes conditions that occur more frequently in patients with a history of current or past IPV.

Screening for IPV includes an assessment of past or current IPV exposures among at-risk but asymptomatic patients. Guidelines for IPV screening in health-care settings vary depending on the recommending organization. Some provider professional organizations such as the American Medical Association (AMA), the American Association of Pediatrics (AAP), and the American College of Obstetrics and Gynecology (ACOG) recommend routine screening of IPV. Other organizations, such as the American Association of Family Physicians (AAFP), recognize the role of primary care providers in being alert for risk factors and signs of violence and recommend that providers be capable of providing appropriate responses to patients affected by IPV, but these organizations do feel there is sufficient evidence to recommend routine screening.

The U.S. Preventive Services Task Force (USPSTF) is a central organization responsible for collecting data to support screening efforts in primary care settings. Currently, the USPSTF has rated the data as insufficient to support or refute IPV screening in primary care settings. The USPSTF uses the highest standards of evidence when considering data to support their medical screening recommendations, focusing on data described in randomized controlled trials. The USPSTF made their recommendations recognizing the prevalence and health-associated impact of IPV, but raised concerns over the lack of evidence that screening for IPV leads to decreased disability or premature death, limited data on screening among older adults and children, insufficient data describing screening instruments, and a lack of evidence describing the potential for harm resulting from IPV screening processes.

Criticisms of the USPSTF recommendations center on the issue of categorizing the assessment of IPV screening from the framework of medical screening (i.e., screening for heart disease or colon cancer) rather than IPV identification as part of a behavioral health assessment. Concerns raised included the USPSTF's suggestion of possible harm while citing that there were no data assessing the presence of harm associated with IPV screening and the exclusion from their review of 750 studies on screening and 650 studies on intervention, including those that looked at pregnant women, as well as studies that examined patients presenting with trauma.

Recently, the Institute of Medicine (IOM) was commissioned by the Department of Health and Human Services (HHS) to review what preventive services are necessary for women's health and well-being and should be considered in the development of comprehensive guidelines for preventive services for women. After reviewing the USPSTF data along with data published since the 2004 USPSTF recommendations, the IOM found sufficient evidence to support recommending the routing screening of women and adolescent girls (Fox & McCarthy, 2011)

New data considered included a large, well-done randomized controlled trial of IPV screening conducted in primary and acute care settings in Canada. While no direct benefit in terms of reduced rates of IPV was demonstrated, screening was associated with improved quality of life. This study was also the first randomized controlled trial that documented that no harm to patients was associated with IPV screening. Other data have emerged documenting significant benefit associated with IPV-related interventions.

Several brief IPV screening instruments have been validated for use in primary care settings. Single-item screening questions have consistently demonstrated poor sensitivity and are not the best screening instruments. Most brief, recommended validated instruments have three to eight questions and vary in sensitivities from 30 to100 percent and specificities from 80 to 99 percent.

Intervention

Once patients experiencing the effects of IPV are identified, physicians are well positioned to address their needs. Provider actions should be guided by efforts to promote the safety, well-being, and empowerment of IPV survivors. Survivor empowerment begins with listening and validating the experiences related to the disclosure while assuring privacy and confidentiality, unless suicidal or homicidal intentions are identified or the state in which a provider is practicing requires mandated reporting. Providers should familiarize themselves with local laws and policies within their health system regarding variations that exist in mandatory reporting laws related to IPV, and all patients should be made aware of mandated reporting requirements *before* they are asked questions about violence and safety so they can make an informed decision about what to disclose. The provider should communicate that no person deserves to be abused and that every person has the right to be respected in all of their interpersonal relationships. Further empowerment can be provided by assessing the patient's preferences for next steps and potentially helping her develop safety planning measures. Survivors are the experts of their situations. Providers should respect the fact that many survivors may stay with their partners out of choice or necessity. Providers can help survivors identify at-risk times and behaviors. Safety planning involves constructing strategies to help facilitate egress from danger by developing plans for safe contacts and by assembling important documents should the patient need to leave quickly. Providers should offer survivors contact numbers and an opportunity to call local IPV-related resources. Most community IPV shelters offer services other than shelter (mental health, legal advocacy, support) that can be helpful to survivors who are not interested or able to leave. Providers should offer close follow-up and documentation of IPV-related incidents to support ongoing survivor advocacy.

Providers should include adequate documentation of incidents of IPV in the medical record. Depending on state and local regulations, provider documentation can be used to help advocate for the patient for IPV-related adjudications. Documentation of subjective content should use wording provided by the patient and quotes when possible. Names, locations, use of weapons, and timing of events can be helpful to document. Providers can offer to take pictures of injuries including rulers to provide a sense of scale and the survivor's face to help verify the identity of the injured patient. Body maps are another means of documenting the location and extent of injury. Finally, providers should document their assessment of the events, clinical impact, plans for safety planning, resource and treatment coordination, and follow-up.

Screening is also a time when providers can provide educational interventions regarding IPV. Discussing how common IPV experiences are and the known effects of experiencing or witnessing IPV can help support survivor decision making regarding disclosure and help-seeking. Patients who do not disclose IPV may not have experienced IPV or may not be ready to discuss the issue at that time. It is important that providers communicate that they will always be available in the future should a person ever want to discuss current or past IPV experiences. Educational interventions may also help patients who may know a person experiencing IPV.

Prevention

Data are lacking to support any particular primary prevention strategy. The screening and intervention strategies described in the preceding sections are designed to help reduce future exposures to IPV and increase the safety of those affected. Patient education can help people in identifying IPV as a problem and build connections between their experiences with IPV and the health of their families.

Breaking cycles of violence is a central tenet of primary prevention and involves addressing the needs of children who have experienced or witnessed IPV. Pediatric providers should screen patients' caregivers for IPV experiences, educate caregivers about the impact of IPV on child health, and provide resources for both survivors and their children. Discussing healthy relationships with adolescent patients also may be beneficial. Identification and engagement of IPV perpetrators in therapeutic treatment programs and criminal justice interventions when necessary also have the potential to address the root cause of IPV. Commonsense strategies support initiatives to provide a clinical environment that promotes disclosure, provides resource information, and addresses behavioral social norms.

See also: Health Effects of Domestic Abuse; Pregnancy and Domestic Abuse; Reproductive Coercion

Further Reading

Abbott, J., Johnson, R., et al. (1995). Domestic violence against women: Incidence and prevalence in an emergency department population. *Journal of the American Medical Association* 273(22), 1763–1767.

Basile, K., Hertz, M., et al. (2007). *Intimate partner violence and sexual violence victimization assessment instruments for use in healthcare settings: Version 1.* Atlanta (GA), Centers for Disease Control and Prevention, National Center for Injury Prevention and Control.

Black, M., et al. (2011). The National Intimate Partner and Sexual Violence Survey (NISVS): 2010 Summary Report. Atlanta, GA, National Center for Injury Prevention and Control, Centers for Disease Control and Prevention.

Bradley, F. et al. (2002). Reported frequency of domestic violence: Cross-sectional survey of women attending general practice. *BMJ, 324*(7332), 2.

Campbell, J. C. (2002). Health consequences of intimate partner violence. *Lancet, 359* (9314), 1331–1336.

Coben, J. H., & Friedman, D. I. (2002). Health care use by perpetrators of domestic violence. *Journal of Emergency Medicine, 22*(3), 313–317.

Coker, A. L., Davis, K. E., et al. (2002). Physical and mental health effects of intimate partner violence for men and women. *American Journal of Preventive Medicine, 23*(4), 260–268.

Fox, M., & McCarthy, M. (2011, July 19). Institute of Medicine report recommends free women's health services. *National Journal.* Retrieved January 30, 2013 from http://www.nationaljournal.com/healthcare/institute-of-medicine-report-recommends-free-women-s-health-services-20110719

Lapidus, G., Cooke, M. B., et al. (2002). A statewide survey of domestic violence screening behaviors among pediatricians and family physicians. *Archives of Pediatrics & Adolescent Medicine, 156*(4), 332–336.

Lloyd, S. (1997). The effects of domestic violence on women's employment. *Law & Policy, 19*(2), 139–167.

MacMillan, H. L., Wathen, C. N., et al. (2009). Screening for intimate partner violence in health care settings: A randomized trial. *Journal of the American Medical Association, 302*(5), 493–501.

Oriel, K., & Fleming, M. (1998). Screening men for partner violence in a primary care setting: A new strategy for detecting domestic violence. *Journal of Family Practice, 46*(6), 493–498.

Rodriguez, M. A., Bauer, H. M., et al. (1999). Screening and intervention for intimate partner abuse: Practices and attitudes of primary care physicians. *Journal of the American Medical Association, 282*(5), 468–474.

Tjaden, P., & Thoennes, N. (2000). Full report of the prevalence, incidence, and consequences of violence against women: Findings from the National Violence Against Women Survey. Washington, D.C: National Institute of Justice.

Waalen, J., Goodwin, M. M., et al. (2000). Screening for intimate partner violence by health care providers. Barriers and interventions. *American Journal of Preventive Medicine, 19*(4), 230–237.

Peter F. Cronholm and Megan H. Bair-Merritt

PIZZEY, ERIN

Journalist and author Erin Pizzey is best known for establishing Chiswick Women's Aid in England, the first refuge for battered women. Pizzey opened her first community center in 1971 to assist families in obtaining government services. Pizzey then established the National Women's Aid Federation to coordinate services specifically for victims of domestic violence, and the organization expanded throughout the United Kingdom. Pizzey's refuge served as the model for the creation of refuges in many countries. She continued to oversee Chiswick Women's Aid until 1981. Despite considerable changes in the organization, leaders of Women's Aid have persevered in the work begun by Pizzey—seeking an end to domestic violence by providing family shelters and advocating for coherent domestic abuse policies and legal protection for families in crisis. Pizzey wrote several nonfiction books, such as *Scream Quietly or the Neighbors Will Hear* (1974), *Infernal Child* (1978), and *Prone to Violence* (1982); her books often address issues of domestic violence. She was frequently criticized for her theories about violence-prone women who seek relationships with aggressive men as a means of continuing their addiction to violent behavior.

At the Chiswick facility, Pizzey met with a persistent stream of abused families. Her first book, *Scream Quietly or the Neighbors Will Hear* (1974), graphically exposed the secret lives of many of the battered women. The book was later made into a film that aired on American *PBS* in 1979. Through her writing, she challenged society to cease its ignorance or excuse of domestic abuse. Finding her voice and an audience, Pizzey continued to write, advocate, lobby, and campaign against domestic violence. Her work directly impacted the establishment of the Select Committee on Violence in Marriage in 1974, which resulted in a comprehensive legislation package called the Domestic Violence and Matrimonial Proceedings Act 1976.

However, Pizzey's wide-range public activities were not always well received. Her outspoken support of traditional marriage and family values set her at odds with feminists who claimed that capitalism and men were responsible for the degradation of women. According to Pizzey, left-wing feminists viewed the role of a father as obsolete. Pizzey, though, included men in her advocacy work, and she often invited men to participate in shelter maintenance. She objected when men were exclusively blamed for domestic abuse. She believed that abusive adults, both males and females, were generally products of abusive parents, not of the capitalist political system. Children who witnessed domestic violence learned to emulate patterns of abuse.

Pizzey also distinguished between types of abused women, and her theories are elaborated in *Prone to Violence* (1982). She suggested that in some violent relationships, men and women were equally capable of violence. According to Pizzey, these "violence-prone women" had a psychological addiction that caused them to seek violent relationships. Her views once again set her in opposition to feminists, who were eager to portray women as innocent and naïve victims of abusive, power-hungry men. Pizzey's opponents verbally attacked her and claimed that she promoted the view that women *wanted* to be beaten. She rejected their accusations, and she was consistent in her belief that the addiction (not the victim) was responsible for reciprocal cycles of abuse between domestic partners.

To test her hypothesis that separate victim categories existed, Pizzey collaborated with Dr. John Gayford in 1975 to design a questionnaire. The forms were distributed to shelter residents, and the results of the study were republished in 2009. These results have often been cited, and the pair's work prompted further clinical investigations into domestic violence. Pizzey and Gayford (as well as other investigators) were able to sort the information using a variety of data, such as age, alcohol use, sex, nationality, and education. A random selection of survey forms showed that 62 percent of the women who filled out questionnaires were both violence-prone and abused as children. Pizzey concluded that intergenerational family violence is more widespread than isolated cases of domestic abuse. In her concluding remarks, she warned that criminal punishment will not solve the crisis of intergenerational violence; instead, successful interventions involving entire families may break the cycle of violence before it overwhelms another generation of children.

The intergenerational violence that Pizzey experienced in her own family eventually led her to formulate many of her thoughts about patterns of abuse. Much of her childhood is detailed in *Infernal Child* (1978). Pizzey has said that she was raised in a loveless family. She and her twin sister, Rosaleen, were born February 19, 1939, in Tsingtao, China. The children's father, Cyril Carney, was a foreign diplomat who had grown up in a large Irish family. Pizzey recalled that her father despised his mother, but he admired his violent father. She also claimed that her mother was physically and verbally abusive to her children, and she often likened Pizzey to her own mother, an alleged prostitute who died in a Swiss insane asylum. Pizzey has acknowledged her own violent tendencies, which once brought her dangerously close to killing her father.

Her mother, Pat Carney, died of cancer when Pizzey was 17 years old. In Pizzey's 2011 memoir, *This Way to the Revolution*, she recalled the impact of the events after her mother's death. Pizzey's father initially refused to allow a burial for his deceased wife. He chose, instead, to lay her body upon the dining room table and established a ritual for nightly viewing of the corpse by himself and his three teenaged children. Pizzey described the psychological trauma of being forced to witness her mother's decomposition for six days. She also writes about her frustration over the neighbors' apathy and their refusal to intervene in the psychological abuse taking place in the Carney household. Pizzey found the community's lack of compassion disturbing. The event was a motivating force behind her future hands-on community assistance model; she writes, "I would never be one of those indifferent neighbours and turn my back on those in need" (2011, p. 245). Although 15 years would pass between her mother's death and the opening of her first community center, Pizzey's unorthodox childhood clearly affected her desire to assist victims of domestic violence.

In 1961, she married Jack Pizzey in the United Kingdom and gave birth to daughter Cleo in Singapore later that year. The family afterward returned to England, where their son was born. As the mother of two small children and wife of a BBC journalist who worked long hours, Pizzey found herself longing for a women's community that would alleviate her isolation. She desired a community in which women could support each other, reminiscent of the extended families that she observed during her travels abroad. Her search for community brought Pizzey into contact with the women's movement, a political liberation organization. Ultimately, however, she believed the feminist movement was founded upon Communist idealism, which Pizzey viewed as destructive to families and which she felt promoted men as oppressors; Pizzey loved her family and husband, and she found no solace in a movement that sought to destroy men.

Through her short-lived involvement with the feminist movement, Pizzey met a number of like-minded women who shared her vision for community. In 1971, the group established a small assistance center at a house on Belmont Terrace. The center became a place where women could solicit advice on navigating the complex government aid systems in England, such as Social Security. Shortly after the center opened, a battered woman arrived. She had been abused and claimed no one would help her. Pizzey was reminded of her own childhood in an abusive family. She felt tremendous compassion for the woman, and the center unexpectedly became a refuge.

The first house was not large, and it could not withstand the pressures of an increasing full-time population. Pizzey was adamant that no woman or her children would be refused, and her "open-door" policy led to overcrowding that quickly became a health-regulations problem. By 1974, the group had procured a larger facility, called the Big House on Chiswick High Road. Pizzey envisioned a dormitory-like, hostel-style environment in which women and children could take responsibility for themselves in a community setting. The model of Pizzey's refuge conflicted with the more popular methods for assisting victims of domestic abuse in which victims were often placed with an accommodating family until independent housing could be provided. Pizzey found such a model to be ineffective because victimized women and children often could not integrate, even for short periods of time, into a nonviolent family. In addition, once the women and children were relocated into private housing, the mothers often experienced social isolation. She discovered that the women's loneliness often prompted them to seek comfort from predatory individuals or return to their abusive partners; in some cases, the victims experienced extreme depression and committed suicide. In Pizzey's refuge design, therefore, she sought to minimize the isolation of the women. The housework, maintenance, and child-care needs were provided by the shelter residents in a cooperative manner. Pizzey believed that through a community-based model, the mothers could better learn to cope with their new lives, while still giving each other social support. Ultimately, she hoped each woman could learn to parent responsibly, and each child could grow up without continued violence.

Pizzey's model of Women's Aid worked well, and it prompted other countries to request her assistance. In 1978, she was invited to New Zealand to share her insights, and the following year, the U.S. Salvation Army invited her to lecture in 21 American cities. In 1981, however, her position within Women's Aid was abruptly altered. The Greater London Council (GLC) offered a substantial amount of public money to maintain the refuge. Pizzey's history with the GLC had been strained, and she suspected that, if the GLC took control of the refuge, her position might be temporary. Despite her concerns, she decided that the shelter residents should make the decision to accept or reject the GLC's offer. She explained that the GLC's funding would bring scrupulous accounting and governmental regulation to the refuge, but she also advised that the money would enable the shelter to continue operating indefinitely. The residents ultimately decided to accept the offer. Late in 1981, a new director informed Pizzey that she was no longer welcome on the refuge's property. She accepted exile from the refuge and took pride in the fact that she had been influential in establishing refuges throughout the world.

Pizzey's exclusion from Women's Aid did not stop her involvement in preventing domestic abuse. After her departure, she wrote novels, traveled, lectured, and wrote about domestic violence issues. She was given the Nancy Astor Award for Journalism in 1983, and she received the St. Valentino Palm d'Oro International Award for Literature in 1994. She spent 15 years away from England, residing in New Mexico, the Caribbean, and Italy. In 1997, Erin Pizzey returned to England, where she continued to work as a family advocate and an author. She currently resides in London.

See also: Europe and Domestic Abuse; Women's Aid Federation of England; Women's Rights Movement

Further Reading

Erin Pizzey: http://www.erinpizzey.com
Fathers for Life on Erin Pizzey: http://www.fathersforlife.org/pizzey/cv.htm
Pizzey, E. (1974). *Scream quietly or the neighbours will hear.* Harmondsworth, England: Penguin.
Pizzey, E. (1978). *Infernal child: A memoir.* London, England: Victor Gollancz.
Pizzey, E. (2009). Practice report: A comparative study of battered women and violence-prone women. *Journal of Aggression, Conflict and Peace Research, 1*(2), 53–62.
Pizzey, E. (2011). *This way to the revolution: A memoir.* London, England: Peter Owen.
Pizzey, E., & Shapiro, J. (1982). *Prone to violence.* Feltham, England: Hamlyn.
Rappaport, H. (2001). *Encyclopedia of women social reformers.* Santa Barbara, CA: ABC-CLIO.
Reece, H. (2006). The end of domestic violence. *Modern Law Review, 69*(5), 770–791.
Worell, J. (2001). *Encyclopedia of women and gender: Sex similarities and differences and the impact of society on gender.* San Diego, CA: Academic Press.

Denice Knight-Slater

POLICING DOMESTIC ABUSE

When domestic abuse escalates to the point of violence, police or other law enforcement officers are often tasked with responding to and resolving these incidents. There are many issues that affect the police response to domestic violence. For example, domestic violence calls are often some of the most dangerous handled by officers, requiring particular attention to officer safety. Additionally, family violence legislation aimed at deterring and decreasing domestic violence impacts the approach, handling, and disposition of domestic violence situations by police. Varying types of relationships and family structures can influence the police response to domestic violence. Another significant factor for the police officer is his or her perceived role in such matters (e.g., enforcement- or service-driven). Further, officers' attitudes, knowledge, and beliefs are also important to consider when discussing the police response to domestic violence. For example, officers would often prefer more flexibility in how they are allowed to handle domestic violence calls, as the legal limitations placed on them are generally viewed as too restrictive. A final issue warranting attention is that officers and laypersons may have disparate perspectives and methods with regard to the handling of domestic violence calls. This entry will review relevant issues in the police response to domestic violence regarding both policy and its application in the real world.

Risk to Officers

Calls for service involving domestic violence are among the most dangerous to which police officers respond. Specifically, data collected by the Federal Bureau of Investigation (FBI), for their Uniform Crime Report (UCR), Law Enforcement Officers Killed and Assaulted (LEOKA), indicate that 31.3 percent of officers who were assaulted in the line of duty were responding to domestic/general disturbance calls (FBI, 2010). Domestic violence cases pose unique dangers to officers. First, there are usually at least two citizens on the scene with whom police must interact. Also, these encounters often take place inside the homes. The danger for officers is increased because the subject and the victim are both more familiar with the layout of the building than officers. For example, officers may not know where weapons may be hidden or escape routes are located. Such encounters are volatile, due in part to heightened emotions of the parties involved and the often complex nature of these relationships. In particular, there is a danger that if a suspect becomes resistant or violent with police officers, the victim may actually intercede on behalf of the suspect, which could potentially take officers by surprise. Knowing the risks involved in responding to domestic violence cases can influence officers' priorities when handling these situations by forcing them to place a strong emphasis on their own safety.

Domestic Violence Legislation

Once officers have assured their own safety at the scene of a domestic violence situation, they can begin to consider the legal options available to them for resolution of the case. Prior to the 1980s, most considered the issue of domestic violence to be a private family matter, not requiring outside intervention. However, as domestic violence became a more prevalent social issue in the late 1980s and 1990s, legislation requiring or preferring arrest in such situations became more common. Under these laws, officers are now encouraged or even required to make an arrest in cases of domestic violence. These laws were created to deter abusers from engaging in violence against their spouses and to protect victims from harm. In one of the classic studies in outcomes of police intervention in domestic violence cases, Sherman and Berk (1984) found that arrest led to the least amount of recidivism. Since that time, some investigations of the effects of these laws on deterrence have revealed that there is no significant impact. However, Garner and Maxwell (2000) have argued that the reason for this could be inadequate methodological rigor in previous studies. For example, Hirschel, Buzawa, Pattavina, and Faggiani (2007) used data from the National Incident Based Reporting System (NIBRS), and analyzed it using hierarchical general linear modeling techniques. Their investigation revealed that mandatory arrest laws increased arrest rates among offenders and mediated disparities in arrest rates based on gender, race, and other variables. Hirschel et al. (2007) propose that mandatory arrest legislation compel police officers to take a more mechanistic approach to law enforcement in domestic violence, as opposed to using their own discretion. Many advocates and victims view this as positive change, maintaining that use of police discretion previously led to inaction in such cases. Additionally, Garner and Maxwell (2000) also found that arrest does, in fact, tend to deter repeated domestic violence. However, the frequency with which police were required to respond to domestic violence cases was not reduced. Finally, Garner and Maxwell (2000) found that mandatory and preferred arrest laws were efficacious in protecting victims from harm.

A criticism of mandatory and preferred arrest laws has been that they can lead to dual arrest situations, in which the domestic violence victim is arrested in addition to the perpetrator. Hirschel et al. (2007) found that, although mandatory arrest effectively increased offender arrest rates, it also increased dual arrests in some situations. Finn and Bettis (2006) sought to determine officers' rationales for arresting both parties in cases of domestic violence. They found that officers most often reported arresting both parties because it was required under the law and/or they felt it was the best way to connect both parties to needed resources (e.g., therapy, child and family services). Mandatory and preferred arrest laws, like many laws, cannot account for all possible circumstances in their enforcement. Specifically, these laws often require responding officers to determine the primary aggressor, or primary perpetrator of violence. In cases in which the victim has defended him/herself vigorously, or in which both parties appear to participate equally in attacking each other, making such a determination can be quite difficult. If officers are forced to make an arrest in these situations, arresting both parties may be the only fair course of action at the time.

Diversity in Domestic Violence

Domestic violence traverses many lines that divide the general public. Domestic violence can and does occur regardless of socioeconomic status, race, sexual orientation, religion, or other demographic factors. Thus, when police respond to domestic violence, they must be prepared to address it in the context in which it occurs. These differences can affect how police officers respond to domestic violence cases. One example is the police response to domestic violence in same-sex couples. Often, same-sex couples are not included in the verbiage of domestic violence legislation. Further, there has been a fear within the gay and lesbian community that homophobia might lead police to respond differently to domestic violence among gay and lesbian couples. Research conducted in California illustrated that officers in that state did not perceive a scenario involving domestic violence differently based on sexual orientation of those involved. It must be noted, however, that in California the domestic violence legislation specifically includes same-sex couples. Thus, the research findings suggest that in states that include same-sex couples/families in their domestic violence legislation, homophobia on the part of police officers does not seem to impact their ability to fairly enforce the law. Of course, the relationship of potential biases to same-sex relationships is more complex and likely to vary by state, police department, and even the officer.

Officer-Level Factors

Several factors influence how individual officers will respond to domestic violence situations.

Perceived Roles

Officers have different ideas about their role in responding to domestic violence. How an officer conceives his or her role and responsibility in responding to domestic violence can have a serious impact on the type of response that is provided. For example, if an officer views his/her role as being an enforcer, he/she might place emphasis on making arrests or finding violations of the law. However, if the officer sees protecting victims as the most important aspect of the job in domestic violence response, he/she might focus on referrals to social services. Researchers have theorized that officers' perceptions of their role can be viewed as a continuum. These perceived roles can range from strict enforcer (e.g., legalistic, enforcement driven) to more of a service officer (e.g., social service related, service driven). Within these two roles is a balance between enforcement and service that Balenovich et al. (2008) refer to as the "integrated investigator." They maintain that this latter role is the optimal perception for officers to hold when responding to domestic violence. However, the enforcement-driven role was most common among police officers.

Officer Attitudes and Beliefs toward Response to Domestic Violence

Police officers have disparate views regarding response to domestic violence situations. Overall, they recognize the importance of responding to domestic violence in their communities to protect victims and prevent future violence when possible. Research by Gover, Paul, and Dodge (2011) suggests that police officers feel they need more flexibility in their ability to utilize their own discretion in responding to domestic violence. Officers believed that many of the recent laws regarding domestic violence were too restrictive of their actions to operate as effectively as they would like. Further, officers acknowledged the risk to police intervening in domestic violence cases. In addition, officers in this study were quite knowledgeable about domestic violence trends and statistics.

Mandatory and preferred arrest laws have not been shown to significantly impact the beliefs officers have about domestic violence. Overall, officers who were hired and trained prior to enactment of such laws reported similar presentations regarding domestic violence cases as officers who were hired and trained subsequent to their passage. Although legislation does not appear to impact attitudes per se, it does affect the actions and outcomes of police responses to domestic violence cases.

The attitudes and beliefs held by police are often different from the public, or even across law enforcement agencies or groups. There are disparate perceptions of what methods of intervention are effective in domestic violence cases. Specifically, Stalans and Finn (2006) found that rookie officers, experienced officers, and laypersons all have different views on domestic violence response by police. Their research revealed that laypersons were less likely to believe that any of the police interventions would be effective. In particular, laypersons reported that asking one party to leave or arresting the man as less effective strategies than did rookie or experienced officers. Interestingly, laypersons and rookie officers found threatening to arrest, doing nothing, and letting the couple handle it to be more effective than did experienced officers. A likely interpretation of this finding is that experienced officers, having tried these interventions early in their careers, have found them less efficacious over time, preferring to take more decisive action.

Summary

Police officers are often called upon to respond to domestic violence incidents. Many issues affect their response to such situations. For example, domestic violence calls are more dangerous than many other types of calls handled by officers. Additionally, legislation intended to deter and decrease domestic violence influences the way police respond to domestic violence situations. Differing kinds of relationships also affect the way in which domestic violence is handled. The officer's perceived role in such matters (e.g., enforcement or service driven) impacts the way in which domestic violence cases are handled by police. Further, officers' attitudes, knowledge, and beliefs are important to consider when discussing the police response to domestic violence. Finally, officers and laypersons may view methods of handling domestic violence situations differently.

See also: Legislation and Policies, Domestic Abuse; Mandatory Arrest Policies

Further Reading

Balenovich, J., Grossi, E., & Hughes, T. (2008). Toward a balanced approach: Defining police roles in responding to domestic violence. *American Journal of Criminal Justice, 33,* 19–31. doi: 10.1007/s12103-007-9028-5

Buzawa, E. S., & Buzawa, C. G. (1996). *Domestic violence: The criminal justice response* (2nd ed.). Thousand Oaks, CA: Sage.

Centers for Disease Control and Prevention. http://www.cdc.gov/ViolencePrevention/intimatepartnerviolence/

Domestic violence: Best practices for law enforcement response; A model policy manual prepared under the Violence Against Women Act: http://www.ncgccd.org/pubs/dvproto.pdf

Federal Bureau of Investigation (2010, October). Law enforcement officers feloniously killed and assaulted: Percent distribution by circumstance at scene of incident, 2000–2009. In

Law enforcement officers killed and assaulted, 2009 (Figure 4). Retrieved from http://www2.fbi.gov/ucr/killed/2009/data/figure_04.html

Finn, M. A., & Bettis, P. (2006). Punitive action or gentle persuasion: Exploring police officers' justifications for using dual arrest in domestic violence cases. *Violence Against Women, 12,* 268–287.

Garner, J. H., & Maxwell, C. D. (2000). What are the lessons of the police arrest studies? *Journal of Aggression, Maltreatment, & Trauma, 4,* 83–114.

Gover, A. R., Paul, D. P., & Dodge, M. (2011). Law enforcement officers' attitudes about domestic violence. *Violence Against Women, 15,* 619–636.

Hirschel, D., Buzawa, E., Pattavina, A., & Faggiani, D. (2007). Domestic violence and mandatory arrest laws: To what extent do they influence police arrest decisions? *Journal of Criminal Law & Criminology, 98*(1), 255–298.

Law enforcement response to domestic violence calls for service: https://www.ncjrs.gov/pdffiles1/nij/grants/215915.pdf

Rominson, A. L. (2000). The effect of a domestic violence policy change on police officers' schemata. *Criminal Justice and Behavior, 27,* 600–624.

Sherman, L. W., & Berk, R. A. (1984). The specific deterrent effects of arrest for domestic assault. *American Sociological Review, 49,* 261–272.

Stalans, L. J., & Finn, M. A. (2006). Public and police officers' interpretation and handling of domestic violence cases. *Journal of Interpersonal Violence, 21,* 1129–1155.

Younglove, J. A., Kerr, M. G., & Vitello, C. J. (2002). Law enforcement officers' perceptions of same sex domestic violence: Reason for cautious optimism. *Journal of Interpersonal Violence, 17,* 760–772.

Kori A. Hakala, Samuel L. Browning, and Vincent B. Van Hasselt

PREGNANCY AND DOMESTIC ABUSE

Each year in the United States approximately 14–35 percent of women visiting an Emergency Department and 12–23 percent of women in Family Medicine settings reported having been physically abused or threatened by their partner within the previous year. Generally, obstetric and gynecological physicians (ob-gyns) have reported even higher rates of abuse. Annually, an estimated 324,000 pregnant women are abused, which makes domestic violence during pregnancy more common than preeclampsia and gestational diabetes. In 2005, the CDC reported that homicide is now a leading cause of death for new and expectant mothers, second only to auto accidents. Homicide accounted for 31 percent of maternal injury deaths. One study found that 77 percent of abused pregnant women were killed by their abusers during their first trimester. The majority of domestic violence homicides of pregnant women involve firearms.

Teens are particularly at risk. The 2011 CDC Youth Risk Surveillance Study found 14.5 percent of female twelfth-graders had been forced to have sex. As many as two-thirds of pregnant adolescents endured physical or sexual abuse in their lifetimes. No less than 25 percent, with some estimates as high as 80 percent, of pregnant teens are in violent, abusive, or coercive relationships before, during, and/or immediately after their pregnancy. Pregnant teens are the highest-risk age group. Abused pregnant women are most often killed early in their pregnancy.

Bill Clinton and Candice Slaughter, who was physically abused while pregnant. (AP Photo/ Wilfredo Lee)

Similarly, women of color are more vulnerable to experiencing abuse while pregnant. Black women had a maternal homicide risk seven times that of white women, with black women ages 25 to 29 at a shocking 11 times greater risk.

Women with lower socioeconomic status are at greater risk for enduring abuse during pregnancy. Women in these social classes also tend to lack the same degree of social support as middle- and upper-class women, hence may stay in abusive relationships longer.

The problem of abuse during pregnancy is true outside the United States as well. Arslantas et al. (2012) studied 253 pregnant women in Turkey. They found that 24.1 percent had experienced domestic violence previously, and 11.1 percent saw the abuse continue into their pregnancy. Women with less education and whose pregnancy was unintended were more likely to suffer abuse. In India, studies show 13 to 16 percent of pregnant women endures domestic violence. Research by Mahapatro, Gipta, Gupta, and Kundu (2011) found domestic violence to be prevalent during pregnancy and far worse when the husband or the wife believed the baby to be a female. Women's Aid workers in the United Kingdom have also reported an increase in incidents of women being abused during pregnancy.

Sometimes, women who are being abused prior to getting pregnant believe that their pregnancy will stop the abuse. The reality is typically the opposite: that is, for approximately 70 percent of women, the abuse continues during the pregnancy. In many cases, the abuse increases in frequency or intensity.

Many women become pregnant with abusers' babies due to birth control sabotage, often referred to as reproductive coercion. One study found two-thirds of women who experienced domestic abuse also had been victims of birth control sabotage. Women may be beaten or coerced to submit to unwanted abortions. Several studies have shown that the risk of enduring abuse during pregnancy increases when the baby is not planned. One study found women with unintended pregnancies were four times more likely to endure physical violence than those whose pregnancies were planned. Nearly one in seven women who sought abortions at a large family planning clinic in Iowa (13.8 percent) reported at least one incident of physical or sexual abuse in the past year, usually by an intimate partner. The prevalence of physical and sexual violence by an intimate partner was 9.9 percent and 2.5 percent, respectively, according to the study, published in the *American Journal of Public Health*. Possible explanations for this include that the abusing partner is jealous of the unborn child or that the baby will reduce the woman's ability to care for her spouse or partner. Additionally, given that abuse is about control, perhaps some male abusers are upset that they felt they could not control the pregnancy. The risk for enduring abuse while pregnant is also greater for younger women.

Research has shown pregnant women are among the least likely to report abuse. A study of more than 16,000 women who gave birth in Texas found 5 percent had experienced abuse but only 1 percent had reported it.

Both physical and verbal abuse during pregnancy has been linked to a host of complications, ranging from low birth weight to premature labor to miscarriage and infant death. Pregnant women who are enduring abuse often delay seeking prenatal care, resulting in a variety of complications. Abused women are twice as likely to delay prenatal care as women who are not abused. Women who are abused during or just prior to pregnancy are 60 percent more likely to have high blood pressure, vaginal bleeding, severe nausea, kidney or urinary tract infections, and hospitalization during pregnancy compared to nonabused women.

Several studies have found correlations between domestic violence and other detrimental maternal behaviors, including smoking and alcohol and drug abuse. Women who are enduring abuse may eat unhealthily, suffer from depression, have poor weight gain, and experience anemia.

Experiencing domestic violence during pregnancy can affect overall reproductive health, as it might bring about gynecological disorders, sexually transmitted diseases, or HIV/AIDS. A study of families in India published in 2006 found that a mother's experiencing domestic violence significantly increases the risk of infant death The study found almost one in five prenatal (28 weeks of pregnancy to the first seven days after birth) and neonatal (first month following birth) deaths could be prevented if abuse is prevented. The study found nearly 18 percent of participants had been physically abused by their husbands during pregnancy. Michael Koenig, coauthor of the study and associate professor in the Bloomberg School's Department of Population and Family Health Sciences, noted, "Our results underscore the need for public education and awareness programs in developing countries such as India that highlight the serious and negative consequences of domestic violence, not only for women but for their children as well. The prevention of domestic violence may be an important, but largely overlooked, intervention for improving child survival in such settings."

Data suggest that few primary care providers screen for IPV. Rates of screening tend to range between 10 percent and 25 percent of providers. Yet fewer than half of pregnant women are screened. Providers cite a variety of barriers to screening related to a perceived lack of time, training, comfort, and access to effective resources. Providers have also raised concerns over the possibility of harm related to screening that might include fear of offending the patient, possible retaliation and police involvement, as well as cultural differences. Medical professionals who deal with pregnant women are ideally suited to screen for abuse and to provide victims with resources and support, however. Physicians and their staff should be trained about domestic violence.

The Affordable Care Act was passed in the United States in 2010 and included provisions to support America's Healthy Futures Act, a $1.5 billion, five-year national initiative to support maternal infant and early childhood home visitation programs. It also included new requirements for states to enact home visitation programs to reduce domestic violence.

In addition to providing funds to support these services, the legislation also included new benchmark requirements for states. One such benchmark requires home visitation programs to measure a reduction in "crime or domestic violence."

Futures Without Violence provides a wealth of data and important tools for addressing domestic violence during pregnancy. Its Healthy Moms, Healthy Babies Train the Trainer Curriculum can be used by state and local entities as well as non-profit groups as part of their home visitation processes.

Additionally Futures Without Violence offers numerous tools for health-care professionals to help them understand the connections between domestic violence, pregnancy, and other health-related issues. The organization also helps sponsor an annual Health Cares About Domestic Violence day the second Wednesday in October and an annual National Conference on Health and Domestic Violence.

Another useful guide called *Addressing Intimate Partner Violence, Reproductive and Sexual Coercion: A Guide for Obstetric, Gynecologic, and Reproductive Health Care Settings* is available at http://www.KnowMoreSayMore.org. That website also features the stories of women who have endured reproductive coercion or abuse during pregnancy, as well as fact sheets and resources for teens, parents, educators, and health-care professionals.

See also: Health Effects of Domestic Abuse; Physicians, Health-Care Providers, and Domestic Abuse; Reproductive Coercion; Types of Domestic Abuse

Further Reading

Arslantas, H., Adana, F., Ergin, F., Gey, N., Bicer, N., & Kiransal, N. (2012). Domestic violence during pregnancy in and eastern city of Turkey: A field study. *Journal of Interpersonal Violence, 27*(7), 1293–1313.

Ascribe Newswire. (2006, August 1). Domestic violence during pregnancy increases risk of early childhood mortality. Retrieved April 27, 2012, from http://www.ncdsv.org/

images/DV%20during%20Pregnancy%20Increases%20Risk%20of%20Early%20Childhood%20Mort.pdf

Family Violence Prevention Fund. (2010, January 26). Study: Many victims of partner violence experience reproductive coercion. Retrieved June 21, 2012, from http://www.ncdsv.org/images/SpeakingUp_ManyVicimsofPVExpReproductiveCoercion_1-26-10.pdf

Futures Without Violence: http://www.futureswithoutviolence.org

Harvard School of Public Health. (2006, June 28). Violence from male partners associated with serious health threats to pregnant women and newborns. Retrieved June 20, 2012, from http://www.ncdsv.org/images/Violence%20from%20Male%20Partners%20Associated%20with%20Serious%20Health.pdf

Huggins, C., (2005, August 31). Women's domestic abuse risk rises after childbirth. Retrieved June 21, 2012, from http://www.ncdsv.org/images/WomensDomesticAbuseRiskRisesAfterChildbirth.pdf

Jasinski, J. (2004). Pregnancy and domestic violence: A review of the literature. *Trauma, Violence, & Abuse,* 5(1), 47–64.

Know More Say More: http://www.knowmoresaymore.org

Leiderman, S., & Almo, C. (2006). Interpersonal violence and adolescent pregnancy: Prevalence and implications for practice and policy. *Healthy Teen Network.* Retrieved January 30, 2013, from http://www.healthyteennetwork.org/vertical/Sites/%7BB4D0CC76-CF78-4784-BA7C-5D0436F6040C%7D/uploads/%7B035E2659-FD00-41B8-A195-49CDBA3059DF%7D.PDF

Mahapatro, M., Gupta, R., & Gupta, V. (2012). The risk factor of domestic violence in India. *Indian Journal of Community Medicine,* 37(3), 153–157.

Moore, A., Frohwirth, L., & Miller, E. (2009). Male reproductive control of women who have experienced intimate partner violence in the United States. *Guttmacher Institute.* Retrieved June 20, 2012, from http://www.guttmacher.org/pubs/journals/socscimed201002009.pdf

Norton, M. (2005, July 20). Abused pregnant women at risk of complications. Retrieved April 25, 2012, from http://www.ncdsv.org/images/AbusedPregnantWomenRiskComplications.pdf

Revel, J., & Hobson, J. (2004, May 23). Pregnancy can spark violence by partners. *The Observer* (UK). Retrieved June 21, 2012, from http://www.ncdsv.org/images/Pregnancycansparkviolencepartners.pdf

St. George, D. (2005, February 23). CDC explores pregnancy-homicide link: Killings cited among top causes of trauma death for new, expectant mothers. *Washington Post.* Retrieved April 27, 2012, from http://www.ncdsv.org/images/CDCExploresPregnancy-HomicideLink.pdf

World Health Organization (2002). Intimate partner violence. Retrieved January 30, 2013 from http://www.who.int/violence_injury_prevention/violence/world_report/factsheets/en/ipvfacts.pdf

Laura L. Finley

PREVENTION INSTITUTE

Prevention Institute was founded in 1997 to serve as a focal point for primary prevention practice—promoting policies, organizational practices, and collaborative efforts that improve health and quality of life. Much of the work of the institute addresses domestic violence. Located in central Oakland, California, the organization is committed to investing in the city's development and to promoting nonviolent solutions to problems both inside and outside of city limits.

As a national nonprofit organization, the institute works to prevent illness and injury, to foster health and social equity, and to build momentum for community prevention as an integral component of a quality health system. It synthesizes research and practice; develops prevention tools and frameworks; helps design and guide interdisciplinary partnerships; and conducts training and strategic consultation with government, foundations, and community-based organizations nationwide and internationally.

Taking a comprehensive, integrated approach to solving complex health and social issues, the institute advances prevention efforts that address multiple problems concurrently. It catalyzes prevention strategies that are well designed, reflect and respond to diverse community needs and assets, and achieve far-reaching outcomes. The institute helps practitioners and decision makers achieve outcomes that are enduring and sustainable. It maintains a core focus on promoting health equity, and primary emphases include preventing violence, traffic injuries, and chronic disease.

Prevention Institute has inspired a broad, comprehensive approach to systematizing prevention as a distinct discipline and attempts to provide more than simply an educational message. It infuses a community and policy orientation into prevention practices, and it emphasizes the importance of *quality* prevention strategies—ones that are well designed, achieve far-reaching outcomes, and incorporate these six key elements, as presented on its website:

- Advances Solutions Rooted in Community Wisdom—the combined knowledge, assets, and skills of community members which is the foundation for a stronger, healthier community environment and successful, sustainable prevention efforts.
- Pursues Comprehensive Action to solve complex problems and achieve far-reaching gains in health and safety. Applies a layered framework of mutually supportive community prevention strategies to improve social and physical environments.
- Taking Two Steps to Prevention, tracing a pathway from medical concerns to the community conditions, norms, and root factors leading to poor health and inequality in the first place. Finds community solutions supporting prevention and wellness for everyone.
- Promotes Norms That Support Equity, Health, and Safety. Norms are "behavior shapers," levers for effective prevention. Altering policy is a vital tipping factor for changing norms, leading to supportive behavior and improved health and safety.
- Encourages Interdisciplinary Partnerships to help break down silos; synthesize and integrate knowledge, perspectives, and tools across disciplines; and construct shared comprehensive solutions.
- Catalyzes Innovative Strategies and Analysis that change community-wide systems and foster a new way of thinking where prevention is primary.

Prevention Institute currently supports five key initiatives: Strategic Alliance for Healthy Food and Activity Environments, UNITY, Healthy Places Coalition, Convergence Partnership, and Joint Use Statewide Taskforce.

The Strategic Alliance for Healthy Food and Activity Environments (Strategic Alliance) is a coalition of nutrition and physical activity advocates in California. The Strategic Alliance is shifting the debate on nutrition and physical activity away from a primary focus on personal responsibility and individual choice to one that examines corporate and government practices and the role of the environment in shaping eating and activity behaviors.

UNITY builds support for effective, sustainable efforts to prevent violence before it occurs so that urban youth can thrive in safe environments with supportive relationships and opportunities for success. Young people are severely impacted by violence, and those who live in urban areas are disproportionately affected. Thus, Prevention Institute aims to address urban violence in ways that are both practical and sustainable. This work is not exclusively focused on domestic and dating violence but those issues are included.

The Healthy Places Coalition advances public health involvement in land-use and transportation planning to ensure that all neighborhoods in California promote the opportunity to live a healthy life. The coalition consists of practitioners from the planning, public health, parks and recreation, and other related fields, community advocates, academics, and concerned individuals committed to social and health equity from around the state. Although not directly related to abuse, the promotion of a healthy lifestyle can serve to protect or insulate people from various forms of violence.

Prevention Institute provides ongoing guidance, strategy development, and policy analysis for the Convergence Partnership. The Convergence Partnership is a collaborative of funders in the United States that have come together to jointly advance equity-focused efforts to create environments that support healthy eating and active living. The Convergence Partnership aims to strengthen and accelerate collaboration among practitioners, policy makers, funders, and advocates. The steering committee includes representatives from the California Endowment, Kaiser Permanente, Nemours Foundation, the Robert Wood Johnson Foundation, the W. K. Kellogg Foundation, and the Kresge Foundation. Representatives from the Centers for Disease Control and Prevention serve as critical technical advisors.

Established in May 2008, the Joint Use Statewide Taskforce (JUST) includes organizations representing health, civil rights, community collaborative, planners, local elected and appointed officials, park and recreation officials, school board administrators, academic researchers, and a growing list of groups interested in ensuring that all children have a safe place to play and be active within easy reach. Again, such activity is protective of abuse.

Prevention Institute brings cutting-edge research, practice, and analysis to address important health and safety issues. Determined to achieve health and safety for all, to improve community environments equitably, and to serve as a focal point for primary prevention practice, the institute asks what can be done in the first place, before people get sick or injured. In regard to abuse, Prevention Institute coordinates webinars and other educational programs to help develop knowledge and disseminate best practices to practitioners and communities. This is one of the organization's most wide-reaching efforts to address domestic and dating violence.

See also: Educational Programs; Social Change Campaigns

Further Reading

Centers for Disease Control. (n.d). Teen Dating Violence. Retrieved January 30, 2013 from http://www.cdc.gov/violenceprevention/intimatepartnerviolence/teen_dating_violence.html

Peacock, D. (2003). Building on a legacy of social justice activism: Enlisting men as gender justice activists in South Africa. *Men and Masculinities, 5*(3), 327–330.

Pollack, W., & Shuster, T. (2000). *Real boys' voices: Listening to boys speak out—about drugs, sex, violence, bullying, sports, school, parents, and so much more.* New York: Random House.

Prevention Institute: http://www.preventioninstitute.org

Jennifer Rey

PRISONS AND DOMESTIC ABUSE

According to the Bureau of Justice Statistics, more than 50 percent of the women in jail in 2007 reported they were physically or sexually abused before their imprisonment. This rate far exceeds that of imprisoned males, which was slightly more than 10 percent. Other studies have found much higher rates: A 1999 study by Browne, Miller, and Maguin found that 82 percent of women at New York's Bedford Hills Correctional Facility had a childhood history of severe physical and/or sexual abuse. More than 90 percent had endured either physical or sexual abuse in their lifetime.

According to a report by the Avon Global Center for Women and Justice at the Cornell Law School and the Women in Prison Project of the Correctional Association of New York, an estimated 9 out of 10 women in New York prisons are survivors of physical and sexual abuse. A shocking 93 percent of women in New York's prisons for killing their intimate partners were themselves abused by an intimate partner in the past.

Women who fight back against abusers may be arrested and in many cases are convicted. A study conducted by the Michigan Women's Justice & Clemency Project in 2007 found that, of all homicide convictions and sentences in Oakland County between 1986 and 1988, domestic violence victims had higher conviction rates (78 percent) and longer sentences than all others charged with homicide. Even those with previous violent criminal records were less likely than domestic violence victims to be convicted, at 62 percent. African American women were convicted at a higher rate (80 percent) than all others (62 percent). The study found that a white female defendant who killed another white person could expect an average sentence of 10–30 years. If the woman was a victim of domestic violence, however, she was most likely to receive a life sentence. Although U.S. law allows killing in self-defense, it is rare that women who kill their batterers are successful in self-defense claims, resulting in 75–80 percent of women who killed in self-defense being convicted or convinced to plead guilty.

In 2012, the case of Marissa Alexander garnered attention in Florida and beyond. Alexander was sentenced to 20 years in prison for firing a warning shot at the wall as a way to stop her husband from abusing her. He was not in any way injured from the shot. Alexander, who had never been arrested before she fired the warning shot in 2010, had tried to use Florida's "Stand Your Ground" law, asserting that she was in danger, and, under the law, those in fear for their life have no duty to retreat. A jury deliberated just 12 minutes before finding her guilty as charged: aggravated assault with a deadly weapon. Because she fired a gun while committing a felony, Florida's mandatory-minimum gun law dictated the 20-year sentence. This is the same controversial law that gained attention in 2012 when George Zimmerman shot and killed 17-year-old Trayvon Martin in Sanford, Florida, and was not immediately arrested because he was said to be standing his ground. On August 1, 2010, Alexander thought her husband, Rico Gray, against whom she had a restraining order, would not be there, so she went to their former home to obtain some things. She and Gray had had a baby together just nine days earlier. Gray was home, however, and the two argued. Alexander feared for her life and went to her vehicle to obtain her legally owned gun. When she came back inside, she still felt threatened and fired the shot into the wall, which ricocheted into the ceiling. Gray claims Alexander was the aggressor and that he had repeatedly begged her to put the gun away.

Many of the women in jails and prisons are there for drug-related offenses. Between 1996 and 2002, the number of women in prison for drug-related offenses rose 37 percent, making these offenders the largest group in jails. Domestic violence victims often use alcohol or drugs as a way of coping with the abuse. According to a 1999 report by the U.S. Department of Justice, 89 percent of women prisoners who report having been abused before arrest had used drugs regularly before their imprisonment.

Scholars and advocates have called on the judicial system to take this into account when sentencing female drug offenders, although it seems that most judges do not. In some cases, judges will look for a duress link, or some reason why the crime was not truly of one's own volition. Yet a duress link is very difficult to prove, and it is not exactly duress but the desire to self-medicate that drives many victims of domestic violence to abuse drugs or alcohol. In other cases, victims are too ashamed to bring up the issue of abuse in court.

Elizabeth Brundige, Associate Director of the Avon Center, adjunct professor of law, and one of the coauthors of the Avon Center's report, explained that "New York state has an obligation under international law to respect the human rights of survivor-defendants by taking their experiences of abuse into account. The reforms recommended by the report would help New York to realize this international law obligation and to ensure that survivors are treated with fairness and dignity." She and the other authors made a number of recommendations to address the issue of domestic violence victims in prison:

- Allowing judges to sentence domestic violence survivors convicted of crimes directly related to abuse to shorter prison terms and, wherever possible, to community-based alternatives to incarceration;
- Providing domestic violence survivors currently in prison the opportunity to appeal for resentencing;

- Allocating funds to expand and establish more alternatives to incarceration, court advocacy, and reentry programs for survivors;
- Allowing individuals incarcerated for violent crimes, including domestic violence survivors, to earn merit time credits;
- Expanding eligibility for temporary work release to include domestic violence victims;
- Allowing individuals incarcerated for violent offenses, including domestic violence survivors, to have parole release decisions about them made not solely on the nature of the offense for which they are incarcerated but also by weighting their public safety risk and their confinement history.

The report also supports enactment of the Domestic Violence Survivors Justice Act, a bill pending in the New York State Legislature.

The American Bar Association issued a statement in 2007 urging "bar associations and law schools to develop programs that encourage and train lawyers to assist victims of domestic violence with applying for pardon, restoration of legal rights and privileges, relief from other collateral sanctions, and reduction of sentence" (ABA Resolution 120, 2007).

Founded in 1987, the National Clearinghouse for the Defense of Battered Women "is a resource and advocacy center for battered women charged with crimes related to their battering. Through its work, the organization aims to increase justice for—and prevent further victimization of—arrested, convicted, or incarcerated battered women" (http://www.ncdbw.org/about.htm). It provides a wealth of information and coordinates legal help for battered women.

Some prisons have implemented unique programs for victims of domestic violence. Artspring in Homestead is one example. Artspring Inc. is a 501(c)3 nonprofit organization with the mission of using "arts-based educational programming to develop self-growth and effective life skills for incarcerated women, men and youth as well as other at-risk populations in underserved communities." Operational since 1994, Artspring has been recognized as the longest ongoing arts-based correctional program in Florida. It provides educational and arts-based workshops to some 600 inmates and juveniles each year.

The Michigan Coalition Against Domestic Violence has developed a toolkit of the best practices for working with survivors who have criminal histories. The toolkit recommends the use of trauma-informed strategies for both criminal justice practitioners and domestic violence advocates. Such strategies involve understanding how women have experienced and cope with trauma, helping trauma victims restore a sense of power, providing a feeling of safety, and empowering without overwhelming. Given the overrepresentation of women of color as both domestic violence victims and incarcerated persons, it is essential that both groups maintain culturally competent services. The toolkit is available at http://www.ncdsv.org/images/MCADSV_BestPracticeToolkitWkgDVSurvivorsCriminalHistories_12-2011.pdf. Harden and Hill's (1998) book *Breaking the Rules: Women in Prison and Feminist Therapy* is another useful tool for working with battered women in prisons and in reentry efforts. Some domestic violence shelters also help coordinate support groups in prisons for abused women.

See also: Battered Woman Syndrome; Drugs and Domestic Abuse; Self-Defense, Homicides and Domestic Abuse; Self-Defense, Legal Issues

Further Reading

Alexander, C. (2012, May 7). Battered justice: Domestic violence victim's life after prison. *KOMU*. Retrieved June 21, 2012, from http://www.komu.com/news/battered-justice-domestic-violence-victim-s-life-after-prison/

American Bar Association Resolution 120. (2007). Retrieved January 2013, from http://www.bradycampaign.org/xshare/pdf/resolutions/workplace/ABAresolution0207.pdf

Bible, A. (2011). Issues to consider when facilitating groups with battered women in jail or prison. NCDSV. Retrieved June 21, 2012, from http://www.ncdsv.org/images/NCDBW_IssuesConsiderWhenFacilitatingGroupsBWInJailOrPrison_3-2011.pdf

Browne, A., Miller, B., & Maguin, E. (1999). Prevalence and severity of lifetime physical and sexual victimization among incarcerated women. *International Journal of Law and Psychiatry*. 22, 301–322.

Hairston, C., & Oliver, W. (n.d.). Safe return: Domestic violence and prisoner reentry: Experiences of African American women and men. Retrieved June 21, 2012, from http://www.idvaac.org/media/pubs/SafeReturnDomesticViolenceAndPrisonReentry.pdf

Harden, J., & Hill, M. (1998). *Breaking the rules: Women in prison and feminist therapy*. New York: Haworth.

Jacobson, C. (2007). When justice is battered. *Solidarity*. Retrieved June 21, 2012, from http://www.solidarity-us.org/node/729

Muscat, B. (2008, December). Domestic and safety programs in women's prisons and jails: Addressing prevention, intervention and treatment. Retrieved June 21, 2012, from https://www.ncjrs.gov/pdffiles1/nij/grants/225342.pdf

National Clearinghouse for the Defense of Battered Women: www.ncdbw.org

Stacy, M. (2012, May 19). Marissa Alexander gets 20 years for firing warning shot. *Huffington Post*. Retrieved June 21, 2012, from http://www.huffingtonpost.com/2012/05/19/marissa-alexander-gets-20_n_1530035.html

Zheng, J. (n.d.). The abuse-incarceration connection. Retrieved June 21, 2012. from http://nyunewsdoc.wordpress.com/drug-abuse/the-abuse-incarceration-connection/

Laura L. Finley

PSYCHOLOGICAL EFFECTS OF DOMESTIC ABUSE

Domestic violence includes physical, sexual, verbal, and/or psychological abuse that impacts the mental health of battering victims and children that witness such abuse. This article will focus on the psychological consequences of domestic violence on battered victims and their children and psychotherapeutic interventions to assist survivors in the recovery process.

In the past, women in violent relationships were diagnostically labeled as masochistic by the mental health community for remaining in and/or returning to an abusive relationship. However, the efforts of victim's advocates, feminist scholars, social workers, and psychologists led to research that challenged previous conceptualizations of battering victims and explored the dynamics of abusive relationships and the psychological effects of violent relationships on the victim. According to

Deaton and Hertica (2001), "A thorough reading of the literature on victims indicates that victims are well-adjusted individuals whose maladaptive symptoms occur after experiencing marital violence rather than antecedents or concurrent factors" (p. 9). Physical and psychological abuse are methods used by batterers to increase their power and control over the victim by degrading one's sense of self and self-worth in order to increase dependency on the batterer. Psychological abuse includes criticizing and ridiculing, social isolation, and restricting access to resources. According to a study by Sackett and Saunders (1999), psychological abuse had a greater impact on victim's feelings of fear and self-worth and results in greater psychological distress for the individual than physical abuse.

The seminal work of Dr. Lenore Walker on the battered woman syndrome (BWS) and the cycle of violence further challenged the way the mental health community perceived male batterers, female victims, and violent relationships. Dr. Walker's BWS applied the theory of learned helplessness to women who were battered and proposed that victims of domestic violence learned that their lack of autonomy and power to change their environment resulted in perceptions of helplessness that affected their thoughts, feelings, and behaviors. Dr. Walker's research led to the establishment of BWS as a subcategory of post-traumatic stress disorder (PTSD). It is now widely accepted by the mental health community that the psychological effects of abuse include PTSD, depression, anxiety, sleep disorders, eating disorders, substance abuse, suicidality, intrusive thoughts, somatization, victimization of others, and hypervigilance. Further research indicates that the psychological effects of physical abuse include higher levels of depressive symptomatology, anxiety, PTSD, social withdrawal, and low self-esteem for individuals who experience a history of domestic violence.

Domestic violence also has negative consequences on the mental health of children who experience violence in the home. According to Edleson (1999), a child's experience of adult domestic violence may include "hitting or threatening a child while in his or her mother's arms, taking the child hostage to force the mother's return to the home, using a child as a physical weapon against the victim, forcing the child to watch assaults against the mother or participate in the abuse, and using the child as a spy or interrogating him or her about the mother's activities" (p. 4). Social learning theory posits that children who witness violence in the home may learn violent behaviors through modeling and imitation of parental figures. As a result, children may learn to use aggressive and violent methods to get their needs met. The psychological impact of witnessing parental violence can include the child demonstrating difficulties with externalizing behaviors such as aggression and delinquent and oppositional behaviors, and internalizing behaviors such as anxiety, depression, social withdrawal, and somatic complaints. In addition, research has shown that children exposed to violence in the home have difficulties with academic and social performance and low self-esteem.

Psychotherapeutic treatment models emphasize the development of rapport, trust, and empathy within the therapeutic relationship in order to improve treatment outcomes. A review of the literature indicates that there are numerous therapeutic models for working with victims of domestic violence. Most treatment models focus on crisis intervention, short- and long-term counseling, and relapse prevention. Crisis intervention includes psychological assessment, the development of a safety plan, and psychoeducation regarding psychological effects of abuse. Short- and long-term counseling include improving self-esteem, decision making and life skills, and focusing on empowerment and client strengths.

According to the research, "The process of leaving an abusive relationship typically involves numerous stressors, such as relocation, economic instability, legal actions, child custody issues, disruption of social networks, and possibly difficulties involved in terminating the emotional connection with the batterer. If a woman either inaccurately perceives or minimizes the difficulties that she may experience throughout this process, she is likely to be unprepared for the feelings that may arise during these struggles and may be more vulnerable to making a sudden decision to return to the batterer" (Griffing et al., 2002, p. 306). Therefore, it is essential during the therapeutic process that individuals are encouraged to explore these issues and the possible feelings that may arise as a result of leaving the batterer. Group therapy can also help victims of domestic violence feel validated in their shared experience with others and allows for mutual support and healing. Another important feature of therapeutic work with survivors of domestic violence includes trauma recovery and grief work. According to Russell and Uhlemann, "the process of leaving an abusive partner shares many characteristics with the grieving process such as depression and guilt. These are not considered pathological" (Deaton & Hertica, 2001, p. 6).

Children who witness domestic violence are often not identified as victims of trauma. However, it is essential that children receive psychotherapeutic services in order to help heal and recover from the psychological distress caused by violence in the home environment. Individual, group, play therapy can be effective to help children express their feelings and process their experiences related to the abuse.

Domestic violence has negative psychological effects on battering victims and children who witness violence in the home. Psychological interventions must be individualized in order to meet the particular needs of these individuals and must focus on crisis intervention, short- and long-term counseling, and relapse prevention. Research shows that interventions based on psychoeducation, empowerment, improving self-esteem, validation of experiences, and trauma recovery are essential to help victims recover from these abusive relationships. Studies indicate that group therapy may promote the recovery process through shared experience and mutual support, and children may benefit from therapeutic modalities including individual, group, and play therapies in order to develop coping skills, learn new behaviors, and process their experiences.

See also: Battered Woman Syndrome; Biological and Psychological Theories about Domestic Abuse; Effects of Domestic Abuse; Therapy and Counseling for Domestic Abuse; Walker, Lenore

Further Reading

Deaton, W. S., & Hertica, M. (2001). *A therapist's guide to growing free: A manual for survivors of domestic violence*. New York, NY: Haworth Maltreatment and Trauma Press.

Edleson, T. (1999). Children's witnessing of adult domestic violence. *Journal of Interpersonal Violence. 14*(8), 839–870. doi: 10.1177/088626099014008004

Griffing, S., Ragin, D. F., Sage, R. E., Madry, L., Bingham, L. E., & Primm, B. J. (2002). Domestic violence survivor's self-identified reasons for returning to abusive relationships. *Journal of Interpersonal Violence, 17*, 306. doi: 10.1177/0886260502017003005

Kohn, R., Pearlstein, T., Peterson, J., & Zlotnick, C. (1998). Partner physical victimization in a national sample of American families: Relationship to psychological functioning, psychosocial factors, and gender. *Journal of Interpersonal Violence, 13*(1), 156.

Sackett, L. A., & Saunders, D. G. (1999). The impact of different forms of psychological abuse on battered women. *Violence and Victims, 14*(1), 105–117.

Street, A. E., King, L. A., King, D. W., & Riggs, D. S. (2003). The associations among male-perpetrated partner violence, wives' psychological distress and children's behavioral problems: A structural equation modeling analysis. *Journal of Comparative Family Studies, 34*(1), 23–40.

Walker, L. E. A. (2009). *The battered woman syndrome* (3rd ed.). New York, NY: Springer.

Kathryn Goesel

REPRODUCTIVE COERCION

In some abusive relationships, men have pressured women to become pregnant. Or the male partner may sabotage the woman's birth control or physically hurt her to end a pregnancy. These actions or behaviors are often employed by men on their intimate partners in order to maintain control and power over them. Violence against women is an ongoing problem, and young women are at greater risk. Violence has the potential to limit a woman's ability to be in control of her reproductive health. It also prevents women from making their own choices concerning pregnancy. Reproductive coercion is often present in abusive relationships, leaving women little to no options but to satisfy their partner's demands.

Reproductive coercion is a form of abuse in which women's partners force or threaten them into adopting the partner's reproductive intentions. Two forms of reproductive coercion are pregnancy, coercion or pressure to become pregnant, and birth control sabotage, in which the partner interferes with contraception. These male partners can use verbal threats and even physical or sexual violence to pressure their female partners into becoming pregnant, resulting many times in unintended pregnancies. Other partners resort to sabotaging their female partner's birth control. These behaviors are often associated with abusive relationships as women in these relationships are more likely to fear the consequences of resisting their partner's demands. Intimate partner violence (IPV) including sexual, physical or emotional abuse, together with reproductive coercion, does not give women the liberty to make reproductive choices.

Reproductive control and the behaviors that accompany it can occur before sexual intercourse, during sexual intercourse, and after conception. Before sexual intercourse, women may experience pressure of verbal threats from their partner to become pregnant. During sexual intercourse, men interfere with contraception, such as removing condoms or forcing sex on their partners. After conception, male partners can influence the outcome of the pregnancy by forcing either birth or an abortion. Men can also be violent against their female partners in order to kill the fetus or cause a miscarriage if pregnancy is unwanted. Women who endure forced intercourse and those who are unable to use contraceptives because of their abuser's control are at greater risk of becoming pregnant unintentionally (Miller, Jordan, Levenson, & Silverman, 2010).

According to Miller, Jordan, Levenson, and Silverman (2010), in the United States, an estimated one in four women and one in five teen girls report abuse. The Bureau of Justice Statistics estimated that in 2008, females age 12 or older experienced about 552,000 violent victimizations by an intimate partner. A study titled

Pregnancy Coercion, Intimate Partner Violence and Unintended Pregnancy examined the relationship between reproductive coercion, intimate partner violence, and unintended pregnancy. A survey was given to 1,278 females ages 16 to 29 who were seeking care in family planning clinics. For women to be classified as having experienced unintended pregnancies they had to have been pregnant one or more times when they didn't want to be. If a woman was hurt physically because she did not agree to get pregnant, was pressured to become pregnant, or their partner said he would leave her if she would not get pregnant, then she was deemed to have experienced pregnancy coercion. Birth control sabotage was measured if the women answered yes to questions like, "Has someone you were dating taken your birth control away from you so that you would get pregnant? Or made you have sex without a condom?" Results from the study showed that approximately 683 women reported intimate partner violence. Out of that number, 237 women, or 35 percent, also reported reproductive coercion. According to the study, pregnancy coercion was reported by one in five females, birth control sabotage by one in seven females, and at least one unintended pregnancy by more than two in five females. This study documented the high prevalence of partner violence, pregnancy coercion, and birth control sabotage among young women who attend family planning clinics. This study was one of the first quantitative studies concerning reproductive coercion in the domestic violence literature. Reproductive control was more common among women who were physically and sexually abused than women who did not experience partner violence.

Male Reproductive Control of Women, Who Have Experienced Intimate Partner Violence in the United States, a study conducted in 2007, gathered the reproductive histories of 71 women ages 18–49 who had a history of IPV. In-depth interviews were conducted for these women, who were chosen from a family planning clinic, an abortion clinic, and a domestic violence shelter in the United States. Reproductive control in the study was defined as the women's ability to make independent choices or decisions about their reproduction. Reproductive control was presented in different forms: economic, emotional, and physical. An example of economic reproductive control was not giving women money to buy birth control or to obtain an abortion. Emotional reproductive control could take the form of accusing her of infidelity if she chooses birth control or denying being the father of the unborn. Physical reproductive control can range from beating her up if he finds she is using birth control to threatening to kill her if she has an abortion. The types of reproductive control perpetrated by men on females were examined along three stages discussed earlier; before sexual intercourse, during sexual intercourse, and after conception.

Women were asked to describe their relationship histories of birth control use, abortions, and miscarriages. The interviews also dealt with the female's ability to negotiate sexual encounters with male partners and decisions about pregnancy. Out of 71 respondents in the study, 53, or 74 percent, reported experiencing reproductive control, and most respondents were between the ages of 20 and 29, African American, and had completed at least high school. Women often began their story of reproductive control prior to sexual intercourse by explaining how their male partners verbally threatened and forced them to become pregnant. Women respondents said their partners often told them they wanted to impregnate her so she could be tied to him forever. Respondent 1 said her partner told her, "I should just get you pregnant and have a baby with you so that I know you will be in my life forever" (Miller, Decker, et al., 2010). This same male partner refused condoms, accused her of being unfaithful if she tried to use birth control, and denied being the father of the baby when she became pregnant. When discussing incidences like these, women stated that their partner had no regard for their own feelings or thoughts about pregnancy.

Before engaging in sexual intercourse, other respondents reported their partner continuously flushing birth control pills down the toilet and refusing to use condoms. As is common in intimate partner relationships, men stated that they were emotionally rejected when their women partners protested against becoming pregnant. To avoid abuse, their female partners would reassure the men of their feelings, which sometimes included having unprotected sex. During sexual intercourse, respondents experienced violent rape. Respondent 3 in the study told the interviewer that she could not say no to sex with her partner. She was with this abusive partner for eight years, and he would force her to have sex and not use a condom. Some women during sexual intercourse were at risk of unwanted pregnancy. Birth control sabotage occurred in different ways among respondents. Some male partners manipulated the condoms by taking them off, biting holes in them, or not telling their partners when the condom broke. Other male partners resorted to persuading the women that birth control had very harmful side effects that could affect them (the men) or render them sterile. One male even pulled out a contraception ring from inside of his female partner.

When pregnancy became reality for these women, their vulnerability increased, and so too did men's controlling behaviors, like manipulating the outcome of the pregnancy to their desire. The female partners in this study described the men pressuring them to resolve the pregnancy the way they wanted, without regard for the women's concerns. Some men forced their female partners to terminate the pregnancy, while others refused to let them have an abortion. When respondents wanted to terminate the pregnancy, their male partners were completely opposed to the idea. According to respondents, these abusive partners would make them feel guilty about going through with an abortion. The men would also beg and assure that they would support the baby in order to convince the women to give birth. When the men were the ones who wanted to terminate the pregnancy, female respondents reported they were threatened with being thrown down the stairs or punched in the stomach to end the pregnancy. Men who refused to let their partner have an abortion would deny her the ability to have the procedure done. They would accomplish this by denying her the money to pay for the abortion or sabotaging her abortion appointments. Some respondents in the study faced threats to harm or kill them if they had an abortion. Even though some women did not follow their partner's rules, the acts of resisting were seen less frequently than adherence to the partner's demands. This study gives insight into the lives of women who experienced reproductive coercion and how these behaviors have a strong association with abusive relationships.

The studies described above shed light on an issue that needs to be addressed in order to effectively help women who find themselves in abusive relationships. Health-care providers or support systems, such as family planning clinics, need to address the issue of reproductive coercion with efforts to reduce IPV, in turn decreasing the number of unintended pregnancies. Planned Parenthood Federation of America, along with the Family Violence Prevention Fund, has been working on tools and strategies to address reproductive coercion. They include posters that educate women about reproductive coercion, methods of birth control that male partners cannot interfere with, access to emergency birth control, and training providers on how to offer referrals to domestic violence shelters. Experts suggest education and counseling for teens in order for them to recognize behaviors that are abusive or coercive and not misinterpret them as evidence of love. Counseling can encourage women to speak up and recognize when they are in an unhealthy relationship, one that affects their ability to make their own reproductive choices.

Women who have experienced intimate partner violence are consistently found to have poor sexual and reproductive health compared to nonabused women (Miller, Moore, & Frohwirth 2010). Studies have found a link between IPV and what is known as reproductive coercion. Often present in abusive relationships, coercive behaviors, such as pregnancy coercion or birth control sabotage, are behaviors that provide men the power and control over their partner's reproductive health. These behaviors often leave women vulnerable and susceptible to abuse and at a higher risk of unintended pregnancies. Research and studies have suggested that in order to tackle the issue of reproductive coercion, we need to first focus on the larger problem underlying these behaviors, the problem of partner violence.

See also: Pregnancy and Domestic Abuse; Teen Victims; Types of Domestic Abuse

Further Reading

Catalano, S., Smith, E., Snyder, H., & Rand, M. (2009, October 23). Bureau of Justice Statistics: Female victims of violence. Retrieved from http://bjs.ojp.usdoj.gov/content/pub/pdf/fvv.pdf

Miller, E., Decker, M. R., McCauley, H. L., Tancredi, D. J., Levenson, R. R., Waldman, J., Schoenwald, P., & Silverman, J. G. (2010). Pregnancy coercion, intimate partner violence and unintended pregnancy. *Contraception, 81,* 316–322.

Miller, E., Jordan, B., Levenson, R., & Silverman, J. G. (2010, June). Reproductive coercion: Connecting the dots between partner violence and unintended pregnancy. Retrieved from http://www.arhp.org/publications-and-resources/contraception-journal/june-2010

Miller, E., Moore, A. M., & Frohwirth, L. (2010). Male reproductive control of women who have experienced intimate partner violence in the United States. *Social Science and Medicine,* 1–16. doi:10.1016/j.socscimed.2010.02.009

Vanessa Marquez

RESTRAINING ORDERS AND PERSONAL PROTECTION ORDERS

Many people think of physical violence when they hear the term domestic abuse. While physical battery is certainly a large aspect of domestic abuse, one cannot diminish the negative impact other forms of abuse have on a victim. The FBI's Uniform Crime Reports include domestic violence as a "series of behaviors"—including but not limited to threats, intimidation, mental and/or verbal abuse, and isolation. In 2003, the American College of Emergency Physicians reported that for American women between the ages of 15 and 44, domestic violence is the "single largest cause of injury." One potential means of protection is a restraining order or personal protection order. Unfortunately, some studies purport that restraining orders are becoming overused and are either unnecessary or even completely false in some instances. For this reason, it is imperative that a victim precisely follow the proper protocol when seeking a restraining order.

When a person is in danger of continued domestic abuse, she or he may choose to get a restraining order, sometimes called a protection order. Restraining orders differ somewhat from protection orders, and it is important to differentiate between the two to better understand the reasoning behind obtaining one. Resource 4 the People, a legal help website, explains further: A protection order is specifically designed to prevent family violence in protecting a "family member from imminent physical harm." A restraining order is most often used during a divorce or the end of a long-term relationship. Restraining orders can prevent the offender from clearing out joint bank accounts, selling real estate property, or cancelling credit cards. We must also understand that restraining orders do not apply to nonphysical types of abuse such as mental, verbal, and/or emotional abuse.

The Gay Men's Domestic Violence Project outlines what is needed in order to obtain a restraining order. While this organization is intended for the gay community, it offers a very specific overview of the process. We must also be aware that that the legal information included there pertains to the Commonwealth of Massachusetts in particular. This material, while Massachusetts-specific, will still provide a general idea of the procedure en masse. In certain states, a restraining order only means that the attacker can't come within a certain distance of the abused. A protective order is really a "no abuse" order, explicitly worded to prevent any further violence from occurring. Oftentimes, these two orders are combined to provide the most success for the abused. There are also several stipulations that can be added to a restraining order, depending on the circumstances of the abused. In situations where the accused and the abused live together, a vacate order forces the abuser to move out of the shared home. In this instance, the police department will serve the vacate order and then oversee the abuser's departure from the residence. If the abused and accused share custody of minor children, the victim may be granted full custody on a temporary basis. During this time, a child support order may be granted, compelling the accused to supply child support on a temporary basis. A restitution order would reimburse the abused for any wages lost, medical bills incurred, or other payments for damages stemming from the suffered abuse.

If the accused violates any part of a restraining order, he or she may be subject to any or all of the following: instantly being remanded to police custody or jail, charged with an additional felony or misdemeanor crime (if convicted of these new charges, the accused may have to pay a fine or even be sentenced to prison time), or required to attend therapy such as a "batterer's intervention program."

Once a restraining order is granted, the abuser is to have no contact with the victim. One reason restraining orders fail is that often the abuser will violate the order and initiate contact with his/her abuser. If a victim is not willing to have the abuser arrested and charged if he/she breaks the rules of the order, then there is little reason to obtain one in the first place. For this reason, anyone considering securing a restraining or protection order should weigh the pros and cons.

The first pro of acquiring a restraining order is that most abusers tend to respect the restraining orders. Time away from an abuser can be quite beneficial to the victim while he/she decides what to do next. However, there are those accused who do not respect the protection order. Some would say a protection order is simply a piece of paper providing no protection whatsoever. One large benefit stemming from a restraining order is that if the accused breaks the order, the victim or anyone in the victim's support system can call the authorities and even have the accused arrested. If the restraining order includes a strict no-contact order, this will also protect the victim's children from the abuser as well.

Some advocates would argue that there are more cons than pros to restraining orders. Many abusers refuse to respect a restraining order, which naturally, is likely to make the abuser even more irate and therefore more dangerous—potential jail time or not. If a victim's abuser is the mortgage or leaseholder of a primary residence, a vacate order may prompt him/her to violent retribution against the victim. Such violence may be more severe and could even be fatal in extremes. Domestic abuse victims must carefully examine their abusers' likelihood of becoming more violent if a restraining order is issued against them. There are several things to look for to determine this. If the abuser has weapons, has ever intimidated the victim with threats of using weapons, or has a fascination with weapons, then he/she is much more likely to become more violent after a restraining order has been issued. If the abuser already has a history of violence or a criminal record, the chances of violence against the victim increase significantly. Also, if the abuser has a fear of courts or law enforcement and then is served with a restraining order, he/she could become so incensed that fatal violence will occur.

Break the Cycle, an antidomestic abuse organization, claims that by law, restraining orders are free in all 50 states. But while the cost or fee of a restraining order is waived if—and only if—there is evidence of physical violence, many victims may be bogged down with the process of obtaining one. In most situations, a victim will need to go down to the local courthouse to initiate the process. The abused must then complete an affidavit to request that a formal restraining order be served to the perpetrator. After this paperwork is complete, the victim will have to appear before a judge. The judge will then ask several questions about the victim's safety. It may be necessary for the victim to provide the judge with evidence of abuse, such as any pertinent police reports and/or medical records. Unfortunately, some victims do not have this type of evidence. Some never go to the hospital or to a doctor's office following an attack—there are those abusers who know just how far to go to prevent medical assistance from being necessary. After this first appearance before the judge, the victim will be given a copy of a temporary restraining order that she/he should carry at all times. It is suggested by the Gay Men's Domestic Violence Project that the victim also make copies of the restraining order and keep a copy in different locations—at work, in the car, and with a friend or trusted family member. They also recommend the victim keep a photo of the attacker with each copy of the order in case it becomes necessary to involve the police. It may also be a good idea to provide a copy of the restraining order as well as the perpetrator's picture to any service providers like therapists, child-care providers—schools of the victims' children, coaches, day care centers—as well as lawyers or victim advocates.

In addition to medical records and police reports, victims should also bring as much information as they have on their attacker. Information that the judge may find helpful includes the perpetrator's locations—work, home, as well as family members' locations or any other places where he/she may be found—and also the abuser's Social Security number if known. After the temporary order has been given to the abused, the court system will notify the police department that the order has been granted. It is advised, however, that the victim also go to her/his own local police department to personally provide them with a copy of the restraining order. Only after this will the police serve the accused with the restraining order.

If a vacate order is included, the police will go to the victim's home and give the accused a set amount of time in which to gather his or her belongings from the shared home. The police will remain in the accused presence at all times, but a victim may choose to be absent while this occurs. After the initial 10 days of the temporary restraining order, the abused must appear before the judge once more for an additional hearing. At this second court appearance, the accused has the legal right to be there and tell his or her side of the story. The abuser is also granted legal counsel for the hearing. This hearing will certainly be extremely difficult for the abused. It is highly recommended that the victim have a support system accompany him or her to the hearing. This support system should include a victim advocate to provide both emotional and legal support, legal counsel to protect the victim's rights, and any family members or friends. A victim will have the chance to tell his or her side of the story as well, but this will most likely be the hardest part of the process. Harsh words, false accusations, and intimidating looks from the abuser are all sure to heighten the stress level of any victim.

The judge will then need to decide if the victim has shown a "substantial likelihood of immediate danger and abuse" and if the abuse fits at least one of the following categories: Was the abuse intended to cause physical harm? Did the abuse cause physical harm? Has the abuse made the victim afraid of impending serious physical harm? Has the abuse forced you to involuntarily engage in sexual relations—either by force or threat of force? After this hearing, the judge may decide to extend the temporary restraining order for a year's time. Following that year, if a restraining order is still needed, the victim may have to repeat this process. For this reason, a victim must carefully weigh her/his own personal pros and cons of obtaining a restraining order. In the end, the time and emotional stress of the legal process may prove too taxing on a victim.

Although only a piece of paper for some, a restraining/protection order may prove quite useful and invaluable. The restraining order may provide the victim with the time she/he needs to get a survival plan in order and to obtain desperately needed help. Restraining orders are only as good as the enforcement of them, however.

In 2011, the Inter-American Commission on Human Rights determined that the U.S. Supreme Court had erred when it ruled that victims are not entitled to the enforcement of their protection orders by police. The ruling came from the case of

Jessica Gonzales, whose three daughters were murdered by her husband in Castle Rock, Colorado, when he violated a restraining order. Police had been contacted multiple times and failed to act.

See also: Castle Rock v. Gonzales Case; Courts and Domestic Abuse; Lesbian, Gay, Bisexual, and Transgendered (LGBT) Victims; Policing Domestic Abuse

Further Reading

Jessica Gonzales v. the United States of America: http://www.jessicagonzalesvsunitedstates.com/Jessicas_Story.html

Mabrey, V., & Peterson, C. (2010, March 15). When restraining orders cannot stop a killer. *ABC News.* Retrieved May 31, 2012, from http://abcnews.go.com/Nightline/restraining-orders-stalkers-domestic-violence-victims-call-enforcement/story?id=9999086#.T8jhGlLl8xM

Protection orders, restraining orders, protection from abuse orders. (2011, March 6). AARDVARC. Retrieved May 31, 2012, from http://www.aardvarc.org/dv/orders.shtml

Kristin Franklin

RUNAWAY AND HOMELESS YOUTH

The Office of Juvenile Justice and Delinquency Prevention in the U.S. Department of Justice estimated in the year 2002 that there were approximately 1,682,900 homeless and runaway youth in the United States. Some studies indicate that the number of homeless youth is increasing and may be as high as two million. Family conflict has been identified as one of the most important causes for homelessness among teenagers. The most common types of family conflict reported by homeless teenagers are domestic violence, child abuse, sexual activities, relationship with stepparents, pregnancy, sexual orientation, academic problems, and substance abuse. A study conducted by the U.S. Department of Health and Human Services (1997) showed that 46 percent of runaways and homeless youth have been subjected to physical abuse, and 17 percent have been sexually assaulted by someone in their household. More than 50 percent of teenagers in shelters reported that their caregivers ordered them to leave their homes or demonstrated that they did not care if they left.

Reports regarding the gender and ethnicity of homeless youth show different results depending on the source. While shelter samples tend to indicate an equal number of males and females, samples of street youth show a majority of males. Some studies show that young minorities are more likely to be homeless than white teenagers. However, other studies report that the homeless teenagers' ethnic makeup is consistent with the demographics of the areas where they are located.

Approximately 20 percent of homeless girls become pregnant. The high rate of pregnancy is due to different factors, including sexual assaults, survival sex, forced prostitution, and lack of access to contraceptives. Teen pregnancy among homeless youth has been associated with belonging to an ethnic minority, not finishing high school, being homeless for significant periods of time, having a sexually transmitted disease, seeing oneself as abandoned by family members, having a history of maternal emotional abuse, and having been raised by a single parent.

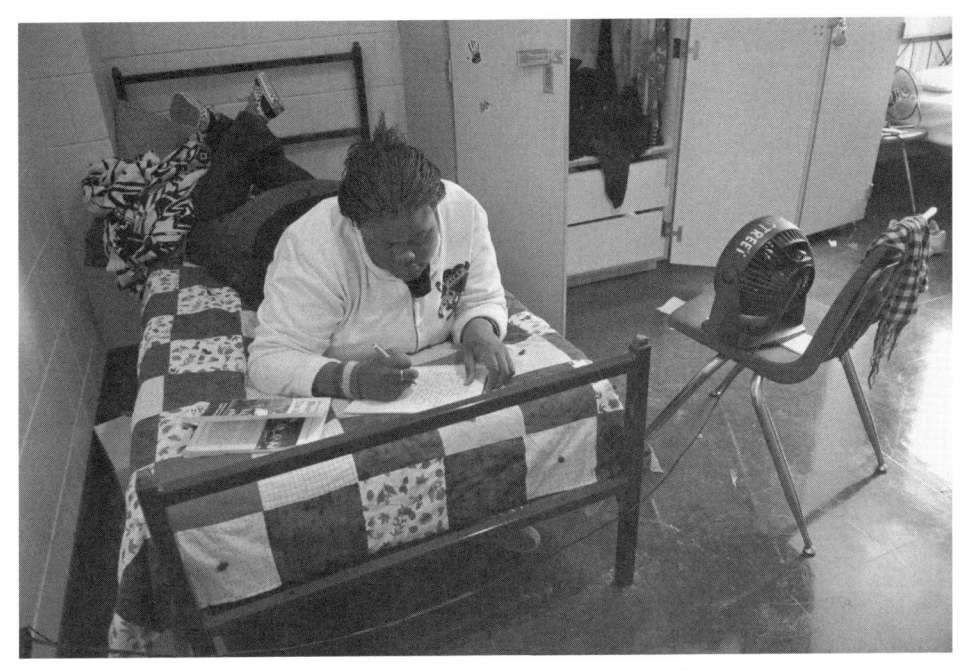

A homeless teen writes in her journal at the Hope Street Shelter for homeless teens in Minneapolis on December 22, 2009. The homeless shelter was her only option after her mother repeatedly stole money from her that she was using to save for college. (AP Photo/Dawn Villella)

Most homeless teenagers were raised by families that were poor or middle class. Further, the majority of homeless teenagers report having stepparents or being raised by one parent and having no contact with the other biological parent. Residential instability is another common characteristic in their upbringings. Indeed, homeless teenagers' families have a tendency to move significantly more often than other families.

Teenagers who live on the streets or in homeless shelters report high levels of physical and psychological problems. The most common psychological disorders reported by homeless youth include post-traumatic stress disorder, depression, suicidal behavior, substance abuse, and conduct disorder. Further, homeless teenagers are significantly more likely than their housed peers to be victimized physically or sexually, and they have alarming rates of repeated victimization.

GLBT Youth

It has been estimated that 20 to 40 percent of American homeless teenagers are gay, lesbian, bisexual, or transgender (GLBT) even though only 4 percent of U.S. teenagers identify as GLBT. As in the case of straight teenagers, family conflict is the main reason behind GLBT homelessness. Soon after disclosing their sexual orientation, 50 percent of GLBT teens experience rejection by their families, 33 percent get physically assaulted, and 26 percent get thrown out of their homes. According to a study published in the *Journal of Sex Research*, about 58.7 percent of

GLBT homeless youth report that they have been sexually assaulted, while 33.4 percent of straight homeless youth report that they have been sexually assaulted.

A report published by the National Gay and Lesbian Task Force in 2006 indicated that many GLBT homeless teenagers suffer from discrimination, harassment, and assaults while residing in the shelters due to lack of protective policies toward GLBT youth. The report claimed that homeless shelters that are faith based, particularly the Covenant House, were often unfriendly toward GLBT youth and that they refused to admit transgender teenagers unless they dress according to the gender that appears in their identification. Claims regarding these issues led the Covenant House, a chain of shelters for homeless and runaway youth with locations across the nation, to implement GLBT-sensitive regulation. There are shelters that have been especially designed to respond to the needs of GLBT youth. However, their capacity is often very limited, and there are only available in a few U.S. cities.

Street Survival Behaviors

A study conducted in four U.S. cities—Los Angeles, Austin, Denver, and St. Louis—showed that homeless youth engage in five main types of survival behaviors: dealing drugs, commercial sex, selling blood or plasma, stealing, and panhandling. The authors identified certain individual characteristics that appear to increase the teenagers' engagement in the aforementioned survival behaviors. These characteristics included being transient, addicted to drugs, unemployed, and reliant on peers for help. Further, those teenagers in the transient subsample who were white and who were victimized in the past were found to be significantly more likely to engage in these survival behaviors.

Teenagers who get involved in illicit survival behaviors are at high risk of being victimized by others and of developing physical and psychological problems. Risky sexual behaviors can lead homeless teens to suffer from sexually transmitted diseases, HIV, AIDS, and unplanned pregnancies.

Foster Children

Research has found that about 30 percent of homeless adults have a foster care history. Approximately 11,000 foster youth run away from their placements, and 24,000 foster youth age out of foster care each year. A study conducted by Reilly (2003) indicated that up to 36 percent of former foster children experience homelessness after aging out of the system.

Youthful Offenders

Approximately two-thirds of boys and three-quarters of girls who are arrested and detained in the United States suffer from a psychological disorder. Nearly 200,000 individuals aged 10 to 24 get released annually from juvenile detention centers and other correctional facilities. The majority of them do not have a high school diploma, do not have any employment history, and do not receive proper services while detained. As a result, they have high rates of unemployment, poverty, and homelessness. It has been estimated that nearly 30 percent of the teenagers who received services at Covenant House have been previously detained or incarcerated, 80 percent of the offenders do not have a high school diploma or a GED, and 41 percent abused substances.

Interventions

The interventions that are used to help homeless youth include brief motivational interventions, intensive case management, cognitive-behavioral interventions, living skills/vocational interventions, supportive housing, peer-based interventions, and independent living programs.

Some studies suggest that family-focused interventions could be used to help homeless youth. Due to the fact that most homeless youth return to live with their families, the use of systems therapy seems to be particularly important. Indeed, positive results have been reported by Thompson, Pollio, and Bitner (2000). Even though family-focused interventions can be effective, they are counter indicated in cases where the children have been subjected to extreme neglect or abuse. Taking into account the severity of trauma suffered by the teenager is fundamental while choosing the appropriate intervention.

Services

The National Runaway Switchboard (NRS), founded in 1971, is the national hotline for U.S. homeless and runaway teenagers. The NRS was the first communication system of its kind in the world. It receives about 100,000 phone calls per year. The services it offers include crisis intervention, education and prevention services, and referrals to different local resources. The NRS crisis hotline is 1-800-RUNAWAY.

There are a number of organizations in the United States that offer shelter for homeless youth. The largest is the Covenant House, which serves 55,000 children per year. The Covenant House was founded by Father Bruce Ritter in 1971 in New York City, and it later expanded to other areas around the United States, Central America, and Canada. Father Ritter, a Catholic priest, served as director until he resigned in 1990 after three former residents accused him of sexual abuse. Since then, the organization has been under the leadership of Sister Mary Rose (1990–2003), Sister Tricia Cruise (2003–2008), and Kevin Ryan (2008–present).

Prevention Programs

Due to the research conducted about homeless youth, it has been determined that there are two major at-risk groups that must be targeted: children aging out of the foster care system and children in the juvenile justice system. The most common prevention strategies include parenting skills training, support groups for caregivers, and conflict resolution skills training. Programs designed to help children aging out of the foster care system are mainly funded by the John Chafee Foster Care Independence Program (CFCIP). The CFCIP provides grants to states and tribes that submit projects that help foster youth continue their education, find employment, find housing, receive life skills training, mentoring, health education, and case management.

See also: Lesbian, Gay, Bisexual, and Transgendered Victims; Teen Victims

Further Reading

Covenant House Statistics: http://www.covenanthouse.org/homeless-teen-issues/statistics

Ferguson, K. M., Bender, K., Thompson, S., Xie, B., & Pollio, D. (2011). Correlates of street survival behaviors in homeless young adults in four U.S. cities. *American Journal of Orthopsychiatry, 81*(3), 401–409.

Fernandes, A. L. (2007, January 8). Runaway and homeless youth: Demographics, programs, and emerging issues. Washington, DC: Congressional Research Service. Retrieved from http://assets.opencrs.com/rpts/RL33785_20070108.pdf

Hammer, H., Finkelhor, D., & Sedlak, A. (2002). Runaway/thrownaway children: National estimates and characteristics. Washington, DC: Office of Juvenile Justice and Delinquency Prevention.

National Runaway Switchboard: http://www.1800runaway.org/

New York City Association of Homeless and Street-Involved Youth Organizations. (2005). *State of the city's homeless youth report.* New York, NY: New York City Association of Homeless and Street-Involved Youth Organizations.

Ray, N. (2006). *Lesbian, gay, bisexual and transgender youth: An epidemic of homelessness.* New York, NY: National Gay and Lesbian Task Force Policy Institute and the National Coalition for the Homeless.

Reilly, T. (2003). Transitions from care: Status and outcomes of youth who age out of foster care. *Child Welfare, 82*(6), 727–746.

Roman, N. P., & Wolfe, N. (1995). *Web of failure: The relationship between foster care and homelessness.* Washington, DC: National Alliance to End Homelessness.

Teplin, L. A., Abram, K. M., McClelland, G. M., Dulcan, M. K., & Mericle, A. A. (2002). Prevalence of psychiatric disorders in youth in juvenile detention. *Archives of General Psychiatry, 59,* 1133–1143.

Thompson, S. J., Bender, K. A., Lewis, C., & Watkins, R. (2008). Runaway and pregnant: Factors associated with pregnancy in a national sample of runaway/homeless females. *Journal of Adolescent Health, 43*(2), 125–132.

Thompson, S. J., Pollio, D. E., & Bitner, L. (2000). Outcomes for adolescents using runaway and homeless youth services. *Journal of Human Behavior in the Social Environment, 3*(1), 79–97.

U.S. Department of Health and Human Services. (1995). *Youth with runaway, throwaway, and homeless experiences: Prevalence drug use, and other at-risk behaviors.* Silver Spring, MD: National Clearinghouse on Families & Youth Silver Spring.

U.S. Department of Health and Human Services (1997). National Evaluation of Runaway and Homeless Youth. Silver Spring, MD: National Clearinghouse on Families & Youth.

Whitbeck, L. B. (2009). *Mental health and emerging adulthood among homeless young people.* New York, NY: Psychology Press.

Whitbeck, L. B., Chen, X., Hoyt, D. R., Tyler, K. A., & Johnson, K. D. (2004). Mental disorder, substinence strategies, and victimization among gay, lesbian, and bisexual homeless and runaway adolescents. *Journal of Sex Research, 41*(4), 329–342

Maria F. Espinola